THE AMERICAN SOUTHWEST

Its People and Cultures

Lynn I. Perrigo

UNIVERSITY OF NEW MEXICO PRESS
Albuquerque

Reprinted 1975 by the University of New Mexico Press
by arrangement with Holt, Rinehart and Winston, Inc.
Library of Congress Catalog Card Number 76-146926
International Standard Book Number 0-8263-0403-6
Manufactured in the United States of America

Second printing, University of New Mexico Press, 1979

PREFACE

The Southwest has experienced such variety in definition that it is now an elusive entity.

Early usage referred to "The Old Southwest." When the western frontier had penetrated only to the Mississippi River, the southwestern part of the occupied area included the present states of Tennessee, Alabama, and Mississippi. Therefore that was the Southwest of that era, and in historical perspective it has become "The Old Southwest."

Next west of that region lies a group of states including Arkansas, Oklahoma, Louisiana, and Texas. Often regarded as *The* Southwest, especially in Texas, it, too, has a proper appellation, "The Gulf Southwest."

Then there are some residents of southern California and western Arizona who aspire to be at the center of the Southwest, and again there is an appropriate name for their region— "The Pacific Southwest."

Another name, "The Greater Southwest," also has a basis in fact and in usage. The scope of this definition is the entire quadrant southwest of two lines dissecting the nation midway east to west and north to south. That quadrant includes ten southwestern states. The history of that region once was traced in a book by Rupert N. Richardson and Carl C. Rister, entitled *The Greater Southwest*.

That is not all. When archeologists write about "digging in the Southwest," they refer especially to New Mexico and Arizona. Highly developed Pueblo cultures exist in those present states, and their pre-Columbian antecedents were also centered in the same locality, with a shading off into southern Utah and western Texas. Therefore that region is "The Aboriginal Southwest" of the archeologist and the anthropologist.

There was a time when geographers divided the nation into groups of contiguous states for convenience in descriptive treatment. Those groupings, however, did not embrace entire quadrants. They were smaller, so that the geographers would have a Middle West, a Great Plains, and a Far West, as well

iii

as a Southwest and a Northwest. Upon the adoption of the regional approach, geographers ceased describing a "Southwest." Instead, they divided the West into fairly homogenous regions including the High Plains, the Rocky Mountains, the Intermontane Basins, and the Pacific Coast, each of which extends into the Southwest. Nevertheless, the southern portions of those regions do have common factors in the generally prevalent aridity and high altitudes.

A definition oriented to one corner of a modern nation has no point of reference, of course, in an era before the emergence of the nation. Among the Amerinds there were many tribes and linguistic families in the region and no rationale for such a concept. Furthermore, in the Spanish colonial period our Southwest was a northern frontier, known officially as "Interior Provinces."

Nevertheless, assuming that the present nation will long endure, the historian can anticipate that the term "Southwest" will have an orientation for generations to come. For his analytical approach the more fruitful concept is a cultural definition, "The Old Spanish Southwest," or Herbert Eugene Bolton's "The Spanish Borderlands." This Southwest may be defined as the region once occupied by Spanish colonists and still retaining evidences of the Spanish heritage. The localities qualifying under that definition extend from central Texas westward through New Mexico and Arizona to southern and central California. When the history is continued into the modern political units, for convenience in handling of data, that "Old Spanish Southwest" becomes a "New Southwest" comprising four modern contiguous states—Texas, New Mexico, Arizona, and California.

Though there was once a Spanish outpost on the east coast of Florida, obviously that location is too far removed for inclusion in the southwest. Likewise for forty years Spain had a seat of colonial government in Louisiana, but Spanish influence there did not displace the predominant French culture. Moreover, Spanish colonization penetrated into southern Colorado, but not far enough or early enough to bring all of present Colorado within the scope of this definition.

The significance of the cultural definition lies in the unity which it provides for historical study. First, the Aboriginal Southwest, centered in this Spanish Southwest, contributed much to the cultural background. Next, under Spain the entire region was crisscrossed by expeditions of exploration and thus became the locale of institutions having essentially common characteristics. Later, the Southwest experienced its peculiar trends and troubles during the Mexican Period, which terminated in a war between Mexico and the United States and extended across the whole region. Likewise, the Civil War had its effect all through these Borderlands. Meanwhile common problems of acculturation appeared throughout, and they were accompanied by the ultimate subjugation of the nomadic Indian. Development of the transportation lines, of the cattle industry, and of agriculture by irrigation continued the unity in the story beyond the Civil War. Thenceforth industrial development and its accompanying trends contributed to a parting of the ways. The four states since 1900 have acquired respective distinguishing characteristics; yet this recent era of emerging individuality is quite brief in contrast with the three centuries of essential unity. The historian finds the common experiences of the past helpful in interpreting the recent superstructure of diverging development.

The transition from Spanish to English in the Southwest has created a few problems in writing. Although certain proper names, such as Mexico, Santa Barbara, and Rio Grande, once bore accent marks, they now have become anglicized. Names like Gómez may also appear without an accent mark without confusing the experienced Southwesterner; yet elsewhere such names may be uncommon in English usage. The guiding rule, therefore, is the extent to which such names may be considered anglicized. On the other hand, some reviewers still criticize an author for omission of an accent mark on Santa Fe, whereas its use on certain monosyllables has been ruled as incorrect in Spanish usage for fifty years.

In the employment of italics, the same rule — the extent of adoption in English — may also be applied. Thus such common terms as "padre," "fiesta," and "peso" need not be italicized, while others like *audiencia, vara,* and *alcalde,* still essentially foreign, are printed in italics.

Confusion has arisen also in the abbreviation of Spanish family names. Some early writers in English mistook the final word in a name for the last name and thus wrote about Coronado and Cárdenas. Now an understanding of the Spanish custom of creating a compound last name is becoming more prevalent. Often the final part is the mother's name, added for one generation, whereas the continuing paternal name appears to be a middle name. Sometimes the second part of the surname is the location of the ancestral

home, as the village of Coronado in Spain was for the Vásquez family. Therefore, if a shortened form for Coronado or Cárdenas is to be employed, it should be Vásquez or López, respectively. In the case of such long-established errors, it is difficult now to make a semantic correction. Nevertheless, at least in the use of less familiar names, for which no such error has become ingrained, the correct designation can be employed.

Certainly one person alone cannot produce a text of regional coverage. Extensive use of numerous sources has been necessary, and all have been listed among the titles included in the classified bibliography. Reference assistance has also been contributed by several libraries. An obligation thus has accrued to staff members of the Thomas C. Donnelly Library of New Mexico Highlands University, of the Library of the State Museum of New Mexico, of the Bancroft Library at the University of California, and of the libraries of the state universities in Arizona, New Mexico, and Texas.

In addition, my gratitude is extended to Dr. LeRoy R. Hafen, Professor of History at Brigham Young University, to Father J. F. Bannon of St. Louis University, and to Dr. C. L. Sonnichsen, Professor of English in the University of Texas at El Paso, for reading the entire manuscript and suggesting some needed improvements.

Lynn I. Perrigo

Las Vegas, New Mexico
January 1971

CONTENTS

LIST OF
MAPS AND CHARTS

A PHOTO ESSAY ON
THE AMERICAN SOUTHWEST

1
BEFORE COLUMBUS

To comprehend the arid and beautifully strange Land of Desert, Mesa, and Mountain, one begins by studying its sky. As source of the intense heat and frugal moisture, Sky Determines climate, and climate determines flora, fauna, and the general aspect of the country. The sky has, since long before the dawn of history, exercised compelling potency in shaping the destiny of the human inhabitants, and this fact permeates all southwestern anthropology, history, and economics.

Ross Calvin, Sky Determines *(Albuquerque, 1965), p. 9.*

THE ENVIRONMENT

Brilliant sunshine, tempering altitude, and periodic aridity characterize most of the region now known as the Southwest.

From the Red Prairie of central Texas the elevation increases gradually to four or five thousand feet above sea level on the plains of western Texas and eastern New Mexico. Even higher elevation is encountered in north central New Mexico, where the hogback foothills and granite ranges of the Rocky Mountains extend southward from Colorado. West of this range the Intermontane Region is represented first by the Colorado Plateau, where the average elevation of the tableland is four thousand feet and high-

lands rise to eight thousand. This region also includes basins which are near sea level. The largest is known as the Mojave-Gila Desert.

High altitudes prevail in parts of the Pacific coastal region, especially in the north-south ranges of the Sierra Nevada of eastern California. There is also the lower, round-top Coastal Range, broken off precipitously in places by the cliffs overlooking the ocean. South of these two ranges lie the transversal, or east-west, ranges of the San Bernardino and San Gabriel Mountains. They separate the low-lying Central Valley of California to the north from the Los Angeles Lowland to the south. High altitude

1

thus prevails throughout much of the Southwest.

Although the mountain ranges themselves attract precipitation, they also cause much of the aridity of neighboring localities. Moisture in wind currents is condensed into precipitation whenever those winds rise, as they are forced to do in passing over mountains, or whenever they encounter cooling influences, as they may do by movement either northward or into higher altitudes. In the winter season, especially, the prevailing westerlies lose their moisture on mountain slopes as they move inland toward higher altitudes. Then as they cross a lowland or plateau, with most of their moisture lost, they blow dry the rest of the way.

If the Southwest were dependent solely upon moisture drifting across from the Pacific Ocean, obviously the eastern parts would be a desert. That extremity is prevented by another movement of air currents. The prevailing westerlies have storm centers of low atmospheric pressure, which attract inward movements of currents from the surrounding area of higher pressure. As those storm centers move eastward across the Rocky Mountains, they cause moisture-laden currents of air to move inland from the Gulf of Mexico. As those currents rise, their moisture condenses and falls as rain or snow on the high plains and the higher mountain ranges.

The contour of plains, plateaus, and mountains stands out distinctly on a map of precipitation in the Southwest. Rainfall of thirty to forty inches annually in eastern Texas decreases inland to the west. The valley of the Rio Grande in southern New Mexico, the Mojave-Gila Basin bordering the Colorado River in western Arizona and southeastern California, and the Central Valley of the latter state have below ten inches annually. Those lowlands, therefore, are the deserts of the Southwest—the land of cactus, yucca, mesquite, and creosote bush. The higher altitudes of the plateaus and highlands causes those localities to fare somewhat better. The Staked Plain of eastern New Mexico, the Big Bend country of western Texas, the Colorado Plateau of western New Mexico and eastern Arizona, and the coastal ranges of Southern California have precipitation amounting to from ten to twenty inches annually. On the mesas, or tablelands, the moisture is sufficient to sustain grass, sagebrush, and wild flowers, while in the highlands it produces a growth of juniper, piñon, fir, and pine trees.

Precipitation is even more bountiful, ranging from twenty to thirty inches annually, in the Sacramento Mountains and Sangre de Cristo ranges of New Mexico, and from twenty to fifty inches in the Sierra Nevada of California. Up to timberline at about ten thousand feet, the slopes of those mountains bear heavy stands of pine, fir, and spruce, and, in California, giant redwood trees. The mountains, therefore, become the focal point of activity in the Southwest. They provide the playgrounds for those who like to go fishing, hunting, skiing, and camping. They produce the timber for the building of cities in their vicinity, as well as minerals and grazing land to help sustain the economy. Moreover, most of the rain and snow of the Southwest falls in the mountain elevations, and the trees and grasses hold much of it there. The water in mountain streams flows to lower lands, where it is used to irrigate the fields and to supply the cities. Ross Calvin in *Sky Determines* has aptly summarized the role of the mountains, at present and through the ages:

Mountains are the authentic abode of the Sky Powers, who in the beginning determined the function of lofty ridges and peaks in the economy of nature. There, in majestic councils, they deliberate upon such basic matters as rainfall for the valleys and grazing lands, coolness for tempering the desert heat, frost for ripening the corn, winter snows for feeding the trout streams.[1]

The present physical and climatic features have prevailed since the time of Christopher Columbus, with some periodic variations. After all, five centuries comprise a relatively short period in the evolution of the cosmos. Geologists have uncovered evidence that twenty thousand years ago this region was a cold, moist zone of pine forests dotted with lakes, swamps, and glacier-covered mountains. The fauna then included mammoth, giant bison, antelope, mastodon, and the eohippus, a small primitive horse. Such was the environment of the earliest men who arrived in the present Southwest; the warming and drying trend did not set in until about ten thousand years later.

EARLY INHABITANTS

Weapons, tools, and remains of the campfires of Ice Age hunters have been found at two locations in the Southwest, one in the Sandía Mountains of New Mexico and another near Midland in Texas. Recently remains of a similar age have been found at the Tule site in the southern tip of Nevada. By measurement of the faint radioactivity emanating from burnt remains, scientists have dated the time of origin of all three sites at more than twenty-thousand years ago.

Next in age came the hunters of the transitional era about ten thousand years later. They were the Folsom Man of northeastern New Mexico and the Cochise Man of southeastern Arizona. Unfortunately their campsites reveal little beyond the fact that they, too, were nomadic hunters. The artifacts include spear-throwers, hammer stones, bone needles, and projectile points made of stone. Nearby are the discarded bones of game which they had killed and consumed.

EMERGENCE OF VILLAGES

About 3000 B.C., the cultivation of corn introduced a significant change in the pattern of life. The Indians settled down in villages, where the men became farmers rather than hunters and the women learned to make baskets and handwoven fabrics. The people of that era are known today as the "Basket Makers," whose culture reached its zenith from about 100 to 700 A.D. At first they built one-room shelters of logs, twigs, and mud, located either inside caves or out in the open. Later they constructed individual stone dwellings. With their digging-sticks they cultivated small patches of corn, beans, and

[1] Sky Determines, p. 63.

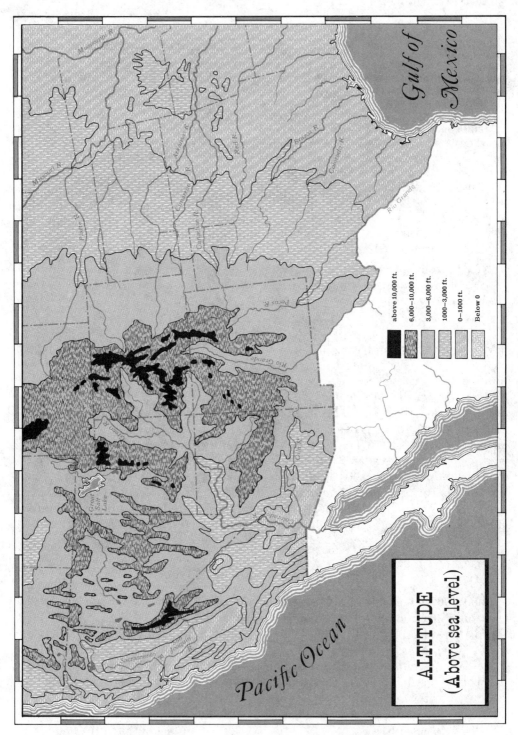

Gulf of Mexico

Pacific Ocean

above 10,000 ft.
6,000—10,000 ft.
3,000—6,000 ft.
1000—3,000 ft.
0—1000 ft.
Below 0

ALTITUDE
(Above sea level)

4

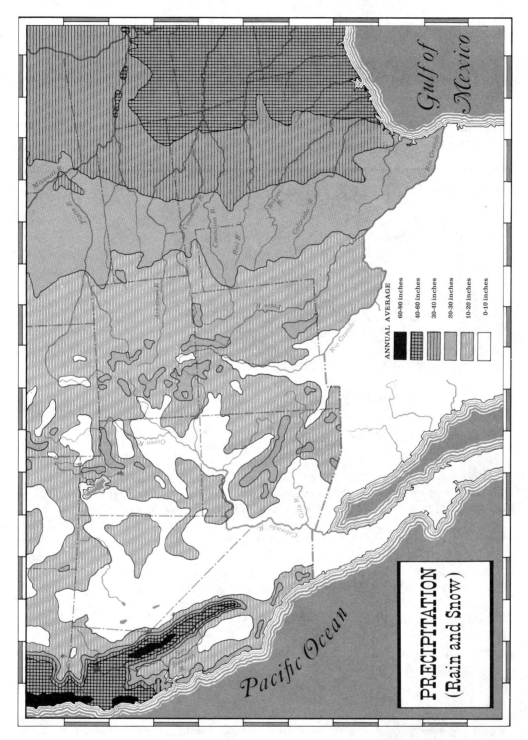

PRECIPITATION
(Rain and Snow)

ANNUAL AVERAGE

60-80 inches
40-60 inches
30-40 inches
20-30 inches
10-20 inches
0-10 inches

Gulf of Mexico

Pacific Ocean

Rio Grande

Missouri R.

Platte R.

Arkansas R.

Cimarron R.

Canadian R.

Red R.

Brazos R.

Colorado R.

Pecos R.

Rio Grande

Green R.

Gila R.

Colorado R.

5

pumpkins, which they supplemented by gathering wild vegetables. They had domesticated dogs and possibly also raised turkeys. Their highest developed art was basketry, both coiled and plaited. They used baskets of several sizes and shapes for storage vessels, as cooking utensils, and transport containers. Other artifacts found at their village sites include arrowheads, battle clubs, spears, spear-throwers, stone knives, grinding-stones, clay pipes, plaited sandals, fabrics woven from yucca fiber, and robes made of rabbit furs and turkey feathers.

When the Spaniards who later came found Indians living in villages, they referred to them as *pueblo* or "community" Indians, and that name has continued to the present. The typical Pueblo people, however, were round-headed invaders who had come among the long-headed Basket Makers and presently displaced them in some localities. Even so, they seem to have borrowed from and built upon the achievements of the preceding Basket Makers. One of their innovations was the molding of pottery. After an introductory epoch, known as Pueblo I, came the period from about 700 to 1000 A.D. known as "Developmental Pueblo" or "Pueblo II."

Archeologists have located three principal areas of early Pueblo activity. Apparently the earliest, known as the Mogollón-Mimbres culture, emerged in the locality of the Cochise hunters. Around 500 A.D., the Mogollón-Mimbres people began building small groups of pit houses with earthen floors sunk a few feet below ground level and with roofs supported on posts. They made stone weapons and tools as well as a plain brown pottery, and they had domesticated dogs. By about 1000 A.D. their descendants were living in adjoining rectangular rooms built of masonry on top of the ground. The walls, made of boulders plastered with mud, supported roofs of brush and grasses. Some villages had as many as forty rooms surrounding a central open space or plaza. The rooms had no windows or doors and were accessible only through openings in the roofs. A few large, round, partly subterranean rooms apparently served as "kivas," or meeting places like those that appeared later in the northern pueblos.

By this time the potter's art had superseded that of the Basket Maker. The Mogollón-Mimbres pottery is a beautiful black-on-white with near-perfect geometric designs. The decorations sometimes include natural, lifelike figures. The ruins of their dwellings have yielded stone bowls, grinding-stones, arrowheads, stone axes, hammer stones, hoes, spears, knives, and drills. Because charred corn has been found, obviously the cultivating of corn provided some of the food, supplemented by hunting and gathering.

West of the Mogollón peoples, or in central and southern Arizona, appeared a similar culture now known as "Hohokam." Its emergence dates back to the first century A.D., when these people were living in rectangular pit houses larger than those of the Mogollóns but lacking the kivas. Corn had become their staple food, so that there was less dependence upon hunting.

After a thousand years of relatively sedentary life, the Hohokam people were joined by others known as "Salados," who moved in from the central part of present Arizona. At first their pueblo structures were only one story high, but later some of them were multi-room, rectangular adobe dwellings of several stories. The Casa Grande in Arizona stands today as an example of the later type of pueblo.

In their villages the two groups of people seem to have intermingled peacefully. They dug great irrigation canals for extensive production of cotton and food crops, including corn, squash, and beans. They, too, had a well-developed pottery. The most common characteristic was the application of red paint to create decorative rectilinear figures. Their tools included stone axes, picks, saws, hammers, hoes, drills, knives, and polishing implements. Remains of finely woven cotton garments and twilled matting also have been found.

In economic achievement, the Hohokam people by 1000 A.D. certainly had surpassed their neighbors, the Mogollóns; yet their success was of little consequence, for around 1400 A.D.

both the Hohokam and Mogollón cultures collapsed. Perhaps the causes were exhaustion of the soil and failure of their irrigation system. The latter explanation is supported by stunted tree rings for the years from 1276 to 1299 A.D., indicating that the entire Southwest experienced a serious drought enduring through those twenty-three years. At any rate both the Mogollóns and Salados moved out. Some anthropologists believe that they went southward into Chihuahua, where they may have merged with other peoples to become the present Tarahumara Indians.

As for the Hohokams, they apparently deserted their larger dwellings and reverted to the simpler practices of earlier years. They may have merged with others to survive today as Pimas and Pápagos, or they may have become extinct. It was the Pimas who later told the Spaniards about their predecessors whom they called *Hohokam* or "vanished people."

A CULTURAL CENTER

A third large area of early Pueblo culture, known as the "Anasazi," was located northward from the two just described. The zone of highest development encircled the present "four corners" where Arizona, New Mexico, Colorado, and Utah now join. At about 200 A.D., a Basket Maker culture emerged in that locality, with features apparently borrowed from peoples to the south. Later, however, the Anasazi influence was destined to overshadow the neighboring cultures and to make contributions to their development.

In the Anasazi area the Pueblo I era

emerged about 700 A.D., and a little after 1000 A.D. the transition was made through the Pueblo II period to Pueblo III, the Golden Age, that endured for about two centuries. Some of the people of that era were medium long-headed, while others were round-headed, with skulls flattened on the back. Some lived in cliff dwellings, of which Mesa Verde is a well-known example, and others dwelt in large towns out in the open, as in Chaco Canyon. Those towns were comprised of a terraced series of adjoining rooms built of stone and plastered with mud mortar. The rooms, connected by means of small doorways, were covered on the top story by a thatched roof laid on poles. Each town had small or large kivas built underground and accessible only by ladders. The kivas were used by the men for religious ceremonies.

The Pueblo III economy had advanced considerably beyond that of the Basket Maker era. The fields were larger and now they were planted in cotton, beans, and pumpkins, as well as several varieties of corn. The bow and arrow had become an effective weapon for defense and for hunting wild game. By that time the animals available for stalking were much the same as in that locality today—the bear, elk, buffalo, deer, sheep, wolf, and rabbit. Interesting articles found in the ruins of the townsites include bracelets, beads, combs, brushes, bells, whistles, canes, buttons, needles, dice, pendants, rope, and stone tools. For containers some coiled baskets were in use, but pottery was much more prevalent and now it had become highly specialized in design. There was the Mesa Verde pottery with its bands of geometric designs, the Chaco Canyon type with its fine-line decorations, and the Kayenta design of zigzag lines, all with black painted on white. In addition there were several kinds of colored pottery and even some of polychrome, decorated with two or more colors.

After about 1300 A.D., most of the great cities of the Pueblo III era in the Anasazi region were abandoned. Perhaps a plague caused those superstitious people to move away from the "evil spirits," or perhaps the invasion of hostile, nomadic tribes was a contributing factor. However, again a likely cause was that long drought of the late thirteenth century, followed by conditions even more arid than previously. Today in some of the abandoned pueblos irrigation ditches originate in arroyos where water flows only occasionally after a heavy rain.

Whatever the cause, the Pueblo people entered upon their fourth period in which they moved to new locations and revised somewhat their techniques.

HISTORIC PUEBLOS

Two of the early sites, at Oraibi in Arizona and at Ácoma, the "sky city," in New Mexico, continued to be occupied.

Elsewhere the Anasazi people reassembled in pueblos which have been classified in linguistic families, as follows:

KERES	TIWA	TEWA	TOWA	HOKAN	AZTEC-NANOON
Ácoma	Isleta	Nambé	Jémez	Hopi	Zuñi
Santa Ana	Picurís	Santa Clara	Pecos	(Same	(Same
Cochití	Sandía	San Ildefonso		as	as
Santo Domingo	Taos	San Juan		Yuma	Pima)
San Felipe		Tesuque		and	
Zía				Sioux)	

For a simpler analysis, a division into river pueblos and desert pueblos is possible. The former group includes all of those in the valley of the Rio Grande and one to the east on the Pecos River, while the latter group is comprised of the Ácoma, Hopi, and Zuñi villages, with the later addition of Laguna.

At the desert settlements laborious dry farming produced corn, beans, squash, tobacco, and greens. The houses were single-story stone structures built close together around the village plaza. Many of the practices were similar to those of the earlier Pueblo III peoples. Among others was the creation of pottery typical of each village. For the Zuñi pueblos it was a greenish glaze over a white geometric design on an orange background, or a purplish black on a white base, and in the Hopi villages it was a black and red geometric design on a yellow base.

The women of the desert pueblos wore square sleeveless garments made of a cotton cloth, while the men wore cotton kilts and yucca sandals. Both also wrapped themselves with woolen blankets when needed. They lived in closely knit villages in which the women did the work of the household, while the men tended the fields and conducted the religious rites. Marriage was strictly monogamous, but a divorce was easily obtained. Descent was matrilineal. The woman owned the house, and newly-weds resided in a room provided by the bride's mother. The father's role was more like that of a friendly counsellor for his children than a severe patriarch.

The religion of the desert pueblos explained in simple terms their presence on earth and required their observance of worshipful ritual. The Hopi *Kachinas* (masked rain-beings) and supernatural clowns danced in the village streets, and Zuñi priests entertained the new-year spirits who came to bring their blessings. The organized priesthood offered the only hope for cure from illness, because communication with the controlling spirits could be maintained only by their ceremonial intercession. Government was controlled by organized societies in which the ceremonial chief was selected according to traditional rules. In other words, control of society both in religion and government was restricted to a select few.

The river pueblos differed in many respects from the desert villages. They had water for irrigation, which greatly facilitated agricultural production. They also had clay suitable for the construction of hand-molded adobe buildings. Moreover, in the northern pueblos, where cotton could not be grown, clothing was made of buckskin. Each pueblo had its own type of pottery, but all of it had a common characteristic in the use of geometric polychrome designs and the application of a glaze paint.

In contrast with the restrictions of the desert pueblos, those in the river valley maintained societies and activities which were open to anyone, and a young man could work his way up without relying upon inherited advantages. Resort to warfare was more frequent, perhaps due to the greater individualism. In family organization a distinct difference prevailed in some pueblos, where descent was patrilineal. Despite the social individualism, land ownership and management was communal.

The government of each river pueblo was controlled by a council comprised by rotation of the leaders in social groups and organized clans. The council selected a political chief and a war chief. Although religious functions were closely intertwined with those of the government, there was a separate religious leader, or cacique, who was chosen to serve through his lifetime.

Their religion expressed a serious concept of God and Nature with a dual principle of female and male in everything. This concept found expression in all arts and activities. Religious beliefs also called for prayerful corn dances and other ceremonies devoted to productivity.

SPANISH CONTACTS

The Anasazi peoples had not disappeared like the Mogollón and Salados; instead they were still present when the Spaniards came. In fact, their numbers were relatively large, perhaps fifty thousand in the river pueblos at the time of the conquest. One group of desert villages, the Zuñi, heralded as the "Seven Cities," provided a stimulation for early exploration, and the presence of people in such numbers offered opportunities for conversion of the heathen to Christianity. The Spanish conquerors admired especially the advanced culture of the river pueblos and recorded what they observed. Thus they provided posterity with documents useful in reconstructing a view of pueblo life in that era. As one illustration, Hernán Gallegos, who accompanied the Rodríguez expedition in 1581, wrote as follows of the Pueblos whom they called the "Tigua":

We entered the settlement where the inhabitants gave us much corn. They showed us many ollas and other earthenware containers, richly painted, and brought quantities of calabashes and beans for us to eat. . . . In these pueblos there are also houses of three and four stories similar to the ones we had seen before, but the farther one goes into the interior, the larger are the pueblos and the more numerous its people.

These people are handsome and fair-skinned. They are very industrious. Only the men attend to the work of the fields. The day hardly breaks before they go about with hoes in their hands. The women busy themselves only in the preparation of food and in making and painting their pottery and pans in which they prepare their bread.[2]

Gallegos wrote much more about all the sights he saw, as did also his companion, Pedro de Bustamante. The latter described in third person, for example, a Pueblo called "Puaray" near present Bernalillo with glowing praise:

These were the finest people of all they had met, possessing better pueblos and houses, and were the ones who treated them best, giving them most generously of what they had. They have well-built houses of four and five stories, with corridors and rooms twenty-four feet long and thirteen feet wide, white-washed and painted. They have very good plazas, and leading from one to the other are streets along which they pass in good order. Like the others they have a good supply of provisions. Two or three leagues are other pueblos of the same nation, and consisting of three or four hundred houses, built in the same fashion. They dress in cotton like the foregoing nations.[3]

[2] George P. Hammond and Agapito Rey, ed. and trans., *The Rediscovery of New Mexico* (Albuquerque, 1966), p. 84.

[3] Herbert Eugene Bolton, ed., *Spanish Exploration in the Southwest* (New York, 1949), p. 146.

There were other less sedentary Indians in that locality, however, as Bustamante and Gallegos soon saw. When they traveled eastward to verify the presence of bison on the plains, they found some nomadic Indians who elicited less admiration. Those people they called *ranchería* Indians to distinguish them from the Pueblos. Here is the observation of Gallegos, as translated by Agapito Rey:

We came upon a ranchería on this river in which we found fifty huts and tents made of hides with strong white flaps after the fashion of field tents. Here we were met by more than four hundred warlike men armed with bows and arrows who asked us by signs what we wanted. . . .

These semi-naked people wear only buffalo hides and deerskins for covering for themselves. At this season they live on buffalo meat, but during the rainy season they go in search of prickly pears and yucca. They have dogs which carry loads of two or three arrobas, and they put leather pack-saddles on these animals, with poitrels and cruppers.[4]

Indeed there were many tribes and families of nomadic and semisettled Indians in the Southwest, as other Spaniards would find as they pursued their explorations.

NOMADIC INVADERS

Somewhere near 1200 A.D. a group of nomadic peoples had migrated from the north to the fringe of the Pueblo world. Their frequent raids caused the abandonment of outlying settlements, and soon some of the nomads had taken over vacant spaces between the areas of Pueblo concentration. Thereafter the rival groups engaged in a running contest of raiding and warfare.

The newcomers, whose original habitat had been western Canada, were taller on the average than the Pueblo Indians, and they spoke a singsong Athapascan dialect. The Pueblos called them "Apaches," meaning "enemies." One tribe, which penetrated into the vacated Anasazi center in the present four-corners area, came to be known as *Apaches de Nabahú*, which was later contracted to one word, *Navajo* (sometimes spelled *Navaho*). Other tribes were the Jicarilla Apaches of northern New Mexico, the Mescalero Apaches of the southeastern part of the same state,

the Lipán Apaches of the Big Bend country, the Mimbreño Apaches west of the Rio Grande, and across the line in what is now Arizona were the Western Apaches, or the Chiricahua, San Carlos, Tonto, White Mountain, and other tribes.

Originally the Navajos were rather primitive hunters, but from the Pueblos they stole sheep and horses, after these animals had been introduced by the Spaniards. In time they also learned to weave woolen blankets and to make silver jewelry. A shorter, stockier physique among some of the clans resulted from intermarriage with the Pueblos. The typical dwelling was the hogan, a several-sided structure of stones or logs, covered with earth. Because the clans were matrilineal, women had an important role in their society. These people were very religious and pleasant, intelligent, and artistic as well. They wor-

[4] Hammond and Rey, p. 89.

shipped their nature gods with much mythic lore, including hundreds of formal songs and prayers.

While this one tribe was acquiring many of the sedentary traits associated with corn culture, the others continued to be essentially nomadic hunters and raiders. They dwelt in brush shelters and remained in one place only temporarily. From the Spaniards they had obtained horses, and then they soon acquired a reputation as exceedingly elusive, fierce, warlike predators. Their roving existence discouraged the development of the arts beyond the feminine skills in making the necessary baskets and buckskin clothing. A leader of one of the larger, wealthier clans usually served as chief of the tribe.

East of Apacheland another band of warlike, nomadic people came to the high plains of western Texas but a little later than the time of the Apache migration into New Mexico. These Indians, the Comanches, were also rather large in stature but slightly more corpulent than the lanky Apaches. They were an offshoot of the Shoshonean people of the northern plains. Now they had become nomadic buffalo hunters, camping at any one location only briefly in their moveable tipis. They obtained their food, clothing, tools, and tipi skins from the product of their hunting and had developed their social and ceremonial life around the ritual of the buffalo hunt.

Such a society lessened the role of women and enhanced, instead, the social standing of the brave young warriors. After the Comanches had acquired horses from the Spaniards, they became some of the most skillful and hardy riders of the Southwest.

OTHER TRIBES

A family of tribes known as the Caddo occupied the southeastern part of present Texas. These Indians were a semi-settled people who lived partly by growing corn and vegetables and partly by hunting the buffalo. They occupied villages of conical huts made of poles thatched over with grass; and they made their garments of cloth woven from vegetable fibers. Most of them wore decorative rings in holes pierced through the nasal septum. As a rule members of one tribe could be distinguished from the others by characteristic types of tattooing. The chieftainship of a tribe was hereditary, and descent was matrilineal. Their religious ceremonies were devoted both to the hunting of game and to the raising of corn. In them the Caddo emphasized the value of truth and honesty as well as the future reunion of kin in an after-life.

Ten or twelve divisions, composed of many subtribes, made up the Caddo confederacy. Among them the Asinais, or Hasinai, was the largest group, numbering perhaps five thousand souls. According to Spanish legend it was they who greeted the explorers as *tehas*, meaning "friends" or "allies." Mistaking this salutation for the name of the tribe, the Spaniards called those Indians the *Tejas*, which could also be spelled *Texas*. However, some students of history believe that the *tehas* greeting came not from the Hasinai but from a group of Jumano Indians residing in the western part of what is now Texas.

Of all the numerous tribes located in particular localities in the Southwest, only a few more can be singled out for a brief description in this introductory sketch. Because of their role in history, certainly the Pima and Yuma deserve inclusion.

The Pimas occupied the region of the former Hohokam and used their ancient irrigation system to draw water from the Gila River for irrigation of their fields of corn and vegetables. They had a legend that they once had lived in pueblos but had been forced out, and upon their return later they had not rebuilt their former houses. Instead, they resided in thatched huts and engaged in a semi-settled existence based upon hunting and agriculture. For the one their weapon was the bow and arrow, while for the other their principal tool was the planting-stick. This tribe had five divisions, in which descent and authority was patrilineal. Marriage was arranged easily, and polygamy was approved if a warrior could support several wives. Women performed most of the laborious tasks, as was characteristic of cultures based upon hunting, including the making of their tightly plaited, waterproof baskets. Each village had a council and a chief, and the several chiefs chose one to head the tribe. These formerly warlike people were rather peaceably inclined when they were first encountered by the early explorers.

To the west of the Pimas, the Pápagos, also semisettled, managed to subsist in a rather harsh environment. More significant in early history were the Yumas, because their domain straddled the lower Colorado River. They had several subdivisions, including the Mojave; but attention is given here to the Yuma proper. Although they had a social organization like that of other hunting societies, they were corn growers. When they first became known to the Spaniards, they had, apparently, only recently settled down to sedentary ways. The men were tall and strong, whereas the women were more corpulent. Since they counted descent in the male line and also practiced polygamy, a warrior resided with his several wives and his male offspring and their children in one large family house — a sort of communal lodge constructed of cottonwood logs. The women wore only a small apron and the men a breechcloth, and both bore extensive tattoo marks. They exalted their warriors and medicine men, who relied heavily upon "dream power." In other words, they believed that revelations derived from dreams gave them wisdom and strength. They even chose their war chief upon his demonstration of superior dream power. The hereditary civilian chief served only in an advisory capacity. The Yumas cremated their dead. Annually all the relatives assembled for an elaborate mourning ceremony consisting of speeches, songs, and the burning of an effigy.

VARIETY IN CALIFORNIA

Although some anthropologists contend that the Pueblo Indians must have migrated northward from the Aztec center in what is now Mexico, a more commonly accepted theory is that the Indians of North America migrated southward in wave after wave, through many centuries, after having originally crossed from Asia. If the latter theory is the sound one, then wave after wave must have left a tribe residing in California while the main body pushed on to the south or in some cases to the east. Within the bounds of the area now known as California there were approximately fifty tribal groups speaking twenty-one dialects and representing five major linguistic families. Many of the tribes were quite small, while others filled rather densely the place where they resided. Estimates have placed the total number at over one hundred thousand.

The Yumas of the valley of the Colorado River already have been mentioned. To the west and north were several tribes which had little in common except their practice of gathering roots and herbs for food. Hence they acquired the appellation "Digger Indians." Some such tribes, that had been "reduced" into missions by the Spaniards, came to be known as "Mission Indians." Five tribes of central California spoke the Penutian language, which was related to the Sahaptin of the Intermontane Plateau. Others in California were linguistic cousins of the Navajo of the Southwest, of the Sioux of the Great Plains, and of the Algonkian of the northeast coast.

Among the Penutian people, the Maidu and Miwok were the more numerous. Their location was inland from present Sacramento. They exercised care to stay within their established localities in order to avoid warfare with their neighbors. They had medicine men, but no war chiefs. Legend has it that in case of a dispute the tribes each chose a champion and let those two representatives fight it out. The economy of these people was based upon both hunting and gathering. They were Basket Makers to perfection. The basketry of some tribes was noted for its superior construction with decorations of colored beads and feathers. Like the Yumas these Indians wore little clothing, counted descent through the father, emphasized dream power, and cremated their dead. Their dwellings, on the other hand, were partially excavated pit houses, different from those large log homes of the Yuma.

Among the Mission Indians the Luiseño of the Mission San Luis Rey may be considered as typical. They lived between the coast and the San Jacinto River, and they spoke a dialect related to the Shoshonean of the region which later became Wyoming. Otherwise they shared some similarities with the Yuma. They wore little clothing, had father clans, valued dream power, cremated their dead, and conducted mourning ceremonies. On the other hand, like some of their neighbors in California, they lived in pit houses covered with thatching, and they traded with shell money. Their pottery and basketry was rather crude, and they combined some hunting with the gathering of roots, nuts, and herbs. Among them an

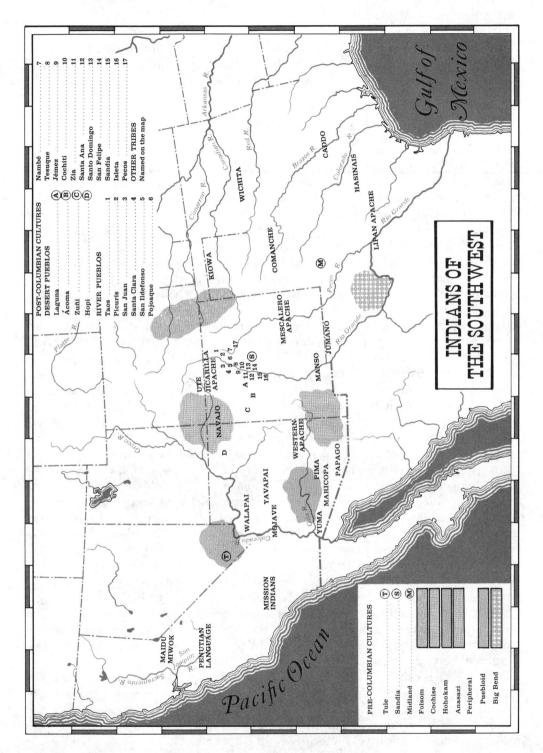

INDIANS OF THE SOUTHWEST

POST-COLUMBIAN CULTURES

DESERT PUEBLOS
- (A) Laguna
- (B) Ácoma
- (C) Zuñi
- (D) Hopi

RIVER PUEBLOS
1. Taos
2. Picuris
3. San Juan
4. Santa Clara
5. San Ildefonso
6. Pojoaque
7. Nambé
8. Tesuque
9. Jémez
10. Cochiti
11. Zia
12. Santa Ana
13. Santo Domingo
14. San Felipe
15. Sandia
16. Isleta
17. Pecos

OTHER TRIBES
Named on the map

PRE-COLUMBIAN CULTURES
- Tule
- Sandia
- Midland
- Folsom
- Cochise
- Hohokam
- Anasazi
- Peripheral
- Puebloid
- Big Bend
- (T)
- (S)
- (M)

Gulf of Mexico

Pacific Ocean

interesting ritual was the use of ground paintings for instruction of girls and boys at adolescence. This practice may have come from the distant Navajo or Pueblo people, or perhaps it could have been the other way around.

ABORIGINAL CULTURES

This summary of several representative aboriginal cultures reveals that nearly all bear evidence of earlier migrations and diffusion of traits. Some apparently had appeared only recently in their pre-Columbian locations, while others had a long history of evolution to a relatively advanced stage. In Arizona and New Mexico corn culture under irrigation had created a village life which encouraged an advanced artistry and a complex social organization. Difficulty of subsistence elsewhere discouraged a sedentary existence and its cultural attainments. Everywhere cultural traits were closely associated with the environment. On the plains the bison provided the means and inspiration of life, while in coastal valleys vegetal matter provided the source. Everywhere, therefore, one can only marvel at the aboriginal success in converting a semiarid land into a domicile for rich, primitive cultures.

All tribes left place names. All resisted conquest, and that in turn had its effect upon the conquerors by steeling them for a hard, physical contest, which eliminated weaknesses and emphasized material achievements. All tribes, too, stimulated exploration and investigation as missionary objectives. In the more favorable localities this produced a heritage of monumental mission landmarks.

On the role of the Indian in the Americas a provocative interpretation has been advanced by Charles C. Griffin in a collection of essays entitled *Concerning Latin American Culture.* The essence of it is that different outcomes for the Indians were due not so much to differences between their English, French, and Spanish conquerors as to variations in the levels of Indian culture. The advanced groups were more easily understood and had a larger population; therefore they were assimilated and became a fertile field for acculturation. The nomadic and semisettled peoples, on the other hand, could not be readily absorbed. Instead, they became decimated by the struggle for possession of the land.

In the story of the Southwest it will be seen that the Spaniards themselves developed different policies for the two types of Indians. For the nomads they seldom were able to operate missions successfully for long; instead, they resorted to endless defensive warfare under a policy of retaliation. Among the Pueblos, on the other hand, they were able to apply successfully most of the time a policy of assimilation, whereby those people kept their villages and some of their land. Admittedly, many became *peones* in the Spanish system, but at least they did survive.

Gradually, by intermarriage and by fusion of the cultures over the years of their coexistence, a great deal of the Pueblo heritage was assimilated into the Spanish culture.

2
THE
SEVEN CITIES

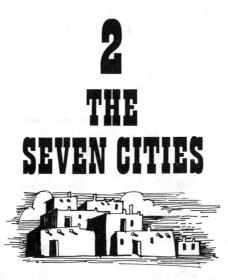

It now remains for me to tell about the Seven Cities, the kingdom
and province of which the father provincial gave your Lordship an
account. To make a long story short, I can assure you he has not told
the truth in a single thing he has said, for everything is the very opposite of what he related except the name of the cities and the large
stone houses. However, although they are not decorated with tur-
quoises, nor made of lime or good bricks, nevertheless they are very
good houses, three, four, and five storeys high.... The Seven Cities
are seven little villages, all having the kind of houses I have described, and all within a space of four leagues.

Francisco Vásquez de Coronado, quoted in Herbert Eugene Bolton,
Coronado on the Turquoise Trail (Albuquerque, 1949), p. 128.

From the birth of Christ to the fission
of the atom the event of greatest consequence to the modern world was the
discovery of an entire new continent
named America. Actually the event
of 1492 was not so much a discovery as
it was a spreading of timely news by a
good salesman, Christopher Columbus,
or Cristóbal Colón, to give him his
Spanish name. The new continent had
been found perhaps fifteen or more
times before Columbus, but Europe
had not been prepared for overseas
expansion. Such a startling idea had
even been difficult to accept by people
steeped in medieval superstition.

SPAIN IN AMERICA

By 1492, however, Spain had become a unified nation, one of the first in modern times. The medieval order was yielding under the pressures of maritime commerce, the profit motive, and religious unrest. Moreover, ships and instruments were ready for the task, and printing presses were available to spread the news. The Portuguese were ready, too, though they were pursuing their exploration of a route around Africa. Therefore Spain became the nation first interested in the proposal of Columbus and in the possibilities of capitalizing upon his findings.

After a Spanish colony had been founded at Santo Domingo in 1493, the center of activity soon shifted to La Habana in Cuba. From Habana, Juan Ponce de León ventured northward to explore the coast of Florida in 1513 and Francisco Hernández de Córdova sailed to Yucatán to capture a cargo of Indian slaves in 1517. Columbus had already explored the coast of Central America in search of a passageway through to India. Now to investigate further, another explorer, Alonzo Alvárez de Piñeda, embarked from Jamaica in 1519 with a fleet of four caravels. He circled the Gulf coast and made a map of it. Consequently he must have been the first European to see a part of our Southwest—the coast of present Texas.

At about that time Hernández de Córdova had brought back tales of great and rich inland cities, which he had heard about in Yucatán. This report persuaded the governor of Cuba that he should send forth a conquering expedition. Hernando Cortés led the band of four hundred and fifty soldiers who found the Aztec capital at Tenochtitlán in 1519 and soon conquered it. Renamed Mexico City in 1522, it became the capital of the province of New Spain. From it the conquest proceeded northward and southward.

A lieutenant of Cortés, one Nuño de Guzmán, conquered a little kingdom of his own on the northern frontier in 1531 and founded therein the town of San Miguel de Culiacán. Many other frontier outposts had been established, but Culiacán is singled out here because of its historic role in relation to the frontier of the "Seven Cities" of Cíbola, the "promised land" of the Indians.

FIRST ON THE FRONTIER

In 1536, Álvar Núñez Cabeza de Vaca and three companions wandered into Culiacán after making an astounding journey on foot across our Southwest. This man, whose appropriate paternal name, Núñez, has been slighted in history in favor of the distinguished family name of Cabeza de Vaca, came of illustrious Spanish ancestry noted for prior services to the king. In 1528, he had accompanied the ill-fated expedition of Pánfilo de Narváez, which set sail for Florida in search of riches like those already found in Mexico. After suffering defeat at the hands of hostile Indians in Florida, this band of conquerors found their plight serious, for Narváez had ordered his ships to sail away after the men had landed. In an effort to work their way around the Gulf coast, the two hundred and fifty survivors built rafts of logs lashed together with thongs of horsehide. A crew sailed the rafts westward near the coast, while their companions scouted ashore for food. Slowly they worked their way past the mouth of the Mississippi, only to have their crude rafts wrecked in a storm off the coast of Texas. About eighty of the men survived this disaster, but most of them soon became victims of disease and of Indian raids. Núñez was one of a few who were forced into slavery by the Indians. Presently, he made contact with three others, Alonso del Castillo Maldonado, Andrés Dorantes, and a Moorish slave known as Esteban or Estevanico.

Núñez soon learned the local art of herb-healing and became famous as a medicine man. As one tribe after another sought his services, he and his companions wisely worked their way westward, for somewhere in that direction they believed that they might ultimately reach Mexico. In the journal which Núñez later wrote from memory it is difficult to trace his path, for the Indian placenames which he mentioned are now unknown. Ten scholars who have tried to map his route have advanced several versions. A few conclude that he crossed northern Mexico without ever setting foot in the region which was to become New Mexico and Arizona. On the other hand, the majority favor the conclusion that he crossed central Texas to the Pecos River and thence to the Rio Grande beyond the Big Bend — that he followed it to a point above present El Paso be-

fore turning west again through southern Arizona to the Sonora River in northern Mexico and finally worked his way southward until he and his companions met a party of slave hunters near Culiacán. The Spaniards found it hard to believe that these three haggard, bronzed, almost naked men, accompanied by a Negro and a large escort of Indians, were also Spaniards. Likewise the Indians were incredulous at first, for, as Núñez related afterward, the Indians said

> ... that we cured the sick, while the others [Spaniards] killed those that were healthy; that we went naked and shoeless, whereas the others wore clothes and went on horseback with lances. Also that we asked for nothing, but gave away all that we were presented with, meanwhile the others seemed to have no other aim than to steal what they could, and never gave to anybody.[1]

In Mexico City the newly appointed viceroy, Antonio de Mendoza, listened with much interest to the story of the four adventurers. Then Núñez returned to Spain, where he wrote his book about his experiences. In it he gave a description of seven great cities which according to the Indians were located not far north of his pathway across the frontier. Dissemination of this news stimulated great interest. Here was another Marco Polo to arouse Europe to activity!

Certainly Álvar Núñez Cabeza de Vaca deserved some kind of a reward for his contribution. At that time reports of trouble with Indians were arriving from a place called "Asunción" in South America. Therefore the king

[1] Quoted in Morris Bishop, *The Odyssey of Cabeza de Vaca* (New York, 1933), p. 147.

appointed this friend of the Indians as governor of Asunción to replace a less-trusted man, Domingo Irala. En route to his new post in Paraguay, Núñez discovered the great waterfalls of Iguassú while he went on foot inland across Brazil. In Paraguay, however, he encountered opposition to his decrees banning slavery and polygamy. Irala and others conspired against him for thus revoking "the liberties of Spaniards." They filed formal charges and sent him in irons back to Spain to stand trial. After several years he was cleared of the charges, but his health and fortune had been sacrificed.

Thus ended the official career of this eminent explorer and indefatigable pedestrian; yet his influence continued long afterwards. Prospective explorers studied his guide book, and several colonists bearing his name, shortened to C. de Baca or even to Baca, later came as pioneers to the northern frontier of New Spain, where their descendants now reside.

SPANISH MOTIVES

From 1536 to the end of the century the Spaniards sought to find and conquer the Seven Cities. That overt goal, however, served as a symbol of factors more complex. Certainly an objective in the early years was the acquisition of quick wealth. As a result, a great lust for gold has been attributed to the Spaniards, and it is true that spectacular expeditions traveled afar in search of it. However, such behavior is not abnormal for any human beings when great riches are in sight. In the early years the English and French adventurers simply did not find any great deposits of precious metals to spur them on, otherwise they too no doubt would have spanned the continent rapidly. They had to seek other sources of wealth until gold was found in California, and then the Forty-Niners demonstrated that they were as avaricious as the Spaniards. Likewise those Spanish colonists who failed to find gold or silver also sought other sources of quick wealth. One which was extensively exploited was the Indian captives who were rounded up for sale into slavery. In those early years another motive also spurred on the Spaniards, and that was the opportunity for adventure and personal glory. In addition religious motivation cannot be dismissed lightly. In 1492, Spain had concluded successfully a great Catholic crusade against the Moors, and the crusading spirit was still alive. Under a king who had been honored by the Pope as "Our Holy Catholic Majesty," a sure path to glory and reward lay in professing a burning religious ambition. Therefore, whether they were sincere or not in those early years, nearly all conquerors took missionaries along with them and proclaimed that they intended to expand the Kingdom of God.

Quite early the lay conquerors and the religious leaders became engaged in a Great Debate as to whether the Indians were to be treated as mere work animals or as human beings with souls to be saved. After the clergy had won the king over to their viewpoint, from 1542 on the religious motive found a more sincere expression and resulted in greater evidence of effectiveness.

For the founding of missions and the conversion of natives, certainly those populous Seven Cities offered great promise.

After exploration had failed to uncover great deposits of precious metals, the lust for gold gave way to a lust for land. Especially did that desire motivate the younger sons of aristocratic families, because the rule of primogeniture barred them from inheriting a part of their father's estate. Land was the main emblem of wealth in those days, and a great estate abounding in serfs or slaves to do the work made a man an *hidalgo*, eligible to display his coat-of-arms and to revel in the luxuries of life.

Later, as rumors spread of the approach of the English, French, and Russian interlopers, another motive appeared. The Spaniards should establish outposts as distant as possible in order to intercept and frustrate their rivals. Therefore the early pattern of motives—wealth, adventure, and religion—prevalent from 1500 to about mid-century became transformed by 1600 into a new pattern—religion, land, and rivalry.

PROBING NORTHWARD

In the time of the able viceroy, Mendoza, the early set of motives produced a great flurry of activity. From 1538 to 1542 those rumors about the Seven Cities inspired no less than eight expeditions, three by sea and five by land. Perusal of the surviving documents reveals that in those years the Spaniards thought that North America was pear shaped with the broader part surrounding Mexico City. To the north it surely became narrower, so that the great cities might be reached as well by sea from either side as by travel overland to the north. And a little farther north there must be a passageway through from sea to sea; in fact, they were so certain about it that they had a name for the passageway: the "Strait of Anian." This mistaken concept explains why they attempted to converge upon the great cities from three sides. Asunción and Nadal, Fray Marcos, Díaz, and Coronado backtracked over the route of Núñez Cabeza de Vaca, while Ulloa, Alarcón, and Cabrillo, and Ferrelo sailed up the coast of the "South Sea" and Soto penetrated overland from Florida.

First, in 1538, two Franciscan friars, Juan de Asunción and Pedro Nadal, journeyed from Mexico City through Culiacán and northward in an effort to find the legendary "Seven Caves of Chicomoztoc" or "Aztlán," from which the Aztecs of Mexico believed their ancestors had come long ago. They also hoped to convert some of the Indians of Sonora. Upon their return they claimed to have traveled about seven hundred miles to a great river located at thirty-five degrees north latitude. That would put them on the lower Colorado River. They, too, heard reports of great cities inland, but did not claim to have seen them. Otherwise they brought back such unfavorable reports of a barren land that had the other Spaniards heeded them, exploration would have ceased then and there.

Meanwhile Mendoza had been seeking someone in whom he could trust for an investigation of the accuracy of the rumors about the Seven Cities. In the person of one Marcos de Niza he thought he had found his man, for it was Fray Marcos who had written a report about the despoiling of the Incas of Peru by Francisco Pizarro. The friar accepted the assignment, and by now the Moor, Esteban, was the only one of the companions of Núñez who was available to serve as guide. Therefore he should go along together with Fray Honorato and an escort of friendly Indians.

Early in 1539 the party departed from Culiacán, where Fray Honorato had dropped out due to illness. Soon Fray Marcos became alarmed at the conduct of Esteban, who was enjoying the venture quite heartily. Because the Indians regarded the strange Moor as a medicine man and magician, Esteban sought to exemplify the role by wearing bells on his ankles and elbows and carrying a gourd rattle decorated with feathers. Fray Marcos concluded that it would be wise to part company with his guide. Therefore he instructed Esteban to head an advance party which should send back a messenger carrying either a large cross or a small one as an indication of the magnitude of his discovery. Thus flattered, Esteban boldly went ahead as the "king" of a band of some three hundred Indians, while Fray Marcos followed cautiously several leagues behind.

Esteban and his party did find some Indian villages, the Zuñi Pueblos. As he approached the first town, Háwikuh, he arrogantly rattled his gourd and demanded gifts of turquoise and women. Because the Zuñi men protected the chastity of their women and the rattle was of a type carried by enemies of the Zuñi, Esteban found himself in a hornets' nest. As he fled, he was overtaken and killed, along with most of his Indian escort.

A few survivors bore the stunning news to Fray Marcos. He returned hastily to Mexico City for presentation of the report which was expected of him. In it he claimed that he had advanced within sight of the pueblo, which was a "very beautiful city,... bigger than the city of Mexico,... situated on the brow of a roundish hill." By describing it as one of the "Seven Cities of Cíbola" he introduced the use of the word *cíbola* (buffalo cow) in the title of these towns. He feared that if he became too bold, he might not survive to carry home the news; therefore he explained that after erecting a cross on a distant hill to establish a claim to those cities in the name of God, the Emperor, and the Viceroy, he had hastened homeward. Later historians have concluded that he must have fled faster than he cared to admit, without even viewing the pueblo. In his report he had not allowed enough time to travel the full distance to Háwikuh from where he said he had been encamped when the messengers arrived. Moreover, Háwikuh was located on a flat mesa and it was but one-sixtieth the size of Mexico City. Apparently Fray Marcos had drawn upon his imagination for part of his report.

While Marcos de Niza was making his reconnaissance, two other parties were on their way. One, aboard three ships under the command of Francisco de Ulloa, had sailed from Acapulco in southern Mexico up the west coast in July, 1539. As Ulloa came to the headwaters of the Gulf of California, he entered the Colorado River. However, the dangerous sand bars and the pitching of the ship in the tidal waves so frightened him that he abandoned his quest of the Seven Cities. Instead, he returned to the tip of Lower California and then worked up the Pacific coast to about twenty-eight degrees north latitude. Somewhere in the vicinity of the present Vizcaíno Bay in Lower California he put in for three winter months in 1539–1540. Then one ship returned to Mexico with news of the exploration of the Gulf.

This report established that Lower California, which had been earlier explored by Cortés, was not an island; but that conclusion soon was forgotten and had to be confirmed again later. With the two other ships Ulloa sailed on northward, but no record of that journey has ever been found.

BOLD EFFORTS

Another expedition already on the way when Fray Marcos returned was headed by Hernando de Soto. After accompanying Pizarro to Peru, he had become restless and hoped to find another such source of wealth in the land explored by Núñez Cabeza de Vaca. Therefore he had obtained a commission to conquer Florida, where he arrived in May of 1539. While he was en route, his secretary had learned that bids were being received by the viceroy of New Spain for the conquest of the Seven Cities. Consequently Soto's agent presented an application in his behalf, inasmuch as he was already on the way. That appointment, however, was granted to Coronado.

Near Tampa Bay, Hernando de Soto found Juan Ortiz, a survivor of the Narváez expedition who had been living among the Indians. Because Ortiz could converse with the Indians and had heard reports of gold somewhere in the interior, Soto took him along as a guide. Rapidly this expedition traveled through present Georgia, South Carolina, North Carolina, Tennessee, Alabama, Mississippi, and on across into Arkansas. Soto came within three hundred miles of Coronado's army, without either one knowing of the other until too late to make contact. No gold had been found; Juan Ortiz, guide and interpreter, had died; and now Soto himself was suffering from illness. Therefore he returned to the Mississippi River, where he died in May of 1542. His companions lowered his body into the river and told the Indians that he had gone on a visit to heaven, in order to maintain the fiction that Spaniards were immortal.

Soto had pushed his men onward with great determination. For emergency rations he had brought along some swine, which were driven slowly at the rear of the procession all the way from Florida. The hogs had multiplied until there were nearly seven hundred of them. Upon the death of the commander, discipline became relaxed and the zeal for exploration spent. The men chose for commander one Luis de Moscoso, who was more easy going. He would lead them out of this strange land, they hoped; but first he put the swine up for sale and the soldiers enjoyed a grand barbecue. Then Moscoso led the soldiers westward into present Texas, where at first they found the Indians numerous and the corn abundant. They talked to an Indian woman who had been held captive briefly by Coronado's men, and they found evidence that Álvar Núñez Cabeza de Vaca had traveled that way long before them. That reminded them that according to his report the Indians farther west "lived like arabs," meaning that there would be no corn to buy or confiscate. Therefore they again returned to the Mississippi River, where they built seven small boats for their return journey. As they floated down the river they ran the gauntlet of several Indian assaults. Finally, after an arduous journey around the Gulf coast, three hundred of the men arrived at the Spanish settlement of Pánuco (now Tampico). They had failed in their main objective, but they did return with information—in part accurate and in part fanciful—for European cartographers to use in their revision of the distorted maps of America. Meanwhile in New Spain, Antonio de Mendoza had been making preparations methodically for the conquest of the Seven Cities. In 1539, he sent a company of cavalry under the command of Melchior Díaz, *alcalde* at Culiacán, to explore the route and to analyze the reaction of the Indians. This advance party traveled to the desert south of the Gila River in present Arizona. Like Asunción and Nadal, Díaz had meagre praise for the country he had seen.

Next the viceroy instructed Hernando de Alarcón to sail three supply ships up the Gulf of California and into the lower reaches of the Colorado River. He was to provide logistic support for the main expedition; that he failed was not his fault. Undaunted by the bore of the Colorado River as Ulloa had been, he entered that "very mighty river, which ran with such great a fury of a stream, that...[he] could hardly sail against it."

He found numerous unfriendly Indians but no land party. He tarried a while, but not long enough to find Díaz who ultimately did arrive in that vicinity. Finally he sought to leave a message as proof that he had fulfilled his assignment and then sailed back to New Spain.

THE CORONADO EXPEDITION

At the same time the great expedition led by Coronado was also in the field. From among the applicants, Mendoza had selected as commander his young friend, Francisco Vásquez de Coronado. As in the case of Núñez, an error pertaining to the last name has become ingrained in English usage. His paternal name was really Vásquez, but he has been mistakenly called "Coronado" for so long that a correction now is not readily accepted. Vásquez had served ably as governor of the province of Nueva Galicia. Now he became the commander of an expedition of two hundred and twenty-five cavalrymen and sixty foot soldiers. Some were battle-scarred veterans, but more were eager young *caballeros,* "the most brilliant company ever collected in the Indies." With them they took five friars, their servants and military guard, nearly a thousand Indian escorts, and reserve mules, horses, and cattle numbering close to fifteen hundred. Vásquez and the viceroy had invested the equivalent of two million dollars in present United States currency in the organization of this expedition and, for assurance of success, Mendoza had persuaded the reluctant Fray Marcos to serve as a guide.

It was a gala day in Campostela when the soldiers proudly paraded in review before the viceroy. Because the leaders then knew no other route than the one backtracking that of Núñez, they led the expedition to Culiacán in February of 1540, and thence northward into the Sierra Madre Occidental of New Spain. En route Vásquez de Coronado met the returning party of scouts led by Melchior Díaz. Despite the depressing report of Díaz, Vásquez pressed onward with an advance guard. The main army followed slowly under the command of Tristán de Arellano. In July, the advance couriers entered Háwikuh, the first of the Zuñi towns. The fabled Seven Cities turned out to be ordinary Indian pueblos. Neither gold, nor turquoise, nor emeralds! The disappointed conquerors so taunted the chagrined Fray Marcos about this that he took advantage of an opportunity to return hastily to Mexico City.

If riches were to be found, the Spaniards must explore further. Vásquez sent the friar Juan de Padilla and the soldier Pedro de Tovar with a small company of men westward. They found the Hopi villages and claimed that they conquered them. Vásquez also sent Díaz back to the Sonora River from which he was to explore westward in an effort to make contact with Alarcón's supply ships. He reached the Colorado River, where he only found Alarcón's message. He crossed the river into California only to suffer a severe injury in a hunting accident. For twenty days

his men carried him on the return trail; he then died and was buried in the desert.

Meanwhile Vásquez learned from Tovar that a great river could be found somewhere west of the land of the Hopi. Therefore he sent Captain García López de Cárdenas and a company of twenty-five cavalrymen to search for the stream. This party discovered one of the marvels of America—the Grand Canyon of the Colorado River. Three of the men tried to work their way down the cliff to the stream bed; but they returned exhausted after making it only about a third of the way. All were greatly impressed by the grandeur; yet they still had not found the treasures they were looking for.

Vásquez next considered exploration eastward, where the Indians said there was a great pueblo high on a mesa (Ácoma). Then came two chiefs from the distant Pecos Pueblo with presents for these strange interlopers. With the Pecos chiefs as guides, Captain Hernando de Alvarado and Fray Juan de Padilla headed a small detachment of cavalry for a reconnaissance to the east. They traveled past the impressive Sky City, visited the Tiguex Pueblos on the Rio Grande near the site of present Bernalillo, went north through other towns to Braba (Taos), and finally went southeast to Cicuye (Pecos). They arrived there in the autumn of 1540 and found that pueblo to be one of the more populous and thriving of any they had visited. Alvarado conversed there with two Indian captives, one a Pawnee called El Turco and the other a Wichita named Isopete. Those two obtained a release long enough to lead Alvarado onto the plains along the tributaries of the

Canadian River in order to see the herds of buffalo. They mentioned casually that farther east was Quivira, a land of gold and emeralds. Promptly Alvarado returned to Tiguex with the two Plains Indians and the two Pecos chiefs as his prisoners in order to await the arrival of Vásquez de Coronado and convey the exciting news to him.

At Tiguex the vanguard of the Spanish forces, under the command of López de Cárdenas, already had arrived. López persuaded the Indians to vacate the southernmost village, named Alcanfor, for occupation by the invaders as winter quarters. There Vásquez and his band found the housing comfortable, and the view of the blue Sandía mountains quite inspiring, while the news transmitted by Alvarado was at least hopeful. All might have gone well if the Indians had remained friendly that winter, but they became antagonistic by the Spanish appropriation of their women and their blankets. They drove the visitors out, and then the Spaniards counter-attacked. This campaign of siege and attack that lasted most of the winter finally resulted in the destruction of those pueblos and most of their inhabitants.

Finally the winter quarters of the Spaniards were free of harassment; but now the winter had passed and a distant fortune beckoned. With El Turco and Isopete as guides, Vásquez led forth his entire expedition of thirteen hundred persons. Eastward they marched, across the Pecos River, past the camps of *ranchería* Indians, and out onto the *Llano Estacado* or "Staked Plain." Presently some friendly Indians, through an interpreter, revealed to Vásquez the truth about the dismal country ahead. Then the two guides confessed that they deliberately had led the Spaniards into a barren land instead of on the route to Quivira. The Pecos people had offered to grant their two captives their freedom if they would entice the intruders to almost certain doom on the arid plains. Vásquez placed the two guides in irons and veered northward. Presently the expedition found Quivira, some villages of impoverished Indians residing near the site of Lyons in present Kansas. Again, no gold nor jewels. As the disappointed captains led their army back toward Pecos, Isopete revealed that El Turco was conspiring with the Wichita Indians to lay an ambush for the party. For this treachery, El Turco paid with his life.

In Kansas, the expedition of Vásquez was not far from that of Soto, then on the Arkansas River. What would have happened if the two explorers had met? They might have engaged in a bloody battle for dominance in this field of conquest or they could have joined forces to establish a permanent settlement on this frontier of New Spain.

INGLORIOUS OUTCOME

The dejected conquerors returned to Tiguex by a more direct route, going up the valley of the Canadian River and over the pass near Pecos. Once again they made winter camp on the banks of the Rio Grande, where failure was climaxed by disaster. While Vásquez was riding with some companions, his saddle girth broke and, after he fell, his head was trampled upon by the hoof of a horse. For weeks he remained an invalid, unable to muster the strength to lead his army back to Mexico. When he did finally depart, three friars chose not to return with him; instead they remained as missionaries among the Indians. Juan de la Cruz stayed at Tiguex, Luis de Escalona went to Pecos, and Juan de Padilla retraced the route to Quivira. All died as martyrs to their faith. However, one Andrés do Campo, a Portuguese lay brother who had accompanied Padilla to Quivira, escaped the fate of his companions. He wandered southward over the plains, across the Rio Grande, and through the mountains to Pánuco. Finally he straggled into Mexico City five years after the return of the expedition. Across this northern frontier he had made a remarkable peregrination alone, whereas his illustrious Spanish predecessor had had three companions.

After resting briefly in Mexico City, Vásquez de Coronado returned temporarily to his former post as governor of Nueva Galicia. In 1544, he had to stand trial for some charges brought against him by malcontents in his expedition. As a result, he was indicted for alleged mismanagement, but the *Audiencia,* or superior court, which reviewed the case, exonerated him. However, because Vásquez was a wealthy man, he suffered persecution by those who sought to divert that wealth into their hands. Officials in Spain revived the charges, and he was brought to Madrid as a prisoner for retrial in 1548. Two years later the Council of the Indies found him guilty, banned him from returning to New Spain for ten years, fined him two hundred ducats, and sentenced him to serve the king for a term of a year at a small town on the southern coast of Spain. For his services, Vásquez lost his health, considerable wealth, and his intrepid spirit. He died a broken man in 1556. Although he had failed to find great riches, he did provide detailed information concerning the true nature of the northern frontier. After his disappointing revelations, the desire for conquest of the Seven Cities took a deserved recess for about forty years.

UP THE WEST COAST

Gradually the vastness of North America was becoming apparent to the Spaniards, even though they still held to the hope that a passageway by a strait through the continent could be found. Consequently amid the frenzied activity of the early 1540s one more expedition was undertaken. Under the captaincy of a Portuguese sailor, Juan Rodríguez Cabrillo, it set sail in June of 1542 to find that elusive strait. The two small, poorly outfitted vessels departed from Puerto de Navidad on the western coast of New Spain and worked laboriously up the coast of California. At one port, which Cabrillo named San Quentin, the sailors brought aboard some friendly Indians who by sign language said that about five days' journey inland they had seen other men like these Spaniards "who wore beards and who brought dogs, and crossbows, and swords." Probably they had encountered the Díaz branch of the Coronado expedition. The captain gave the Indians a letter to deliver to them, but there is no evidence that the letter ever reached its destination.

On up the coast the Rodríguez Cabrillo crew spent the winter on San Miguel Island, where the captain died on January 3, 1543. His pilot, Bartolomé Ferrelo, continued the exploration. On March 1, he recorded that the ships had come to the mouth of a large river at about forty-two degrees north latitude. Probably it was the Rogue River in present Oregon. This was the turning point. A severe storm and a depleted supply of food gave warning that the return voyage should be begun. More severe storms were encountered off the coast of California; for three weeks the two ships lost sight of each other, but finally, in April of 1543, they arrived at their home port. Cabrillo and Ferrelo had found no passageway, but they had contributed more information about the vastness of the continent.

This expedition up the west coast introduced an era of activity in the Pacific area as a kind of compensation for disappointment about the Seven Cities. Even while Cabrillo was sailing northward, Ruy López de Villalobos was crossing the "South Sea" to the San Lázaro Islands, which had been discovered previously by Ferdinand Magellan. Now Villalobos laid claim to them in the name of the Spanish Emperor, Philip II, and renamed them the Philippine Islands. Later, in 1565, Miguel López de Legazpi led another expedition from New Spain to these islands and completed the subjugation of the natives. The Philippines then became a part of New Spain, and a profitable trade was carried on across the Pacific by means of the Manila galleons. From New Spain the voyage west was abetted by the trade winds, but for the return trip a more practicable route lay northward following the course of the Japan current and the prevailing westerlies. This route carried the traders to the California coast, where the hazards of cold, storms, fog, and rocky shoals had to be surmounted in the coast-wise voyage southward to the ports of New Spain. The Manila trade therefore made desirable Spanish control of the coast of California.

RIVALRY ON THE PACIFIC

Interest in the Pacific area caused the Spaniards to be alarmed when they heard that an English freebooter, Sir Francis Drake, was trying to appropriate the California coast. In 1577, with five ships Drake had initiated a devastating campaign of raids on Spanish ships and cities all around South America. In the spring of 1579, he sought refuge for his one remaining vessel in a harbor on the west coast at about thirty degrees north latitude. There he observed the Indians with interest and erected a marker claiming the land in the name of Queen Elizabeth. A bay north of the Golden Gate now bears his name, and an old engraved plate suggesting that Drake's harbor was San Francisco Bay may have been transplanted there. Soon the *Golden Hind* had been repaired and restocked and in July of 1579 Drake sailed out onto the Pacific. Over a year later he and fifty of his original crew of one hundred and sixty-four arrived at Plymouth, England, after having circumnavigated the globe.

Drake had hoped to return with colonists to California, but that was a dream never realized. Instead, another Englishman, Thomas Cavendish, next appeared in the Pacific. He left England in 1586, raided the coasts of Peru and New Spain, and dropped anchor in San Bernabé Bay in California. When a great ship of the Manila galleon approached the coast, Cavendish took it as a prize and then, like Drake, crossed the Pacific on his return voyage to England.

Obviously, if the Spaniards were to secure the coast of California, it was urgent for them to do something about it. Therefore the then viceroy, Luis de Velasco, requested a reconnaissance of the coast with a view to improvement of its defense. This task he assigned to a Portuguese navigator, Sebastián Rodríguez Cermenho, who was captain of a ship engaged in the Manila trade. On his return trip from the Philippines in 1595, he came in sight of the west coast at about forty-one degrees north latitude. Using a small launch for coastal explorations, he worked his way southward. As usual, the trip along that rocky coast proved to be a perilous one. Somewhere near Drake's Bay a storm wrecked the large ship, drowning two of the crew and leaving the valuable cargo submerged. The survivors crowded into the launch and continued their observations of the coastline southward. With their maps and notes they finally reached Mexico City in April of 1596.

Shortly before the arrival of Rodríguez Cermenho in 1596, another merchant engaged in the Manila trade had embarked from New Spain with a commission for development of a colony on the Gulf of California. This captain, Sebastián Vizcaíno, hoped to establish a base for pearl-fishing from which information about the region might be sent

back to the interested authorities. Because he encountered winter storms, he left his colonists and flagship at La Paz in Lower California while his two smaller ships went on exploring. A battle with Indians, the loss of a ship, and the plight of the colonists caused the abandonment of this project, but Vizcaíno promptly returned for further exploration. The successful conclusion of this latter reconnaissance revived Vizcaíno's hope for the future of California.

After a delay caused by the threat of two Dutch ships cruising in the Pacific in 1599 and 1600, Vizcaíno finally organized his second expedition. This time he had authorization only to do some more exploring. His select crew of two hundred, including three Carmelite priests, embarked from Acapulco in May, 1602. In November they entered a good harbor, which Vizcaíno named San Diego, and a month later they found Monterey Bay. The captain praised the latter location. He described it as the best port yet found, well sheltered, and having access to a fertile land abounding in Indians and gold. Despite the cold weather, a shortage of provisions, and the illness of many of the sailors, Vizcaíno sailed two of his ships on northward to Cape Mendocino. Upon his return to Acapulco in March of 1603, he and his diarist, Padre Antonio de la Assensión, turned in glowing reports, especially about that bountiful harbor of Monterey. The viceroy concluded, however, that it would be both dangerous an unprofitable to plant a colony so far up the coast; therefore attempts to expand northward were postponed for a hundred and sixty years.

While attention was being concentrated temporarily upon California, a steady and less spectacular movement pushed the area of settlement northward on the central plateau of Mexico. In the 1540s, a few cattlemen and friars led the way and the trickle became a flood after a rich silver lode was opened at Za-catecas in 1546. Then more lands were granted for grazing, new roads were opened, and the wild tribes of Chichi-meca were pacified. By 1580, a frontier village had been founded at Santa Bárbara on the Conchos River and, by 1584, at Monterrey in Nuevo León.

A NEW OVERLAND ROUTE

Now finally the border of settlement was advancing closer to the Seven Cities and a new route had been found. To reach the pueblos the Spaniards could follow the Conchos River from the central plateau to the Rio Grande and follow it northward. That was a route much less difficult than the early trail from Culiacán over the rugged western range. Presently, in 1579, some frontier slave-hunters brought back to Santa Bárbara an Indian who told of large cities beyond the Rio Grande where the people raised cotton and corn. Once again the Spaniards became excited about those Seven Cities.

The first to investigate the report was a Franciscan lay brother, Fray Agustín Rodríguez. Accompanied by two other friars and a squadron of soldiers commanded by Francisco Sánchez Chamuscado, Rodríguez departed from Santa Bárbara in June, 1581. After passing numerous pueblos along the way, the explorers reached the Tiguex villages where Vásquez de Coronado twice had spent a winter. They traveled to the east to get a view of the buffalo plains and to the west to visit the desert pueblos. Then the soldiers returned home, but the two friars remained as missionaries in the Pueblo of Puaray in the Tiguex group located near the site of the present Bernalillo.

The returning soldiers confirmed the report that the pueblos could be reached by the new route following the Conchos River. Moreover, fear was aroused concerning the safety of the two friars who had stayed among the Indians without soldiers for protection. Therefore a wealthy resident, Antonio de Espejo, offered to finance and lead a rescue party, and the viceroy approved his proposal. With Fray Bernaldino Beltrán and a small group of soldiers and servants, Espejo set forth on the Rodríguez trail in November of 1582. They made it to the pueblos with little difficulty, only to find that the Indians already had killed the two friars, Agustín Rodríguez and Francisco López. Thwarted in his announced objective, Espejo concluded that he could at least do some exploring. He led his party two days east to the buffalo country, then back and northward from one pueblo to another along the Rio del Norte (Rio Grande), and finally west past Ácoma to Zuñi. Indian guides led him about a hundred miles farther west to some mines. Espejo wrote: "I found them, and with my own hands, I extracted ore from them, said by those who know to be very rich and to contain much silver." Back again on the Rio Grande, he found some more mines from which he claimed to have extracted some samples of "shining ore."

For his return trip he tried a different route, down the Pecos River, past the Jumano villages to the Rio Grande, and then across to the Conchos and back to Santa Bárbara in September, 1583.

Espejo drafted a somewhat exaggerated report about the pueblos and mines to the north and thereby revived momentarily that early motive — the quest for quick wealth. This report reached the ears of Gaspar Castaño de Sosa, lieutenant governor of Nuevo León. In 1590, upon his own initiative Sosa organized the mining camp of Nuevo Almadén (now Monclova) into an expedition of one hundred and seventy colonists. Without bothering to apply for official authorization, he led his party up the Pecos River to the pueblos and conquered Pecos, Taos, and Tiguex. Spanish officials had been wanting that region subjugated and now the job was done. But such a demonstration of private enterprise had no proper place in the Spanish colonial system. Therefore Captain Juan Marlete and a company of soldiers traveled northward along the same arduous trail, arrested Sosa and his entire party, and returned them to Nuevo León.

Disregarding the fate of Sosa, two other adventurers led forth another unauthorized expedition in search of any kind of treasure that could be found. These two were Francisco Leyva de Bonilla and Antonio Gutiérrez de Humaña. Of all the bands of explorers who braved the dangers of the northern border, this was the only one that failed to return. Years later news of its fate was obtained from two survivors.

According to fragmentary reports, the Leyva-Gutiérrez expedition established headquarters among the Pueblos and then marched eastward to Quivira, where it veered northward to a large river, probably the Platte. While en route, the two captains quarreled and Gutiérrez murdered Leyva. Among the Indian aides who then deserted was a certain Jusepe, who had been a captive of the Apaches for a year and who finally escaped and returned to the Pueblos. In 1598, he related his story to Juan de Oñate, the colonizer of New Mexico. The remainder of the party under Gutiérrez had been ambushed by Indians and only one soldier, Alonso Sánchez, survived. He was adopted by a tribe of Indians, who finally came to regard him as their chief. Ultimately his story of the fate of the expedition was transmitted in a round-about way to the Spanish officials.

In view of the revival of interest in the potential of the Pueblos, certainly a properly authorized conquest of them seemed imminent. The frontier of settlement had approached the Rio Grande and a new, easier route had been found. This would facilitate advancement with new motivation — the acquisition of land and the founding of missions. This new combination of concepts in fact determined that New Mexico should soon become the first part of our Southwest to acquire a successful Spanish colony.

3
NEW MEXICO

Of arms I sing, and of that heroic son,
Of his wondrous deeds and of his victories won,
Of his prudence and his valor shown when,
Scorning the hate and envy of his fellow men,
Unmindful of the dangers that beset his way,
Performed deeds most heroic of his day.

I sing the glory of that mighty band,
Who nobly strive in that far distant land,
The world's most hidden regions they defy,
"Plus Ultra" is their ever battle cry.
Onward they press, nothing will not dare,
Mid force of arms and deeds of valor rare.
To write the annals of such heroic men,
Well needs the efforts of a mightier pen.

Gaspar Pérez de Villagrá, trans. Gilberto Espinosa in History of New
Mexico *(Los Angeles, 1933), p. 41. By permission of the translator and
editor.*

PREPARATION FOR COLONIZATION

In the Spanish colonies the launching of a major expedition required the observance of a routine of formalities. First, the provincial officials had to be persuaded that a certain project merited its undertaking, and the king and Council of the Indies had to grant approval. Second, bids were called for. The applicants stated their terms—what they would take along, how much they would contribute, what they expected the royal treasury to provide, what share of any profits would accrue to the king, and what titles and gains they would like to reserve for themselves and their heirs. Presumably the contract would then be awarded to the highest bidder, but that was not always the case. The

32

king would consider also the experience and reputation of the applicants, the influence of their family connections, and his own obligation to some of them for favors rendered in the past. Once the contract had been awarded, the king sent his inspectors to the point of departure in order to ascertain that the appointee was fulfilling his promises.

In 1595 pursuit of the formal procedure for conquest of the pueblos led to the selection of Don Juan de Oñate, who had many favorable qualifications. He was a veteran of Indian campaigns on the northern frontier and was a personal friend of the viceroy, Luis de Velasco. His father had acquired wealth from the exploitation of rich mines, and his wife had a dowry as a descendant of Cortés. Moreover, in his letter to the viceroy the Don outlined his terms clearly and favorably. He had offered to enlist and outfit at his own expense an expedition of two hundred men for the purpose of establishing the colony "by peaceful means, friendliness, and Christian zeal." He had agreed to provide and transport to the new land five hundred pesos' worth of "wheat for sowing," three thousand sheep, a thousand goats, a thousand head of cattle, and such tools as sledgehammers, plowshares, picks, wedges, hoes, axes, adzes, angurs, saws, chisels, and sickles. Moreover, when the expedition finally got under way, some of the men would be accompanied by their families. Obviously these Spaniards were going to the frontier primarily for the founding of a permanent settlement. A new motive had superseded the earlier frenetic quest for gold.

Oñate requested that the Crown send and sustain six friars for the "conversion and pacification of the natives." Then, as compensation for his own expenses and efforts, he asked that he be appointed governor and captain-general of the new province, with the title of *adelantado* for himself and for two generations of heirs. That title was one which had originated in Spain on the granting of extraordinary responsibilities to a governor who was "sent forward" into a frontier zone as the representative of the king. He also sought for himself and heirs the title of "marquis." Further, he asked and obtained the right to designate and acquire for himself thirty square leagues of land, "including all the subjects who may live within the said territory." But his additional request for an annual salary of eight thousand ducats and a loan of twenty thousand pesos was pared down to six thousand of each. For the officers under his command he obtained the title of *hidalgo* and the privilege of acquiring *encomiendas* of Pueblo Indians and other "vassals." Under the prevailing system this meant that his captains would become the lesser nobility to whom allotments of Indians would be granted in trust. The *encomenderos* would supervise and protect their vassals in exchange for a tribute which could be collected from the subjects. The medieval European pattern, therefore, was to be transplanted to this frontier, as it was being done elsewhere in the Spanish colonies.

Upon acceptance of his terms, Oñate began his preparations, but unanticipated troubles caused delay. His friend Velasco was replaced by a new viceroy who revised the contract in petty and annoying ways. Even so, Oñate mustered his two hundred men in readiness for departure, only to receive orders to hold back. The Council of the Indies was preparing to cancel his contract in order to award it to a new and more eminent candidate, Don Pedro Ponce de León. Soon, however, the new favorite fell ill and ran short of funds. Thereupon the royal favor reverted to Oñate, who finally received authorization to proceed when ready and able to pass inspection.

Formal review by the royal agents took two weeks in December and January of 1597 and 1598. The long delay had decimated Oñate's volunteers from the original two hundred and five to one hundred and twenty-nine, but Oñate promised to enlist eighty more as reinforcements to follow later. In the sworn statements taken by the royal inspector, the ordeal of the long wait and the dramatic moment of a lifetime are expressed tersely. For example, Gerónimo Marquéz avowed that, "Because of the great hardships that we have endured in the delay of the expedition, most of the goods that I had brought have been consumed, lost, or pilfered," and Juan Pérez listed along with his meagre equipment "Further, my wife, seven daughters, and two grown sons." Alonso Sánchez appended this explanation:

In addition to what is listed here, I declare that I brought from my home for the support of my household and family seventy quintals of flour and hardtack, which has been consumed and used up because of the long delay. When this food gave out, which must have been four months ago, the governor furnished provisions without ever failing.[1]

Because of his determination to succeed, Oñate had become more and more involved financially, as is indicated by the number of enrollees who reported simply that "I have nothing to manifest, because the governor, Don Juan de Oñate, is giving me the arms, horses, and other necessary things." As the roll call was concluded, it listed, besides the soldiers and settlers, seven Franciscan friars, two lay brothers, and their administrator or "commissary," Fray Alonso Martínez.

An interesting sidelight is found in Oñate's agreement to take along "200 pesos' worth of paper," symptomatic of the centralization prevailing in the Spanish system. Much paper would be needed for the filing of reports and requisitions. At a later date, one officer complained that in order to get nails for horseshoes he had to file a formal request and wait for months until he received the approval of the bureaucracy. Further, the friars and captains would consume much paper in the writing of their diaries. One, Captain Gaspar Pérez de Villagrá, wrote his in the form of an epic poem relating, in thirty-four long stanzas, the story of the conquest. Even though he exalted the role of the Spaniards with superlative praise, his account has become valuable as one of the sources for later historical writing.

[1] George P. Hammond and Agapito Rey, *Don Juan de Oñate Colonizer of New Mexico* (Albuquerque, 1953), I, p. 248.

OÑATE'S JOURNEY

When preparations had been completed early in 1598, the assemblage advanced in a long procession across Chihuahua to the Rio Grande. At that point Oñate claimed formal possession of all

lands, pueblos, cities, towns, castles, fortified and unfortified houses which are now established in the kingdoms of and provinces of New Mexico,... the mountains, rivers, fisheries, waters, pastures, valleys, meadows, springs, and ores of gold, silver, copper, mercury, tin, iron, precious stones, salt,... with power of life and death, over high and low, from the leaves of the trees to the stones and sands of the river.[2]

A little farther up the river, near the site of present El Paso, the governor, the commissary of the friars, and a small group of soldiers went on ahead. Presently they came upon one pueblo after another, and as they did, they cajoled the Indians into submission, which was affirmed in a formal procedure. At Santo Domingo on July 9, for example, Oñate through an interpreter described the purposes of the visitors and requested obedience. He explained something about the new religious faith which they would introduce, and then the chiefs knelt and kissed the hands of the governor and the father commissary.

On July 11, the vanguard arrived at the Pueblo of Ohke on the east bank of the Rio Grande near its confluence with the Chama. This site they chose as headquarters. They renamed it San Juan Bautista and, after the main body

of colonists arrived on August 18, they began work on their shelters and a church building. Simultaneously some of the friars went out to the neighboring pueblos.

Soon Captain Vicente de Zaldívar and sixty men traveled eastward through Pecos to satisfy their curiosity about the buffalo on the plains. Simultaneously Oñate and another company of soldiers backtracked southward to the pueblos near present Bernalillo, whence they turned west to visit Ácoma, Zuñi, and the Hopi villages. From the latter place Oñate sent a squad under the command of Captain Marcos Farfán de los Godos westward across present Arizona. Near the Big Sandy River they found an old Indian mine, staked out some claims, and returned with a jubilant report about what they claimed was "the richest ore in New Spain."

Meanwhile Oñate had been awaiting the reinforcements that had been following under the leadership of Juan de Zaldívar, a brother of Vicente. However, when Zaldívar had sought some provisions at Ácoma, he and twelve of his party had been killed by the Indians. Thus only a handful of survivors overtook Oñate, and together they sadly returned to San Juan in December of 1598.

Soon afterward Vicente de Zaldívar marched seventy soldiers to Ácoma in order to avenge the death of his brother. While his main force attracted attention by climbing the cliff on one side of the Sky City, a small party carrying a cannon scaled the cliff at another point. Their surprise assault, supported by the cannon, diverted the defenders

[2] Hammond and Rey, p. 335.

long enough for the others to gain the heights. With the Indians holed up in their kivas, Zaldívar set a torch to the city and destroyed most of it. Although many of the Ácoma men were killed and others escaped, about seventy-five men and five hundred women and children were taken as captives. Later those who had escaped returned and built a new village at the foot of the cliff, and not until 1680 did their descendants reoccupy the original site. Consequently the claim that Ácoma is the oldest continuously occupied city in the United States must be qualified to allow for an absence of eight decades. During that interval, however, the pueblo was not far distant.

Those captives taken by Zaldívar were removed to San Juan, where they were put through the formality of a trial and then severely punished. The men under twenty-five drew a sentence condemning them to a term of twenty years as personal servants, while the older men received a similar sentence besides having one foot cut off. The women and children were assigned to the Spanish officials for supervision, which amounted to condemnation to slavery. Perhaps it was due to the severity of this punishment that no other serious uprising occurred for eighty years.

After a year in San Juan the colonists chose a new site for their homes across the river at Yunque, which was renamed San Gabriel. They somehow persuaded the Indian occupants of that village to trade places with them. In the summer following, in 1600, seventy-three colonists and seven friars arrived as welcome reinforcements. Then Oñate became interested in the story of Jusepe, the Indian who had survived the Leyva massacre, and concluded that he must find the fabulous Quivira. So in June of 1601, with seventy soldiers he traveled eastward past Pecos to the buffalo plains. However, the hostility of the Wichita Indians caused this band of explorers to turn back with nothing to report except that the land appeared to be fertile.

UNSETTLED SETTLERS

Two hundred colonists had come to New Mexico for the unmistakable purpose of making their homes and tilling the land. Within three years their leader had demonstrated that he was about fifty years behind the times, for he was still eager to find gold and glory. In the midst of their work the men had been interrupted several times by orders to march forth to the west or the east, and they became unhappy about this. Thus by 1601 most of the colonists and several of the friars had deserted. They had taken with them some sworn statements testifying as to the lack of conversions, the poverty of the land, and the imminence of starvation. The few who remained sent to Mexico some counter-claims about the wealth of the province and the good administration of the governor. Oñate, realizing that his future was at stake, sent Zaldívar to Spain with an appeal to the Council of the Indies for reinforcement by three hundred more recruits. Then in a desperate effort to mark up some spectacular accomplishment to his credit, Oñate led forth about thirty soldiers on yet another journey of exploration.

For his final fling, Oñate retraced his earlier route through the desert pueblos, beyond them to the Colorado River, and then down it to the Gulf of California, and returned to San Gabriel by April in 1605. There bad news awaited him and he could report no discovery of sufficient magnitude to counteract it. In Spain, some serious misgivings had been aroused by the adverse report of a friar concerning the colony of New Mexico. Consequently the Council of the Indies recommended that Oñate be recalled, that his army be discharged, and that his conduct should be investigated. All this the king ordered in June of 1606. Faced with the prospect of removal, Oñate resigned in August of the following year.

While the disappointed captain was awaiting the arrival of his successor, the *Audiencia* (Council) of New Spain considered what should be done for the few baptized Indians. With abandonment of the colony imminent, should those Indians be colonized elsewhere or allowed to revert to heathenism? While the fate of New Mexico hung in the balance, a friar, Lázaro Ximénez, arrived with a report more favorable than previously had been received. He claimed that seven thousand Indians had been converted. Therefore the *Audiencia* recommended to Emperor Philip III that he take over New Mexico

as a royal colony under a new governor supported by a company of soldiers. Further that young Cristóbal Oñate should not be allowed to inherit his father's privileges nor have anything to do with the colony. They advised also that New Mexico should be designated a missionary field with friars maintained at royal expense. Adoption of this proposal meant that New Mexico had been saved from abandonment only by emphasis upon the religious motive. It meant, too, that a project launched largely by private enterprise would be nationalized, much like the conversion of the distant English colonies from private to royal control.

As for Oñate, he experienced degradation comparable to that which befell many other Spanish conquerors. Investigation of his conduct begun in 1612 led to his conviction for indulging in immoral conduct, for punishing Indians with excessive severity, for misrepresenting the wealth of New Mexico, and for mistreating the officers under his command. He was deprived of his titles, assessed a fine of six thousand ducats, and banished from Mexico City for four years.

Oñate appealed to the king for exoneration, and finally in 1622, according to the meagre evidence available, it appears that his petition for leniency and restoration of his titles was granted.

NADIR IN NEW MEXICO

Don Pedro de Peralta succeeded Oñate as governor and captain-general at an annual salary of two thousand pesos. He arrived in the autumn of 1609 with instructions to reorganize the

colony and to remove it from proximity to the Indian pueblos to a new Spanish *villa* to be founded for the accommodation of the settlers. Possibly he selected the site still farther south that autumn, but more likely during the next spring. In 1610, the colonists completed the transfer of their possessions to the new capital named La Villa Real de la Santa Fe de San Francisco, which soon was shortened to Santa Fe.

In its early years the new colony maintained a precarious existence, and a report of 1617 enumerated only forty-eight settlers. Nevertheless, out among the Pueblos the few friars pursued valiantly their work of pacification and conversion. In one village after another they supervised the labor of the Indians in the building of adobe mission churches. Sometime between 1614 and 1617 the Franciscan Chapter advanced this mission field from a *comisario* to a *custodia*, meaning that it had become a more important administrative area in the province. The first custodian was Fray Estevan de Perea, who served as supervisor and provincial judge from 1617 to 1622. In 1625 a new custodian, Fray Alonso de Benavides, assumed supervision with added responsibility as commissary of the Holy Office of the Inquisition. The usual pomp and ceremony heralded his arrival. The governor and town council met him on the outskirts of the village and accompanied him to the small church, while the soldiers were assembled in the plaza to salute his arrival. On January 25, 1625, he read the Edict of the Faith for the first time in the Santa Fe church.

In Mexico City, in 1629, Benavides prepared a report which he sent to Spain a year later. It is often cited as a source on conditions in the colony at that date. His descriptions may have been accurate for the most part, but his claim that over sixty-three thousand Indians living in ninety pueblos had been converted certainly seems an exaggeration. On the other hand he gave the number of friars as about fifty, which was approximately correct. Another source reported sixty-six in 1631. At that time this was essentially a colony of scattered missions supported by a company of soldiers. For maintenance of those missions, the friars exacted tribute of the Indians in the form of labor. Supplementary supplies came up from Mexico City on the royal caravans every third year, starting in 1609. The wagon train brought provisions and ecclesiastical equipment. On the return trip a year later the caravan transported hides, textiles, salt, and other products to be marketed in Mexico City. Incoming custodians, governors, and traders usually came with the caravan, and those departing returned with it. This was the only regular contact, the only means of communications between this isolated colony and the outside world.

The route of travel followed an unimproved road which came to be known as *El Camino Real* (King's Highway). The journey was a memorable experience, especially over that arid, hazardous portion in southern New Mexico known as *La Jornada del Muerto* (Journey of the Dead).

CONFLICTING JURISDICTIONS

While the missions were expanding and prospering, the lay colony also grew by the addition of traders and the soldiers' families. Now the stage was set for a conflict. Impoverished colonists grew envious of the affluent missions, and governors sought to assert their jurisdiction over friars as well as over their lay subjects. The very first custodian, Fray Esteban, clashed with the governor, Juan de Eulate, who served from 1618 to 1625. The friars complained that Eulate boasted that the emperor's authority was superior to that of the pope, therefore as representative of the emperor, he could arrest and judge the clergy if need be. Further, the friar alleged that he denied them military protection, insulted them publicly, deprived them of the service of the Indians, and encouraged the latter in their continuation of heathen practices. According to the complainants, Eulate defended the colonists in their rounding up of Indians for forced labor on their farms without remuneration. The authorities in Mexico City investigated these charges and sent out new detailed instructions defining the fields of responsibility more clearly. France V. Scholes, writing in the *New Mexico Historical Review*, has concluded that the revised rules represented "a severe reproof to the clergy" and "a sort of Magna Carta of secular rights." Thenceforth both religious and civil officials were ordered to stay away from the pueblos, when the Indians were electing their governors, in order to eliminate undue pressure. Friars and laymen both were warned to refrain from employing Indian labor in illegal ways, and the friars were to permit the collection of tribute from the Indians by the *encomenderos* to whom it was due. Further, the custodian was to refrain from taking any action affecting laymen "except it be ecclesiastical matters according to law," and the friars should employ Indian labor only with moderation in "things necessary for the church."

Despite the delineation of jurisdictions, the conflict erupted again with greater severity during the administration of Luis de Rosas, who served as governor from 1627 to 1644. An incoming governor customarily conducted an investigation, called a *residencia*, concerning the conduct of his predecessor. While the latter was still "in residence," because the caravan had not yet departed, the new governor gathered complaints and conducted a trial over his predecessor. The clergy filed an accumulation of complaints against the man being replaced by Rosas, for which he was let off easy, apparently by bribing his prosecutor. Then Rosas forced the Indians of several pueblos to weave blankets for him, and he brought in captured Apaches to labor as slaves in his own workshop in Santa Fe. Moreover, the friars alleged that Rosas engaged in a profitable trade with the unsubdued Apaches, who now were pressing close in the foothills to the east, and that he failed to provide the missions and pueblos with protection against those marauding Indians. Presently Rosas violated ecclesiastic privilege by having a friar arrested. For that the custodian retaliated by excommunicating the governor. The *cabildo*, or town council, investigated and issued a report emphasizing economic causes. According to these laymen, the friars possessed thousands of sheep, numerous horses, and abundant firearms, far beyond their needs and excessive in relation to the poverty of the laymen. They proposed that secular priests under the nearest bishop should replace the Franciscan friars. During the interval required for this change, they recommended that the missions temporarily be placed under the supervision of Father Juan de Vidania, who happened to be a close friend of Rosas. Naturally this latter proposal antagonized the friars against Vidania. They had him excommunicated and then when they sent two of their number to negotiate with Rosas, he beat them with a club. In retaliation, someone murdered Rosas.

Affairs in Santa Fe were in a critical state when in 1642, a new custodian and a new governor arrived. The latter, Alonso de Pacheco y Heredia, presided over a hasty investigation, pardoned many of the offenders, and reported that "the entire realm is at peace." However, he and the new prelate, Fray Hernando de Covurrubias, soon were arrayed against each other in a renewal of the conflict. Again new appointees replaced them.

The smoldering antagonism erupted again in 1659 when Bernardo López de Mendizábal arrived as governor and ordered immediately that the Indians should be paid one *real* a day for their labor, instead of half a *real*. Both colonists and friars resented this decree, and the latter complained to the Holy Office of the Inquisition that López himself was using Indian slave labor

for the production of goods which he was preparing to ship out and sell for his own profit. Further, the friars alleged that his laxity made even more critical the problems of Pueblo discipline and the Apache raids. The Franciscans even threatened to withdraw entirely from this mission field.

Soon a new governor, Diego de Peñalosa, arrived in Santa Fe, where he lasted only three years—from 1661 to 1664. He held his predecessor in jail while conducting the usual *residencia*. And, as usual, he saw an opportunity to start his own accumulation of wealth by soliciting a bribe from his predecessor. For ten thousand pesos he would let López off easy; but López rejected the offer and Peñalosa proceeded with the prosecution. He filed thirty-three charges with the *Audiencia* in New Spain. With no spokesman to defend him, López was convicted on several of the counts, for which he was fined three thousand pesos and ordered to pay the claims assessed against him by signing over some of his own property.

In the procedure against López, the avaricious Peñalosa had garnered personal gains. For that the custodian, Padre Alonso de Posada, publicly denounced the governor, who then locked the friar in jail. Further, he ordered that Indians must not be employed in weaving blankets and shawls for the friars without a license from the governor, for which he would collect some fees. When the friars protested, he made derogatory remarks about the Church and its Inquisition. For that he was brought to trial before the Holy Office and found guilty of heresy. He was fined heavily, disqualified from holding office, ordered to march barefoot through the streets of Mexico City while carrying a green candle of penitence, and finally exiled forever from New Spain. The embittered Peñalosa (who incidentally had made a journey of explora-tion to the Mississippi River in 1622) soon appeared in Paris with a scheme for retaliation against Spain. His part in promoting an invasion of the northern frontier by a French expedition will be observed later.

THE PUEBLO REBELLION

Insufferable exploitation and endless internal conflict brought dire consequences for both colonists and friars in New Mexico. First, the nomadic Indians got out of hand. The Navajos destroyed the Zuñi town of Háwikuh in 1672, and simultaneously the Apaches sacked Gran Quivira and other pueblos on the eastern border of settlement. Three years later a friar at San Ildefonso charged some Indians with witchcraft for which forty-seven medicine men were arrested. After four had been hanged, a delegation of Indians demanded that the governor release the remaining forty-three. Frightened by the threats of the petitioners, the governor acceded. Among those released was an Indian named Popé. Although he had come from San Juan, he now made his headquarters in Taos and began secretly to foment a general uprising. A custodian, Fray Francisco de Ayeta, who had only recently arrived, became so alarmed at the plight of the missions and colonists that he hastily returned to Mexico City. He obtained reinforcements and a relief caravan of supplies, but his return journey in the autumn of 1680 came too late to prevent the catastrophe which he foresaw.

The causes of the disastrous Pueblo Revolt of 1680 were manifold. The Indians who had been converted had good reasons to be resentful. Among the laymen they owed tribute first to one and then to another of three authorities. The nonresident *encomendero*, a conqueror or one of his heirs, levied tribute in the form of blankets, shawls, or labor; the local *alcalde*, or justice of the peace, had to have his fees and fines; and the governor, himself, usually appropriated all the Indian products which he could command for shipment to outside markets, and in some instances even maintained a workshop where Indian slaves labored for his profit. Then there were the friars, who required the Indians to herd sheep, to build and maintain churches, and to assist with the religious services. The Franciscans, too, became triple-headed task masters in the persons of the Custodian, the Treasurer of the Crusade, and the Commissary of the Holy Office of the Inquisition. Moreover, the friars sought to repress the pagan dances and idolatrous worship of the primitive cultures, whereas some of the governors, especially Rosas and López, viewed those ceremonies and rather enjoyed the spectacle.

Little wonder that the Pueblos became skeptical about the advantages of being "civilized"; besides, they observed that the Indians in those remote villages which had not been "reduced" continued to be free from tribute and able to retain their old customs. Meanwhile the Navajos and Apaches were developing a profitable commerce with the lay colonists and then stealing pueblo flocks and crops with brazen immunity. While the Spanish officials who were responsible for protecting the pueblos were either impotent or unconcerned, the raids became so devastating as to cause periodic famine in the villages. Amid all this distress the friars cleverly invoked an old practice for condemnation and punishment of those Indians who returned to their pagan worship. By accusing the medicine men of witchcraft, they could have them condemned to death. That was the customary punishment of such aberration in that era.

RETREAT TO EL PASO

Popé emerged as the spokesman of resistance. He claimed to be in communication with supernatural powers which would give him and his followers guidance. Cautiously he enlisted support in all the pueblos and kept in communication with them by means of secret emissaries. Through his loyal runners he sent a message by means of knotted cords informing the pueblos that the date of the slaughter was to be August 11, 1680. When two of the runners were caught, Antonio Otermín, the governor, sent out a warning to the colonists. Popé then hastily changed the date to the 10th, when the Indians arose in unison as planned and seized the soldiers' arms. Then in village after village they massacred men, women, and children, with especial brutality reserved for the friars. Only Santa Fe held out against the assault. To the capital some surviving colonists fought their way from Santa Cruz de la Cañada, where they were joined by a few survivors from other outlying settlements. Additional survivors gathered in another refuge center at Socorro. In Santa Fe the soldiers tried twice to drive away the besieging Indians, but without success. Therefore on August 21, the Spaniards abandoned the capital and retreated southward. When they came to Socorro they found that the other group had gone on ahead of them, but they succeeded in overtaking the others on September 13. Just above El Paso the refugees met Father Ayeta's supply train. Across the river was a mission which had been founded in 1659. Around it, in the village of El Paso del Norte, the New Mexicans settled temporarily. Some remained there permanently while others later moved across the river to the site of present El Paso. As will be seen, the city south of the river ultimately was renamed Ciudad Juárez. In the evacuation the Spaniards had not entirely abandoned New Mexico, for El Paso then was considered to be within that province. The continuity of the settlement was maintained, although the location of the capital had been changed.

Over four hundred Spaniards had been slain in the uprising, or about one-sixth of their total number, and only eleven of the thirty-three friars had survived. The Indians methodically destroyed churches, houses, and other buildings, along with all the books and records. They were going to live a life of freedom and revive their old customs with no visible vestige of the former Spanish mastery!

Because many of the transplanted Spaniards wanted to return and rebuild their homes, Governor Otermín soon undertook the reconquest. In November, 1681, with an expedition of one hundred and forty-six soldiers, one hundred and twelve allies from friendly Indian tribes, and four Franciscan friars, he marched up *El Camino Real* past some deserted pueblos to Isleta. It was still occupied by rebellious Indians. On December 5, Otermín reconquered Isleta, whereupon the Indians disclaimed responsibility for the rebellion. They said that they had merely followed orders of chiefs to the north who had commanded them to destroy all religious articles and to return to their old customs.

From Isleta, Otermín sent forth Captain Juan Domínguez de Mendoza with sixty cavalrymen. The captain obtained the submission of a few pueblos, but he found that others had been abandoned and that their occupants had fled into the mountains. Confronted with a conspiracy to ambush and massacre his company, he retreated to Isleta, whereupon Otermín concluded that he should abandon this attempted reconquest. Of about sixteen thousand apostates, only a little over five hundred had been restored to the Faith. Captain Domínguez was convinced that the Indians were hopeless "traitors and idolaters at heart."

Father Ayeta, upon his return from this expedition, testified that the Pueblos had suffered no "stings of conscience" and were rejecting "all the conveniences of civilization" by returning to their original paganism, "completely dominated by the devil" and determined "to die rather than yield to the Spaniards."

LOOKING EASTWARD

With the reconquest thus postponed, the colonists in El Paso turned their attention eastward where possibly they might recoup their fortunes. Texas had long been neglected. From New Mexico Coronado and Oñate had explored that land, and their investigations had been followed by those of Friar Juan de Salas in 1632, Alonzo Baca in 1634, and Herman Martín with Diego del Castillo in 1650; but the results had been insignificant. More recently, in 1675, another party led by Fernando del Bosque and Friar Juan Larios had crossed the Rio Grande from Coahuila and had returned with a recommendation that missions should be founded in Texas; but they elicited no response. Now, oddly enough, a delegation of Jumano Indians appeared in El Paso to extend an invitation for missionaries to take up residence among them. It seems that they thought missions meant aid with defense, and this they needed in their contest with marauding Apaches. At that time the pioneers in El Paso were also interested in rumors of pearls to be found farther east in the land of the Tejas Indians, and in the possibility that an overland route might be opened to a seaport for trade with Havana. Consequently the new governor, Domingo Petrís de Cruzate, authorized the exploration of Texas. He sent forth Captain Domínguez de Mendoza and Fray Nicolás López with a dozen soldiers and one other friar. They crossed the Pecos and Concho Rivers to another river in central Texas, probably the Colorado. They stayed six weeks, erected a combined fort and chapel, and baptized many Indians. This field they abandoned in order to journey to Mexico City and present a plea for support in founding more missions, but again the appeal was in vain.

The Spaniards had much else to do before they could get around to Texas.

In 1689, Governor Petrís attempted a reconquest of the pueblos. He led an expedition to Sía, or Zía, which he took after a severe battle. Hundreds of the occupants were killed, and many preferred to die in their burning houses rather than to surrender. After this demonstration of will to resist, Petrís returned to El Paso. Soon he was replaced by a new governor, Don Diego de Vargas, who came with determination to effect the reconquest.

RECONQUEST BY VARGAS

The new appointee was one of the illustrious Vargas family of Madrid, who long had been advisers and soldiers of the emperor. His father had been knighted in the Order of Santiago, and his wife was a Ponce de León. Don Diego consequently possessed a vast estate—mansions, land, and rentals—in both Spain and New Spain. For him certainly the acquisition of wealth was not an objective; therefore he must have been motivated solely by a desire to serve God and the Crown. Something was impelling him forward, and no doubt to the surprise of the dismayed colonists, this newcomer with such a gilded heritage proved to be a vigorous and capable governor.

The settlement of El Paso del Norte was near starvation and suffering also from harassment by the Indians of that locality. First Don Diego de Vargas drove the wild tribes away from that vicinity, and then he organized an expedition for subjugation of the pueblos. In August, 1692, he set forth with about two hundred men, including Indian

auxiliaries. Along the Rio Grande he found most of the villages deserted and met no resistance until he came to Santa Fe on September 13. The ruins of that *villa* were surrounded with entrenchments, which swarmed with Indians. After negotiations had failed, Vargas laid seige. When he cut off the supply of water in the town ditch, his final ultimatum demanding surrender was heeded. Then Vargas and his men repossessed Santa Fe in the name of Charles II, his Catholic Majesty, and the friars absolved the natives of their heretic defection. Soon neighboring pueblos also submitted peaceably. After the death of Popé, their fiery leader, in 1690, apparently the Indians had lost their enthusiasm about basking again in primitive "freedom." Moreover, existence for them had been hard after they had destroyed most of their own pueblos.

Vargas marched his army east, north, and west to accept the submission of one pueblo after another. Finally, he went west to the Hopi, who were bluffed out of their insolence by the sheer boldness of Vargas. While returning as a reconqueror he paused at Inscription Rock to carve under Coronado's famous inscription his own record of achievement. In short order twenty-three pueblos had been recovered, at least superficially, and the only bloodshed had resulted from skirmishes with some Apaches. The drive and determination of Vargas had proven to be effective in overawing the faltering natives. His tactics were described by Don Carlos Sigüenza y Góngora in this passage about the Hopi:

The general made a halt and forced the Indians, who were most conspicuous in their impudence and insults, to come up to where he was, and he said to them: "Oh, Indians, oh, you dogs of the worst breed that the sun warms! Do you think that my tolerance is owing to fear of your numbers and arms? Pity is what I have had for you in not killing you, for by a single threat on my part, you would all perish. . . .

The crash of a thunderbolt would have left them less awestruck than these words and, no answer to give, they laid down their arms and knelt on the ground to worship Most Holy Mary in her image, striking their breast many times.[3]

In El Paso, now that the way had been prepared, many of the colonists packed their belongings for the journey back to the former homes. For reinforce-ments, Vargas recruited some soldiers elsewhere in New Spain. When finally ready the expedition was comprised of one hundred soldiers, seventy families, eighteen Franciscan friars, and numerous Indian allies and servants. With appropriate pomp and ceremony, they departed on October 4, 1693. This time, however, the *entrada* was not made so peacefully. The first alarm came from the chief of the friendly Pecos Pueblo. He had traveled all the way from Pecos out onto the road below Santa Fe in order to warn Vargas that seven towns were preparing to resist occupation. Rumor had spread among the Indians that Vargas would not respect his promise of forgiveness and would execute all the leaders of the revolt. In mid-December, when the expedition approached Santa Fe, the occupants refused to admit the Spaniards. Vargas again sought to negotiate. In two weeks, while the colonists were camping out in the cold, twenty-one died of exposure. His resolution aroused, Vargas stormed the walls of the *villa*, battered down the gates, and occupied the city with the loss of only one man. Immediately his soldiers singled out seventy of the Indian leaders, for whom a prayer was offered by Padre Juan de Alpuente, and then they were promptly executed.

PACIFICATION OF THE PUEBLOS

To launch the New Year of 1694 the seven hundred colonists and soldiers were resettled in Santa Fe, only to become aware that surrounding ene-

[3] Irving A. Leonard, trans., *Mercurio Volante of Don Carlos de Sigüenza y Góngora* (Los Angeles, 1932), p. 82.

mies made their position precarious. The friendly pueblos included only Pecos, Santa Ana, Sía, and San Felipe. Vargas promptly set out to subdue the others in rapid series of marches and assaults. First, in April he and his band of soldiers dislodged the Cochití from a high butte. Then he attacked the Indians of San Ildefonso, whose position proved to be too strongly fortified. Passing them up temporarily, he carried his campaign up the Rio Grande to the border of present Colorado, where he had a skirmish with the Ute Indians. On the return march he overcame the Jémez warriors, who held a strong defensive position on a high *mesa*, and then attacked San Ildefonso again, with success this time.

Once more Spanish settlement spread out in the vicinity of Santa Fe, and the friars undertook assignments among the pueblos. A group of fresh arrivals founded a settlement at a place which they named the "New Villa of Santa Cruz." At the capital a newly appointed *cabildo* tried to cope with many problems, including both deficient supplies and hostile Apaches. Presently a warning came of another Pueblo conspiracy, but amid so many urgent problems, the tip was disregarded.

Another revolt did occur in June, 1696, when the Indians of six pueblos arose with renewed fury and killed five padres and twenty-one colonists. Again Vargas called out the soldiers and raged up and down the valley, battering down resistance with a vengeance. By the end of his term of office that year, he reported all hostiles suppressed except at Ácoma and the Hopi villages. He felt that he had earned reappointment; but before the viceroy received his petition, a successor had already been named.

As soon as the new governor, Pedro Rodríguez Cubero, arrived in July, 1697, he initiated the customary *residencia* in a manner designed to humiliate his predecessor and to profit from his deposition. Now that the resolute Vargas was out of power, latent grudges came out into the open. The *cabildo* alleged that Vargas had been domineering, that he had embezzled royal funds, that he had deprived the colonists of their Indian slaves, and that he had recklessly provoked the Indians into hostility. Rodríguez Cubero as judge of the *residencia* jailed Vargas, found him guilty, fined him four thousand pesos, and ordered his property confiscated. However, the custodian, Fray Francisco de Vargas, who was no relation to Diego, saw that an injustice was being done and made a special trip to Mexico City in behalf of Don Diego. As a result, he was ordered released. Meanwhile the king had received and granted the petition of Vargas for reappointment.

In July, 1700, the order for release and the news of reappointment arrived in Santa Fe simultaneously. The chagrined *cabildo* immediately recanted. Therefore the charges were withdrawn, the fine was cancelled, and the governor's property was restored. The deflated prosecutor, Rodríguez Cubero, departed from the province immediately.

After three years in jail, Vargas was back in office again. Now he reported chaotic conditions, which he blamed on the maladministration of the interim incumbent. Once again he marched forth his soldiers for a campaign of retribution against hostile Indians, this time the Apaches. Unfortunately his physical condition, undermined by imprisonment, precipitated an illness while he was in pursuit of the enemy in the Sandía Mountains. He died at

Bernalillo on April 14, 1704. During his regime the pueblos again had been subjugated and churches had been rebuilt. Retribution for treachery had been so thorough and so prompt that the Pueblo Indians remained pacified for many years. One contributing factor no doubt was the decision of Vargas not to permit the restoration of the exploitive system of the *encomiendas* of prior years. The colony in New Mexico had survived a century of precarious existence, and now this foothold was assured.

TROUBLESOME NEIGHBORS

In the next century the principal sources of trouble were the unpacified neighbors. They included the Hopis, Navajos, Utes, and Apaches, as well as some newcomers, the Comanches, who were pressing westward from the high plains. The friars were especially dejected over the defection of the Hopi (sometimes called Moqui) from the ranks of civilized tribes. They had reverted to their old customs and ignored the entreaties of visiting missionaries and governors. The thirty families who did accept conversion were considered renegades by the Hopi; therefore they were resettled at a separate site at La Laguna. There they created a new pueblo.

Of the nomadic Indians, only the Jicarilla Apaches were inclined to be friendly. Since they dwelt close at hand, in the mountains around Santa Fe and Taos, they engaged in a regular commerce with Spanish traders. In 1723, a royal decree ordered that all such commerce should be restricted to official trading posts in Pecos and Taos. The friars then founded a few missions out among the Apaches, but those Indians were unresponsive. Meanwhile all frontier garrisons since 1707 had been pulled in and concentrated at Santa Fe, because the Apaches, Utes, and Comanches were crowding close to the settled area. The garrison, however, was rather impotent in intercepting the surprise raiding parties of the Apaches, who it seemed would trade one day and raid the next. Legend has it that they practiced wise forethought, because whenever they stole livestock they were careful to leave a few behind so that they would breed more for them to steal the next year. After 1747, the Apaches became even more formidable because of their acquisition of arms by barter with French fur traders approaching from the northeast.

Against the nomadic Indians it seemed that the Spaniards could win a battle but never the war. After suffering a devastating raid, the colonists would muster all their strength for a campaign of retaliation. They would find some wild Indians, and bring back prisoners for impressment into slavery, only to find that next year the marauders were swarming down upon their settlements again. The principal events recorded for the short term of each governor were his campaigns against the Indians: against the Suma near El Paso in 1712, against the Navajos west of Taos in 1709 and 1713, against the Hopi farther west in 1715 and 1747, against the Utes to the north in 1714, 1719, and 1745, against the Apaches south and east in 1704, 1714, 1783–1786, 1795, and

1800, and against the Comanches on the plains in 1706, 1719, 1735, 1762, and 1779.

At times Spanish expeditions ventured far into distant Indian country in a desperate effort to get at the source of the menace. Back in 1664 when a few Pueblo families had escaped oppression by flight to the northeast, Juan de Archuleta with a small company of soldiers pursued them into western Kansas. There they had found refuge with some Apaches in a village which Archuleta named El Cuartelejo. He apprehended the escapees and returned them to their proper jurisdiction. In 1696, some more Pueblos fled to the same place with Vargas in pursuit. He overtook some of them en route, and in 1706 Juan de Ulibarrí led an expedition after the rest. He traveled east from Taos and then north to the Arkansas River, which he followed across present Colorado. At Cuartelejo he took possession in the name of the Crown, appointed an Apache chief as an official representative, and obtained news of French encroachment from the east. He returned sixty-two of the fugitive Pueblos, who, he reported, had been "living as apostates, slaves of the devil, and as captives of the barbarity of the Apache."

Three subsequent expeditions sought to intercept the French and ward off the Comanches. In 1719, Governor Antonio Valverde y Cosio led forth about six hundred men comprised of the Santa Fe garrison and militiamen. He followed the route of Ulibarrí to Cuartelejo, where he learned that French trading posts had been opened on the Platte River. When he returned, he advised further reconnaissance;

therefore another expedition retraced his line of march in 1720. Led by Captain Pedro de Villasur, it was comprised of forty-two soldiers, a friar, an interpreter, and sixty Indian allies. It traveled beyond Cuartelejo into the Pawnee country in the valley of the North Platte. In camp there Villasur's party was ambushed at dawn by a vicious assault of well-armed Pawnees and French traders. Villasur fell, and only twelve Spaniards and forty-eight of the aides escaped. Stunned by this severe blow, Spanish officials considered establishing a *presidio*, or fort, out at Cuartelejo; but they concluded instead that the friendly Apaches might serve as an adequate barrier against further French inroads. Therefore no other expedition went far to the east until 1750, when Bernardo de Bustamante y Tagle led an exploring party down the Arkansas River to the land of the Wichita Indians.

In Santa Fe, a friar, Sylvestre Vélez de Escalante, became interested in opening a trail to the west coast. In 1776, he and another friar, accompanied by eight laymen, including the veteran explorer and engineer, Bernardo Miera y Pacheco, traveled northwest from the capital by way of the Chama valley across the San Juan River through what is now southwestern Colorado to Utah Lake. They turned southwest to Sevier Lake and thence back southeast because of the imminence of winter weather. On their way to the Hopi villages they found a crossing of the Colorado River at Glen Canyon near the present boundary of Arizona and Utah. They had not reached their goal and no immediate results accrued; but their explorations did prepare the way for the later development of a trading route to the west,

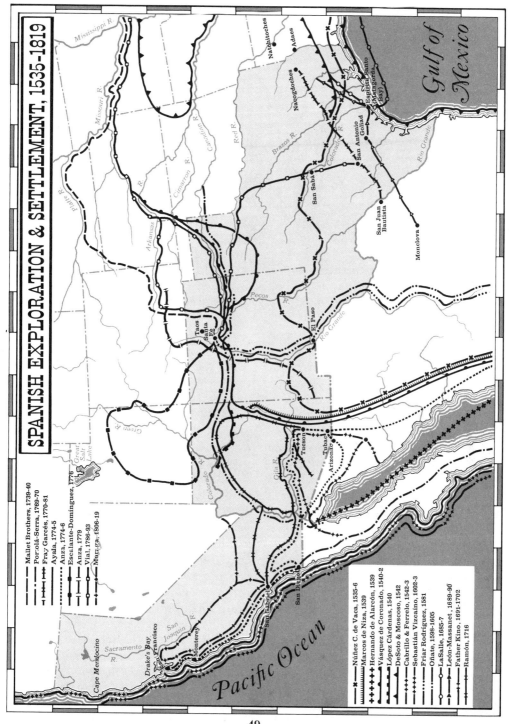

to become known as "The Old Spanish Trail."

In those years the Comanches became a serious menace. In 1779 Governor Juan Bautista de Anza waged a campaign against them with immediate, if not lasting, success. With six hundred and forty-five men, both regulars and volunteers, he marched north through Taos, past present Alamosa, and eastward in Colorado until he found the enemy. In the battle which ensued the Spaniards killed Cuerno Verde, the celebrated Comanche chief, and thirty-eight of his braves. The governor returned a hero.

Again, in 1780, Anza went off in the opposite direction in an effort to open a trail to Sonora, where he had seen action earlier in his career. This time he had in his command about three hundred soldiers and Indian allies. They traveled down *El Camino Real* and turned west through the Mimbres Mountains to the Sonora road in the upper Gila Valley. There a detachment from Sonora met his army, and together they dealt some effective blows upon the troublesome Mimbreño Apaches. He had found a trail which could be used for cooperation in defensive action, and his campaign had pacified the Indians of that region momentarily; but the route was not as direct and practicable as he had hoped. As in the case of Escalante's trail, this one had a potential that would remain dormant until a later time.

A FIRM FOOTHOLD

Although the strenuous drive for security had not removed the Indian menace, the repeated act of retaliation did contribute a greater degree of safety for expansion in central New Mexico. Among the new villages founded in this era was one of thirty families located about sixty miles south of Santa Fe and authorized in 1706 by Governor Francisco Cuervo y Váldez. He named it Alburquerque (now spelled Albuquerque) after the viceroy, a Spanish duke of that name. Accretions to the Spanish population in New Mexico increased the number from about 5,200 (including El Paso) at mid-century to approximately 24,000 by 1800. Pueblo population had been decimated by warfare to about 13,500 in 1750. Due largely to the ravages of a plague of smallpox in 1779 to 1780, their numbers decreased further to about 10,000 in 1800. Meanwhile new governors came and left. Some served briefly and retired with whatever wealth they could salvage from their *residencia*. A few served long enough to give some attention to the improvement of conditions. Notable in this latter group were Juan Domingo de Bustamante, 1722 to 1731, and the aforementioned Juan Bautista de Anza, 1778 to 1788. Incidentally, Anza once ordered the *villa* at Santa Fe moved south of the river in order to improve its defensive position, but twenty-four of the settlers raised such a protest that the *comandante general* in Arizpe set aside Anza's order.

In its second century New Mexico witnessed less serious conflict between the civil and ecclesiastical authorities, but the basis for conflict was still present. Now it had assumed a new form. The *cabildo* in Santa Fe once had recommended that secular churches be established. In 1725, during the administration of Bustamante, the Bishop of Durango had visited this province and expressed a desire to bring the Spanish *villas* under his jurisdiction. Three more *visitas* by bishops followed during the next thirty-five years. Everywhere the prelates were cordially received, though the friars had misgivings. Theoretically they were supposed to evacuate their territory and yield to parish clergy once they had effectively "reduced" the Indians in their missions. In practice, they became jealous of their vested interest and resisted eviction. Sensing that the visit by bishops would lead to their displacement, they contended for retention of their communicants and property. Despite their opposition, parish churches were established in 1797 to serve the Spanish population in the larger towns — El Paso, Albuquerque, Santa Fe, and Santa Cruz de la Cañada.

In the second century of its existence New Mexico had become the home of a heterogeneous population comprised of a few full-blooded Spanish soldiers and *alcaldes*, many Creoles born in New Spain of Spanish ancestry, a growing body of *mestizo* citizens blending Spanish and Indian blood, many Apache household servants held as prisoners of war, and a declining number of subdued Pueblo Indians. Colonial society finally had become adjusted with some stability to the isolation and hardships of this frontier.

At the time of its origin in 1598, the colony in New Mexico antedated both that of the English at Jamestown, founded in 1607, and that of the French at Quebec, founded in 1608. Santa Fe represented a continuation of the original colony, and its founding by 1610 makes it now the oldest capital in the United States, because its only predecessor, Jamestown, was burned and abandoned in 1675. Even the abandonment of Santa Fe from 1680 to 1693 does not impair its continuity, because the location was vacated only temporarily by removal of the settlers to another location within the province.

For a century New Mexico had been the sole Spanish wedge penetrating this northland; in the second century other wedges were entering what is now Arizona, Texas, and California; yet for a long time afterward those fellow colonists would be too far removed for neighborly cooperation.

4
MORE BORDERLANDS

Father Garcés is so well fitted to get along with the Indians and to go among them that he appears to be but an Indian himself. Like the Indians he is phlegmatic in everything. He sits with them in the circle, or at night around the fire, with his legs crossed, and there he will sit musing two or three hours or more, oblivious to everything else, talking with them with much serenity and deliberation. And although the foods of the Indians are as nasty and dirty as those outlandish people themselves, the father eats with them with great gusto and says that they are good for the stomach and very fine. In short, God has created him, as I see it, solely for the purpose of seeking out these unhappy, ignorant, and rustic people.

—Fray Pedro Font, translated in Herbert Eugene Bolton, Anza's California Expeditions *(Berkeley, California, 1930), IV, p. 121.*

OUTPOST IN ARIZONA

For two years beyond a century New Mexico stood alone on the northern frontier before an outpost appeared in Arizona. Several explorers had crossed that area, but permanent occupation would be difficult until the mission frontier of New Spain approached closer. That approach was made by Father Eusebio Francisco Kino, a pioneer Jesuit missionary.

The Society of Jesus, commonly known as Jesuits, had been founded by Ignatius Loyola in 1534 to help counteract the defection resulting from the Protestant Revolt in northern Europe. The order adopted a militant discipline for aggressive missionary activity sustained by education. Much later, in 1664, Kino became a member. A native of the Tyrol in the Alps, he had been educated in Germany, where the Jesuits recruited many of their able teachers. In 1683 Father Kino began work in Lower California and four years later he founded a mission in Sonora. There, at Nuestra Señora de los Dolores, he made his headquarters, alone for six years and with companions for another eighteen years. He had a deep affection for the Indians and enthusiastically taught them elementary lessons in religion. To reach as many as possible he lived constantly in the saddle, often riding twenty or thirty miles a day for weeks at a time. It seems strange that this man, who seemed so durable, often complained in his diary that he did not feel well. Regardless of his infirmities, he demonstrated, too, that he was a good manager. He brought in fruit trees for the planting of orchards at his missions, and he inaugurated cattle grazing on a large scale in about twenty localities of northwestern New Spain.

At that time northern Sonora and southern Arizona were considered to be one province, *Pimería Alta,* or Upper Pima land. Kino found a natural route for his travels down the valley of the Santa Cruz River, which flows northward from Sonora into the Gila River. While devoting himself primarily in the 1690s to his neophytes in the Magdalena Valley, near his base, he also found time for visits among the Pimas of the Gila Valley. On one of his journeys, the Pimas gave him such a cordial welcome that he returned in 1699 and selected a site for a mission. The next year he laid the foundation for his principal base in Arizona, San Xavier del Bac, located nine miles south of present Tucson. In his diary he recorded that on April 28, 1700, "we began the foundations for a very large and capacious church and house of San Xavier del Bac, all the people working with much pleasure and zeal...." He added,

"that house with its great court and garden nearby will be able to have all the water it may need running to any place or workroom...." To the south along the Santa Cruz he soon built two more missions, San José de Tumacácori and Los Angeles de Guevavi. For each his subordinates provided a herd of cattle, and from each they served *visitas,* or branch missions, in neighboring localities.

With their herds, orchards, and workshops, these outposts of New Spain were almost self-sufficient out of necessity in that isolated location. Any tools and ecclesiastical supplies from the outside had to be transported by pack trains over long trails from Guadalajara by way of Dolores, across the mountains, and down the Santa Cruz.

One of Father Kino's good friends, Father Juan María Salvatierra, who had been serving a group of missions in Lower California, crossed the Gulf for a visit with Kino in about 1699. Later Kino found among the Pima Indians some blue shells like those he had once picked up along the California coast. If the Pima had obtained them by barter, surely there must be a land route to Lower California, which then was thought to be an island. Possibly he could open overland communication with Salvatierra's missions. For investigation of this conjecture, he traveled down the Gila to its confluence with the Colorado River in 1700 and retraced that route twice in the next two years. Finally, in 1702, he penetrated far enough into Lower California to satisfy himself that he had rounded the head of the Gulf. In a scholarly treatise, which he sent back to Mexico City, he presented his proof that the "island" actually was a peninsula. That conclusion had also been reported by Ulloa long before, only to be forgotten in the intervening period.

In the course of Kino's long and notable career he founded twenty-nine missions in Sonora and Arizona. One of his compadres wrote that his death in 1711 came "as he had lived, with extreme humility and poverty"; and his deathbed, "as his bed always had been, consisted of two calfskins for a mattress, two blankets such as Indians use for covers, and a packsaddle for a pillow."

NEW LEADERSHIP

After the going of Kino, Padre Luis Velarde succeeded him at San Xavier del Bac, and others followed, but none could quite compare with Kino in austere devotion to the task and friendly reception by the Indians. The task was growing more difficult, too, because hostile Apaches were invading the Pima domain, and even the once friendly Pimas were becoming rebellious against their new taskmasters in the missions.

Another location in Pimería Alta soon attracted attention. In 1736, a rich mine was opened at a place called "Arizonac," just below the present international border. Rumor had it that the deposit was so rich that some miners had found large balls of silver. Immediately hundreds of miners and prospectors rushed there; but within five years those mines, nearly exhausted, were closed by royal order because many of the miners were suspected of carrying away the ores without paying the "royal fifth" into the treasury. Even so, this mining rush gave Arizona its name and brought a northward scattering of transient prospectors.

In subsequent years the Indian menace became more critical. The Pimas rose in rebellion in 1751 and plundered the missions. Temporarily the Jesuits and their aids withdrew into Sonora, but with a company of soldiers for support they returned within a year. At Tubac near Guevavi the soldiers built a *presidio* or fort. They brought with them a few settlers, including the first Spanish woman to make her home in Arizona. Because the Apaches had become a serious threat, the colonists hovered close to the protective walls of the *presidio*. For several years the reports from this outpost revealed that the missions were languishing.

In 1768, two events changed the course of Arizona history. Back in Spain an "enlightened" monarch, Charles III, had launched a series of reforms for improvement of conditions in the colonies, and one of them pertained to the missions. In Spain advisers had persuaded the emperor that the Jesuits were disdainful of royal supremacy. By its great works this Order had grown wealthy, powerful, and international in spirit rather than subservient to the sovereignty of any one nation. Therefore, Charles III became convinced that he was introducing a desirable reform when he issued a decree in 1767 that banished the Jesuits from the Spanish realm and that confiscated their property. After news of this decree had reached the frontier a year later, the Jesuits sadly departed. Although their mission field was transferred to the Franciscans, this "reform" inevitably precipitated a serious setback. During the period of readjustment in Arizona, the missions were slow to recover, and elsewhere in the colonies, where Jesuits were the principal educators, the schools and colleges had to close down. Even before the Franciscans had actively assumed control, the second blow fell. While the little garrison of fifty soldiers at Tubac stood by, unable to lend effective assistance, the mission of San Xavier was raided and burned down by hostile Apaches.

If Arizona were to be brought to life again after 1768, energetic measures would be required. Two capable men responded. One was a Franciscan missionary, Fray Francisco Garcés, and the other was a military captain, Juan Bautista de Anza.

The young, energetic, devoted Garcés arrived at the ruins of San Xavier in 1768. Like Kino, he had a winning way with the Indians. First he brought the Pimas back to the Catholic faith and inspired them to rebuild a new and beautiful edifice for their mission at San Xavier. He even brought in a Spanish architect, Ignacio Gaona, for supervision of this work. Completed in 1797, the mission has been occupied almost continuously and stands out today as the "White Dove of the Desert," one of the remarkable landmarks of the Southwest.

Garcés extended his efforts beyond the realm of the Pimas. In 1770 he explored southwestern Arizona, and the next year he traveled southward to Dolores, Father Kino's former headquarters. Soon afterward he twice accompanied expeditions into California; but that is getting ahead of the story.

The other competent leader who helped revive Arizona was Juan Bautista de Anza, captain of the *presidio* at Tubac. He had been born and raised in Pimería Alta, where both his father and his grandfather had been loyal servants to the Crown. After a spell in Mexico City for formal education, he returned as a soldier to the frontier whose problems he well knew. He also was aware that the defense of California had become important for Spanish commerce and that a feeble colony had been planted at San Diego in 1769. Because of the hazards of travel by ship along the rocky and stormy coast, he concluded that an overland route should be opened through Arizona to California. In 1772, his proposal was received favorably by the viceroy. In order to comprehend more fully its significance, a review of the antecedents will be helpful.

The enlightened monarch, Charles III, had sent to the colonies some new appointees better qualified and more consecrated than many of their predecessors. Among them was José de Gálvez, who served as the royal *visitador general* in New Spain from 1765 to 1771. He conceived the offensive-defensive strategy which had as one objective the occupation of California. Now that England had succeeded in acquiring French Louisiana east of the Mississippi in the French and Indian War, the aggressive English vanguard might imperil Spain's northern border. Morever, since Russia had been sending expeditions to Alaska since 1741, Russian fur traders might soon invade California. Although both threats were then rather remote,

Gálvez capitalized upon them in order to obtain approval for occupying the "wonderful" Bay of Monterey which Vizcaíno had praised so highly. Then Gálvez proceeded with his preparations. He sent military forces into Sonora for pacification of hostile Indians and personally supervised the transport of ships, men, and supplies to the chosen base of operations at San Blas, whence the expedition would cross the gulf to Lower California.

COLONY IN CALIFORNIA

In 1769, two expeditions advanced up the peninsula by land and two ships of supplies and colonists embarked for a voyage by sea to California. Fernando de Rivera y Moncada and the distinguished friar, Juan Crespí, headed the overland vanguard. Gaspar de Portolá commanded the larger land party, which was accompanied by the president of the projected Franciscan missions, Junípero Serra. On April 11, after a voyage of fifty-five days, one of the ships, the *San Antonio*, arrived at San Diego, and two weeks later the other one came in. All of the crew and passengers on both ships were ill with the exception of two friars, and all but two of the crew of the second ship had died from scurvy. Rivera's advance party spent fifty-one days on the march of four hundred miles. It arrived in mid-May, and the larger expedition of Portolá and Serra reached its destination on July 1. San Diego, however, had been selected only as a point of rendezvous; the combined expedition was supposed to move on to Monterey Bay. Therefore Portolá dispatched the *San Antonio* back for provisions, with only eight of the crew well enough to go on board. At San Diego, Father Serra remained to care for the ill and to build a mission, while a party of about sixty, including Portolá, Rivera, and Father Crespí, moved overland toward Vizcaíno's Monterey.

The explorers marched thirty-eight days through an "ungracious" country to Monterey Bay, which was so inauspicious as to escape recognition. Portolá led them on to the Golden Gate, where he found "nothing worthy of description." By that time the men were so famished and exhausted that he concluded he should return to San Diego. There Portolá held on doggedly in the face of near starvation while awaiting the return of the *San Antonio*. Finally the ship arrived with essential provisions. Even though nearly all his crew died during the return journey, the captain agreed to sail on to Monterey. Leaving eight soldiers with Father Serra at his Mission of San Diego, Portolá had only sixteen left to take with him. Undaunted, they embarked for Monterey, where they built a mission and a *presidio*. After Portolá had presided at its formal dedication on June 3, 1770, he left Pedro Fages in command and returned to New Spain.

Only two feeble missions and settlements had been founded thus far in Upper California, and their survival hung in the balance. In fact, in 1772, only a successful bear hunt organized by Fages saved the colonists from starvation. By the next year the friars had built four more missions, at San Gabriel, San Luis Obispo, San Antonio, and San Carlos. Here, however, the Indians were different from those in New Mexico. They were so primitive that it was difficult for them to comprehend elementary instruction about Christianity. Elsewhere offers of food often enticed the Indians to the missions, but even that trick failed here. The simple tastes of these Indians had too long been satisfied by the food prepared from the nuts, herbs, and roots which awaited gathering in abundance in the forests. Besides, seldom did the friars have much food to offer; therefore progress was more disappointing than among the Pueblos of New Mexico. In five years only four hundred and ninety-one baptisms were recorded at all five missions; and that number included not a single adult.

A CONNECTING LINK

The plight of the missions in California became serious. Any supply ship sent north spent weeks on the way and arrived battered by storms and crippled by illness aboard. It is no wonder, then, that Anza's proposal for investigation of the overland route received favorable consideration. Besides, another factor was propitious. Although the energetic Gálvez no longer was present in New Spain as *visitador general*, California had another strong partisan in the person of a new viceroy, Antonio María Bucareli y Ursua, who from 1771 to 1779 gave New Spain its best administration since Mendoza. While he was pondering Anza's proposal Father Serra had arrived in Mexico City and urged adoption. That clinched it. Anza received authorization to take twenty volunteers from his *presidio* at Tubac, with Padre Garcés as guide, for exploration of a route across the deserts and mountains to Monterey and for cultivation of the friendship of the Indians along the way.

Anza and his party departed from Tubac on January 8, 1774. Besides Garcés and twenty soldiers, the expedition enlisted Father Juan Díaz, three guides, and some laborers. The livestock included, besides the necessary horses, sixty-five head of cattle and thirty-five pack mules carrying provisions. One soldier even took along his violin, which later served a useful purpose in entertaining the Indians. Anza traveled west across Sonora, past the ruins of some of Padre Kino's missions, to Altar, the outermost *presidio*. Here he veered northwest through the desert country of the Pápago Indians. That was a difficult leg of the journey. The party made it, nevertheless, by virtue of Anza's good management, the friars' earnest prayers, and the natives' water "tanks" found on the slopes of the hills.

Upon arrival in the land of the Yuma Indians, Anza lingered a while in order to cultivate the friendship of Chief Salvador Palma. His good will would be essential for continued access to the ford across the Colorado River near its confluence with the Gila. Palma was won over by a speech by Anza, a gift of some medals, and presents for his tribe. Ahead lay the sand dunes above Laguna Salada, that proved to be a test even more severe than the crossing of the Sonora desert.

Hindered by excessive impedimenta, the party failed in its first attempt to cross the dunes. Anza returned to the Yuma and left a few soldiers and most of his pack train in the care of Chief Palma. Thus, by traveling light, he was able to skirt the deserts and toil through mountain passes to San Gabriel, north of San Diego. His arrival on March 22 sparked justifiable joy in the missions.

In pursuit of his orders, Anza made a rapid journey to Monterey, and back at San Gabriel he sent a favorable report to Bucareli. On May 3 he set out on his return trip. When he arrived at the Colorado River, he found that Palma had taken good care of his pack animals and provisions, but that the soldiers he left there had deserted. On the homeward journey Anza tried a route up the valley of the Gila and found it less difficult than crossing the desert of the Pápago country. Padre Garcés took leave of the expedition at Yuma and wandered about among Indian tribes of his acquaintance north of the Gila. Therefore it was Anza who arrived first at Tubac on May 26. By a journey of only four and one-half months, and without mishap, he had opened a difficult but passable trail to Monterey.

That fall he reported in person to the viceroy, who promoted him to the rank of lieutenant colonel of cavalry as a reward for his "special merit."

Meanwhile Bucareli had been encouraging other undertakings for the development of California. First he approved an instrument of government for the colony in 1773, and the next year he sent Juan Pérez to explore the coast up to fifty-four degrees north latitude. Simultaneously he arranged for Juan Manuel de Ayala to reconnoiter San Francisco Bay in preparation for a colony to be brought there by the new governor of upper California, Fernando de Rivera y Moncada. In 1775, another expedition under Bruno de Heceta sailed on up the coast, and one of his captains made a survey to a point about fifty-eight degrees north, farther than any Spaniard yet had ventured. But still there was no colony at San Francisco. In 1774, Rivera had brought to San Diego a small group of settlers from Lower California, but that was enough of a journey for them. Therefore, for the purpose of founding a *presidio* and a colony at San Francisco, Anza received authorization to lead a second expedition overland across Arizona.

TO THE GOLDEN GATE

Anza's colonizing expedition was ready to leave Tubac late in October of 1775. It was comprised of two hundred and forty persons, one hundred and forty mules carrying provisions, and four hundred and fifty saddle horses and mules. Padre Garcés went again along with two other friars. Of the thirty soldiers, only one was unmarried; the rest had their families with them, as

did most of the colonists. For the pack train to carry, Anza had overseen the gathering of an abundant stock of supplies. There were tents, tools, provisions, presents for the Indians, spare clothing for everyone, including such items as four pair of stockings and six yards of ribbon for each woman.

The California-bound colonists traveled down the Santa Cruz to the Gila and along the latter to the Colorado River. There they were received as guests by the Yuma Indians, whose Chief Palma was presented with a gorgeous suit of clothes sent by the viceroy. As a result of the friars' instructions of the preceding year, Anza observed that these formerly naked polygamists now wore a little clothing and that each brave now had only one wife. With the aid of the stalwart Yumas, the expedition was forded safely across the Colorado River. Beyond lay the severe trial of the desert and dunes, but all made it across safely. Remarkably, upon arrival at San Gabriel on January 3, 1776, this expedition could count four more persons than at the start, owing to the birth of babies en route.

Anza's arrival proved to be a timely godsend for the California missions. The Indians of that locality, perturbed by the invasion of their land, had organized a conspiracy for eviction of the Spaniards. Already they had attacked the Mission San Diego, and soon they expected to wage a general campaign which might have been as devastating as the earlier revolt of the Pueblos in New Mexico. At that critical moment, two supply ships hove into port and Anza's expedition arrived. This timely demonstration of unexpected support overawed the Indians and so prevented a massacre.

Previously Anza and others had pioneered the opening of a trail near the coast, which came to be known as the *Camino Real* of California. By that route he led the colonists northward to Monterey, where they arrived on March 10 in a steady downpour of rain. Governor Rivera then accompanied Anza on to San Francisco Bay for the selection of a site. That done, Anza concluded that his mission had been accomplished. He turned over the command to José Joaquín Moraga and departed on his return journey to New Spain. His companions part way were only a dozen soldiers and Fray Pedro Font, but at the Colorado River they were augmented by the addition of Chief Palma and some Yuma chiefs. In response to Anza's persuasion they went along for a visit in the great city of Mexico.

Father Garcés took off on his lone way, as he had done on his previous trip. First he explored the Colorado River to its mouth, then he returned northward to the Mojave River and west through Cajón Pass to San Gabriel. Soon he backtracked over the pass to the Mojave villages and set out east in an effort to find a new trail. He succeeded in finding his way across present Arizona to the Hopi villages. Everywhere he was encouraged by the reception extended by the Indians, except among the Hopi. Like his contemporaries in New Mexico, he found those Indians rather adamant about accepting reconversion.

Back in Monterey the governor, Rivera, had lost what little enthusiasm he had had about colonizing at San Francisco Bay and refused to lend further assistance. Nevertheless, Anza's Lieutenant, Moraga, set out with the colonists on June 17. Ten days later they arrived at the Bay, where they camped at a place they called Dolores. Within a month they were able to move to a *presidio* which they were building. In a small chapel Fray Francisco Palóu conducted the first mass on July 28, and on September 17 the log *presidio* was ready for dedication in honor of the feast of San Francisco. Meanwhile the colonists had erected log cabins for their homes and a warehouse for storage of provisions that were to be brought in by sea. Finally, in the same year when the English colonists on the distant eastern seaboard were launching their struggle for independence, the Spaniards had made more secure their claim to California by the founding of a colony near the Golden Gate. Five years later they strengthened their hold on the coast by founding another settlement at another bay named Los Angeles. So the project initiated by Gálvez, Portolá, and Serra had been brought to fruition by another capable trio, Bucareli, Anza, and Garcés.

As *visitador general*, Bernardo de Gálvez had recommended that the entire northern frontier be designated the "Interior Provinces" and united for coordinated defense under one *comandante general*. The first appointee to that post, Teodoro de Croix, prepared plans for the establishment of a

fort and settlement at the strategic Yuma crossing of the Colorado River and of a regular supply service and overland mail on Anza's route. This plan had been abetted by the visit of Chief Palma to Mexico City, where this swarthy guest was baptized by the archbishop and granted an audience by the viceroy. Palma asked that missions and settlers be sent to his realm and, because that coincided well with the desires of the viceroy, his wish was granted. The officials failed to comprehend that in Palma's experience missions also meant presents for his tribe.

Soon, in 1779, Croix undertook this project though he was able then to send to Yuma only a dozen soldiers and two friars, Garcés and Díaz. They crossed over the Colorado River to the west side, where Garcés founded Puerta de la Concepción, a small log mission, while Díaz built his, San Pedro y San Pablo, eight miles down river. At each mission they added a small cabin to house some soldiers.

THE YUMA MASSACRE

The Yumas soon learned that although the missionaries had benevolent desires, the soldiers did not. They taunted the Indians about their primitive practices and appropriated the best of their lands. Garcés employed his good offices in an effort to keep the natives placated. Then the settlers came. For their supervision the able, tactful Anza was not available, as he had been rewarded in 1778 by an appointment as governor of New Mexico. Instead, the man sent to Yuma in 1781 was Rivera, the faltering former gover-

nor of California. He brought two more friars, some additional soldiers accompanied by their families, and no presents for the Yumas. As these additional intruders settled among the natives, they only provoked more antagonism. The Indians learned quickly enough what a settlement in their midst really meant. On July 17, they rose in revolt and massacred all except the women and children, who were taken as captives. Afterward some of the survivors related how Chief Palma came to the ruined mission, lifted the body of Padre Garcés in his arms and wept. This seemingly undeserved fate as a martyr had brought to an end the labors of Arizona's second great missionary.

Colonel Pedro Fages and a company of soldiers came up from Sonora in September, 1781, with the determination of avenging the Yuma Massacre. However, overawed by the numbers of the aroused Indians, they engaged only in negotiations to obtain the release of the women and children and the recovery of the bones of the friars. For many years afterward, the hostility of the Yumas effectively disrupted all traffic on the overland trail from Arizona to California.

In Tubac, where the *presidio* and missions had bustled with activity in its few years of association with California, the severing of the trail brought back the isolation of earlier years, even though Anza had brought about a few changes. Before he left for his post in New Mexico he had recommended that the *presidio* be moved. As he had observed that the Apaches usually came to San Xavier del Bac from the north, he proposed that the garrison at Tubac be relocated nearer the Gila River. At a site known as Tucson the padres already had established a *visita*. When the *presidio* was built there in 1776, a

Spanish colony of soldiers' families along with a few ranchers and traders made their homes at Tucson.

From New Mexico, in 1780, Anza waged a campaign westward against the Apaches in Arizona, bringing some relief for the colonists there. In fact, a time of relative peace prevailed until after 1800. That breathing spell encouraged expansion of the area for ranching around the missions and for prospecting in the mountains. However, the loss of contact with California had a deadening effect, and throughout the remainder of the Spanish colonial era, little news was heard from Arizona.

Out on the coast after the Yuma Massacre the colonists again became dependent upon the hazardous coastwise contact with the cities of New Spain. For a few years the venerable Father Serra continued his labors. By the time of his death in 1784 he had founded nine missions along the King's Highway connecting the islands of settlement between San Diego and San Francisco. As Father-President his successor was Fermín Francisco de Lasuén, who was to serve until his death in 1803. In his time nine more missions were added. He had the distinction, too, of being appointed as the first ecclesiastical judge and commisary of the Inquisition in Upper California.

ROMANTIC CALIFORNIA

As in New Mexico, the civil and religious authorities came into conflict. In the early years the very survival of feeble California had been kept in hazard by the dispute of Father Serra with Pedro Fages about jurisdiction over the soldiers assigned for pro-

tection of the missions. Later a serious dispute arose when the zealous Felipe de Neve replaced Rivera as governor in 1777. Immediately he advocated that, henceforth, each new mission should be assigned only one friar, who should attend strictly to spiritual matters without having any economic enterprises to oversee. Father Lasuén so vociferously deplored the imposition of "grievous desolation" upon the missions that the governors who succeeded Neve after 1782 dropped that proposal. Now Father Lassuén had a free hand in the development of the missions, that already were active centers of farming and ranching. Then he introduced instruction in crafts, which enabled the friars to employ the Indians in a rebuilding of the missions with innovations in architectural design known later as the characteristic "mission style." The improvement of the missions and the devotion of their unfettered leadership yielded encouraging results. By 1806 the friars could boast of twenty thousand Mission Indians responsive to their surveillance.

By 1800, California had—besides the "reduced" Indians—about twelve hundred *mestizo* and Spanish settlers in the several villages scattered mainly along the King's Highway. Attention next turned to exploration and expansion inland. One governor after another almost every year sent expeditions over into the Central Valley and sometimes into the mountains beyond. In 1806, for example, no less than four expeditions were in the field. One of them, led by Gabriel Moraga, penetrated to the foothills of the Sierra Nevadas. For that year the Father-President, Estevan Tapis, reported visits to twenty-four villages of natives having a total population of fifty-three hundred In-

dians. Thirteen years later the veteran Moraga led an expedition around the southern tip of the Sierra Nevada and on across the Mojave Desert. By that time a few missions had been added at inland locations.

After 1790 English and Yankee ships began putting in at California ports. Soon the Russians also appeared. In 1806, Nikolai Rezánof sailed into San Francisco Bay in quest of supplies to take back to a famine-stricken Russian colony of fur traders at Sitka in Alaska. While there he courted young Concepción Argüello, the attractive daughter of the *presidio comandante*. He had to finish his errand first, but he promised to return. Concepción waited faithfully, but he did not reappear. Finally she became a nun and devoted her remaining years to charitable work. It was in 1842 that she learned that Rezánof had succumbed to illness while crossing Siberia.

This romance is often mentioned as an illustration of the isolation, during the years from 1780 to about 1820, known as the "romantic period" in Upper California. The colonists, undisturbed by the events of the outside world, had to rely upon their own resources for winning a livelihood and finding entertainment. The nearest neighbor was the Russian fur-trading post of Fort Ross which had been established in 1812 on Bodega Bay not far from San Francisco; but with those threatening rivals there was only intermittent intercourse.

RIVALS IN TEXAS

With the story of colonial expansion in Arizona and in California now recounted, attention turns next to Texas. Actually the first permanent settlement in central Texas came chronologically between those of the two far-western provinces. However, the temporary relationship of Arizona with California provided a logical continuity from one to the other, just as the sequence of events will lead conveniently from Texas out to the Louisiana frontier.

As related previously, Texas had been penetrated by Spanish explorers several times before 1700, but no lasting foothold had been gained. The motive that finally impelled colonists across the Rio Grande was the encroachment of French rivals in that province. Specifically, they were alarmed by the activities of the noted French entrepreneur, René Robert Cavelier, Sieur de La Salle.

In the region of the Great Lakes, La Salle had first founded a fur-trading empire, and this seemed only to arouse his desire for further adventure. With Henri de Tonti, he descended the Mississippi River to its mouth in 1682. In the mistaken belief that he was the discoverer of the Delta, he claimed possession of the entire river basin in the name of Louis XIV, for whom he named the valley "Louisiana." Upon his return to Quebec he sailed for France in order to promote the occupation and exploration of the southern reaches of Louisiana.

In Paris, the exiled former governor of New Mexico, Peñalosa, already was seeking French aid for an expedition which he might lead to the Rio Grande and inland. He held out the inducement that rich mines awaited conquering; but the fact was that he bore a grudge for his eviction from New Spain. Already he had interested the French court in his proposal and now, lest he be pushed aside in favor of La Salle, he proposed a joint project. With one fleet La Salle could plant a colony at the mouth of the Mississippi while he would occupy Pánuco (Tampico). La Salle had proposed that the king provide two ships and two hundred men for the planting of a colony at the mouth of the Mississippi; he would then enlist Indians for assistance in conquering those "rich mines" of Nueva Vizcaya which Peñalosa had described. This the king accepted with such enthusiasm that he granted four ships instead of two. According to Father Nicolás de Freytas, the expedition of La Salle was to be a preliminary thrust in preparation for the invasion of New Spain by Peñalosa.

La Salle embarked from France on August 1, 1684, with three hundred men on the four vessels. After a delay in Santo Domingo caused by sickness aboard, three of the ships finally headed westward in the Gulf of Mexico in December. Another misfortune befell them when La Salle's pilot lost his bearing, passed the Mississippi Delta, and landed at Matagorda Bay on the coast of Texas in January, 1685. There the ferocious Karankawa Indians took as captives the first group of men sent ashore and, while La Salle was rescuing them, one of the ships foundered. With it went a cargo of provisions. Soon

La Salle quarreled with his pilot, who then sailed away with one of the remaining seaworthy vessels. Soon a large number of the men who had gone ashore with La Salle became ill because of the unsalubrious conditions at their camp.

One misfortune after another had decimated the colony and discouraged the survivors. However, a new campsite proved more satisfactory, and food was found in abundance in the wilderness. Now in an effort to determine his location, La Salle explored eastward to a river which he thought might be the Mississippi. To guard that escape route he left at the river a small detachment of soldiers who never afterwards were found. When he returned to the others at their makeshift camp, he found that Indians had massacred all the crew of the only ship that remained afloat and that the vessel had then drifted out to sea. Again La Salle took some of the colonists eastward in an effort to find the Mississippi River. By this time they had become overwrought with hatred and dissension. In an encampment somewhere near the Brazos River, disgruntled conspirators assassinated

La Salle and plundered his personal possessions. The young explorer, then only forty-three, had blundered into an unfortunate end to an illustrious career. One of his followers, Henrí Joutel, attempted to explain how this had come about:

> He had a capacity and talent to make his enterprise successful; his constancy and courage, and his extraordinary knowledge in arts and sciences, which rendered him fit for anything, together with an indefatigable body, which made him surmount all difficulties, would have procured a glorious issue to his undertakings, had not those excellent qualities been counterbalanced by too haughty a behavior, which sometimes made him unsupportable, and by a rigidness towards those that were under his command, which at last drew on him implacable hatred and was the occasion of his death.[1]

Most of La Salle's colonists perished, but Joutel and seven others made their way overland to the Mississippi, up it by canoes to the Great Lakes, and finally to Quebec. There, in July of 1688, they brought the news of the disastrous end of the lost Mississippi colony.

CONTINUED COMPETITION

It was inevitable that the Spaniards should hear that the French had planted a colony in Texas, but rumor failed to describe the outcome. Therefore, the Spaniards became aroused about this intrusion in a land which by prior exploration they claimed was theirs. In 1686, Alonso de León was sent from Coahuila with a company of men to the Rio Grande in search of La Salle's colony. The next year he probed far-

ther, to the Nueces River. In 1689, after León had been promoted to the governorship of Coahuila, he led forth another expedition with Father Damian Massanet as chaplain and a French deserter from La Salle's colony as a guide. This time he found the site of La Salle's former camp on the Bay of

---

[1] Quoted in Isaac J. Cox, *Journeys of Rene Robert Cavalier, Sieur de La Salle* (New York, 1905, 1922), II, p. 127.

Espíritu Santo, as the Spaniards named it. There they found nothing but ruins and desolation—"a wooden fort made from the hulk of a wrecked vessel,... a great lot of shattered weapons, broken by the Indians,... two unburied bodies,... many torn-up books, and many dead pigs." However, León picked up a report from an Indian that the French colonists had founded a settlement farther inland, where they soon would bring their families and more colonists.

False rumors obtained from loquacious Indians and the occasional appearance of a Frenchman among the natives still impelled the Spaniards onward. In 1690, León and Massanet crossed Texas to the Trinity River, where they built a *presidio* and mission at a site about forty-five miles southwest of present Nacogdoches. They named it San Francisco de los Tejas. Three padres and a few soldiers remained there while León returned to Coahuila. The Indians here, like those in California, proved to be unreceptive. The padres sought to bring the natives into the missions where they could be "reduced" from barbarism under their close supervision; but the plan failed. Then the few soldiers grew restless and this mission was abandoned. A year later Father Massanet and Domingo Terán led another party to the site of the mission. Terán hoped to find and expel any French intruders and also to build more missions for the nine friars who accompanied him. However, because the winter weather in that location turned out to be more severe than was anticipated, he withdrew without accomplishing either objective. This early effort to hold Texas by the founding of missions far out on the eastern border had failed; but it, too, would be renewed later.

During the next twenty years, while the Spaniards neglected Texas, the French approached closer. In 1699, they achieved La Salle's goal by planting a colony at Biloxi, near the Delta of the Mississippi, and in 1718 they found a suitable site near the mouth of that river for the founding of New Orleans. Meanwhile at the Spanish Mission of San Juan Bautista on the Rio Grande, Father Francisco Hidalgo had been begging for greater support, but in vain. If the Spaniards were not interested, he would try the French, for they, too, were Catholic. Therefore he addressed a plea for aid to Antoine de la Mothe Cadillac, governor of New France. It was a propitious moment, for the king of France had granted a contract to Antoine Crozat for trade with the Indians of lower Louisiana. In 1713, Crozat sent a representative, Louis Jucherau St. Denis, to establish a trading post at Natchitoches on the Red River. Information about Father Hidalgo's request was transmitted to St. Denis. Therefore, he crossed through the land of the Hasinais Indians to the Rio Grande in an effort to confer with Hidalgo, only to find him temporarily absent from his mission. The captain of the soldiers, Diego Ramón, then held St. Denis at San Juan Bautista and requested instructions from the viceroy.

Now St. Denis either indulged in some clever duplicity or concluded that he should join the opposition for his own benefit. He courted and wed Manuela, the granddaughter of Diego Ramón, and after he had been taken to Mexico City, he divulged voluntarily the plans of the French for development of trading posts among the Caddo Indians of Texas. Consequently, the viceroy decided to renew efforts for the planting of a Spanish outpost in eastern Texas. For that purpose he authorized an expedition under the leadership of Captain Domingo Ramón, son of the *presidio* captain, and entrusted St. Denis with the responsibility as guide.

The Ramón expedition was comprised of sixty-five persons, including nine Franciscan friars, and it carried along about a thousand head of livestock. In April, 1716, it traveled north from Coahuila and thence east across Texas to the Neches River. There the colonists and friars built a *presidio* and five missions, one of which was located at Nacogdoches near the French post of Natchitoches. At the latter place St. Denis retrieved a cache of hidden wares sent to him by Crozat for bartering with the Indians. Now he claimed the goods as his own and returned to San Juan Bautista to try to sell them there.

Meanwhile the wary Spanish officials had intercepted a letter which St. Denis had written to French authorities recommending that they occupy and fortify the bay at Espíritu Santo; therefore St. Denis was arrested and taken to Mexico City. He managed to break out of jail and on a stolen horse he fled ahead of his pursuers to San Juan Bautista. Accompanied by his wife, he escaped to New Orleans. Immediately the French governor returned him to his former command at Natchitoches, where he promoted trade with the Indians until his death in 1744.

PRECARIOUS COLONIES

Due to harassment by both the Indians and the French, the remote Spanish colonies in eastern Texas were in a precarious situation. The Spaniards concluded that communication and defense might be facilitated if a "half-way house" were established on the Texas *Camino Real* leading to those missions. Therefore in 1718, the year of the French founding of New Orleans, Martín de Alarcón, governor of Coahuila, led a party of seventy-two persons to the San Antonio River in central Texas. They founded the Presidio of San Antonio de Bejar on May 5 at a site Ramón had located two years earlier and recommended to them. Near the *presidio* Fray Antonio Olivares directed the building of the Mission of San Antonio de Valero. Because war broke out on the eastern border in 1720 between the Frenchmen and the Spaniards, the exposed missions in the east withdrew to San Antonio. This interruption of continuity in the east meant that San Antonio was to become the second oldest permanent settlement in what is now Texas, counting El Paso as the oldest.

For the reoccupation of eastern Texas, another governor of Coahuila, the Marquís de San Miguel Aguayó, advanced into that region with eight companies of cavalry maintained largely at his own expense. He reopened the eastern missions and beyond them, only fifteen miles from the French at Natchitoches, he built the Presidio of Pilar to protect the mission of Adaes, which was made the first capital of the province of Tejas. He also sent a garrison to man a new *presidio* at Matagorda Bay, and in 1722 near that bay the friars founded the missions of Espíritu Santo. Then additional missions also were opened near San Antonio, which the Spaniards referred to by the latter part of its name, Bejar. At that location the civil settlement was organized in 1731, then known as the Villa of San Fernando. Incidentally, in that settlement it was the large chapel of the Mission of San Antonio de Valero which became the famous Alamo of later history.

Texas, with its first capital at Adaes, became an organized province attached to Coahuila for administration and development. The first governor was Pérez de Almazán, but there is little to record for his term of office. In fact, most of the reports for the first fifteen years pertained to the disturbing rivalry with French traders for influence over the several tribes of Indians. There is a record, too, of the effort of the Franciscans to maintain their missions and to establish more of them farther inland. Discouragement and instability are the themes of the story of the founding of missions and then of moving or abandoning them. For example, the Mission of Espíritu Santo was removed to the Guadalupe River in 1727, only to be relocated again in 1749 on the San Antonio River. There it became the nucleus of a settlement, known as Goliad, at that site southeast of San Antonio. Also, in 1747 three missions were founded on the San Xavier River in the Apache country, only to be abandoned soon afterward in favor of a new site at San Sabá, near present Menard.

At first the friars had great hopes for the mission, but this display of interest in the Apaches antagonized their traditional enemies, the Comanches, who destroyed the mission the year after it had been founded. To avenge the loss, Diego Órtiz Parrilla marched a hundred soldiers to that frontier, but when he attacked the Comanches and Wichitas, in camp on the Red River and flying a French flag, his attack was repulsed with heavy losses. He had to give up, but the struggle continued. As a general rule, the Spaniards maintained the friendship of the Hasinais and occasionally of the Apaches, while the French retained influence over some Caddo and Wichita tribes.

In Texas the poor progress with conversion of the Indians was discouraging. Here, where there were no great pueblos like those of New Mexico, the friars tried to create something like them. By offering gifts, they sought to bring the Indians together in "reductions" where they could supervise their instruction and employ their labor in support of the missions. As in California, these primitive tribes did not respond very well. Offers of food and gifts brought in some, but they could not comprehend the new religion, or they did not want to. Moreover, the imposition of duties created restlessness and often led to rebellion. By 1762, the friars could claim surveillance over only about two thousand Indians. Twenty years later according to Padre Juan Morfi, the number had diminished to about five hundred. By that time the Spanish soldiers and settlers in Texas numbered approximately twenty-six hundred.

The settlements grew slowly, and

governors came and went, submitting to the customary *residencia* before departing. As in New Mexico and California, jurisdictional conflicts arose to complicate other difficulties. The friars contended that the soldiers were vicious and unmanageable; in response the civil authorities at times threatened to remove protective support. Moreover, the friars protested that the settlers wanted to appropriate their Indians for impressment into slavery; the colonists replied that the friars commer-

cialized their advantage by requiring the neophytes in the missions to produce surpluses for sale in competition with the lay producers. In the 1740s this conflict became quite serious, and much to the distress of the friars in the next decade Governor Jacinto de Barrios y Jáuregui issued decrees favoring the soldiers and settlers. More commonly, however, the attention of the governors was diverted from this rivalry by the more serious problem of the intrusion of the French.

FRENCH TRADERS

As the fur traders of New France approached the outposts of the frontier of New Spain, a few boldly crossed the vague borderline in an effort to open commerical relations with the Spaniards. In 1739, Peter and Paul Mallet, with six companions, traveled up the Platte River, crossed southward to the Arkansas River, and ascended it until they found an Indian guide who could lead them through the Sangre de Cristo range into Santa Fe. The viceroy, however, denied their petition for the opening of trade, and in 1740 the frustrated party returned to the headwaters of the Canadian River. There they divided. Some of them went down the Arkansas and Mississippi to New Orleans, while the others traveled across to Illinois.

News that a trail to Santa Fe had been opened encouraged others to renew efforts for commercial contacts. However, the Spanish monopolistic policy would permit no trade with foreigners. From 1748 to 1752 several French traders made futile trips to Santa Fe. One of those ambitious attempts was made in 1751 to 1752 by Jean Chapuis

and Louis Feuilli. Their pack animals carried quite a load of wares, including two hundred and ninety-five ells of cotton cloth, two hundred and sixty ells of melton, one hundred and thirty-five ells of linen cloth, one hundred strips of narrow ribbon, thirty-three cotton caps, twelve beaver hats, thirty pairs of men's hose, seventy-four blankets, twenty-six knives, sixteen hatchets, and thirty-one jugs of aguardiente. On the headquarters of the Canadian River they, too, found an Indian guide who led them across the mountains to Santa Fe. However, like the others they were denied trading privileges. Spanish officials confiscated their goods, sold them at auction, and sent the two Frenchmen to prison in Mexico City, whence they were later removed to Spain.

In 1762, suddenly and rather unexpectedly, the cause for conflict with the French vanished. With Spain as an ally, France had been waging a war against the British from 1754 to 1763. At stake was colonial supremacy in both America and India, and France lost. As the contest neared its end, the French expected Britain to lay claim to all of French Louisiana. In order to keep at least part of it out of the reach of Britain, if that were possible, in 1762 France had ceded Louisiana west of the Mississippi to her ally, Spain. When the change was effected formally, the Spanish border moved over to the Mississippi River, with the British as neighbors and rivals east of the river until the English colonies won their independence.

SPANISH LOUISIANA

By the acquisition of Louisiana, Spain had been relieved of conflict with French traders in eastern Texas, only to acquire problems of administration in Louisiana. In 1766, when Antonio de Ulloa arrived in New Orleans as the first Spanish governor with only ninety soldiers for support, the French officers there refused to heed his orders. Antagonism increased when he prohibited all trade with France in line with established Spanish monopolistic policy. The French settlers broke into open insurrection and expelled him from Louisiana.

Spain responded with vigorous measures. Alexandro O'Reilly, a naturalized Irishman who had become a distinguished Spanish officer, arrived in New Orleans in 1769 with a large expeditionary force aboard twenty-one vessels. After conducting the ceremony of formal possession, he arrested the leaders of the rebellion. He condemned six to death and six to prison sentences, and sent into exile twenty-one others who refused to take the oath of allegiance to Spain. After O'Reilly had broken down all open resistance, he turned conciliatory. He established a *cabildo*, or council, on which Frenchmen were represented, and he appointed several Frenchmen to other important offices. Then he yielded control to Luis de Unzaga as civil governor.

Unzaga made further concessions. He permitted trade with Britain and France in violation of traditional Spanish policy, and he permitted the continuation of familiar French institutions instead of substituting typical Spanish *presidios* and missions. In further deviation from Spanish policy, he sent an agent to Kentucky with an invitation for some of the resident aliens there to settle in Louisiana. On the frontier he even retained French fur traders and made Spanish Indian agents of them. Management of an established colony of people of a different nationality was a new experience for Spanish colonial officers. They soon revised their policies to meet this test, and the common Catholic faith of both ruler and the ruled facilitated the readjustment.

On the frontier at Natchitoches the Spaniards retained as commander a Frenchman, Athanase de Mézières. Previously he had cultivated for France the friendship of the Indians along the Red River; now he had to reverse his tactics and do the same for his Spanish superiors. That was not an easy assignment, but the skill and tact of Mézières were adequate for it. He even employed his abilities in behalf of Spain by traveling among the Indians far to the west near present Waco, Texas. After a visit among the Apaches on the upper Red River in 1778, he crossed southward to San Antonio. There this French Spaniard received a letter rewarding him with appointment as governor of Texas. His immediate illness and death, however, prevented his assumption of the office.

In the formerly contested border zone some significant changes were effected. Because the distant outposts in eastern Texas no longer were needed for defense against the French, the friars and most of the colonists were removed to San Antonio in 1773. Nevertheless some of the settlers longed to return. In their behalf Antonio Gil y Barbo obtained approval, and in 1792 several did return to the vicinity of Nacogdoches, where Gil y Barbo became a responsible Indian agent. He and others represented a revision in Indian policy. Much earlier, in 1767, the Marqués de Rubí had found the frontier of Texas in chaos due largely to the hostility of the Apaches and Comanches. He recommended a realignment of the *presidios* and a war for subjugation of the nomadic tribes. As the military campaign

pacified more and more of the frontier, the Spaniards now borrowed a leaf from the French book. Instead of attempting to corral the Indians into missions, the new policy entrusted Indian relations to bonded agents. While promoting trade, these agents also cultivated friendship for Spain and instilled hatred of the English, who had become the new and dreaded threat.

Back in the older portion of Texas the existing missions, excepting those at Refugio and Espíritu Santo, were secularized. Their lands were sold, their buildings fell into decay, and their former communicants in the larger settlements were organized into parishes. The first such secular church had been established in 1793 in the Villa of San Fernando. By that time the *presidios* and defensive organization had come under the control of Teodoro de Croix, as *comandante general* for the Interior Provinces. In Texas, however, he had made little headway with his plans for reorganization before Spain became involved in the American Revolution.

AN UNCOMMON CAUSE

Once more as an ally of France, Spain became involved in a war against the British. This time the allies had unharmonious objectives. The French court sought to weaken Britain by aiding her colonies in America in their struggle for independence, whereas the Spanish crown sought acquisition of Florida and the Mississippi Valley. This might mean wresting those lands away from the new nation whose independence France was abetting; therefore Spain never entered into an alliance with the Thirteen Colonies. Even so,

the Spanish campaigns directed against the British were helpful to the American colonial cause.

In 1779, Bernardo de Gálvez, governor of Spanish Louisiana, led a strong force up the Mississippi and occupied the British post at Natchez. When the British tried to retaliate in 1780 by taking St. Louis in Spanish Louisiana, they were repulsed by the able defensive campaign conducted by Captain Fernando de Leyba. Then from St. Louis a Spanish expedition marched overland to the southern tip of Lake

Michigan, where they surprised a British contingent at St. Joseph and destroyed the supplies stored there. The Spaniards also occupied Pensacola in British West Florida and provided supplies to George Rogers Clark during his campaign against the British occupants of Kaskaskia and Vincennes.

By helping in the elimination of Great Britain from the Mississippi Valley, the Spanish officials hoped to win the support of France, their ally, in obtaining for Spain an extension of territory into West Florida and the region northward, possibly to the Ohio River. In the final treaty of 1783, Spain did get all of Florida, but by astute diplomacy the representatives of the independent English colonies wrested from Britain all of the West to the Mississippi, except for New Orleans and Florida. At the conclusion of that war, therefore, and for twenty years thereafter, Spain faced at its Mississippi border a new competitor for empire—the young United States of America.

EASTERN CONTACTS

During those forty years when Spain held western Louisiana, trade with New Orleans and St. Louis was not proscribed, for they were within the colonial realm. Therefore intercommunication again was promoted. In the autumn of 1786 the governor of Texas authorized exploration of a trail to Santa Fe. The man selected for this task was a former Frenchman, Pierre Vial, who as a naturalized Spaniard came to be known as Pedro Vial. He went north to the Red River and traveled up it and across the mountains to Santa Fe. This aroused the interest of the governor of New Mexico, who sent José Mares back over Vial's trail for improvement of the route. He arrived in San Antonio in 1787. The next year Vial traveled over much the same route to Natchitoches instead of San Antonio, and then returned to Santa Fe. The governor proposed that he open a trail to St. Louis. Therefore in 1792 he traveled down the Canadian River, crossed over to the Arkansas, followed it eastward, angled across to the Big Bend of the Missouri, and followed that river to St. Louis. On his return trip the next year he followed the Arkansas River west and cut across overland to Santa Fe.

Pedro Vial had charted the path of the later Santa Fe Trail, but conditions were not yet favorable for a profitable commerce. St. Louis did not have available at that early date the products of eastern industry for marketing in Santa Fe. Moreover, Spain soon lost possession of the eastern terminus, and that put St. Louis outside the realm, where Spaniards were forbidden to trade.

Spanish possession of western Louisiana was yielded reluctantly to Napoleon Bonaparte, Emperor of France, by the Treaty of San Ildefonso in 1800. Following the purchase of Louisiana by the United States in 1803, the Stars and Stripes were raised over New Orleans and St. Louis. Once more the border north and east of New Spain became a vague zone somewhere beyond Texas and New Mexico, but now the occupants on the other side were the aggressive frontiersmen of the United States.

For a century New Mexico had stood

alone as an isolated outpost on the northern border of New Spain. In the second century, from 1700 to 1800, the motives of land, religion, and rivalry had impelled Spaniards onward into other borderlands — Arizona, Texas, Louisiana, and California, in that order. That was the zenith in Spanish colonial expansion. Subsequent adjustments of the boundary and relations with new neighbors will be discussed in a later chapter.

5

THE COLONIAL PATTERN

Lands and vicinity to be settled shall be chosen in every way possible for their fertility, abundance of pasture, wood, timber materials, fresh water, transportation, entrances and exits, and that no lakes were nearby, nor swamps in which poisonous animals were bred, nor contamination of the air and the water.... The settlers must arrange that the lots, residences and outhouses shall be in the form which will be an ornament to the settlement, and so that they may benefit from the north and south winds, uniting them in order that they may serve as a defense and strength against whosoever may seek to disturb or harass them; they must so provide that the outhouses will contain their horses and service animals, with yards and corrals of the greatest dimensions possible, in order that they may enjoy health and cleanliness.

Recopilación de Leyes de Los Reynos de Las Indias, *Antonio Balbas,* *ed. (Madrid, 1756), II, pp. vii and xii.*

In New Spain the conquerors and colonists unconsciously sought to reproduce the pattern of institutions and the way of life of the homeland, for that pattern was all they knew. However, there were some inherent variations in the different provinces of Spain, so the pattern was not absolute and, as well, adaptation had to be made to the environment of the frontier. In fact, in colonial government, as described by Marc Simmons, the early pattern was quite simple; but the complexities introduced later almost defy definitive description. With the passing of time, readjustments brought progressive changes; yet a degree of uniformity did prevail and makes possible some generalizations about the pattern of colonial institutions.

LAND SYSTEM

After the early feverish search for precious metals had subsided, the economy settled down to a basis essentially agricultural and pastoral, which necessarily relied upon a system of land ownership. That system included several types of grants. The early conquest in New Mexico was encouraged by the awarding of small *encomiendas,* which were a medieval combination of vague title to land and jurisdiction over the natives residing on it. The Indians, as the American equivalent of Spanish "serfs," retained some land near their villages and tilled their fields, but also rendered services for the *encomendero* as their tribute in payment for the instruction and protection which the master was supposed to provide. The "Dons" as holders of *encomiendas* laid claim to land surrounding Indian villages. Elsewhere in New Spain usually they occupied large houses on their *haciendas,* but in New Mexico the typical *encomendero* was an absentee, residing in Santa Fe. As related previously, after the reconquest these grants were cancelled by Vargas. Elsewhere in the realm the king had been trying to eliminate this type of exploitive privilege since 1542, but in some localities the practice continued until about 1720.

After the *encomiendas* had been abolished, the principal types of land grants employed on the northern frontier were the community grant, the town proprietary grant, and the *sitio,* or ranch.

In the community grant, the title was held by ten or more families who obtained the charter. The typical grant was four square leagues—more than seventeen thousand acres. For the laying out of the towns the royal ordinances gave explicit instructions. After the plaza was located, a lot for the church was to be reserved on an eminent site near the plaza. Small plots for the residences were to be distributed by lot, and in the construction of their residences the settlers were given specific rules as to uniformity and proper ventilation. Near the village a common wood lot and common pasture were to be reserved for use by the entire community. Additional lands were divided into two kinds—fields which could or could not be irrigated—and each head of a family received strips of land in each category. Each settler and his heirs were to have title to the ownership of those fields. This pattern will be recognized as having a uniformity much like that of New England towns. However the pattern in New Spain was imposed by ordinance, whereas in New England it became established by custom.

In New Mexico, where the Indians also resided in villages, the king awarded the pueblos community grants, which came to be known as pueblo grants. For need of another name, the organized Spanish towns were called *villas,* and that name for the Spanish communities also was employed in Texas. In California and Arizona, however, where there were few Indian villages comparable to those of New Mexico, the Indians were gathered into missions for "reduction," and the Spanish villages holding community grants were called *pueblos.* Further, community grants were sometimes awarded also to a *presidio* where soldiers were stationed for a long period of time and wanted to bring out their families.

The proprietary grant vested title in a "Don" who assumed responsibility for the founding of a new settlement. He was authorized to take at least thirty families to the location, where he would lay out the town, distribute the arable lands, build a church, and support a priest.

The *sitio*, on the other hand, was a grant for a ranch without any specifications about supervising its settlement. There were two sizes, small and large, and the practice under this plan progressed from "small" *sitios*, about one league square in the early years, to lavish concessions of hundreds of thousands of acres to prominent favorites of the politicians in the Mexican Period. The owner of a productive *sitio* was the lord of an extensive estate with means for enjoying a life of greater lux-ury than was the lot of the townsmen.

Where a community grant had been awarded, those townsmen owned some land, tended their own flocks, tilled their own fields, and had some voice in the management of the community projects. They were better off than the rural laborers, because of a new system which had been adopted after the *encomienda* system had been discarded. That system was known as "debt servitude." It made *peones*, or serfs, of the rural workers by resort to a subterfuge. The proprietor recorded on his books his transactions with his laborers, and usually only he could read his record. He sold provisions from his stock at high prices and paid the workers low wages. At the end of each year the books showed each tenant still heavily in debt, which bound the laborer to remain and work off his obligation. As a rule, he never got out of debt and continued in a state of peonage.

FRONTIER SOCIETY

The source of the labor supply for peonage usually was derived from a growing *mestizo* population—the propertyless offspring of soldiers who had married Indians. Another source of labor for Spanish "Dons" and affluent townsmen was provided by the acquisition of Indian servants. The law would not allow the overt enslavement of Pueblo or Mission Indians; but it did approve the sale of captured "wild" Indians into slavery. Thus these personal servants usually were captive Apaches. In the missions, of course, the labor was contributed by the neophytes. Often these Indians were pushed hard in a manner not far removed from slavery, so that the missions might have surplus products for sale in the open market. Moreover, missions which were well-blessed with abundant Indians sometimes assigned allotments of them to assist with public works and to labor on private ranches.

While seeking a supply of labor in the early years, the colonists found subsistence uncertain at times. For that reason the Crown provided subsidization in the form of supply caravans sent to *presidios* and missions. In California, for a while, that was supplemented by payment of annuities to help the settlers get started.

As time passed, the colonial outposts

attained a greater degree of self-sufficiency. In fact, each ranch and each mission became nearly a self-contained economic unit. Each had its cattle and sheep, its garden and orchard, its shop and tools. The settler constructed his own house, usually of adobe blocks made from a clay found ready at hand. Wooden beams, or *vigas*, cut from forests nearby, supported a flat dirt roof. Skins and hand-woven rugs and mats covered hard-packed earthen floors. Native pine or oak provided the materials for the making of the few items of furniture, often bearing distinctive designs carved by hand. Few of the poorer households had much furniture beyond a worktable and some storage chests. Beds which were spread on the floor at night were rolled up along the wall to serve as a sofa in the daytime.

The ingenious pioneer and his family, aided sometimes by Indian craftsmen, processed or fabricated most of the necessities for subsistence. Sheep and cattle provided hides and meat. The cowhides made available leather for tanning and shaping into boots, saddles, and harness. Sheep yielded wool which was spun and woven into cloth for the making of garments. The fat of the butchered animals provided shortening for cooking and tallow for home-dipped candles. Corn or wheat from local fields, ground into flour on a stone *metate*, and pinto beans from the garden, became the staple foods, which the ingenious housewife prepared in a variety of ways. Essential utensils were wrought from scrap iron melted down for that purpose, and tableware was moulded from native clay.

An economy based on corn and livestock employed donkeys, oxen, and horses for transportation. Because travel was expensive, slow, and difficult, the poorer classes once they became settled in a given locality did not go far away except for those men who joined a military or exploring expedition. Friars, government officials, and wealthy citizens made astonishingly long journeys across mountains and deserts to distant cities. As they traveled, the "Dons" and the military parties were supported by an impressive entourage of armed guards, personal servants, pack animals, and spare mounts.

Horses, introduced in the colonies in the early years, multiplied rapidly until they became quite abundant. Larger ranches and missions had hundreds of them, and those which escaped bred bands of wild steeds which roamed the countryside. Once at San José, California, horses became so superabundant and pestiferous that the settlers rounded up and slaughtered about seventy-five hundred of them in one month in 1806. Long experience with horses made the Spaniards skillful riders, proud of their fast, dependable mounts. In the early years this gave them a great advantage over the Indians, but as soon as the natives obtained horses, partly by theft and partly by catching some of the wild ones, they too became daring horsemen and formidable foes. Some of the Indians, notably those of the high plains in eastern New Mexico and western Texas, became sly horse traders. Spanish itinerant traders, known as *comancheros*, would move about the countryside to meet these Indians at certain customary places of rendezvous in order to trade weapons and other wares for horses and buffalo hides. This illicit traffic, of course, at times exasperated the soldiers and settlers who greatly feared these native warriors.

On the whole, however, this self-sufficient society depended very little upon commerce. A few traders brought in loads of goods with the presidial and mission supply caravans, and some others brought their goods by sea and put into the ports of California and Texas. They bartered cloth and hardware for hides and wool. Trading in any form usually was by barter, because very little coin of the realm found its way out to the frontier. The *manta*, or shawl, was an item commonly used for expression of value in New Mexico, while a blanket was the unit of value among the Indians, and cattle and hides at the ranches.

Profession and economic status divided the colonial population into four classes. The professional category included the friars and soldiers. The numerous Franciscans and few parish priests enjoyed the prestige of their profession, augmented by the pervasive role of the Church. The soldiers and their families lived a life apart in the settlements surrounding the *presidios*. Many acquired an *esprit de corps* which gave them a feeling of superiority over ordinary colonists.

The economic factor, related also to hereditary titles and standing or the lack of it, divided the remainder of the colonial establishment into proprietors and landless, masters and servants. In California, the upper class prided themselves on being *gente de razón*, in contrast with the childlike aptitudes of their Indian wards. There and elsewhere the proprietors of estates were addressed as Don. Spanish blood, a degree of literacy, government office, and land ownership usually went hand in hand as the prerequisites for entitlement as Don José or Don Juan, whatever the given name might be. Some of these were the aristocratic owners of great estates, while others were only moderately well-to-do. One in New Mexico, for example, owned four farm lots in community land grants and grazed ninety-one head of cattle. He and his family enjoyed the luxury of a nine-room house, while his eight servants occupied small cottages appraised at about three pesos each, and they owed the Don an average of thirty pesos each. For comparative values, a horse was then worth about eight pesos and a sheep one peso. These Dons, whether they were small or great, were not all alike in benevolence. Some earned the trust and gratitude of their numerous servants, whom they regarded as one large family, while others ruled as cruel taskmasters and ruthless exploiters.

THE FRANCISCAN ORDER

In Spanish colonial society the Catholic faith became an all-pervasive influence. As described previously, its missionary impulse had motivated the effective stage of the conquest after 1600. In that the Jesuits had been active temporarily only in one area, southern Arizona, from 1700 to the time of their departure in 1768. Thereafter in Arizona and originally elsewhere on the northern frontier the Franciscans became the agents for propagating the

Faith. Consequently it is well to know something of the ideals and organization of that Order.

The Franciscans owed their origin to young Giovanni Francesco Bernardone, son of a wealthy merchant of Assisi in thirteenth-century medieval Italy. Taken ill while confined as a prisoner of war, he meditated about religion and became animated with a spirit of charity, piety, and poverty. Upon his recovery he sold some of his father's goods in order to provide the local priest with funds for repairing the parish church. As punishment his father demanded that he either pledge obedience to him or renounce his inheritance; and Francis chose the latter. He swore obedience only to his Heavenly Father, took up residence with the Bishop of Assisi, and went about town in the clothing of a poor laborer. He begged for his living while he helped in the rebuilding of the local church.

The townsmen at first regarded Francis as a foolish lad; but presently a wealthy merchant gave away his goods and became a follower of Francis, and then the canon of the Cathedral of Assisi joined the two.

Francis wrote certain rules for his small society. They were to engage in manual labor with no pay beyond that necessary for their bare sustenance. They would have several periods of fasting annually and would consider penance as a virtue in itself rather than only as an atonement for sin. Moreover they would wander freely wherever their services might be helpful, and never would they own any worldly possessions, not even a "blade of grass." Instead, they would accept only the "use privilege" of any property

pertaining to their work. They vowed that they would preach penitence with a minimum of formal discipline. Because they became itinerants, living by alms, they were described as "mendicant friars."

The first Franciscan order grew rapidly and sent missionaries into lands bordering on the Mediterranean Sea. Soon, in 1212, Clare Favorino, an attractive and wealthy Italian girl, borrowed the Franciscan rules for the founding of a second order known as the Sisters of Clare, or the Poor Clares. Next, after Fray Francis had preached a stirring sermon at Cannara, the entire town wanted to join his order. Therefore he prepared rules for a third, or Tertiary Order, open to both men and women, single or married. The members would continue to live in their own homes and could own property and work for profit. They should live and dress simply, should refrain from quarreling with other Christians, and should give to charity any surplus profits derived from their secular interests. This cleverly devised "auxiliary" for support of the Franciscans grew rapidly and later enrolled many of the famous men of the fourteenth and fifteenth centuries.

In 1223, the rules of the Friars Minor received papal sanction. Three years later the founder died, and in 1228 he was canonized as Saint Francis. In 1289, the Pope granted a charter to the Third Order. Subsequently the first body fell into a schism which split it formally in 1415 into two divisions, and later a third group was added. Thus finally the original order produced three branches, the Friars Minor Observant, the Friars Minor Capuchin, and the Friars Minor

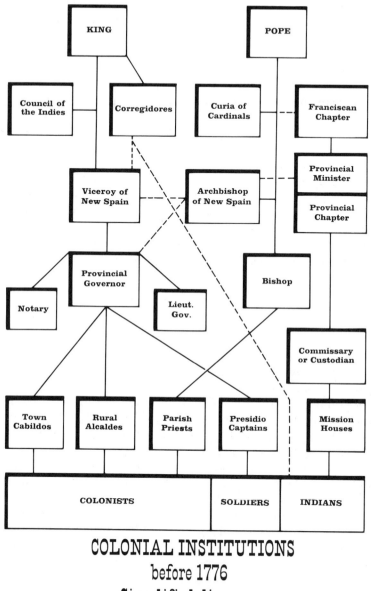

COLONIAL INSTITUTIONS
before 1776
Simplified diagram

Conventual, besides the Sisters of Clare and the Tertiary Order.

Representatives from local areas comprised a general chapter for administration of the work of the Friars Minor. Provinces and custodies were the local units, each including a minimum number of houses, or convents. A guardian headed each convent, and representatives of the convent formed a Provincial Chapter, headed by an elected Provincial Minister. A Commissariat supervised a new frontier area until the number of houses justified the creation of a Custody.

Some Franciscans who came with Columbus on his second voyage opened their first convent in America at Isabella in Hispaniola in 1493. By 1524, they had established a Custody in New Spain which, within ten years, developed into a Province.

A great deal has been said previously about the role of the Franciscans in founding missions throughout the northern borderlands. Although pacification of the Indians was their major objective, they also brought to this frontier the Third Order of St. Francis. Many Spanish laymen and converted Indians became members of local chapters, for which the friars conducted services in their special chapels. In this manner the Franciscans ministered to the non-mission population until the Spanish communities had acquired parish churches with their secular ministry.

RELIGIOUS SERVICES

Near the end of the seventeenth century, a religious society known as the "Penitentes" appeared in isolated rural villages in New Mexico. Members of that society and later observers often have assumed that the rites of the organization originated quite early as a corruption of those of the Third Order. However, Fray Angélico, writing in the *New Mexico Historical Review*, has pointed out that, as late as 1776, Francisco Atanasio Domínguez made no mention of the Penitentes in his thorough survey of the religious institutions of New Mexico. Fray Angélico concluded that the order was patterned after one which existed in Spain, and that it was introduced in New Mexico when the decline of Franciscan activities around 1800 created a religious void.

Whatever the origin, the numerous chapters revived the medieval practice of flogging initiates and requiring them to bear heavy crosses in the ceremony observing Holy Week. Men who became members were classed as Brothers of Darkness (commoners) and Brothers of Light (leaders). The religious rituals of the order usually were performed in *moradas*, or private chapels. The principal exception was the public ceremony performed during the week before Easter. Then the members formed a procession and proceeded silently to a consecrated site for a vivid re-enactment of the events leading to the Crucifixion. Some blood was drawn in the flagellation along the way, but usually without serious injury. Aside from that form of penance, the rules were much like those of the Third Order—to assist at mass, to observe other Catholic rites, and to renounce luxury and litigation. In the colonial era the Penitentes had not yet resorted to secrecy. That came later, after Church officials began to frown upon their practices and curious outsiders became unsympathetic observers.

In the heyday of the Franciscans the Spanish settlers who resided near their convents, even if they were not members of the Third Order, came to the friars for baptisms, marriages, and masses. The fees collected from them helped support the missions. In the larger Spanish *villas* parish churches were supported directly by their communicants. However, these churches, lacking the economic functions of the missions, usually were not so well maintained. They were small, unpretentious buildings, meagerly decorated and inadequately furnished. Nevertheless to them came most of the local Spanish populace to sit on crude wooden benches, or even on an earthen floor, while hearing the mass read in Latin by the scholarly priests. Usually these priests were the only educated persons in the community, upon whom all were dependent for a limited acquaintance with the educational and religious heritage of the Western world. Teachers, lawyers, and doctors were almost universally lacking throughout the colonial era on this frontier.

The Church in the Spanish realm was a state church, closely involved with the civil government. The military provided protection for the friars while the latter aided the military with pacification of the Indians. No heretic expressions or competing religious activities were permitted. Whenever the Office of the Inquisition found someone guilty of heresy, that person was turned over to the civil authorities for punishment. Governors required the *alcaldes,* or local justices of the peace, to keep a zealous watch over their subjects so that they might "be instructed in the rudiments of Our Holy Catholic Faith, ... punishing severely the public and scandalous sinners."

Civil authorities regulated strictly the collection of tithes for the Church. According to one set of instructions circulated on the frontier, the local tithe collector must maintain a list of the number of animals in all flocks and herds in his locality. He had to send his list to another collector if one of the owners moved. He was required to observe all flocks closely in order to make collections at wool-cutting time and to watch over the fields of vegetables and grain so as not to miss anything, not even the produce "which they consume without awaiting harvest time." From all income and production it was his duty to exact the tithe by taking "one from each ten measures or one from each ten whole parts," without allowing the producer to "deduct the cost of the seed, rent, or any other expense, nor pay any debt." Then the collector had to render a sworn account to the treasury officials, and if any citizen had refused to make full payment, he would take that case before the local *alcalde.* In this way the political arm sought to aid the religious establishment in obtaining its means for support.

LIFE IN THE MISSIONS

Among the Indians, the source of support—besides alms and subsidies—came from the product of Indian labor in the missions. These houses were operated, not by the secular clergy, but by the orders in which the priests lived under strict rules, or *reguli*. Therefore these priests have been designated as "regular clergy." In the Franciscan houses, isolated as much as possible from worldly affairs, the friars supervised a little world of their own. The lands surrounding the missions still were technically Indian lands, although they soon came to be looked upon as mission lands. The friars observed their rule that they own nothing themselves but rather should regard the usufruct as theirs in trusteeship. They also managed the house and the land so thoroughly that they gave the appearance of ownership.

Whenever a new convert was baptized, he learned that his services now belonged to God, whom the friar represented. Henceforth he was disciplined by the patriarchal management as if he were part of the property of the mission. Where the neophytes were numerous, however, the tasks were not too severe. Starting with mass at sunrise, the convert had to undergo a periodic routine of religious rites and duties. In addition, during the forenoon and afternoon he labored in the fields or helped with construction of buildings or worked in the shops of the mission. Ordinarily he had time left for participation in a social hour set aside for music, dancing, and games.

A report from the friars in Texas in 1762 described life in the missions there. All the Indians recited in concert twice daily the "text of the Christian doctrine according to the catechism of Repalda." The priests instructed the Indians in the "mysteries of our holy faith and the obligations of Christians with similes and arguments adapted to their inexpressible rustic simplicity." The Indians received allotments of beans, corn, pumpkins, melons, pepper, salt, and sugar. The latter, made from sugar cane at the missions, the friars suggested as "the best thing to regale the Indians and the most pleasing to the appetite." In the missions the Indians wove cotton and wool into coarse cloth, shawls, scarves, and blankets for their own covering. Any surplus products were sold for "secured bills," which were sent to the father guardian in order to establish credit for obtaining any clothes, hats, knives, or tools which were needed.

At the missions in Texas, the labor of the Indians was employed in the planting of fields, the grazing of cattle, the watering of crops, the cutting of weeds, the harvesting of grain, and the construction of buildings. This work was done, the friars complained, "with such slowness and carelessness that it was always necessary for some Spaniard to be directing them." They plaintively added that "four of them are not sufficient for what could be done by one." They had no criticism of the work of the women and children who combed cotton and spun thread. All this labor, according to the missionaries, "constituted no impediment to their spiritual welfare or the help due their families," but was "very moderate" and in harmony with "their want of culture, little talent, and great sloth."

Far to the west, in San Luis Rey in California, life in the mission was described by a visitor from France. The building, he observed, was elevated about ten feet above the ground and was two stories in height, built around an interior *patio*. Opening on the gallery were small workshops, schoolrooms, storehouses, and the sleeping rooms of the friars, of the "major domos," and of any visitors. Young Indian girls, called "nuns," resided in halls called the "monastery," where they had to be secluded for security from "outrage by the Indians." Under the care of trusted Indian matrons, they learned to make clothing of cotton, wool, and flax. They could not leave the monastery until they were married. The Indian children mingled in the schoolroom with those of the Spanish settlers of the vicinity. Those who displayed the "most intelligence" learned chanting and instrumental music.

Those men who showed greater talent in the carpenter's shop of San Luis Rey, or in agricultural labor, became *alcaldes*, or overseers, who supervised a group of Indian workmen. The friars said that they employed only as many Spaniards as were absolutely necessary. "To maintain morals and good order," they had found that "the influence of the latter was wholly evil and that association with them develops gambling and drunkenness."

The mission buildings represented the finest accomplishment of the colonists in art and architecture. In the supervision of their construction the padres copied a style they had known in Spain but adapted it to building materials locally available. The style had features drawn from several antecedents. The massive wall, round arch, and ground plan were Romanesque; the long corridor and occasional use of the horseshoe arch were Arabian; the plain exterior, the interior court, and the type of cupola ornamenting some of the structures were Moresque. Here and there features were drawn from Aztec sources or from local pueblo style. The combination presented massive beauty in harmony with the local landscape.

Artistic adornments decorated the mission chapels impressively. Oil paintings, either produced locally or imported, hung in wooden frames on the walls; hand-carved designs appeared upon beams, door posts, and altar pieces; and colorful frescoes applied by native artists decorated the walls of some missions. Nearly all the churches displayed *santos*, or religious images, made of native materials in colorful representations of saints and Biblical characters. Some were carved and painted by the friars; others were produced by professional *santeros* who peddled their craftwork from church to church. In nearly all cases the *santeros* now remain anonymous, but recognizable style-groups characterize the work found in different localities.

FOLK ART

The folk play and folk song also expressed the religious influence. A cast drawn from the village enacted dramas appropriate to religious anniversaries. Whether the plays were originally written in Spain or in New Spain, the friars found them to be an effective means for penetrating the language barrier in order to reach the Indians. Likewise such plays carried a message effectively to the Spanish populace, and many of them were rewritten in part for adaptation to local traditions. One play, *Los Pastores*, had several versions built around the theme of shepherds, accompanied by a choir, going from house to house in search of lodging for Mary and Joseph. At the climax the Christ Child was greeted with the chorus, *duérmete niño lindo en los brazos del amor*, or "Sleep, perfect child in the arms of love." In another plot, a brutal Cain's assault upon the life of a good Abel was built up with great religious sentimentality.

Only a few of the village plays and folk songs had a secular theme. Some ballads told the tragic story of a dying lover, or lauded the deeds of a hero like Robin Hood, or condemned the mistakes of an unfaithful wife. One drama, *Los Comanches*, was enacted annually in some villages of northern New Mexico throughout the nineteenth century and on into the twentieth. It commemorated the victorious campaign in 1779 of Governor Anza against Cuerno Verde, the Comanche chief, but somehow heroes and events of other campaigns often intruded in the stanzas.

Folk songs known to everybody were rendered to the accompaniment of violin or guitar played by local musicians. Often troubadors accompanied expeditions and armies in their distant travels. Those who had talent for originality provided entertainment at the balls, where they regaled the dancers with some lines of witticism composed *ad libitum* about one or another of the prominent persons present. The object of the poetic barb then tossed a coin to the troubador; the crowd enjoyed the entertainment and speculated about the probable factual basis of some of the humorous stanzas, which were not always complimentary.

LITERATURE AND LANGUAGE

Although rich in folk art, the frontier of New Spain produced little indigenous literature. Friars and explorers filled rolls and rolls of parchment with descriptive writing, but these authors had been raised and educated elsewhere in the Spanish realm. They prepared diaries and reports ostensibly for the dissemination of information but often also for the advocacy of a cause or the justification of their own role. In California, for example, where a number of well-educated Spaniards migrated late in the colonial era, the Dons subsequently filled many sheets of manuscript with their personally slanted "History of California." Friars and captains, too, wrote extensively and favorably concerning their experiences. Such diaries and recollections comprised the principal literature of the time, and today they are valuable sources for historical writings.

The language of the distant frontier was a richly archaic Spanish. It seems that the early forms introduced in this isolated area did not undergo the evolution characteristic of language in centers of greater interchange. Moreover, the pronunciation was Andalusian, giving an *s* sound to a *c* or *z* before an

e or *i* and including some other variations from the classical Castilian of Madrid.

People took pride in what they believed to be the correctness of their local language, and the literate officials who kept records wrote with a clear, firm script, adding their own original flourishes. In their messages, they observed well the established Spanish rules of courtesy and formality.

SOCIAL CUSTOMS

A pleasing politeness in formal social relations pervaded upper-class society. Any request was preceded by an expression of personal concern about the health and well-being of the person addressed, and women and elders were greeted and treated with appropriate deference. Most cordial hospitality was extended to a guest, and no pay could be accepted for services rendered to a friend or a visitor.

Customary observances marked the milestones of life. Baptism called for the designation of godparents, who were to be the spiritual guardians of the child and henceforth members of the large family group on social occasions. The event was solemnized at the church and followed by a feast, an open house, and a dance. Weddings were contracted by parents often while the children were very young. After the marriage ceremony in the church, that event, too, called for a dinner and a *baile*, or ball. When a death occurred, the neighbors and relatives of the deceased assembled for an all-night "wake," with a paid chanter of prayers reciting from his copybook. Following the funeral and high mass in the church, the body

was carried to its resting place in the *campo santo*, or holy ground, which had been properly dedicated as a cemetery.

The family was the unit for most social and economic activities. It was a large unit, too, including all the relatives and sometimes the godparents. The elder male of the larger group was respected as a patriarch, while in the more intimate family group the male head exercised complete control. Young people thus were reared in a constantly observant primary group in which they were admonished to respect stern authority and to regard highly the advice of many elders. Informal instruction also emphasized "sticking together" for mutual helpfulness. In such a society there was almost no crime, very little juvenile delinquency, and continued respect for old customs.

In the family and community many occasions provided opportunities for spontaneous recreation. The religious fiestas, family feasts, and village balls have been mentioned. In addition the children had their games, men competed in contests requiring skillful horsemanship, crowds applauded the bullfights, and everyone crowded into the marketplace at the time of the village fair. For social events the poor, of course, wore such coarse clothing as they had. By contrast, the wealthy women wore their expensive, long-skirted, hand-embroidered dresses, and the affluent men donned their colorful riding costumes. They also adorned their horses with a silver-studded saddle and bridle, a fancy blanket, and an embroidered cushion. The contrast in costumes in colonial California led one discerning and amused observer, Richard Henry Dana, to remark that "every rich man looks like a grandee, and every poor scamp like a broken down gentleman."

LOCAL GOVERNMENT

The protective shelter under which these frontiersmen lived, labored, and played was provided by a government which was authoritarian, like the family. The viceroy in New Spain represented the distant emperor; the two collaborated in the appointment of provincial governors, who were assisted by notaries, or secretaries. As a rule the governors were outsiders, haughty and exploitive. On the other hand, the secretaries often were men who had resided in the province much longer and understood better its problems and needs. They heard more sympathetically the entreaties of the citizens and endeavored to give the governor sound advice. In later years the governor usually named a lieutenant governor who shared with him the administration of a geographic division of the province, and *alcaldes mayores* supervised subdistricts.

Heads of three types of administrative units served under the governor. One was the *presidio* captain who exercised control over the soldiers and laborers in the fort under his jurisdiction. Prior to 1776 he was responsible to the governor, but in pursuance of the reform measure of that date he was placed under the direction of the *comandante general*, and the governor became only a political head.

In the rural areas, *alcaldes ordinarios* supervised the Spanish settlers of their districts, and some *alcaldes* had deputies in charge of outlying villages. These local officers heard the claimants in disputes, supervised Indian relations, enforced orders and statutes emanating from the office of the governor or viceroy, and rendered periodic reports. One, who was appointed an *alcalde* in New Mexico in 1819, was instructed by the governor to "deal with cases and matters which arise, civil, and criminal, prosecuting them until passing judgment." The town crier was requested to announce his appointment "with good public notice through all parts of the neighborhood," so that all would be alerted to "obey and keep his oral and written orders." A Don who obtained an appointment as an *alcalde* indeed was an important person. He was the agent of the governor, perhaps his willing tool in aggrandizement, and an appeal from his orders was difficult and costly. Such an appeal could be addressed to the governor or to the distant Audiencia of Guadalajara, a kind of appellate court for northern New Spain. Only the more affluent could afford the expenditure of time and money required for such an appeal. All others had to submit dutifully.

A third type of administrative unit appeared in some of the towns near the end of the colonial period. These towns normally would have two or three *alcaldes*. A few *regidores* or councilmen also were appointed, and with the *alcaldes* they comprised a *cabildo*, or town council, sometimes also referred to as the *ayuntamiento*. The laws provided that the town council should carry out the provisions of royal ordinances, direct public works, administer justice, and distribute irrigation rights. However, any ordinance which the *cabildo* might originate was subject to approval by the governor. If he was obstreperous, the council was stymied. Usually time at the meetings was consumed in petty, ineffectual discussion, but occasionally a town council would emerge as a representative administrative body in time of crisis or, at least, as the advisory body of a cooperative administrator. Sometimes *alcaldes* were natives of Spain sent to the frontier to fill that office; but often the *regidores* were prominent local men. Such a council, then, was a germ of democracy which, although it functioned feebly in colonial times, might emerge at a later

date in a more responsible role.

For successful operation the officers of government had to have funds sufficient to pay for maintaining the *presidios*, to provide for salaries of the governor and assistants as well as the salaries and pensions of army officers and soldiers, and to advance the stipends owed to the friars for their work. For such purposes funds were derived from the *alcabala*, or sales tax, many other petty and annoying taxes, duties paid by the operators of mines, the government monopoly on the sale of tobacco, and the *media anata*, which was the customary "kickback" of one half of the first year's salary of newly appointed officials. As a rule, the income was never enough to meet all of the needs.

In some few towns improvement of education as the handmaiden of democracy was sought after, but the results were meagre. In 1789, the Villa of San Fernando at San Antonio, Texas, launched a prolonged movement for the opening of a local school, but without success in the colonial era. However, in 1817 and 1818 the pueblos of Los Angeles and San José in California did succeed in establishing local schools. This achievement negates the popular notion of a later day that this need was overlooked entirely.

THE PRESIDIAL SYSTEM

The towns relied to some extent upon their own manpower for defense against marauding Indians. They became better prepared near the end of the eighteenth century when they were permitted to maintain an organized and armed militia for that purpose. Even so, defense was primarily the

responsibility of the *presidios*. In the early years colonial policy called for the making of treaties of peace with the Indians whenever possible, followed by such punitive measures as might be required by violations of the peace. As a supplement to that plan, *presidios* were located in a haphazard pattern wherever colonies and missions appeared to need protection.

The *presidios* were frontier forts. The one in Tucson for example, was built with adobe walls about two feet thick and twelve feet high surrounding an interior area about seven hundred and fifty feet square. Two towers pierced with loopholes stood on opposite corners. Inside the walls a firing platform about eight feet high served also as a roof over barracks, shops, storerooms, and stables. At the center of the interior area stood the more pretentious house of the officers.

The garrisons of the fort at Tucson and others elsewhere were comprised of twenty-five to seventy-five tough soldiers. Off duty their professed religion did not interfere at all with their gambling, swearing, and carousing; yet in battle they fought effectively and courageously with their arquebuses, carbines, lances, and broadswords. Outside the walls of some of the forts families of the soldiers occupied presidial towns. Although maintained in part by supply trains, the soldiers in such towns engaged in supplementary farming and stock raising. For this they received community grants of land. Beyond their four square leagues the land was reserved as the "king's farm" for pasturage of spare military mounts.

The presidial system had serious defects which became more and more apparent when the Apaches or other hostile tribes became aggressive. Some of the forts lay in unsupportable, exposed locations. Some also had outlying pastures where the Indians could easily make off with the horses. Purchasing agents obtained supplies in distant towns, where merchants raised their prices when they saw them coming. As the increased cost of goods for the soldiers made their pay sadly inadequate, their officers managed to reduce them practically to a state of peonage and they became resentful and sullen. Moreover, according to Teodoro de Croix, the officers were "undependable in the execution of their orders and in the accuracy of their reports." Further, he complained that they indulged in "abominable excesses of drunkenness, luxury, gambling, and greed."

UNIFIED DEFENSE

In 1766, the Marqués de Rubí made a study of the defensive system in a special tour of inspection. He recommended that many of the *presidios* be relocated to form a line of fifteen extending from Altar in Sonora to Bahía in Texas. Hugo Oconor carried out that plan of reorganization rather effectively between 1773 and 1775, and then he waged a successful campaign against the Apaches in western Texas.

Many of the faults in frontier defense still awaited correction. Therefore in 1776, the Council of the Indies adopted the recommendation of the *visitador general*, José de Gálvez, that all of the northern "Interior Provinces" be placed under one military commander independent of local governors and even of the viceroy. As related before, it was in 1777 that Teodoro de Croix became the first *comandante general* of the *Provincias Internas*.

Croix selected a competent staff,

including the eminent Father Juan Morfi as chaplain, and established his headquarters in Arizpe, Sonora. Then he made a tour of inspection of frontier posts. From seven councils of war, which he convened from time to time, he obtained criticisms and recommendations. He relocated some of the *presidios* so as to develop a second line of defense. He never succeeded in getting the full appropriations which he requested, but he did obtain means for increasing the size of the garrisons and for the improved training of recruits. He also obtained approval for the organization of companies of militia at some of the towns. Unfortunately these supplementary units were ineptly commanded, poorly trained, and inadequately armed, often only with bows and arrows.

In addition, Croix proposed reforms in the presidial system: horses were to be pastured close to the fort, adjutant paymasters should be appointed for stricter management of finances, and expeditions were to take fewer spare horses and to travel light for greater mobility. Before his recommendations were acted upon, he was promoted in 1782 to the viceroyalty of Peru. As noted earlier, the effort of Croix to establish a settlement at the Yuma crossing for maintenance of a line of communication with California ended in disaster. For that he received considerable criticism. Yet, on the whole, he demonstrated comprehension of the problems, injected new life into the defensive establishment, brought the hostile Comanches into a peaceful alliance, and

increased the number of men under arms on the northern frontier to about five thousand. Certainly, in view of the accumulated faults of two centuries of maladministration, he had contributed a great deal in his brief term of five years.

The successors of Croix usually filled the office too briefly to gain a comprehension of the task or to lead in effective action. In 1786, the Interior Provinces had been divided into two commandancies, and seven years later they were again consolidated into one. Such vacillating policies also further hampered the pursuit of the policies of Croix. Nevertheless, the third *comandante*, Jacobo Ugarte y Loyola, who served from 1786 to 1791, almost succeeded in pacifying the Apache frontier, despite the handicap of divided jurisdiction, the inadequacy of his poorly equipped force of soldiers, and his own advanced age.

The attention of Spain soon was diverted to other frontiers by the American Revolution and the subsequent conflict with the United States on the borders of Louisiana and Florida. Then the Spanish society of the northern frontier began to feel the stimulating, sometimes disrupting, influence of the vanguard of another culture. Instead of waging a frontal assault, like the Indians, the so-called "Anglo-Americans" filtered into the Spanish settlements and created a problem of internal adjustment. That, along with the attainment of independence by Mexico, marked the beginning of a new period in the Spanish Borderlands.

6
INFILTRATION

Some thirty days in the fierce moon haze
  I have travelled the Desert prairie
And some thirty more are yet in store
  Ere our life so lorn can vary.
A life of Romance, Adventure & Chance
  Hath its charms to bewitch and bedevil,
But nought we admire and sometime may tire,
  And our best pleasure change to evil
The Night-Guard is a thing not poetic to say,
  Nor is it delightful to serve on
Rain, hail, dark or light, to get up in the night
  Requires a man's best coat of nerve on. . . .

And closer still and nearer now
The sun sinks o'er the mountain brow.
Behold! Is there no God of bliss
To praise for such a scene as this?

Matthew C. Field, Matt Field on the Santa Fe Trail. © *1960, University of Oklahoma Press,* pp. 21, 48.

Spain retained control over her colonies to about 1810, when the wars for independence challenged that control. Up to that time, therefore, Spanish colonial policy prevailed insofar as it could be enforced. That policy, called "mercantilism," was designed to strengthen Spain in competition with rival nations by the maintenance of controls over economic activities in both the mother country and the colonies. One such control reserved the commerce of the colonies as a monopoly for favored Spanish subjects. Originally trade was also restricted to a few specified ports, but an enlightened emperor, Charles

III, encouraged greater freedom of trade by opening more ports and by eliminating some of the controls. His new "free trade policy," however, still sought to exclude foreigners from colonial commerce.

BREACHES IN MONOPOLY

In 1713, Britain was the first to penetrate the barrier by obtaining consent to send one "permission ship" annually for trade with New Spain. Soon the merchants of several nations found channels for contraband trade with Spanish subjects in the colonies. The opportunities were greater on the fringe of the empire, where the danger of detection was slight and the remote market was not well served within the Spanish system.

As early as 1774, a few British ships dropped anchor in Texas ports and some even sailed up the Trinity River to feel out the possibilities. The inland colonies of Texas, however, proved to be more difficult of access than the coastwise settlements of California.

On the Pacific coast the first intruders were exploring expeditions. In 1786, a French captain, Comte de Lapérouse, anchored his ship for supplies in Monterey Bay for ten days. Two years later, the *Lady Washington* and the *Columbia*, commanded by captains James Kendrick and Robert Gray, coasted along California on a voyage around the world, but they kept out of the Spanish ports. Next, between 1792 and 1794, British vessels under Captain George Vancouver made three visits in California coastal cities, where he obtained a favorable impression of the commercial possibilities. In 1796 the *Otter*, commanded by Ebenezer Dorr, became the first ship from the United States to call at a California port, but it paused only briefly in Monterey Bay to take on supplies.

After the preliminary contact several more Yankee traders visited California in quest of otter and seal for the profitable disposal of the furs in China. These contacts caused the Spanish colonists to speak of "Boston," when they really meant the United States. In the years around 1800, the Spanish governors restricted the visitors to the procuring of necessary provisions, but the callers nevertheless made some keen observations and became eager to return for the opening of trade. After the long struggle for independence started in 1810, the regular supply ships no longer came from Mexico to California. Then the governors ceased enforcing the royal restrictions, and conditions favored illicit trade.

Back on the eastern fringe of the Borderlands, the first relaxation of Spanish policy occurred in Louisiana while that province was under Spanish rule. Royal officials sought to strengthen the colony by increasing its population. Settlers were brought in from the Canary Islands, and offers of land grants were extended to German and French Catholics and to British Loyalists displaced by the American Revolution. In 1786 the Americans were also invited to come, on the supposition that they could be converted into loyal Spanish subjects. As the result of the work of an agent sent to Kentucky, a considerable immigration poured into Spanish Louisiana, West Florida, and Missouri. However, in 1802 the king put an end to the granting of land to Americans, because they seemed to have little affinity for adjustment to Spanish political and religious institutions.

In the period of temporary relaxation on the eastern border, some of the Americans who came to Louisiana trickled westward into territory that would become part of eastern Texas. As early as 1791 Edward Murphy took up a land grant on the Arroyo Hondo, and soon several Anglo-Americans settled in the vicinity of Nacogdoches. By 1821, when Stephen Austin's "first" colonists arrived, already there were about eighty American families in eastern Texas.

THE FIRST FILIBUSTER

Prior to the independence of Mexico in 1821, the restrictive policy prevailed in most of the Borderlands, and unsettled conditions encouraged violations of the restrictions. Several of the filibustering expeditions had some connection with General James Wilkinson, who was a paid secret agent of the Spanish king while serving as commander of the American forces in the Southwest. He engaged in intrigue with Spanish officials in a scheme to wrest Tennessee and Kentucky from the United States and attach them to Spanish Louisiana, and he maintained contact with American soldiers-of-fortune who sought to detach Texas from New Spain.

What influence General Wilkinson may have had upon Philip Nolan, one of the earliest of the adventurers, has never been clearly established; but at least he knew Nolan and was in communication with him when he was planning his ill-fated expedition into Texas. Ostensibly Nolan's purpose was to catch and sell wild horses, and he did round up three hundred of them along the Brazos River in 1800; but then he continued to linger in Texas. This aroused the suspicion of the governor of Spanish Louisiana. He dispatched a warning to the *comandante*

in Chihuahua that Nolan was preparing a map for General Wilkinson and that he might try to instigate an Indian uprising. Then from a man who had deserted Nolan came the warning that Nolan was building a fort among the Caddo Indians for use as a base in the conquest of Texas. The *comandante* sent out a force of one hundred soldiers, who defeated Nolan's little band in a battle which was fought near present Waco. Nolan was killed, and ten of his men were taken as prisoners.

Spanish orders provided that one of each five of Nolan's men was to be chosen by lot for execution. Because one of the ten prisoners had died, the selection of one of the remaining nine was decided upon as sufficient for fulfillment of the order. That unfortunate lot fell upon a Quaker, one Ephraim Blackburn, who was hanged in Chihuahua on November 11, 1807. For years the assumption has been that Nolan's name and mysterious plans inspired Edward Everett Hale's story, *The Man without a Country*, but in that story Philip Nolan was sentenced to spend the rest of his life on board ships at sea. However, recent investigation suggests that Hale's use of the name Nolan may have been only coincidental.

DISPUTED BOUNDARY

After the purchase of the Louisiana Territory by the United States in 1803, the border of New Spain moved from the Mississippi westward to a boundary not clearly specified. Because the treaty of purchase failed to locate the exact boundary, the government at the new capital on the Potomac could assert claim to boundaries as France might have defined them. Thus Texas could be included in the claim as a result of La Salle's short-lived settlement on Matagorda Bay. Northward the western border presumably should follow a line connecting the headwaters of the several streams which drained into the Missouri and Mississippi Rivers. That would place the border in the foothills of the Rocky Mountains—a definition which certainly could be disputed. Spanish officials could lay prior claim to much of western Louisiana by virtue of permanent settlements in Texas, extensive exploration of the high plains, and suzerainty over some of the Plains Indians who had been trading with the Spanish agents.

The disputed border almost precipitated a clash on the frontier in 1806. Simón Herrera marched twelve hundred Spanish soldiers east to Nacogdoches and announced that he intended to send patrols as far as the Arroyo Hondo. Simultaneously an American captain posted at Natchitoches proclaimed that his soldiers would protect American citizens as far west as the Sabine River, and news of the impending conflict enflamed the war spirit on both sides. General Wilkinson brought reinforcements to the Sabine, where he encamped on the east side across from Herrera. Presently, in November, 1806, the two commanders agreed that the area between the Arroyo Hondo and Sabine should be a neutral zone which would be vacated by both armies pending a settlement by their respective governments. Wilkinson's soldiers, eager for battle, felt that he had let them down, and Wilkinson's critics became suspicious that the Spaniards had bought him off. The rumor had it that he had been offered three hundred thousand pesos, of which he had succeeded in collecting one hundred and twenty thousand. At that time convincing proof that he was a pensioner of the Spanish Crown had not yet come to light.

Temporarily, war on the Spanish border had been avoided. Therefore, in 1806, President Thomas Jefferson sent Thomas Freeman and a party of thirty-seven men up the Red River with advice to withdraw if challenged. This expedition was seeking a clarification of the exact location of the headwaters of the Red River, which could be considered as the southwestern extremity of the Louisiana Purchase according to the American version. Spanish officials had alerted the governor of Texas to be on the lookout for any such "invasion." Therefore when Freeman and his party had advanced to a point six hundred and thirty-five miles west from the Mississippi River, they met a large force of Spanish soldiers under the command of Francisco Viana. When he ordered the Americans to withdraw, they courteously retreated. Thus the full extent of the Red River still remained unestablished and the true boundary of the new territory undetermined.

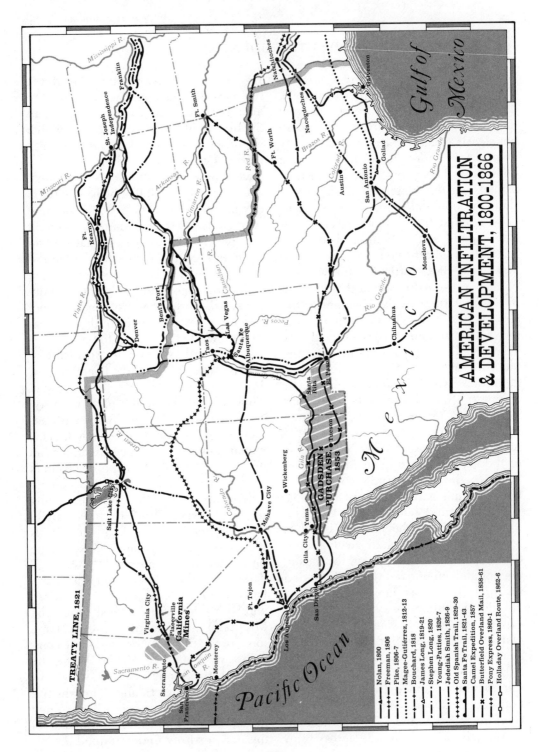

AMERICAN INFILTRATION
& DEVELOPMENT, 1800-1866

TREATY LINE, 1821

GADSDEN
PURCHASE,
1853

Gulf of Mexico

Pacific Ocean

M e x i c o

Legend:
— Nolan, 1800
—+— Freeman, 1806
······ Pike, 1806-7
—··— Magee-Gutiérrez, 1812-13
—△— Bouchard, 1818
—···— James Long, 1819-21
—··— Stephen Long, 1820
—◆— Young-Patties, 1826-7
—✚— Jedediah Smith, 1826-9
—✦✦— Old Spanish Trail, 1829-30
—✛✛— Santa Fe Trail, 1821-43
—×— Camel Expedition, 1857
—+++— Butterfield Overland Mail, 1858-61
—·+·— Pony Express, 1860-1
—○— Holladay Overland Route, 1862-6

94

PIKE'S ADVENTURE

In the year of Freeman's expedition, Zebulon Montgomery Pike was leading another party west. It, too, was one of those mysterious affairs associated with Wilkinson. Pike always disclaimed any ulterior motive, and he later gave his life in the service of his country during the War of 1812; yet, in the journey of 1806, his objectives certainly remain obscure. He went forth under orders from Wilkinson with instructions to escort some Osages and Pawnees to their own country and then to explore the upper Arkansas and Red rivers. Pike and his party of twenty-two left St. Louis in June, with Wilkinson's son as a companion for part of the trip.

In a Pawnee village on the Republican River in what is now Kansas, Pike learned that a Spanish army was out to intercept him. That report was correct, for the governors of New Mexico and Texas had been alerted, and already Facundo Melgares had marched six hundred Spanish soldiers out onto the plains. He had visited the Pawnees and had presented them with small Spanish flags as emblems of their proper allegiance. They insisted that Pike turn back, but instead he gave them American flags and traveled on toward the mountains. Already he had fulfilled the ostensible purpose of his journey; yet he continued westward.

While Pike was on the upper Arkansas River he sent some of his men, including Wilkinson's son, back to St. Louis, and with the remaining few he wandered about in the high Rockies in the winter. When he tried to climb the peak which now bears his name,

he found upon reaching the summit that he was atop a neighboring peak. Undaunted, he pushed onward. At Christmas time he was in the vicinity of present Salida, Colorado, and in January he was encamped near Canyon City. Because food supplies were short and the men were near exhaustion, Pike broke out of the mountains, not homeward, but to the south.

On the Conejos, a tributary of the upper Rio Grande, Pike's party built a small stockade. While the men were recuperating, Dr. John Robinson traveled down the Rio Grande to Santa Fe on an errand for William Morrison of Kaskaskia, Illinois. Two years earlier, Morrison had sent Baptiste La Lande to Santa Fe with a pack train of goods, but La Lande had remained in New Mexico without remitting payment for the merchandise. Now Dr. Robinson was going to investigate La Lande's conduct, and his instructions from Pike indicate that he also went ahead in the role of spy.

Because Robinson knew which way to go to reach Santa Fe, obviously Pike was aware that he was on the Rio Grande in territory claimed by Spain. Instead of withdrawing promptly, he waited in camp until the Spaniards came after him. Soon a hundred cavalrymen appeared under the command of Bartolomé Fernández. Pike expressed embarrassment upon learning that he was on Spanish soil, whereas he had thought, so he said, that he was on the Red River. Fernández politely requested that the Spanish flag be hoisted over the stockade in place of the Stars and Stripes. After this exchange of courtesies, Pike surrendered quite "reluctantly" and went along as a prisoner with Fernández to Santa Fe.

In the provincial capital the governor, Joaquín del Rael Alencaster, suspected that Pike's expedition was but the forerunner of an anticipated massive invasion by the agressive "Yankees." While he was preparing his defense, Pike avoided Dr. Robinson. Because he was uncertain whether Robinson had betrayed his real mission, Pike disclaimed any acquaintance with him. In the meantime, Pike had been trying to hide his journal and other papers, but the Spaniards found and seized them and sent them to Mexico City. There they were found in the Mexican archives by the historian, Herbert Eugene Bolton, a century later.

In Santa Fe the prisoner displayed a suavity which stood him in good stead. He won the friendship of the governor, who presented him with some fine clothes and began to treat him as a guest. Yet the conclusion was inescapable that Pike should be sent to the *comandante* at Chihuahua. Again his escort part of the way on that journey was Fernández, who by now had become cordial. He revealed that the New Mexicans wanted to open trade and to be friendly, if it were not for the dread suspicion that the Americans had war-like intentions.

For the final leg of the journey to Chihuahua, Fernández turned over his "guest" to another escort commanded by Melgares, the officer who had tried to intercept Pike out on the plains. Now this captain also became a genial "host," who entertained Pike and his men at *fandangos* arranged for them. In Chihuahua City the *comandante*, General Nimecio Salcedo, also treated Pike as a guest and then released him and his men for the return journey overland across Texas to the American outpost in Natchitoches.

Upon his return Pike wrote Wilkinson that he had gathered valuable information which would "open a scene for the generosity and aggrandizement of our country." Wilkinson, however, had his own personal use for Pike's information. He replied that already people were associating Pike's expedition with the Burr conspiracy, and for that reason Pike should be "extremely cautious" about saying anything to anybody. Moreover, publication of his report might "excite a spirit of adventure adverse to the interests of our government." Nevertheless, Pike did prepare a report from memory. Its publication in 1810 stimulated a new and widespread interest in the Spanish Borderlands that was to bear out Rael's suspicion.

THE BURR CONSPIRACY

The Burr conspiracy which Wilkinson mentioned was another of those shady affairs in which he had had a hand. He had been a willing consultant in the preparation of some kind of plan by Aaron Burr, but apparently the desires of Burr became too ambitious or too dangerous for Wilkinson to help him achieve them. Perhaps it may even have been originally the "Wilkinson conspiracy," for which Burr "took the rap."

Burr, the brilliant but disgruntled and discredited politician, came down the Ohio River in the winter of 1806 to

1807 with gunboats and a party of armed men. He had alienated his former Republican teammate, Thomas Jefferson, and had shot his popular New York rival, Alexander Hamilton, in a duel. Now he was apparently launching a western project for the satisfying of his ambitions. But what those ambitions were remains obscure, for the records reveal that Burr gave different explanations to many interested persons. He sought funds from the British minister to aid him in separating the West from the Union and turning it over to Great Britain. He asked the help of Mexican patriots in exile in New Orleans in a campaign for liberation of the northern frontier from Spanish rule. He requested the Spanish minister to grant him funds which he would use to prevent the separation of the Spanish colonies from the crown. He offered General Wilkinson an office in a proposed western confederacy, and to Henry Clay and Andrew Jackson he proposed the annexation of more territory to the United States. Finally, to the immediate members of his party

he promised generous grants of land in the West. Only one thing is certain— whatever the objective may have been, it had designs upon the area now included within the Southwest.

Again Burr's ambitions were frustrated. Without sound evidence, Jefferson spread the alarm that Burr was engaged in a treasonable plot. Then the slippery Wilkinson deserted Burr, if he had ever been an accomplice, and hastened to New Orleans to apprehend the whole party. Under charges of treason, Burr was sent to Richmond, Virginia, for trial. There the evidence against him was inconclusive until General Wilkinson, himself, arrived with damaging testimony. Nevertheless, the presiding justice, John Marshall, who was a political adversary of Jefferson, found a way out. He declared Burr innocent because he had not been caught in any treasonable "overt" act against his country; mere talk was not proof of treason. Even so, Burr's character was thoroughly besmirched, and Wilkinson's duplicity remained unexposed for long afterward.

OTHER INTRUDERS

General Wilkinson had at least a remote association with the next filibustering expedition, for its leader, Augustus Magee, had once been a lieutenant under his command. Magee obtained the inspiration for his plan by conferring with Spanish exiles in New Orleans. Among them was Bernardo Gutiérrez de Lara, who had been associated with Father Miguel Hidalgo y Costilla in the unsuccessful peasant uprising in Mexico during 1810 and 1811. Gutiérrez was trying to enlist men in New

Orleans for a campaign to sever Texas from New Spain. Magee, who was a graduate of West Point, joined in this project and soon enlisted two hundred riflemen in the midwestern states. As commander, Magee assumed the rank of colonel, with Samuel Kemper serving under him as lieutenant colonel. These two conveyed the impression that Gutiérrez was the leader, in order to create the appearance that this was a Spanish-led expedition for the relief of fellow Spaniards. This strategy attracted additional volunteers from among the exiles in New Orleans and from the Spanish population in Texas.

In the summer of 1812 Magee's cosmopolitan "foreign legion" marched across Texas to Bahía, later known as Goliad, where the invaders were confronted by fifteen hundred soldiers under the command of General Simón Herrera, accompanied by Governor Manuel Salcedo of Texas. In the face of such numbers, Magee agreed to surrender, but soon he was found dead in his tent. His riflemen then fought their way out of the siege with such devastating accuracy of fire that over two hundred of the Spaniards fell in the battle. In March of 1813 Salcedo again hit the intruders at Rosillo near San Antonio. This time the filibusters only lost nine of their own number while mowing down a thousand of the Spaniards. Salcedo and Herrera were taken as prisoners, and the remnant of the routed Spanish army fled. Then the two captured leaders were secretly taken out of the camp and executed under orders from Gutiérrez. Kemper and other Anglo-Americans were so disgusted at this exhibition of bad faith that they abandoned Gutiérrez and returned to New Orleans. José Alvárez de Toledo became the next commander of the decimated band of adventurers. Near the Medina River they were ambushed by a fresh Spanish army of two thousand soldiers. Only ninety-three of the invaders made their way back to Natchitoches, and this campaign for the "independence" of Texas was over.

Two more filibustering expeditions were yet to come, but before they got under way some Anglo-Americans who ventured into New Mexico encountered an unfriendly reception. They were preceded by two outsiders who became the only known exceptions to the rule. One was the aforementioned Baptiste La Lande, a French trader who had come from Illinois in 1804. He was arrested and sent to jail in Chihuahua, but somehow the Spanish officials released him and allowed him to return to Santa Fe. There he married a local *señorita* and raised a large family. Another exception was James Purcell, who had come from Kentucky on a hunting trip in 1805. He took such a liking to Santa Fe that he remained there and became one of New Mexico's prominent citizens.

Then came other men with interest in opening commercial relations, only to find that the governors of New Mexico had become sticklers for enforcing the restrictive policy of the Spanish regime. In 1810, three Missourians—James McLanahan, Reuben Smith, and James Patterson—with a Spanish guide, traveled overland toward Santa Fe for investigation of the market there. On the upper Red River, Spanish soldiers arrested them and took them to the governor. He sent them to jail in Mexico; only after a miserable two years there were they allowed to return to their homes.

In 1812, another party of ten, including Robert McKnight, James Baird, and William Chambers, stimulated by Pike's book about his experiences, traveled up the Arkansas and across to Santa Fe. They were arrested, their goods were confiscated, and despite the plea of the President of the United States, they were kept under guard in Chihuahua for almost eight years, or until Mexico became independent of Spain. These men, like Pike, had been impressed by the friendliness of the natives of New Mexico. Therefore, in the 1820s, after Spanish restrictions had been lifted, McKnight returned to Chihuahua and Baird reappeared in Santa Fe and later settled in El Paso.

Meanwhile a group of trappers and fur traders organized by Pierre Chouteau and Julius de Munn of St. Louis had found an encouraging area for trade among the Indians on the upper Platte and Arkansas rivers. In 1816, De Munn sought approval in Santa Fe for extension of his activities to the upper Rio Grande. Before long he was ordered to clear out of Spanish territory, and thinking that removal to the east watershed of the mountains would be satisfactory, he and the trappers returned to the Las Animas, a tributary of the Arkansas. There they built a small stockade and resumed their trapping.

Now the Spaniards became excited about rumors that twenty thousand men were assembling for an attack upon New Mexico. Consequently the governor sent north a company of soldiers who brought the trappers as prisoners to Santa Fe in May, 1817. The Spaniards permitted the men to return to St. Louis, but confiscated all their furs and equipment, valued at about thirty thousand dollars. The trappers appealed to the State Department of the United States. Through diplomatic channels the claims were pressed against Mexico and thirty years later financial redress was finally obtained.

Two other persons also fell into the hands of the Spanish soldiers patrolling the northeastern border. David Meriwether and his Negro servant were crossing the plains with a band of Pawnee Indians in 1819 when they were arrested by a troop of cavalrymen on the suspicion that they were spies. After due deliberation Governor Facundo Melgares released the suspects in the mountains east of Taos. They had some more harrowing experiences on the plains before they finally returned safely to St. Louis. Incidentally, thirty-four years later Meriwether returned to the city of his brief imprisonment as the territorial governor of New Mexico.

In those years when foreigners were failing to penetrate New Mexico, some others did find weak places on the borders of New Spain. One was at Galveston Island off the coast of Texas. In 1816, Louis de Aury and a motley band of pirates made their base of operations on this island. They plundered the shipping in the Gulf of Mexico and connived with Mexican rebels in assaults on the mainland of New Spain. A Spanish guerilla leader, General Javier Mina, brought his company of two hundred revolutionists to the island, and the entire "army" of pirates and insurgents embarked on a campaign for the liberation of Mexico from Spanish rule. After the failure of this project, De Aury found Galveston in the possession of another pirate, Jean La Fitte. The latter built and fortified a city known as Campeachy, where he maintained his headquarters for four years. When some United States warships appeared in the Gulf, he moved away without offering any resistance.

Foreigners also began trickling into another coastal area without molestation by Spanish officials. Because New Spain was in the turmoil of revolution, enforcement of the restrictions became relaxed in California. Trade with foreign shippers increased, and presently some Anglo-Americans ventured ashore and found that they could stay. The first of record was a young Bostonian, Thomas W. Doak, who took up resi- dence in Monterey in 1816. Within a year Joseph Chapman landed at Los Angeles and Daniel Call came to Santa Barbara, and the Americanization of California had begun.

MORE EXPEDITIONS

Next, it became California's turn to attract a filibustering expedition. While the Mexicans were engaged in their struggle for independence, ships from Boston and Baltimore came into the Pacific Ocean for harassment of Spanish shipping. The Americans sympathized with the Mexican insurgents and claimed that they were abetting the cause of independence, yet most of these sailors were little better than pirates who were profiting from advantageous circumstances. One such Baltimore ship, commanded by a Frenchman, Hippolyte de Bouchard, accompanied by a British vessel, departed from the Hawaiian Islands in the fall of 1818 and approached the California coast. The ships flew the flag of the Mexican independence movement, and their captains proclaimed that they would "bring into the liberal cause the inhabitants of California."

If the Spanish colonists on the west coast had trusted these foreigners and cooperated with them, an independent republic might have appeared in California at that early date. Instead, they suspected that the enterprise was piratical and refused to submit. At Monterey, Bouchard's landing party overcame Spanish resistance and sacked and burned the town. However, as they moved on down the coast, they found that the colonists had rallied for stronger, more effective defense of their other cities. Therefore the filibusters sailed on to Chile and Argentina, where they lent aid to those colonies in their rebellion against Spain. Consequently California continued under the rule of a Spanish governor, Pablo Vicente de Sola, until the independence of Mexico caused his removal in 1822.

A year before the achievement of Mexican independence a party of explorers from the United States skirted the northern frontier of New Spain without being intercepted. In 1820, Major Stephen Long, accompanied by his brother David and a botanist, Dr. Edwin James, led an official government expedition in search of the elusive headwaters of both the Platte and Red rivers. Long traveled up the Platte, discovered the peak in Colorado now bearing his name, and sent a few of his men on the first successful ascent of Pike's Peak. Then he went south into New Mexico, where he turned east on a small stream which he thought might be the beginning of the Red River. That stream, now named Major Long's Creek, turned out to be a branch of the Cimarron River, which led Long in turn to the Arkansas River instead of the Red. One of the contributions of this survey was a report which described the high plains as unsuited for settlement. For years afterward maps of the region bore the caption, "Great American Desert."

While Major Long was in the field, one more, and the final, filibustering expedition of this early era was being organized. It was led by James Long, who was not related to his contemporary, Stephen. This Long had married the niece of General Wilkinson and had become interested in his schemes. Now alarm was spreading through the West over rumors that John Quincy Adams, Secretary of State, was negotiating a treaty which would relinquish any claim of the United States to Texas derived from the Louisiana Purchase. At a protest meeting held in 1819 in Natchez, Mississippi, the local citizens decided that an armed force should occupy Texas in order to keep it from being given away. As leader of the movement, James Long became "General Long" in command of a "regiment" of about fifty men. He promptly occupied Nacogdoches and organized a provisional government for the "free republic" of Texas. Possession of that one town on the border was far from establishing control over the province; therefore he sought an alliance with La Fitte, who at the time had not yet been frightened away from Galveston. That sly buccaneer, however, refused

to become involved in a land campaign which certainly would have provoked the wrath of Spanish authorities.

While Long was in Galveston, Spanish soldiers routed his followers out of Nacogdoches. Undaunted, Long then enlisted a new army which included many Mexican insurgents. Now he proclaimed that he would help the revolutionists in their war for independence. While he was en route in 1821 to "liberate" Goliad, Mexico became independent and Long's excuse for his campaign vanished. Now he was leading a feeble attack upon a Mexican outpost without a plausible justification. At Goliad he had to surrender to a much larger force of Mexicans led by Colonel Ignacio Pérez, who took his captives to prison in Mexico City. They were soon released as a result of the pleas of the American minister; but General Long was no longer among them. He had been shot by a Mexican sentry.

His death brought an end to the machinations associated in one way or another with General Wilkinson. By this time Wilkinson's activities were arousing such suspicion at home that he moved to Mexico City, where he died in 1825.

MOMENTOUS CHANGES

The rumor about relinquishing Texas to Spain proved to be true. The United States could advance a tenuous claim to Texas and Oregon, both of which Spain could also claim, and John Quincy Adams was aware that his fellow New Englanders were interested in Oregon. Therefore in the treaty for the acquisition of Florida, negotiated in 1819 but not ratified until two years later, Adams

did reluctantly give up Texas to Spain in exchange for Spain's renunciation of her claim to Oregon. This was embodied in agreement upon a definite boundary. From the Gulf of Mexico it followed the Sabine River to the thirty-second parallel, thence on north to the Red River, up its south bank to the one hundredth meridian, again due north to the Arkansas River, up its south bank to the source of that river, north again along the mountain range to the forty-second parallel, and westward on that line to the Pacific Ocean.

Finally the vague and disputed border between Spain and the United States had been eliminated by an agreement upon a definitive one, but by then Spain no longer was one of the contenders. In February, 1821, the Mexican reactionary general, Agustín de Iturbide, had met with the insurgent leader, Vicente Guerrero, and agreed upon a joint campaign for independence. By the time the boundary treaty was approved by Spain, her loss of the colonies in New Spain was fairly assured. Since the government of the new nation of Mexico accepted the settlement of the Treaty of 1821, the newly defined line became the border between Mexico and the United States.

In Mexico, both the short-lived empire of Iturbide and the Republic established under the liberal Constitution of 1824 abandoned the monopolistic policy which had been maintained by Spain. The doors now would be open for immigration and trade. Immediately Americans realized that they might venture safely across the boundary into the zone which long had looked so attractive to them. As a result, the year 1821 stands out as a significant date in the history of the Borderlands. In addition to the independence of Mexico and the agreement upon a boundary, described above, the big events of that year included the colonization of Texas, the opening of the Santa Fe Trail, and the admission of fur traders into New Mexico. The year following also marked the beginning of Mexican rule in the Borderlands, thus inaugurating the "Mexican Period." Now the infiltration of *extranjeros* across the border, largely frustrated before 1821, may be followed under the more auspicious conditions prevailing in the Mexican Period, that is, from 1821 to 1846.

COLONISTS IN TEXAS

In the final years of the Spanish regime, the Crown had once more made an exception to its rule banning the immigration of American settlers. The concession was made to Moses Austin of Missouri. After he had lost in a bank failure the fortune which he had made from lead mining, he sought a new opportunity in Texas. In San Antonio he made application in 1820 for a tract of land where he could settle three hundred families, but he became ill and died before word came that his petition had been granted. His son, Stephen F. Austin, then only twenty-seven years of age, inherited the land grant and undertook the trying task of serving as *empresario*, or agent, for the colonization of Texas.

By the terms of the grant the colonists had to agree that they would pledge allegiance to Spain and become converted to Catholicism. Each head of a family would receive a small grant of land, with some additional acres for his wife and for each child and slave, and the fees amounted to only a few cents an acre. In the United States, under the Act of 1820, land on the frontier cost one dollar and a quarter an acre. That higher cost, along with the economic depression following 1819, made Austin's project quite appealing. In December of 1821, after he had settled his first group of a few families along the Brazos River, he learned that the province was now Mexican and not Spanish. His royal grant would be invalid unless he could obtain confirmation of it from the Mexican government.

Austin made the difficult journey to Mexico City, where he continued patient and hopeful negotiations until Iturbide's empire collapsed and the Mexican Congress emerged in control. Finally, in February, 1823, he obtained confirmation of his father's grant along with some additional concessions. Each head of a family would get one *labor* of one hundred and seventy-seven acres for farm land and one *sitio* of one square league for grazing. A square league contained four thousand four hundred and twenty-seven acres—a truly magnanimous grant. Austin was appointed a lieutenant colonel of the militia, with power to supervise the defense against Indians and to administer justice in his colony. As before, the immigrants were required to accept Catholicism, but now the oath of allegiance would

be rendered to Mexico rather than to the Spanish king. The favorable terms immediately attracted more settlers, so that by 1824 two hundred and twenty-two land titles had been issued in Austin's colony on the Brazos.

A colonization law enacted in 1825 by the legislature of the State of Coahuila, of which Texas was then a part, even exceeded in liberality the grant made to Austin. Awards were made to several other *empresarios*, including Dr. John Charles Beale, David C. Burnet, Green De Witt, Haden Edwards, Robert Leftwich, Ben Milam, and James Powers, all from the United States, and Lorenzo de Zavala of Mexico. Up to 1832 the twenty odd grants covered almost the entire area of Texas and allowed for the bringing in of about nine thousand families. Immigrants poured in from New England, the Midwest, and the South, and many of those from the South brought their Negro slaves. Even so, the heavy influx did not fill up the grants of all *empresarios*. The unclaimed lands were grabbed up by eastern brokers and held for speculation.

GROWING PAINS

The problems of the pioneers in Texas were manifold. The remoteness of this frontier, the restlessness of the Indians, the weakness of local government, the lack of good roads, and the presence of many adventurers among the immigrants, all made life hazardous and difficult. As the recognized leader of the *empresarios*, Austin strove strenuously for improvement of conditions while also seeking fulfillment of the settlers' obligation to become good

Mexicans and Catholics. In the first decade much progress was made, and the population increased from about four thousand in 1821 to five times that number in 1830. By the latter date, Austin's colony, alone, had a population over four thousand.

Among the hardy pioneers were many tough, fearless frontiersmen like Big Jim Bowie, who became famous for the hunting knife which he or his brother designed. Bowie is reputed to have employed his skill with the weapon several times in vicious duels in which he overcame opponents armed with guns and swords. He also set out in 1831 with a party of ten in search of the silver mine which once had been opened near the old mission of San Sabá. However, when near the site, his little band was attacked by a war party of perhaps two hundred Indians. The deadly fire of the Texans killed fifty of the Indians and drove away the others. With several of his men wounded, Bowie had to return without reopening the mine. Throughout the years treasure hunters have tried in vain to find that lost mine of San Sabá.

Texas had many resident Spanish Americans who were bewildered by the sudden pouring in of immigrants. As a rule they and the Anglo-Americans enjoyed amicable relations in the early years. In fact, one Mexican observer lamented that his countrymen in Texas showed little interest in the revolution in Mexico and borrowed the habits and customs of the "North Americans" to the extent that they were only "Mexicans by birth," because they even spoke their own language "with noticeable error." A Mexican official, Juan N. Almonte, made a tour of inspection in 1834 and recommended that his government transplant more Mexicans as settlers among the immigrants in Texas. As for economic development, he found the colony to be making sound progress. The district of the Brazos, alone, he reported, had produced two thousand bales of cotton that year and was grazing twenty-five thousand head of cattle.

Almonte estimated the total annual value of imports at six hundred and thirty thousand pesos, and exports at half a million pesos, with additional contraband trade valued at probably two hundred and twenty thousand pesos. He also saw a potential for the development of manufacturing. He concluded that the population at that time was about sixteen thousand Anglo-Americans and four thousand Negro slaves as against less than five thousand Mexicans. Obviously in this borderland the overwhelming infiltration was challenging the old order by creation of a new kind of society.

THE SANTA FE TRADE

While farmers were moving into Texas, traders were penetrating New Mexico. Immediately upon the termination of Spanish rule, in 1821, two parties departed for Santa Fe. One group of nine headed by Thomas James and John McKnight, brother of the McKnight imprisoned in Chihuahua, left St. Louis in May with goods valued at ten thousand dollars loaded on a keelboat. They traveled down the Mississippi, up the Arkansas, and then up the Cimarron until halted by water too shallow for a boat. While scouting around for some wild horses, James met Hugh Glenn of a trapping expedition which was also headed west. The James party then trudged overland, crossing the Canadian River, toward Santa Fe. The hardships of the desert caused the loss of some of the merchandise. Once they were surrounded by Comanches, but a friendly

Indian brought some Mexican soldiers to their rescue just in time. On the first of December they finally arrived in Santa Fe, where they sold the remnants of their cargo at a loss of several thousand dollars.

Because the trail opened by the James party had turned out to be so hazardous, it was not followed by others. Therefore the credit for the opening of the Santa Fe Trail belongs to a more successful rival, William Becknell. On September 1, 1821, he left Franklin, Missouri, with four men and a small cargo of merchandise loaded on pack animals. From Franklin he followed the Missouri River west to the Big Bend and then crossed to the Arkansas. Farther up that river he intended to engage in barter with Indians, but then he decided to try Santa Fe instead. The party moved southward through rugged country where they had to roll big boulders out of the way to get through. Probably they were traversing Raton Pass. In the foothills east of Santa Fe they met a Mexican patrol, which extended a friendly greeting and offered to show the way to the capital. On the 16th they arrived in Santa Fe, where they soon sold their goods at a handsome profit. When Becknell returned to Franklin in February with rawhide bags full of Mexican silver dollars, news spread quickly that the border was open and the trade profitable.

In the summer of 1822, Becknell returned to the trail with twenty-one men and three wagons, which were the first vehicles to be driven across the plains and mountains to Santa Fe. That year four other parties also traveled to New Mexico with loads of merchandise, and all realized a good profit. The trade grew rapidly, and fortunately Dr. Josiah Gregg, who made six trips over the trail, wrote a history and description of the commerce. A table he prepared in 1844 shows that according to the reports he had gathered the amount realized from sale of merchandise increased from about $15,000 in 1822 to approximately $250,000 in 1831, and then after a period of decreased traffic it returned to a quarter of a million dollars again in 1839 and jumped to nearly a half of a million in 1843. He estimated the number of traders at seventy in 1822 and over one hundred in almost all subsequent years, with peaks of three hundred and twenty in 1831, two hundred and fifty in 1839, and three hundred and fifty in 1843. He also included figures for the proportion of the trade that went to Spanish cities other than Santa Fe, amounting to one-third or sometimes to one-half of the annual business.

Wagoners who followed the Trail regularly developed an established routine. Early in May they gathered in Independence on the Big Bend of the Missouri River. Thence in small groups the wagons of merchandise, accompanied by merchants, bullwhackers, freighters, and tourists, traveled separately until they arrived in Council Grove. There the men organized a caravan, elected officers, and prepared for mutual protection against the hazards of the plains. When they were ready, according to Dr. Gregg,

"All's set!" is finally heard from some teamster—"All's set," is directly responded from every quarter. "Stretch out!" immediately vociferates the captain. Then the 'heps' of drivers—the cracking of whips—the trampling of feet—the occasional creak of wheels—the rumbling of wagons—form a new scene of exquisite confusion, which I shall not attempt further to describe.[1]

En route certain favorable spots about a day's drive apart became by custom the camping places overnight. It was a slow, unromantic journey through dust or mud, depending upon the weather. When "Matt" Field, correspondent for the New Orleans *Picayune*, made the trip in 1839, he tried to make it sound romantic by describing the entire journey in a long, stilted poem, in which the ecstatic climax came when mountains were sighted ahead.

As the journey neared its end, the weary men changed to clean clothes and thrilled with a sense of expectation. Curious natives of Santa Fe thronged the narrow streets as the wagoners cracked their bullwhips and pulled up their teams in the plaza at the end of the Trail. While their merchandise was being sold, they had time for exploration of this Spanish community. Some of them, reflecting a Puritan heritage, thought Santa Fe a rather wicked place; others with less straight-laced standards liked the "democracy" of Spanish society. They visited the bars and gambling halls and enjoyed the company of the attractive *señoritas*. The women secretly admired these uncouth traders, but openly they regarded them as "heathens" and called them "burros." The Mexicans were obtaining their first impressions of Anglo-American individualism and freedom from observation of some of the less restrained representatives of the neighboring nation.

The traders brought to Santa Fe much cotton goods, some woolen garments, and a variety of light hardware. On the return trip they took out horses, mules, beaver skins, buffalo robes, and some good hard money. At a time when specie was scarce in the Midwest, the coins introduced in Missouri by this commerce made a valuable contribution to the sound monetary basis of that state. Moreover, Missouri became famous for its mules brought from Santa Fe.

In New Mexico the market was starving for cloth for the making of attractive garments, and now these merchants displayed the colorful prints which appealed to the Spanish lady. Admittedly, the prices were high; goods valued at thirty thousand dollars back East sold for six times that sum in 1824. However, machine-woven cloth even at high prices was still relatively cheaper than the laboriously woven domestic homespun on which most New Mexicans had depended previously. In later years the increased competition reduced the margin of profit to somewhere between ten and forty percent. The traders were supplying a real want in the Mexican towns and were realizing a good profit for their own risk and investment.

ALONG THE TRAIL

As the commerce increased, the Congress of the United States appropriated thirty thousand dollars in 1825 for improvement of the road. Surveyors marked out the trail and persuaded the Kansas and Osage Indians to permit

[1] M. L. Quaife, ed., *Commerce of the Prairies* (Chicago, 1926), p. 26.

the passage of the caravans "without any hindrance or molestation." Farther west the Comanches and Kiowas were less tractable. After they waylaid some of the wagons in 1828, President Andrew Jackson authorized a military escort which no doubt saved the caravans the next year. Most of the time, however, the wagoners had to rely upon their own numbers and efficient organization for protection.

In 1829, when Charles and William Bent brought a load of merchandise from Missouri and were besieged by Indians, Ewing Young of Taos hurried east with a company of one hundred volunteers and rescued the party. In Taos the Bents found an old friend, Ceran St. Vrain. Together they concluded that it would be helpful to have a fort as a "half-way house" out on the trail where the Indians were most threatening. They selected a site near present La Junta in Colorado, and by 1833 their adobe fort, much like a Spanish *presidio*, was ready for service. In Taos, St. Vrain and Charles Bent operated their trading post, while William managed the fort. Bent, St. Vrain & Company sent traders out among the Indians, and often large Indian trading parties were camped outside the walls of the fort while engaged in bartering. Until it was burned down in 1849, this fort served not only as an active outpost of commerce but also as a welcome resting place for travelers on the Santa Fe Trail.

As time passed, the Trail experienced some variations and improvements. The Cimarrón Cutoff from Fort Dodge, Kansas, to the Mora River in New Mexico, proved to be less difficult for wagons than the route over Raton Pass. Quite early, therefore, it became the pre-ferred route for the trip to Santa Fe, whereas the trail up the Arkansas, over Raton Pass, and on to Taos became known as the "Mountain Route." After Las Vegas, New Mexico, was founded in 1835, it became the easternmost point of entry for the caravans. By that time the trail was acquiring extensions. A branch followed the old *Camino Real* south from Santa Fe to Chihuahua, where Samuel and James Magoffin of Kentucky established their trading post. Another extension followed the Old Spanish Trail westward through southern Utah. It was used largely by trappers and by traders, or thieves who obtained their horses in California for sale in New Mexico.

The Mexican War interrupted the profitable commerce temporarily. After that war New Mexico was a territory of the United States; therefore when the trade was renewed it no longer was international in character. Again the commerce by wagon trains grew steadily until it was taken over by the railroad in 1880. In the later years companies in New Mexico also put wagons on the road, so that the trade no longer was a Midwestern enterprise and caravans shuttled back and forth from both ends.

In these years, too, many more branches were added to the Trail in order to reach the newer communities in northeastern New Mexico. Each trail could also become several trails, for, when one set of tracks was worn too deep, the drivers would pull over to make a new, less dusty trail. Several rows of parallel tracks often spread out into a multiple trail a mile wide. Today at several places along the route the deep ruts still can be seen.

THE MOUNTAIN MEN

Back at the time of the opening of the Santa Fe Trail, trappers from the Midwest also were beckoned by the open door in the Borderlands. In 1821, the above-mentioned Hugh Glenn accompanied Jacob Fowler and a party of trappers up the Arkansas to the site of present Pueblo. There Fowler and his men built a stockade and waited while Glenn made inquiries in Santa Fe. It so happened that he and Becknell appeared in the capital simultaneously and, because each was suspicious that they both had the same objective, they avoided each other. But Becknell was seeking permission to trade, while Glenn was soliciting approval for trapping, and each was successful.

When Hugh Glenn returned to the Arkansas with the good news that the trappers could enter New Mexico, the Fowler party established headquarters in Taos and began trapping for beaver along the upper Rio Grande. In 1822, James Baird of Missouri, recently released after some eight years in a Spanish jail, returned to Santa Fe, became a naturalized Mexican citizen, and joined in the quest for beaver. As soon as more trappers came to the Rio Grande, Baird complained to Mexican officials that the "foreigners" were "clandestinely" taking so many pelts that the beaver were becoming scarce and "we Mexicans" no longer could make a profit from the resource which a "merciful God" had bestowed upon "our soil."

The fur traders have been called a "reckless breed" of "Mountain Men." Several made their headquarters in Taos, an adobe village located in a mountain valley at high altitude where the environs were advantageous for trapping and trading. Since well back in the colonial era Taos had been the site of annual fairs that attracted merchants from Santa Fe and Chihuahua for bartering with the Indians. Now the fairs gave way to small stores operated by resident merchants. Here a Canadian, Carlos Beaubien, made his home and became one of the early dealers in pelts and merchandise. Among the trappers were Bill Huddart, Antoine Robidoux, Isaac Slover, Tom Smith, Joe Walker, William Wolfskill, and Ewing Young. They so thoroughly cleared the streams of beaver that in 1824 the governor of New Mexico banned trapping in the area. Thenceforth they would have to travel farther afield.

In 1825, Ceran St. Vrain of Taos formed a partnership with François Guerín of Missouri, and a certain Bernard Pratte advanced goods on credit for sale to the trappers. Guerín, however, soon became discouraged and sold out to St. Vrain. Then Pratte's son, Sylvester, brought out another party that included Sylvester and James Ohio Pattie, a father and son. They traveled on to the upper Gila River, where Pratte gave up trapping in favor of a lease for the operation of the old Spanish copper mine at Santa Rita del Cobre.

COMMERCE WESTWARD

In 1826, another noted Mountain Man, "Bill" Williams, former preacher and interpreter among the Indians, came to Taos with the government party which was surveying the Santa Fe Trail. Now St. Vrain obtained the approval of the governor for a group of these trappers to work the streams far across the Borderland. In his party were Williams, Young, the two Patties, and Miguel Robidoux. They traveled down the Rio Grande, crossed westward through the Mogollón Mountains, and came out upon the upper Gila River. Separated into four bands, these men covered most of Arizona. The Patties even crossed Southern California to San Diego, where the Mexican officials refused to accept their trapping license as valid and threw them in jail. There the elder Pattie died, but his son, James Ohio Pattie, ultimately returned to the Midwest. Later he told his story to Timothy Flint, whose imaginative writing made the book one of the most exciting to come out of the early Far West.

In 1826, another well-known trapper, Jedediah Smith, also ventured into California. As a partner in a trapping operation in the central Rockies, he worked the region over to the Great Salt Lake, and then with a party of eighteen men he set out for the west coast. This group followed up the Sevier River in Utah to its source, crossed over to the Colorado River, followed it down to the Mojave Indian villages, and then crossed the desert and mountains to San Diego. Although the padres in the mission made the visitors welcome, the Mexican authorities were less cordial. They ordered "Jed" and his men out of California.

Smith returned across present Nevada to the trading rendezvous on Bear Lake in Utah. Again, in 1827, he retraced the trail down the Colorado River to San Gabriel. This time the Mexicans arrested him and took him to the governor in Monterey. There John R. Cooper and some other merchants advanced the incredibly large sum of thirty thousand dollars as bond for the release of Smith and company. They departed by a northerly route to Vancouver and thence eastward across the mountains. In those early years this party had engaged in some extensive exploration which later would prepare the way for overland emigration to California.

In 1826, the year of the St. Vrain and "Jed" Smith expeditions, Christopher Carson arrived in Santa Fe. Young Kit, as history knows him, had been lured from his home in Franklin, Missouri, by reports brought back by Santa Fe traders. After joining the trappers in Taos he soon earned a reputation for his courage and skill. Trading and trapping for furs, he worked north in the mountains and sometimes east into Texas. Like his colleagues, he made money readily only to lose it easily in the pleasures of Taos society—then back to the streams again. In 1829, Carson was one of a party of forty trappers led into Arizona by Ewing Young. Lacking a permit, this group circled northwestward first, in order to deceive the Mexican officials, and then turned south past the Zuñi villages to the Salt and Verde rivers. Some of the men returned to Santa Fe, but Ewing, Carson, and a few others went on through the Mojave country to San Gabriel. Arrested by the Mexican authorities in Los Angeles, they managed to escape and on the return trip they trapped along the Gila River until they arrived at Santa Rita. Young left a cache of furs there while he went to Santa Fe for a permit to trap in Arizona. With that secured, he and Carson and the others returned to Taos in 1830 with pelts valued at about thirty thousand dollars.

While Young and Carson were in the Gila country, Antonio Armijo, head of a trading company in Santa Fe, sent a company of Mexican traders over Escalante's old route through Utah and thence on to California. Thus they opened what came to be known as the "Old Spanish Trail." Over that same route William Wolfskill led a party of trappers in 1830. Three years later William Walker with another group worked west from Utah in 1833 in search of a trail to California more direct than the one followed by Jedediah Smith. They ascended a stream now named after Walker, crossed the Sierra Nevadas, and traveled down the Yosemite River into the San Joaquin Valley. In San Francisco, this trapper fared better than had his predecessors in California, for the Mexicans granted him permission to trap along the San Joaquin. That done, he returned by ascending the

Kern River, crossing through Walker Pass, and heading east across Utah to the Great Salt Lake. He and Armijo both had opened trails to California by routes to be followed frequently in later years.

As alien traders filtered into New Mexico, they became influential in the economy and society of the province. Yet they never had the force of overwhelming numbers as did the immigration into Texas, for only sixty to eighty of the newcomers could be counted as residents at a given time. Meanwhile, in 1828 new mines, called *Placeres*, were opened south of Santa Fe and stimulated a rush to that region. From New Mexico prospectors and trappers rediscovered Arizona, which had almost been deserted by the Spaniards. The Mission of Tumacácori was evacuated in 1824, and San Xavier del Bac was abandoned temporarily by 1829. The presidial villages of Tubac and Tucson were the only centers of Spanish activity remaining in the vaguely defined region of Arizona.

To that region the transient trappers of the 1820s and 1830s brought no permanent accretion, but they did explore trails to California and arouse interest in the resources of the Gila Valley. Their pioneer work would be useful in the later development of Arizona.

MIGRATION TO CALIFORNIA

Although some of the Mountain Men had penetrated to California, their success there was discouraging, and the more consequential early infiltration came by sea. Even before 1820, a few aliens had gone ashore at the

coastal towns, as earlier related. Soon, in 1823, a Boston ship captain, John R. Cooper, obtained a trader's license from the Mexican governor, Luis Argüello. The profits derived from Cooper's enterprises so impressed the governor that he sent a ship under his command to Canton, China. Cooper brought back a cargo of silks and other merchandise valued at about twelve thousand dollars. That was the beginning of the lucrative China trade conducted largely by New Englanders in their famous clipper ships. From the eastern states some of them brought cutlery and cotton goods to California, obtained a cargo of beaver and other pelts, traded them in China for tea and silks and returned with them to Boston. Usually they realized a profit of ten to twenty percent of their original investment. Other shippers, after disposing of their merchandise in California, took on cargoes of tallow and hides produced by the growing cattle industry on the numerous *ranchos*. The tallow was sold in Mexico, Peru, and Chile, while the hides were taken to New England for processing by the rising boot and shoe industry. As a result several mercantile firms opened offices in Monterey and in other California ports. When the Yankee ships anchored in the harbors, the Californians went aboard and "shopped" for cutlery and light hardware, cloth and clothing, and staple groceries. To those early supermarkets afloat, they came to gaze upon and purchase the fascinating products of another world.

Competitors temporarily challenged the supremacy of the Yankee traders in California. At Fort Ross, north of Bodega Bay, the Russians had a post which they used as a base for trade in furs, cattle, grain, and tallow. In 1813, their commerce was valued at fourteen thousand dollars; but thenceforth the Californians became less cordial and in 1841, the Russians sold out and withdrew. In the same year agents of the Hudson's Bay Company came down from Fort Vancouver and opened a store in Yerba Buena, a village later absorbed into San Francisco. At that post they sold merchandise and bartered for beaver skins, while also engaging in intrigue in an effort to wrest California away from Mexico. However, the trade languished and the intrigue failed.

On the other hand, the Yankee merchants enjoyed a brisk business. As Richard Henry Dana observed, "Having more industry, frugality, and enterprise than the natives, they soon got nearly all the trade into their hands." Prominent among those merchants on the coast were William Goodwin Dana, William E. P. Hartnell, Thomas A. Larkin, Alfred Robinson, David Spence, Abel Stearns, Alpheus B. Thomas, and the clipper captain, John R. Cooper. Some of the aliens also took up ranching. Although Mexican law restricted land ownership to native and naturalized Mexicans, and allowed only Catholics to have access to local courts and legal proceedings, some of the immigrants acquired ranches without first becoming naturalized and converted. The officials either overlooked their transgression or accepted a bribe, and the Americans kept hoping for a change in Mexican policy which would favor them. Eminent among the ranchers were Dr. John Marsh, who began the practice of medicine in Los Angeles in 1836, and later acquired a ranch in central California, and John Sutter, a Swiss-American who, in 1840, obtained permission from Governor Juan Alvarado for the acquisition of a large ranch in the Sacramento Valley. It was he who, a year later, bought out the neighboring Russian post at Fort Ross.

By 1840, the foreign-born population had grown by slow infiltration to approximately four hundred as against about two thousand Mexicans. Up to that time most of the immigrants had come by sea, but soon more were to arrive by the overland routes explored by the trappers. In the year 1840, Antoine Robidoux conveyed to the Missourians his enthusiasm for California, where he had found the land fertile, the climate mild, and the people hospitable. Consequently, a school teacher, John Bidwell, organized the Western Immigration Society, which enrolled several hundred members. By 1841, sixty-nine of them were ready to start west. Under the leadership of John Bartleson they traveled up the Platte River and that fall braved the Walker Pass through the Sierra Nevada to the ranch of Dr. John Marsh in the San Joaquin Valley. The Mexican officials imprisoned them, because they lacked permits. They soon obtained their release and scattered out among the Mexican residents.

Another band of immigrants arrived soon after those of the Bartleson party. It was comprised of about twenty-five Mexicans and Anglo-Americans led by William Workman and John Rowland. They came from New Mexico and traveled by way of the Old Spanish Trail through southern Utah. In 1843, two more groups of settlers arrived, one led by Joseph B. Chiles and the other by Lansford W. Hastings.

It is remarkable that so many of the emigrants traveled the long, arduous trails to California safely, and only one group of seventy-nine persons blundered into disaster. That was the Donner party of 1846. It had poor management, lost precious time along the way, then tried a "short-cut" over an untried route through the Sierra Nevada and encountered an early storm on the Humboldt. Bogged down in ten feet of snow in November, this party suffered from starvation and frigid cold while encamped by Donner Lake. Four rescue parties were required to extricate the forty-five enervated survivors and transport them to the nearest ranches in California. Several other groups did make the journey safely that season, so that by 1846 the Anglo-American population of Mexican California was approaching one thousand, or double the number of 1840.

In the coastal province, near the end of the Mexican Period, the aliens made up less than one-third of the population. In New Mexico they comprised only a handful in contrast with the numerous Mexicans and assimilated Pueblo Indians. In Texas, on the other hand, they outnumbered the Mexicans five to one.

People who pulled up their roots and made the long, difficult journey to the Borderlands would be by nature enterprising and aggressive. As they filtered in among the Mexican residents, the stimulation of intercultural contacts would threaten the tranquility of established Spanish institutions. Especially was this true in Texas, where the immigrants so greatly outnumbered the Mexicans.

7

THE
LONE STAR REPUBLIC

The naturalized North Americans . . . maintain an English school and send their children north for further education; the poor Mexicans not only do not have sufficient means to establish schools, but they are not of the type that take any thought for the improvement of its public institutions or the betterment of its degraded condition. . . . The colonists murmur against the political disorganization of the frontier, and the Mexicans complain of the superiority and better education of the colonists; the colonists find it unendurable that they must go three hundred leagues to lodge a complaint against the petty pickpocketing that they suffer from a venal and ignorant *alcalde*, and the Mexicans with no knowledge of the laws of their country, nor those regulating colonization, set themselves against the foreigners, deliberately setting nets to deprive them of the right of franchise and to exclude them from the *ayuntamiento.* . . .

Manuel Mier y Teran, quoted in Richardson and Rister, The Greater Southwest *(Glendale, Calif., 1934), p. 90.*

Young Stephen F. Austin strove conscientiously to solve the problems of the Anglo-American colonists in Mexican Texas and at the same time patiently reminded them of their pledge to become good "Mexicans." He held them in line reasonably well until 1835, but finally the destiny of Texas arose beyond his control. The grievances of the colonists and of the Mexican officials became rapidly more difficult to reconcile because of complications in the home countries. The real causes, therefore, lay not so much in unsolved grievances as in the ramifications of a revolutionary struggle in Mexico and a spirit of Manifest Destiny on the American Frontier. From opposite directions these movements swept into the frontier province of Texas and swirled up the bewildered colonists in the vortex of a political whirlpool.

MEXICO IN TURMOIL

In Mexico reformers drew inspiration from European philosophers and revolutionary crises. They sought to improve the lot of the common man by an abrupt adoption of republican institutions along with curtailment of the wealth and political influence of the aristocracy and of the Catholic Church. In this, of course, they had to contend against the opposition of big landowners and high clergymen.

After Mexico had become independent and had found Iturbide's imperial rule unsatisfactory, the liberals drafted a constitution in 1824 embodying many of their ideals. It outlined an organic law so remarkably similar to that of the United States that it appeared to have been copied, but Vito Alessio Robles subsequently insisted that "the conception of the one and the other differed absolutely." At any rate, it did establish an elective bicameral legislature, a system of federal courts, and a president indirectly elected. The nineteen states also were to have their own representative governments, and the four territories, including Texas, could aspire to later achievement of statehood. Although trial by jury and religious toleration were omitted, this constitution did provide for a separation of powers in a federal system wherein the states had considerable leeway in managing their own affairs, and it affirmed personal rights and guarantees for the citizens of Mexico. It became, therefore, the political platform for the rallying of liberals against conservatives throughout the violent strife of several succeeding decades.

Mexicans by and large were ill-prepared for so abrupt an immersion into the intricacies of self-government. After the adoption of the federal Constitution of 1824, they chose as their first president General Guadalupe Victoria, a hero of their wars for independence, and allowed him to serve a full term of four years amid constant harassment. After his term, constitutional government succumbed to political feuds, with the result that in the succeeding decade there were twenty presidents. In that era Joel F. Poinsett, United States minister to Mexico, observed that British agents were siding with the conservatives; consequently he gave encouragement to the liberals. He organized five York Rite Masonic lodges, which became schools for instruction in democratic strategy for prominent politicians, including Vicente Guerrero, Lorenzo de Zavala, and Antonio López de Santa Anna. It was in that era, too, that the central government of Mexico and the legislature of the state of Coahuila made liberal land grants to *empresarios* in Texas, including Zavala. Immigrants who poured into Texas in those early years also regarded that liberal constitution as their greatest source of hope, for it encouraged them to look forward to statehood as soon as their numbers sufficed. In their own state, under that constitution, they could control the local courts and build their own roads and schools, for they had learned under the American system how to do those things for themselves. But meanwhile, as residents of a mere territory, they would have to look to the Mexican central government for aid in the solution of their problems.

MANIFEST DESTINY

Simultaneously the situation in Texas was complicated further by the spirit of Manifest Destiny which animated many Americans. It was a spirited version of liberal thought on the role of popular sovereignty in the attainment of better government. Sufficient time had passed since the winning of American independence to bolster the conviction that the American experiment was a success. Democracy was Man's greatest hope, and under it many reforms could be effected for improving the lot of the Common Man. Further, the United States was then predominantly Protestant, and the evangelical, individualized faith propagated by a popular ministry seemed to harmonize with the democratic spirit, or so thought the Protestant spokesmen.

Many Americans became convinced that democracy and Protestantism were the hope of the world and that the United States as chief exponent of this new order had a "high duty to mankind." By contagion this new way of life would spread naturally among other peoples who would see the advantages and would want to be absorbed into this progressive society. Originally, therefore, this "chosen people, beacon to mankind" concept of the national destiny contemplated only an inevitable but peaceful absorption of neighboring areas into the United States until the nation reached natural boundaries in the hemisphere. Later it acquired the additional conviction that if other people, like the Mexicans, were blinded by dictatorial control and thus unable to learn by "remote example," they would have to be "liberated" first in order to be schooled in democracy. In Albert Weinburg's study of Manifest Destiny, he defined it as a "spiritual exaltation" derived from a belief in the "superiority of American institutions and a zeal for expanding the area of freedom by example and expansion." William Gilpin, who was one of the original enthusiastic exponents of the movement, expressed the spirit of Manifest Destiny as follows:

The untransacted destiny of the American people is to subdue the continent—to rush over this vast field to the Pacific Ocean—to animate the many hundred millions of its people and to cheer them upward—to set the principle of self-government at work—to absolve the curse that weighs down humanity, and to shed blessings around the world.[1]

The colonists in Texas personified Manifest Destiny. They insisted upon self-government as a prerogative and hoped in vain for realization of their ideal within the Mexican system. One observer remarked that they carried a constitution with them in their hip pockets.

[1] *Mission of the North American People* (Philadelphia, 1873), p. 124.

TROUBLES IN TEXAS

Mexican misgivings about the aliens in Texas were aggravated by a rebellion which occurred in 1826. Haden Edwards, an *empresario* in eastern Texas, found some Mexican and Anglo squatters on his land grant and evicted them. This precipitate action led to a disputed election which created an alignment in two bitter factions. After the settlers had persuaded the Mexican officials in San Antonio to annul the Edwards grant, he and his brother enlisted the aid of a band of Cherokee Indians and proclaimed the creation of the "Fredonian Republic." Their rebellion for "Independence, Liberty, and Justice" collapsed after Mexican soldiers and militia defeated their motley army. The Mexicans drove Edwards and his allies out of Texas and transferred his land grant to Joseph Vehlein and David G. Burnet. Although in this campaign against insurrection, Austin and his militia loyally supported the authorities, this uprising aroused even further the suspicions of Mexicans about the motives of the immigrants in Texas.

Soon afterward, in 1829, President Guerrero (the second president of Mexico) precipitated another crisis by issuing a decree abolishing Negro slavery throughout the Republic. Naturally the slaveholders in Texas regarded this as a serious blow. Actually they were in a minority among the colonists, and Austin himself was opposed to slavery in any form, yet the privilege of bringing Negro slaves into Texas had been embodied in the original grant to Austin. Therefore when Austin addressed a protest to the president, enforcement of the decree was suspended in Texas.

In 1829 other sources of estrangement also arose. In that year Andrew Jackson, an avowed expansionist, became President of the United States. Previously the Secretary of State, Henry Clay, had undertaken negotiations with Mexico for purchase of territory west of the Sabine River, but the Mexicans had been unresponsive to his argument that cession of some territory would contribute an improvement by making Mexico City nearer the center of the country. When Jackson assumed office, he renewed the negotiations through his minister to Mexico, Anthony Butler, who offended the Mexicans by his artless overtures accompanied by wholesale bribery.

During this period, General Manuel Mier y Terán was in Texas making a survey of boundaries, and in 1829 the central government made him commander of frontier defense. He saw nothing but trouble and danger in Texas, where colonization appeared to him as only a well-designed forerunner of annexation by the United States. He recommended that his government should try to prevent that outcome by garrisoning more soldiers in Texas and by transplanting Mexican settlers among the Anglo-American colonists.

MEXICAN MEASURES

Matters were made worse by the seizure of government in Mexico by Anastasio Bustamante, the vice president, whose conservatism made him anti-American. His foreign secretary, Lucas Alemán, proposed that Texas be made into a penal colony for the resettlement of Mexican convicts, that immigration of non-American foreigners be encouraged, that the colonization act of 1824 be rescinded, and that efforts be made to improve trade relations between Texas and Mexico. Pursuant to these recommendations, an act adopted in April of 1830 suspended *empresario* contracts, banned further importation of Negro slaves, placed heavy duties upon goods imported into Texas, and prohibited the admission of any more Anglo-Americans excepting at Austin's colony and two others. For enforcement of the new measures, Bustamante increased the strength of the Mexican garrisons in Texas to about thirteen hundred soldiers, many of whom were conscripted vagabonds. Two years later supplementary legislation provided that Mexican colonists should be settled upon the unoccupied parts of the canceled land grants.

Certainly by 1832 the Mexican government was committed to measures which would crack down upon the Texans, despite their vociferous protests. In that year a glimmer of hope appeared. Dr. Valentín Gómez Farías, a physician, who came to be known as the "Father of Reform," became a candidate for the presidency on a liberal platform. He advocated redistribution of wealth, suppression of the monasteries, termination of the Church mo-

nopoly of education, freedom of speech and press, and assurance of territorial integrity for colonies having Mexican culture. However, a professed liberal, General Santa Anna, had a greater popular appeal due to his military exploits. Subsequently these two teamed up, and in 1833 Santa Anna became president with Gómez Farías as his vice president. The president immediately retired to his plantation, while the doctor tried to carry out his reforms. As could well be anticipated, Gómez Farías encountered strong opposition. Then Santa Anna, the unscrupulous opportunist, emerged from retirement and as the champion of the clergymen and army officers staged a coup d'état whereby he ousted Gómez Farías and reconquered his own presidency.

Before Santa Anna turned reactionary, the first clash occurred in Texas. Colonel John Davis Bradburn, a Kentuckian employed in the Mexican service, commanded the garrison posted in Anáhuac on Galveston Bay for enforcement of the collection of import duties. He seemed meddlesome beyond the call of duty, and his soldiers were unbearably arrogant. In 1832, after a local woman had been mistreated by some of the soldiers, a mob of angry Texans was preparing to tar and feather a suspect when Bradburn's troops arrested several of them, including William B. Travis. Thus at Anáhuac the Texans were rallying against Bradburn and the *presidio* in the name of Santa Anna's cause at the very moment when Santa Anna was leading liberals in Mexico into battle against Bustamante. With a schooner bearing a cannon and forty good marksmen, the "Texians" routed the garrison out of the *presidio* and forced Bradburn to flee from Texas. Next, under the leadership of James Bowie, they marched upon Nacogdoches and defeated the Mexican garrison posted there. They made their Mexican prisoners declare in favor of Santa Anna's cause and then paroled them to return to their homes. If Santa Anna had failed in his campaign, the Texans would have found it difficult to explain their deeds; but Santa Anna fortunately came out victorious and soon would become president. Thus under the guise of loyalty to the "liberal" victor in Mexico, the Texans had removed all Mexican troops from their province.

The majority in Texas still remained loyal to Mexico, even though they desired some reforms. Since 1824 the frontier province had been supervised by the *ayuntamiento* of San Felipe and, although some subdivisions in local government had been created in 1828, the adjustments were inadequate in proportion to population growth. In 1832, Austin complained that there was not one civil court in all of Texas, so that appeals from decisions of the

Mexican *alcaldes* had to be carried to distant Saltillo. In effect that denied justice to persons of meagre means. "In short," he concluded, "you may say that Texas needs a *government*, and that the best she can have, is to be created a State in the Mexican Federation." Hopefully the Texans in 1833 sent delegates to a convention, drafted a constitution for the proposed state, and adopted a request for better mail service, tariff reform, and the restoration of a liberal immigration policy.

In behalf of the colonists Austin traveled to Mexico City, where Santa Anna received him cordially. The president agreed to the repeal of immigration restrictions, but denied the application for statehood. Evasively he referred tariff reform to the Treasury Department and political reform to the State of Coahuila. The state legislature did respond by dividing Texas into three departments, including six new municipal governments, and by adopting some judicial reforms. The latter included the creation of a supreme court, the introduction of trial by jury, and permission for the use of the English language in judicial proceedings.

FROM REFORM TO RADICALISM

Austin could return home with gratification that he would be able to report some favorable accomplishments. While on his way back, however, he addressed a letter to the council in San Antonio to continue with steps toward the organization of a state government. His letter was intercepted by agents of Santa Anna and, because it plainly represented defiance of the decision denying the Texans statehood, Austin was returned to Mexico City and imprisoned until December, 1834.

In the critical year of 1834 the chief proponent of conciliation remained in enforced inactivity, where he could only write appeals for patience to friends back home. In the absence of Austin's restraining hand, a new leader, Sam Houston, grew in influence. In his youth he had lived among the Cherokees as the adopted son of a chief, and in the war of 1812 he had served with distinction under General Andrew Jackson. His home state, Tennessee, then had selected Houston governor, but when his bride deserted him soon after their wedding, he had resigned the governorship. He returned to live with the Cherokees, who had by then been removed to Indian Territory (now Oklahoma). That brought him in close proximity to Texas, where he appeared in 1832. He made a tour of observation with James Bowie and immediately wrote his old friend Jackson, who then had become President, that most of the people in Texas desired union with the United States. At that time actually only a minority were so inclined. Houston soon became the vigorous spokesman of that minority, whereupon the movement for independence from Mexico and annexation to the United States rapidly gained ground.

When Santa Anna, once the standard bearer of the liberals, turned reactionary, this unexpected reversal played into the hands of the agitators in Texas. In 1834 and 1835 Santa Anna installed a conservative puppet in the presidency of Mexico, abolished the state legislatures, divided the country into administrative departments, denied the plea of Texans for statehood, ordered their militia reduced to only one man for every five hundred people, and sent an army to Texas for enforcement of collection of the customs duties. Those import duties had become a serious source of contention. Mexico had imposed them in an effort to force the Texans to trade with Mexico; but the Texans wanted and needed the manu-

factured wares available in New Orleans and St. Louis; consequently they had resorted to smuggling, which by 1834 had grown in value to over two hundred thousand pesos annually, according to Juan B. Almonte. Evasion of the customs collectors would soon grow into open defiance, as Captain Antonio Tenorio learned when he brought a detachment of soldiers to Anáhuac. In June, 1835, Travis and a band of irate "Texians" drove them out. Consequently Santa Anna sent up a larger force, six hundred men, under the command of his brother-in-law, General Martín Perfecto de Cos.

General Cos also had orders to arrest Lorenzo de Zavala. That *empresario* formerly had been a close friend of both Poinsett and Santa Anna, and he had accompanied Austin when he presented his plea for reforms to Santa Anna. After the latter had betrayed his erstwhile liberal supporters, Zavala had hastened back to Texas and there issued a statement charging the dictator with treason. Now that an army was coming to arrest him, it was in his personal interest to encourage resistance on the part of the Texans. That helped further the cause of the restless agitators.

When James Bowie reported that a large force of Mexicans under General Cos was disembarking at Matamoros, a convention of Texans assembled on October 15, 1835, in Washington-on-the-Brazos. By that time Austin had returned. He sought to reassume leadership and to counsel moderation; yet even he was becoming aware that a clash of arms was imminent. To the committees of safety organized in town after town he sent a circular letter proclaiming that "War is our only recourse. We must defend our rights, ourselves, and our country, by force of arms." Even so, he still said nothing about independence, and the majority of the delegates at the Consultation sided with him on that issue. They voted down the radical minority, who wanted to break abruptly with Mexico. Instead, they pledged allegiance to the liberal Constitution of 1824, if it were restored and respected. Then they declared for independence only if restoration of federal govern-ment should be denied them. Finally, the delegates made preparations for the latter contingency by organizing a provisional government. They named Henry Smith as governor, James W. Robinson as lieutenant governor, Sam Houston as commander of the army, and Austin as an agent for solicitation of aid in the United States. The latter could be considered an important as-signment for Austin, yet in a sense they were promoting him out of the way.

CONCILIATION DENIED

By leaving an opening for overtures from Mexico, the delegates at the Con-sultation had been conciliatory, but no overtures came. Instead, a Mexican army was approaching. James Bowie, now Colonel Bowie, harassed the in-vaders in some preliminary skirmishes, but he was unable to prevent the oc-cupation of San Antonio by General Cos. Soon the Texan army grew to ap-proximately eight hundred by the en-listment of recruits from the vicinity and by the arrival of a company of volun-teers from New Orleans. Finally on December 5, 1835, the Texans assaulted the Mexican forces in the city and in the Alamo, an old mission chapel which had been converted into a for-tress. In the unorthodox fighting which ensued, the Mexicans in four days lost nearly three hundred men and the Texans only two. Then General Cos surrendered. Upon his promise never again to oppose constitutional govern-ment, the Texans permitted him and his few hundred survivors to return to Mexico.

For the battle of San Antonio the Texans had rallied heroically, and certainly the war had begun in earnest; yet immediately both the army and gov-ernment in Texas collapsed. Volunteers had returned home, and with the remnant of an army a few spirited officers set out to invade Mexico. In their momentary exuberance they as-sumed that liberals below the Border would rise in rebellion against Santa Anna and join them in a triumphal restoration of constitutional government. General Houston rode hard in order to overtake the runaway army and halt it at Refugio. Then he received reports that another Mexican army was coming and sent Colonel Bowie back with orders to demolish the Alamo so that it could not be occupied and held again as a fortress.

Meanwhile, the Consultation, still in session, had deposed both Governor Smith and General Houston. Colonel Bowie, left in temporary command, received reinforcement by a company of Tennessee volunteers led by David Crocket. Bowie and Crocket, with only one hundred and eighty men, then prepared to defend the Alamo rather than to destroy it. As Bowie said, "the public safety demands our lives rather than evacuate this post to the enemy."

While the military and political leaders were working at cross purpose and Austin was eliciting only a lukewarm official response in the United States, the Grand Army of perhaps close to four thousand Mexicans under the command of General Santa Anna advanced upon Texas. The vindictive dictator proclaimed that he would crush the rebellion, punish the leaders, free the Negroes, annul the land grants, and colonize Mexicans among the refractory Texans. Now with all hope for conciliation abandoned, the only alternative was a war for independence. In late February of 1836 a second convention met in Washington-on-the-Brazos and on the second of March it adopted a declaration of independence. The delegates drafted a constitution for the Republic of Texas, elected David G. Burnet and Lorenzo de Zavala as provisional president and vice president, and reappointed General Sam Houston to the military command. Finally the issue was drawn, and on April 13 General Houston issued a plaintive appeal:

TO THE CITIZENS OF TEXAS

You have suffered panic to seize you. You will now be told that the enemy have crossed the Brasos, and that Texas is conquered. Reflect, reason with yourselves, and you cannot believe a part of it. . . . The force of the enemy does not exceed nine hundred men. With a semblance of force sufficient to meet him, his fate is certain. If, then, you wish your country saved, join her standard. Protect your wives, your children, and your homes, by repairing to the field, where alone, by discipline and concert of action, you can be effective. . . . Those who do not aid Texas in her present struggle, but flee and forfeit all the rights of citizens, will deserve their fates.[2]

CAUSES OF THE CONFLICT

Now that the incidents leading to the open conflict have been reviewed, consideration of the basic causes is in order. At that time an allegation was advanced about slavery as a possible cause. Almonte thought that he detected evidences of a conspiracy on the part of the slaveholders, who were migrating to Texas in order deliberately to seize that frontier province for the South. He corresponded about this with Abolition leaders in New England, who in turn raised an alarm about this "disgraceful conspiracy" on the part of the slavocracy in the South. The investigation conducted by the late Eugene C. Barker has convincingly disposed of that contention. No evidences of a conspiracy could be found; instead, Texas was settled by a normal westward movement which naturally brought some slaveholders to the rich lands of this new frontier. The majority of the colonists actually opposed slavery and, when threatened by Mexican decrees, those who depended upon the system

[2] Amelia W. Williams and Eugene C. Barker, eds., *Writings of Sam Houston* (Austin, 1938), I, pp. 408-409.

merely converted to retention of their slaves under labor contracts.

Only later, after Texas became independent, did the hard-pressed Southern leaders become aggressive in their desire to acquire Texas for the strengthening of their political position within the Union. It is true that the government in Washington did then renew efforts to purchase Texas, and this has been cited as further evidence of infidelity. Such efforts were made partly to correct the "error" of Adams in trading off Texas in 1821 and partly to provide the means whereby Mexico could pay some unsettled claims advanced by American citizens. Evidence is lacking that this desire in any way caused the government of the United States to foment a revolution in Texas, and when the conflict broke out officials in Washington regarded it as detrimental to their pursuit of peaceful negotiations.

Some historians have attributed the outbreak of the revolution to cultural estrangement and racial distrust. However, the distrust which existed was more between the leaders of the colony and the opportunistic politicians of a distant, ineffective government than it was between the residents of Spanish and Anglo heritage in Texas. A search through Austin's correspondence from 1828 to 1834 fails to yield a single reference to inter-cultural conflict, whereas he did complain that his own colonists were the "most obstinate and difficult people to manage that live on earth." Furthermore, when war started a Mexican became provisional vice president and twenty-one others joined in the fight for autonomy by organizing a volunteer company of their own, commanded by Juan N. Seguín.

As a reflection of the divergence in culture, religious conflict has been suspect. The Texans did neglect to become good Catholics, and they did welcome the arrival of Protestant missionaries, but some of the fault can be attributed to the Mexican Church for failure to provide an adequate number of priests. The Texans filled the void by continuation of their previous faith, and a contemporary observer, Benjamin Chase, lamented that religion was suffering more from general indifference than from an overt conflict between Protestants and Catholics.

In the final analysis the fundamental causes were derived from the Mexican federalist movement and the American spirit of Manifest Destiny, as noted previously. Immediate causes were the unsolved problems of the colonists, the abrogation of the liberal Mexican Constitution of 1824 by Santa Anna, the agitation by radicals in Texas, and the final punitive measures adopted by the Mexican government.

Through it all there were many circumstances similar to those of the American War for Independence. A period of "salutary neglect" was followed by the abrupt imposition of controls. Then the contention of loyal subjects for their rights under the existing government was converted into open resistance when soldiers were sent to enforce the collection of customs duties. Further military intervention by a "Tory" government soon transformed resistance into a war of independence. In both instances liberals in the home government encouraged the colonial patriots in their efforts to secure their freedom.

FROM DEFEAT TO VICTORY

By February of 1836, war had come in earnest. While the courageous delegates at the Convention were preparing a declaration of independence, the Mexican army laid siege to the Alamo. At the old mission chapel in San Antonio, Colonel W. B. Travis assumed command of the valiant little band of one hundred and eighty-two men after Colonel Bowie had been incapacitated by an unfortunate injury. In his final message to his fellow patriots Travis pledged that he would never surrender nor retreat, but would contest the enemy to "Victory or death." Since no reinforcements could be rallied in time to save the defenders of the Alamo, they all died as martyrs, including Travis, Crockett, and Bowie. However, during the long siege that lasted from February 23 to March 6, their frontier marksmanship cut down so many Mexicans that, coupled with desertions, Santa Anna's effective force was reduced to somewhere in the neighborhood of two thousand men. Therefore they had contributed an invaluable service by their heroic resistance, and by death had inspired that memorable battle cry, "Remember the Alamo!"

Part of the Mexican army had been sent out in search of a force of about four hundred Texan volunteers led by Colonel James W. Fannin. Soon after the fall of the Alamo, this detachment suffered defeat near Goliad and surrendered under terms allowing them to lay down their arms and disband. Instead, Santa Anna ordered the prisoners executed and, on March 27, some three hundred and seventy-one of them were massacred. This wanton butchery gave rise to another spirited battle cry, "Remember Goliad!"

Meanwhile Houston had undertaken the task of enlisting and organizing an army and, by this time, had gathered together about four hundred men at Gonzales. Because he needed more time, he concluded that he would have to retreat eastward. Many frightened Texans around San Antonio, left to the mercy of pillaging Mexican soldiers, loaded their belongings in wagons and followed after the retreating army. Likewise the officers of the provisional government moved the capital temporarily to Harrisburg, near Galveston Bay.

Houston's tactics proved to be sound. As he retreated, his army grew steadily by the accretion of recruits coming from all over Texas and by the arrival of other volunteers from the United States. Attracted in part by the Texan cause and in part by Houston's offer of land in return for their services, full companies of volunteers came from Mississippi, Kentucky, and Ohio.

Afterwards the Mexican government lodged protests with the foreign offices of both Great Britain and the United States concerning the alleged improper intervention by the United States in this insurrection. It is true that President Jackson refrained from issuing a neutrality proclamation and that law officers were lax in enforcing the restriction about the organization of hostile expeditions on American soil for intervention in the affairs of a friendly state. But no regular United States soldiers went to the aid of Texas, while the volunteer companies claimed that they were not yet "organized." Moreover, the hovering of an American army on the border of Texas was explained as a precaution against an Indian uprising. A British agent in Texas investigated the basis of the Mexican complaint and reported to his government that the aid which came was by individual choice and that no official assistance was lent by the government of the United States "or connived at in any way."

Houston's army grew to over a thousand soldiers by the end of March, whereas Santa Anna, following in pursuit, had lost many men by desertion. Moreover, he had overextended his line of supplies and had divided his force. In another month Houston also had lost some of his followers, who had grown impatient with his Fabian tactics. He had about eight hundred men when on April 20 he turned about at the San Jacinto River and attacked Santa Anna's fifteen hundred surprised Mexicans. In the brief battle, the Texans killed six hundred and thirty of the invaders, wounded two hundred and eight more, and took seven hundred and thirty prisoners, while they lost only six killed and twenty-five wounded.

Santa Anna had fled from the field of battle, but soon he was found and returned to Houston's camp. He then signed the Treaty of Velasco in which he agreed to withdraw the other divisions of his army and to recognize the independence of Texas. President Jackson promptly extended recognition to the new republic and invited Santa Anna to Washington for a visit. Jackson treated the distinguished prisoner as a guest, conferred with him about unpaid claims against Mexico, and released him. After his return to Mexico he repudiated his agreement to recognize the independence of Texas, for the reason that he had been forced to sign the Treaty of Velasco "under duress." The Texans thought that they had won their freedom; but obviously they were going to have trouble in maintaining it.

PROBLEMS OF THE REPUBLIC

While Mexico was withholding recognition, the Texans proceeded with the organization of a government. In July of 1836, David G. Burnet, the provisional president, proclaimed an election for the first Monday in September. Matters to be voted upon were adoption of the constitution drafted by the Convention, the election of officers, and a proposal for annexation by the United States. To be president for a term of two years the voters cast over five thousand ballots for Sam Houston, the popular hero of San Jacinto. His opponents, Austin and Henry Smith, garnered only a few hundred votes each. Likewise the decision in favor of annexation was nearly unanimous.

Almost insuperable difficulties would tax the ability of the first president of the Lone Star Republic. Mexican warships were choking off commerce by sea, and a Mexican army was harrassing the border. The patriot army became restless from lack of pay, and there was no money in the treasury. Adventurers attracted to Texas by the lively activity of the past year would be hard to keep under control. Finally, amid all this a

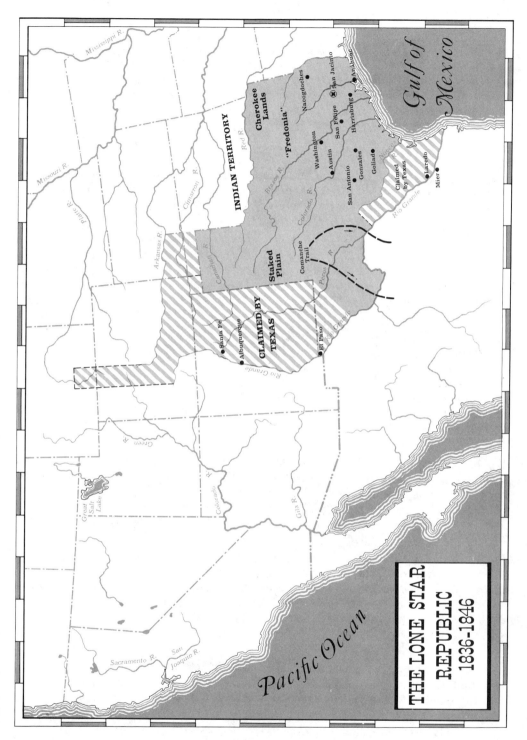

THE LONE STAR REPUBLIC 1836-1846

125

new government had to be organized.

When the refined General Mirabeau Buonaparte Lamar succeeded Houston in command of the army, the unruly volunteers refused to obey his orders and forced his retirement. Then Houston dismissed from service about three-fourths of the soldiers and placed the remainder under the command of the competent and respected Albert Sidney Johnston. The retired veterans were pensioned by grants of land which within a year amounted to about three million acres.

Simultaneously naval defense required attention. In fact, there was no navy, because only one of the four ships of the revolution had survived, and early in 1837 it was demolished in a storm. Yet coastal shipping badly needed protection. Consequently in 1839, the congress purchased a steamship, the *Zavala*, which was converted into a warship, and further authorized the construction of four more vessels. Under the command of Commodore E. W. Moore, the feeble navy undertook a blockade of Mexican ports. Because Texas had insufficient funds for maintenance of the ships, the little navy was lent to Mexican revolutionists for service in their cause. Later, when the president of Texas sent orders for the navy to return, Commodore Moore disregarded that request and continued the ships in service as privateers. Then the congress of Texas voted to sell the navy, but Moore still would not yield control. After Texas was annexed by the United States, the maverick fleet reluctantly submitted to absorption into the navy of Uncle Sam.

Solution of the financial problems of Texas also proved difficult. The congress voted an issue of bonds up to five million dollars, paying ten percent interest. Even though public lands were pledged as security, the bonds found no buyers. Simultaneously the congress levied heavy taxes upon commerce and property, but trade was stagnant and no revenues were yielded from these sources. In desperation, the congress then resorted to the issue of paper money, but with nothing to establish its value it deflated rapidly and sent prices soaring. Meanwhile the expenses of the new government piled up. To the cost of the navy was added the expense of a reorganized army. In December, 1836, the congress enacted measures providing for the enlistment of a "battalion of mounted riflemen" for defense of the border and protection of the frontier. In the following June, President Houston took a leave of absence for thirty days so that he could "organize and set on foot" the corps of troopers who were to become the illustrious Texas Rangers.

In those early years the principal resource of the Republic was its public lands, amounting to one hundred and eighty million acres, but even that advantage was frittered away. When eleven land offices were opened, returns from cash sales provided little revenue. Instead, in exchange for land the land offices accumulated mostly land scrip issued to veterans and other certificates forged by unscrupulous persons. The speculative mood then led to the chartering of a grandiose venture in the form of the Texas Railroad, Navigation, and Banking Company. This corporation was granted a charter allowing a capital stock of five million dollars for the building of railroads and canals connecting the water-ways of Texas from the Rio Grande to the Sabine. The scheme was so devised that the principal stockholders would have become the "feudal landlords" of a large part of the Republic. However the project failed, because the stockholders could not even raise the initial capital necessary for the launching of the bank.

The greatest disappointment in Houston's program was the rebuff received in Washington. The Texans had come out strongly in favor of annexation, and if President Jackson ever had encouraged Houston to strive for that objective, he certainly reversed himself now. Because the conflict of North and South over slavery was becoming critical, the Abolitionists were raising alarm about the alleged conspiracy of the slavocracy. "Texas," said William Lloyd Garrison, "is the rendezvous of absconding villainy," determined "to extend and perpetuate the most frightful form of servitude the world has ever known and to add crime to crime."

Jackson sensed that if he were to lay the proposal for annexation before Congress, it might be voted down, or at least it would provoke a spirited debate which might split his Democratic party; consequently he tabled the application. Texas would have to wait for more propitious circumstances.

SPIRITED STRATEGY

In Houston's first term of two years, the public debt of Texas had grown to almost two million dollars. Although for that sum Houston could point to no spectacular achievements, actually he was gradually laying a solid foundation. The import duties were being collected, and salaries were being paid; immigration was increasing, and Britain and France were preparing to grant commercial treaties. The electorate, however, grew impatient and elected as his successor, for a three-year term, the sophisticated Lamar. He promised a radical departure from the cautious policies of his predecessor, whom he regarded as a rather vulgar intimate of Indians and rowdy adventurers. In his inaugural address in December of 1838, Lamar held up a high destiny for Texas as an independent nation. Moreover, he would lead the way in adorning the land with the fine graces and stern virtues of a noble culture. (The "Great Society" of a later era!) Almost immediately Lamar moved the capital from Houston to a new city, Austin, located on the frontier of that time but at a site which would be more centrally located in later years. Then he embarked upon domestic, Indian, and foreign policies which rapidly increased the public debt to seven million dollars and brought Texas to the brink of disaster.

To support his foreign policy Lamar had the Texas Rangers increased to eight hundred and forty men by means of an issue of promissory notes amounting to seven hundred thousand dollars. Soon another company of about five hundred was added by underwriting an outlay of another seventy-five thousand. Simultaneously more expenditures were authorized for the acquiring of the four ships for the Texas Navy.

With a strengthened military establishment, Lamar first gave attention to the critical Indian problem. Two years earlier, in April of 1836, the Comanches had overwhelmed Parker's fort, located west of Waco. They had massacred John Parker and seven others and had taken into captivity five children, including Cynthia Ann Parker. General Edward Gaines regarded the massacre as justification for leading American troops across the border of Texas for the "defensive" occupation of Nacogdoches. Because Mexico was refusing recognition of the independence of Texas and was hoping to reconquer that province, the Mexican government claimed that the occupation of a Texas town constituted military intervention on the part of the United States and broke off diplomatic relations temporarily. In as much as Parker's fort was far removed from Nacogdoches, the Texans also resented the violation of their border by the United States. Therefore Lamar considered his election to the presidency as an expression of a rising Texas nationalism which, if it could not challenge the United States, could at least eliminate the excuse for the brief, odious occupation of Nacogdoches by taking punitive action against the Red Men.

The first blow fell upon the Cherokees. Previously, by consent of the Mexican government, many of them had settled in the upper Trinity and Neches valleys, where they labored peacefully as farmers and even assisted the Texans in their troubles with hostile tribes. Houston, an adopted Cherokee, had negotiated a treaty which confirmed the rights of the Cherokees to the lands they occupied. Under Lamar's guidance, the congress abrogated that agreement, and Lamar then proclaimed that the Indians would be removed either "by friendly negotiations or by the violence of war." When a commission failed to obtain their peaceful departure, Lamar sent against them a thousand soldiers under the command of General Thomas J. Rusk and Colonel Edward Burleson. The outnumbered Cherokees fought valiantly and then retreated across the Red River into Indian Territory. Houston bitterly condemned this shameful campaign, but his denunciation went unheeded.

Some Comanches were the next victims. In March, 1840, a party of thirty-two warriors with their women and children came to San Antonio, under a promise of safety, in response to an invitation for negotiating a treaty of peace. While twelve of the chiefs were in the courtroom for discussion of the liberation of one of their captives, Colonel William S. Fisher tried to arrest them. They resisted and were slaughtered. As those remaining outside tried to flee, they too were massacred.

The treachery of the "Council House Fight" set the Comanches on the warpath. Four hundred of them ravaged Texas from San Marcos to the coast, where they hoped that Mexican forces would join them. Disappointed in that expectation, they moved inland toward the capital. General Felix Huston and the Texas army halted them at Plum Creek. Forty braves fell, and the survivors fled into western Texas. Then, in retaliation for Mexico's failure to give assistance, they went on a destructive raid down the Comanche Trail four hundred miles into Coahuila. One

Texan detachment succeeded in finding a Comanche village on a branch of the Colorado River and slaughtered one hundred and twenty-eight of the surprised occupants. However, that was the only feeble success achieved by Lamar's policy of extermination. Hundreds of elusive, embittered Comanches would pillage the frontier mercilessly for many years to come.

Intensification of Indian warfare was accompanied by a renewal of hostilities with Mexico. Colonel S. W. Jordan led a company of Texans across the border in 1840 for the purpose of joining with Mexican Federalist insurgents and detaching the northern provinces of that country from Centralist control. Together they would create a large "Republic of the Rio Grande." The Mexicans then failed to cooperate. As the Texans approached Saltillo, the two companies of Mexicans who had joined them deserted to the Centralist army commanded by General Mariano Arista. Jordan soon found his little band of one hundred and ten men besieged in an old stone house by a force of approximately twelve hundred Mexicans. Nevertheless, the "Texian" riflemen broke out of this trap. Their devastating accuracy left four hundred of the enemy dead on the field of battle.

After the failure of that ambitious revolutionary scheme, Lamar organized an expedition for the invasion of New Mexico. Texas claimed the Rio Grande as the southern boundary, and now that claim was interpreted to mean the Rio Grande all the way up to its headwaters. That would bring into Texas the eastern half of New Mexico, including the cities of Taos, Santa Fe,

and Albuquerque, as well as that part of El Paso on the Texas side of the river. (Present Ciudad Juárez was then known as El Paso.) Ostensibly the purpose of Lamar's expedition was to open a route of commerce to Santa Fe. By 1841 the Santa Fe trade was thriving and the import duties levied upon the traders were providing considerable revenue for the governor of New Mexico. If the New Mexicans could be persuaded that they lived in Texas, that revenue could be diverted to the empty treasury of the Lone Star Republic. However, when a band of two hundred and seventy armed men set out from Austin in June, 1841, it became obvious that, if necessary, force was to be employed for persuasion of the New Mexicans. Under General Hugh McLeod the volunteers advanced in high spirits onto the Staked Plain. They were accompanied by an editor of the New Orleans *Picayune*, George Wilkins Kendall, who was destined to write, not an account of a glorious conquest but of an adventure into disaster. More will be said about that a little later.

Although Lamar's Indian and foreign policies failed, he can be accredited with at least one constructive measure. For the elevation of culture among the Texans, he recommended the founding of a system of schools. To that end the congress in 1839 and 1840 reserved four square leagues of land in each county for the benefit of local public schools and a total of fifty leagues as an endowment for two colleges. Although little else was done immediately, these measures did provide a foundation for the later development of a good public school system and a major state university system.

PAYING THE PENALTY

When election time arrived again, in the autumn of 1841, the voters had had enough of Lamar's spirited and expensive administration. They abandoned the poet and violinist and turned overwhelmingly again to Houston. Reinstated in the presidency, that cautious strategist had to cope with the consequences of the overextended ambitions of his predecessor.

First, Houston had to announce the saddening news that the Texas-Santa Fe expedition had been intercepted in New Mexico and that the men all had been captured and imprisoned. Even so, Texans still eyed jealously the lucrative Santa Fe trade. If the terminal city could not be taken, at least they might divert the trade at a point northeast of Santa Fe where the wagons crossed territory claimed by Texas. To that end the Texas government gave approval for Colonel Jacob Snively to set out for the Arkansas River with one hundred and eighty men in the spring of 1842. They would pillage the caravans for whatever profit could be garnered for Texas. When Snively found that an escort of four hundred Mexican cavalrymen was coming out to meet the caravan, he put that force to flight. However, when he turned about he encountered an unexpected escort of about two hundred United States dragoons who were guarding the caravan. Because the Texans wanted to retain the friendship of the United States, Snively was frustrated in reaching his goal. He conferred with the commander of the dragoons, Captain Philip St. George Cooke, and tried to explain that the Texans were not trespassing upon United States territory; but Cooke would not accept that excuse. After relieving the Texans of their arms, except for ten muskets needed to shoot wild game, he sent them home in humiliation.

Next came a war with Mexico as an outcome of the transgression of the border back in Lamar's term. In January, 1842, General Arista invaded Texas and even occupied Goliad and San Antonio. However, he well remembered having faced Texas rifles before and he hastily withdrew. Later in that year Texas was threatened with reconquest again. An army of fourteen hundred soldiers under General Adrian Woll invaded the Republic and again occupied San Antonio. The Texas militia soon rallied in defense of their capital and after three sharp engagements forced Woll's withdrawal.

For defense of the border, seven hundred and fifty of the volunteers marched southward. At the Rio Grande they refused to return home, but instead they plundered Laredo. When General Alexander Somerville took their loot away from them and returned it to the inhabitants of Laredo, a third of the spirited Texans elected Colonel William S. Fisher as commander and crossed the river for a campaign of retaliation in northern Mexico.

In December, 1842, this maverick Texan detachment laid siege to Mier, a Mexican village which was occupied by General Pedro de Ampudia. By Christmas day they had almost taken the town, only to be thwarted by the arrival of Mexican reinforcements. In the battle ensuing they inflicted about six hundred casualties upon the enemy but finally had to surrender to a force which they estimated at five times the strength of their own. By orders received from Santa Anna, seventeen of the Texas prisoners were chosen by lot for immediate execution. The others were marched all the way to Mexico City, where they languished in prison for a year. Finally the one hundred and twenty who still survived were released.

While contending with the distressing outcome of misadventures on the border, Houston also coped with the critical problem of finances. At his suggestion the congress pledged the confiscated Cherokee lands as security for an issue of two hundred thousand dollars in treasury bills, but that paper money soon declined in value to twenty-five cents on the dollar. Meanwhile Houston had ordered severe retrenchments. Offices were abolished and salaries were cut, so that the annual cost of government was reduced to one-tenth of what it had been under Lamar. Nevertheless, other expenses in excess of the meager income increased the public debt year after year.

IMMIGRATION ENCOURAGED

In his endeavor to encourage immigration Houston met with greater success. Back in his first term, in 1836, the congress of the Republic had authorized an extravagant grant of over one thousand acres of land for each immigrant, but a year later the acreage had been reduced to six hundred and forty. Next, in 1838, the congress also adopted a homestead act, which gave title to one hundred and sixty acres to each settler who could prove occupation and advance evidence of improvements made upon the land. With such inducements available, Houston now began the solicitation of European immigration. In 1842, he sent Henri de Castro to Paris as consul general with authorization for the granting of lands for colonization. Castro recruited nearly five hundred families and about as many single men in France and Germany. In 1844, they founded a settlement of hardy pioneers at Castroville on the Medina River.

Interest in Texas spread throughout Germany, where several members of royal families formed the *Mainzer Adelsverein,* a colonization society. This organization obtained a grant of three million acres along the San Sabá River and designated Prince Carl von Solm-Braunfels as the leader of the emigrants. In May, 1844, he brought to Texas over one hundred and fifty families, who founded New Braunfels. A serious epidemic soon threatened the survival of this first colony, but presently it abated and thousands of other Germans came to the region north of San Antonio. There they transplanted their folkways and contributed their strength and skill to the progress of the young, troubled republic. Thus in the very same province where the Mexicans formerly had failed to assimilate a large Anglo-American immigration, the newcomers founded institutions which accommodated quite successfully the influx of many people of a different cultural heritage. By 1847, immigration along with natural increase had boosted the population of Texas to one hundred and forty thousand, including nearly forty thousand Negroes.

The three-year second term of Houston would terminate at the end of the year 1844. Therefore that autumn brought around election time again. As Houston's successor the Texans chose the methodical Dr. Anson Jones, an influential cotton planter who had been closely associated with the government of the Republic in one capacity or another ever since the achievement of independence. He had little opportunity to demonstrate his capability as an administrator, because the principal event of his brief administration was the culmination of the movement for annexation. Consequently he won claim to fame merely as the "last president of Texas."

STATEHOOD OR INDEPENDENCE?

After the bid of Texas had been tabled in Washington early in Houston's first term, Lamar had sought, instead, a glorified independence. Nevertheless one after another of the Texas ministers in Washington kept alive some discussion of the subject. However, the prospects grew even dimmer in the term of Jackson's successor, Martin Van Buren, who was quite indifferent. Therefore the Texans sought a settlement of their differences with Mexico and welcomed British and French recognition of their Republic.

For several reasons the British took a special interest in the fortunes of Texas. They had a mutually advantageous commerce with the South, where they could obtain cotton for English mills and in exchange export manufactured products. However, if the United States, under pressure from the North, should ever erect a high tariff barrier, that commerce with the South would suffer. It would be advantageous, then, to prepare for such an exigency by cultivating a similar exchange with another cotton-growing region, namely Texas. Moreover, the Mexican residents of California and New Mexico were growing restless under the centralist regime in Mexico. Although rebellions in both of those provinces had failed, in 1836 and 1837, hopefully they might yet strike out upon an independent course. If so, the British likely would recognize their independence, as had been done for Texas. Already Oregon was partly British, under the agreement providing for joint occupation. With the cultivation of an independent California, New Mexico, and Texas, the British Empire would have a friendly borderland from Texas to Oregon serving as a buffer zone between the United States and Mexico. Even the Abolitionists in England hoped to reap an advantage from the independence of Texas, for they might persuade the Texans to liberate their slaves. Possibly in this way they could demonstrate to the South that cotton could be produced profitably with freedmen as laborers.

An independent career, however, was proving to be a hazardous course for the Lone Star Republic. Therefore Houston again proposed annexation after John Tyler became President of the United States. The Secretary of State, Abel Upshur, embraced the proposal with enthusiasm, and the chances appeared to be good until Upshur met a tragic death in an accident aboard a warship in February, 1844. Meanwhile some support in Washington was lost as a result of a proclamation by the Mexican government that annexation would mean war. Then when James C. Calhoun succeeded Upshur as Secretary of State, the submitting of Upshur's treaty to the Senate by that champion of slavery appeared to bear out the "conspiracy" allegations. By a vote of thirty-five to sixteen the treaty was rejected.

When Anson Jones became president, therefore, he had cause to believe that the best, and perhaps the only, course for Texas would be independence under the most favorable terms which Mexico would accept, and he initiated negotiations. Simultaneously and rather unexpectedly the political situation in the United States took a favorable turn. James K. Polk, a "dark horse" Democratic nominee, won election to the presidency upon a platform advocating the "re-occupation" of Oregon and the "re-annexation" of Texas. Therefore when Jones was being inaugurated in Austin in December, the Congress in Washington was considering a resolution which would give effect to that part of Polk's platform pertaining to Texas. In order to obviate the necessity of getting a two-thirds majority in the Senate, as required for the ratification of a treaty, this time the friends of Texas introduced a joint resolution in both houses. In that form the proposal for annexation carried in the House by a vote of one hundred and twenty to ninety-eight and barely squeaked through the Senate, twenty-seven to

twenty-five. Because Polk's victory in November was considered a mandate of the voters in regard to Texas, the Congress responded by adoption of that resolution in January and February, 1845, even before Polk had yet assumed office. (Prior to World War II inaugurations were held in March instead of January.) Therefore it was President John Tyler who signed the joint resolution on March 1, 1845.

Meanwhile in Mexico a conciliatory candidate, José Joaquín Herrera, had seized the presidency by ousting and imprisoning Santa Anna. Immediately the British Foreign Office began applying pressure upon that new government. The gist of it was that Mexican recognition of the independence of Texas might head off annexation by the United States. The pressure was effective. Soon Herrera's government agreed to recognize Texas if that Republic would agree never to become annexed by any other nation.

So it came about that in Texas when the congress convened in June, President Jones presented two proposals, one from Mexico and one from the United States. The Republic could choose to continue upon an independent career under conditions more favorable than those prevailing during the past nine years. As an alternative, Texas could become a state in the Union by accepting the terms proposed in the joint resolution. The Republic would transfer title to all public buildings, posts, harbors, and forts to the United States. The new State of Texas would assume the debts of the Lone Star Republic but it would retain possession of the public lands as a source of revenue for retiring those debts. In addition, four new states might be created by a division of Texas, with the consent of the original state, and slavery would be permissible south of the parallel of thirty-six and one-half degrees. Both the United States and Mexico proposed in their simultaneous overtures that any disputed boundaries should be submitted for later negotiation.

ANNEXATION ACHIEVED

Almost unanimously the members of both houses of the Texas Congress voted in favor of annexation. The question then was referred to a popularly elected convention, which gave approval on July 4, 1845, and a state constitution was adopted in a referendum on October 13. When the first state legislature met in February, 1846, Dr. Anson Jones delivered a farewell address in behalf of the Republic:

The lone star of Texas, which ten years since arose amid clouds over fields of carnage, and obscurely shone for a while, has culminated, and, following an inscrutable destiny, has passed on and become fixed forever in that glorious constellation which all freemen and lovers of freedom in the world must reverence and adore—the American Union.[3]

William C. Binkley, in his summary of the Texas Revolution, has shown that the purposes went through three distinct stages, the political organization through five steps, and military operations through four stages. Then in the brief period of the Republic, administrative policies shifted rapidly from one extreme to another, under Houston, Lamar, and Houston again. Meanwhile the fortunes of the annexation proposal were experiencing similar ups and downs. If this becomes complex and confusing to the student of history, it must have been even more baffling to the participants; yet in good Anglo-Saxon tradition they "muddled through" to ultimate success. However, upon the achievement of annexation, some unfinished business was carried over. The Republic had transferred to the United States a large territory fertile for development, but along with that it transmitted to the federal government responsibility for two unsettled disputes which would provoke a confrontation with the unyielding government of Mexico on the one hand and, on the other, a conflict with the unsubdued Indians of western Texas.

[3] Quoted in Herbert M. Gambrell, *Anson Jones* (Garden City, 1948), pp. 418–419.

A PHOTO ESSAY ON THE
AMERICAN SOUTHWEST

Of all the clearly definable regions of the United States the American Southwest is the most varied. It is the home of traditional Indian societies that have some customs dating back a thousand years. It is also the location for the control center for moon shots. It has the most populous state and the least populous state. It has towering mountains and deserts like Death Valley. Contrasts are everywhere. The American Southwest has vast riches and abject poverty. It is at once the most progressive and forward-looking part of the United States and the section that is without equal for the intensity of its conservatism and that is in closest touch with the past.

This limited photo essay cannot begin to show the vast sweep of the Southwest. It can only hint at its variety.

A Navajo herdsman tends his sheep. (Paul Conklin, PIX, Inc.)

Above. Tribal leaders treating a sick boy in the ceremonial chamber of the Zia Pueblo, New Mexico. (Smithsonian Institution, National Anthropological Archives, Bureau of American Ethnology Division)

The modern world obtrudes into the life of the Indians of the Southwest but ancient ways remain vital.

Opposite, top left. A Navajo woman stands at the door of her kitchen. (Paul Conklin, PIX, Inc.)

Opposite, top right. A Pueblo father and his daughter in the traditional clothes that are worn on some occasions to this day. (Smithsonian Institution, National Anthropological Archives, Bureau of American Ethnology Division)

Opposite, bottom. A chapter meeting on the Navajo reservation in Arizona. These men have gathered in their meeting hall to hear an Office of Economic Opportunity official explain part of his program. (Paul Conklin, PIX, Inc.)

Spanish culture has left an enduring imprint on the American Southwest.

Opposite, top. Franciscan fathers are depicted converting Indians in Father Pablo de Beaumont's *Crónica de Mechoacán.* (New York Public Library, Rare Manuscripts Division)

Opposite, bottom. San José de Tumacácori Mission in Arizona. (The Bancroft Library, University of California, Berkeley)

Below. San Xavier del Bac Mission in Arizona. (The Bancroft Library, University of California, Berkeley)

Missions were the center of Spanish colonial life as well as of Indian life on the borderland.

Opposite, bottom. The mission of San Carlos Borromeo near what is now Carmel, California. The Spanish citizens together with the Indians are shown participating in a festival. (De Young Museum)

Below. An old flour mill operated by a water wheel located near Mora, New Mexico in an area where Spanish settlers grazed vast herds of sheep. (Courtesy of H. F. Thatcher)

Opposite, top. Pasturing vast herds of cattle was the principal occupation of settlers in the Spanish borderland. This painting shows *vaqueros* apparently of both Spanish and Indian origin. (Courtesy of Dr. Carl Dentzel)

Settlers from the United States into what had newly become the "American" Southwest adopted almost completely Spanish-American cattle raising procedures. The typical "American" cowboy learned his trade from the Spanish-American *vaqueros* who came before him.

Opposite. The spring house of the Spur Ranch in Texas. (Library of Congress)

Below. A chuck wagon on the Shoe Bar Ranch in Texas. (Library of Congress)

Economic activities of all kinds intensified when the Southwest became American.

Opposite. Early mining operations in California. (Denver Public Library, Western Collection)

Below. Settlers who homesteaded in New Mexico in the period after the Civil War. (Library of Congress)

Transportation was of crucial importance in tying together the vast reaches of the Southwest.

Above. A photograph of the stage coach that ran between Independence, Missouri and Santa Fe, New Mexico. (The Santa Fe Railroad)

Opposite. A Wells Fargo Express Company Freight Wagon. The heavily armed guards indicate that the material being transported was of some value. (Library of Congress)

The main square in San Antonio, Texas in the period before American penetration. (Charles Phelps Cushing)

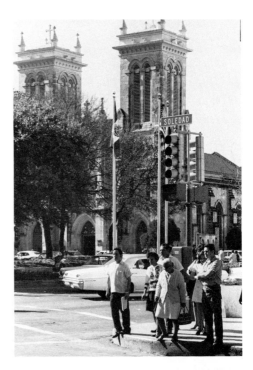

At right. A corner today very near the same spot in San Antonio shown on the preceding page. There have been many changes but much that is old has remained. (Michal Heron)

Below. Some Spanish American citizens of San Antonio, Texas. (Michal Heron)

8
THE
MEXICAN PERIOD

As obedient sons of the mother country, and faithful defenders of your dear liberties, you swore solemnly before God and men to be free, and to die rather than to be slaves. In this spirit you adopted forever, as a social compact to direct you, the federal Constitution of the year twenty-four, your government was organized at the cost of immense sacrifices which unnatural sons trampled upon, ignoring them in order to found upon your ruins their fortune and criminal advancement, and when it seemed that you were already the sure patrimony of the aristocratic tyrant, you boldly waved the banner of the free. "Federation or Death is the destiny of the Californian."

Juan B. Alvarado, quoted in California Historical Quarterly, XV, 2 (June, 1936), pp 354-355.

Following the independence of Mexico in 1821, the era known as the Mexican Period lasted in Texas only to 1836. In the remainder of the Borderlands, Mexican administration continued ten years longer, or from early 1821 to the autumn of 1846. One of the characteristics of that era was the infiltration by Anglo-Americans, as described previously, and in Texas that migration created problems which cut short the Mexican Period. In California and New Mexico revolutions also occurred; but as will be seen, the "foreigners" had only an incidental relation to them, and they failed to achieve independence.

SEPARATION FROM SPAIN

Out on the coast as soon as news of the independence of Mexico arrived in January, 1822, Pablo Vicente de Sola convened a *junta*, or committee, which recognized the empire of Iturbide. On April 11 the citizens of the capital, Monterey, formally swore allegiance to the new government and then celebrated with a joyous fiesta. On the other hand, in New Mexico the celebration occurred on January 6, immediately upon receipt of the news. In Santa Fe the townsmen participated in a parade and fiesta, followed by a grand ball in the old Palace of the Governors. In 1824, in both provinces the change from an empire to a republic elicited another enthusiastic celebration.

The happiness and hopefulness generated by the changes in government were a natural response after the long period of neglect under Spain. The secular arm of the Church had done little toward serving the spiritual needs of the colonists, the government had failed to provide public improvements, and the military establishment had been unable to cope adequately with the Indian menace. The Crown sent out local officials who were in the main natives of Spain and who regarded with arrogant disdain the poverty-stricken *mestizos* who resided on the frontier. Too often they came merely to exploit their subjects so as to extract as much wealth as they could cart away. Many demonstrated no real interest in the improvement of conditions in these remote provinces far from home.

With the change in government the colonists hoped that all their ills would vanish. Soon they were doomed to disappointment, for the change brought only some minor revisions in the structure of local government without introducing revolutionary improvements. Moreover, Mexico as an independent nation turned out to be much more unstable and ineffective than the colonial administration of New Spain. Consequently the colonists were destined to endure twenty-five years of turmoil and uncertainty in the Mexican Period.

Under the new regime the official title of the governor was changed to "political chief," and the executive continued to have arbitrary and comprehensive powers like those in the colonial era. Since 1812 the Spanish provinces each had had an appointive "Deputation," which served as a rather ineffective legislative council. Under Mexico that body became elective, but the law specified that the incumbent colonial members be re-chosen. The *alcaldes* and *cabildos* of the old regime were incorporated intact in the new system. The principal innovation came in 1824, when provision was made for an elected delegate to represent each territory in the Mexican Congress. Another new practice, which the citizens welcomed, was the frequent appointment of one or another of their own eminent citizens as political chief instead of sending in outsiders.

MEXICAN CALIFORNIA

Under the Mexican Republic the first governor of California, Louis Argüello, had to cope with a serious Indian rebellion. At the mission of Santa Inés in 1824, after a soldier had flogged an Indian, the neophytes set fire to the buildings. News of this insubordination spread rapidly to the other missions, where the Indians seized arms and held the soldiers at bay. Several small battles were fought in the neighborhood of Santa Barbara before the Indians finally were brought under control again.

The next governor, José María Echeandía, a radical republican, assumed control in 1825. Immediately he encountered difficulties. A plan for promotion of the colonization of California by settling convicts among the colonists had been inaugurated by the Mexican government. Over a hundred came within a year, and the residents began protesting against the development of a penal colony in their midst. Simultaneously the friars became aroused. They suspected rightly that a radical republican administration sooner or later would undertake the secularization of the missions and the expropriation of their lands, therefore they refused to swear allegiance to the Constitution of 1824. After some persuasion, however, the governor issued a compromise decree in 1826 whereby the confiscation of the mission lands would be postponed until those Indians who were capable could be resettled in villages away from the missions. That resolved the conflict only temporarily, because the procedure was too slow to satisfy some avaricious reformers.

RADICAL REPUBLICANISM

Soon a radical agent, José María Padres, disciple of the Mexican reformer, Dr. Valentín Gómez Farías, arrived in California. His ardent persuasion won over to radical republican principles several of the leading local citizens, whose names weave in and out of the story of troubles in California through the next two decades. Deriving their inspiration from old Mexico, these converts to radicalism expected to facilitate the advent of republicanism locally by expropriating Church property, which in this case would be the mission lands. In the process the profits from redistribution of the lands would accrue to the new regime and to themselves as official custodians.

The Franciscans employed their influence to get a governor more favorable to their cause. The new appointee was Manuel Victoria, formerly commander of Mexican troops in Lower California, who came to succeed Echeandía in January, 1831. The aroused Padres faction persuaded Echeandía to issue a last minute decree of secularization before Victoria took over. He did, and Victoria was justifiably angered by that hasty act.

In this way the issue of secularization became a prime cause of a preliminary revolt in California in 1831; but there was another provocation. Echeandía, a cautious and easy-going former professor, had neglected the punishment of criminals and the maintenance of good order. Victoria now pledged to remedy this forthwith. He called for action on several pending cases, with applause from the friars and "foreigners," and he proceeded from this to the arbitrary arrest and banishment of liberal opponents, namely Abel Stearns, Antonio Carrillo, and Mariano Duarte. Furthermore, he suspended the Territorial *Diputación* and the local *ayuntamientos,* or town councils, because he suspected correctly that they were controlled by liberals and would oppose his administration. Being an army officer, his way to order and good government was quite simple; he would obtain it by strict military control.

The liberals held some secret meetings, sent a complaint to Mexico, and then collaborated with Carrillo and Stearns, the exiles, who had slipped back into San Diego and were organizing the opposition. They enlisted the former governor, Echeandía, to head the movement, while their representative in the Mexican Congress, Juan Bandini, supported their cause at the capital. In November, 1831, the revolutionists issued a statement charging Victoria with "crimes," "scandalous acts," and "tyranny," and they proclaimed, "let the rights of the citizen be born anew; let liberty spring up from the ashes of oppression, and perish the despotism that has suffocated our security." The liberal "army" of one hundred and fifty men soon sallied forth to contest the issue with the governor and his thirty soldiers, approaching from the north. On the fifth of December, in an exchange of many words and a few shots, the governor was wounded and his soldiers deserted to the opposition; on the sixth Victoria abdicated.

Juan Alvarado and Mariano Vallejo, prominent in Monterey, hastened south to meet with the *Diputación* in Los Angeles, where this body designated Pío Pico as political chief; but Echeandía refused to recognize Pico, who retired without contesting the issue. However, the former secretary of Victoria, one Agustín V. Zamorano, did contest Echeandía's supremacy. Zamorano, with the aid of William Hartnell, merchant in Monterey, enlisted a company of fifty foreigners, who had found Victoria's strict rule advantageous to their business interests. They challenged Echeandía, and by March, 1832, a compromise was effected whereby Zamorano would rule in the north and Echeandía in the south until the central government sent out an official appointee. When in April, 1832, José Figuaroa arrived as the new political chief, both claimants yielded to him and this revolt was at an end. The Californians had deposed an autocratic, reactionary governor and had restored their rights to limited self-government in their *Diputación* and *ayuntamientos.*

SECULARIZATION OF THE MISSIONS

This preliminary success may be set down as one of the causes of revolt five years later when the liberals again faced a similar threat. In the meantime Figuaroa won favor, not only because he restored the institutions of local autonomy, but also because he proceeded conservatively with plans for secularization of the missions. Good fortune abetted the cause, for soon Gómez Farías was elected vice-president of Mexico and served briefly as acting president. Juan Bandini, delegate in Congress, obtained from him the decree of secularization of August 17, 1833, which also provided that the nationalized lands should be opened to colonization. Simultaneously José María Padres obtained for himself and his colleague, José María Híjar, appointments as directors of colonization. Because Figuaroa was ill and requesting retirement, Híjar was designated political chief for California, with Padres as military commander. By an offer of liberal subsidies they induced two hundred and fifty colonists to go with them to California. They purchased a ship, the *Natalia*, and departed northward with a warship as escort in August, 1834. Some of the colonists went ashore at San Diego, while others went on by sea to Monterey.

Before the expedition arrived in Monterey, a special courier came by land with the news that Santa Anna had assumed the presidency in Mexico and was ordering Figuaroa to retain his position as combined *jefe* and *comandante*. Nevertheless, the two *empresarios* still held titles as directors of colonization, which Figuaroa duly recognized. The two ambitious liberals, deprived of their full glory, were deserted by other local liberals, like Alvarado and Vallejo, because these Californians had agreed earlier that they themselves should reap the fruits of secularization, and now Padres was bringing in colonists to administer the mission lands. Therefore, the *Diputación* permitted continuation of the colonization scheme, but with the provision that Padres and Híjar should keep their hands off the missions.

At this juncture some Sonorans led a revolt in Southern California, which, although seemingly unrelated to the colonization project, aroused the suspicions of Figuaroa. On the supposition that Padres and Híjar were secretly fomenting trouble, Figuaroa ordered the titles of both *empresarios* suspended, whereupon they returned to Mexico. The governor also had Vallejo arrest and deport some suspects among the new colonists, but over two hundred did remain to augment the sparse population of California. Consequently this radical scheme for the expropriation of lands and the revolutionizing of California was thwarted by Santa Anna's coup and his retention of Figuaroa, along with local sentiment against the aggrandizement of newcomers.

After making a tour of the missions, Figuaroa became convinced that immediate release of the Indians would be disastrous for them. He favored, instead, a gradual secularization. However, he had received a decree which required completion of the change within four months after April of 1834. Yet he applied the order first to only ten of the missions, with a provision that about half of their assets should be bestowed upon the displaced Indians. He placed the remaining mission properties under secular administrators, with the friars remaining only for supervision of religious instruction.

The death of Figuaroa in 1835 prevented his completion of his conservative plan. Alvarado eulogized him as a "beneficent father" who had given an "incalculable impulse" to the prosperity of California by "preventing this virgin land from being sprinkled with the blood of its children." The president of the missions, Father Narciso Durán, had the ex-governor's body interred in a vault in Santa Barbara as evidence of the Franciscans' appreciation for his services. At that time a foreign merchant remarked that the Texans were engaged in a revolution and now the death of Figuaroa probably would precipitate similar trouble in California.

Within the next year the remaining eleven missions were secularized, with a haphazard distribution of part of the property among the neophytes. Some Indians submitted to practical slavery on the private ranches created from former mission lands, while others joined bands of horse thieves who were doomed to ultimate extinction.

One of the fundamental causes of discord in California was this issue of secularization, or more specifically the issue of how it was to be carried out and who was to profit by it, which aroused avarice and suspicion. Richard Henry Dana observed that the property of the friars was being preyed upon by "The harpies of the civil power," who went forth as "administrators" and soon ended up "by making themselves fortunes." However, there were other causes of unrest, and prominent among them was the ambition of proud local men to govern themselves rather than to submit to the incompetent and erratic governors, excepting possibly Figuaroa, who had been sent up from Mexico.

Mariano G. Vallejo, prominent in the revolutionary movement, wrote afterwards that because of poor administrators who lacked the necessary attributes for "ennobling them" to their subjects, "what man of good sense could blame an entire populace for rising up with majesty to reestablish the dignity of the law?" Worse yet, the Constitution of 1835 made California a "department" subdivided into districts, ruled by a governor and prefects, respectively, to be appointed by the central administration. This drastic change, accompanied by some petty provocations, was the immediate cause of revolution in 1836.

CENTRALIZED ADMINISTRATION

To Colonel Mariano Chico fell the disagreeable task of inaugurating the centralist regime in California. Formerly a congressman from Guanajuato, he now received the appointment as *jefe político* for this northern territory, where he arrived in April of 1836, and immediately issued a proclamation requiring all officials to take an oath to support of the new constitution. All complied, with few protests; yet his mission made him unpopular from the start, and the Californians soon would find ways to make known their displeasure. The opportunity came when the governor appeared in public accompanied by his mistress and her friend who was under arrest at the time. Respectable ladies arose and left the audience in disgust, whereupon the resentful Chico quarreled with the *alcalde* and then jailed him. Popular excitement was so aroused that the governor deemed it prudent to stay inside his house for several days. He dispatched an order south for troops to come to his support and, while awaiting their arrival, he suspended Cosmé Peña, a customs official, for taking sides with his foes. Frightened by the fury he had kindled, Chico then decided to embark for Mexico, but before his departure he designated Nicolás Gutiérrez, *comandante*, to act as governor.

Gutiérrez took over on September 6, 1836, and because he was regarded as the heir of Chico, he inherited also the animosities aroused by the abdicated ruler. Immediately he quarreled with the *Diputación*, to which body he asserted that he had no need of deputies of "pen and wind," because he had on his side "deputies of saber and musket." Thereupon he dissolved the *Diputación* and ordered guards to keep watch over the customs collections.

When one of the clerks, Juan Alvarado, protested, Gutiérrez ordered him arrested.

In the meantime the dissident elements had received the heartening news that Santa Anna had been defeated and captured by the Texans. Encouraged by this news and by a memory of their successful resistance in 1831, the Deputies met secretly in the former mission of San Juan, where they debated what they should do. David Spence, a merchant with an eye on his business, proposed that they do no more than to address a complaint to the central government; this was voted down. Juan Alvarado insisted, instead, that the delegation of authority by Chico to Gutiérrez was illegal and that it was their duty to resist. The adoption of a motion to that effect precipitated a revolution against the Mexican dictatorship.

REVOLUTION OF 1836

Young Alvarado, once secretary and now president of the *Diputación*, formerly a clerk at the customs house and an avid reader of contraband books, emerged as the leader of the revolution; yet to some he appeared to be merely an ambitious manipulator who sought out pretexts deliberately. Be that as it may, Alvarado sent a messenger to Monterey to bear the news that the "people of California and their representatives have taken upon themselves the responsibility for public order and the preservation of federal institutions and that they are preparing their own defense with all of their military power."

Soon Alvarado entered Monterey secretly for consultation with Isaac

Graham, a hunter from Tennessee, who promised to raise a company of "two dozen good riflemen." According to Vallejo, many Americans in California were willing to help because they were disgusted with their treatment by the Mexican authorities, but one of them later attested that a stronger motive was the promise of three dollars a day during service, grants of land, and citizenship, which Alvarado held out as inducements.

In Monterey, Alvarado was apprehended by some soldiers, but he escaped on Graham's horse. He fled northward to Sonoma, where his young uncle, Mariano Vallejo, was an influential rancher and *comandante* in charge of defense on the frontier. Vallejo, lukewarm at first, finally agreed to enlist two hundred soldiers; but this he found difficult because before they could depart they had to make provision for their families for two or three months. According to Vallejo, all had a "swarm of children, since the women of California were very fertile." While Alvarado awaited the support of Vallejo, an impatient friend suggested that they liberate the Indians from "slavery" at the missions and arm them to bolster their forces, but Alvarado was of the opinion that freeing the Indians was not their objective.

Finally, in early November, the little army of about seventy-five natives, armed with lances and a few muskets, flying the Mexican flag, and supported by Graham's company of twenty-five Anglo-American riflemen, approached the *presidio* in Monterey and demanded its surrender. The rebels had gotten hold of a cannon for which they found one cannon ball, and by a lucky shot they dropped it through the roof of the governor's residence. That was enough. Gutiérrez and his force of fifty-five men gave up and agreed to embark for Mexico on a ship then in port, *The Clementine*, as soon as it sailed. In a burst of jubilation the populace shouted "California is free." Then Alvarado and William Hinckley, a foreign trader, brought out a new flag with "stars and letters of gold," but one of the more judicious soldiers insisted that they continue to display only his Mexican flag, and his arguments prevailed.

In a long document justifying his abdication, Gutiérrez contended that the "foreigners" were to blame and that they overwhelmed him by means of men and cannon and ammunition lent by four or five merchant ships then lying in port, and one of his staff supported him, adding that a United States warship also appeared and threatened to intervene for protection of American commerce. Therefore the first news of the event which reached the outside world via the *Honolulu Gazette* attributed the revolt to the instigation of foreigners who were trying to establish an independent California. However, the narratives of the participants, already referred to, have established the fact that, except for Hinckley, the foreign merchants abstained from participation; Vallejo denied flatly that any aid was received from the ships, and Bandini insisted that the few who favored independence were mostly native Mexicans. The only consequential support by *extranjeros* was provided by Graham's company of former Midwestern squirrel hunters who were more interested in land titles than in political autonomy. As has been shown previously, this was no Indian rebellion nor peasants' revolt; it was rather a feud of the Dons, and it is notable for the number of "histories" which it evoked in later years. No less than nineteen of the participants penned in eloquent Spanish their versions and their justifications.

After Gutiérrez had been deposed, the victors celebrated with a triumphal parade, and then the *Diputación* drafted a preliminary manifesto: "California is free and severs all relations with Mexico until the mother country ceases to be oppressive under the present dominant faction entitled the central government." Alvarado also issued his personal proclamation of November 6 to the people of California, whose destiny would be "Federation or Death."

Next the *Diputación* prepared a formal and more reserved declaration of independence, which proclaimed California independent "until such time as the Federal system that was adopted in the year 1824 shall be re-established." The declaration converted the *Diputación* into a constituent congress for drafting of a constitution, affirmed faith in the Roman Catholic religion, with the qualification that none should be molested for religious opinions, and designated Vallejo as *comandante*. José Castro, president of the *Diputación*, acted as political chief until December 7, when Alvarado was elected. Admittedly all this went further than many

had anticipated, but the citizens stood by and more decrees followed.

The state was divided into two cantons with Monterey and Los Angeles as the two capitals. Each canton was to have a political chief to be appointed by the governor from a trio to be nominated by the local *ayuntamiento*. Actually this Bolivarian scheme never was put into effect because of unexpected interruptions, which, as Alexander Forbes related, precipitated civil war between North and South while impotent Mexico paid little heed and left California to shift for itself, "to have a government of its own manufacture, or to live without a government at all."

REACTION UNDER ALVARADO

Trouble arose at once owing to the disaffection of citizenry of Los Angeles. They did not desire independence and so proclaimed their own provisional government, loyal to Mexico. Then the Indians on the northern frontier began depredations that required Vallejo's presence there to restore peace. As a result of these events, Alvarado had to delay organization of the government while he took command of the troops for a campaign in the south. Graham's company went along. In Los Angeles, Alvarado spent the winter and spring of 1837 in negotiations with the local leaders. Once he had obtained their agreement on the principle of federalism under a native governor; but soon his adversaries, convinced that they had been tricked into submission, raised an army and prepared again to resist. At this point a Mexican officer, Captain Andrés Castillero, with troops, landed

at San Diego and required all to pledge allegiance to the centralist Constitution of 1835. He repeated this procedure in Los Angeles in June, with little resistance, and then met Alvarado in Santa Barbara in July.

At this conference Alvarado, too, took the oath of allegiance, agreed to give up the idea of independence, and to restore California to Mexico. Since he was the senior officer of the *Diputación*, this automatically made him the legal governor *ad interim*. He then sent Castillero to Mexico to obtain confirmation of his status, while he circulated a decree promulgating the departmental system. For this apparent about-face he received much criticism. At first his militia refused to take the new oath, because this was not what they understood they had been fighting for; but Alvarado later insisted that his acts all were consistent with his principles and in the best interest of all Californians.

The new governor, who thought that he was consistent in his principles, certainly was not so in his policy toward foreigners. Since he suspected that they might not support him loyally in his new role, he turned on his former benefactors, confiscated their property, and called them "heathens" and "Jews." In 1840, he arrested Graham and approximately one hundred other aliens, put them in chains, and shipped them to Mexico. Then he proclaimed that he had saved California from this peril. Yet Graham was permitted to return in 1842, and many of the others came, too. Due to the alarm raised by Alvarado, the central government in Mexico City became concerned about the influx of foreigners, but Alvarado, himself, did not respond further to it.

During the administration of Alvarado, which continued to 1842, secularization of the mission lands was completed. In 1839, the governor appointed the capable William P. Hartnell as supervisor of the mission properties, but the spoilsmen raised such a protest that Hartnell resigned. Soon the remaining property was disposed of, and a few years later Father Durán reported that nearly all the missions had been closed. Meanwhile, in 1840, another Franciscan, Father Francisco García Diego, had been appointed bishop of a new diocese comprised of Upper and Lower California. In Santa Barbara—one of the last of the active missions—the bishop established his see in 1842 and began the slow work of building up the secular church. After his death in 1846, Santa Barbara also passed into private ownership. How-

ever, the Franciscans reserved some rooms in the building for use in maintaining an apostolic college. In this way Santa Barbara continued to be occupied by friars, who kept the building from falling into a state of disrepair as that which had occurred at so many of the other missions.

When immigrants from the United States began arriving in larger numbers by the overland routes, the central government in Mexico became alarmed at the leniency of Alvarado, who was now making them welcome. For this reason, and also because Alvarado and his *comandante*, Vallejo, had fallen out, the officials in Mexico concluded that both men should be removed. The new appointee as governor was General Manuel Micheltoreno, who was directed to take with him an army of three hundred and fifty ex-convicts to force the eviction of the numerous foreigners.

While Micheltoreno was traveling to Monterey, some of the "foreigners" almost deprived him of his capital. Commodore Thomas Ap Catesby Jones, commander of the small United States fleet in the Pacific, had become alarmed concerning British designs on California. When he heard a false report in 1842 that war had broken out between the United States and Mexico over Texas, he sailed rapidly from Peru to California in order to get the jump on Great Britain. On October 20, he took possession of Monterey, hoisted the Stars and Stripes, and proclaimed California annexed to the United States. However, he immediately discovered his error, apologized to the government, and withdrew.

FREEDOM TO FEUD

Although Californians were weary of their political feuds and the new governor, Micheltoreno, had turned out to be a genial gentleman, his convict soldiers — hungry, wretched, almost naked, and addicted to night marauding — proved intolerable. Moreover, he failed to check the rising tide of immigration, and he refused to move the capital to Los Angeles. Therefore California was destined to experience one more revolution in which Alvarado again played a leading part. Forces in the south, augmented by some recruits from the north, arose in rebellion in 1844, and after some futile negotiations, stood for battle at Cahuenga Pass on February 20, 1845. This time, as could be well expected, Isaac Graham and his sharpshooters joined Micheltoreno against Alvarado, but the revolutionists also succeeded in enlisting a contingent of Anglo-American riflemen. One spectator has told how the crowds gathered on a hill to watch the battle:

The scene on the hill was a remarkable one. Women and children with crosses in their hands, kneeling and praying to the Saints for the safety and protection of their fathers, brothers, sons, husbands, lovers, cousins — that they might not be killed in the battle; indifferent to their personal appearance, tears streaming from their eyes, and their hair blown about by the wind, which had increased to quite a breeze.[1]

At the last minute the Anglo-Americans, who had discovered that some of them were marshaled on each side, talked it over, decided to withdraw, and became spectators. This so weakened the governor's defense that after an exchange of artillery fire, which killed two rebel horses and wounded a government mule, Micheltoreno capitulated and agreed to abdicate, taking his impotent army of *cholos* back to Mexico with him.

Again the Californians had deposed a governor; a native, Pío Pico, senior officer of the *Diputación*, succeeded automatically to the post as interim *jefe*. Again old strife between north and south was renewed, but Alvarado now retired into the background. The Californians had confirmed their freedom to go on feuding among themselves, which they did without delay. Soon the foreigners would easily be able to take the lead in encouraging one of the local factions in the creation of the Bear Flag Republic, as will be related later on.

NEW MEXICO UNDER THE REPUBLIC

As in California, the immediate problem of the New Mexicans following the winning of independence by Mexico arose from Indian disturbances. As their first political chief, the settlers petitioned for and secured the appointment of Colonel José Antonio Viscarra, who had commanded the garrison in Santa Fe for several years. In his two-year term, from 1822 through 1823, he waged a campaign against the troublesome Navajos. They yielded to an agreement whereby they would surrender

[1] William Heath Davis quoted in *Calif. Hist. Soc. Quarterly*, XIII, 3 (September 1934), p. 230.

several captives and pay for damages inflicted upon the ranchers by their raids.

From 1823 to 1825 Viscarra's successor as political chief, Bartolomé Baca, had at his call only one company of one hundred and twenty soldiers for defense of the entire territory. Yet with that small force he served rather effectively in the continuous warfare with the hostile tribes. In 1824, a large band of Comanches raided the settlements along the Pecos River. They seized as captives one American and four Spanish women, one of whom was the daughter of a former governor. Baca immediately called out the garrison and enlisted the aid of Sylvester Pattie and a group of Anglo-American fur traders. Together they overtook the Comanches, rescued two of the captives, and put the Indians to flight. In this brief but serious clash, the Americans lost ten men and Pattie was severely wounded. Naturally this courageous assistance won favor for the fur traders in Santa Fe. The next year the governor granted Pattie a license to operate the mines at Santa Rita and to trap for beaver along the Gila River.

The next governor, Colonel Antonio Narbona of Chihuahua, continued the campaign against the ever-restless Navajos. His successor, Manuel Armijo of Albuquerque, who served as political chief from 1827 to 1829, tried to strengthen the military establishment. He and his inspector-general of defense, Colonel Viscarra, concentrated upon a reorganization of the local units of militia and provided an escort for the Santa Fe caravans from the Arkansas River into New Mexico.

In 1828, during Armijo's brief first term, some prospectors had found a rich vein of gold at a location known as *El Placer* in the mountains south of Santa Fe. The rush of miners to the area included also a few of the alien residents until an official order reserved the mines for native citizens only, each of whom could work a claim ten paces square. Most miners realized only a few *reales* a day for their labors, but occasionally one would pick up a rich nugget, of which one was said to have been worth thirty-four hundred pesos. A few years later, in 1839, after a new strike opened other mines near *El Placer*, the town of Tuerto mushroomed to such proportions that for a while its twenty-two stores did more business than those in Santa Fe. Like most mineral deposits this one too soon played out. A short time before, in 1838, the hostility of the Western Apaches had forced the abandonment of copper mining at Santa Rita del Cobre.

The brief mining boom injected a shot of prosperity for a few years, and then conditions settled back to the normal struggle for subsistence. Conditions in those years may well be sensed by perusal of a set of revised statutes drafted in 1826 by a special committee of citizens in Santa Fe. First, the committee apologized for the need to impose higher penalties than those prevailing before, because they were fully aware of "the lamentable state of affairs." Then they proposed a new schedule of penalties, and after each ordinance the political chief entered his marginal notes of approval or disapproval.

The ordinances provided as follows: for traders who come to sell goods, one peso for each load; for violation of curfew at night, one peso; for failure to join an expedition sent in pursuit of Indians, three pesos; for stealing rationed irrigation water, or for allowing the ditches to overflow on the roads, one peso; for contaminating a community well, four *reales;* for failure to help with public works, four *reales;* for damages caused by one's cattle in a neighbor's field, two *reales;* and for making insulting remarks to the authorities, one peso. Those "authorities" were the *alcaldes* who had the responsibility for enforcing the ordinances and collecting the fines. Incidentally, at that time one peso was the value of one head of sheep, and eight pesos would buy a cow or horse.

The early 1830s in New Mexico, as in California, was the era of secularization of the missions. Secular churches and schools were needed to take their place. Therefore in the administration of José Antonio Chaves, Santiago Abreu, and Francisco Serracino, greater attention was given to religious and educational needs. Back in 1826 the Bishop of Durango had sent Agustín Fernández de San Vicente to New Mexico as vicar-general. He had designated parish priests to serve in five towns, and had prepared plans for the founding of a Franciscan college in Santa Fe. The college never materialized, and when Juan Rafael Rascón arrived in 1829 as the next vicar-general, he found that the churches were too few and too poorly supported by their parishioners, with the result that they were in a "deplorable, almost ruinous condition." Although he met with meagre success in his efforts to remedy those conditions, he did fill a serious need. For the first time, he, as vicar-general, had the

authority to confer the sacrament of confirmation upon the children. Previously that rite had been reserved for ministration only by a bishop; and no bishop had visited New Mexico since 1760.

Finally, in 1832, awareness of religious needs brought another visit by a bishop in New Mexico. In February the Rt. Rev. José Antonio Laureano de Zubiría, Bishop of Durango, was received with great enthusiasm in Santa Fe. After his tour of inspection, his departure was clouded by sadness, he said, because he lacked resources for improvement of the disheartening conditions. He found poorly supported churches in the few existing parishes, and only two of them were maintaining parochial schools. To fill the educational void, the principal towns were trying to establish public primary schools, in harmony with the radical republican ideals then prevailing in Mexico. However, in 1832 only eighteen such schools were reported to be in operation; but they had not lasted long, owing to a shortage of funds and a dearth of qualified teachers.

Again the normal routine was disrupted by a serious rebellion. California had three of them in the 1830s and 1840s, whereas New Mexico had only one; but this one broke more suddenly and violently than those of the Dons out on the west coast. Moreover, this one developed no profound political philosophy, yet it was a direct outcome of the imposition of centralism by Santa Anna in Mexico.

There were some underlying reasons for discontent. One was the constant and serious harassment by the nomadic Indians, for which Mexico had failed to provide adequate defense.

In outlying villages some of the farmers quit planting crops, because the Indians so often hindered their work and robbed them of their products. Many left their homes and went to the towns, where they subsisted in poverty and discontent. Some of them once sought permission to move to California, but this was denied. Only three small companies of regular soldiers were provided by the central government and they were posted at Santa Fe, San Miguel del Bado, and Taos.

Local resources were inadequate to maintain and equip properly the militia; consequently it was only natural to blame Mexico for the annoying conditions.

CENTRALIZED ADMINISTRATION

For many years the political chiefs often had been local men; therefore, when a Mexican was sent out in 1835 to fill the office, it become another cause of dissatisfaction. Four years previously, Padre Antonio José Martínez of Taos, who had become inbued with the new liberal doctrines while attending the seminary in Durango, had attracted considerable attention by making a speech before the *Diputación* in which he had warned Mexico that this territory had men capable of filling local offices. Nevertheless, a distinguished Mexican army officer, Albino Pérez, came in April, 1835, and his personal qualifications might have been acceptable under ordinary circumstances. With appropriate ceremonies and festivities the citizens celebrated his inaugural, at which he commended them for their "docility, love of order, and a real perfection of so many civic and moral virtues." According to Kirby Benedict, "He was in person, tall and graceful. His address was courteous and polished. He was a man of education and of middle age. He was fond of social life, and prodigal of expenses in procuring its gratification. This was one source of this disaster."[2] Worse yet, Pérez had a low opinion of the New Mexicans, whom he defied and irritated on many occasions, and his policies favored a privileged few, widening the breach between them and the distressed populace. He did, however, promulgate the first statute for the founding of a system of public schools in this territory in July of 1836, and in that year he also led a campaign against the Navajos. Despite his low opinion of New Mexicans, he had married Trinidad Trujillo of Santa Fe, who bore him a son, Demetrio, on December 22, 1836. Occasionally he met with the *Diputación* in Santa Fe for consultation on various petitions and problems of defense which came before that small legislative body. In fact, there is no indication whatever in the minutes of the *Diputación* that trouble was brewing, and Pérez was accepted for two years even though there was latent sentiment against submission to this non-resident.

When it became the obligation of Pérez to give effect to the decrees of 1836 for introduction of the new centralized system by which New Mexico

[2] Santa Fe *New Mexican*, December 24, 1863.

was to be reduced to a department and the *Diputación* converted into a mere *Junta*, or committee, things seemed to go smoothly at first. In May, 1836, Juan Felipe Ortiz was duly elected as deputy to the national Congress, and seven distinguished citizens, including Padre Martínez of Taos, were chosen to form the new Departmental *Junta*. Then, as required by a Mexican law, the *Junta* nominated a trio (excluding Pérez!) from whom the central government was to name a political chief, who henceforth would be entitled *gobernador*. Perhaps the citizens even welcomed the new machinery of government as an opportune device by which they could eliminate Pérez legally; but if so, this slow process was overtaken by other developments. Pérez was called upon to announce and enforce another innovation, a direct tax, which heretofore had never been exacted in this territory (excepting the tithe, and the people had had some relief from arbitrary collections of it since 1833). In view of the prevailing distress it is easy to see how this direct tax could be regarded as a means to exploit the poor even further for the benefit of the aristocrats.

The stage was thus set for ambitious and unscrupulous local politicians to enflame the masses against Pérez, and in this case Manuel Armijo, who lived near Albuquerque, was said to be the leader. At a later date George Kendall of the New Orleans *Picayune* heard rumors in New Mexico that Armijo had built his fortune originally by gambling and stealing sheep, but by 1837 he had become a distinguished and influential citizen—one who had been a member and president of the *Diputación* and had served a brief term as *jefe político*.

Armijo also had now a personal grudge against Governor Pérez. When the chief customs officer and some others had been arrested in 1836 for misappropriating funds, two of the three judges on the District Court had been disqualified because of their implication in the affair, and the remaining judge, Juan Estevan Pino, had pronounced the culprits "guilty." Then Armijo had obtained the appointment as collector at a salary of four thousand *pesos*, which made this the richest "plum" in the territory. But before long Pérez had intervened and by connivance with the two passive judges had obtained the reinstatement of the former officers, which put Armijo out and left him in ill humor. When a new statute made the governor responsible for reviewing the statements of the customs office, Armijo was loudest in criticism of this gubernatorial power. Soon the new direct tax became the object of general discontent among the citizenry. Rumors spread that the governor would even tax away the eggs which hens laid, and according to contemporary accounts, Armijo and his friends had provoked this feeling of unrest by sending out agents into all parts of the territory.

REBELLION OF 1837

In August, 1837, the growing agitation brought results with a vengeance as the outgrowth of an incident which occurred north of Santa Fe at Santa Cruz de la Cañada, then a village of some three hundred persons, mostly Pueblo Indians. When a local *alcalde* dismissed a suit for the collection of a debt of one hundred pesos, Governor Pérez ordered the prefect to suspend and jail the *alcalde*. This act fired the smouldering hatred of these Indians, who regarded it as but the entering wedge for the levying of all sorts of unbearable taxes. A mob released the *alcalde*, and the revolt spread to Taos, where Padre Martínez, who originally had sympathized with the rebels, now sought in vain to quell the threatening disturbance. At a meeting of the leaders from several *pueblos* in Santa Cruz on August 3, a proclamation was prepared and published. It declared laconically and bluntly:

Viva, God and the nation, and the faith of Jesus Christ; for the principal points which we defend are the following:
1st. To be with God and the nation, and the faith of Jesus Christ.
2nd. To defend our country until we spill every drop of blood in order to obtain the victory we have in view.
3rd. Not to admit the departmental plan.
4th. Not to admit any tax.
5th. Not to admit the disorder desired by those who are attempting to procure it.
God and the Nation.
— Encampment.[3]

Santa Fe was duly alarmed at this uprising. The governor called out the militia; yet even with reinforcements of friendly Indians from two pueblos, he could muster only one hundred and fifty men. With these he marched north, but near San Ildefonso most of his force deserted to the rebels. Pérez and about twenty-five of his men fled to Santa Fe and on south. In the valley of the Rio Grande he found his way blocked by more rebellious Pueblo Indians. He retraced his path to the home of a friend about three miles south of Santa Fe, and there he was apprehended, murdered, and beheaded. His head was carried to the camp of the insurgents, where, according to Josiah Gregg and George Kendall, it was kicked around like a football. Five other prominent citizens, loyal to Pérez, were also overtaken and murdered, and their property was confiscated. On August 9 about two thousand of the insurgents occupied the capital, where the leaders held a meeting the next day to organize a provisional government. About Armijo, Kendall related later:

Shrewdly conjecturing, now that he had raised a whirlwind, that he might easily direct the storm to his own personal advancement, Armijo, after the manner of his great prototype, Santa Anna, suddenly left his hacienda and made his appearance at Santa Fe.[4]

He had fully expected to be elected governor, and one can well imagine his chagrin when the rebels chose José González, the illiterate but capable and popular chief of the Taos Pueblo!

[3] Quoted in Ralph E. Twitchell, *Leading Facts of New Mexico History* (Cedar Rapids, Iowa, 1912), II, p. 61.

[4] M. M. Quaife, ed., *Narrative of the Texas Santa Fe Expedition* (Austin, Texas, 1935), I, p. 346.

González called in the *alcaldes* of the adjoining towns, who, meeting as his *asemblea*, approved the provisional government, drafted a statement of grievances, and professed loyalty to Mexico. In this action Armijo participated, but without his original enthusiasm for the revolution.

COUNTER-REVOLUTION

Foiled in his scheme, but not yet eliminated, Armijo returned to Albuquerque and soon appeared at a mass meeting in Tomé on September 8, where the residents of the lower valley resolved to raise and equip a band of men to suppress the rebellion. One of the speakers nominated Armijo to lead them, and since no other name was presented, he was chosen. Immediately, he and five others drafted their "Plan of Tomé," which refused to recognize the incumbent in Santa Fe, pledged obedience to Armijo until the supreme government should act, authorized him to meet the necessary expenses of a military campaign by "whatever measures may to him appear convenient," urged the Pueblo Indians to refrain from participation, and provided that a messenger should carry news of this action to Mexico.

In Santa Fe, González fled before Armijo's approach and, while Armijo and his men stopped there to await the arrival of reinforcements from Mexico, they held a meeting in the Palace of the Governors on September 14. There his officers pledged allegiance to the Plan of Tomé and recognized Armijo as *interim* governor, all of which he boastingly reported to Mexico forthwith. For his "valiant" restoration of order and his "loyalty" to the centralist regime he won the gratitude of conservatives in Mexico, who for years afterward commended his "integrity" and "sincere patriotism." On the other hand, Kendall ferreted out a less complimentary version of Armijo's deeds, including a report that he had bribed his officers to proclaim him governor.

Upon the arrival of two hundred or more dragoons from Mexico, the combined regulars and militia moved northward under Armijo's command. At Pojoaque they met González and his band of insurgents who, according to one Mexican historian, numbered one thousand three hundred against Armijo's six hundred. Armijo became frightened by the size of the Indian mob, but a captain of the Vera Cruz dragoons asked permission "to oust the rabble" and then led the attack. In the "battle" which ensued the rebels fled and their leaders surrendered. They promised allegiance if relieved of the obnoxious direct tax. Most of them, however, were imprisoned, and four were summarily court-martialed and executed. Not González. He was shot down on the field of battle upon the orders of Armijo. According to one version, González approached Armijo with the greeting, "How do you do, comrade?" Whereupon Armijo responded with a similar greeting and then turned to his soldiers and said, "Now shoot my comrade." Against the subsequent execution of the other prisoners many protests were raised in Santa Fe, but Armijo turned a deaf ear. Kendall explained this afterwards as an indication that they had been co-conspirators with Armijo in his original plot.

Now, finally, Armijo was in undisputed command, and, as in California, a local feud had resulted in a contest between south and north, in which the southern forces in this instance had obtained control. As in California, too, the alarm had spread meanwhile that the original rebellion was inspired by the foreigners — the Anglo-American traders — and that this was to be another "Texas affair." Actually the merchants in Santa Fe had loaned money to Pérez to help sustain the hastily enlisted army which went forth to challenge González, and on this account they were fearful of retribution when Armijo later left the capital unguarded while on his campaign northward. Afterwards several of the traders filed claims with the Mexican government for the funds which they had advanced to the loyal officials. As for the support of Texas, at one time some of the insurgent leaders considered denying the authority of Mexico and appealing to Texas for aid; but after investigating this angle Hubert Howe Bancroft concluded that although the revolt in Texas may have had some effect directly or indirectly upon the events in New Mexico, there is no evidence of actual collaboration.

In appreciation of the "loyal services" of Armijo, the officials of the central government in Mexico appointed him governor. With only one brief interruption, he held that post for eight years, that is, to the end of the Mexican Period. In that time, like Alvarado in California, he condemned the foreigners, blamed them for the troubles in New Mexico, and in some cases confiscated their property.

He expressed his grudge further by levying a duty of five hundred pesos upon each wagon arriving over the Santa Fe Trail, which also happened to be a convenient way of bolstering his revenues. When he found that the traders were loading a few wagons to the sky and leaving those emptied outside the town, he sent an armed escort far out on the trail to make the collections. He also strengthened the militia in the several towns, with the explanation that he anticipated an invasion by Texas or the United States.

THE TEXAS EXPEDITION

Armijo had an opportunity to swagger forth at the head of his militia when the Texan expedition sent to Santa Fe by President Lamar arrived in New Mexico in the summer of 1841. Actually the poorly managed band of Texans had almost gotten themselves lost on the high plains. Indians had stolen most of their horses, the stock of food had become exhausted, and the men had straggled aimlessly into the eastern villages of New Mexico. All thoughts of commerce or conquest had become subordinate to a desire merely to survive.

When Armijo heard rumors of the approach of the expedition, he became suspicious that his own people might seize upon it as an opportunity to rebel against him. For his own security he spread propaganda about the evils that would be suffered by homes and churches if the foreigners should conquer New Mexico. This passionate appeal to patriotism so aroused the people that they became rude and insulting to the resident alien traders. Some of the foreigners even sent an alarm to Washington about the danger of their losing both their property and lives.

Armijo marched his militia east on the road to Las Vegas and intercepted a trio of negotiators sent ahead by General Hugh McLeod, commander of the Texans. Next he picked up a party of scouts, one of whom, a Captain Lewis, could speak Spanish. Armijo offered him inducements if he would serve as his interpreter and special emissary. In that role, or put more bluntly, as a traitor, Lewis met the main body of the expedition, explained the hopelessness of resisting an army of six hundred Mexicans, and conveyed Armijo's offer of amnesty if they would lay down their arms and surrender.

The exhausted Texans accepted the terms offered by Armijo, only to learn that he had deliberately deceived them. They were rounded up, tied together by ropes in small groups, and driven relentlessly on a cruel march of two thousand miles to prison in Mexico City. The starvation diet, the lack of warm clothing, the worn-out boots, and sleeping out in the cold at night so weakened some of the prisoners that they lagged behind. Then the guards shot them down and cut off their ears to present to their officers as evidence that none of the laggards had escaped. On the first lap of the journey to El Paso, the cruelties were so flagrant that the commander at that post court-martialed Captain Damasio Salazar, who had thus far managed the expedition.

In Mexico City some of the captives escaped from prison, others were released upon the intercession of foreign ministers, and the remainder finally were turned loose by Santa Anna in June of 1842. After nearly a year in prison they returned dejectedly to their homeland. This incident unfortunately aroused a long-lasting distrust, even hatred, between the Texans and the native New Mexicans.

TYRANNY AND PARTIALITY

As the defender of his country Armijo garnered great glory from his victory over the Texans. Now he seemed secured even more invincibly in his oppressive rule as governor. George Wilkins Kendall, the journalist from New Orleans who accompanied the Texas expedition, saw General Armijo at the zenith of his power. He wrote this description of him:

His appearance certainly was imposing, even unto magnificence. On this occasion he was mounted on a richly caparisoned mule of immense size and of a beautiful dun colour. In stature Armijo is over six feet, stout and well-built and with an air decidedly military. Over his uniform he now wore a poncho of the finest blue broadcloth, inwrought with various devices in gold and silver, and through the hole in the centre peered the head to which the inhabitants of New Mexico are compelled to bow in fear and much trembling. Armijo is certainly one of the best appearing men I met in the country, and were he not such a cowardly braggart, and so utterly destitute of all moral principle, is not wanting in other qualities of a good governor....[5]

[5] *Narrative*, I, p. 394.

He concluded that the New Mexicans were "far more dissatisfied with his administration than they were with that of Pérez," so that "even his sycophantic favorites would prove his bitterest enemies were he once in adversity."

Evidently some of those "favorites" were humored by the bestowal of generous land grants. In New Mexico, and in California, too, a lavish distribution of land occurred in the dying years of the Mexican regime. Altogether about eight hundred grants were made in California and approximately three hundred in New Mexico. In the latter territory the more recent grants were so extravagantly generous that nineteen of them exceeded one hundred thousand acres each. Moreover, there were thousands of claimants to small tracts in the large community grants awarded in the Mexican Period.

Armijo himself bestowed several grants of enormous tracts of land. One, the Rayado, or Miranda-Baubien Grant, subsequently acquired by Lucien Maxwell, covered much of northeastern New Mexico. Another, known as the Sangre de Cristo grant, included about a million acres in present Colorado north of Taos. East of it, also in Colorado, lay the expansive Las Animas Grant. Several others, though lesser in size, were still quite extensive.

When a grant had been awarded, according to custom a local official, usually the *alcalde,* would survey the boundaries of the tract. Then the grantee would walk around the border of his land, snapping twigs, pulling up grass, and tossing up handfuls of earth, as tokens of his possession. In case of some of the grants made by Armijo, the local *alcalde* claimed that he had properly surveyed the perimeter, but the dates given on the documents allow insufficient time to encircle so vast a tract on horseback. Another evidence of collusion came to light later when Armijo claimed in his will that he owned a share in both the Rayado and Las Animas grants. Apparently some favored citizens, sensing the imminent demise of the Mexican regime, hastened to appropriate to themselves the remainder of the public domain, and under a governor who would bestow the grants and wink at any evasion of the legal requirements, they could well afford to share their booty with him.

In the Mexican Period, gross neglect and misrule had weakened the hold of the central government upon the northern frontier. Revolutions had occurred in all three of the principal territories, but only that in Texas had resulted in complete loss of the province by Mexico. In all three the causes of unrest were similar—a local desire for a degree of autonomy and the imposition of centralist rule under a dictatorship in Mexico. That slavery and religion and culture conflict may not have had much of a role in Texas is indicated by the fact that the peoples of the other two territories thought that they had ample cause for contemporaneous rebellions with no hint of such factors as causes. Moreover, if conspiracy by foreigners had any influence, certainly the conspirators failed to follow up their advantage in all three instances. In fact, in Texas the revolution had been essentially conducted by the Anglo-Americans with the support of some of the Mexicans; in California it was a Mexican uprising with aid lent by the few foreigners; while in New Mexico it was Mexican and Indian with discouragement on the part of the aliens.

Even so, now that the latter two territories seemed on the verge of falling away from Mexico, the proponents of Manifest Destiny in the United States admittedly had their eyes on them. Moreover, in those two territories the citizens had shown an interest in self-government and a revulsion against tyranny that soon would lend a helping hand to Manifest Destiny.

9
NEW ALLEGIANCE

We come amongst you as friends, not as enemies; we come to you as protectors, not as conquerors; we come amongst you for your benefit, not for your injury. Henceforth I absolve you from all allegiance to the Mexican government, and from all obedience to General Armijo. He is no longer your governor. I am your governor. I shall not expect you to take up arms, and follow me, to fight against your own people, who may be in arms against me; but I tell you now that those who remain peaceably at home, attending to their herds, shall be protected by me in their property, their persons, and their religion, and not a pepper or an onion shall be disturbed or taken by my troops, without pay or without the consent of the owner! But listen! He who is found in arms against me I will hang.

Gen. Stephen Watts Kearny, quoted in G. R. Gibson, Journal of a Soldier under Kearny and Doniphan *(Glendale, Calif., 1935), p. 75.*

By the annexation of Texas the United States inherited a war which already was being waged between Mexico and Texas. In 1836, the Mexican Congress had repudiated Santa Anna's recognition of the independence of the Lone Star Republic. In 1841, Mexico had undertaken unsuccessfully the reconquest of Texas. Two years later the Mexican government had warned that the acquisition of Texas by the United States would mean war between that country and Mexico, and in 1844 Santa Anna had renewed hostilities with Texas.

When annexation was consummated a year later, the United States assumed responsibility for defending the Texas border, and war followed within a year.

THE ROAD TO WAR

Closer analysis reveals that the causes of the war involved more than the Texas border. For several years relations between the two governments had been strained by the haggling over unpaid debts and other issues. During the revolutionary disturbances in Mexico, citizens of the United States had accumulated claims for losses they had incurred that, in 1840, were adjudicated at about two million dollars by an international arbiter, the King of Prussia. Mexico had accepted this decision and had paid a few installments, but a shortage of funds prevented payment of the balance. As the officials in Washington became interested in acquiring some Mexican territory, the outstanding debt served as a basis for bargaining. With funds offered by the United States for purchase of Texas or California or both, Mexico would be able to pay the balance of the debt owed to American citizens. However, a proposal for the concession of any territory became so unpopular among the Mexicans that they would likely oust from office any government which would engage in such negotiations.

Governments fell easily in Mexico. A coup d'état removed Santa Anna because of his renewal of hostilities with Texas. Allegedly for his prosecution of the war, he sought taxes, loans, and gifts in such an amount that he provoked a rebellion and had to hasten into exile in Cuba. On the other hand, his successor, José Joaquín Herrera, was forced out of office by a revolution because he had offered Texas a recognition of independence and had hinted to the American minister that he would re-

ceive a commissioner for discussion of the boundary dispute. Texas claimed the area to the Rio Grande, while Mexico contended that the boundary of Texas as a Mexican province always had been at the Nueces River, a short distance north of the Rio Grande.

The President of the United States, James K. Polk, was eager to obtain possession of California before the British should acquire it; yet he hoped to do so by peaceful means. To that end, before advancing troops to the Rio Grande, he sent John Slidell to Mexico in the autumn of 1845 for discussion of all current issues. Slidell was authorized to pay up to twenty-five million dollars and to assume the debts owed to American citizens in exchange for California up to the Golden Gate. Although Slidell's mission was supposed to be shrouded with secrecy, Mexican newspaper reporters got wind of it and upbraided their "vile government" for engaging in negotiations with "usurpers." Herrera then refused to see Slidell, because of the fact that he came as a "minister plenipotentiary" for negotiation of all issues, which could include the concession of territory, instead of coming as special commissioner merely for discussion of the Texas boundary. Despite Herrera's abstention from actual negotiations, the uproar swept him from office. As could be well expected, his successor, General Mariano Paredes y Arillaga, was even more belligerent.

In the United States the neglected payment of an acknowledged debt, followed by the refusal to negotiate, could be taken as an affront justifying war with Mexico. On the other side, the annexation of a rebellious province, Texas, accompanied by a blockade of some Mexican ports, could be regarded as ample cause for war with the United States. On both sides, therefore, a war fever flared up. Already Polk had sent a messenger with secret instructions about California to Commodore John D. Sloat, commander of the United States squadron in the Pacific, and to Thomas A. Larkin, American consul in California. Now he ordered General Zachary Taylor to transport about three thousand of his troops from camp in Corpus Christi to the north bank of the Rio Grande. Meanwhile Mexican border reinforcements sent by Paredes were moving northward. Then when news came to Mexico City that Taylor had advanced into the disputed zone, the Mexican Congress on April 23 approved a proclamation of a "defensive war" against the United States.

In case of war with Mexico, President Polk had cause for anxiety about the effect upon California. Following the revolutions in that territory it had become almost independent of Mexico. Would California become fully independent in case of war, and would it be ripe for annexation by some other power? If so, then the British could be expected to move in. Already Great Britain had a claim upon Oregon, and British agents had meddled in California's factional strife. Furthermore, while the dispute with Mexico was becoming critical, Polk seemed to be leading his country to the verge of war with Great Britain over Oregon. Because of his campaign promises about Texas and Oregon, now that Texas had been "re-annexed" he was obligated to do something about "re-occupying" Oregon.

Therefore he gave the British notice of the termination of joint occupation and advanced a claim to all territory to the southern boundary of Russian Alaska. It was this claim which later inspired the slogan, "Fifty-four forty or fight!"

Although a negotiated settlement soon disposed of the dispute with Great Britain, the apparent crisis of 1846 helped cause the war between Mexico and the United States, because it made the Mexicans overconfident. When their congress declared war, they were encouraged to believe that Britain would be their ally, so that the United States would be involved in a war on two fronts. They also had been led to believe that even if Britain avoided war with the United States, they would at least have some support from overseas in their contest with the United States. Foreign observers had complimented them upon the superior strength of their standing army of thirty thousand men, which they believed to be well trained. Although much of that army was filled up with rabble on relief and its officers were ineffective and its equipment inadequate, the Mexicans had unjustified confidence in their "numerous and veteran forces, burning with a desire to gain immortal renown." They thought that the United States would fall apart in the face of a real war, because southern Negroes would rebel and New Englanders would secede from the Union. The Americans, their newspapers boasted, "could not resist artillery, . . . are without steadiness under reverses, they cannot march on foot." Moreover, because the United States would "grow stronger" in the future, the Mexican press clamored for an immediate war, while their country still had the "advantage." Recent research in Mexican sources by Gene M. Brack affirms that two Mexican presidents in succession, although dubious of the claims about the military superiority of Mexico, were forced to maintain a warlike, arbitrary stance in response to local public opinion and pressure by Catholic clergy who feared the predominantly Protestant United States.

Nevertheless, President Polk gambled upon one more chance for a "peaceable conquest." Now that Santa Anna was in exile in Cuba perhaps he could be induced to influence opinion in Mexico in favor of negotiations, if he were assisted in regaining power. First, Polk had the Secretary of the Navy send orders to the naval squadron in the Gulf of Mexico to let Santa Anna through if he should attempt to run the blockade. Next he had Commander Alexander Slidell Mackenzie confer with Santa Anna in Cuba. The opportunistic exile agreed that if he were given assistance in returning to Mexico, he would negotiate a treaty disposing of all current issues, including the cession of territory, in return for "ample consideration in money." He did return to Mexico, where he soon regained supremacy, but he assumed leadership in the war against the United States instead of seeking peaceable negotiations.

TAYLOR ON THE RIO GRANDE

Even while the fruitless deal was being arranged with Santa Anna, events on the border precipitated war. On March 28, General Taylor's army had taken a position on the banks of the Rio Grande in the disputed zone. At a bend in the river his men erected Fort Texas, where from their entrenchments along the river they could observe the Mexicans in their comfortable quarters in Matamoros on the opposite bank. On April 12, General Pedro de Ampudia sent a warning to Taylor that he would attack the Americans if they remained in the disputed zone. Taylor responded by ordering the fleet in the Gulf to blockade the mouth of the river in order to prevent the landing of supplies for the Mexican army. When Ampudia protested that the blockade was an "act of war," Taylor responded with a proposal for an armistice pending disposition of the disputed area by a negotiated settlement.

The Mexicans insisted upon withdrawal of the American troops as the prelude to an armistice, but Taylor would not budge. On April 25, General Mariano Arista arrived at Matamoros with two thousand reinforcements and crossed the river immediately for defense of the Mexican claim to the disputed territory. That large Mexican army easily overcame the small detachment of dragoons which Taylor had sent out for investigation of the reported "invasion." Taylor promptly sent a report about this engagement to President Polk.

On Sunday, May 9, President Polk had informed his Cabinet about the rebuff which Slidell had received in Mexico City; but the meeting was adjourned without a firm decision as to action which should be taken. That very evening Polk received Taylor's dispatch reporting that the Mexicans had crossed the Rio Grande and had attacked an American patrol. Immediately the Cabinet reassembled for approval of Polk's war message. In an effort to unify the nation by an appeal to patriotism, Polk placed emphasis in his message, not on the refusal of Mexico to negotiate the unpaid debt, but upon the "shedding of American blood on American soil." On Monday the House of Representatives applauded the President's message and promptly granted appropriations for a war which existed "by the act of the Republic of Mexico." As previously noted, Mexico had declared war first, on April 23.

The war message diverted attention from the fundamental causes by playing up an incident in which the United States had a weak case. Abolitionists challenged the accuracy of the statement about "American soil," when it was in fact territory which was in dispute, and this gave them reason to raise a protest about a "Southern conspiracy" and a "war of aggression." In that era when Southerners were making American history and Northerners were writing it, the version which got into the books and persisted for several generations was the Abolitionist interpretation that Polk had deliberately precipitated an "unjust war." As a tool of the slavocracy, this view asserted, he had filched territory from a weak neighbor for the creation of additional slave states—an act which was a "black spot" on the American flag. Not until long afterward was Polk given due credit for his patriotic effort to uphold the Monroe Doctrine by peaceful acquisitions, if possible, in the thwarting of British designs upon the Borderlands.

Even before the Congress acted, Taylor was at war. With only twenty-seven hundred men against perhaps eight thousand, his position was none too secure. Especially must he hold Point Isabel on the coast, where his supplies came by transport ships. Therefore he left the Seventh Infantry, comprised of about five hundred men under Major Jacob Brown, to defend the fort, while he marched the remainder of the army to Point Isabel. On May 3, the roar of cannon in the distance brought realization that Fort Texas was under attack. Although Major Brown was fatally wounded, the outnumbered garrison held on doggedly during the siege. Afterward, in commemoration of the Major, the fort was renamed Fort Brown, from which Brownsville, Texas, subsequently derived its name.

On May 6, Commodore David Conner sent ashore five hundred marines for the defense of Point Isabel. Then Taylor's force of about twenty-two hundred men started the return march toward Fort Brown. Two days later his expedition of men and supply wagons encountered Arista's army stationed across the road on the plains of Palo Alto. At first the Mexican artillery blasted serious gaps in the American lines; but as soon as Taylor's battery came into position, it retaliated effectively. When darkness forced a cessation of the firing, two hundred and fifty of the Mexicans lay dead and wounded, whereas Taylor had lost only nine killed and forty-four wounded.

The next day Taylor's men pursued Arista's army into the chaparral and found the Mexicans again drawn up in battle position in *resacas*, or dry depressions surrounded by dense chaparral.

This time the American infantrymen hacked their way through the brush and hit the enemy in a frontal assault. Soon Arista's flanks gave way and the Mexicans fled toward the Rio Grande with the Americans in pursuit. In this Battle of Resaca de la Palma, Arista lost two hundred and sixty killed and three hundred and forty-five wounded, against Taylor's thirty-nine and eighty-two respectively. The date of this engagement was May 9, the same day as the Cabinet meeting in Washington for consideration of a war message, but with no knowledge of Taylor's victory.

With war now a reality, President Polk called for the enlistment of twenty thousand volunteers and entrusted the superior command to General Winfield Scott, a veteran of the War of 1812. Although the strategy was to be revised later, the first plan called for a three-prong attack across the Rio Grande. General Taylor would advance from Fort Brown, General John E. Wool from San Antonio, and Colonel Alexander W. Doniphan by way of Santa Fe. The first to cross was Taylor, who occupied Matamoros on May 18. Thus far his force had been comprised of well-disciplined regular soldiers, but now he was overwhelmed by the arrival of six thousand untrained and ill-equipped volunteers.

Then, as he put it, he was "embarrassed by numbers." Moreover, his camp no longer was in the field, but in the outskirts of Matamoros, which was converted suddenly from a quiet Mexican city to a den of newly arrived saloonkeepers, gamblers, vaudeville actors, and other adventurous characters. While awaiting the arrival of transport ships, the soldiers became restless; they consumed too much liquor, quarreled with each other, and annoyed and plundered the Mexican countryside.

ON TO MONTERREY

In August, by means of twenty steamboats, Taylor finally was able to transport his army upstream to Camargo. There the equipment was transferred to nineteen hundred pack mules, loaded and driven by Mexicans who had been employed for that purpose. In September the army was moving toward Monterrey, one hundred and fifty miles to the southwest. Near that city, the capital of Nuevo León, Taylor divided his army into two commands. He led the direct approach from the east, while General William J. Worth, with two thousand men, encircled the city in order to advance upon it from the west. On September 21 the Battle of Monterrey began, and four days later General Pedro de Ampudia capitulated.

At Monterrey, incidentally, a young officer who earned commendation for courage under fire was destined to emerge much later as a presidential candidate. His name was Ulysses S. Grant. The Texans, too, made a significant contribution to Taylor's campaign. The first state governor, J. Pinckney Henderson, took personal command of the contingent of two regiments of infantry and two of cavalry. At Monterrey the Texas Rangers under Colonel Jack Hays won renown as courageous cavalrymen and versatile scouts. At last the earlier humiliations suffered at Mier and at Santa Fe had been avenged!

A week after the occupation of Monterrey the second prong of the campaign, four thousand men of the "Army of the Center" under General Wool, left San Antonio by way of the old *Camino Real* to cross the Rio Grande and meet Colonel Doniphan in Chihuahua. At Monclova, however, Wool received revised orders. He was to continue to Parras, instead of Chihuahua, and to hold that position as the west flank of Taylor's command.

While the third prong, comprised of Doniphan's Missouri Volunteers, was advancing toward Chihuahua, another change in strategy was adopted. From Monterrey the Americans started moving toward Mexico City in accord with Taylor's original instructions. Now, however, the officials in Washington concluded that such a campaign would be very slow and difficult. Besides, Taylor, a Whig, had suddenly emerged as a national hero and had consented to run for the presidency as his party's candidate in the election of 1848, much to the chagrin of the Democratic administration. The commander-in-chief, General Winfield Scott, was also a Whig, but at least the making of another Whig hero might divide the party and detract somewhat from Taylor's glory. Therefore Scott received orders to relieve Taylor of a large part of his army in order to make a landing at Vera Cruz. From that port an army crossing the mountain range toward Mexico City could be provisioned with much greater facility than one marching overland the long distance from Monterrey.

When Scott came to Camargo on the Rio Grande for consultation about division of the troops, Taylor bluntly informed Scott that he could not meet him there because he was "too busy" in Monterrey. Then, when Scott ordered Taylor to concentrate all of his forces in Monterrey, Taylor refused to do so "without orders from the proper authorities." Nevertheless, Scott did finally prevail upon Taylor to allow the transfer of a large part of his command to him for the campaign in central Mexico. Taylor grumbled that this left him with only six thousand men, mostly green volunteers, to face four times as many men who were approaching Saltillo. Meanwhile in Mexico, Paredes had been ousted from the presidency by a revolution, and the new government had turned to the recently exiled Santa Anna for defense of the northern border. Therefore it was Santa Anna who challenged Taylor at Buena Vista. There, on February 22, Taylor won a decisive victory, which contributed further to his political popularity. Soon Scott's landing at Vera Cruz drew Santa Anna back to the south, and Taylor thenceforth saw no more action around Monterrey. He rested on his laurels there while holding that city as a mere defensive position.

THE ARMY OF THE WEST

Through that summer of 1846 a campaign had also been carried into New Mexico. In June, volunteers assembled at Fort Leavenworth to make up the companies of the Army of the West. It was commanded by Colonel Stephen Watts Kearny, also a veteran of the War of 1812 and an efficient disciplinarian, who was promoted to the rank of brigadier general while he was en route to New Mexico. He had been instructed by President Polk to occupy the northern territories of Mexico by means of peaceful persuasion, if at all possible. The recent restlessness of the Mexican people in both New Mexico and California indicated that the occupation might easily be effected; but if Kearny encountered unexpected resistance, he should be prepared to overcome it by force. While his objectives were New Mexico and California, he also was accompanied by Doniphan and the regiment of Missouri Volunteers who were to proceed from New Mexico into Chihuahua.

By late June, Kearny had his army of seventeen hundred men and his supporting supply train on the road. West of Independence the expedition picked up the Santa Fe Trail and followed it westward toward Bent's Fort. Immediately he sent a detachment ahead in an effort to overtake a shipment of arms destined for New Mexico. Governor Manuel Armijo, when he became aware that war had started, had sent a Santa Fe merchant, Albert Speyer, to St. Louis for the purchase of guns and ammunition, and now his two wagons were reported to be headed homeward. Two companies of dragoons under Captain Benjamin D. Moore tried to intercept those wagons, but they had too much of a head start. However, Moore did overtake and detain about four hundred other wagons on the trail and required them to form a caravan in the wake of the military expedition.

In the remarkable time of twenty-nine days the Army of the West made the march to Bent's Fort, where Kearny ordered a halt for a brief rest. At that point three Mexicans who had been apprehended on the trail were encouraged to observe fully the strength of the encamped army, whereupon they were allowed to depart for Santa Fe. Then Kearny sent ahead a proclamation which he hoped would be received and heeded by the citizens of New Mexico. In it he urged them to submit to his superior arms. A little later, on August 1, he sent ahead two messengers with a letter for Governor Armijo. He wrote with assurances that he came with the intention of treating "All Mexicans and others as friends who will remain quietly and peaceably at home and attend to their own affairs." They would not be disturbed "either in their Persons, their Property, or their Religion." He stated that by the annexation of Texas the United States had acquired the Texas claim to all territory east of the Rio Grande, and that if anyone should resist his occupation of that area, he was well prepared to take possession forcefully.

As the bearers of his message he chose James W. Magoffin, a Kentuckian who had become an influential merchant in Chihuahua as well as a familiar figure in Santa Fe, and Captain Philip St. George Cooke, an officer of considerable experience on the Santa Fe Trail. Magoffin was chosen for the task of exercising some tactful persuasion, while Cooke was the bearer of a warning of the ill consequences which would follow if the negotiations should fail. In Santa Fe these two emissaries obtained a private interview with the governor. First, Cooke presented Kearny's ultimatum. Next, Magoffin sought to smooth the way for Kearny's *entrada* by persuasion that resistance would be futile.

Governor Armijo was in a jam. He was responsible for the defense of the province, yet he was unpopular among his own people, who might now find courage to rebel. By calling out the militia, he could muster several hundred men, but they were untrained and poorly armed. Governors had always been reluctant to let the militia have more than bows and arrows, lest the weapons be used in an uprising against their own despotism. Now that the shortage of arms had been relieved somewhat by the arrival of Speyer's two wagon loads of rifles, even the untrained militia could offer effective resistance by occupying the narrow defile of Apache Canyon southeast of Santa Fe. That is, they could if they would heed loyally the governor's orders. In order to get the populace aroused and in a mood to respond to his orders, Armijo had spread word about the heathenish intentions of the barbaric invaders, just as he had done when threatened by the Texan expedition of 1841. In addition he had appealed for, and collected, donations of money and silverware for the purchase of arms.

Although no record of the negotiations conducted by Kearny's two messengers is available, evidently they conceded that the governor at least would have to make a show of resistance but they seemed to succeed in persuading him to withdraw at the last minute. That some money may have changed hands is suggested by the claim which Magoffin later submitted in Washington for fifty thousand dollars for his "expenses" in conducting these negotiations. With Armijo pacified, the emissaries still had to contend with Colonel Diego Archuleta, next in command. According to all reports he was more belligerent than Armijo. Allegedly Magoffin explained to him that because the United States was laying claim only to the territory east of the Rio Grande, it would leave headless the western part of New Mexico. Possibly Archuleta would like to emerge as the new ruler of that vast area. By thus catering to Archuleta's ambition, Magoffin and Cooke cooled off the colonel, but only for the time being.

While the way was being prepared for his *entrada*, Colonel Kearny led his army over Raton Pass and down the Santa Fe Trail into New Mexico. He decided against going by way of Taos, because an entry by that route might arouse the Pueblo Indians. That this decision was a wise one came out later when a Pueblo delegation called on Kearny in Santa Fe and welcomed him as the "good ruler" whom their legends told them might some day come from the east to deliver them from Spanish "injustice and oppression." By staying on the main route of the Santa Fe Trail, the Army of the West entered Las Vegas as the first outpost of Mexican settlement. There on August 15 the citizens assembled fearfully in the plaza and heard Kearny's proclamation that he was their new governor who came as their protector, not as a conqueror. At the conclusion of his speech, he had two local *alcaldes* take the oath of allegiance to the United States and pledged them his support.

When the Army of the West departed from Las Vegas, the commander, now promoted to the rank of general, had not received any news of the outcome of the negotiations in the capital. Consequently he moved forward cautiously in anticipation that he might have to do battle with a Mexican force, possibly in Apache Canyon. However, when the army came to the canyon, the ramparts were there but no defenders. Armijo had made quite a bluster about his patriotism and the terrors which would be inflicted upon Mexican women and churches if the invaders were allowed to take possession. He had had earthworks prepared, the artillery moved into position, and several hundred men marshaled in defensive positions in the pass. What happened then is not clearly established, because contemporary observers recorded only some hearsay reports. The plausible version is that Armijo called one council after another for consultation with his officers, to whom he kept putting the question as to whether they were ready to fight. Finally, in disgust, some of them allegedly disputed Armijo's statements about the evil intentions of the invaders, whereupon he shouted "Cowards!" and ordered the men to break camp. One account even had it that when Armijo and some of his colleagues fled southward they took along wagons loaded with the silverware and other valuables which he had commandeered ostensibly to defray the expense of protecting Mexican homes and churches. Certainly, he could not have carried away all the loot, because he had sent at least some of it to St. Louis with Speyer. At any rate, in his report to the central government, he was able to boast about his own "courage" and "loyalty," while shifting the blame for his failure upon his "cowardly" soldiers.

KEARNY IN SANTA FE

Upon Kearny's bloodless occupation of Santa Fe, he appeared immediately before the townsmen assembled in the Plaza and repeated the address that he had delivered in Las Vegas. Again he assured the New Mexicans that those who submitted would be protected, not molested. Juan Bautista Vigil y Alarid, the territorial lieutenant governor, responded by requesting his people "to obey and respect the established authorities, no matter what may be our private opinions." He regretted that they had been plagued by "domestic troubles" which had contributed to this outcome, and he expressed satisfaction that they were being conquered by "a great and powerful nation" whose representatives were courteous and kind, in contrast to what might have been their fate if they had been invaded by some European nation.

For a full month General Kearny remained in Santa Fe for the management of reorganization. He appointed Charles Bent of Taos to serve as civil governor until a territorial government could be organized, and he directed the drafting of a code of civil law which embodied some established Spanish principles. For improvement of defense he selected a site on a hill not far from the plaza and started work on the construction of Fort Marcy. Then he marched seven hundred of his men down the lower valley as far as Tomé, and upon his return he reported to Washington, somewhat prematurely, that the people of the entire territory were friendly and "contented with the change of government."

Naturally, during the sojourn of the Army of the West in New Mexico, the old capital experienced some appropriate social festivities—dinner parties for select guests and grand balls for the officers. All this was witnessed and recorded by Mrs. Susan Shelby Magoffin, the young bride of Samuel, brother of James Magoffin. In preparation for this trip, she had studied Spanish before departing from Kentucky. The couple then had followed in the wake of Kearny's march; but before proceeding to their new home in Chihuahua, they had to wait until Colonel Doniphan's regiment was ready to lead the way. In Santa Fe the sometimes ill, but always alert, young bride found herself the first Anglo-American woman to be seen and feted in that ancient city. She admired the politeness of the people, liked the Mexican food, and found the *bailes* quite entertaining; but she was rather uncomplimentary about the Catholic church services, where the priest "neither preached nor prayed," and merely "repeated some latin neither understood by himself or by his hearers." She concluded, therefore, that this was "a strange mode of worship to a protestant." Later, as time approached for continuation of their journey, she and her husband became concerned about rumors that Armijo planned to return with four or five thousand men for reconquest of New Mexico.

DONIPHAN'S EXPEDITION

Despite the ominous rumors, Colonel Doniphan prepared for the march southward into Chihuahua. However, because General Kearny had departed for California on September 25, Doniphan had to hold Santa Fe until relieved by reinforcements. When another regiment of Missouri Volunteers, commanded by Colonel Sterling Price, arrived early in October, Doniphan was free to depart. However, because the Navajos had become troublesome during the period of confusion, Kearny had requested that Doniphan pacify them. The thousands of Navajo warriors conceivably could have obliterated Doniphan's regiment, but, ignorant of the risk they were running, the soldiers marched directly into the heart of the Navajo country. The Indians mistook the Missourians' ignorance for courage, and courage they respected. Therefore,

fourteen of their chiefs responded when Doniphan requested their presence for a council at Bear Springs. They expressed astonishment that the Americans should want them to cease making war upon the Mexicans, when the Americans were engaged in such a war themselves. Nevertheless, they yielded to Doniphan's persuasion and agreed to keep the peace. However, after Doniphan's departure, they soon forgot about that agreement.

By mid-December the Missouri Volunteers were ready for the advance toward Chihuahua. Accompanied by the Magoffins and a caravan of traders' wagons, they moved southward through Albuquerque and across the dreaded *Jornada del Muerto* to the village of Doña Ana, where they arrived on December 22. There they learned that a Mexican force of two thousand soldiers under Colonel Antonio Ponce was coming up to stop them, and the two armies met at El Brazito. Doniphan's men held their fire until the Mexicans were nearly upon them, and then they blazed away with such deadly accuracy that the battle was ended in half an hour. The Mexicans left forty-three dead on the field, while the Americans had only seven men wounded.

Doniphan proceeded to El Paso without encountering any further resistance. While the men rested and went sightseeing and indulged in too much drinking and gambling, Doniphan became puzzled about the lack of news of the approach of General Wool. Actually Wool's instructions had been revised so that he would not advance into Chihuahua, but Doniphan did not know this. When some badly needed cannon arrived from Santa Fe early in February, Doniphan concluded that he should wait no longer. As he marched his men southward, he did pick up reports along the way that Wool was headed in a different direction, yet he deliberately advanced into strange territory with little knowledge of what lay ahead.

On February 28, a few days after Taylor's victory at Buena Vista, the regiment from Missouri encountered fortifications erected across the road at Sacramento, eighteen miles north of the City of Chihuahua. Back of the barricades the Mexicans had ten pieces of artillery and two thousand men under the command of General José A. Heredia. Rapidly Doniphan moved his cannon into position and poured a heavier fire into the Mexican lines than they were able to return. Because the enemy powder was punk, some of the farm boys from Missouri said afterward that they were able to dodge the cannon balls as they came bouncing toward their lines. After an hour of bombardment, Doniphan's men charged the ramparts and routed the Mexicans. Again the American sharpshooters with their squirrel rifles proved to be the better marksmen. In a few hours one hundred of the Mexicans were killed with the loss of only one American. Here and at El Brazito and Buena Vista originated the contention of critics of this war that a big powerful nation overwhelmed a poor weak neighbor; but before the battles such a one-sided outcome could not have been anticipated.

After the victory at Sacramento, Doniphan proceeded unimpeded in his occupation of the City of Chihuahua, where he received orders to join General Wool near Saltillo. In May, the Invincible Thousand arrived at Buena Vista and, after being reviewed by General Taylor, they were transported to New Orleans. There they received the first pay that had overtaken them since their departure from Missouri. In one of the most remarkable campaigns in American military history, over unfamiliar ground and without logistic support, they had covered over five thousand miles in a year's time.

RESISTANCE IN NEW MEXICO

Both Doniphan and Kearny had departed from Santa Fe in confidence that New Mexico was pacified and that Colonel Price had control in his hands. However, they failed to make allowance for the disaffection of Colonel

Archuleta, who had hoped to emerge as governor of the western half of the territory. The initial American claim to only the eastern half somehow had been expanded subsequently into occupation of the entire province. Consequently the disgruntled Colonel and Tomás Ortiz organized a conspiracy and enlisted the aid of some of the Pueblos for expulsion of the conquerors. When Colonel Price heard rumors of this in December, he promptly arrested some of the conspirators. However, he was not able to apprehend the instigators, Archuleta and Ortiz, because they had fled to Mexico.

In this conspiracy, the Taos Indians had been aroused, and the absence of the Mexican leaders did not deter them. While Governor Bent and five other officials were in Taos, on January 19 the Indians struck in vengeance for the arrest of three of their members for theft. First they killed the Anglo-American sheriff and the Mexican prefect, and then they broke into Bent's house and brutally murdered the governor and his companions. Before it was over, the infuriated Indians had slaughtered all but two of the Americans who then resided in Taos. Moreover, at Arroyo Hondo, several miles to the north, eight more had succumbed at the hands of the Pueblos.

To avenge the massacre, Colonel Price started north with his infantry and cavalry on January 23. He soon encountered and routed a disorganized concentration of Indians near Santa Cruz de la Cañada. In the Taos pueblo, on February 3, he overtook a band of the insurgents and directed cannon fire into the buildings. Then his men assaulted the main stronghold, the church, and killed most of its defenders. On the next day, with one hundred and fifty occupants of the pueblo dead, the remaining four hundred capitulated. Six of the leaders were arraigned before Judge Carlos Beaubien, whose son had been murdered in the massacre, and he sentenced them to be hanged on February 9.

The uprising in Taos enflamed the village of Mora, east of the mountains, where a band of rebels murdered five American merchants. In Las Vegas, Captain J. R. Hendley enlisted a number of Americans who had gathered there for safety, and on February 25 he led them in an attack upon Mora. Although Captain Hendley fell, mortally wounded, in the street-fighting which ensued, the others killed fifteen Mexicans and nearly destroyed the village of Mora. Soon afterward a conspiracy was detected near Las Vegas. In June, a detachment of American soldiers entered that town, killed ten or twelve Mexicans, burned the mill belonging to the *alcalde*, and took about forty prisoners to Santa Fe. Subsequently six of them were executed.

The legend that the occupation of New Mexico was peaceably accomplished has a foundation only in the circumstances surrounding the original *entrada* of Kearny. Before the territory was brought fully under American administration the conquest precipitated considerable bloodshed. Altogether at Santa Cruz, Taos, Mora, Las Vegas, and El Brazito, nearly three hundred Mexicans had been killed and thirty-some Americans lost their lives. Moreover, of the eight skirmishes fought in the

Southwest, three had occurred in New Mexico (Santa Cruz, Taos, and El Brazito). Two had taken place near the Rio Grande in Texas, and three more were yet to come in Southern California.

FRÉMONT IN CALIFORNIA

As General Kearny proceeded down the Rio Grande on his route to California in late September of 1846, he met Kit Carson and some other scouts who had come from the west coast with a message for President Polk. The gist of it was that under the leadership of John C. Frémont the Californians had won their independence and had established a republic. Because Kearny had instructions to conquer California, it appeared that he had better get there promptly if he were to have a hand in it. He persuaded Kit Carson to join him as his guide, while he dispatched the letter on to Washington by other messengers. To make as much speed as possible, he sent back to Santa Fe all baggage that he could spare and all but one hundred of his dragoons and a core of topographical engineers. Then he headed west and drove man and beast as rapidly as possible toward California. He even by-passed the settled portion of Arizona, with the expectation that another regiment soon could follow and occupy that territory.

Now it is necessary to survey the developments in California, starting back even before Kearny had departed from Leavenworth. Prior to the outbreak of hostilities, President Polk had sent Lieutenant Archibald Gillespie of the Marine Corps with secret instructions for Commodore Sloat and Consul Larkin. This emissary crossed Mexico, delivered his memorized message to Sloat in port at Mazatlán, and arrived in California on April 17, six days before Mexico declared war. After he had transmitted his message to Larkin, he conferred with Captain Frémont, who was in California with what purported to be an exploring expedition. Afterwards Frémont stated that Polk had authorized him to swing the sentiment of the Mexicans of California "in favor of the United States" in order to counteract "the designs of the British upon that country." He contended, therefore, that this authorized his "taking possession of California."

Frémont's designs were abetted by local political trends. With war imminent, Governor Pío Pico of California called a convention to meet at Santa Barbara on June 15 for the purpose of proclaiming independence and soliciting the protection of some nation other than Mexico. Immediately Sir George Seymour, commander of the British Pacific Squadron, sailed toward California so as to be on hand when that province fell away from Mexico. Simultaneously the aged Commodore Sloat, who had received news of the skirmishes in Texas, also sailed up the coast to blockade the California ports. He had been instructed to take that step in case of war. However, the imminent clash with Britain for control of California was forestalled by the fiasco in Santa Barbara. The convention erupted into a conflict between northern and southern Californians because of disagreement over the location of the capital. With independence delayed, the British maneuver was frustrated. On the other hand, with Comandante Castro and Governor Pico aligning their forces for civil war, circumstances were propitious for intervention by Frémont. If Californians were to gain their independence, it appeared that someone was going to have to step in and take the lead.

Frémont's fortuitous presence in California at this critical moment requires explanation. As the son-in-law of the eminent Senator Thomas Hart Benton of Missouri, Frémont had been able to obtain appointments for the conducting of two exploring expeditions into the West, and this was his third. With experienced trappers as guides, he had traveled over trails well known to the Mountain Men. Moreover, with a wife having literary talent and with friends in prominent positions, he was able to get reports of his explorations published for wide distribution. In that manner he acquired a reputation as the "Pathfinder of the West," which Allan Nevins later reinterpreted as the "Pathmarker of the West." At any rate, the publicity made him a rapidly rising prospect for high political office, unless someone could soon deflate his image.

In the spring of 1845, on his most famous expedition, Frémont had crossed the Rockies by way of Utah to Sutter's Fort in California. He had official United States government authorization to conduct this party of sixty-two men, with Kit Carson as a guide, into California for exploration, but he lacked the consent of Mexico. Therefore,

through Consul Larkin, he obtained the permission of the *comandante* for the pursuit of "scientific" observations in California, with the qualification that he should not go near the coast. As soon as he ignored that proviso by approaching Salinas, Castro ordered him to depart. He retired not to the east, but slowly northward until Lieutenant Gillespie overtook him at Klamath Lake with that "message" from President Polk.

Immediately Frémont turned back, paused at Maryville Butte on the Sacramento River, and explained that he was preparing to return to St. Louis. Actually he was cautiously observing the turmoil precipitated in California by the "independence" convention in Santa Barbara. As groups of frightened settlers came to his camp for protection and counsel, he advised them as to the procedure which they might follow. In effect, he directed a revolution while keeping himself in the background.

Inspired by Frémont, Ezekiel Merrit and thirty-four others seized the Mexican post at Sonoma, confiscated the livestock and military supplies, and took as prisoners eighteen of the occupants. Among them was Mariano Vallejo, the founder of the settlement. Next, at Sonoma on June 14, Americans under the leadership of William B. Ide proclaimed the independence of California and hoisted a new flag displaying the figure of a grizzly bear as the emblem of their "Bear Flag Republic." On the next day Frémont sent a request to the commander of an American warship offshore for money and supplies, because he claimed he needed both for his long journey back to Missouri. The commander responded with generosity. Instead, with augmented resources, Frémont moved into Sonoma, assumed active leadership in the independence movement, and made plans for extension of control throughout California.

It was news of this coup d'état which Kit Carson was carrying east when he met Kearny in New Mexico on his way west, causing Kearny to hasten his march to the scene of the action.

OCCUPATION OF THE SEAPORTS

Before General Kearny could arrive in California, the Pacific Squadron of the United States occupied the principal ports. On July 2, 1846, Commodore Sloat's flagship dropped anchor in Monterey Bay, and five days later a landing party was in control of the capital. Sloat then proclaimed the possession of California by the United States and promised the inhabitants protection of their personal interests and freedom from arbitrary restrictions. Two days later the commander of a warship took possession of San Francisco and sent a detachment of men to Sonoma, where they lowered the Bear Flag and raised the Stars and Stripes. A British man-of-war, commanded by Sir George Seymour, appeared in Monterey Bay on July 16, and a conflict appeared imminent. However, when another United States frigate arrived and prepared for action, the British ship soon sailed away. This American frigate brought in Commodore Robert F. Stockton as a replacement for Sloat, who had reached retirement age. Because José Castro was hastily organizing a defensive force, Stockton obtained the collaboration of Frémont by making him commander of the California Battalion of Mounted Riflemen comprised of sixty of Frémont's followers. When opposed by this company, Castro's little band evaporated. As yet southern California remained unconquered; therefore

Stockton sailed for Los Angeles while Frémont followed by land.

On August 7, Stockton landed an "army" of three hundred and sixty sailors, and soon they were joined by eighty cavalrymen under Frémont. Together they took possession of Los Angeles on the 12th, without opposition. Stockton proclaimed California annexed to the United States and declared martial law, with himself acting as governor until a civil government could be established. He directed the drafting of a new code of laws, the opening of a school, and the preparations for the selection of municipal officers in an election to be held on September 15. Then, like Kearny in New Mexico, he reported prematurely to Washington that he had "restored peace and harmony among the people."

The blockade of California ports, which Stockton had imposed, and the severity of his police regulations under martial law so annoyed the Mexican Californians that they organized an insurrection. On September 24, Captain José María Flores with an army of about five hundred men made camp near Los Angeles. On the next day, when Kearny was departing from distant Santa Fe, Flores closed in on the city and forced the surrender of the small detachment of American occupants. Because Commodore Stockton in great confidence had sailed on up the coast, leaving

Marine Captain Gillespie in charge, it was Gillespie who suffered the humiliation of this surprising reversal. From San Francisco, Stockton immediately sent a warship to San Pedro, but the Californians repulsed the landing party. Then they named Captain Flores as their governor and commander. In this first skirmish in southern California the Mexicans had won the advantage.

KEARNY IN COMMAND

While Frémont was maintaining control in central California and Stockton was preparing another expedition, Kearny was hastening westward. He led his picked company down the Gila route and crossed the Colorado into California on November 25. Before the dragoons and their horses could recuperate from the crossing of the desert, they encountered a superior force at San Pascual under the command of Andrés Pico. On December 6, Kearny sent his weary dragoons into battle with the Mexican Californians at night in a downpour of rain. In this encounter everything was in confusion, and the next morning both sides withdrew to their camps. Although thirty of the Californians had been killed, Kearny had lost nineteen killed with about as many wounded. He himself was among the wounded. In effect, then, the Mexicans had won this skirmish. Kearny was halted and pinned down.

On the day following the battle at San Pascual, Kearny's forlorn survivors carried their wounded to the nearest ranch, while the courageous Kit Carson stole through the enemy's line in quest of relief. In response, Stockton in San Diego sent eighty marines and a hundred soldiers to extricate the Army of the West. This done, Kearny then boasted that he had won a victory at San Pascual, but it certainly was rather dubious triumph. Why Kearny ever rushed into battle under such unfavorable conditions remains a puzzle, especially when an alternate route to San Diego by way of Cajón Pass lay open to him.

Kearny's surviving dragoons united with four hundred sailors and marines and sixty volunteers for a march from San Diego to Los Angeles. The Mexicans under Flores came out to halt the Americans but wilted away under the assault made upon their position. In this third skirmish in southern California, the army of occupation had finally emerged victorious. Over the City of the Angels the Stars and Stripes were raised once more on January 10, 1847. Meanwhile from the north Frémont had been approaching with about four hundred mounted riflemen. Near Los Angeles, on January 13, he met Andrés Pico and a company of the Californians who had halted Kearny at San Pascual. This time, far outnumbered, Pico capitulated without a contest. In the Treaty of Cahuenga, Kearny permitted the insurgents to remain in California if they so chose, and he guaranteed them all the rights and privileges of American citizens.

The armed conflict between the Californians and their conquerors had terminated, only to give rise to personal conflicts involving Stockton, Frémont, and Kearny. Under orders received from the Navy Department, Stockton contended that he had full authority both on land and sea, and he appointed Frémont as governor *pro tempore*. On the other hand, citing his orders from the War Department, Kearny insisted that he was responsible for the management of California. He established his capital in Monterey, while Frémont set up his in Los Angeles. Emulating the earlier *politicos*, these rival leaders threatened to divide California, until the conflict was resolved in February by the arrival of Colonel Richard B. Mason. Under instructions agreed upon in Washington, he brought word that the Navy under Stockton was to control port regulations, whereas the senior Army officer, Kearny, was responsible for administration ashore. As soon as Mason had the support of a newly arrived company of New York Volunteers, Kearny left him in charge. Then Kearny ordered Frémont to turn over to him his records. When Frémont refused, Kearny arrested him and returned him in custody to Washington. In court-martial proceedings Frémont faced charges of mutiny, insubordination, and prejudicial conduct. The prolonged trial ran up a burning political fever back in the States; nevertheless the court adjudged Frémont guilty and recommended his dismissal from military service. President Polk approved the verdict except for the alleged mutiny, though he afterward restored Frémont to his rank.

In protest, Frémont resigned from the Army and his father-in-law, Senator Benton, gave up the chairmanship of the Senate Committee on Military Affairs. Frémont's growth as presidential timber may have been set back momentarily, but he soon recovered popularity. In 1856, he became the first presidential nominee of the new Republican Party.

THE MORMON BATTALION

In his rapid march to California, Kearny had traveled the Gila route without pausing for a visit in the sparse Mexican settlements of southern Arizona. That chore he assigned to the Mormon Battalion. At the outbreak of the war the Mormons, under the direction of Brigham Young, had moved from unfriendly Nauvoo in Illinois to a temporary encampment at Council Bluffs, Iowa. They were preparing for a trek to some isolated location, perhaps in the remote northern part of the territory then still held by Mexico. Because considerable prejudice against these Latter Day Saints had been arising back in the States, this "flight," at a time when the United States was engaged in a war with Mexico, might well be given an adverse interpretation. To counteract contention about unpatriotic motives as well as for economic reasons, Brigham Young offered to send a battalion for participation in the military conflict under an arrangement whereby the men would send him their monthly paychecks. Consequently, while General Kearny was still at Leavenworth, he sent Captain James Allen to the Mormon camp as enlisting officer. Volunteers soon filled five companies, which were mustered in at Fort Leavenworth on August 1 and arrived in Santa Fe in two detachments on October 9 and 12.

Captain Philip St. George Cooke

took command of the four hundred and eighty Mormon recruits, of whom he sent back eighty-six as unfit for active duty. He had orders from Kearny to take possession of Tucson and to find a passable wagon route to southern California. The battalion left Santa Fe on October 19, and in November it crossed from the Rio Grande through the mountains to Arizona by a route south of the one followed by Kearny. As the expedition approached Tucson in December, Cooke sent a courier into the Mexican village for negotiations. Because the garrison in the *presidio* numbered only a few over a hundred men, the *comandante*, Antonio Comadurán, agreed to an armistice and withdrew. Without firing a shot, therefore, the battalion entered Tucson on December 17. Cooke described the village as having somewhat the appearance of Santa Fe. He found it "containing about five hundred," which was "more populous" than he had expected.

On December 18 the battalion went north to the California trail which followed down the valley of the Gila River. It crossed the Colorado River at the Yuma junction on January 9 and arrived in San Diego twenty days later. The Mormons remained on uneventful garrison duty in several California towns until they were discharged on July 16, 1847. The battalion had marked the first wagon road to California and had laid claim to the settled portion of Arizona. In his report, Cooke boasted quite justifiably that,

History may be searched in vain for an equal march of infantry. Nine-tenths of it has been through a wilderness where nothing but savages and wild beasts are found, or deserts where, from want of water, there was no living creature. There, with almost hopeless labor, we have dug deep wells which the future traveler will enjoy.... With crowbar and pick and axe in hand we have worked our way over mountains which seemed to defy aught save the wild goat, and hewed a passage through a chasm of living rock more narrow than our wagons.... Thus marching half naked and half fed, and living upon wild animals we have discovered and made a road of great value to our country.[1]

THE CONCLUSIVE CAMPAIGN

The ultimate effect of the campaigns of Cooke, Doniphan, Kearny, Taylor, and Wool in the Borderlands hinged upon the final outcome of the campaign conducted by Scott in central Mexico. On March 9, two months after the pacification of California, Scott landed ten thousand men at Vera Cruz, the port which served Mexico City. A siege and bombardment of Vera Cruz forced the surrender of that city on March 29. Soon afterward the invading army moved out onto the road toward the mountains which had to be traversed in order to reach the Valley of Mexico. With confidence as to the outcome, President Polk appointed Nicolas P. Trist as his special envoy for negotiation of a treaty of peace, and immediately Trist departed for Vera Cruz.

Scott advanced rapidly and relentlessly. On April 18, he defeated Santa Anna at Cerro Gordo and took as pris-

[1] Quoted in R. P. Bieber, ed., *Exploring Southwestern Trails* (Glendale, Calif., 1938), p. 239.

oners three thousand soldiers and officers, or almost half of the vanquished army. Santa Anna rounded up recruits and made another stand at Churubusco. Again, on August 20, Scott overwhelmed this defensive force and took another three thousand as prisoners. Finally on September 13, the Americans stormed and occupied the "Halls of Montezuma" in the weakly defended Palace of Chapultepec, and Santa Anna evacuated the capital.

This final campaign produced another national hero, General Scott, who became the third presidential aspirant, after Taylor and Frémont, to emerge from the Mexican War. He was chosen by the Whigs as their candidate for the presidency in 1852, but he lost to another veteran of the war, General Franklin Pierce, the Democratic candidate. Pierce had been one of Scott's able subordinates. Moreover, just as Grant had distinguished himself in the Battle of Monterey, so did another young officer, Jefferson Davis, win acclaim for his brilliant maneuvers in the action in central Mexico.

While the campaign was proceeding so successfully, a wave of enthusiasm for the acquisition of all of Mexico swept over the Midwest of the United States. Under the accepted rules of warfare, if one nation occupied the capital of another it could lay claim to the entire defeated country. When this proposal began to receive some consideration in Congress, southern senators under the leadership of John C. Calhoun killed it.

They feared, rightly, that if they approved the taking of so much territory, they would be blamed for having supported this war for the extension of slavery, and they contended that continued military occupation of Mexico would be too expensive. Certainly this final self-abnegation should have spiked the propaganda about despoiling a neighbor for the benefit of the slave states; but it failed to have that effect.

THE TREATY

After some annoying delays in the negotiations, Trist finally obtained agreement upon the terms of the Treaty of Guadalupe Hidalgo, which was signed on February 2, 1848. Meanwhile, Polk had become impatient at the delay and had recalled Trist. Nevertheless, with the conclusion then in sight, Trist finished the negotiations and returned to Washington with the signed treaty. Although Trist experienced humiliation for having disregarded Polk's notice of dismissal, his treaty turned out to be quite acceptable; therefore, the Senate approved it quite agreeably on March 10, 1848.

In the final settlement the United States did not annex all of Mexico, but rather only the Borderlands. In effect, Mexico was forced by war to sell some territory on terms similar to those rejected before the resort to arms. The United States agreed to pay fifteen million dollars to Mexico and to assume the unpaid, validated claims which American citizens had against Mexico, to the extent of three and a quarter million dollars. In return the United States obtained clear title to all of the area which Texas had claimed, as well as cession of the territory which later was subdivided into the states of Nevada, Utah, California, Arizona, New Mexico, and a part of Colorado. The treaty provided that the boundary would follow the Rio Grande to the southern border of New Mexico, thence to the headwaters of the Gila River, down it to its confluence with the Colorado River, and across California to a point one league south of San Diego. This definition left room for a dispute over the Mesilla Valley in New Mexico, and it clearly conceded to Mexico possession of the settlements in Arizona south of the Gila River. Those omissions soon would give rise to agitation for correction of the southern boundary so that the achievements of the Mormon Battalion in occupying Tucson and in opening a wagon road would not have been in vain.

Mexican citizens residing north of the line could choose to remove to their motherland, where the Mexican government in a subsidiary act offered them homesteads. Approximately two thousand accepted that offer, but a far larger number elected to remain in their familiar environment. Those who stayed had one year in which to choose either Mexican or American citizenship. Nearly all made the latter choice, and then "all the privileges and guarantees, civil, political and religious, which would have been possessed by the inhabitants of the ceded territories, ... would be enjoyed by them." In other words, besides the rights and duties of American citizenship, they would have some special privileges derived from their previous customs in language, law, and religion.

In view of the current contention about old Spanish land grants, the provisions pertaining to property are of special interest. In the original draft, Article X made a comprehensive declaration guaranteeing all prior and pending titles to property of every description, but the Senate of the United States refused to ratify the Article. Thus, in subsequent copies of the Treaty, a blank space appears under "Article X." Because the Mexican administration objected to that deletion, the American emissaries drafted a statement in the Protocol of May 26, 1848, in order to obtain ratification by that government. The appended provision reads as follows:

The American government by suppressing the Xth article of the Treaty of Guadalupe Hidalgo did not in any way intend to annul the grants of land made by Mexico in the ceded territories. These grants ... preserve the legal value which they may possess, and the grantees may cause their legitimate [titles] to be acknowledged before the American tribunals.

Conformably to the law of the United States, legitimate titles to every description of property, personal and real, existing in the ceded territories, are those which were legitimate titles under the Mexican law of California and New Mexico up to the 13th of May, 1846, and in Texas up to the 2d of March, 1836.[2]

A protocol, however, is merely an explanation, or an executive agreement, which is not permanently binding. Another statement, which appears in Article VIII, guaranteeing property rights of "Mexicans not established there," obviously was meant to apply only to

[2] *Compilation of Treaties in Force* (U. S. Government Printing Office, 1899), p. 402.

Mexicans owning property in the ceded area but still residing in Mexico. Nevertheless, still another provision, in Article IX, guarantees that those Mexicans who remained in the territory should enjoy "all the rights of citizens of the United States," including "free enjoyment of their liberty and property." Court opinions based upon this article have interpreted it as protecting land titles and water rights of former Mexicans and their heirs who continued to reside in the United States, as well as the rights of others who obtained legitimate titles to such property by transfer from the original owners.

By the terms of this treaty the United States acquired from Mexico a vast territory, then rather sparsely populated but rich in resources as yet untapped. In any objective summary of the events leading to that outcome, the blame for the consequences do not fall upon one nation alone. Instead, the conflict has to be interpreted in terms of national interest amid the power politics of that era. Just as the United States, with a surprising demonstration of strength, took advantage of Mexico in that young nation's most chaotic era in order to acquire Borderlands that might otherwise have fallen into the hands of Great Britain, so had the Spaniards previously taken advantage of the disorganization and military weakness of the Indians to conquer those same Borderlands lest the French or Russians beat them to it.

If one were to consider only the long range preservation of friendly relations of the United States with the emergent Mexican nation, then allowance must be made for an alternate course of events. First, in view of the state of affairs in Mexico in that era, it is likely that the rebellious northern frontier would have been lost soon, one way or another. Second, Texas would have been required to continue as an independent buffer state between the two larger neighboring nations, as Mexico then finally had conceded. Third, Sir George Seymour would have been unimpeded by the United States in his effort to establish British dominance in California, so that not the United States but somebody else would have been the "spoiler" in that coastal region. Fourth, New Mexico, including Arizona, might have followed up the Rebellion of 1837 by the creation of an "Aztlán" as another small buffer state, which in turn might have been conquered by a second, more successful Texas-Santa Fe expedition. Finally, at the end of the Civil War, the existence of small nations between the United States and Mexico certainly would have made this nation less concerned about the continuation of the French occupation of that country. All told, the ultimate destiny of the Borderlands, and even of Mexico, cannot be envisioned with any certainty in this hypothetical revision of history.

10
ACROSS THE SOUTHWEST

Everywhere run the stage-coaches, of the type with which you are familiar; everywhere are relays, taverns, and barns.... On the roads opened partly by nature and partly by men, and very poorly maintained by the latter,... the dust rises in a thick cloud, when the coach moves rapidly, at the gallop of its six horses. One is literally powdered, blinded, especially in the country, where not a drop of water falls in more than six months. At the coach stations a hand-basin and a pot of water await you, along with some soap and an endless towel turning on an elevated roller. Mirrors, combs, and brushes are there; brushes of all kinds, even the toothbrush attached to a long string so that each one who uses it will not carry it away. At Paris, you are going to laugh at these democratic ways, here they are accepted by everyone and are even welcomed, except perhaps the toothbrush, which one regards with a suspicious glance.

L. Simonin, Le Grand-Ouest des Etats-Unis (Paris, 1869), pp. 65-67. Author's translation.

Immediately upon conclusion of the war with Mexico a great flurry of activity swept the Southwest, and in some instances, clear across the continent. The animating factors of peace and gold discovery sparked a rush to the mines, a revival of interest in Arizona, experiments with camel transportation and pony express, and the launching of express and stagecoach lines.

GOLD IN CALIFORNIA

On January 24, 1848, even before the Treaty of Guadalupe Hidalgo had been signed, gold was discovered at John Sutter's mill in central California. Then the ardent exponents of Manifest Destiny, especially those of fervent Protestant conviction, could exclaim with E. L. Cleveland:

Why, Sir, did God preserve this whole country more than a century after its discovery for the English, turning the foot of the Spaniard to the sunny region of the tropics? ... In fine, why were the immense treasures of California hidden from the world until she was annexed to this Republic? And tell me, if anyone can, why it was that the title deed of transference had no sooner passed into our hands than she gave up her mighty secret and unlocked her golden gates?[1]

John Sutter's dream of maintaining a tranquil home at his *rancho* on the Sacramento River were rudely shattered after one of his workmen, James Marshall, detected some yellow flecks along the tailrace of a mill that was being built at Coloma on the American River. Sutter sought to discount and hush up the significance of the discovery until he could acquire title to more land in that locality. Nevertheless, news leaked out and feverish prospectors overran his lands, broke down his gates, butchered his cattle, and "stole everything," so he said. Because his ranch had been "taken over," he appealed to Congress for compensation, but his claim was disregarded.

[1] Quoted in C. B. Goodykoontz, *Home Missions on the American Frontier* (Caldwell, Ida., 1939), p. 271.

News of the discovery first appeared in the newspapers of San Francisco on March 15, 1848; but it was a mere casual comment, not wholly believed as yet. At first only a few curious persons went out to Coloma, but as soon as some of them returned with pouches of precious gold dust, the real rush broke loose. Along the coast houses were abandoned, stores were closed, ships were deserted, and Monterey and San Francisco practically became ghost towns. As the populace rushed to the inland district, the field of operations began to spread to other localities. Then the good news reached out farther and depopulated more of the coastal settlements. Some prospectors went to the Yuba River, where they averaged about one hundred dollars a day; others hastened to the Feather River, where they took out about forty pounds a week, and still others went to Dry Diggings, or "Hangtown," where fortunate miners averaged five pounds a day. Soon other mines were opened on the Stanislaus River to the south of the area of the early discoveries and, there, some miners averaged two or three hundred dollars a day.

In the discovery gulches the prospectors and early miners worked the sands along the creeks by the placer method. They carried dirt from the dry diggings to the water or scooped up gravel along the banks of a creek, placed it with water in the prospector's pan, and rotated it slowly. By centripetal force the heavier gold particles gravitated to the grooves in the center of the pan, where they amalgamated with a few drops of mercury. Then by means of a simple retort, the mercury could be vaporized and separated from the gold. At a good location the miners soon rigged up rockers and sluice boxes, which operated upon the same principle as the pan but could process more of the sand. These larger contraptions required the digging of a ditch to provide running water.

Before the first summer had passed, the reports of rich returns had attracted miners from Oregon on the north and Mexico on the south, increasing the number to close to ten thousand. In that first season the excitement was limited mainly to the west coast; but the next year it stimulated a transcontinental rush to California.

THE RUSH OF '49

When letters bearing the news of the discovery were published in eastern newspapers in the autumn of 1848, the glowing reports at first were regarded dubiously. After a representative of Governor Richard B. Mason of California had arrived in New Orleans with gold valued at about three thousand dollars, doubts soon gave way to excitement. Soon a rush of fever-stricken Easterners departed for California by way of all the routes then known to be passable. At first the safer and easier journey was by sea down the east coast of South America, around Cape Horn, and up the west coast to San Francisco. Another popular route went most of the way by ship but with a land-crossing at the Isthmus of Panama. A third and more difficult course was by sea to the mouth of the Rio Grande and then up that river and overland on the Gila Trail near the Mexican border. Two additional routes were entirely overland. One took the Forty-niners down the Santa Fe Trail to New Mexico and continued along the Gila to southern California, and the other followed the Mormon Trail into Utah and then branched off onto the Walker Trail to central California.

At first the heavier traffic went by the sea routes, which had a natural appeal to New Englanders, many of whom organized stock companies for the purchase of ships and supplies. Altogether over five hundred ships arrived in San Francisco Bay in the summer of 1849. Those travelers from the East who took the Panama route found that with good fortune they could make faster time than those going around the Cape; but at the height of the rush some were unable to get immediate passage on any of the fully loaded ships traveling up the west coast, so they often remained stranded on the Isthmus for several weeks.

The route by sea to Brownsville, Texas, traversed the Southwest. From Brownsville the emigrants traveled on a "fast-sailing, high pressure steamboat" up the Rio Grande to Roma or to some other landing place as far as the seasonal flow of water would permit navigation. Thence they followed the river on up to El Paso, where they sometimes could join parties which had come by land from San Antonio. In that summer of 1849, over four hundred wagons passed through El Paso on this route. No estimate is available as to how many safely made the remainder of the journey, down the Gila route, through the domain of the sinister Apaches, and then across the sand dunes on the blistering desert of southern California.

The overland trails attracted the heavier traffic as the rush gathered full momentum. On the well-worn Santa Fe Trail many Forty-niners joined with parties of veteran traders or else formed caravans of their own. From Santa Fe some of them veered off to the northwest on the Old Spanish Trail; but a far larger number, about eight thousand in 1849, chose the route down the Rio Grande, across the Mimbres Mountains, and down the Gila River to southern California. One who made that journey remarked afterwards that anyone who did it successfully could "throw himself on his knees and thank God."

In the summer of 1849, a company of United States dragoons arrived at the Yuma crossing on the southern route to the mines and erected Fort Calhoun on the California side, at the site of the former mission founded by Padre Garcés. Although the dragoons had been sent out originally for protection of the commissioners who were to survey the new boundary as designated in the Treaty of Guadalupe Hidalgo, they also proved to be a godsend to the emigrant parties in the big rush that year. Besides lending all kinds of assistance to troubled travelers, the dragoons under the supervision of Lieutenant Dave Couts constructed a large raft that was operated as a ferry. Private entrepreneurs then took over the ferry service, but the next year the Yumas massacred them and closed the crossing. By the intervention of another detachment of soldiers, commanded by Major S. P. Heintzelman, the ferry was reestablished, and soon

Louis J. F. Jaeger became the successful proprietor. During the years 1850 to 1851, he transported an estimated forty thousand persons across the river. In 1852, the Yumas disrupted this service again, but once more the soldiers pushed them back and restored the ferry. Meanwhile Fort Yuma had been built at the Yuma crossing. Now, for the security of this vital crossing, the defensive force was strengthened and a paddle-wheel steamer was put into operation on the Colorado River for improvement of the supply service.

The hazards of the southern route contributed to a concentration of traffic on the central route, which became favored as the more direct line of travel from the Midwest to the mines in central California. The distance was approximately two thousand miles, which required about a hundred days by pack mule or by wagon. As a rule, ten to twenty wagoners organized into a caravan for the crossing of the plains and then wended their way through South Pass at an elevation of about seven thousand feet. The Mormon oasis at Salt Lake provided a mutually advantageous "half way house." There the weary travelers could rest and make repairs to their equipment, and the Mormons could make profit by serving the needs of their visitors. Beyond Salt Lake the Argonauts traveled through the arid, inhospitable country of Utah and Nevada and crossed through a difficult pass in the Sierra Nevada. On this central route the Indians initially were more curious than hostile, but there were other perils. Many parties started with so much baggage as to impede their progress and then would discard too much of it for a successful journey. Such difficulties could delay the time of arrival in the Sierras until there was danger of getting caught in an early snowstorm.

By August of 1850, at Fort Laramie on the central route, about forty-five thousand persons and nine thousand wagons had been counted, and the drivers had reported over three hundred deaths en route, mostly from cholera. That was a year of the decennial census, but the people-counters in California were baffled by the pouring in of the Argonauts and their constant mobility. They moved about rapidly as rumors spread of richer diggings elsewhere. Consequently the census report of ninety-three thousand for California could at best be only a reasonably good estimate. Even so, in a land where there had been only fifteen thousand persons a few years previously, the new figure attests to the great transformation which had taken place.

The transformation in central California swept down upon San Francisco with breath-taking rapidity. That place grew almost overnight from a quiet Mexican town to a cosmopolitan city. Flimsy structures of frame and canvas arose rapidly as shelters for inns, stores, and gambling halls, while lusty miners and curious visitors from the States and abroad thronged the streets. Prices rose in a business boom as speculative as mining. Whenever ships came to port, glutting the market with goods, prices would fall temporarily, only to soar to the sky again in a spell of scarcity. Moreover, when a miner flushed with money wanted something to satisfy his needs or whims, little did he care about the extravagant cost.

FEVERISH CONFUSION

Simultaneously the mining region became a scene of feverish confusion. Hugo Reid found the camps "loaded to the muzzle with vagabonds from every quarter of the globe." Nevertheless the majority of the miners retained their sense of justice and order, which they drew upon for the improvisation of their own government. At the moment there was none. Mexican authority had lapsed upon the transfer of the territory at the end of the war, and the United States would not be able to get the state government organized immediately. To fill the void, the miners spontaneously organized each camp into a mining district. Taking a cue from the "claims clubs" of the Midwest and borrowing some features from Mexican mining laws, they staked out their claims, elected a secretary to record them, adopted appropriate laws, and established miners' courts for the adjudication of disputes. Although the miners' governments were derived from no superior legal authority, they were generally effective in creating some order out of anarchy. They demonstrated the propensity of American frontiersmen for self-government and their ingenuity in devising it when the circumstances so required.

While many miners found continued working of the placers profitable, others less fortunate or adept prospected for the veins from which the paydirt had washed down along the streams. When such veins were found embedded in rock formations, they required a different type of mining operation known as "quartz mining." Then the miners had to break up the rock and cart it out to a mill erected for the crushing of the ore. At first some constructed a simple Mexican *arrastra*, which was comprised of a large stone rotated upon another one by means of horses or oxen hitched to a pole and driven in a circle around the stones. As soon as a stamp mill could be brought in, it functioned more efficiently. In it the ore was crushed by steel stamps attached to a revolving crankshaft operated by waterpower or a steam engine. After the quartz had been crushed, sometimes it could be washed by a gravity process similar to that of the sluice box; but more than likely the gold would be found in combination with other minerals. Then it could be removed only by means of a chemical process in an expensive refining plant.

From the placers and lodes in California the miners extracted a fabulous production in the early years. The figure jumped from an estimated yield of ten million dollars in 1849 to forty-one million the next year and then to a peak of twice that magnitude in 1852. In the first seven years the total production was about three quarters of a billion dollars' worth of gold. Meanwhile placer mining had begun to play out and quartz mining became more stabilized. Then as disappointed prospectors turned to other employment in the cities, life in them also readjusted to the routine of the new era.

The early period of mining in California contributed immensely to the world's stock of gold, thereby stimulating an improvement of economic activity in distant commercial centers. In the coastal region itself, the gold rush created a new, or second, California. The old center of activity lay south of Monterey in the region of Spanish ranches and missions. Now a new region of mining and commerce had risen spectacularly inland from San Francisco. Moreover, the rush of immigrants and the increase in population created a demand for improvement of transportation facilities not only in California but all across the newly acquired Southwest.

For communication between the east coast and California, the ocean route was employed at first. As early as 1847, the Congress approved the awarding of contracts for the building of four steamships which would carry the United States mail as well as passengers and freight around Cape Horn and up the west coast. The first of those ships, the *California*, departed from New York in October, 1848, and arrived at San Francisco in time for the transporting of men and supplies along the coast during the first rush to the mines.

To shorten the distance, the construction of a railroad across the Isthmus of Panama was undertaken in 1851 and completed four years later. Meanwhile about three hundred thousand pounds of mail was being transported across the Isthmus annually in wagons at a cost of about fifty thousand dollars a year.

EARLY TRANSPORTATION

The first overland stagecoach and mail line was inaugurated on the central route, which was heavily traveled by 1850 and passed through the Mormon settlement in Utah. For this reason, and because the route went more directly to the mining region, it seemed to have advantages over the southern route, especially when a government subsidy could be obtained. Such a subsidy was forthcoming in 1850, when the government offered a contract for the carrying of mail from Independence, Missouri, to Salt Lake City in Utah. The successful bidder was Samuel Woodson, who received fourteen thousand dollars annually for making one trip each month. The next year a similar contract was awarded to George Chorpenning and Absolom Woodward for carrying the mail from Salt Lake City to Placerville in California. The rather slow, monthly service on those lines did not satisfy the needs of the miners very well; consequently they kept hoping for the awarding of a subsidy for a faster, more frequent service for the carrying of their mail.

Within California a network of local lines transported passengers and freight from San Francisco to neighboring cities and inland to the mining region. John Whistman provided the first local service in 1849 by hitching some mules to an old French omnibus and running it on the road from San Francisco to San José. In 1850, he sold his line to Jared B. Crandall and Warren F. Hall, who obtained a government contract for hauling the mail on this route. By 1853, twelve stagecoach lines terminated at Sacramento, which then had become the transportation center of the northern valley. By that date the service had also been extended on down the Central Valley. Harris Newmark, a Prussian immigrant who rode on one of the southern lines, complained that the roads had "never been cared for" and were "abominably bad." The coaches had four rows of seats, which could accommodate up to sixteen persons, including the "oft-bibulous drivers." Drawn by four to six broncos, the vehicles "tore along at breakneck speed."

Local enterprise also provided the first express service to the mines. For the convenience of the miners Alexander H. Todd inaugurated a delivery service in 1849, and soon he had a list of two thousand customers. With headquarters in Stockton, he operated a daily delivery service between San Francisco and the mining camps. In 1852, an eastern firm, Adams & Company Express, bought up Todd's profitable business and some of the other local lines. Soon this company became the leading business firm in California, with assets then appraised at close to two million dollars.

Simultaneously, in 1852, another eastern firm, Wells, Fargo and Company, opened a forwarding office in San Francisco. Soon it, too, had a network of express lines serving several cities in California. In the cutthroat competition between the two companies, Wells, Fargo and Company emerged triumphant in 1855, when the rival company folded up. Thenceforth in central California and all up and down the west coast, Wells, Fargo remained preeminent in the express business.

SOUTHERN ROUTE AND BORDER

Intense competition also threatened the early hegemony of the central overland trail. As tension mounted between the South and North in the 1850s, every proposed public enterprise became an issue between the two sections. If the North should acquire a serviceable stagecoach line to the mining region, this no doubt would contribute unduly to the prosperity and political influence of that section. Therefore the South should get that stagecoach line. Moreover, if federal aid were to be forthcoming for the building of a transcontinental railway line, whichever stage route became established as the preferred one, it would likely also become the route of the first railway. Neither section could let slip the opportunity to grasp a boon of such magnitude. In this rivalry the South had the momentary political advantage, because the Democratic Party, guardian of pro-Southern policies, controlled the presidency, the cabinet, and the senate, down to 1860. Furthermore, in the early 1850s certain advantages could be claimed for a southern route crossing the newly acquired Southwest. Centers of settlement were more numerous and closer together than on the central route; the mountain passes were less difficult; the climate was more equable; and, as will be shown presently, after 1850 all of the area along the southern border was organized under either state or territorial governments. On the central route prior to 1854, a long span lay in unorganized Indian territory.

In 1853, a noted scout, François X. Aubry, led an exploring party from the Colorado River across northern Arizona to Albuquerque and proclaimed that that route along the thirty-fifth parallel would be an excellent one for the building of a transcontinental railway. However, some investors who had Southern backing were partial to a route farther south, along the thirty-second parallel, where the Mormon Battalion had opened a wagon trail to southern California. However, the Treaty of Guadalupe Hidalgo had drawn the boundary line at the Gila River, and a considerable part of that road lay south of the river, that is, in Mexico. Moreover, Tubac and Tucson, the principal settlements in Arizona, also were located south of the Gila, and in southern New Mexico a serious dispute had risen over the location of the boundary line. The commissioners for the survey of that line had come into disagreement about the disposition of the Mesilla Valley, a valuable area northwest of El Paso. The governors of Chihuahua and New Mexico were almost at arms in their contention for possession of this valley. Therefore for the abatement of that conflict and for the development of a favorable southern route, pressures mounted within the United States for revision of the treaty line.

As the official envoy of the United States, James Gadsden opened negotiations in 1853 for the purchase of a strip of land which would bring Mesilla, Tubac, Tucson, and the Mormon wagon road definitely north of the Border. At that time Santa Anna had returned once more to the presidency of Mexico and, fortunately for the United States, he had urgent need of funds for the continuation of his regime. Therefore, for ten million dollars he sold the desired territory in a treaty signed by Gadsden at Mesilla on December 30, 1853. This cession of more territory to the United States so aroused the liberals in Mexico against Santa Anna that they forced him into exile once again, and permanently, within two years, or as soon as his funds again were exhausted. Nevertheless, the treaty had been executed and was binding. By its terms the boundary was revised to a line south of the Gila, where it remains today.

This acquisition placed Mesilla, Tucson, and Tubac on the north side of the line, and it added about thirty thousand square miles to the area of the United States. Further, it eliminated another source of contention by freeing the United States of responsibility for the forays of Indians across the Border into Mexico.

AWAKENING IN ARIZONA

Since 1826 Arizona had been crossed and re-crossed by some of the Mountain Men, and in the four years preceding the Gadsden Purchase the Gila trail had been followed by thousands of emigrants bound for California. In addition, a few ranchers had driven herds of cattle along that trail to the mining camps. Now the acquisition of the area south of the Gila encouraged local development. A few Anglo-Americans stopped off in Arizona and became pioneer settlers. Among them was Peter Kitchen, who arrived in 1854 and became a successful, respected rancher at Nogales.

Some of the pioneers in Arizona came for the promotion of mining. One of them, Charles D. Poston, accompanied by a German miner, Hermann Ehrenberg, began prospecting in 1854 in the vicinity of Tubac and soon found rich deposits of copper at Ajo. Two years later, he interested investors in incorporating the Sonora Mining and Exploring Company for the working of the mines at Ajo. His success aroused the interest of others, so that Tubac soon became a lively center of prospecting and mining. In addition, while traveling to California in 1854 he laid out streets and lots for a town which he called "Arizona City." Located on the east bank of the Colorado River at the Yuma crossing, this speculative townsite did not pan out for Poston; but later a city, the present Yuma, did arise upon that site. Poston's energetic promotion earned for him the title of "the Father of Arizona." Moreover, as *alcalde* in Tubac he offered a free marriage service which attracted there many couples from Sonora who came to evade the twenty-five dollar fee charged by the priests. At that time most of the women in Tubac and Tucson were Mexicans from Sonora, who, according to Poston;

> could keep house, cook some dainty dishes, wash clothes, sew, dance, and sing. Moreover, they were experts at cards, and divested many a miner of his week's wages over a game of monte.[2]

More prospectors and traders rushed to Arizona after a rich gold discovery was made by Jacob Snively, a Texan. He made his strike in 1857 at a loca-

[2] Quoted in Edwin Corle, *The Gila* (New York, 1951), p. 201.

tion about twenty miles above Yuma, where the town of Gila City immediately sprang up. In that camp, before the gold began to play out in 1861, about twelve hundred miners were averaging close to a hundred dollars a day. By 1864, Gila City was a ghost town, but meanwhile another rich mine had been opened at Wickenberg in 1863.

SURVEY FOR RAILROADS

The transitory boom in gold mining in Arizona strengthened the contentions in favor of the southern stage route. Before yielding to sectional pressures, however, the Congress sought to settle upon the best route by scientific investigation. Expert surveyors surely could sift fact from propaganda and select the practicable route. Therefore, in 1853, the Congress made an appropriation for surveys of the five proposed railway routes to the west coast. Isaac Ingalls Stevens, governor of the Oregon Territory, was designated as the surveyor of one route near the Canadian boundary. Farther south, E. G. Beckwith would survey the pass through the mountains near the forty-second parallel, and Captain J. W. Gunnison would explore the central route. In the Southwest the survey of the route approximating the thirty-fifth parallel was entrusted to Lieutenant A. W. Whipple, while the Mormon Road south of the Gila would be traced piecemeal by a relay of three separate parties.

Lieutenant Whipple was well qualified for the task of making the principal survey across the Southwest. From 1844 to 1849 he had served as one of the surveyors of the Maine boundary, and during 1850 to 1851 he had been a member of the commission, headed by John R. Bartlett, which established the boundary between Mexico and the United States. In addition he could draw upon the prior reports of lieutenants J. W. Abert and William Emory, who had accompanied General Kearny, and of Colonel Cooke, who had commanded the Mormon Battalion, as well as those of Lieutenant James H. Simpson, who had accompanied an expedition into the Navajo country in 1849, of R. B. Marcy, whose dragoons had escorted an emigrant party to Santa Fe in that same year, and of Captain Lorenzo Sitgreaves, who had explored a trail across Arizona.

Whipple's company was comprised of ten able scientists in addition to a military escort, and in Albuquerque he employed as guide Antoine Leroux, who had served in a similar role with the Sitgreaves expedition. This party left Albuquerque in November, 1853, and surveyed a route which is now followed rather closely by the Atchison, Topeka, and Santa Fe Railroad. Upon completion of the task in California in the spring of 1854, Whipple transmitted a comprehensive report to Washington. His conclusion was that the route along the thirty-fifth parallel was not only practicable but quite favorable for the building of a railway.

To the consternation of those who were relying on the surveys for an objective selection of a route, all five of the surveyors reported their routes feasible. That tossed the problem of decision right back into the hands of the prejudiced politicians. Now that the southern routes were known to be suitable, with several natural advantages in their favor, champions of the central route needed desperately to improve their position. One way would be to create a governmental organization in the Indian country west of Missouri and Iowa. This is believed to have been one of the motives which prompted Senator Stephen A. Douglas of Illinois, as the agent of Chicago railway interests, to lead in the sponsorship of the Kansas-Nebraska Act of 1854. That Act seemed to offer a compromise whereby the North would get Nebraska as a free state and the South might get Kansas as a slave state. The outcome is well known; the Act precipitated a violent struggle for Kansas which postponed the admission of that state until after the coming of the Civil War.

THE CAMEL EXPERIMENT

In the late 1850s, the advocates of the southern route did all they could to capitalize upon their momentary advantage. One of their projects for that purpose was the famous camel experiment. Although others may have originated the proposal, the persistent proponent of it in Washington was Jefferson Davis, Secretary of War. One who is often given credit as the original sponsor was Edward Fitzgerald Beale, who had traveled to the west coast in 1848 and had returned there five years later as Indian agent for southern California. His travels on the overland trail across the semi-arid portions of New Mexico and Arizona suggested to him that in that country camels would be the most durable beasts of burden. He became an ardent promoter of the camel experiment. Others who lent support were John R. Bartlett of the boundary commission, Major Henry C. Wayne of the United States Army, and George R. Glidden, formerly the American consul at Cairo, Egypt.

In 1853, the Congress failed to approve the first recommendation of Jefferson Davis for an appropriation for the importation of camels; but two years later his repeated request was granted. Then a navy storeship, the *Supply*, was converted for transportation of the animals and was sent to the Levant under the command of Navy Lieutenant David D. Porter. He was accompanied by Major Wayne, who was sent for supervision of the business transactions. In the Near East and North Africa these agents purchased thirty-three camels, which were loaded on the *Supply* in February, 1856, for the voyage to Texas. That ocean journey turned out to be quite an ordeal for the crew and attendants, who had to scrub the deck daily, feed the animals according to a prescribed formula, and give extra attention to some camels which had the itch as well as some which bore calves en route. In May, after this first cargo was unloaded at Indianola, Texas, the ship returned for another load of thirty-six, which arrived in Texas eleven months later.

The camels were taken to Camp Verde near San Antonio for a period of training and acclimation. Major Wayne wrote to the War Department enthusiastic reports about the preliminary tests; but the enlisted men who had to load and feed and drive the beasts had less affection for them. They found it difficult to master the art of securing a pack on the backs of the animals, and they became "sea-sick" while riding on them. Moreover, the camels had a nasty disposition and a repugnant odor. They nibbled on soldiers' clothing and hands, and they could kick hard enough to kill a mule. Sometimes, when the soldiers had them out for a trial run, a few of the more vicious beasts would fail to return. Probably they were pushed over a cliff, but the reports said that they "died from causes unknown."

Finally the camels were ready for a test on a long drive. They were sent out under the direction of Lieutenant Edward F. Beale for a military survey of the already-surveyed wagon road from Albuquerque west along the thirty-fifth parallel. The strange procession left San Antonio on June 25, 1857, and in El Paso a month later Beale wrote to the Secretary of War that thus far the experiment had been an "entire success." He continued;

Laboring under all the disadvantages arising out of the fact that we have not one single man who knows anything whatever of camels or how to pack them, we have nevertheless arrived here without an accident and although we have used the camels every day with heavy packs, have fewer sore backs and disabled ones by far than would have been the case traveling with pack mules.[3]

[3] Quoted in Harlan D. Fowler, *Camels to California* (Stanford, Calif., 1950), p. 55.

As he continued with the journey he became even more laudatory. Upon his arrival at the Colorado River in October, he wrote in his report: "Without the aid of this noble and useful brute, many hardships which we have been spared would have fallen to our lot; and our admiration for them has increased day by day." The expedition crossed the California desert without mishap to the terminal point at Fort Tejón, and then Beale returned to Washington.

In California the Army used the camels for transportation of supplies, and the officers recommended acquisition of more of them. The new Secretary of War, John Floyd, then sought in vain to get congressional approval for more extensive use of camels by the Army. The atmosphere in Washington had by then become clouded by the imminence of civil war, and when that conflict did come in 1861, the Southerners left Washington. Then, of course, a Congress of Northerners showed little interest in an experiment which had been launched by Jefferson Davis. An order went out for sale of the camels at auction. Some were purchased for transportation of supplies to the mines, others were acquired by circuses, and a few were bought for novel beasts of burden on ranches. Those in private service died off rapidly; but the few which remained in the possession of the Army showed up in the inventories until 1885, when they were turned out in the desert. For many years afterward some appeared occasionally as a startling apparition to a dazed prospector.

STAGECOACH LINES

In the year of the launching of the camel experiment, the Post Office Department also gave a boost to the southern route. A contract was let to James Birch, formerly President of the California Stage Company, for carrying the mail from San Antonio, Texas, to San Diego, California. For semimonthly service on a thirty-day schedule he was to be paid one hundred and fifty thousand dollars a year. He put his coaches on the road in July, 1857, and because they were drawn by mules instead of horses, his passengers began to call his line the "Jackass Mail." Even though Birch soon was drowned in an accident at sea, his stagecoach line continued in operation under new management. With a military escort through the Apache country, this line transported passengers the fifteen hundred miles for a fare of two hundred dollars each.

For improvement of the transcontinental service, Congress, in 1857, enacted a special appropriation offering up to six hundred thousand dollars a year for "good four horse coaches" to operate on a twenty-five day schedule and with suitable stage stations along the way. The Postmaster General, Aaron V. Brown, announced that one eastern terminus would be at St. Louis and the other at his own home town, Memphis, Tennessee. From those two cities the branches would converge at Fort Smith. The route for the remainder of the journey would be southwest to El Paso, across southern New Mexico and Arizona through Tucson and Yuma to Los Angeles, and finally on up the San Joaquin Valley to San Francisco. The total distance of two thousand seven hundred and fifty miles made this the longest stagecoach line in the world. It came to be known as the "Ox-bow Route," because of the curve far to the south between the terminal cities.

John Butterfield of New York, founder of the American Express Company, became the successful bidder for the new mail contract. He agreed to start service in September, 1858, on a semi-weekly basis, for payment of the maximum sum of six hundred thousand dollars a year. He organized the stagecoach service into divisions and built altogether one hundred and thirty-nine small stations averaging eighteen miles apart. Depending upon materials available locally, some of the stations were frame structures and others were built of stone or adobe. He ordered new Concord coaches, purchased mules and horses, and employed the requisite number of drivers, attendants, and managers.

The first stagecoaches on the Butterfield line took to the road in mid-September, with one starting from each end of the line. The only passenger on the first westward journey was Waterman L. Ormsby, a New York newspaper reporter. He wrote interesting articles about his experiences and sent them back for publication. The coach had three seats with hinged backs so that they could be let down at night for conversion of the day coach into a "sleeper." While the weary mules were being replaced at the way stations, he had an opportunity for a brief rest. Twenty-one days after the time of departure from St. Louis, this first coach came over the hill into downtown San Francisco. According to a report published in the San Francisco *Bulletin,*

As the coach dashed along through the crowds, the hats of spectators were whirled in the air and the hurrah was repeated from a thousand throats, responsive to which the driver, the lion of the occasion, doffed his weather-beaten old slouch, and in uncovered dignity, like the victor of an old Olympic race, guided his foaming steeds toward the Post Office.[4]

Despite the improved service offered by Butterfield on the southern route, the miners in central California continued to be partial to the more direct central route. In addition, that route had meanwhile been acquiring more arguments in its favor. Kansas and Nebraska had been organized as territories in 1854, and five years later the "Pike's Peak" gold field in central Colorado and the rich Comstock silver strike in western Nevada brought a rush of travelers up the Platte River to the mountains and created two new centers of settlement. Relay stage lines were operated by John Hockaday to Salt Lake City and by George Chorpenning on to Placerville, California. Although they demonstrated that they could carry the

mail through to the mines in a week's less time than could Butterfield on his deluxe but roundabout southern route, Postmaster General Brown would grant a contract for no more than a weekly service on the direct line. Worse yet, Brown's successor canceled the Hockaday and Chorpenning mail contracts. This forced the ruined proprietors to sell out. The freighting firm of Russell, Majors, and Waddell bought the two lines, but without a subsidy the partners were able to operate their "Central Overland California & Pike's Peak Express" only as far as Salt Lake City. By 1860, then, the populous cities and mining camps of central California had no mail or stagecoach service on their preferred route. By that time California had a population of three hundred and eighty thousand people who were clamoring for service; moreover, Colorado, Utah, and Nevada were enjoying rapid growth, which would provide subsidiary business. Yet the operation of a stagecoach line across the intervening vacant spaces would not pay without a subsidy for the carrying of mail.

THE PONY EXPRESS

Proponents of the central route desperately sought ways of attracting attention to the need for service. One of them, William H. Russell of the freighting firm, now conceived the idea of inaugurating a pony express for carrying mail rapidly to the mines. Although one partner, Alexander Majors, expressed objection, Russell continued his

promotion of the project and thought that he had lined up some support in Washington for the granting of a subsidy by Congress. Because he heard rumors that Butterfield was going to establish a "Horse Express" on the southern route, Russell concluded that he should work fast. After he had an encouraging interview with Senator William M. Gwin of California, he acted without consulting his partners.

[4] San Francisco *Bulletin,* October 11, 1858.

On January 27, 1860, he telegraphed this announcement from Washington: "Have determined to establish a Pony Express to Sacramento, California, commencing the 3rd of April. Time ten days."

Because Russell already had committed the company, his reluctant partners concluded to go along. Then Russell hastened with his preparations in order to be ready on the scheduled date. For riders he selected light, sinewy youngsters of good character. He required them to swear that they would refrain from drinking, and he provided small, leather-bound Bibles to serve as reminders of their pledge. For their steeds he purchased fleet mustangs which could outrun most Indian ponies. In fact, his instructions specified that the riders should try to outrun their pursuers rather than to stand for a shoot-out.

The letters to be carried on the pony express had to be written on tissue paper. They were packed in leather bags, known as *mochilas*, which could be swung quickly from one saddle to another. At distances of ten to fifteen miles relay stations were provided for change of ponies, but the rider continued for about seventy-five miles before he was relieved. Then on his next jaunt he back-tracked to his starting point. With the riders and ponies thus shuttling back and forth, the mail was rushed through from east to west to east simultaneously. In summer the relay of riders covered the two thousand miles from St. Joseph, Missouri, to San Francisco in about ten days, as Russell had promised; but in winter the trip required about two weeks.

The skillful performance of the riders thrilled the spectators at relay stations. Often while both ponies were going at a gallop, the rider coming in would toss the *mochila* over the back of the remount and swing from one saddle to the other without touching the ground. Mark Twain once observed the pony express in action while he was traveling the same route by stagecoach. He marveled at this miracle of horsemanship:

Away across the endless dead level of the prairie a black speck appears against the sky, and it is plain that it moves. Well, I should think so. In a second or two it becomes a horse and rider, rising and falling, rising and falling—sweeping toward us nearer and nearer—growing more and more distinct, more and more sharply defined— nearer and still nearer, and the flutter of the hoofs comes faintly to the ear—another instant a whoop and a hurrah from our upper deck, a wave of the rider's hand, but no reply, and man and horse burst past our excited faces and go swinging away like a belated fragment of a storm.[5]

At first the fee for a letter weighing one-half ounce was five dollars, but soon the rate was reduced to one dollar. The lower fee increased the volume, but not enough to meet the expenses of operation nor to provide any profit on the investment. The pony express might have been sustained, but only temporarily, if a lucrative subsidy had been forthcoming. In 1861, after secession left only Northerners in Congress, the federal government did appropriate a million dollars for the maintenance of a semiweekly pony express and a daily overland mail on the central route, but that assistance came too late. By that time even more rapid com-

[5] Samuel Clemens, *Roughing It* (New York, 1913), p. 54.

munication by telegraph was on the way, and it put the Pony Express out of business after a brief life of only eighteen months. The freighting company never made public the amount of its loss, but the figure may have been close to a quarter of a million dollars.

The pony express could carry only concise messages, which could be transmitted with much greater rapidity by telegraph. In 1858, a wire service had been extended west as far as Kansas City, and the next year the California legislature advertised an offer of six thousand dollars a year for the stringing of an extension line to the west coast. A year later the Congress appropriated funds for payment of forty thousand dollars a year for ten years for use of such a line by the government. That offer brought an immediate response. In 1861, the Pacific Telegraph Company set poles rapidly for the stringing up of the "talking wires," as the Indians called the magic line. At Salt Lake City, on October 24 of that year, the wires of the eastern and western divisions were connected, and Chief Justice Stephen J. Field of California dispatched the first transcontinental telegraphic message to President Abraham Lincoln.

FROM BUTTERFIELD TO HOLLADAY

By 1861 the South had seceded from the Union and the government in Washington could encourage the development of facilities on the central route without sectional complications. First, the Postmaster General ordered Butterfield to discontinue service on the southern route, and then Butterfield obtained the million dollar contract for operation of stagecoach service on the central route. He moved his equipment north and sublet both the eastern and western divisions of the line. The first coach departed from St. Joseph on July 1, 1861, and arrived in San Francisco on the 18th. Through the remainder of that summer the service was good; but when winter came, the snow and mud caused annoying delays. Then Russell, Majors, and Waddell, the operators of the eastern division, went broke. Because of losses incurred in the operation of the pony express, that firm had obtained heavy loans from Ben Holladay, who had grown prosperous in the freighting business. When Holladay insisted upon a settlement, the three partners sold out to him for one hundred thousand dollars.

Ben Holladay reigned as "stagecoach king" of the West from 1862 to 1866, when he transferred his holdings to Wells, Fargo and Company. He relocated and improved the road to Salt Lake City and, because Butterfield's subcontractor continued in control of the division from that city into California, Holladay extended his line northwest nearly a thousand miles to Dalles on the Columbia River. He developed an efficient corps of loyal employees, and twice a year the tall, black-bearded proprietor made a fast trip of inspection by traveling the entire length of his line in a luxurious coach drawn by the finest and fastest horses on the road.

At distances of ten to fifteen miles along the route Holladay maintained way stations for the comfort of the passengers and for the servicing of the rolling stock. The vehicles were the sturdy Concord coaches, which had become an institution on the western highways. The body was suspended on two long leather straps, which did to some extent absorb the jars and bumps; but they also caused the coach to sway from side to side and back and forth. This constant motion made some passengers "sea-sick." As Mark Twain remarked, "Our coach was a great swinging and swaying stage of the most sumptuous description—an imposing cradle on wheels." With a mixture of disgust and humor other travelers described their experiences riding the western stagecoaches. Demas Barnes wrote that a passenger obtained "A through ticket and fifteen inches of seat, with a fat man on one side, a poor widow on the other, a baby on your lap, a bandbox over your head, and three or four persons immediately in front, leaning on your knee. . . ."

L. Simonin, a French visitor, remarked that

The coach goes at full speed down the steepest slopes, over great stones and other obstacles. Unmoved on his box the coachman drives with a steady hand the six steeds that are entrusted to him. . . . Inside, the travelers suffer, bruised, broken by the jolts. Some are even made sea sick by this rolling and pitching so novel to them.[6]

Nevertheless, the service provided was regarded as ultra-modern in the 1850s and 1860s. By means of stagecoach the mail and passengers reached all parts of the newly acquired Southwest, and these lines of communication served as bonds uniting those distant lands with other parts of the nation. Moreover, they broke the trails which later would become the approximate routes of transcontinental railways.

[6] *Le Grand-Ouest*, p. 67.

11
AMERICANIZATION

It may be asked whether the native Mexicans have been benefitted by the country coming into possession of the United States, and having our institutions extended over them. From my observation, I believe that they have been improved in both a social and political point of view. They live under certain and written laws, and are protected in the enjoyment of their rights, instead of trusting to the caprice of an irresponsible individual as before. There is a decided improvement in the style of dress and mode of living; they wear a greater quantity of American goods, and tea, coffee, and sugar are becoming more common in use among the peasantry. Many are dispensing with the *serape* [blanket] as an every-day garment, and are wearing coats instead; and buckskin is giving way to woolen and cotton goods, and moccasins to leather shoes. There is also an improvement in the mode of building, and their houses are made more comfortable than before.

William W. H. Davis, El Gringo *(Santa Fe, 1938), p. 253.*

By the terms of the Treaty of Guadalupe Hidalgo most of the Mexicans of the Borderlands became citizens of the United States of America. The name of this nation throughout its history has not lent itself well to any sort of distinctive modification as a descriptive term, for indeed "America" also refers to two entire continents. Because "United Statesians" is awkward and cumbersome, the last word of the name has long been employed for reference around the world to the nation and to its citizens. Therefore, with apologies to the other peoples of the two continents, the term "Americanization" is employed here in its national sense, for want of a better term describing the process of acculturation of other peoples within this one nation. In this

195

instance it refers especially to efforts made for rapid conversion from Spanish to "American" institutions. In order to bring practices in harmony with those then prevalent in the United States, revisions were undertaken in forms of government, land policies, school, and religious institutions.

EARLY HEADWAY IN TEXAS

By 1848, Texas already had a head start toward Americanization, in so far as it had been acquired three years earlier and already was well-populated by Anglo-Americans. In 1845, the Texans had drafted a constitution which corresponded closely to those of the other states. The electorate would choose a governor for a two-year term, but he could not continue in office more than four years out of six. With the confirmation by the state senate, the chief executive would appoint the secretary of state, attorney general, and state judges. The legislature would have a house with representatives elected for two-year terms and a senate with members chosen for terms of four years. One unique feature, which probably was derived from Midwestern sentiment against financial institutions, was the provision that the legislature could not charter any banks. Another one, which was a little ahead of the times, legalized the separate ownership of property by women.

The first governor of Texas, J. Pinckney Henderson, immediately facilitated a smooth transition to federal ownership of its public buildings, its postal system, its military installations, and its navy. That was done just in time for the Texans to concentrate next upon their effective participation in the war with Mexico, as described in Chapter 9. Near the end of that war, they elected as governor Peter H. Bell, who was an ardent devotee of the Southern cause and a vigorous champion of the claim of Texas to the eastern half of New Mexico. That claim was compromised satisfactorily in 1850. After Bell had served a second term, his successor was Elisha M. Pease, who concentrated his attention more upon the improvement of roads and schools and the promotion of railroad building.

During the Pease administration Sam Houston was representing Texas as one of the state's two senators in Washington, where he vigorously supported Union measures instead of voting with the South. As Texans took sides for and against Sam Houston, two political parties emerged. Soon a third faction formed the "Know Nothing" party, a secret society of rabid pro-Americans who aroused antagonism against Catholics and recent immigrants. This organization grew so rapidly in influence that for a time even Houston, an avowed Democrat, astutely endorsed its patriotic principles. A majority of the Democrats in Texas, however, rallied to the support of Pease, whom they reelected in 1855 by a margin of only about eight hundred votes. In that contest the Know Nothing contenders had made their most energetic bid for control of the state and, following their defeat, the party disintegrated rapidly.

In the late 1850s, the dominant Democratic party became even more seriously torn by factionalism derived from Houston's policies. The Unionists in the state applauded him for voting with the North on slavery issues, whereas those of pro-Southern inclinations condemned him. In 1857, when Houston returned to seek election as governor, he lost by an overwhelming margin. However, during the term of his victorious opponent, Hardin R. Runnels, the crisis over slavery and secession became so serious that many Texans began to weaken in their support of the extreme pro-Southern leadership of their Democratic party. This reaction provided an opportunity for Houston, who now bolted the party and ran for governor as a Unionist independent. This time, by virtue of support lent by ex-governor Pease and by his own vigorous campaigning, he won election to the governorship by a wide margin. This victory placed him in a strategic but extremely critical position when the southern states seceded from the Union in 1860 and 1861.

Although the achievement of statehood had brought the Texans into a Union which was about to break apart, it had salubrious effects otherwise. By the terms of annexation, Texas retained possession of the public lands within the state, from which the revenue could be used to pay off the public debt of the previous Republic. Then with assistance from the federal government that debt was consolidated in a new issue of bonds for payment over a period of years. In fact, after those annual payments were made, the state came out with a financial surplus, which made possible some public improvements. The state provided an endowment for the public schools and returned some taxes to the respective counties for use in the improvement of roads and the construction of public buildings.

The clarification of the political destiny of Texas, along with the improvement in the fiscal condition, encouraged immigration. By 1850, old settlers and new had occupied the great prairie region on a frontier extending from Corpus Christi in the south to Fort Worth and Dallas in the north. To this region, where soil and climate were favorable for cotton culture, naturally a heavy immigration continued to come from the Southern states, especially from Alabama and Tennessee. The total population of the state had grown to a little over six hundred thousand in 1860, or a threefold increase within one decade, and of the total nearly one-third were Negro slaves. In this way the economy and political alignment of Texas were leading that state rapidly in a direction that diverged from the course followed in the remainder of the former Spanish Borderlands.

PROBLEMS IN CALIFORNIA AND NEW MEXICO

As Texas was undertaking political Americanization, California also began a career as a state in the federal union. Soon after that territory was transferred to ownership by the United States, the local newspapers fired a round of criticism both at the arbitrary rule of the *alcaldes*, inherited from the Spanish regime, and at the temporary military administration instituted following the war with Mexico. When an assembly of four or five hundred citizens in San Francisco endeavored to organize a city government in February of 1848, the military governor, General Persifer F. Smith, expressed disapproval. The next year when the Forty-niners were arriving by the thousands, meetings were held in other towns and in the mining camps and petitions were drafted calling for a constituent assembly. By that time California had a new military governor, General Bennett Riley, who responded by issuing a call for the election of delegates to a convention.

Forty-eight elected delegates assembled in San Francisco in September, 1849. Only ten came from the old southern region of the *ranchos* and missions; the remainder represented the new concentration of immigrants in central California. Among them were José Antonio Carrillo, Thomas A. Larkin, Abel Stearns, and Mariano G. Vallejo, all of whom had been active in the public affairs of Mexican California. In recognition of the great increase in population, the delegates undertook the framing of a constitution for a state rather than for a territorial organization. This was a bit irregular, because the Congress had not yet given them even a territorial government, nor had it adopted an enabling act. Nevertheless, they proceeded, and in their document they copied many of the features of the constitutions of the states of New York and Iowa, which they happened to have at hand. The location of the eastern boundary of the proposed state became a bone of contention. The "large state" and "small state" factions presently compromised upon the line

which is the present boundary. The issue of slavery, on the other hand, provoked no contention. The delegates voted unanimously in favor of an article prohibiting slavery in their projected state. When the constitution was submitted to the electorate in November of 1849, it received almost unanimous approval by the small number of voters who had turned out in a deluge of rain.

The unauthorized preparation for statehood in California was not the only problem pertaining to the Southwest which came before the Congress in 1849. Upon the conclusion of the Mexican War, a convention of delegates had met in Santa Fe and had drafted a memorial asking for the immediate organization of territorial government for New Mexico, without slavery. When this petition came up for consideration in Washington, Southern congressmen challenged the legality of it. Because New Mexico lay due west of the tier of southern states, it too should be open to slavery, according to the Southern viewpoint, or else they never would get additional senators to compensate for those to come from new prospective free states. Distressed by the delay, delegates assembled in another convention in Santa Fe in December, 1849, drafted a plan of government, and elected Hugh N. Smith as New Mexico's delegate in Congress; but the Congress refused to seat him.

While New Mexicans were awaiting the provision of a government by Congress, the interested portion of the population divided into two camps, with one favoring territorial government and the other seeking immediate statehood. Both factions were animated by a desire to be rid of military administration, one way or the other. Presently they both united in presenting a petition to the military governor, Colonel John Munroe, for the summoning of another convention. He finally assented reluctantly, and the delegates again assembled in Santa Fe in May, 1850. It took them only ten days to frame a constitution modeled after those of other states and, like the Californians, they adopted a clause prohibiting slavery. Next, without even awaiting the adoption of an enabling act by the Congress, they organized a state government. In the election of Dr. Henry Connelly as governor and Manuel Álvarez as lieutenant governor, they set a precedent which was followed for many years after New Mexico finally did become a state; the cultural groups compromised by advancing an administrative team comprised of an "Anglo" from the lower valley and an "Hispano" from the northern region. They also chose representatives to a legislature which convened in Santa Fe in July, and it, in turn, selected two senators. When news of this reached Washington, the Congress faced another question like that presented by California. Should approval be granted for a state government already established by irregular procedure?

Consideration of the disposition of the petition from New Mexico was complicated by another issue. The State of Texas had assumed the claim of the previous Republic to all of the territory westward to the upper Rio Grande, a claim which seemed to have been confirmed by the wording of the Treaty of Guadalupe Hidalgo. Therefore as early as March, 1848, the legislature of Texas created the County of Santa Fe as the

political unit for eastern New Mexico and sent thither Spruce Baird as the organizer of this new unit. However, he encountered such opposition in Santa Fe that he gave up and returned to Texas in July, 1849. Nevertheless the Texas legislature was insistent. It delineated four new counties in eastern New Mexico and instructed another commissioner, Robert S. Neighbors, to effect their organization. The townsmen of Santa Fe and Albuquerque refused to acknowledge his authority, but in El Paso they were more receptive. He was able, therefore, to carry out his instructions only in the latter city, where the citizens cooperated in the organization of El Paso County in the State of Texas. Soon afterward the New Mexicans in their proposed state claimed a boundary to the east on the Staked Plain.

The unsettled boundary dispute almost precipitated a war. The legislature of Texas resolved that the state militia should be marched to the Rio Grande, whereupon President Millard Fillmore threatened to send a detachment of the United States Army for defense of New Mexico's claim. Congressional intervention for settlement of this dispute became urgent, therefore, at a time when the lawmakers were considering the petitions of New Mexico and California for statehood. At the same time other problems, not originating in the Southwest, were clamoring for attention. The thriving colony of Mormons in Utah needed a federal government, the Abolitionists were urging the closing of the slave markets in the national capital, and the Southerners were demanding that Northern aid for runaway slaves be outlawed.

COMPLICATIONS COMPROMISED

The several issues were disposed of in September, 1850, by a series of congressional acts which, taken together, are known as the Compromise of 1850. The Congress abolished the slave trade in the District of Columbia, made assistance to the "Underground Railroad" a federal offense, and authorized the organization of a territorial government for Utah, including present Nevada, with the provision that when ready for statehood the question of slavery should be decided by the voters. In its disposition of the Southwestern problems, the Congress admitted California as a free state without its ever having gone through the territorial stage; but it denied a similar status for New Mexico because most of the numerous residents were as yet "un-Americanized." Instead, the Congress granted a territorial government for New Mexico, including Arizona, with provision for disposal of the slave question by "popular sovereignty," as in Utah.

For settlement of the boundary dispute, the government of the United States would assume the public debt of Texas amounting to about ten million dollars, for relinquishment of the claim to eastern New Mexico, except that El Paso would be granted to Texas. The compromised southern and eastern boundaries of New Mexico were drawn where they remain today. However, the original large Territory of New Mexico included a strip in the northeast which was given to Colorado in 1861 and a triangle in the northwest which went to Nevada in 1866.

STRIFE IN CALIFORNIA

In California, the news that statehood had been granted elicited a celebration that lasted for two weeks, and in subsequent years September 9, the date of congressional acceptance, has been observed appropriately as the state's birthday. Although the Constitution of 1849 generally is conceded to have been a sound document, the political performance of the Californians under that fundamental law has been accorded less praise. The first legislature spent most of its session in an acrimonious debate over the location of the capital. The original seat of government had been at San José, and some wanted it continued there. Others contended in behalf of Monterey, while still others proposed various favored locations. When Mariano G. Vallejo offered a spacious site north of San Francisco, the governor, John McDougal, and the legislature accepted it. However, after the location at Vallejo was found to be disadvantageous, the legislature moved the capital to Sacramento in 1852, only to transfer it temporarily to Benicia the following year and again back to Sacramento permanently in 1854.

The incidence of taxation provoked another conflict in which the older southern region was arrayed against the newer central settlements. The adoption of a typical American levy of taxes upon real and personal property placed a heavy burden on the ranchers,

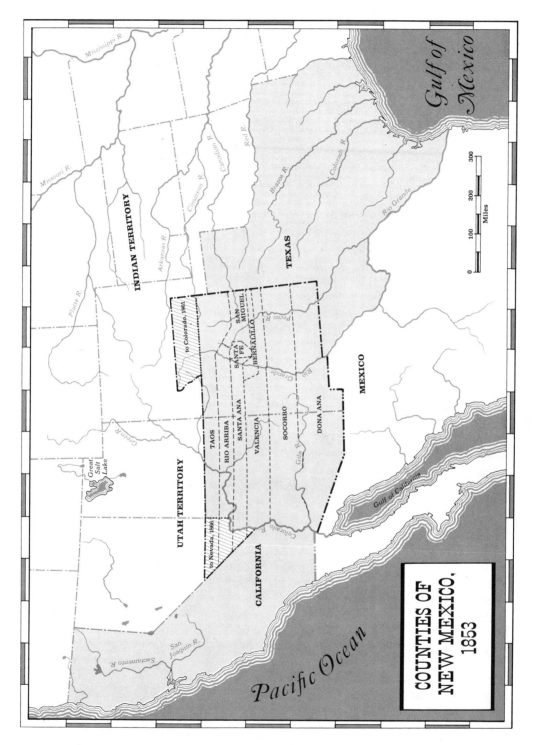

COUNTIES OF
NEW MEXICO,
1853

whereas the populous commercial centers, with a smaller proportion of their wealth invested in tangible assets, escaped payment of their fair share of the cost of government. In 1851, delegates from the southern counties met at Los Angeles and formally expressed their complaints about political neglect and inequitable taxation. Then they adopted resolutions in favor of secession and the organization of a separate state. Throughout the 1850s this agitation continued, and finally near the end of the decade the legislature granted approval for the division of the state. In 1859, the counties from San Luis Obispo on southward agreed upon reorganization as the "Territory of Colorado," but this secession movement was stifled by the upsurge of Union sentiment in California upon the outbreak of the Civil War.

Erosion of state government by political turmoil left local communities almost in a condition of anarchy. According to Hubert Howe Bancroft, in the five years following the gold rush there were four thousand two hundred murders in California, for which there were few convictions. He found evidence also of extreme liberality in the granting of pardons to those few who were convicted. In San Francisco, in 1851, when rowdy elements became rampant, the more prosperous citizens under the leadership of Sam Brannon organized a vigilance committee. Immediately it held a public trial for one John Jenkins, who had been caught robbing a safe, and hanged him from a derrick on the wharf. In defiance of the regularly constituted but inactive tribunals of justice, this First Vigilance Committee tried ninety other suspects, of whom three were hanged, one was whipped, twenty-eight were deported, and only fifteen were turned over to the local authorities.

Soon vigilance committees were organized in other towns. For example, in Los Angeles the mayor and city council took the leadership in forming such a committee, which hanged two murderers and three suspects in the fall of 1852. That tamed down the criminal element for a while, but again in the mid-1850s it got out of hand. Once more the Los Angeles committee, then called the "Ranger Company," went into action and executed twenty-two alleged criminals in the years 1853 to 1855.

In San Francisco, the First Committee had adjourned after its effective cleanup in 1851, but a new one, the Second Vigilance Committee, was organized in 1856 after the editor of the *Bulletin*, James King, had been murdered. In his newspaper he had been exposing graft and corruption involving some city and county officials. That they would oppose extralegal action and might call upon the militia for protection was to be expected; consequently the leaders of the Vigilance Committee quietly built up great strength before acting. Then three thousand men stormed the jail, removed the murderers of King, and lynched them. Next the Committee conducted a vigorous campaign against crime and vice on all fronts. In opposition to the extralegal action of the Vigilantes, the law officers organized a group which they called the "Chivalry." When one of the latter faction attempted to murder a member of the Committee, the Chivalry became discredited and the Vigilantes proceeded without opposition. As soon as they came to the conclusion that they had thoroughly cleaned up San Francisco, their six thousand members paraded through the streets and then disbanded.

In the cities the criminal element included rough characters of all nationalities, among whom some exconvicts from the Australian penal colonies had been notoriously bad. The rural areas, too, suffered a scourge of banditry and cattle-stealing by Mexicans and Spanish Americans. They indulged in this rather uncreditable enterprise in retaliation, as they considered it to be, for some real and some imagined offenses committed by the recently arrived Anglo-Americans. General James H. Carleton expressed the opinion that the newcomers did not seem disposed to grant to the native Californians "the same civil rights which they claim for themselves," and the Spanish-Americans, "unacquainted with the existing Judicial system," resorted to "art and deceit." Some adopted the role of a Robin Hood, by stealing from the rich for the benefit of the poor of their own cultural group. One of them, a son of the respected Carrillo family, assumed the sobriquet of Joaquín Murieta and terrorized the residents of the Central Valley until he was finally overtaken and killed in 1853.

Others, notably Francisco García and Juan Flores, also led bandit gangs in depredations on the cattle ranches and in the mining towns; but before long the gangs such as these were broken up and their leaders apprehended.

During the tumultuous 1850s a majority of the Californians maintained affiliation with the Democratic party; but within that party two senatorial factions engaged in a bitter conflict, again arraying the Old California against the New California. Dr. William M. Gwin, a Jacksonian Democrat who had come from Tennessee, represented the southern section in the United States Senate, while John C. Frémont of the central region occupied California's other seat in the Senate. Soon a Tammany Democrat, David C. Broderick, emerged with sufficient strength as political boss in San Francisco that he began challenging Gwin's leadership. The Know Nothing party, taking advantage of this schism, elected J. Neely Johnson as governor in 1854, but soon afterward the former alignment reappeared. In 1857, the San Francisco machine sent Broderick to Washington as Gwin's colleague in the Senate.

Because he met with an uncordial reception in Washington, he returned to San Francisco in 1859. Quite embittered, he then indulged in a campaign of tirades directed at Gwin, with the result that one of Gwin's supporters challenged Broderick to a duel and fatally wounded him. Nevertheless the well-organized Broderick following remained in control in the central region; in 1860, they joined the young Republican party and helped elect Abraham Lincoln to the presidency.

THE TERRITORY OF NEW MEXICO

Meanwhile New Mexico and Arizona, combined under one territorial government, had been readjusting to the demands of Americanization. James S. Calhoun became the first territorial governor in March, 1851, after having been in charge of Indian affairs in New Mexico since 1849. When the first territorial legislature met in Santa Fe in June, the representatives elected Father Antonio José Martinez of Taos as presiding officer and then gave attention to the stubborn problems of Indian depredations, lack of schools, and shortage of funds. On other fronts, they enacted legislation continuing Mexican customs concerning irrigation, herding, fencing, and mining; they also established local courts and authorized the holding of annual commercial fairs in eight towns.

In 1852, the legislature reorganized the Mexican *condados* into a new pattern of nine counties, of which six extended westward to include strips across Arizona to the Colorado River. After the conclusion of the Gadsden Purchase the next year, the newly acquired territory south of the Gila River became part of Doña Ana County, the southernmost, with its seat of government in Mesilla. That county then became the largest in New Mexico and the one which introduced American political procedures in the settlements of southern Arizona.

In 1852, William Carr Lane succeeded Calhoun as territorial governor, and he was followed in 1853 to 1857 by David Meriwether, who once had been jailed briefly in Santa Fe near the end of the Spanish regime. During his term William W. H. Davis served the territory as United States attorney. Since he became territorial secretary in 1857, he also served briefly as interim governor after the departure of Meriwether and until the arrival of the new appointee, Abraham Rencher, who was governor from 1857 to 1861. Of these early administrators, Davis showed the greatest interest in New Mexico. A keen observer, yet withal an annoying moralist, he wrote a book on the history of the territory and kept a diary of his experiences which also was published under the title, *El Gringo, or New Mexico and Her People.* In it he recorded his impressions of the towns, homes, customs, and morals of the territory. For example, he described in detail the old Palace of the Governors. In his time the legislative council met in a room to the right of the entrance, where "a portion of the wisdom of New Mexico annually assembles to make the laws." The house of representatives met in a larger room nearby, and adjoining it was the governor's office, which was characterized as having "republican simplicity." Davis observed that whenever the legislature met, the members who had long been oppressed by a "rod of iron" were embarrassingly ignorant of the proper procedures for governing themselves. The western end of the portal of the Palace of the Governors sheltered an open market place where, according to Davis,

the country people sell their meats, fruits, and vegetables they bring to town.... The supply is scanty enough and hardly sufficient to meet the limited demand of Santa Fe....

The various articles are brought in on burros, or carried on the backs of the Pueblo Indians; and it is often the case that one of them will come several miles with less than a dollar's worth of marketing. The meats are hung upon a line made fast to two posts of the portal, while the vegetables are put on little mats or pieces of board on the ground, beside which the vender will sit and wait for customers with a patience that seems to rival Job; and if they do not sell out today, they are sure to return with the same stock tomorrow.[1]

In the western part of the Territory of New Mexico the Anglo-American settlers south of the Gila River became dissatisfied with a local government administered from the county seat in distant Mesilla. In August, 1856, they sent delegates to a convention in Tucson and petitioned for a separate territorial government for Arizona. They chose Nathan P. Cook as their emissary for the presentation of their petition in Washington. The next year President James Buchanan responded by recommending that a new territory be organized in Arizona because of the increase in population. Then Senator Gwin of California introduced a bill in behalf of Arizona; but, despite appeals coming from subsequent conventions in Tucson, the bill died in committee.

Again, in 1860, thirty-one delegates assembled in Tucson, and this time they drafted a constitution for their territory, for which they drew boundaries that would have included all of New Mexico and Arizona south of the parallel of 33° and 40'. This aggressive procedure almost got results. First, the New Mexico legislature divided Doña Ana County into two parts, thereby creating Arizona County with the seat of government in Tucson. That reorganization never was carried out, however, because the Congress now seemed ready to respond. Another territorial bill for Arizona was introduced in 1860; but it failed of passage owing to the confusion arising then from the secession of southern states. Thus the division of New Mexico Territory was postponed until 1863, during the Civil War. Then the North had complete control in the Congress and wanted to bind Arizona securely to the Union.

THWARTED AMBITION

While conversion to territorial government was being effected in New Mexico and Arizona, many proponents of Manifest Destiny in the neighboring southwestern states enthusiastically advocated the extension of Americanization to more of northern Mexico and even to Central America. In California, in 1851, Joseph C. Morehead enlisted a band of several hundred filibusters for the conquest of Sonora and Lower California. After they crossed the Border into Mexico, most of the men deserted and Morehead had to pretend that he was there only for the purpose of founding a colony. Then the government of Mexico made a mistake by extending an invitation to some French Forty-niners to come south as colonists. A group, which entered Sonora in 1852 under the leadership of Count Gaston de Raousset-Boulbon, turned

[1] *El Gringo*, p. 47.

itself into an expedition of conquest and took possession of the city of Hermosillo. This band, however, soon had to surrender to a superior force of Mexican soldiers; but Raousset did not give up. Back in San Francisco, he tried to enlist a thousand men for the invasion of Sonora, but he failed in that as well as in his efforts to obtain financial support. Next he cooked up a conspiracy for the promotion of a revolution by Mexicans in Sonora, but Mexican officials found out about this and intervened. Finally, in 1854, Raousset did lead a party of four hundred colonists to Guaymas on the west coast of Mexico, but there he soon got into trouble with the local authorities. When he resorted to force, his little army was defeated by the Mexicans in the Battle of Guaymas on July 13. Raousset was taken prisoner and soon afterward was executed.

While the French filibusters were fizzling out in Sonora, another adventurer, William Walker, was making preparation for a similar fiasco. With forty-five men, mostly Californians, he occupied Lower California in 1854 and seized the Mexican governor; but the hostile natives quickly forced his withdrawal. Undaunted, he promptly enlisted another company of Californians in 1855 and occupied Nicaragua in order to control the route of transportation across that republic. This adventure brought him into conflict with Cornelius Vanderbilt, whose resources overwhelmed him. The shipping magnate had agents enlist an army of Costa Ricans, which defeated Walker's company and turned the restive leader over to a firing squad in 1860.

In the 1850s a boundless expansionism prevailed in Texas, too. Right after the war with Mexico the Texans became insistent upon occupying the eastern half of New Mexico but they were bought off by the federal government in 1850, as has been related previously. Later, when Sam Houston became governor in 1859, he formulated a plan which, according to Walter Prescott Webb, was "the boldest and most daring filibustering expedition that his fertile brain ever conceived." First, he would gradually increase the number of Texas Rangers to about ten thousand men, and then he would lead them into Mexico and establish a protectorate over that nation with himself in charge. So spectacular an achievement should cause the South and North to forget their differences over slavery and states' rights, and they no doubt would join in enthusiastic support of Houston and perhaps even elect him president!

Border difficulties provided an excuse for Houston's preparations. Because the Indians on the frontier were harassing the settlements, that provided a plausible reason for enlisting more Texas Rangers. Then in southern Texas some Anglo-American freighters waylaid and burned the wagons of Spanish-American competitors. They confiscated the cargoes and killed the drivers. This "oxcart war" of 1857 came to an end when other Texans began lynching the ruffians who had assaulted native wagoners.

The strife between competing freighters was followed by raids made on settlements in south Texas by bands of outlaws coming from below the Border. They were led by Juan N. Cortina, a charming but cunning native of Brownsville, who resented the manner in which his fellow Mexican-Americans were being cheated by Texas land-grabbers and bamboozled by local politicians. As the self-appointed champion of his people, he crossed from Matamoros in 1859 with a hundred Mexican recruits. Shouting "Death to the Gringos," they took possession of Brownsville. The citizens of that city then appealed to the state government for help, and since no response came immediately, they turned to the Mexican officials, who sent a company of soldiers across the Border to Brownsville.

Rather than engage in a battle with a Mexican force, Cortina removed his headquarters to Matamoros, where the Mexicans lionized him for defying the Texans. To his fellow Spanish-Americans across the Rio Grande he addressed a bold promise: "Mexicans! My part is taken; the voice of revelation whispers to me that to me is entrusted the breaking of the chains of your slavery. . . ."

Soon a company of Texas Rangers led by John S. Ford and some federal troops under Major S. P. Heintzelman converged upon Matamoros and chased Cortina up the river. In December the Americans overtook and routed the outlaw band, but Cortina himself escaped and continued to be a threat. He and a remnant of his original band fled to the mountains in the interior of Mexico where neither the American nor Mexican army could find him.

At this critical juncture Colonel Robert E. Lee assumed command of the United States military establishment in the Department of Texas and strengthened the border defense. To Mexican officers he sent firm notes charging them with responsibility for policing any outlaw bands operating from their side of the river. Although the threat of another invasion then was rather remote, Houston had a plausible excuse for building up the Rangers in preparation for a punitive campaign against Mexico.

After Houston had increased the Texas Rangers to about one thousand men, he requested each captain to enlist "six good Mexican guides." Then he confided in a few others about his plan. He explained to John B. Floyd, Secretary of War, that his Rangers would "make reclamation on Mexico for all her wrongs" without resorting to any deeds which would be "dishonorable" or would "embarrass" the administration in Washington. When he sought the cooperation of Colonel Robert E. Lee, Lee firmly but politely declined. Finally Houston sent Ben McCulloch to seek financial aid from some representatives of the London holders of Mexican bonds, but the desired aid was not granted. Then the outbreak of war between the states made Houston's plan hopeless and useless. He had failed in his grand design just as his predecessor, Lamar, as president of the Republic, had failed in his plan for creating a "Greater Texas."

REMOVAL OF TEXAS INDIANS

Meanwhile the Indians of Texas had been continuing their depredations. At the conclusion of the Mexican War the federal government had sent General David E. Twiggs with twenty-two companies to forts Polk and Brown from which they manned smaller stations on the frontier. Even after their arrival two hundred settlers were killed in a single year and the property loss was estimated at close to a hundred thousand dollars. Thereupon every town in Texas began clamoring for the manning of a military post in the neighborhood. In response the government built up forts Mason, Belknap, and Phantom Hill, and sent Indian agents west for negotiations with the unruly Red Men.

Texas had several tribes of partially assimilated Indians, a number of "adopted" bands which had recently moved in as a result of pressure on the frontiers elsewhere, and some roving tribes of Apaches and Comanches, who never located anywhere for very long at a time. Among the adopted Indians was a band of Seminoles who had come from Florida. Their chief, Wild Cat, was a scheming troublemaker. While pretending to be making a new home for his people, he provoked trouble all along the border and also secretly maintained an "underground railroad" for transporting runaway slaves across the border to freedom in Mexico.

One of the Indian agents, John H. Rollins, traveled through the Indian country and conferred with several chiefs, including Wild Cat. By December of 1850 he had interested thirty chiefs in attending a conference at Spring Creek, and there he negotiated treaties of peace. The government would give the Indians presents, would establish trading posts, and would create a frontier line, if the Indians would restore captives and stolen property and turn over their own troublemakers to American officers.

Unfortunately the leaders on neither side were able to produce what was promised in the pact agreed upon in the pow-wow at Spring Creek, and the depredations were renewed. In 1853, another Indian agent, Thomas Fitzpatrick, again resorted to treaty-making, with no better results. In fact, the raiding parties seemed to grow more defiant and troublesome according to the reports; but admittedly some citizens did resort to exaggeration in order to get the economic benefit of having military posts, with their purchasing agents, located close by their towns.

Meanwhile a movement for settling Indians on their own reservations and making farmers of them had won converts among the Indian agents all across the Southwest. In Texas, Agent Rollins had advanced such a proposal after conferring with some of the chiefs in 1850, and soon several state newspapers lent their support. In 1854, after the legislature had set aside up to twelve leagues of public lands for this purpose, Major Robert S. Neighbors of the Indian Office and Captain R. B. Marcy of the United States Army selected one tract on the Brazos and another on the Clear Fork tributary of that river.

The Congress appropriated eighty-six thousand dollars for colonizing the Texas Indians, and in 1855 Neighbors rounded up and moved over a thousand of the peaceful Indians to the two reservations. Comanches were assigned to the Clear Fork Agency and a miscellaneous assortment to the Brazos Agency. For each reservation the Indian agents employed an interpretor, a teacher, a farmer, a blacksmith, and a physician. The agents were gratified at the beginning they made in the rehabilitation of the Indians. The latter built log cabins, raised corn and cattle, and according to Captain John S. Ford of the Texas Rangers, were making progress toward "becoming civilized."

Unfortunately some wild Indians remained at large, and as they continued their forays, the frontier became enraged against all Indians. The state enlisted more Rangers for frontier service, and harassed communities organized supplementary companies of "minute men." In 1858, when Hardin R. Runnels became governor, he made Captain "Rip" Ford commander of the Rangers and instructed him to "follow all trails of hostile Indians and if possible overtake and chastise them." Ford divided the Rangers into four detachments, which swept across the frontier in 1858, but without much immediate effect. Then the baffled Texans became aroused against the reservation Indians as the result of an unscrupulous campaign of derogation instigated by John R. Baylor, who had been dismissed as agent at the Comanche Reservation. When the threats of violence indicated that the Indians would have to be removed for their own safety, Neighbors led fourteen hundred of them from the reservations across the Red River, "out of the heathen land of Texas," as he put it. A tragic outcome eliminated that champion of the peaceful tribes. When he returned to Fort Belknap, an embittered Texan shot him in the back.

After the reservation Indians had been expelled from Texas, a vigorous campaign was launched against the wild tribes. Soldiers commanded by Brevet Major Earl Van Dorn overtook a marauding party of four hundred Indians across the line in Indian Territory and chastised them with a severe defeat. In that same year, 1859, he found another party near Fort Atkinson and won another decisive victory. From across the northern boundary, however, forays into Texas continued to endanger the frontiers of settlement. Nevertheless, the heartland of Texas had been relieved of harassment, and in 1860 three thousand regular soldiers stood guard on a thousand miles of the northern and western frontier and a thousand miles of Mexican border. The Texans seemed to be on the way toward a solution of their Indian problem simply by forcing the removal of most of the Red Men from their state.

RESERVATIONS IN CALIFORNIA

In California most of the Indians were sedentary. They remained at peace as long as they were free of provocation, and as Averam B. Bender summed it up later, the problem was really "defense of the Indian against the white man." Immediately after the occupation of California, General Kearny became concerned about the welfare of the Indians and appointed Mariano G. Vallejo and John A. Sutter as agents for the region inland from San Francisco. Kearny's successor, Colonel Mason, designated J. D. Hunter as agent in the south. Soon the Bureau of Indian Affairs sent out a trio of new agents, who divided California into three districts and undertook a study of the Indian problem. Simultaneously the United States Army also posted infantrymen and dragoons near coastal towns, for their protection, and built forts Yuma, Jones,

Lane, Humboldt, Reading, Miller, Tejón, and Umpqua in the interior.

Conflicts with the Indians of California became serious when gold seekers overran the countryside. In the encounters with the numerous small tribes, no campaign could be dignified by calling it a "war." Instead the contestants engaged in an endless series of raids and counterraids. As the Argonauts —the gold-seeking adventurers of 1849— overcame and displaced tribe after tribe, the Indians scattered into bands of renegades who pillaged the ranches. In retaliation the settlers organized a posse or called out the militia for pursuit and chastisement of the Indians. During one such punitive chase in 1851, the Mariposa Battalion under the command of John D. Savage accidentally discovered the Yosemite Valley and spread the news which advertised its spectacular beauty.

While the Red Men were being pushed back, killed off, and sometimes enslaved, the three agents sought unoccupied lands where the tribes could be relocated and indemnified with allowances of blankets, beef, and other provisions. They negotiated about twenty treaties wherein they granted about one-fourteenth of the area of the state to twenty-five thousand Indians. Those agreements committed the government to spend over seven hundred thousand dollars for acquisition of the land, whereas the Congress had appropriated only fifty thousand dollars. The Indian Bureau had to repudiate all of the treaties, and all the patient work of the agents was lost.

In 1852, the Congress established a Superintendency of Indian Affairs for California, and soon Lieutenant Edward Fitzgerald Beale arrived for assumption of his duties as the first superintendent. When he learned that many of the Indians once had been peacefully settled in the self-sufficient Franciscan missions, he concluded that somehow they could be rehabilitated. He proposed that the Indians should be gathered upon reservations where they would be under the protection of military detachments while they were being instructed in farming and handicrafts. For this purpose he requested a congressional appropriation of five hundred thousand dollars. In March, 1853, the Congress provided him with only half of that sum for the development of five reservations. On the first one, which Beale founded in Tejón Pass, within a year over four hundred Indians were farming the land and herding cattle. After that promising beginning, the program bogged down in a morass of mismanagement by some of Beale's subordinates, confounded by political interference by outsiders.

Beale had become the "father of the reservation system" by demonstrating that under favorable conditions the plan could succeed. His successor, Thomas J. Henley, extended the operation. By 1858, he was managing the rehabilitation of about eleven thousand of the state's sixty thousand Indians on these presumably constructive reservations. But to the consternation of Congress, over a million dollars had been expended on this experiment, and then an investigation revealed some glaring abuses. Sanitary conditions were deplorable, Indians who refused to work were whipped into submission, and Henley was taking a kickback from private vendors from whom provisions were being purchased at extravagant costs.

Therefore, in 1859, the Congress became stingy with funds, causing the abandonment of some of the larger reservations. The remaining tracts were too small for the sustenance of thousands of the displaced Indians, who then were parceled out as laborers on private ranches. Disease and murder decimated the Indian population rapidly, and those who survived were debased economically and broken in spirit. The Californians were indeed liquidating their Indian problem, but in a manner not very constructive or creditable.

DEFENSE IN NEW MEXICO

In New Mexico the exposed frontier was dependent upon the federal government for protection, and the response was more vigorous than that territory ever had experienced under Spanish or Mexican rule; yet destructive forays continued regularly. In 1849, when James S. Calhoun came to Santa Fe as the first Indian agent, he was appalled at the conditions which he found there. The peaceful Pueblo Indians were being preyed upon constantly by the nomadic tribes, and these could be checked, he concluded, only by providing improved means for their sustenance. Previously the New Mexicans had resorted to reprisals by going forth upon raiding expeditions among the Apaches and Navajos and by the taking of prisoners into captivity as slaves. Now that the federal government was requiring a cessation of this practice, Calhoun well knew that the war had become onesided.

In 1851, Colonel Edwin Vose Sumner became commander of the military district in New Mexico and immediately conducted a campaign into the Navajo country. As he analyzed the problem of defense, he found that the posting of a small cavalry company in each community was a mistake. The men were exposed to the "vices of the towns," and the total force was too scattered for a display of effective strength when needed. He decided that he should concentrate the available soldiers at new headquarters, one, Fort Union, to be erected on the Santa Fe Trail north of Las Vegas, and another, Fort Defiance, to be located in the Navajo country.

As work progressed on the construction of the log buildings of Fort Union in 1851, Sumner tried an experiment. Because provisions freighted over the Santa Fe Trail or purchased from local farmers and ranchers cost dearly, he proposed that the soldiers when off duty should do some farming and herding on the side, for the fort was located in a valley suitable for that purpose. The enlisted men, however, were averse to this interference with their time for relaxation, and Sumner's plan failed. Nevertheless, the concentration of control did facilitate centralized purchasing, which of itself was advantageous. The providing of hay, wheat, meat, and other supplies, at good prices, stimulated the development of ranching and merchandising in northeastern New Mexico through following years. Simultaneously the soldiers in the old fort, even though they slept with bedbugs under leaking roofs, rode forth courageously time and again in pursuit of Indians who had raided a town or ranch. Other posts built in the 1850s included forts Fillmore and Conrad on the Rio Grande below Albuquerque and Fort Webster near the copper mines at Santa Rita.

Of the bloody conflict with the Indians a record of personal experiences has been preserved in the diary of one of the volunteers, James A. Bennett. Before Fort Union was built, the writer had served under Kit Carson at a cavalry post in Rayado, near Cimarron, New Mexico. He described the thrills and tragedies of one foray after another in pursuit of bands of hostile Red Men. Sometimes they overtook and defeated fleeing raiders; at other times they met in conference with Indian tribes — Bennett acting as interpreter — and were able to recover stolen livestock. However, once when signs of numerous Indians were found on all sides, while they were on an expedition along the distant Gila River, Bennett recorded his disgust when his superiors deliberately avoided an encounter. On another occasion, when the officers ordered the entire command of three hundred men to stand watch all night, while they were sleeping in their tent, Bennett could not restrain his wrath. He exclaimed in his diary, "Oh, that our government only knew the courage of some of her officers."

On most occasions the officers and soldiers manning the Southwestern posts displayed indomitable courage, but their numbers and resources were insufficient to cope with the Indian problem which Uncle Sam had inherited from the equally distressed Spaniards. When nearly three hundred New Mexicans were slaughtered by Indians in the years 1859 and 1860, Colonel Thomas T. Fauntleroy, then in command in this military district, undertook an elaborate program of military reorganization. Before his plan became effective, the secession of the southern states precipitated an even greater crisis for the military establishment.

In the western portion of New Mexico Territory, also known as Arizona, the feeble settlements suffered from frequent harassment by the Apaches. For the protection of the towns the building of Fort Defiance in 1852 far away in the Navajo country was of little assistance. In 1856, therefore, Fort Breckenridge was founded on the San Pedro River and four companies of dragoons were posted in Tucson. In the next year Camp Moore, later known as Fort Buchanan, was built about twenty-five miles east of Tubac, and in 1858 Fort Mojave was established on the Colorado River.

On the Gila Trail to California the Apaches and Mojaves massacred the Oatman family in 1851, except for two girls who were taken into captivity. Five years later the rescue of Olive Oatman from her Indian captors created quite a sensation and the incident has become one of the thrilling legends of early Arizona history. After 1858, however, the Mojaves and some of the smaller tribes were pacified, but the Apaches and Navajos continued their depredations. In 1857, Colonel Benjamin L. E. Bonneville inflicted a severe defeat upon a band of Apache warriors and obtained from them pledges to remain peaceful. His campaign had made safer the route through Apache Pass in the eastern part of the territory.

Other southern tribes of Apaches, led at first by Mangas Coloradas and later by Cochise, grew more belligerent as travelers and settlers increased in numbers. After James H. Tevis moved from Fort Buchanan to a stage way station in Apache Pass, he had several encounters with Cochise and his warriors, who extracted much booty from travelers, as well as from the Mexican settlers and American ranchers. Tevis described one Apache raid among the Navajos in which Cochise lost many braves but returned to his base with perhaps ten thousand sheep. According to Tevis the indomitable Chief Cochise was "as fine a looking Indian as one ever saw," six feet tall and superb in physique.

PACIFICATION OF SOME TRIBES

The perplexing problem of the wild Indians in the expansive Territory of New Mexico created some interest there in the kind of Indian reservation that was being tried in Texas and in California. In the territory the Indian agent most closely associated with the experiment was Dr. Michael Steck. He moved about, working first with the Jicarilla Apaches in northern New Mexico, then with the Apache tribes west of the Rio Grande, and later with the Mescalero Apaches in southeastern New Mexico. In all cases he sought agreements whereby the Indians would settle on a consigned tract of land and become farmers. However, in most instances he found that a treaty made with one small band did not commit an entire tribe. With one band settled, others would continue their depredations and, when all of the attention of the agents and the military became diverted to the troublemakers, the original group would get out of hand. Also, the storekeepers around the established Indian agencies used their influence to disrupt this experimentation with constructive reservations. The Indians would hang around the agency and trade at the stores, to the good profit of their proprietors, and thus removal to a farm would disrupt this trade. Despite the difficulties, Steck achieved something bordering on success in his efforts with the Mescaleros. In 1855, he concluded a treaty which promised them $72,000 to help them get started as farmers, but again Congress failed to come through with the money. Nevertheless, Steck did gather about five hundred of these Indians around Fort Stanton and fed them on Army rations as they learned to till the soil.

In 1855, Governor David Meriwether made a treaty with the Navajo Indians. It fixed the boundaries of their reservation and offered aid in the purchase of seeds and tools, for which Congress did appropriate $30,000. However, raids and counterraids between the Indians and the nearby settlers continued in an even worse way than before.

Farther west, the peaceably inclined Pima Indians accepted a reservation in 1859, and their neighbors, the Pápagos, had the equivalent of a reservation, as, undisturbed, they dwelt on desert lands which nobody wanted. To aid in the conversion and rehabilitation of the Pápagos, the Franciscans reopened their old mission at San Xavier del Bac in 1859.

LAND TITLES IN LITIGATION

Almost as baffling as the problem of Indian relations was the maze of Spanish and Mexican land grants. Especially was this true in New Mexico. In Texas and California, the transition could be effected with less difficulty.

The problem was threefold—involving, as it did, records, surveys, and fraud. For many of the grants the person who was assumed to be the owner could find no legal proof of it. Sometime back in the many years of ancestral occupation of the land, the certificate of title had been lost. In other instances, families had resided on a plot as *peones* on a large estate and perhaps never did have a valid title; yet they felt that they were justified in claiming the land by a principle something like "squatters' rights" on the American frontier. If a search were made for a title, it involved the expensive procedure of research in some distant archive for a copy, and then often none could be found. Or if it were found, the difficulty continued in the method of survey by "metes and bounds" then in vogue for lack of a better method. The tracts were measured in *varas* and *cordeles* and bounded in terms of hills, rocks, cliffs, lakes, canyons, and big trees. With the passing of time some of the landmarks had changed location or disappeared entirely. Given such conditions, a natural concomitant was the fabrication of fraudulent papers by some claimants who could not find the original copy and by others who saw an opportunity to profit from all the confusion.

In Texas, the problem of land titles was less serious than elsewhere in the Southwest because the Spanish individual grants had been few, whereas over twenty million acres had been distributed through the agency of the *empresarios*, most of whom were Anglo-Americans. The majority of the titles in Texas, therefore, had been acquired either from the *empresarios*, or later from the Republic or from the State, under conditions readily understood by American frontiersmen. Records were kept in good order, and the locating of claims had had some supervision. Consequently most of the conflicts which arose were derived from the filing of fraudulent claims or payment in forged scrip, and those conflicts had been rather well disposed of by local boards of land commissioners created under the Republic.

In California, the process of clarification was facilitated by the prompt admission of that territory as a state, so that the task was delegated to local investigators who were familiar with the technicalities and within reach of the claimants. The Congress immediately authorized the appointment of a commission of three members, who opened hearings in San Francisco in 1852. Within four years it received eight hundred and thirteen claims and approved five hundred and twenty-one of them.

The Californians were on the way toward a fairly expeditious settlement, unless they became involved in litigation. Because the findings of the commission were subject to appeal to the courts, sharp lawyers took advantage of this opportunity. They persuaded over a hundred of the claimants to appeal their cases, and government attorneys appealed over four hundred more. Finally six hundred and four claims were validated, but in the process the cost of litigation had impoverished many of the appellants, and the uncertainty of titles had discouraged the making of any improvements on the land.

The process was complicated further by the inrush of miners and farmers who occupied many disputed claims and insisted upon "squatters' rights." Often they refused to give up even after the owner had proven his title. In behalf of these interlopers the state legislature passed an act in 1856 requiring the land owners to remunerate the squatters for any improvements made by the latter. Dissatisfaction also arose from the tendency of the courts to be influenced by trivial details. For example, title to some lands granted to Vallejo in exchange for provisions was held invalid because Mexican law had authorized a governor to "grant" land but not to sell it.

The pueblo, or community, land grants in California became the issue at stake in an especially prolonged litigation, owing to the high value of the town lands involved as well as to the flaws and irregularities in the records. In the case of San Francisco, the legal contention clouded the title of city lots for thousands of citizens until, finally in 1867, the Congress confirmed the municipal ownership of a pueblo grant of four square leagues.

In New Mexico, an even longer period of confusion and suspense clouded the titles to much of the land. Because this territory had no delegate in Congress in the early 1850s aggressively pressing for action, nothing at all was done until 1854. Then, instead of setting up a commission for the territory,

as in California, the Congress authorized the appointment of a surveyor-general who was expected to gather up the claims, investigate them, and report his findings to a congressional committee. The first surveyor-general, William Pelham, established a base line for his survey at a point on the Rio Grande, from which his crew proceeded slowly with their task of providing an accurate basis for the description of land holdings. Meanwhile Pelham collected the claims along with whatever evidence could be presented in support of them. In two years he had gathered together one thousand and fourteen claims; but three years later only twenty-five of them had been surveyed.

Meanwhile the Congress did act promptly upon the claims of seventeen of the Indian pueblos, which received confirmation of their community grants in 1858, and later two more were approved. Although some of the documents describing those claims were questionable, they were accepted because of confirmation that the Spanish emperor once had ordered such grants to be made. As for other claims, they came in slowly because of the requirement that they should be surveyed first. In three decades the Congress received only a little over two hundred of the private claims, of which one hundred and forty-one had been approved and thirteen had been rejected, leaving fifty-one still pending. At that time about nine hundred additional claims were being held in abeyance in New Mexico while awaiting completion of surveys and the gathering of evidence. The entire procedure, so vital to the welfare of the territory, had been hampered inexcusably by lack of understanding, inadequate staff, and absentee management, so that final disposition of many of the claims was delayed until around 1900, thereby retarding seriously the economic development of New Mexico. More will be said about this later.

IMPROVEMENT OF EDUCATION

The American system traditionally called for a literate citizenry; therefore the transition in the Southwest would require improvement in educational facilities. In this endeavor the record was better than in the handling of the Indian and land problems.

Due to the earlier beginning of Americanization in Texas, that state made encouraging headway. Among the pioneers some tutors traveled from one plantation to another in order to give elementary instruction to the children. Because they accepted remuneration in kind, often in corn, their private classes were called "cornfield" or "old field" schools. Under the Republic, the legislature upon the instigation of President Lamar had set aside four leagues of land from which the revenue would be used for common school purposes and fifty leagues for the maintenance of three colleges and a university. Ultimately this foresight provided supplementary resources that aided materially in the founding of the state university at Austin in 1883.

In the earlier days, however, the first creditable schools were privately supported. In 1840, a Methodist missionary, Martin Ruter, started a preparatory school near La Grange, and the next year it became Rutersville College. About the same time McKenzie College was established near Clarksville and a year later the University of Augustine was founded. These schools flourished for a few years, but soon, in 1845, they yielded leadership to a Baptist institution, Baylor University, which was chartered at Independence and later removed to Waco.

After annexation, Texans proceeded with the founding of public schools. In 1853, the City of San Antonio opened four tax-supported schools, and simultaneously some of the German colonists organized associations for the provision of free schools. The legislature, in 1854, created a uniform state system with a portion of the United States indemnity bonds earmarked for its support. At first any group of parents who opened a school and employed a teacher was eligible to receive sixty-two cents for each pupil in the first year and about twice that much the next year. Because the funds provided were inadequate for the maintenance of good schools, the private institutions continued to thrive better than did the public schools. In the first fifteen years following statehood, the state legislature chartered one hundred and seventeen private schools, including thirty colleges and seven universities, most of which were church-supported. In Texas, therefore, education was making such creditable progress that the rate of illiteracy for adults had been reduced to about five percent by 1860.

California also achieved statehood soon after its acquisition, with a resultant early progress in educational services. As in Texas, the first schools were opened by private tutors and missionaries. When the state constitution was drafted, a provision was included for the creation of school districts in which public instruction should be provided for at least three months annually. In 1851, the legislature took steps for effectuating that provision, and two years later it reserved by law sections sixteen and thirty-six in each section of land for support of schools. These measures brought results promptly, especially in the more populous localities; in fact, as early as 1856, the San Francisco district even opened a public high school. By 1860, the California system was shaping up in a pattern typical of that of other states.

Church support made possible the opening of the first institutions of higher learning in California. In 1851, the Baptists founded the College of the Pacific at Stockton and the Catholics opened the University of Santa Clara. The College of California, chartered in 1855, was destined later to become the nucleus of the state university system. The legislative act of 1853, which reserved land for public schools, also set aside two entire townships for the maintenance of a "seminary of learning," but the founding of the state-supported university was delayed until 1868, after the Civil War.

In the Territory of New Mexico the census-takers could find only one school in 1850, the one maintained by Padre Martínez in Taos. In 1852, the Sisters of Loretto established an academy in Santa Fe, and seven years later the Christian Brothers founded St. Michael's College in the same city. Much later some of the experiences of a pupil enrolled in the Sisters' Academy were described in the reminiscences of Marian Russell. In the year of the opening of that school she had been enrolled as the only Protestant pupil among ninety-nine Catholics. She recounted how the Sisters had tried to teach poise and self-reliance, as well as academic fundamentals. In addition, while the pupils were receiving instruction in "fine bead and needle work," the Sisters told them stories — "the sweetest and best ever told to little boys and girls."

In New Mexico, in 1853, two sections of land in each township were set aside for the support of public schools, but in this territory little benefit was derived from that measure. Because the survey of lands had not even been started yet and private claims would not be cleared up for many years, nobody then knew where sections sixteen and thirty-six were located and few persons cared to risk the leasing of lands which had insecure titles.

In 1854, the legislature called for a referendum on a proposed tax for the support of public schools in four counties. Many of the Dons opposed it, because they did not look with favor upon education for the masses; and the priests spoke up against it, because they preferred parochial schools. With such influential opposition, the proposal was defeated at the polls by the astounding margin of about five thousand to thirty-seven.

A few years later, in 1859, the legislature did enact a public school law, which provided funds amounting to fifty cents annually for each pupil, and vested in the local justices of peace the responsibility for the employing of teachers. By 1860, this act had encouraged the founding of seventeen public schools. In addition, there were some parochial schools and three privately supported academies. The total enrollment was only about fifteen hundred in 1860, and up to that date none of those schools was serving the part of the territory which was known as Arizona.

REVITALIZED RELIGION

In the Mexican era the Roman Catholic Church in the Borderlands had continued in effect to be a state church, even though some efforts had been made to separate church and state. The transfer of ownership opened the Southwest to missionaries of other denominations. In Texas, three Methodist missionaries, including the above-mentioned Martin Ruter, began the work of organizing churches and of forming circuits immediately after the achievement of independence. The Methodists continued to increase and build, even though the church split into Northern and Southern branches in 1844 on the issue of slavery. By 1860, the total membership of over thirty thousand made the Methodists the strongest denomination in the state.

The Baptists, who began missionary work as early as 1835 in the Lone Star Republic, had about five hundred churches by 1860. The Presbyterians entered this field in 1837 and had erected seventy-two church buildings by 1860. By that date the Episcopalians, who had started in 1838, had nineteen buildings; the Disciples of Christ, beginning work in 1842, had thirty-nine buildings. Strong leadership overcame distressing obstacles, and typical Protestant union meetings, preaching, Sunday schools, and sociables emphasized morality, good order, and religious fellowship. A collaborating institution was the Masonic Order, which had founded a Grand Lodge as early as 1837 and had enrolled nearly ten thousand members in Texas by 1860.

In California, a similar proliferation of Protestant denominations followed upon the acquisition of that territory. In 1848, the citizens of San Francisco designated the Reverend Timothy Dwight Hunt to serve as their city chaplain. In the next year the missionaries began arriving. In 1849, the Presbyterians organized a congregation in Benicia, the Congregationalists in Sacramento, and Baptists, Methodists, and Episcopalians in San Francisco. In 1850, the Methodists also inaugurated services in Monterey, the Episcopalians in Stockton, and the Presbyterians in San Francisco. By 1852, the latter city, alone, had thirty-seven churches. This Protestant influence was supplemented by the work of the Masons, as in Texas. The first unit was founded in California in 1849, the Grand Lodge a year later, and more than a hundred lodges by 1856.

In New Mexico, the Protestant missionaries found a less fruitful field prior to the arrival of Anglo-American settlers in large numbers. In Santa Fe, in 1849, the Reverend Henry W. Reed started a Baptist mission and a year later the Reverend E. G. Nicholson began preaching at Methodist meetings. Nicholson soon gave up, but the Baptists continued active and in 1854 erected the first Protestant building in the territory. By 1860, they had three churches with a seating capacity of six hundred and fifty. Concerning the difficulties encountered, one Methodist missionary, the Reverend Thomas Harwood, lamented:

What can I do, a lone missionary in this vast field, unacquainted with the languages and customs of the people, except a few American men, and they nearly all married to Mexican women, apparently going back into the dark ages, morally and religiously. . . . I am almost the only republican in the neighborhood.[2]

In the western part of the territory, or Arizona, the only non-Catholic work in those early years seems to have been limited to the missionary activities of a Mormon, Jacob Hamblin, who visited the Hopi Indians in 1858. Really productive Protestant activity in New Mexico would have to await the arrival of more immigrants after the Civil War.

Many Catholic priests had forebodings about the effect on their Church of the transfer of the Borderlands to the United States. They feared that their work and influence would be curtailed seriously in a nation which was then predominantly Protestant and always insistent upon guarantees of religious freedom. Actually, however, the Catholic Church gained strength by the change. Under Spain and Mexico, the neglect of this remote frontier by the ecclesiastical authorities in the homeland had become chronic. As soon as the transfer of the territory called attention to the need for a reorganization of jurisdictions, the work of the Church in in the Southwest became revitalized by new leadership.

[2] *History of New Mexican Spanish and English Missions* (Albuquerque, 1908), I, pp. 76-77.

In the Texas Republic, the Reverend J. M. Odin assumed supervision of Catholic churches in 1844. Four years later, when a diocese was created for Texas, the Reverend Odin became the first bishop and supervised the construction of a cathedral in Galveston. In 1838, the Catholics had only two church buildings in Texas, whereas the number had increased to thirty-three by 1860.

In California, as related previously, a diocese had been created in the Mexican Period; nevertheless, the Church was still weak at the time of acquisition of the territory by the United States. Then, to serve the numerous Catholic miners, churches soon were founded in the central region. For the San Francisco area, a separate diocese was formed in 1850 with the Reverend Joseph S. Allemany as bishop. He became archbishop three years later, and growth continued apace. In a region where there had been only fifteen priests in 1850, twenty-five years later there were over two hundred thousand communicants served by one hundred and twenty-one priests and three bishops.

In the Territory of New Mexico, where the Church was in a sad state in 1846, a new diocese was delineated in 1850 and Father Juan B. Lamy of the See of Cincinnati assumed supervision as bishop. Because his jurisdiction included Arizona and part of Colorado, he assigned those territories to Father Jean B. Salpointe and Father Joseph B. Machebeuf, respectively. For revival of the work of the Church in New Mexico, Bishop Lamy recruited several priests in France and invited the Sisters of Loretto and the Christian Brothers to found schools. By 1865, he was able to report the building of forty-five churches. Altogether, in his entire diocese thirty-seven priests were serving nearly one hundred churches and mission chapels in 1865, in an area where he had found only ten priests in 1850. He estimated that there were one hundred thousand communicants in New Mexico and five thousand more in Arizona. The revival experienced by the Church indeed had been remarkable and laid the basis for the important role it was yet to play.

TRANSFORMATION OF THE SOUTHWEST

As for the general effects of "Americanization," certainly poor headway had been made in the solution of the problems of Indian relationships and land ownership; but definitely more churches and schools had been founded and a new form of government had been imposed. However, within a mere decade the slow process of acculturation could hardly be expected to have progressed with little more than observable effects. In the 1850s, W. W. H. Davis observed a "noteworthy improvement in the style of dress and mode of living," and a little later, in 1867, James Meline was impressed by the "new look" of the Southwest. He observed that American-made trousers, overcoats, shawls, dresses, and even hoop skirts were being worn, in place of the *serapes* and native costumes, and he only wished that the new costumes might be "always as healthy and beneficial" as the old. These observations are in accord with the accepted principle that in acculturation the physical and economic traits are the more readily borrowed, while deeply rooted social practices resist change. In the Southwest the process would continue through many generations, and ultimately it would not be all a onesided "Americanization."

FACTS AND FIGURES, 1850

	California	New Mexico and Arizona	Texas
Total population	92,597	61,547	212,592
Negroes	1,678	22	58,161
Churches	28	73	316
Schools	8	1	349
Newspapers	7	2	34
Acres in farms	110,748	124,370	639,117
Cattle	304,706	20,720	214,868
Sheep	35,867	377,271	100,530

12

SECESSION AND REUNION

Instantly the ranks closed up, the cavalry took open orders by fours, and we rushed forward on the double-quick. Knap-sacks, canteens, overcoats, and clothing of all kinds were flung along the road as the boys stripped for the encounter. How our hearts beat! That tremendous event, the burden of history and song, a battle, burst on our hitherto peaceful lives like an avalanche on a Swiss village. Were we worthy of the name we bore? A few minutes would tell. . . . Battle brings all speculation to a point. Life and death stare each other in the face. Life, however miserable, against death that ends it all. Until actually engaged, the most of men suffer excessively from suspense. In the midst of the fight they partake more or less of the demoniac spirit surrounding them.

Ovander J. Hollister, Boldly They Rode *(Denver, 1949), p. 61.*

In 1848, the Spanish Borderlands had become the southwestern part of a Union which soon was to be plunged into civil strife. Throughout the decade of the fifties one controversy after another drove deeper the wedge between the northern and southern states until finally, after the election of Abraham Lincoln as president by a new sectional party in the autumn of 1860, seven states seceded from the Union. Early in 1861 they united as the Confederate States of America, and soon four more states joined the original seven. The Southerners hoped to go their own way unmolested, but Lincoln felt obligated to protect federal property and preserve the Union. When he proclaimed a blockade of Confederate ports and issued a call for the enlistment of volunteers, the "inevitable" conflict erupted, with effects felt throughout the divided nation.

UNION CALIFORNIA

Although the major theatre of military campaigns would lie east of the Mississippi River, the war would also call for a decision and evoke some strife in the distant southwestern states and territories. As California remained aligned with the Union and Texas joined the Confederacy, the way was prepared for the Southwest to have its own little Civil War, with New Mexico becoming the borderland in which the opposing forces would contend for supremacy.

In California the state legislature adopted resolutions favoring the Union, whereas the governor, John B. Weller, spoke in opposition to military participation, on the ground that he did not believe that the Union "could be preserved by a coercive policy." As an outgrowth of a division in the Democratic party in 1860, the Republicans had won in the election of that year and had turned in their electoral votes for Lincoln. Obviously the gubernatorial campaign of the next year would be decisive. In it a Unitarian minister, David Starr King, and the influential Colonel E. D. Baker campaigned vigorously for Leland Stanford, a Republican. When Stanford emerged victorious, that brought in a governor who was in accord with the legislature and assured the continuation of California in the Union.

Despite the official verdict, many Californians continued to be outspoken "Secesh" sympathizers. Especially in Los Angeles, San Francisco, and the Central Valley, the diehard pro-Southern faction criticized President Lincoln, ridiculed the Union Army, and even conspired to give assistance to the Confederacy. One group in San Francisco acquired a schooner, loaded it with arms, and planned to take possession of one of the federal Pacific Mail steamships, which they intended to convert into a privateer. Federal men, however, heard about this scheme for harassment of Union shipping and intercepted the schooner.

On the other hand, the supporters of the Union were zealous, too; they condemned the secession fanatics and in some instances ran them out of town. They also responded well to the appeals of the Reverend Mr. King, who headed the campaign for support of the relief work of the United States Sanitary Commission. The loyalty of the majority of the Californians, especially in the mining region, is attested by their contribution of over one million dollars, or about one-fourth of the total amount raised by the Commission.

When war became a certainty, Colonel Albert Sidney Johnston, a Texan, resigned his command of the Department of the Pacific in order to make available his services and, as it turned out, to give his life too, in the cause of the Confederacy. Some others of the pro-Southern faction also returned to the states of their nativity in the South for enlistment in the Confederate Army. As commander, Johnston was succeeded briefly by General Edwin Vose Sumner, who had been transferred west and promoted after he had supervised the building of Fort Union in New Mexico. In October, 1861, he was replaced by General George G. Wright, who remained in command in California for three years throughout most of the war.

When President Lincoln called for

volunteers, the response so over-whelmed the available facilities in California that new training camps had to be built hastily. Altogether, sixteen thousand eager young men volunteered for duty in the course of the war and were drilled and equipped for action, but very few were sent to the eastern theater. Some served on garrison duty along the trail to Salt Lake City and in Washington Territory, while some others marched with the regiment that was sent across Arizona to the Rio Grande; but most of them never were called upon for service outside of their own state.

The disaffection around Los Angeles along with the interruption of stage-coach service on the Gila route indicated that the presence of a strong detachment of the California Volunteers was needed in the southern part of the state. General Wright heard rumors that the pro-Southerners there were "organizing, collecting supplies, and evidently preparing to receive a force from Texas," therefore he concentrated defensive units at Camp Wright on Warner's Ranch, at Fort Yuma on the lower Colorado River, and at other posts in the region.

In October, 1861, this area was designated as the "Los Angeles Military District" and assigned to the command of Colonel James H. Carleton. Because the expected difficulties there did not materialize, the Union had available in southern California some inactive reserves who could be marched to the Rio Grande whenever word came that their services were needed.

CONFUSION IN NEW MEXICO

East of the Colorado River in the expansive Territory of New Mexico, the southern towns, especially Tucson and Mesilla, harbored a few avid pro-Southerners, whereas in the valley of the upper Rio Grande many of the Anglo-Americans were staunch Unionists. However, a great majority of the people were the Spanish Americans, who were initially indifferent as to the major issues of the war. As for the Union, they had been denied immediate statehood in it and thus felt that they had not been accepted yet as full-fledged citizens. Concerning the slavery issue, they could not get overly excited, because there were very few Negro slaves in the entire territory. Moreover, these recently naturalized citizens understood little as yet about the form of government or the problems of the nation which had so recently taken them in. Until aroused by a local threat, the Civil War to them would be somebody else's war.

Encouraging to the South were the confusion and suffering which had prevailed in New Mexico during 1861. In the preceding two years serious droughts had brought distress to the countryside, and people in distress are prone to welcome any kind of change that may promise relief. Moreover, the Kiowas and Comanches to the east were riding into the territory almost at will, stealing cattle and looting wagon trains. Additional soldiers for this remote frontier could not well be spared by the Union which faced a major crisis in the East, and those soldiers already on duty were far more concerned about the effect of the crisis upon their own future than they were about the troubles of New Mexico. To make matters worse, most of the officers resigned their commands at the Southwestern posts and accepted commissions in the Confederate Army. Among those who transferred their allegiance were several whose names were destined to loom large in the annals of the Confederacy: Captain Richard Stoddard Ewell; Major Henry Hopkin Sibley; colonels George Bibb Crittenden, Thomas T. Fauntleroy, William Wing Loring, Albert Sidney Johnston, and William James Longstreet; and General David E. Twiggs. Their departure left vacancies which had to be filled by hasty promotions; and one—Colonel Loring, Department Commander—was found to have transferred to the Confederacy valuable munitions and equipment which he had stored at some of the posts, ostensibly for that purpose. Immediately Colonel Edward R. S. Canby, brother-in-law of Sibley but nevertheless a loyal Union officer, was promoted to the departmental command. When he came to Santa Fe from Fort Defiance in June, 1861, he found the defensive forces weak and demoralized.

Troubles multiplied rapidly for Colonel Canby. With a weakened staff and a shortage of men he had to contend against more serious Indian depredations. When the Red Men saw the whites fighting among themselves, they surmised that this was their opportunity for retaliation. In addition to the Kiowas and Comanches, now the Utes, Navajos, and Mescalero Apaches became restless and troublesome. Moreover in that critical time the Departmental paymaster was receiving no funds from the distressed Union for paying the soldiers, who had been protecting this frontier for months without remuneration. At that time the cooperation of the civil government was not very good either. The pro-slavery faction in the territorial legislature pushed the adoption of a slave code through the territorial legislature.

On that account the territorial governor, Abraham Rencher, who was a native of North Carolina, became suspect as a Confederate sympathizer, though Calvin Horn has found meagre evidence implicating him. Nevertheless, at the time the Union officers distrusted him. Moreover, Canby had little time for reorganization of the defense, because immediately upon assuming command he had received reports that a Texan invasion was imminent.

CONFEDERATE TEXAS

In Texas, back in 1859, a pro-Southerner, H. R. Runnels, had been defeated by a strong Unionist candidate for governor, Sam Houston. That election, however, did not reflect accurately the sentiment of Texans about secession, since the defeat of Runnels could be attributed to his unpopular Indian policy along with the magnetic personality of his opponent.

Houston had said at his inaugural in January, 1860, that when Texas had been annexed, "Her connection was not sectional but national." Soon he received a copy of the South Carolina resolutions on state and federal relations, which he duly transmitted to the Texas legislature with his own expressed conviction that "the union was intended as a perpetuity." On the other hand, many Texans were of the opinion that because their state had entered the Union voluntarily they could equally well choose to withdraw. That summer the Texas delegates walked out of the National Democratic Convention in protest against a resolution which opposed the extension of slavery into the territories. As could be anticipated, therefore, neither Douglas nor Lincoln won any electoral votes in Texas. They went instead to John C. Breckenridge and John Bell, the Southern candidates. Meanwhile secession sentiment was being propagandized by local "castles" of the Knights of the Golden Circle, a secret society which was despotically controlled by its pro-Southern superior officers.

The election of Lincoln precipitated a crisis in Texas, as it did in the other southern states. At public meetings in many localities the aroused citizens resolved that they would never submit to rule by "Black Republicans," and they maltreated any avowed Unionist whom they could find. Because Governor Houston refused to call an election for the choice of delegates to participate in a state secession convention, the Knights of the Golden Circle issued the call. Although the ensuing election conducted in January of 1861 was irregular, it did garner thirty-two thousand votes for secession delegates. According to the observations of a former Texas Ranger, Corporal James Pike, the Unionists were the older citizens, those of "property and character," while the secessionists were mostly the younger

men, "ambitious and fanatical." He alleged that the secessionists had obtained their victory by intimidating the voters. Nevertheless the agitators had sufficient influence to persuade the legislature that the irregular election should be legalized. Then the assembled convention adopted a secession ordinance by a vote of one hundred and sixty-seven to seven and submitted it for popular approval at a special election to be held on February 23, 1861.

The secession convention also created a Committee on Public Safety which undertook the accomplishment of secession without even awaiting the outcome of the special election. Under the sponsorship of that Committee, Ben McCulloch with three thousand Knights of the Golden Circle invaded San Antonio on February 16 and prevailed upon General David E. Twiggs to remove all Federal troops from Texas. Twiggs evacuated his three thousand men and surrendered arsenals, forts, and military stores valued at over a million dollars. For his willing capitulation he was dismissed from the Federal service and rewarded by the South with an appointment to a Confederate command.

As the Union troops were being withdrawn from Texas, the Knights took as prisoners three hundred of them in San Antonio and held them for later exchange, if the occasion should arise. In this hostile demonstration the Texans who participated flew the Lone Star flag. In fact, up to that time the seizure seems to have been motivated more by enthusiasm for a restoration of independence than by friendliness toward the Confederacy. Once again Texas would become an independent nation, and it would be expanded into a Great Texas by conquest of the northern states of Mexico or, perhaps, all of that nation.

In their momentary enthusiasm for independence the Texans voted three to one in favor of secession, and the convention reassembled on March 2 for a declaration two days later that the state was once more independent. To that time it appeared that the secessionists themselves were bent upon carrying out Houston's Grand Plan for the glorification of Texas, but then the pro-Southern faction got the upper hand. Within a month it obtained in the convention the adoption of a resolution by a vote of one hundred and nine to two in favor of joining the Confederate States of America. Then when Governor Houston protested that that action had not been authorized, the convention adopted a resolution requiring all state officials to take an oath of allegiance. When Houston refused, he was removed as governor. President Lincoln offered him military assistance if he would oppose the convention with force, but Houston felt compelled to decline because he did not want to engage in warfare against the people of his own state.

TEXAS AT WAR

The deposition of Houston elevated the lieutenant governor, Edward Clark, to the governorship. He formally transferred to the Confederacy all Union property and arms in Texas and offered Jefferson Davis, President of the Confederacy, the services of a volunteer regiment of cavalry. In acknowledgment of gratification for the support of Texas, Davis appointed John H. Reagan of that state as Postmaster General in the Confederate Cabinet.

Texans prepared energetically for their participation in the war. The enthusiastic majority sought immediately to enforce conformity by requiring all citizens to register and to swear allegiance to the Confederacy. This forced the Union sympathizers either to comply or to flee. One group of sixty Germans who tried to escape to Mexico was overtaken by the zealots, and forty of them were executed. That many Unionists, nevertheless, did evade interception is attested by the fact that almost two thousand Texans served in the Union Army.

In 1861, the incumbent, Clark, was defeated in a close race for governor by Francis R. Lubbock, who cooperated loyally with the Confederacy throughout his two-year term. At that time the chief channel of the South's trade with Mexico lay through Texas, and to facilitate this commerce the Texas Military Board bought cotton with state bonds and exchanged it in Mexico for imported clothing, arms, and machinery, which then was transshipped to the other southern states. In addition, Texans drew generously upon their own resources. They built numerous new industrial plants for the manufacture of guns, wagons, textiles, leather goods, and other articles. After the war had taken many of the men away from their farms, the women supervised the labor of the Negro slaves or even did much of the work themselves. The bustling activity made the first year of the war a prosperous one for the Texans; consequently they generously donated clothing and food for the soldiers at the front, and this state was one of the few in the South which cooperated wholeheartedly in the payment of the Confederate war tax levied in 1861.

The first consequential military action in which the Texans participated was directed against New Mexico, wherein lay the key to control of the southern route to California. If the Confederates could gain possession of the forts in this territory, they would be able to open communication with southern California, whence came encouraging reports about sympathetic citizens eager for an opportunity to give the South their support. At Los Angeles the Confederacy would also then have a port which was not hampered by the Union blockade. Moreover, the occupation of New Mexico would give the Confederates a base for a campaign into Colorado for interception of the gold and silver shipments on the central route. With the product of the mines of Arizona, California, Nevada, and Colorado diverted from the North to the South, the Confederacy would have the gold so badly needed for the support of its monetary system and the acquisition of industrial wares abroad. In fact, in the early stage of the war, gold exchanged for munitions in Europe could conceivably have changed the outcome of the conflict. The campaigns conducted from Texas into New Mexico were therefore of more than marginal significance.

"SECESSION" OF ARIZONA

Early in 1861, Colonel John R. Baylor of the Confederate Army enlisted four hundred Texans and occupied Fort Bliss near El Paso. With two hundred and fifty of those volunteers he started up the river on July 23 toward Fort Fillmore, which was held by Major Isaac Lynde and about seven hundred Union troops. Because Lynde feared that he could not hold Fort Fillmore against Baylor's artillery, he came to the conclusion that he should abandon it and withdraw to Fort Stanton about one hundred and fifty miles to the northeast. According to one version, the troopers could not stand it to see some kegs of whisky and brandy wasted; consequently they poured the water out of their canteens and replaced it with liquor. As they marched across the desert and ascended into the Organ Mountains, the liquor only parched their dry throats. Captain Alfred Gibbs, who was in charge of the rear guard, reported that "the infantry had been marched up to noon 20 miles without water, and that under the bushes by the side of the road over 150 men were lying, unable to rise or to carry their muskets, and useless and disorganized in every way." Baylor overtook the Union column in San Agustín Pass and found that "The road for five miles was lined with fainting, famished soldiers, who threw down their arms as we passed and begged for water." Then Major Lynde surrendered his entire command, comprised of eight companies of infantry and four of cavalry, with four pieces of artillery. As a result of this capitulation the small Union force at Fort Stanton abandoned the post, and Baylor sent a detachment to occupy it.

Since the Union soldiers at Fort McLane already had been removed for the strengthening of Fort Fillmore, Baylor now held undisputed possession of all of New Mexico below Fort Craig. Therefore, on August 2, he proclaimed the "secession" of that part of the territory lying south of the thirty-fourth parallel, which also would include southern Arizona. He declared himself, then, to be the military governor of the "Confederate Territory of Arizona," with its capital at Mesilla. While he was organizing the administration of the conquered territory, another campaign by Texans was in preparation. It would determine the disposition of the entire Southwest and to some extent influence the outcome of the war in the East.

INVASION OF NEW MEXICO

The second invasion of New Mexico was organized by H. H. Sibley, a former major in the Union Army who had become a Confederate general. By virtue of his previous experience he well understood the weakness of New Mexico and comprehended the value of occupying that territory. When he presented his proposal for its conquest to Jefferson Davis in Richmond, Virginia, the Confederate President concurred in the conclusion that it should be done; but without troops that could be spared, Davis authorized Sibley to enlist some in Texas. He did, and soon he filled out a full brigade of about three thousand men, which he drilled at Fort Sibley near San Antonio.

Near the end of October, 1861, the first detachment of Sibley's brigade left camp for the westward march, and Sibley followed with the remainder of his force about a month later. From El Paso in December he addressed to the people of New Mexico a proclamation which was quite similar in wording to the one used by General Kearny fifteen years previously. In it he said, in part:

Upon the peaceful people of New Mexico the Confederate States wage no war. To them we come as friends, to re-establish a governmental connection agreeable and advantageous both to them and to us; to liberate them from the yoke of a military despotism erected by usurpers upon the ruins of the former free institutions of the United States, to relieve them of the iniquitous taxes and exactions imposed upon them by that usurpation; to insure and to revere their religion, and to restore their civil and political liberties. . . .

To my old comrades in arms, still in the ranks of the usurpers of their Government and liberties, I appeal in the name of former friendship. Drop at once the arms which degrade you into the tools of tyrants, renounce their service, and array yourselves under the colors of justice and freedom![1]

From El Paso, Sibley detached a company of a hundred cavalrymen under the command of Captain Sherod Hunter for occupation of Tucson. They entered the town on February 28 without encountering any resistance, and Captain Hunter promised the citizens of Arizona peace and prosperity if they would adhere to the cause of the Confederacy.

On the Union side, the occupation of a part of Arizona and New Mexico elicited defensive measures. In Sep-

[1] U. S., *War of the Rebellion* (Government Printing Office, 1882), I, 4, pp. 89–90.

tember, President Lincoln removed Governor Rencher and appointed a loyal resident of New Mexico, Dr. Henry Connelly. At the instigation of the new governor the legislature soon repealed a statute protecting slave property and enacted a war measure which authorized the governor to muster all the resources of the territory, even to proclaim martial law if need be, in order "to repulse and drive from the soil, the now invading army."

To bolster the Union defense, two companies of Colorado volunteers hastened south for strengthening the defensive force in Fort Craig. In addition, the governor's call for volunteers brought a rush of recruits. The hitherto unconcerned Spanish Americans became aroused when they heard that the Texans were invading their land again. In the course of the war over four thousand of them enlisted in the Union Army, and those who volunteered early in 1862 were concentrated at Fort Craig. Then Colonel Canby also went to Fort Craig to take command of the twelve hundred regulars and nearly three thousand volunteers posted there.

Assistance for imperiled New Mexico was also available in California. General Wright had proposed in December, 1861, that Colonel Carleton's regiment, along with a battery of artillery and a company of cavalry, be sent east for the reopening of mail service on the southern route and the reoccupying of the lost forts in southern New Mexico. In January, 1862, after that offer

had been approved in Washington, Carleton began organizing and equipping an expedition of two thousand men, six hundred cavalry and artillery horses, and nine hundred draft mules. The assembling and equipping of a column of this size at Fort Yuma would require several months, so that Carleton would not be able to start the march up the Gila Valley until some time in May, 1862.

Long before the California Column could arrive in New Mexico, Sibley advanced up the Rio Grande. On February 16, the twenty-six hundred men of his brigade were encamped across the river just below Fort Craig. On the 20th, Union scouts reported that a long line of wagons was moving northward on the other, or east, side of the river, as though Sibley was going to bypass the fort. Unfortunately Canby was ill that day and could not take charge in the field; therefore he issued orders from the fort for an attack on the enemy column. In order to intercept Sibley, the Union troops had to ford the river under fire, and this proved to be so difficult that the men scattered and camped in clumps. On the next day, when more Union men tried to charge through the shallow river, they were repulsed with heavy losses. Then Union cannon were brought across the river upstream, ahead of the Confederate brigade, and from that advantageous position the artillery fire forced the Confederates to withdraw from the river to the sand dunes farther to the east.

THE APPEARANCE OF VICTORY

Late in the afternoon of February 21 the Texans boldly charged against the Union battery and overwhelmed it.

Afterwards Theophilus Noel of the Texas Cavalry wrote his account of this encounter. He said that "for a few moments the strife was terrific beyond description," but the charge "routed the enemy," who rushed to the river "more like a herd of frightened mustangs than like men." With their cannon out of commission, the Union troops fled to the fort. In this Battle of Valverde, Sibley had emerged victorious. Canby reported two hundred and sixty-three men killed, wounded, or missing, and he blamed the green volunteers for the debacle:

> The battle was fought almost entirely by the regular troops (trebled in number by the Confederates), with no assistance from the militia and but little from the volunteers, who would not obey orders or obeyed them too late to be of any service. The immediate cause of the disaster was the refusal of one of the volunteer regiments to cross the river and support the left wing of the army.[2]

Subsequently his statement has been interpreted as betraying his prejudice against the Spanish Americans, whom he made the scapegoat; but obviously any group of hastily assembled volunteers would be ill-prepared for the carrying out of rapid maneuvers while under fire.

While the Union men waited in Fort Craig, expecting an assault by Sibley, the latter marched on up the river instead. Consequently Canby sent a message to the garrison of soldiers in Albuquerque ordering the destruction of all of their military supplies. They burned their warehouses and withdrew to Fort Marcy at Santa Fe. Meanwhile Canby back at Fort Craig was drilling his men so as to be better prepared if he should have a second opportunity. He was

hoping, too, that the Confederate invasion would fizzle out because of the problem of logistics. It would be difficult for an army to hold out very long while attempting to subsist by foraging in a desert countryside.

The Confederates occupied Albuquerque on March 2, and Sibley determined that he should remain there while organizing the occupation and celebrating his victory. The next day all but a small detachment of his brigade resumed the northward march toward Santa Fe. Because the city would be difficult to defend, Major James L. Donaldson at Fort Marcy came to the conclusion that he should abandon the capital, and Governor Connelly concurred. On March 4, a caravan of one hundred and twenty wagons loaded with movable supplies departed for Fort Union, and the immovable equipment was burned. Governor Connelly temporarily transferred the territorial offices to a hotel on the plaza in Las Vegas.

As the Confederates advanced they had to send foraging parties far afield in search of provisions which could be confiscated for the maintenance of the army and its livestock. Ranchers fled to distant places of refuge, leaving the contents of their houses and barns a prey to the invaders. Governor Connelly learned that his own ranch house about ninety miles below Santa Fe "was despoiled of its entire contents, including a valuable stock of goods, together with everything in the way of subsistence." While the main force under the command of Colonel William R. Scurry made camp at Galisteo, an advance company took possession of Santa Fe on March 23 and occupied the barren

[2] *War of the Rebellion* (1888), I, 8, p. 668.

Fort Marcy. Immediately·a detachment marched to the southeast for a reconnaissance in Apache Canyon on the road which crossed the mountains to Las Vegas and Fort Union. The methodical removal and destruction of military supplies ahead of them had made the situation of the Confederates daily more precarious, but if only they were able to reach and occupy Fort Union with its abundant store of supplies, valued at over a quarter of a million dollars, they would be in a secure position.

In this dark hour in New Mexico, the Confederates had conquered all but Fort Union, and now everything seemed to depend upon the garrison there, commanded by Colonel Gabriel R. Paul. Because he feared that the original log fort was vulnerable, he began work on the construction of a new "star fort" of earthen parapets surrounding dugouts which could house close to five hundred men. However, he was short of manpower; therefore in response to an appeal sent out by Governor Connelly, the Governor of the Territory of Colorado, William Gilpin, rushed a regiment of Colorado Volunteers to New Mexico. Despite a heavy snowfall, thirteen hundred eager "Pikes-Peakers" under the command of Colonel John P. Slough left Denver on February 22, crossed Raton Pass on March 7, and covered the last leg of ninety-two miles in the incredible time of thirty-six hours.

While the weary Colorado Volunteers rested briefly at Fort Union, the two colonels discussed strategy. Colonel Paul had orders from General Canby to defend the fort and harass the enemy, which he interpreted to mean that he and his reinforcements should stay right there in that underground fort. On the other hand, Colonel Slough, knowing that his men were eager for action, insisted that they could better harass the Confederates by going forth to meet them. To resolve their differences, they compared their commissions. Although Colonel Slough was a recently recruited officer, his commission as colonel antedated by a few days that of Colonel Paul, who was a regular Army man of considerable experience. Therefore Slough asserted his rights as senior officer and led his regiment forth on March 22. Two days later the Pikes-Peakers passed through Las Vegas on the way toward the pass through the Sangre de Cristo range.

DEFEAT AND RETREAT

In the race for the strategic advantage of occupying Apache Canyon, advance detachments of both armies arrived there simultaneously. While Slough encamped with the main body of the Colorado regiment at Bernal Springs, he sent ahead Major John M. Chivington with about four hundred men for a probe into the canyon and possibly a surprise attack on Santa Fe. Already Major Charles F. Pyron with his Texas detachment was also approaching from Sante Fe, and the two armies met in the canyon on March 26. Ovander J. Hollister of the Colorado Volunteers described the battle vividly:

On turning a short bend we entered the canyon proper and came full on two howitzers, less than two hundred yards off. These were attended by a company of mounted men displaying a saucy little red flag emblazoned with the emblem of which Texas has small reason to be proud. . . . On seeing these "lions of the path," the infantry divided, a wing flew into either hill, and the fight commenced. . . . The regular officers plunged wildly here and there. . . . The infantry came down on them like a parcel of wild Indians. . . . In half an hour after the charge, the enemy had disappeared and the firing ceased.[3]

A Texan, writing to his wife, expressed surprise that instead of encountering "Mexicans and regulars," they had met up with "regular demons, upon whom iron and lead had little effect." The Pikes-Peakers, he said, "were upon the hills on both sides of us, shooting us down like sheep."

Because darkness halted that first skirmish, both detachments returned to their camps — the Coloradans at Pigeon Ranch and the Texans at the Johnson Ranch. Both majors immediately reported to their commanding officers, who then brought up their respective armies and joined the advance detachments. Both Colonel Slough and Colonel Scurry waited a day for the other to attempt to march through the canyon, and then on the second day, March 28, both advanced. This time they met near Pigeon Ranch for the major battle, which raged all day. And this time the Confederates outnumbered the Union men by four or five hundred, and further, they had learned a trick from the previous skirmish, for now they took to the hillsides and fired down upon the Coloradans. By evening they had occupied Pigeon Ranch and had pushed the Union

[3] *Boldly They Rode*, p. 61.

force back to Koslowski's ranch. Then, much to the surprise of the hard-pressed Pikes-Peakers, a Confederate messenger bearing a flag of truce overtook them and asked for time for his comrades to bury their dead before evacuating. Although the Coloradans had lost the battle in the canyon, they had won a victory after all, due to a strategic maneuver, and the detachment of about three hundred men for that maneuver accounted for the disparity in numbers in the main battle.

In the Union camp, Captain William H. Lewis and Major Asa B. Carey, of the United States Infantry, had conceived a plan for an assault upon the Confederate base beyond the pass. Major Chivington had led this surprise assault, with Lieutenant Colonel Manuel M. Chávez of the New Mexico Volunteers as a guide. The detachment had scaled the walls of the canyon, crossed over the Mesa, and charged down upon the Confederate camp. The Pikes-Peakers surprised and routed the Confederate guard, overturned and burned their sixty supply wagons, and bayoneted most of their six hundred horses and mules. Consequently, when the Texans returned to their camp that evening, they found that they had none and so sent out the messenger with a flag of truce. For this decisive maneuver, Major Chivington, ex-preacher and budding politician, took full credit in his report and was rewarded with a promotion. Incidentally, it was this same Chivington who, two years later, fell into disgrace for directing an impetuous massacre of Indians in camp at Sand Creek in Colorado.

The Confederate officers concluded that without supplies their tired, ragged

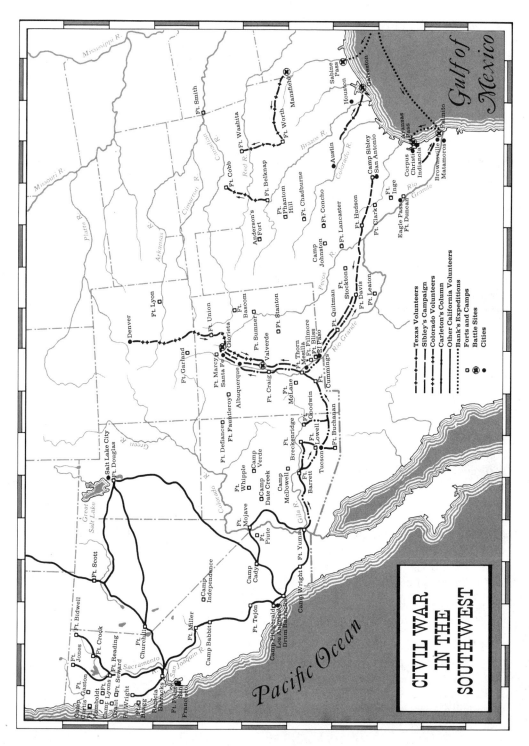

CIVIL WAR IN THE SOUTHWEST

army could not continue the campaign. They had failed in their drive toward the strategic stores at Fort Union, and the valley in their rear had been stripped of everything available. Canby's conjecture about logistics was being borne out. Colonel Scurry retreated to Albuquerque, where he joined General Sibley, and together they prepared for a rapid retreat.

In an effort to intercept the Texans, Colonel Canby emerged from Fort Craig and sent orders to Colonel Paul for him to leave Fort Union, to join forces with the Colorado Volunteers, and to meet him in Tijeras Canyon. However, Sibley's men crossed the Rio Grande, slipped out of camp in the night, and tried to get by Canby. A skirmish ensued, as the opposing batteries fired at each other; but then Canby canceled the battle plans of his officers. Needless to say, they were furious about this, because they had the enemy trapped and thought they could finish him off. Hollister complained that "to see them escape when actually within our grasp, from the stupidity or treachery of our General, effectively kills enthusiasm. . . ." Canby explained that since the Texans were trying to get out of the country, it was better to let them go than to incur more casualties in a futile engagement.

Nevertheless, Canby did follow the retreat, with the armies on opposite sides of the river, and annoyed the Confederates with artillery fire. At Peralta, on April 21, the Texans paused and struck back, in a vain effort to take and silence the Union cannon. Failing in that last stand, Sibley detoured out of sight into the San Mateo Mountains, whence he turned southward for the return march to Fort Bliss. There, on May 4 he wrote in his final report on this campaign, that

we have beaten the enemy in every encounter and against large odds; that from being the worst armed my forces are now the best armed in the country. . . . But, sir, I cannot speak encouragingly of the future, my troops having manifested a dogged, irreconcilable detestation of the country and the people. They have endured much, suffered much, and cheerfully; but the prevailing discontent, backed up by the distinguished valor displayed on every field, entitles them to marked consideration and indulgence.[4]

His withdrawal into Texas spelled valedictory for Baylor's Confederate Territory of Arizona and for all of the strategic advantages which the South might have garnered from the occupation of New Mexico. Although in the battle at Glorieta the casualties had been light— eighty or so on either side—that Union victory had been a decisive one in its effect upon the outcome of the Civil War.

THE CALIFORNIA COLUMN

Sibley already had departed from New Mexico before Carleton and his column were ready to leave Fort Yuma; yet Carleton proceeded up the Gila in order to contribute whatever he could toward recovering Arizona and New Mexico. At Picacho Pass an advance party had a skirmish with some Confederate

[4] *War of the Rebellion* (1890), IX, pp. 511-512.

scouts, who fell back to Tucson. When Carleton arrived in Tucson on May 20th, he found that Captain Hunter's company had evacuated that town and the Southern sympathizers had fled to Sonora. He reported that "Our arrival is hailed with joy by all the people who remain." He exacted an oath of allegiance from all adult citizens and proclaimed the establishment of a separate territorial government for Arizona. That proclamation was premature, because the Congress did not officially divide the expansive Territory of New Mexico until December in 1863.

While zealously apprehending all suspected persons in Arizona, Carleton arrested Sylvester Mowry, formerly an officer in the United States Army, who had become a wealthy miner and an influential citizen. On meagre evidence Carleton's board of inquiry found Mowry guilty of "treasonable correspondence and collusion with well known secessionists," confiscated his property, and sentenced him to prison at Fort Yuma, where he was confined until November, 1864. For vindication and compensation Mowry filed a million dollar lawsuit against Carleton, which was delayed and appealed in the courts for some time afterward with no conclusive outcome.

In general, Carleton's restoration of Arizona to the Union and the subsequent organization of a territorial government had a salubrious effect. New mines were opened, pack trains traveled the trails again, and in the remaining years of the war the population almost doubled. Colorado City (later Yuma) began thriving as navigation was resumed on the Colorado River, and a new city, Prescott, arose at the site selected for the capital by the first territorial governor, John M. Goodwin. Tucson grew in importance, too; but that old city retained much of its Mexican atmosphere, as vividly described in 1864 by J. Ross Browne:

Tucson is a city of mud-boxes, dingy and dilapidated, cracked and baked into a composite of dust and filth, littered about with broken corrals, sheds, bake ovens, carcasses of dead animals, and broken pottery; barren of verdure, parched, naked, and grimly desolate in the glare of a southern sun. Adobe walls without whitewash inside or out, hard earth-floors, baked and dried Mexicans, sore-backed burros, coyote dogs, and terracotta children, soldiers, teamsters, and honest miners lounging about the mescal shops, soaked with fiery poison, a noisy band of Sonora buffoons dressed in theatrical costume, cutting their antics in the public places to the most diabolical din of fiddles and guitars ever heard; a long train of government wagons preparing to start for Fort Yuma or the Rio Grande — these are what the traveler sees. . . .[5]

There, at Tucson, Carleton had tarried for about two months in 1862 before he set out for New Mexico. When he arrived at Fort Thorn on August 7, he found the Stars and Stripes flying again. As soon as he arrived in Fort Bliss he sent a company under Captain John C. Cremony into West Texas for occupation of Fort Quitman and another commanded by Captain E. D. Shirland to take Fort Davis. The Californians found both places deserted. In Santa Fe in September, Carleton succeeded Canby as departmental commander. In his report he included high praise for the California Volunteers for their long march in the summer heat of

[5] "A Tour through Arizona," *Harpers*, Jan., 1864, p. 26.

the Arizona desert without "loss of any kind, but improved in discipline, in morale, and in every other element of efficiency."

The contest at arms in New Mexico had been concluded before the arrival of Carleton. California and Arizona had suffered only minor displacements compared to that incurred in New Mexico. W. F. Arny, writing for the Santa Fe *New Mexican,* described the sad effects of the war as follows:

The destruction caused by the Texan invasion in 1861 and '62 has had a most disastrous effect upon this country. They consumed its substance, caused the loss of almost its entire mercantile and mining capital, and much injured the agricultural interests; it impoverished the whole country. The Indians, seeing that the whites were at war, increased in boldness, and compelled the abandonment of many mines and settlements, while fear of Texans and war induced nearly half the Mexican population of the Mesilla Valley to flee to Mexico, from whence they are slowly returning.[6]

Carleton constantly expected another invasion from Texas and made preparations for meeting it. He maintained a strict military rule and required all citizens to obtain and carry identification cards, because "In times like these, we must *know* who are our friends and who are enemies." But the Texans never came again, and instead, the distressing problem with which Carleton had to deal throughout the remaining years of the war was that of the aroused Indians. How his Indian policy provoked bitter opposition in New Mexico will be explained in the next chapter.

The Texans did not invade New Mexico again because for them the war soon assumed larger proportions. Before the South resorted to conscription in 1862 Texas had contributed about twenty thousand volunteers to the Confederate Army. In the full four years about three times that number saw service, or a large proportion of the ninety-two thousand males who were of military age. About one third of those who served were with the Army of Mississippi and the Army of Virginia, whereas the remainder stayed west of the Mississippi. Famous among the Texas brigades in the eastern and central theatres were those commanded by John B. Hood, Lawrence Sul Ross, and B. F. Terry. Within Texas, during the first year of the war, W. C. Young with an army of two thousand volunteers secured the northern border of the state against invasion by crossing the Red River and occupying forts Arbuckle, Cobb, and Washita.

The regiment of Texas Rangers, commanded by John S. Ford, which was guarding the lower valley of the Rio Grande against a renewal of raids by the Cortina bandits, was converted into a Confederate regiment and assigned to continued defense of the southern border.

TABLES TURNED IN TEXAS

During the first two years of the war Union land forces were busily engaged on other fronts, far from Texas. Their initial approach, therefore, was made by sea. In July of 1861, the Union Navy blockaded the ports of Texas, and gun-

[6] Oct. 13, 1865.

boats bombarded Corpus Christi; but when troops landed, the Texans repulsed them. In October the *Westfield* and three other Union steamers entered Galveston Bay, and a landing force occupied Galveston. Immediately General John B. Magruder organized a countercampaign, which employed three hundred of Sibley's veterans. This operation by land and sea overcame the Union defense and recovered Galveston on January 1, 1863. Three hundred Union soldiers were taken prisoner, and four vessels were captured. A Union blockade patrol also had entered Sabine Pass, and now in January, the Texans also reopened that outlet. Therefore in June 1863, General Magruder could boast that "Texas throughout the broad extent of her vast territory is still free from the presence of the enemy," yet he felt some misgivings because "the people seem to have lost all apprehension for the future and to have been living in a fancied state of security."

A turn in the fortunes of Texas came in 1863 as a result of the fall of Vicksburg, Confederate stronghold on the Mississippi River, and the election of a conservative governor in Texas. First came the severing of the Confederacy at the Mississippi by the relentless campaign of General Ulysses S. Grant. That left the western states to their own resources and interrupted their commerce with the main body of the Confederacy. Immediately General E. Kirby Smith, commander of the Trans-Mississippi Department, called a conference of the four governors at Marshall, Texas, on August 15. They reorganized the Department under several of its own administrative bureaus.

Pendleton Murrah, an advocate of states' rights, was inaugurated as governor of Texas on November 5, 1863. He found himself denuded of powers by the centralization of authority in the military and embarked upon a program of resistance against encroachment upon the rights theoretically reserved to the states. The cause of states' rights, which had disrupted the Union, was arising now as an impediment to the efficient functioning of the Confederacy. Murrah crippled the operation of the Southern conscription laws by giving precedence to service in the state units and by refusing to permit the conversion of those forces to Confederate service. He yielded to General Magruder on that issue in 1864, but he then found that the state militia was inadequate for maintaining order. Robberies, murders, and other outrages became numerous, and the planters in eastern Texas feared a Negro uprising. Fear and confusion damaged morale; desertions became excessively numerous and further reduced offensive strength.

After 1863, Texas had to revert to a strictly defensive role. General Smith sounded the alarm in September of that year; "Your homes are now in peril. Vigorous efforts on your part can only save portions of your State from invasion. You should contest the advance of the enemy at every thicket, gulley and stream." His alarm was occasioned by a major thrust which then was aimed at the heart of Texas. General N. P. Banks and Admiral David G. Farragut had assembled a fleet of four gunboats and several transport ships carrying over five thousand troops for an attack in Sabine Pass on September 8. With the assistance of only two gunboats, about fifty Confederates at the fort, commanded by Lieutenant Dick Dowling, repulsed the entire expedition and took over three hundred prisoners. President Jefferson Davis awarded the defenders unique silver medals for this display of gallantry in the face of extreme odds.

The Texans were less successful against the next assault. This time the Union objective was Brownsville. The naval blockade could not be extended to the mouth of the Rio Grande, because it was an international river; yet Matomoros on the Mexican side had become a vital center of Confederate commerce. Only by occupying the north bank of that river could the trade be intercepted. Therefore, with a combined sea and land expedition of six thousand men, General Banks landed at the mouth of the river on November 1, 1863, and soon occupied Aransas Pass, Indianola, Corpus Christi, and Brownsville. This tightened the blockade.

In the spring of 1864, a strong fleet of gunboats and twenty-five thousand seasoned men under the command of General Banks advanced up the Red River in Louisiana in an effort to humble Texas by an overwhelming inland campaign. Desperately General Smith mustered all the strength he could command, even by filling some of the companies with boys and old men. Even so, the four states could gather only about eleven thousand effectives for interception of this invasion. Nevertheless the Confederates, commanded by General Richard Taylor, met and thoroughly defeated the Union Army at Mansfield, Louisiana, on April 8. Banks won a battle the next day at Pleasant

Hill, but the losses suffered in the first clash made it necessary for him to give up. He abandoned this ambitious campaign without ever having crossed into Texas.

A little later, or in July, 1864, Colonel Ford forced the evacuation of Brownsville by the Union garrison which Banks had posted in that city. The Texans may have lost ignobly in New Mexico, but they had also fended off all threatened invasions. Their land might have remained clear of occupation in any part, if it had not been for a peculiar reversal suffered at the hands of the erstwhile bandit chieftain, Juan N. Cortina. This setback came as the climax in a long and involved drama which can only be outlined here.

Mexico also was absorbed in its own domestic conflict at the time of the outbreak of the Civil War in the United States. At that time Benito Juárez, an Indian reformer, had recently been installed in the presidency; but soon Emperor Louis Napoleon of France sent an army ostensibly for collection of debts owed to French citizens. Instead, the invaders drove Juárez out of Mexico City and installed Maximilian as emperor. Only the conservative faction supported Maximilian; the liberals rallied around Juárez, who established his headquarters in the city now bearing his name, across the river from El Paso. The Confederacy, depending upon Mexican trade and seeking a French alliance, recognized Maximilian, whereas the Northerners regarded Juárez with favor, because he was striving to liberate Mexican Indians while they were fighting to free Southern Negroes.

DISTRESS IN TEXAS

Before the beginning of the war Cortina, outlaw leader and Robin Hood of the Spanish Americans in Texas, had been vanquished from his homeland by the Rangers. Presently he joined forces with Juárez, became a general in his army and the governor of the Mexican state of Tamaulipas. As a long-standing enemy of the Texans, he assumed that the Union would accept him as an ally. Therefore, after the Texans had ousted the Union garrisons from the principal posts in the Rio Grande valley, Cortina led his army across the Border, occupied Brownsville in the name of the United States, and sent news of his victory to the Federal garrison at Santiago Brazos, near the mouth of the river. By this odd set of circumstances, Brownsville was the only city in Texas remaining in Union possession when the war came to an end in the East.

A detachment of Union soldiers started inland for reoccupation of Brownsville, but on May 13, 1865, Colonel Ford met and defeated them at Palmito Ranch. From his prisoners, he learned that General Robert E. Lee, Confederate commander, had already surrendered to General Ulysses S. Grant. This skirmish at Palmito, occurring over a month after the termination of hostilities in the East, was the final "battle" of the Civil War.

When the war came to an end, generals Smith and Magruder were reluctant to quit. Texas still had sixteen thousand troops under arms, and the three remaining states in the Department could count thirty thousand. The Union had about seventy thousand in scattered localities to the northeast; yet the undaunted General Smith still was determined to "secure to our country terms which a proud people can with honor accept." However, the soldiers were weary and disheartened, many were deserting, and all of Texas was in confusion. The governors of the three unconquered states met again in Marshall, Texas, in an effort to salvage whatever they could before the collapse became complete. They requested that the Union recognize the existing state governments, and when that overture was rejected, they tried in vain to concentrate their forces at Houston for a final stand. However, many of the soldiers already had decided for themselves that the war was over and were returning to their homes. On June 2, General Smith finally surrendered the Trans-Mississippi Department. He transferred all Confederate property to the Union and obtained paroles for his eighteen thousand soldiers, the remnant of a formerly proud and determined army.

In the final debacle, economic stress had been the decisive factor. Union control of the lower Rio Grande, combined with the blockade, had left open only Eagle Pass for the shipping of cotton to Mexico, and the cost of marketing it by that roundabout route consumed one-half of the receipts. The interruption of transportation across the Mississippi also ruined Texas commerce after 1863, and near the end of the war even local transportation broke down amid the prevailing confusion.

Financial failure also contributed to the distress in Texas. A market had been found for only one tenth of a bond issue of two million dollars authorized in December, 1863. Thereafter the state treasury accumulated Confederate currency, which depreciated until a dollar was worth only two or three cents. At the end of the war the state had a balance of over three million dollars on the books, but only fifteen thousand of that amount was represented by good, sound specie, and by that time the public debt had grown to eight million dollars.

Heavy taxation and the impressment of supplies also caused distress and dissension. When generous donations were no longer forthcoming, as in the first year, Confederate agents impressed the planters' mules and horses, as well as their implements, clothing, and provisions. They made remuneration in Confederate currency at a schedule of prices very low in contrast to the inflated values then prevalent. Along with this draining away of their means of sustenance, the Texans also saw the income from their labor evaporating, due to the heavy burden of taxation. In four years they paid out over eight million dollars in taxes levied by their state and thirty-seven million dollars collected by the Confederacy.

Under the stress of war a daily ordeal of personal privations was borne heroically by most Texans. Salt, clothing, and manufactured wares became scarce, and a critical shortage of medical supplies caused preventable suffering. A shortage of newsprint curtailed publishing; for example, the Galveston *News* shrank to the size of a handbill, printed on wrapping paper. The deficiencies were numerous, but personal hardships were not the sole cause of defeat. They might have been endured longer if general economic collapse had not followed upon loss of the war in the East. The Texans had not failed in military actions within their own state. Yet to be endured, however, was the ordeal of Reconstruction, which was designed to effect humiliation as a requisite for ultimate reunion.

END OF THE WAR

Upon the termination of the military conflict, a respected Texan and former congressman, A. J. Hamilton, was appointed provisional governor, representing the Union. He would be responsible for the effectuation of President Andrew Johnson's proclamation of June 19, renouncing all acts of the state government since secession, declaring the Negroes free, and paroling all soldiers of the Confederate units in Texas. He was supported by Union troops under the command of General Gordon Granger, whose orders informed him suggestively that there was "not a very wholesome state of affairs in Texas," because the citizens were "generally disposed to be ugly."

At this juncture, relations with Mexico diverted the attention of the Union command. When General Philip Sheridan, Department commander, arrived in Brownsville that June, he found that Confederate soldiers and equipment were being transported across the Rio Grande for support of Maximilian's Empire. He estimated that two thousand soldiers and citizens already had crossed over and added that "Everything on wheels had been run across to the Mexican side." Among the emigrants were many eminent Confederates, including Ex-Governor Murrah and generals Smith and Magruder.

With fresh aid from Texas, the Imperialists were gaining the advantage in the northern states of Mexico, and the ragged army of Juárez was losing ground. Apparently the Confederates who had lost a war north of the Border might win one south of it, and Sheridan wanted to follow them across and chase them out of Mexico. The Department of State in Washington, however, restrained the impetuous Sheridan pending the outcome of negotiations with Napoleon. Even so, Sheridan resorted to some hostile demonstrations, as if he were going to join Juárez, and that frightened the Imperialists enough to cause their withdrawal from Matamoros to Monterrey. Partly in response to pressure from the United States, Napoleon withdrew his troops which had been supporting Maximilian. Then the Empire collapsed and Juárez resumed his presidency in Mexico City in 1867. Finally the North could rest content that a friendly government had been restored in Mexico.

PRESIDENTIAL RECONSTRUCTION

Meanwhile in the era known as "Presidential Reconstruction" manifold problems awaited solution. Because there were not enough Union troops to watch the Border and keep order, too, General Sheridan issued an order on June 20, 1865, holding local neighborhoods responsible for guerrilla bands. Then confusion arose about the ownership of cotton which was piling up at piers and warehouses and awaiting a market. Even more serious was the plight of three hundred thousand Negroes who had been proclaimed free and were roaming about the countryside, crowding into the cities, and swamping the facilities of the newly created Freedman's Bureau. In an effort to control them, the army of occupation devised a contract plan for their return to the plantations, but vagrancy continued.

Governor Hamilton appointed new state officers, issued a revised schedule of taxes, declared invalid all laws passed since the date of secession, and called an election for the naming of delegates to a state constitutional convention. On August 19 registration of voters — only those loyal to the Union — began but proceeded slowly thenceforth due to local animosities. When finally a majority of citizens had become legally qualified to vote, the election was called for January, 1866.

The constitutional convention which met on February 7 divided into conservative and radical factions. The latter embraced the doctrine of *ab initio*, a conviction that secession could not be declared void because it had been invalid from the beginning. A prolonged debate arose, therefore, over the wording of a statement about secession. The same factions also clashed over the disposition of the war debt, the validity of recently enacted laws, and the future status of the Negroes. Finally the delegates drafted articles which annulled secession, established a board to audit the debt and determine what part should be repudiated, and pronounced the Negroes free by force of arms, with a status nearly equal to that of the whites. New state officers would be selected at a special election in July, and at that time the constitutional amendments would also be submitted to the electorate for ratification.

In the special election the voters chose as governor a conservative, J. W. Throckmorton, and approved the changes in the state constitution by a very narrow margin. Then President Andrew Johnson proclaimed that the insurrection in Texas was ended, and the citizens believed that their state had been restored to the Union.

Presuming that they were beyond further military molestation, the proud Conservatives reasserted themselves. In the legislature they chose as United States senators two Texans who could not take the "iron-clad oath" that they had not aided the Confederacy. The Conservatives tabled the proposed Thirteenth Amendment to the Constitution of the United States, freeing the Negroes from slavery, and rejected outright the Fourteenth, which would give the Negroes citizenship. Moreover, they adopted statutes on vagrancy, labor contracts, and apprenticeship much like those of other southern states, but less stringent. Nevertheless in that new code certainly the Abolitionists in the North would condemn the requirements that laborers should not leave home without permission and that they must be "obedient and respectful."

Northerners began to hear reports about disorder and disobedience in Texas. As military and civilian authorities came into conflict, riots and head-on clashes occurred in some localities, especially where the Union Army had posted companies of Negro soldiers. Governor Throckmorton obtained the removal of garrisons from some of the population centers, urged all citizens to respect the rights of the freedmen, and demanded strict enforcement of the law by state officers. Even so, he still failed to get the Freedman's Bureau and the Army administrators to respect his jurisdiction, and this conflict encouraged a continuation of disorder.

RADICAL RULE

Meanwhile in Washington the Radical Republicans had gained control of the Congress. In order to assure their political control, they needed to capture the South for their party. To achieve that, they would have to win the Negro vote, which would require the elimination of conservative restrictions in the South. In effect, they would have to repudiate President Johnson's easy Presidential Reconstruction. Therefore they refused to seat in Congress those conservative representatives and senators recently elected in Texas and other Southern states. They would require, instead, that Reconstruction be started all over again.

The requirements for redoing the process "satisfactorily" were embodied in the Congressional Reconstruction Act adopted on March 2, 1867. This act declared the existing state governments illegal, called for new elections, made mandatory the acceptance of Negro suffrage, required ratification of the Fourteenth Amendment by the new legislatures, and divided the South into five military districts for enforcement of the new procedure. Texas was included in the Fifth Military District, commanded by General Sheridan. He appointed General Charles Griffin as state commander.

The new military boss, Griffin, immediately demanded that Throckmorton pardon over two hundred convicts in the penitentiary, which the governor refused to do. Clashes ensued over the eligibility of persons for jury duty and efforts to restrict the franchise. On July 30, therefore, Sheridan removed Throckmorton from office because he was "an impediment to reconstruction." As provisional governor the new appointee was E. M. Pease, a former governor and one of the more tactful of the Texas Radicals. He obtained the confidence of the military officers without yielding to them subserviently. Therefore he succeeded in obtaining a relaxation in the military policy, so that in the registration of voters the simple "iron-clad oath" was followed instead of the extra-legal set of involved instructions which General Griffin had tried to impose upon Throckmorton. The registration qualified for the franchise about sixty thousand whites and fifty thousand Negroes, and disqualified only about ten thousand former Confederates. The next step would be the election of delegates, in February of 1868, for a second constitutional convention.

As election time approached, the Loyal Union League, as the tool of the Radical Republicans, strove by threats and promises to influence the Negroes and secure their votes. Conservative Democrats retaliated in kind. They organized conclaves of the Ku Klux Klan and borrowed the frightening tactics of that secret society without formally becoming affiliated with the order in other Southern states. The Klan's white-clad horsemen rode through the settlements at night in order to play upon the superstition of the Negroes and frighten them into submission. Sometimes overzealous Klansmen resorted to violence and bloodshed.

In the election fifty-six thousand votes were divided four to one in favor of the convention. Nine Negroes were elected as delegates. When the convention convened at Austin on June 1, 1868, it split into radical and conservative factions, but this time nearly all were Republicans and the division was within the ranks of that party. Once more the *ab initio* doctrine provoked a prolonged debate, so that the convention continued in session all summer and reconvened in December.

The Radicals in the convention made an issue of lawlessness and disorder, which they blamed upon the Conservatives. A special committee dealing with that issue alleged that about five hundred Negroes and as many whites had been killed in the preceding three years. Then a new issue was injected when the Radicals proposed that Texas be divided into two or three states, but that was voted down. In December the delegates finally drafted a new constitution. In it a highly centralized state government was outlined, all adult males not disqualified were given the franchise, and nullification and secession were declared heretical. Especially notable were the provisions for improvement of public education. All receipts from the sale of state lands would be deposited in a school fund for the education of all children from the age of six to eighteen without discrimination as to color or race. In addition, a poll tax was exacted for support of the schools.

The Convention of 1868 had drafted a reasonably conservative constitution, which the Radicals tried to discredit. Failing in that they resorted to intimidation and manipulation in an effort to win the next election. The state commander, General J. J. Reynolds, who had succeeded General Griffin, packed the election boards with Radicals, and the Loyal Union League swung the Negro vote. As a result, the Radicals won control of both houses of the legislature and elected by a narrow margin a Radical Republican governor, E. J. Davis. The new legislature ratified the Thirteenth, Fourteenth, and Fifteenth amendments and selected two senators who would be acceptable to the Radicals in Washington. Therefore on March 30, 1870, President Grant signed the act readmitting Texas, the next to the last of the seceded states to be restored to the Union.

Although political Reconstruction presumably was completed in 1870, the Texans yet had to endure a period of Radical rule under the domination of extremists in the legislature. They arrested and excluded a few Conservative members, and the House removed its presiding officer, Ira H. Evans, because he opposed some of the Radical measures. With all restraints removed, they gave the governor power to impose martial law, authorized him to fill several new offices with Radical bureaucrats, chartered many projected railroads, and granted the railway promoters state lands so generously that soon the public domain of Texas had nearly vanished. Even so, they refrained from resorting to such lavish extravagance as was experienced under "carpet-bag" rule in some of the other Southern states in those years. Considerable progress was made in the building of state roads, in the promotion of railway construction, and in the developing of a creditable system of public schools.

Under Radical rule the Texans complained chiefly about the abuse of martial law. A police force comprised of ill-tempered ruffians, including many vindictive Negroes, handled civilians rudely and sometimes killed prisoners before they could be brought to trial. The participation of Negroes in some of the sordid incidents aroused a bitter race hatred. In one such affair, when whites became threatening after a Negro policeman had killed a citizen, Governor Davis declared martial law in Freestone and Limestone counties and levied a special tax to pay the cost of imposing an unnecessary and bitterly resented surveillance upon the citizens.

Resentment against the roughshod tactics of state police and militia, as well as the unpopularity of much of the Radical legislative program, helped the Democrats gain ground. In 1871, delegates from ninety-four counties, assembling in Austin, adopted resolutions condemning the extravagance of the state administration. In the following year Horace Greeley, Democratic nominee for the presidency, received twenty thousand more votes in Texas than did President Grant, the Republican candidate. In that election the Democrats in Texas recaptured all state seats in congress and regained control in the state legislature. Moreover, the Democratic gubernatorial candidate, Richard Coke, defeated Davis by a margin of two to one.

The banished Republicans challenged the constitutionality of the revised election code, and while a court opinion was pending, Davis tried to prevent the convening of the newly elected Democratic legislature. In January, 1872, Davis and his faction occupied the lower floor of the state house, protected by a company of Negro soldiers, while the legislature met on the second floor, guarded by the state militia. Finally Davis conceded, Radical rule collapsed, and the legislature repealed some of the extreme statutes of the Radical regime. As C. W. Ramsdell summed it up, "Reconstruction had left the pyramid on its apex; it must be placed upon its base again."

At last Texas was relieved of the more odious features of political Reconstruction. Meanwhile, economic recovery also had been partially achieved. With the great plantations partitioned, the wealthy planters no longer were dominant. The Negroes were back at work under a sharecrop system, and cotton production, which in the late 1860s had slumped below four thousand bales annually, climbed above a half million bales in 1873. Immigrants were pouring in, new industries were arising, and railroads were being built.

In one respect, however, Reconstruction remained unfinished. The suddenly liberated Negroes had been forced once more into subjugation of a different kind. Although they no longer were mere chattel, they emerged only as second-class citizens—a minority people. In time the Texans of both races would seek ways to effect gradually the social reconstruction of their state.

13
INDIANS SUBDUED

My heart is filled with joy when I see you here, as the brooks fill with water when the snows melt in the spring; and I feel glad as the ponies do when the fresh grass starts in the beginning of the year.... My people have never first drawn a bow or fired a gun against the whites.... It was you who sent out the first soldier and we who sent out the second.... You said that you wanted to put us upon a reservation, to build us houses and make us medicine lodges. I do not want them. I was born upon the prairie, where the wind blew free and there was nothing to break the light of the sun.... I want to die there and not within walls....

When I was at Washington, the Great Father told me all the Comanche land was ours, and that no one should hinder us living upon it. So, why do you ask us to leave the rivers, and the sun, and the wind, and live in homes?

Chief Ten Bears, quoted in William H. Leckie, The Military Conquest of the Southern Plains *(Norman, Okla., 1963), pp. 60-61.*

For several years after the South and North concluded their conflict at Appomattox Court House, respite from the turmoil and bloodshed of warfare was denied to the people of the Southwest. Indian wars devolved from the civil conflict, when once more the White Man's quarrel encouraged the Red Man to resort to violence in a final and desperate effort to regain primitive freedom.

CONFLICTING POLICIES

On the frontier, responsibility for Indian affairs was divided. The soldiers received their orders from the War Department in Washington, whereas the Indian agencies were under the jurisdiction of the Department of the Interior. Theoretically, the one was to supplement the other, each having its own realm of responsibility. Sometimes that was true, but more often than not the procedures and policies of dual authority came into conflict. To make matters worse, the officials of both departments were dealing with bewildered aborigines, who in desperation often resorted to defiance and duplicity. A tribe might go forth raiding and pillaging in the summer, only to return to the agency in the fall, deny their crimes, profess peace, and beg for government rations for subsistence through the winter.

Distrust and divided responsibilities were encumbered further by indecision and uncertainty as to the national Indian policy. There were several policies to choose from and each had its advocates. Spaniards sought *assimilation* as their original objective: they would convert the Indian, give him some elementary instruction, and absorb him into Spanish society. Much of the time this policy was pursued with some success in the missions, especially in those established among the more highly cultured, sedentary Pueblos. Very few of these missions had survived into the Territorial Period, and then there were others to take up the cause. Eastern churchmen and people of humanitarian inclination became advocates of gradual assimila-

tion. At the time of the Civil War, though they were in the minority, they were gaining in influence. They had the support of some of the more conscientious Indian agents.

Toward the nomadic tribes, which had not responded to the Spanish humanitarian impulse, the Spaniards adopted a policy of *retaliation.* After the Indians had pillaged a settlement, the colonists would go forth and perpetrate acts of retribution upon the camps of the Indians. Indians stole white children for bartering into slavery, and the white man made slaves of Indian captives. In the endless conflict, no one could remember which side had committed the first depredation, and each accused the other. This state of affairs prevailed when the United States acquired the Borderlands, and the Indian agents perceived immediately that a policy of retaliation would never serve as a lasting solution; yet pursuit of the practice prevailed for a long time afterward.

Dealing with an Indian tribe as a *foreign nation* was the traditional Anglo-American policy, which had been inherited from English colonial days. Trade, trouble, war, and treaty, then repeat the cycle—that was the contemporary practice among nations, and wherever the Indians were organized under a chief who could be dealt with, this practice was invoked. Little thought was given at first to the inconsistency of recognizing as a foreign nation a group of persons who were residing upon land claimed by the nation itself. By the time of the Civil War this inconsistency had become more bothersome, especially when it was Americans who wanted the land.

Extermination was the desperate policy of suffering frontiersmen and militant soldiers for bringing an end to the futile treaty-making and the endless retaliations. They regarded the Indians as a hopeless, dangerous obstacle; the Indians were not making good use of American resources and they could not be assimilated. This policy was supported by merchants and ranchers who had found Army contracts quite profitable and wanted the military posts maintained and expanded. This faction was to come into its heyday for a period following the Civil War.

Simultaneously another policy, *segregation*, had been introduced on a trial basis. As wards of the government, a tribe of Indians would be given its own tract of land and would be allowed to retain its own political organization and social customs. Relations of the white man with the Indians would be restricted to traders and missionaries licensed by Indian agents.

The segregation policy was conceived in the 1820s, when it appeared that the Indians could have the "Great American Desert" lying west of the one hundredth meridian, because white frontiersmen were not expected ever to occupy that region. From 1825 to 1835 eastern tribes were moved west to one big reservation beyond that line. Then as frontiersmen began crossing the Great Plains, steps were taken to break up the one big reservation into many smaller ones. This was done by continued resort to treaties promising payment of annuities, under the old foreign nation policy and without much regard for the possibilities of ultimate assimilation.

This practice found stanch supporters among the Indian traders, whose commerce was more profitable when the Indians were at peace and receiving government annuities. Before the Civil War experimentation with small reservations had been undertaken with only spotted success in Texas, New Mexico, and California.

ROUNDUP IN NEW MEXICO

When Carleton and the California Column arrived in New Mexico in 1862, the segregation policy was in vogue, that is, officially; but New Mexicans were pursuing the practice of retaliation. The Apaches, Comanches, and Navajos were doing more damage than the Confederates had in their invasion, and companies of volunteers were resorting to periodic and rather ineffectual punitive action.

Obviously the first requirement would be to halt the retaliatory raids conducted by private expeditions, but to justify

this, the Army would have to demonstrate that it was able to cope with the marauders. When Carleton ordered a campaign against the Mescalero Apaches in the southeastern part of the territory, he gave Colonel Kit Carson explicit instructions:

This making of treaties for them to break whenever they have an interest in breaking them will not be done any more. . . . All Indian men of that tribe are to be killed whenever and wherever you can find them. . . . If the Indians send in a flag and desire to treat for peace, say to the bearer . . .

that you are there to kill them wherever you can find them; that if they beg for peace, their chiefs must come to Santa Fe to have a talk there.[1]

While Carson and his men rounded up the Mescaleros and moved those of peaceable inclinations to Fort Stanton in the winter of 1862–1863, General John R. West campaigned against the Gila Apaches west of Mesilla. Soon the settlers found it safe again to resume farming around Fort Stanton and the miners to return to work in the upper Gila country.

In that same winter Colonel J. Francisco Chávez prepared at Fort Wingate for an assault upon the previously invincible Navajos. He proclaimed July 20, 1863, as the time limit for all of that tribe to come to terms. Thereafter he vowed that "Every Navajo that is seen will be considered as a hostile and treated accordingly."

In the summer of 1863, Carson marched his command of seven hundred troops into the heart of the Navajo country and built Fort Canby to serve as a supply depot. As allies in his forthcoming campaign, Carson enlisted the Ute Indians, who were traditional enemies of the Navajos. Then he confiscated Navajo corn and livestock in order to starve the tribe into submission. The climax came in the following January, when Carson's command marched into Cañon de Chelly, the stronghold of the Navajos, and returned with hundreds of ragged, forlorn prisoners. At Fort Canby, by March 1, twenty-four hundred of the "pitiable creatures" had been rounded up.

Because the Navajo country seemed

barren and unproductive, Carleton conceived a plan for resettling these Indians on more fertile land in pursuit of the segregation policy previously advocated by Neighbors, Steck, and Beale. At Fort Sumner he selected a tract forty miles square, known as Bosque Redondo. He believed that there they would have "arable land enough for all the Indians of this family," and that they would have little opportunity for "lateral contact with settlers." In short, he hoped to convert a seminomadic people into settled but isolated farmers. First he had four hundred of the subdued Mescalero Apaches moved to this reservation, and then he arranged for the dejected Navajos to be marched across the country to join the Apaches. As additional hostiles were rounded up, they, too, endured the forced march over the long trail. Over eight thousand Navajos were confined in the Bosque Redondo by the end of the year 1864.

Carleton boasted that his segregation policy was working successfully, and those officials who visited the Bosque, with Carleton as their guide and informer, also praised his achievements. However, things were not going so well. Because Apaches and Navajos were on bad terms, when the former found themselves greatly outnumbered by unwelcome neighbors, they stole away from the reservation and resumed their pillaging. The Navajos were traditionally pastoral nomads, unaccustomed to sedentary agricultural work; yet the soldiers were under orders to teach them farming methods—a subject in which the soldiers were bad tutors. Moreover, the supply of water for irrigation was inadequate for the sustenance of such large numbers. There-

[1] *War of the Rebellion* (1886), I, p. 579.

fore the Army had to distribute food and provisions, which cost dearly whether purchased locally or hauled in from a distance. The annual outlay ran in the neighborhood of one and a half million dollars. Soon the residents of neighboring towns were complaining that Indians—whom they thought to be Navajos absent without leave from the Bosque—were plundering their fields and stealing their cattle. Moreover, the Navajos themselves were suffering from an unanticipated scourge. With the eastern border of the reservation poorly guarded, these encamped Indians became "sitting ducks" for raids by their traditional enemies, the wild Comanche Indians of the Staked Plain.

A general reaction against Carleton's Indian policy and his martial law spread throughout the territory. Dr. Michael Steck, Superintendent of Indian affairs in New Mexico, disclaimed responsibility for this reservation, which he contended was in reality a concentration camp. The military authorities, he said, had created it; therefore they should be held responsible for the welfare of the Indians there. Although Steck was removed as superintendent, his successor, A. B. Norton, was equally outspoken in behalf of the Navajos. He pleaded: "Let them go back where they can have good cool water to drink, wood aplenty to keep them from freezing to death, and where the soil will produce something for them to eat." Realization that this experiment was a failure finally came through to Washington. In October, 1866, the War Department removed Carleton as commander of this department, and four months later the military relinquished responsibility for supervision of the captive Navajos. Superintendent Norton assumed the burden reluctantly, for the Department of the Interior allowed him only two hundred thousand dollars a year for the sustenance of the seven thousand Navajos at Bosque Redondo, or about ten cents a day for each Indian.

THE PEACE POLICY

The plight of the Navajos and other tribes stirred the humanitarian disposition of Easterners, who obtained the creation of a "Peace Commission" from Congress in 1866. Originally the Commission was comprised of four prominent civilians, including N. G. Taylor, Commissioner of Indian Affairs. This group had instructions to remove, if possible, the causes of the Indian wars in the West; and that in itself was a formidable task, which might require going clear back to Columbus. The charge to the Commission was further complicated by the provision that in removing the causes, the security of the border settlements must not be sacrificed. The method proposed was, in essence, the segregation idea. The Indians should be induced to settle as farmers on two large reservations, one in the Indian Territory (Oklahoma) and the other in the Dakota Territory to the north. The Commission had an appropriation of a half of a million dollars for the execution of this plan.

Within a year the work of the Commission became handicapped by the appointment of four more members—four generals—by President Andrew

Johnson. Among those added was General William Tecumseh Sherman of Civil War fame, now the commander of the Division of Missouri. The generals would let the humanitarians try out their plan, but only briefly. Whenever a hostile action occurred, they would say "I told you so," and then they had sufficient strength on the Commission to undermine its work and resort to their policy of extermination.

When members of the Commission met with representatives of five plains tribes at Medicine Lodge in Kansas, in October of 1867, the Indians accepted reservations in Indian Territory. Among them were the Kiowas and Comanches, who had long been devastating western Texas and eastern New Mexico. However, those Indians were nomads whose braves hunted, raided, and defended their tribe, while the squaws did the work of the camp. As soon as they learned that they were expected to accept a sedentary existence and take up farming, they rebelled against doing "squaw's work." When they again went forth upon their destructive forays, the generals on the Commission took over. The generals condemned the peace policy of the civilian members and organized a punitive campaign under the command of General Sheridan. After a few battles he concluded that he had taught the Indians a lesson; yet some of the bands that had not been apprehended were committing more atrocities at that very time.

While the Commission was seeking reform, and the victorious Republicans were liberating Negroes from bondage, the problem of Indian slavery came before the Congress. Approximately six hundred Indians, predominantly Apache, who had been taken as captives in punitive campaigns, were being held as servants by prominent families in New Mexico. Therefore, in 1867, the Congress passed a law abolishing "peonage," and the next year the Congress authorized General Sherman to enforce the act. J. Francisco Chávez, the territorial delegate to Washington, himself a holder of numerous Indians in bondage, protested that this act violated a long-standing tradition, and he was supported by Governor Connelly and General Carleton; consequently enforcement of the law was long delayed.

Two members of the Peace Commission, S. F. Tappan and General Sherman, visited the Navajo concentration at Fort Sumner. They concluded that retention of that tribe there any longer was a "crime" and that the Navajos should be permitted to return to their homeland. On June 1, 1868, the Navajos happily accepted a treaty giving them a large reservation in northwestern New Mexico and northeastern Arizona. In return for their agreement to keep the peace, the government would establish an Indian agency and provide goats, sheep, seeds, implements, and goods valued at five dollars for each Indian annually for ten years. The government, in addition, would establish a school for every group of thirty children between the ages of six and sixteen, with anticipation that this benevolence would be welcomed.

THE LONG WALK

The Navajos at last would be permitted to trek homeward. They formed a procession ten miles long as they traveled through Albuquerque and on westward to a newly built military post, Fort Wingate. Their joy upon being released was dampened considerably when they first saw the devastation wrought in their native land by the military campaign which had crushed them four years previously. But, hopefully, they spread out to rebuild their homes and reclaim their fields and pastures.

Neighbors of the Navajos had little cause for complaint about their conduct after these formerly troublesome Indians had been resettled. Some small bands eager for vengeance left the reservation to fight the Comanches out on the Staked Plain, and a few hunters did raid some white settlements in Utah, but without doing much harm. Then Jacob Hamlin, a Mormon missionary visited with the Navajo chiefs and persuaded them to restrain their young warriors. In 1872, the Indian agent selected one hundred trustworthy Navajo men and made policemen of them. They succeeded in keeping order much better than any white policemen could have done, and within a year the thieving and other troubles around the fringe of the reservation had ceased.

Previously, in 1869, the flock of sheep promised by the government had arrived. Because their efforts to farm their arid land had not been very productive, more and more of the Navajos turned to the grazing of sheep. For that the land was well suited, and as they built up their flocks they were pursuing an occupation more to their liking and one which offered them some security at their meagre level of subsistence.

In the 1880s the Navajos were grazing over a million sheep and were owners of thirty thousand horses. Because the population was increasing more rapidly than their means of subsistence, they needed more land and water. In 1878, 1880, and 1884 the government made large additions to their reservation until it surrounded one set aside for the Hopi Indians in northeastern Arizona. By 1885, white settlers had taken up land around the reservation, so that there was no room for further expansion.

When the government opened boarding schools on the reservation, only a few Navajo children attended. Their parents did not want to send their offspring so far away from home, nor did they want their children to learn the strange ways of the white man. As a result the government did not fulfill its treaty obligation to establish a school for every thirty Navajo children. At the time that failure was not much noticed or lamented, but later it would have a retarding effect. In some localities, meanwhile, Protestants and Catholics had opened some good mission schools, and both helped to ameliorate the deficiency in educational facilities. By the end of the century the Navajos were a peaceful people, twice as numerous as they had been when they returned from Bosque Redondo, and thus, soon to become the largest of the surviving tribes.

OTHER CONCESSIONS

During those years another numerous family in New Mexico, the Pueblo Indians, had remained at peace. Shortly after the American occupation they had received confirmation of their old Spanish land grants. On them these Indians raised crops in the fields close to their villages and grazed sheep and cattle on the grasslands farther away. Because they were thrifty and industrious, the products of their labor provided a fairly good subsistence for their eight thousand people.

In 1868, the territorial assembly granted the Pueblos the privileges of citizenship, which in effect also made them citizens of the United States. Because they owned their community lands, it could not be said that they were living on government reservations. But they did have the assistance of a government Indian agency established in Albuquerque for their benefit, and by 1885 the government was aiding in the maintenance of three schools for Pueblo children. Meanwhile, in 1879, the War Department had opened an Indian school at Carlisle in Pennsylvania, and within five years nearly a hundred Pueblo youth were enrolled in this school. By 1890, Protestant and Catholic churches were also maintaining mission schools in ten of the pueblos. Although these Indians were still rather segregated in their agricultural communities, they were being prepared gradually for ultimate assimilation.

During the Civil War the Ute Indians residing in northern New Mexico had been kept peaceable most of the time by gifts of food distributed at two Indian agencies, Abiquiú and Cimarrón. In 1863, the Indian agent made a treaty with the Utes, granting them a reservation in southwestern Colorado; but they failed to move there. Another treaty, in 1868, offered them cash annuities and gifts of cattle and money if they would move. Some bands did, but others did not. Finally, in 1874, the government agreed to pay the Ute chief, Ouray, a salary of one thousand dollars a year for ten years and promised the tribe twenty-five thousand dollars annually for maintenance of a Ute agency in Colorado. Soon the remaining Utes joined the others on the reservation.

Then there were the Mescalero Apaches who had run away from Bosque Redondo when the Navajos had been brought there in 1864. The Army rounded up some of those fugitives and confined them at Fort Stanton in 1869. Four years later they accepted a reservation nearby, on the east slopes of the Sacramento Mountains. Even so, some of the Mescaleros would leave the reservation rather regularly and steal food and cattle. The marauding increased after other Apaches were brought to this reservation from west of the Rio Grande in 1879. Then the soldiers confiscated the horses and guns of these Indians. This forced them to settle down as farmers and, when they did, the government opened a school on their reservation. There were a few exceptions. Victorio and a band of renegades remained at large and terrified the countryside, except for a brief period when they were contained on a reservation in Arizona. Finally American and Mexican soldiers combined in a relentless manhunt along the Border and it was the Mexican contingent which killed Victorio and eighty-six of his warriors in October of 1880.

Back in 1874 a treaty had granted the Jicarilla Apaches of northern New Mexico a reservation along the San Juan River to the east of the Navajo lands. The government offered these Indians five thousand dollars a year for five years as annuities and thirty thousand a year for ten years for maintenance of schools, but the Indians would not move from the Indian agencies in the mountains to the valley land. The white settlers objected because they, too, wanted that land along the river.

In 1880, five Jicarilla chiefs accepted a tribal reservation west of Abiquiú. There the seven hundred and fifty people of this tribe were content, but then white settlers began agitating for possession of that desirable land. Therefore, in 1883 the government abrogated the previous treaty and removed the Indians to the Mescalero reservation at Fort Stanton. So far from their homeland the Jicarillas became so dejected that in desperation they returned to the northern mountains without permission. They begged the Indian bureau for the return of their former lands until finally, in 1887, the government gave them back their former reservation.

In California, in the 1850s, many of the displaced Mission Indians had been allotted to farmers as laborers, and for others a few small reservations had been founded. In 1864, Congress created one superintendency of Indian affairs for the state, instead of two. The same act provided for the maintenance of four reservations under the super-

vision of four Indian agents. The four reservations were Hoopa Valley, Round Valley, Tule River, and Smith's River. By 1867, they were serving about three thousand Indians, while California's remaining eighteen thousand were scattered about the state, mostly living as squatters on land claimed by whites. In 1868, the Congress made an appropriation of forty thousand dollars for aid to the impoverished Indians of California and by the same act abolished the Smith's River reservation.

President Ulysses S. Grant undertook some reforms in the Indian Service in 1869. He invited the various church bodies to nominate men for appointment as agents, and in many locations this resulted in the replacement of army officers and political appointees by sympathetic, devoted agents. Two years later the Congress resolved that no more treaties would be made with Indian tribes. This long overdue termination of the inconsistent "foreign nation" policy substituted for it the revised interpretation that Indians were "wards" of the federal government. Next, in California, there developed another concept. In 1873, when John G. Ames was investigating conditions among the Mission Indians, he recommended setting up a number of small reservations in which the grazing lands would belong to the tribe but with each family having its own small farm. He believed that an appropriation of one hundred and fifty thousand dollars for seed, breeding stock, and supervision would help those Indians become self-sustaining. His report quickly gained acceptance among the humanitarians. Why not give all Indians tracts of land "in severalty" and thereby lay the groundwork for ultimate assimilation into American society? Although his proposal was not adopted immediately, it was a harbinger of a reform that would be undertaken later in that century.

CONFLICT RENEWED

While officialdom was pondering the plight of the Mission Indians, attention was diverted briefly to an Indian war in another part of California. In 1864, the Modocs had been removed from the northern part of the state to the Klamath Reservation in Oregon, but they refused to stay there. Led by their chief, Captain Jack, part of the tribe continued to roam their former range near Lost River, whereupon the Army was called upon to evict them. In January, 1873, when the soldiers approached their camp, they hid themselves in the lava beds near Tule Lake.

General E. R. S. Canby, the American commander, arranged for negotiations with Captain Jack, and while the commissioners were conferring with the Modocs, some of the latter suddenly drew knives and guns and murdered Canby and the Reverend Eleazer Thomas. Then the soldiers stormed the lava beds, but to no avail. Presently the Indians were starved into submission. In October, Captain Jack and three other leaders were hanged at Fort Klamath, and the remaining Modocs were moved east to a small reservation in Indian Territory. In this campaign eighty-three American lives had been sacrificed and a half million dollars had been expended rather than concede to the Modocs the reservation that they wanted and which might have cost in the neighborhood of twenty thousand dollars.

After the troubles with the Modocs had subsided, President Grant, in 1875 and 1876, set aside fifteen small reservations in San Diego County for the Mission Indians, who thenceforth would be supervised by the Mission Agency. In 1881, Mrs. Helen Hunt Jackson wrote *A Century of Dishonor*, a book in which she portrayed quite emotionally all the injustices endured by these Indians. This book so aroused public opinion on their behalf that soon eleven schools were established and seeds and equipment for farming were provided. By 1900, the fifteen thousand surviving Mission Indians had been allotted twenty-seven small reservations and considerable headway had been made toward overcoming their former state of degradation.

Back in the Indian Territory the campaign conducted by General Sheridan in 1868 had been ineffectual and the segregation policy had been flouted by the Comanches, Kiowas, Arapahoes, and Cheyennes. Life on a reservation inevitably conflicted with their folkways, and out on the plains the near extermination of the buffalo was eliminating their means of sustenance. Consequently they resorted to pillaging of the ranches, and by 1870 reports of depredations were coming in constantly from western Texas and eastern New Mexico. Finally General Sherman made a tour of the frontier for investigation of the complaints. As if to convince him, the Indians staged raids and massacres while he was in the field, and out of them arose the unfortunate Jacksboro affair.

After gathering specific complaints from some of the settlers, General Sherman inquired at the Wichita Reserve whether any Indians had been absent recently. The Indians themselves answered his question. Chiefs Satank, Satanta, and Eagle Heart came boldly into the reservation office and admitted that they had led a destructive raid. They did it, they said, because their annuity allowances had been stolen from them and the whites were preparing to build a railroad across their hunting ground. After questioning the three chiefs further, Sherman, arresting them instead of the alleged white thieves, sent them to Jacksboro, Texas, where they were to stand trial for their crimes in a white man's court and under his laws.

While being transported southward, Satank prophesied the hour of his death, chanted his parting song, drew a concealed weapon, and was shot by his escort. In July, 1871, the other two were arraigned in court in Jacksboro. In pleading his own cause, Satanta promised that if released he would "wash out the spots of blood and make it [Texas] a white land," but if he were executed, it would "like a spark in the prairie, make big fire burn." The judge found the defendants guilty and pronounced a death sentence, but soon he became fearful of the consequences and changed the penalty to imprisonment for life.

In behalf of the two chiefs, threats of retaliation arose from several tribes, and the Plains Indians sent a delegation to Washington to plead for release of the prisoners. The Commissioner of Indian Affairs gave his assent, if the Indians would promise to desist from their pillaging of frontier settlements. As could be expected, the Texans immediately protested, but finally Governor Edmund J. Davis released Satanta and Eagle Heart with the warning that if apprehended in hostile acts they would be confined in the state penitentiary at Huntsville.

During that year while the two chiefs were in prison, the casualties from Indian depredations in Texas numbered only eighteen, but in the next year, 1874, they increased to sixty-five. For these outrages General C. C. Augur, Commander of the Department of Texas, blamed the Indians at the Fort Sill Reservation, "where they are fed by the government and officially regarded as friendly." He sent to the frontier several punitive expeditions, but the Indians were too numerous and too elusive for apprehension by the soldiers under this one command.

In 1874, the Plains Indians were ravaging the frontiers of Colorado, Kansas, New Mexico, and Texas; consequently the military launched a general offensive campaign. Lieutenant Colonel John W. Davidson operated westward from Fort Sill in Indian Territory, Colonel Nelson A. Miles moved southward from Camp Supply in that same Territory, Colonel R. S. Mackenzie worked northward from Fort Griffin in Texas, and Major William Price marched eastward from Fort Union in New Mexico. Altogether over three thousand regular soldiers were in the field, and in the course of the campaign they fought fourteen pitched battles with the desperate Indians. Incidentally, Colonel Davidson's command included six troops of the Tenth Cavalry of Negro "buffalo soldiers."

By midsummer of 1875 the Red River War, as it was called, had broken down the resistance of the Indians on the plains. The army had captured seventy-five of their chiefs, who were sentenced to prison at St. Augustine, Florida. A few years later they were paroled and permitted to rejoin their tribes; but henceforth the majority of the Indians remained on their reservations and kept the peace. Occasionally a small band of renegades crossed into Texas, committed some depredations, and caused a general alarm, but the era of ceaseless, destructive pillaging had come to an end. Under the threat of extermination, these Indians finally had been segregated from the new society that occupied their land.

CAMPAIGNS IN ARIZONA

After the Plains Indians had been pacified, one more frontier in the Southwest was still suffering from depredations. In 1863, Mangas Coloradas, an Apache chief, had surrendered voluntarily in order to demonstrate his friendly intentions; but he was murdered treacherously under circumstances never clearly explained. This so infuriated the Western Apaches that a general uprising followed. Throughout Arizona the hostile warriors plundered the stage way stations, pilfered the mines, raided the ranches, and in general terrified the populace. In a countryside with which they were quite familiar they could move elusively about in small bands through the canyons and in the recesses of the mountains. Consequently the campaigns waged against them in the 1860s had been quite ineffective, and it appeared that the whites might have to abandon Arizona.

Some of the non-Apache tribes in Arizona were also troublesome. After the Civil War most of the Yumas in the lower valley of the Colorado River were granted a reservation on the California side of the river; but two bands of them, the Yavapais and Walapais, remained in Arizona, unsettled and hostile. The Mojaves, residing in their rather remote homeland in the northwestern part of the territory, as yet had no official reservation, but they submitted to supervision by the Colorado River Agency. As observed previously, back in the 1850s the Pimas and Pápagos had been allowed to continue in undisturbed occupation of their desert homelands in southern Arizona. Many of these formerly proud peoples were now socially disorganized; they resorted to excessive use of alcoholic beverages and depended upon government provisions and allowances distributed at the Indian agencies; but at least they were not so incorrigible as the hostile Apaches.

In 1871, Apache atrocities precipitated the controversial Camp Grant massacre. Indications are that some bands of Indians resorted to Camp Grant as a place of refuge between raids. While in camp they were regarded as peaceable hunters who were entitled to provisions and weapons, but while away from camp they so relentlessly ravaged the countryside in 1871 that most settlements outside of Tucson had to be abandoned. From the town the infuriated citizens sent a request to the Mission of San Xavier for Pápago allies, of whom ninety-two volunteered, for they, too, had suffered from Apache depredations. These warriors along with six Anglo-Americans and forty-eight Spanish Americans attacked the Indians gathered at Camp Grant at dawn on April 30. According to one participant. "They were completely surprised and sleeping in absolute security in their wickiups. . . . The attack was so swift and fierce that within a half hour the whole work was ended and not an adult Indian left to tell the tale."

Although the citizens of Arizona applauded such punishment as justifiable, in Washington, where President Grant's continuation of the peace policy was popular, the massacre aroused some horrified condemnations of the bloodthirsty Arizonans. Immediately Grant notified the territorial officials that if all of those who had participated in the massacre were not arrested and tried, he would place Arizona under martial law. Due to their dilatory response, General George F. Crook, veteran Indian fighter, was placed in command of the poorly garrisoned military posts in the Department of Arizona. Although he was a capable officer, quiet but decisive, he faced a trying task. Back east the reformers were demanding that the Indians be protected against the fury of the whites, whereas in the territory the militant settlers were clamoring for extermination of the Red Men. Moreover, he found that army officers, Indian agents, and traders were working at cross purposes. Without delay, in June of 1871, he traveled across Arizona and consulted with the supposedly peaceful bands of Apaches in order to develop a plan for a punitive campaign against the marauders.

While General Crook was preparing for military action, Vincent Colyer arrived as a special representative of the Board of Indian Commissioners. He had instructions to make peace with the Apaches and segregate them upon reservations. Although Crook and the governor of the territory, A. P. Safford, disagreed with Colyer's proposal and resented his interference, they agreed to postpone the campaign of retribution while he experimented with his approach. They were confident that he would soon find the peace plan unworkable. Colyer did succeed in persuading several bands of Apaches to accept reservations, where army personnel provided food, blankets, and clothing and tried to convert them into peaceable farmers; but depredations by untamed tribes continued and Colyer gave up.

After the departure of the peace emissary, General Crook again prepared for his campaign, only to be interrupted again by the arrival of another agent, General O. O. Howard, sent out for resumption of Colyer's work. This time Crook had to cooperate, because Howard had seniority over him in the military service. Howard visited some of the reservations and called a conference of both citizens and Indians at Camp Grant, where the Americans were persuaded to turn over the Indian children whom they had taken captive during the massacre of adults there. He also enlarged the Fort Apache Reservation, which soon afterward was divided into two reservations—White Mountain and San Carlos.

General Howard obtained the assistance of Thomas Jeffords, a trusted friend of the Chiracahua Apaches, in arranging a conference with Cochise, chief of that band. Accompanied only by Jeffords and three others, Howard traveled far into the Dragoon Mountains and conferred with the famous chief, who explained the reasons for his grudge against the whites. After his "best friend," Mangas Coloradas, had been "treacherously killed" while professing peace, he had retaliated fiercely, killing "ten men for every Indian slain," but now he realized that his braves were hopelessly outnumbered. He would agree to terms of peace, but not to confinement on a reservation. Instead, he begged, "let us go around free as Americans do."

Despite the plea of Cochise, the Chiracahuas did accept a reservation, and they were favored with a commodious one located in the mountains bordering upon Sonora. General Howard also closed the Camp Grant Reservation in 1873 and transferred its Indian charges to the San Carlos Reservation. After he had closed some other small reserves, he concentrated all of the submissive Apaches at three places, Fort Apache, San Carlos, and Camp Verde. Then he considered his mission successfully terminated and returned to Washington.

The pillaging continued, for several hostile bands were still at large, and at last General Crook was able to wage his war against them. He ran down the marauders relentlessly, and in the encounters during 1872 and 1873 his troopers reported that they killed approximately three hundred Indians. Whenever the braves of a hostile group begged for peace, Crook required that they turn over the warriors who had led them in their depredations. If the condemned men refused to come in, he ordered the other braves to bring in their heads, and often they did.

When Apache resistance was broken, General Crook finally made peace with the several tribes in the spring of 1873. He promised to give them food and protection if they would stay on their reservations. Those who remained at large after this agreement were hunted down and forced into compliance. At last the Army had persuaded the Apaches that they must remain secluded on their reservations and abide by the rules or else suffer certain punishment. Arizona therefore enjoyed a brief spell of relief from Indian depredations.

When General Crook was transferred to the Department of the Platte in 1875, General August V. Kautz succeeded him in Arizona Territory. After the departure of the officer whose firmness and reliability had won the respect of both whites and Indians, the former rivalry between officers and Indian agents reappeared and administration of Indian affairs reverted to its normal confusion except at San Carlos.

CLUM'S EXPERIMENT

John P. Clum arrived at San Carlos as Indian agent in 1874. As a recent college graduate he had been serving with the Army Signal Corps in Santa Fe when he had received notification that the Dutch Reformed Church had nominated him for an Indian agency. He had accepted and the Indian bureau

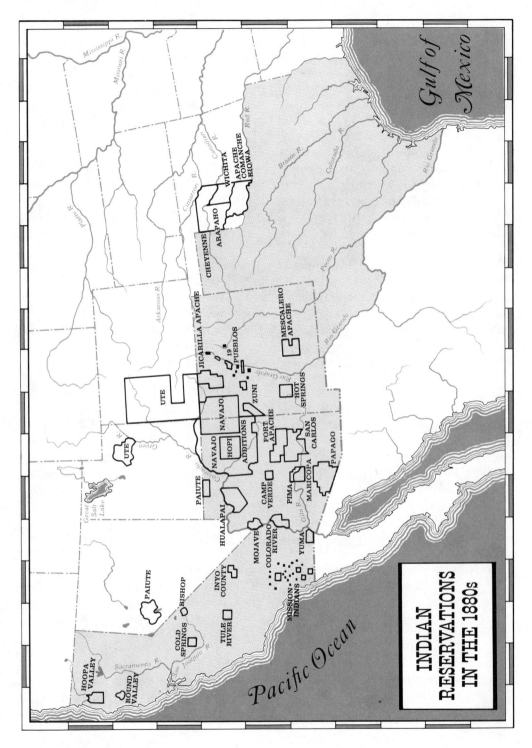

Gulf of Mexico

Pacific Ocean

INDIAN
RESERVATIONS
IN THE 1880s

sent him to San Carlos. Upon his arrival there he investigated thoroughly the problem of Indian discontent. As he related afterward:

Among other things I discovered that the benevolent American government spent thirty-eight million dollars of the taxpayers' money from 1862 to 1871, in its war of *extermination* against the Apaches, and had actually succeeded in exterminating less than one hundred, including women, children, and old men.... I determined that the Apache would get a square deal from that time on, if their new agent had anything to say about it.[2]

The accuracy of Clum's figures can be disputed, but his resolution was firm. At the Agency he soon earned the respect and confidence of the seven hundred Apaches residing there. The four "trustees" whom he selected to serve as policemen proved to be faithful and effective. By promising to relieve the Indians of the odious supervision by soldiers, he persuaded them to turn in their guns. They surrendered their arms reluctantly, and even more reluctantly did Major J. B. Babcock agree to withdraw the soldiers and leave Clum and his four policemen in charge of the reservation. In Tucson the townsmen shivered with fear when they heard that soldiers no longer were patrolling the San Carlos agency. Meanwhile Clum was proceeding with his experiment. He had asked each band of Apaches to choose a representative to serve with him and the others as a governing council, and he found that this sharing of responsibility worked remarkably well. These Apaches learned to farm their land, and a greater

degree of friendliness and contentment prevailed among them.

As Clum's experiment progressed, other roving bands of Apaches also settled at San Carlos, and the white settlers in Arizona became satisfied with his unorthodox administration. Then the Rio Verde tribe, divided into two warring factions, received orders to move to San Carlos, and the arrival of these hostiles threatened to precipitate a crisis in Clum's "peaceful family." However, the Indian policemen presently were able to persuade the Verdes to disarm, and then they were granted representation on the governing council. Trouble was averted.

Because the Indians at the Camp Apache Agency were about to get out of hand, the Indian Bureau ordered Clum to remove the eighteen hundred wards from that reservation to San Carlos. For this mission Clum expanded his police force to about fifty dependable braves and took them along. While the soldiers at the Agency were trying to counteract his persuasion and the officers were insisting the military would have to oversee the removal, Clum's policemen mingled among the other Indians and spread propaganda in favor of San Carlos. They did their work so well that no resort to force was needed for the moving of these Apaches. With their addition, the "happy family" at San Carlos had grown to forty-two hundred. According to Clum's reports, the Indians appreciated his confidence in them and were happy to be freed from annoying supervision by demanding soldiers.

Another assignment soon was thrust upon Clum. After Cochise died in 1874, the Chiricahua Apaches left their res-

[2] *Apache Agent* (Boston, 1936), p. 122.

ervation and began raiding again. For relief of the terrorized citizens of southern Arizona, in 1876 Governor Safford asked Clum to pacify that tribe. For this hazardous undertaking two hundred and fifty of the Apaches at San Carlos offered to serve as Clum's militia. He drilled his volunteers, marched them to Tucson, paraded them through the business district, and staged a sham battle and realistic war dance for the entertainment of the rather terrified townsmen. Then he moved on toward Apache Pass.

For the subjugation of the Chiricahuas, General Kautz had dispatched two companies of cavalrymen to their reservation, but Clum's band arrived ahead of them. Before the military detachment appeared, Clum had the situation under control; but this time it was the sons of Cochise who turned the trick. Out of respect for their father's pledge to keep the peace, they shot the chiefs who had led the uprising. One of the latter, Poinsenay, who was only wounded, surrendered to the Indian policemen and was held as their prisoner. Then Clum met in conference with Geronimo, chief of the southern band of Chiricahuas who were living off the reservation. Geronimo requested that his tribe be permitted to accompany the others in their removal to San Carlos, to which Clum readily assented.

Three hundred and twenty-five subdued Apaches, accompanied by one white man, were journeying from the mountains toward Tucson. On the way they were met by the sheriff, who presented a warrant for the arrest of Poinsenay. Clum yielded custody of his prisoner with misgivings, which proved to be well founded. That very night Poinsenay escaped from the sheriff and thus evaded being brought to trial for his crimes.

By 1876, Clum's wards numbered forty-five hundred, and that summer he selected and rehearsed a troupe of performers for a visit to Washington and to the Centennial Exposition in Philadelphia. Quite impressed by the sights they had seen, the Indians returned directly to Arizona, but their agent detoured alone to Delaware, Ohio. There he wed Mary Dennison Ware, who went with him on a honeymoon by train to San Francisco, by steamship to San Diego, and by wagon across the mountains and deserts of southern California and Arizona to San Carlos.

REMOVAL OF THE RENEGADES

All continued to go well with the reservation Apaches except for the antics of some renegades led by Geronimo. Often they sneaked away with some stolen squaws and then rustled cattle from nearby ranches. They sold both squaws and cattle to traders or ranchers, usually across the border in Mexico. Therefore, in 1877 Clum received orders to apprehend Geronimo. With forty selected Indian trusties, he traveled to Silver City, New Mexico, and near Ojo Caliente in the Sacramento Mountains he and his posse found Geronimo's camp, surrounded it, and forced the surrender of the renegades without firing a shot. Then another outlaw chief, Victorio, came in for a conference, and after some argument he agreed to capitulate. Soon three troops of cavalry arrived to assist in the subjugation of the "savages," but they found the job already done. In May, Clum and his little company of policemen escorted over four hundred of Geronimo's and Victorio's followers on a trek of four hundred miles to the Apache reservation.

Back at San Carlos some bad news awaited Clum, because he found that a company of soldiers had been sent there to make an inspection. This interference was in violation of the long-standing agreement that he had arranged with the War Department for relief from military meddling at this reservation. Forthwith Clum wired the Indian Bureau in Washington: "If your Department will increase my salary sufficiently and equip two more companies of Indian police for me, I will volunteer to take care of all Apaches in Arizona and the troops can be removed." When the officials in the Indian Bureau wavered in their support, Clum resigned in exasperation. After his exciting and fruitful years as an Indian agent, he became a successful newspaper proprietor, first in Tucson and later in Tombstone. He died in 1932 at the ripe age of eighty-one years.

After Clum departed from San Carlos, Geronimo was released from the guard house and allowed the freedom of the other Apaches on the reservation; but he did not merit this trust. He and some other renegades sneaked away in the spring of 1878 and pillaged and murdered at large for eighteen months. He escaped capture by taking refuge across the border in Mexico.

Because of the disintegration of discipline in Arizona, General Crook was returned to this territory for resumption of his vigorous, punitive tactics. Then, in 1884, Geronimo and some other renegades returned to the reservation and professed peaceable intentions. Affairs at the agency degenerated so badly under the administration of H. L. Hart that he was removed. A succession of agents followed him, with little or no better success. Meanwhile management of the Indian police force had been transferred to the military, much to the disgust of the Apaches.

In 1885, Geronimo and his band again left the reservation and resumed their depredations. General Crook hastened in pursuit and apprehended them; but as he was returning with his prisoners, Geronimo and some others escaped. Because Crook was censured for laxity, unjustly he thought, he resigned the command and General Nelson A. Miles succeeded him. Crook had brought twenty-seven of the Apache prisoners to Fort Bowie, and they were now sent to a prison camp at Fort Marion in Florida. Next, in August, 1886, Miles rounded up over four hundred of the Chiricahuas at Fort Apache and put them also on a train for removal to Florida.

General Miles sent Captain H. W. Lawton and a company of cavalrymen in pursuit of Geronimo. After a chase of over a thousand miles, the troopers overtook and defeated his little, exhausted band of renegades. Then Lieutenant Charles B. Gatewood ventured alone into Geronimo's camp and persuaded the treacherous old chief to surrender. He and his companions also were sentenced to prison in Florida; sometime later Geronimo was returned at his own request for imprisonment at Fort Sill in Oklahoma.

Others of the Chiricahuas were released on their good behavior. Some obtained allotments of land in Oklahoma and others at the Mescalero Reservation in southeastern New Mexico. Incidentally, in 1905 at his inauguration as President, Theodore Roosevelt, "Teddy," arranged for Geronimo to be brought to Washington in order to make a spectacular show of the festivities. As he marched in the parade down Pennsylvania Avenue, he was cheered as if he were a returning hero instead of an imprisoned murderer and thief.

In 1886, the apprehension of Geronimo and his band of outlaws had brought an end to the Indian wars in the Southwest. With all consequential resistance crushed, the tribes at last had been confined on reservations in pursuit of the segregation policy. The lessons which could have been learned from Clum's experiment at San Carlos were generally ignored. Dual management continued, but it is true that in the new era of peaceful relations the military became less obtrusive and the agents more responsible and effective. Even so, as Edward Everett Dale concluded, the internal history of the agencies was "a story of petty squabbles" continuing on into the twentieth century.

ASSIMILATION ATTEMPTED

With the Indians finally subdued, the planners in Washington worked toward the adoption of a new policy. Ever since the cessation of treaty-making in 1871, the Indians had been dealt with more as individuals than as organized tribes. From time to time reformers had advanced the proposal that they be further "individualized" and prepared for assimilation by granting them lands in severalty. Finally this proposal was embodied in the Dawes Act of 1887. It provided that the reservations should be divided into tracts of one hundred and sixty acres for parcelling out among the families of each tribe. Those plots would be held in trust by the government for twenty-five years, in order to prevent some unscrupulous whites from trading to the Indians a bottle of liquor for their patrimony. At the end of that long probationary period, the government would deed the Indians titles to their farms and admit them to citizenship.

Any lands remaining after the allotments had been made would be sold and the receipts from that source would be used for maintenance of Indian schools.

Finally Indian policy had come around full cycle. From Spanish assimilation it had gone to retaliation, then to a choice of extermination or segregation as a foreign nation, and finally back to assimilation again, but under American auspices.

In 1906, the Burke Act amended the Dawes Act. Henceforth, without waiting for the lapse of the full twenty-five years, the President could decide when the members of a given tribe had demonstrated sufficiently their responsibility as individuals for admission to citizenship. In addition, the sale of liquor to Indians was prohibited, in order to eliminate that all too common cause of debilitation. In 1924, when one-half of the eligible Indians had qualified for citizenship under the

Burke Act, the Congress passed an act granting citizenship to all of them.

Wherever the land was arable and fairly productive, the provisions of the Dawes and Burke acts were beneficial. The Indians on their allocated lands became good farmers and emerged as dependable citizens. Their children enrolled in Indian schools or even in public schools and became well assimilated by the majority population. Some adults achieved positions of leadership in their states, and a few acquired fabulous wealth when they struck oil on the lands which they had acquired individually.

In the Southwest the assimilation policy did not immediately work out so well. At some few reservations, where the land was good, the Indians all received allotments; at others only a few were provided for, since by then the limited arable lands were filled up. The remainder of the reservation remained undistributed, because no family could subsist on one hundred and sixty acres of boulders and cactus with no water available for irrigation. Thus thousands of Indians, notably the Navajos, remained for a long time an unassimilated, impoverished, pastoral people, crushed in spirit and neglected

by the government. Moreover, because their rights and responsibilities as citizens were dependent more upon state statutes than on federal legislation, the enactment of citizenship for them in 1924 brought little change in status in those southwestern states which failed to respond immediately with extension of full privileges. The unassimilated Indians were destined to continue for a long time as second-class citizens.

By the turn of the century the number of Indians in the Southwest was far less than in the Spanish colonial era. The census of 1900 reported only five hundred living in Texas, about thirteen thousand in New Mexico, fifteen thousand in California, and twenty-six thousand in Arizona. Although assimilation had accounted for some of the depletion, disease and warfare had taken the greater toll. Even with the reduced numbers, the Southwest, due to its impediments hindering assimilation, still harbored the nation's most serious Indian problem. However the problem had outgrown the stage of wars and atrocities into a new type of problem derived from the difficulties in rehabilitating a distressed minority people.

14
THE
CATTLE INDUSTRY

At sundown I saw stretching for miles across the gently rolling and virgin prairie a lately completed barbed-wire fence, four shining strands of galvanized Glidden held up by cedar posts peeled and weathered to the shade of old ivory and set solidly eight feet apart. It was the first real fence I had ever seen, and I had watched the workmen build it wide-eyed with wonder. But at that it was interest mingled with fear instilled by half-heard murmurs against fencing up the country. Men sitting around the general store on Saturday afternoons didn't like it a bit.

During the night a frightful transformation had occurred. Each tightly stretched strand had been cut between each pair of posts, and the wire had curled up about them, giving the line as it led away into the sun a frizzled appearance, as if a vicious animal maddened so that every particular hair stood on end.

> *Roy Bedichek,* Adventures of a Texas Naturalist *(Garden City, N.Y.),*
> *1947, pp. 5-6.*

The Southwest had been a cattle-growing region ever since the time of the Indians, but in those days the cattle were the wild bison of the plains. The region received its first name from that animal — Land of *Cíbola*, or buffalo cow.

SPANISH CATTLE AND SHEEP

The Spanish colonists brought with them cattle, horses, and sheep, and all three helped build the economy of the Borderlands. With them the Spaniards founded a livestock industry long before the Anglo-Americans arrived. Cali-

266

fornians and Texans of the colonial period were predominantly cattlemen who grazed thousands of Texas Longhorns, as they were later to be named, and could have produced more if their market had not been limited to the demand for horns, hides, and hooves. They dried what meat they needed for their own consumption and had to let the remainder go to waste. Their receipts, therefore, from the shipping of the by-products—the "three h's"— were meagre, but good enough to keep them in business. In that early date and in this remote region conditions favoring extensive cattle raising for the production of beef were not yet favorable.

Because the Texans engaged predominantly in general farming, which also included considerable cattle raising, the Californians were the first to specialize in cattle production. From the original stock of a few hundred head brought up from Mexico the Dons bred herds running up into the thousands, which they grazed on their ranches and on the open range beyond. Although they had only the slender-legged, rangy Spanish Longhorns, those animals produced nutritious meat and useful by-products. The hides could be used for the making of leather products, the horns for handcrafting into tools, and the hooves for boiling down into glue. Life on the ranches of the Dons was gracious and leisurely for the proprietors and their families, but trying and toilsome for the Spanish and Indian *vaqueros*, or cowboys.

In early California a system of branding became necessary, because the cattle ran loose on unfenced ranches. With the local *alcalde* each owner registered the brands which distinguished his stock from others—the *señal*, or ear mark, the *fierro*, or iron brand, and the *venta*, or sale mark. At least once annually the cowboys rounded up the herds for separation of one owner's cattle from others and for the branding of calves. Upon completion of the work, the neighboring cattlemen, their families, servants, and cowboys, shared in a joyous fiesta of dancing, horse racing, gambling, and games.

The ranches of California produced the West's first typical cowboys. The men who herded the cattle were skilled horsemen, who rode hard and lassoed adeptly. They equipped their saddles with *armos*, or leather shields, which protected their legs from cactus and thorny brush. They wore short trousers and high buckskin boots fitted with large spurs. They sported short colorful jackets of embroidered satin or silk, and wore broad-rimmed, low-crowned hats, called *poblanos*. Always they wore or carried on their saddle a *poncho*, or cape, made of broadcloth and decorated with a silver or gold fringe.

As each owner and his hands rode in and out among the cattle, cutting his animals from the herd, the costume and skill of the cowboys made the annual roundup a picturesque event. *Vaqueros* became grim and alert as they tested their skill in evading maddened bulls, and they shouted excitedly while they chased escaping steers. Simultaneously the roundup became an occasion for pomp and ceremony, as the *alcalde* ordered the town criers to call out the public announcements, and the cattle judges inspected the segregated herds to make certain that they were properly identified. That was the prototype of the modern rodeo.

The missions in California also became great cattle ranches. In their corrals the *padres* taught the Indian neophytes how to break and saddle horses, throw their lariats, and brand the cattle. The Indians soon became skillful riders and industrious cowhands, and years later, after the missions had been secularized, many of those Indians became the exploited *vaqueros* of private ranchers.

Whereas cattle dominated the economy in Spanish California and also held an important place in Texas, it was the lowly sheep which became the mainstay of New Mexico and Arizona. The colonists drove up from Mexico flocks of small sheep known as *churros*, which multiplied into thousands on the ranches along the Rio Grande. Most of the sheep were owned by only a few families, the *ricos*, who had many servants, or *peones*, for tending the large flocks. Later that peonage was supplemented by a share-grazing system known as the *partido*. Under the latter arrangement the owner, or *patrón*, delegated most of the responsibility to his herders, or *pastores*. The herders responded, therefore, with improved care and industry, and the *patrón* found that he could encourage those qualities by his own kindliness and reliability.

As a rule the *pastor* took over a part of the *patrón's* flock under an agreement whereby he would turn in half of the annual increase, make good all losses, and return the original number of sheep to the owner at the end of a five-year period. The *pastor* drove his flock from one meadow to another, watched for any sickness, and guarded against predators. At night he parked his wagon, or pitched his small tent, or laid out his bedroll wherever he was and slept "with one ear open." The continuous solitude made him shy and taciturn. However, the monotony of his existence was broken by one very busy season—lambing time each spring. Then he had to bring his flock in close to the ranchhouse, keep watch over the ewes day and night, and take good care of the newborn lambs.

Old Mexico provided a market for thousands of the sheep raised in New Mexico. Annually a long caravan journeyed down the Rio Grande, over the *Jornada del Muerto*, across the river to old El Paso, and on south to the cities of New Spain. The number of head driven south ranged between two hundred thousand and half a million annually. In one year, 1839, Colonel Francisco Chávez, New Mexico's leading sheep rancher, sent southward himself a flock of seventy-five thousand, besides the thousands from other ranches. This was the original Long Drive of the region which later would become our Southwest.

Four years after the military occupation of the Spanish Borderland by the United States, the census takers counted three hundred and seventy-seven thousand sheep grazing in New Mexico and Arizona. At that date, 1850, California had three hundred and five thousand head of cattle and Texas about two-thirds of that number. Texas, on the other hand, had seventy-five thousand horses, California sixty-two thousand, and New Mexico and Arizona, combined, only about five thousand.

EXPANSION OF RANCHING

After the Anglo-American frontier moved out farther west in the decade before the Civil War, new markets opened up for beef and mutton. As early as 1842, a small herd of Texas cattle was driven to market in St. Louis and another to New Orleans. Four years later Edward Piper took a larger herd, about a thousand head, to Ohio; but those early long drives hardly paid expenses. Soon afterward the opening of mining camps in California turned the trails westward. The Spanish-American ranchers of southern California were the first to take advantage of the new market in the mining region and realized greater profits from their herds than ever before. Soon the Dons of New Mexico—the Armijos, Bacas, Oteros, Romeros, among others—sent flocks of sheep on the long drive to California, and then some cattlemen of western Texas, James Campbell, John James, John Trimmier, and others, took to that trail, too. The journey through New Mexico, Arizona, and California was hazardous for both man and steer, but if the deserts could be crossed safely and the Indians fought off, considerable profit could be gained by selling cattle worth five to ten dollars a head in Texas for twenty-five to one hundred and fifty dollars in California. This market offered the most in the middle 1850s; thereafter the prices declined and that long drive no longer was worth the risk.

The good profits gained by the sale of cattle for slaughtering encouraged the Texans in their quest for similarly lucrative markets. They began driving herds to Shreveport, New Orleans, and St. Louis. The Galveston *News* estimated that in 1856, over thirty thousand head had been sold in New Orleans, and later reports indicate that even more were being driven to St. Louis. At that time the herds driven to Missouri were taken over the Old Shawnee Trail, which crossed through Cherokee country and southeastern Kansas and thence to the Missouri River and along it to St. Louis. A few herds were even driven on to Chicago or Cincinnati or other cities in the Midwest. Soon, however, the farmers in Missouri became alarmed by an outbreak of Texas cattle fever and then they sent out committees to prevent the herds from crossing their state. This interference caused the drovers to follow the Kansas line north to Kansas City, which soon began to thrive as a marketing center for cattle. In 1859, however, when Kansas also imposed a ban upon the trailing of Texas cattle across that territory, groups of armed farmers met the herds and turned them back. Even so, a few Texans continued to ignore the quarantine and to evade the posses.

Meanwhile the growing market for wool and mutton had stimulated an expansion in the sheep industry, which began taking over much of the high plains of western Texas. Austin's colonists had introduced the grazing of the Spanish white-wooled Merinos, which yielded a finer fleece than the little *churros* of New Mexico. Subsequently a crossing of those two breeds produced a new strain well suited to the climate in Texas. Eminent among the pioneers in this new industry was George W. Kendall, the journalist who had accompanied the ill-fated Texas-Santa Fe expedition in 1841. In 1856, he began grazing a flock of Merinos near New Braunfels, realized a good profit, and improved his stock by importing Rambouillet rams from France. Then more and more frontiersmen in Texas became sheepmen. Simultaneously Spanish Americans from New Mexico were expanding their sheep-raising frontier eastward onto the high plains of western Texas and northward into the mountain valleys of southern Colorado. Then after Juan Candelaria of New Mexico relocated with a large flock at Concho, Arizona, in 1866, the sheep industry grew rapidly in that territory. Likewise, in California, where the missions once had grazed sheep as well as cattle, some Anglo-American settlers acquired ranches for sheep raising. Prominent among those newcomers was Julian I. Williams, who took over the old Chino ranch for the grazing of thirty thousand head.

New Mexico, however, continued to have the greater concentration of sheep. Many of the Dons, as of old, were large producers, and now Anglos also became proprietors of some of the ranches. After Lucien Maxwell acquired the Beaubien-Miranda land grant in 1864, he became one of the largest holders. On his ranch of one million seven hundred thousand acres he grazed about fifty thousand sheep. He built a great manor house at Cimarrón, where he entertained many noted guests. In 1871 he sold his ranch, which soon was acquired by an English company.

By 1880, when the sheep industry had reached its zenith in New Mexico, the sheepmen of this territory owned nearly three million head, from which many of the ranchers then were accruing good profits. At thirty cents a pound the wool, alone, from a thousand ewes brought in fifteen hundred dollars annually, and the proprietor could employ a sheepherder for two hundred dollars or less a year. After 1879, when the Santa Fe Railroad reached Las Vegas, that town in New Mexico boomed for about two decades as the wool-shipping capital of the Southwest.

In Texas, where conditions favored cattle raising, the stockmen were on the verge of tapping a lucrative market when the Civil War interrupted the northward drives and drew many of the able-bodied men into the service of the Confederacy. As a concession to the vital but languishing cattle industry, the draft law of 1862 allowed the exemption of one stockman for each five hundred head of cattle, and by that time the Confederacy was buying cattle at twenty-five dollars a head; therefore the business picked up momentarily. Texans drove herds across Louisiana and Mississippi to the newfound market until the severing of the Confederacy at the Mississippi by Union forces in 1863 interrupted the long drives. To make matters worse, a severe drought had burned up the pastures during the war years. In exasperation, many ranchers turned loose their cattle on the open range, where the Longhorns could forage for themselves. They also multiplied rapidly, so that by the time the war ended, great herds of wild cattle were roaming beyond the frontier. Whenever marketing conditions should again become favorable, they could be rounded up for a revival of the industry.

FAVORABLE FACTORS

When peace was restored, several factors favored the cattlemen. Soon afterward the hostile Indians were subdued and confined on reservations, as has been related in the preceding chapter. Meanwhile a less critical nuisance was also being abated by the near extermination of the bison on the plains. In that era of unheated vehicles and bedrooms, buffalo robes were so much in demand that hunters rode onto the plains to kill and skin countless thousands of bison. The hunt was facilitated by the penetration of the plains country by the railways, and the railways themselves provided an additional incentive because large herds would get on the tracks and stop the traffic. On the Kansas Pacific line in 1868, for example, a train traveled the one hundred and twenty miles from Ellsworth to Sheridan through herds crowded together so closely that the engineer had to stop frequently and wait for the track to clear. If ever the trains were to run on schedule, the buffaloes would have to be removed. The new towns which sprang up at intervals along the tracks became immediately the headquarters of hunters. Dodge City, for example, was a buffalo hunters' town for several years before it became a cow town. Soon it and the other cities attracted sportsmen who rode thither from St. Louis or Kansas City in excursion trains. On the way they shot buffalo from the windows of the train, and at the town of their destination they mounted horses and went forth as members of shooting parties with seasoned buffalo hunters as guides. The slaughtering of thousands of cumbersome, dull-witted bison was a rather dubious sport, but at least the hunters did render a service by rapidly clearing the animals from the plains and removing that hindrance.

As the railways penetrated the grasslands of the plains, they became available for the transportation of cattle. When first one line and then another built westward from St. Louis and Kansas City, they brought terminals for shipping closer to Texas. They were also the vanguard of the new industrial civilization which was then emerging in the East. No longer did the average man engage in subsistence farming, which included the butchering of his own cow or hog. Instead he had become a city dweller, employed in a factory and dependent largely upon others for the production of his meat and vegetables. Those who had the means wanted to dine on good beef. Simultaneously the marketing of fresh meat was facilitated by the development of refrigeration for freight cars and storage facilities and, in 1865, the first large meat-packing plant was built in Chicago.

After the Civil War the wild cattle in Texas were rounded up and branded as the foundation for the building up of new herds. Then H. M. Childress drove some of his steers to Iowa, where he received thirty-five dollars a head; but two others who tried that trail encountered so many difficulties that they gave up. A few succeeded in evading the blockades in Kansas and Missouri, while others followed a safer trail to Shreveport or New Orleans.

In Colorado the mining rushes were creating boom towns, and in New Mexico the government was maintaining forts for defense against the Indians and was feeding the Navajos at Bosque Redondo. Therefore in 1866 Oliver Loving and Charles Goodnight trailed a herd over the former Butterfield stagecoach route to the Pecos River and up it to Fort Sumner, where they disposed of the steers at eight cents a pound on the hoof. Then they drove the cows and calves on over Raton Pass to market in Denver. They had opened access to a new market by a route known thereafter as the Loving-Goodnight Trail, over which they and others sent herds in subsequent years.

Obviously the opportunity was at hand for the making of a great industry if some promoter could conceive a way to capitalize upon the favorable factors — the Longhorn herds of the Southwest, the grasslands of the spacious plains, the expanding market of the East, the new freedom from danger and nuisance, and the available facilities of railway and refrigeration. Moreover, many Confederate veterans were unemployed and restless. They found conditions in their home states depressing, and the Homestead Act of 1862 excluded them from the privilege of taking up free land. In search of something to do, many of the younger men drifted to the West. Some became cowboys and stockmen, and many more would become available whenever the favorable factors might overcome the obstacles of distance and opposition.

As the railroads were built into Kansas, where some of the counties were exempt from quarantine, obviously therein lay the best connecting link; but the businessmen of the new towns displayed little interest. They dismissed as entirely impractical any proposal for the handling of cattle from Texas. At Topeka in 1867 one promoter did make a half-hearted bid for the business. Chester Thomas, president of the Kansas Live Stock Company, sent out a circular about a route over which cattle might be driven without crossing the line of the quarantine. Most Texans, however, distrusted the Kansas "sharpers" and their "flattering reports." Moreover, the few who did respond found that when they arrived in Topeka with some cattle, the company there had no stockyards for handling them. As a result, most Texans who took herds north still risked the blockades on the Old Shawnee Trail en route to Baxter Springs, Kansas.

The promoter who envisioned the possibilities of an improved outlet for Texas Longhorns at a Kansas railway town was Joseph G. McCoy of Springfield, Illinois. In Abilene he conferred with Colonel John J. Myers, a stockman from Dalhart, Texas, who lent encouragement. McCoy then returned to St. Louis, where he approached John T. Perry, president of the Union Pacific Railroad. Perry offered him a commission of five dollars for each carload of cattle which he might ship over that line. Near Abilene, therefore, McCoy selected a site for a stockyard at Solomon City, but the townsmen objected. They did not want great herds of cattle driven through their streets. Although the site which McCoy selected in Abilene was held at a high price, he made a deal for it that summer, 1867, and began preparations. Abilene was sixty miles inside the quarantine zone; but the country south of the town was then only sparsely settled, so that there would be few farmers who could raise objections.

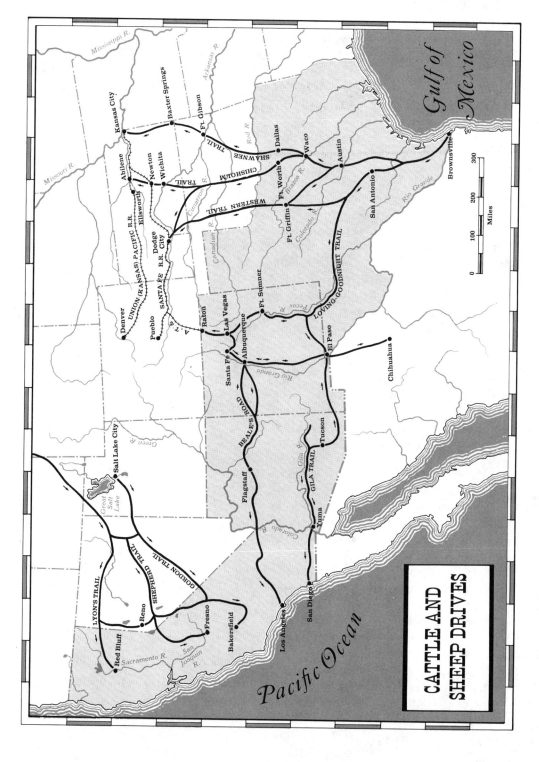

CATTLE AND SHEEP DRIVES

While McCoy was proceeding with the construction of an office, a stockyard, and a new hotel in Abilene, he sent out agents for distribution of handbills among Texas cattlemen. Because the facilities were not to be ready until fall, there was little time left that year; nevertheless a few Texans became interested and sent herds north. Those few profited from the advantages of the new outlet and relayed the good news to others. The next year, when the Texans trailed seventy-five thousand cattle to Abilene, the success of the project was assured and the range industry received a mighty impetus.

THE LONG DRIVE

The route of the Long Drive from Waco and Fort Worth across Indian Territory to Abilene was called the Chisholm Trail. The name was derived from Jesse Chisholm, who had long been a trader among the Wichita Indians and had built a store at the mouth of the Little Arkansas River. From his store he often drove his wagon south into Indian Territory. In that way he had marked out a primitive road, which the drovers were to follow north in 1868 and afterward. Some hands called it the "Texas Cattle Trail"; but it became more popularly associated with the veteran trader, who died in that first big year of the cattle drive into Kansas.

As soon as Abilene began to boom as a cow town, other places in Kansas sought to divert some of the business to their own benefit. Then McCoy advertised Abilene widely in order to keep ahead of his rivals. He brought Illinois cattle buyers to Abilene for a buffalo hunt, and he organized a Wild West show, which performed in St. Louis and Chicago. His campaign succeeded well until a scourge of Texas fever broke out among the cattle on the farms near Abilene and spread into Illinois. By that time the good citizens of Abilene were in an outrage about the saloons, dance halls, and red-light districts which had grown up in their midst. The gunplay and disorder was giving their town a bad reputation. Finally, in 1872, the local Farmers' Protective Association served notice on the drovers "to seek some other point for shipment, as the inhabitants of Dickinson County will no longer submit to the evils of the trade."

Banned from Abilene, some Texans turned to Wichita as their new shipping point, while others took their cattle to Ellsworth. Additional towns built facilities and profited from them; in fact no longer could one or two outlets handle all the trade. In 1872, the peak year, Texans trailed three hundred and fifty thousand head north for loading on the railways in Kansas towns. For a decade after 1875, Dodge City on the Santa Fe Railway held supremacy as the "cowboy capital" of the West. In those years a quarter of a million head of cattle arrived annually from the central and northern plains as well as from New Mexico and Texas.

In the era of the long drive the cattlemen built their industry on the open range. Without paying for a lease, they grazed their cattle on land owned by the state in Texas and by the federal government elsewhere. By homesteading a small tract around a watering place, or by obtaining ownership of it otherwise, they controlled the grazing land for miles around, since nobody else could make use of that land without access to water. Because the cattle of one owner mingled with those of another on the distant hills, the ranchers had to have an annual roundup for the branding of the calves. That procedure was more economical than the fencing of thousands of acres; but the intermingling of cattle on the range would not permit improvement of the stock by selective breeding. However, there was no need to raise premium cattle as long as the scrawny, durable Longhorn was marketable, due to lack of competition by beef of better quality.

THE COWBOY

By 1880, the grasslands of the Southwest were dotted with the cattle of many herds. The central figure in that era was the cowboy, whose garb was both distinctive and practical. Seldom did he wear a coat, but usually a vest, in which the several pockets served for the carrying of tobacco, matches, and other small items. He wore a large brown or grey hat as protection against sun and rain as well as for convenience in carrying water when necessary. Around his neck he tied a bright kerchief, which he could lift over his face as a shield against wind and dust. Over his loose woolen trousers he donned leather "chaps," short for *chaparejos,* for protection against cactus and thorny brush. His embroidered gloves prevented rope-burns, and his high topped, high-heeled boots were designed to fit into stirrups rather than for comfort while walking.

Each cowboy owned his own heavy, durable saddle, which he decorated to suit his own taste. On his saddle horn he carried his rope, called a "lariat," coiled and ready for instant use whenever he needed to "lasso" a steer or horse. In his belt holster he packed a Colt six-shooter for protection against wild animals. Contrary to the legend purveyed by television and motion pictures, the average cowboy could not shoot accurately except at close range and usually removed his holster and gun whenever he entered a saloon, house, or dance hall. Cattle men in their reminiscences typically described the hard work that was done and reported having seen but very little shooting. Of course, among thousands of hands there were some bad ones, and in town many indulged in boisterous relaxation. Moreover, some of them did become involved in vicious range wars at times.

By and large the average cowhand led a rather dull, solitary existence. Because he seldom needed to say much, he had a limited vocabulary, mostly comprised of the jargon of his vocation sprinkled with some rich profanity. He vented his need for self-expression more eloquently in song. In the bunkhouse a group might tune up a guitar and sing some sentimental ballads about home and death. Such songs were useful, too, in calming a restless herd out on the range.

The strenuous work in the routine of the cowboy came at the time of the annual roundup. The riders from several neighboring ranches rounded up the animals out on the open range and drove them to a central spot, where they cut out the steers and cows bearing the brands of the respective owners. Since most of the calves tagged along, they could then be identified, roped, and branded. The "coat of arms" of the cattle baron was the unique combination of letters and symbols which made up his brand, and those of all owners were properly registered and protected by law. In that "heraldry of the range," here is an example of what was made of only one letter: A plain W in a square became a "box W," with wings it was a "flying W," sitting on a curved line it was known as a "rocking W," on its side it was called a "lazy W," and with a straight line below it became a "bar W."

The "long drive," normally organized after the roundup, entailed some more routine riding which could at times be rudely interrupted by the dangers of the trail. A herd of several hundred head required the services of a foreman, a dozen cowboys, the necessary horses and mules, and a chuck-wagon manned by a cook and his helper. The foreman and chuck-wagon led the way, while the cowhands rode on either side of the herd in order to keep the animals from straying. At one side also rode the horse "wrangler" with some spare mounts. The less experienced cowboys who followed the herd, watching for stragglers, had the disagreeable position, because they had to "eat the dust" kicked up by the many hooves ahead.

Much of the time the trailing of a herd was easy and monotonous, until dangers were encountered. A thunderbolt or any other sudden, startling noise could precipitate a stampede, which usually was hard to stop without the loss of some

cattle and perhaps some horses and men. Swimming the cattle across a river involved a risk, too, because they might crowd too closely together and drown. In the early years a source of peril was a surprise attack by Indians, and later another hazard was provided by rustlers, who could be as vicious as the Indians once had been. Those risks of the trade steeled the cowboy for vigorous action on a moment's notice and prompted him to compose a song: "Come along boys, and listen to my tale, I'll tell you my troubles on the Old Chisholm Trail," continuing with many stanzas and several variations.

When a cowboy rode into town at the end of the long drive, he experienced an exhilarating release from tension and crowded into his brief sojourn all of the exciting amusements that he could find and afford. Refreshed by a shave and a bath and thrilled by the possession of some cash as payment for his work, he was ready to patronize the saloons, gambling dens, and houses of prostitution. In the cow towns abundant vendors of such amusements stood ready to relieve him of his hard-earned dollars honestly or otherwise. Soon, with his money spent, he returned to his dusty, smelly, lonely work for another spell of several long months.

Among the cowhands were numerous Negroes, who could not be identified, of course, in the lists of names of employees; yet time and again in available memoirs mention is made of two or three Negroes among the hands on each ranch and in the crew of each long drive.

They had a conspicuous place in the cattlemen's West, according to Philip Durham and Everett L. Jones, who have described their role in the face of blizzards, stampedes, grass fires, and other chores in the "dangerous and hard lives" of the cowhands. Among them, one, Bose Ikard, for example, merited high praise by his employer, Charles Goodnight, who wrote this tribute:

There was a dignity, a cleanliness, and a reliability about him that was wonderful. He paid no attention to women. His behavior was good in a fight, and he was probably the most devoted man to me that I ever had. I have trusted him further than any living man. He was my detective, banker, and everything else in Colorado, New Mexico, and the other wild country I was in.[1]

CONFLICTS WITH SHEEPMEN

As cowboys and cattle owners extended their area of activity on the open range, they came into conflict with sheepmen, who were also expanding their industry. The former complained that the sheep destroyed the grass by cropping it too closely, that their sharp hooves also damaged the turf, that the flocks left a bad odor wherever they grazed, and that cattle would not drink at watering places frequented by sheep. John Muir, the naturalist, called the sheep "horned locusts," and cattlemen alleged that their range land was "going bad" because it had been "sheeped off." Moreover, the cowboy and *pastor* were not congenial, as they had little in common in their contrasting ways of life. Most of the sheepherders were reticent Spanish Americans, whereas the majority of the cowboys were lusty Anglo-Americans.

Serious clashes occurred in the border zone where the two industries overlapped. Some of the conflicts were merely local and inconsequential, but others sparked a serious range warfare. When some New Mexicans pastured their flocks on the Goodnight range in western Texas, several cowboys vindictively drowned four hundred sheep in the Canadian River. After more such clashes had occurred, Goodnight entered into an agreement with the sheepherders for observance of a dividing line on the range. As the conflict spread, the cattlemen elsewhere resorted to intimidation and violence; if a herder was killed, the owner of the flock could have no recourse at law because the influential rancher had public support in his neighborhood. One such conflict in Arizona erupted in a round of violence. Sheepmen who controlled the range from Ash Fork to Seligman trespassed on the lands of some neighboring cattlemen. In the ensuing Graham-Tewksbury feud six sheepmen and twenty-six cattlemen were killed.

Before long the competitors on the Southwestern grasslands reconciled their differences. They found that if sheep were not herded in a dense flock, they grazed lightly and the range actually improved. Their droppings made good fertilizer, and their hooves left imprints in which moisture accumulated. Finally the ranchers realized that cattle and sheep could thrive on the same pasture, and in that discovery they also found an economic advantage. When the market for one was in a slump, the profits from the other might tide the owner through a lean period. As Wini-

[1] Quoted in J. Evetts Haley, *Charles Goodnight* (Norman, Okla., 1949), p. 242.

fred Kupper remarked, "Economics will always get the better of sentiment." When the cattlemen began grazing some sheep on the side, they forgot "that sheepmen were once a low breed to be shot at" and that the wool-producers were "scabby pests" which must be "run off the bluff or drowned in a river." The fencing of ranches also helped separate the bitter rivals of earlier years.

THE BIG RANCHES

The building of fences was facilitated by the invention of barbed wire, and its use was stimulated by the boom in the cattle industry. In 1882, the Chicago stockyards paid nine cents a pound for cattle, which meant that Texas steers, that would have been worth about five dollars a head in 1865, were selling for seven times that sum. Good profits attracted investors, including several Scottish and English capitalists. As large companies entered this field, the competition became keen for acquisition of all available pasturage. Land was purchased from the government or obtained by fraudulent abuse of the Homestead Act and the Desert Land Act. Sometimes large tracts were fenced without the filing of any kind of papers for legal ownership.

Some of the companies of investors fenced in ranches which became enormous "spreads" running into thousands, even millions, of acres. The greatest of them all was the mammoth X I T Ranch in the Texas Panhandle. It originated in an offer by the state legislature of an appropriation of three million acres in exchange for the building of a new state capitol in Austin. In addition, fifty thousand acres would be granted for the surveying of the tract. The only bidder was Mattheas Schnell of Rock Island, Illinois, who transferred three-fourths of his interest to Taylor, Babcock, and Company of Chicago. By 1888, the con-

tractors had expended close to three and a quarter million dollars on the building of the capitol, which then stood out as one of the more imposing state buildings in the nation. As work on it had proceeded, the company had received title to the promised acreage in a wide strip of land extending along the western boundary of the Panhandle from Yellow Houses to Texline.

At first the owners of the X I T considered opening the ranch for settlement; but because that frontier had not yet developed adequately for the attraction of farmers, they agreed upon the raising of cattle as an intermediate stage. They opened a company office in London for the soliciting of investment by English capitalists. Then they employed John V. Farwell as managing director of the ranch and Colonel B. H. Campbell as foreman. Next came the task of building the line fences, as described by Lewis Nordyke:

The surveyors moved ahead, determining the line and marking the post locations. Behind them came the post setters, pounding holes two to three feet deep and tamping dirt around the posts. The bracers followed, and behind them were the wire-stretchers and the staplers. . . . Slowly the fence crept across the prairie and by late December (1885) the fencers reached the center of X I T's northern axis. There they were days away from the nearest settlement and had to haul water 35 miles for themselves and their work animals.[2]

Enclosing the X I T required fifteen hundred miles of fencing, and then it was ready. In 1885 to 1886 thousands of head of Texas cattle were purchased and driven to this ranch, which for management had to be subdivided, with a centrally located "camp" serving as the headquarters of each division. As the ranch became fully developed, it grazed one hundred and sixty thousand head of cattle.

Stockmen laid out several other mammoth ranches in Texas. In the southern part of the state Colonel Richard King owned eight hundred and fourteen thousand acres, on which he grazed sixty-five thousand head of cattle. Nearby was the ranch of Mifflin Kenedy, who had acquired one hundred and forty thousand acres. The Prairies Land and Cattle Company had one hundred and fifty thousand head of livestock on seventy-nine hundred square miles of ranchland in Texas, New Mexico, and Oklahoma. John Hittson grazed fifty thousand head on a big ranch on the Brazos River, and west of it lay the spread of John Chisum, who owned a herd of thirty thousand. Subsequently Chisum built up holdings extending for one hundred and fifty-five miles along the Pecos River in New Mexico and moved his headquarters to Fort Sumner.

The famous Maxwell Ranch in northeastern New Mexico supported a herd of ten thousand cattle and a flock of fifty thousand sheep. East of it lay the Bell Ranch, formerly the Pablo Montoya land grant. At its peak that cattle kingdom encompassed two million acres. In Arizona, Henry Clay Hooker bought a vast tract in Sulphur Springs Valley in 1872, and later the Aztec Land and Cattle Company grazed sixty thousand head on its ranches lying between Flagstaff and Holbrook. Another later spread, and a large one, was the old Babocomari land grant, which was acquired by American investors in 1880. Those cattlemen in Arizona drove their herds to market by way of the old Beale wagon road to Albuquerque or by a branch of the Loving-Goodnight Trail, which went east through El Paso.

In California the great cattle industry developed by the Dons on grants of land obtained in the colonial era or in the Mexico Period had declined due to some severe droughts before and during the Civil War. Thereafter in the dry summer months the raising of cattle was shifted to the mountain valleys. After the war a new center arose in the San Joaquin Valley, where Henry Miller and Charles Lux became the proprietors of a large ranch in the 1870s. They grazed a herd of over a hundred thousand head of cattle on land fronting on the river for forty miles.

TRANSFORMATION OF THE INDUSTRY

One of the reasons for the fencing in of the formerly open range arose from the transformation experienced by the

cattle industry. First, the invasion by many investors and competition from abroad caused overproduction, which in turn led to a slump in the market beginning in 1883, when the export of

[2] *Cattle Empire* (New York, 1949), p. 110.

American beef declined by fifty percent. By 1887 the stockyards were offering only three cents a pound for cattle
on the hoof. That decline alone caused
some of the big outfits to go broke, and
even more troubles were ahead. In the
years from 1885 to 1890 summer
droughts were followed by severe winters. Forage which was scarce even in
summer time became buried under
deep snow in the winter, and bad blizzards stranded the cattle. In the words
of Ray Allen Billington,

In the past cattle had withstood tempests
by drifting before them; now they piled up
against fences to die by the thousands. On
the heels of the storm came a numbing cold
which drove temperatures to sixty-eight
degrees below zero. Ranchers, huddling
about their stoves, did not dare think of
what was happening on the range—of help-
less cattle pawing at frozen snow in search
of a little food or fighting to strip bark from
willows and aspens along streams, "dogies"
floundering in drifts, whole herds jammed
together in ravines to escape the frosty
blast and die by the thousands. When spring
finally came cattlemen saw a sight they
spent the rest of their lives trying to forget.
Carcass piled upon carcass in every ravine,
gaunt skeletons staggering about on frozen
feet, heaps of dead bodies along the fences,
trees stripped bare of their bark—those
were left as monuments to the thoughtless
greed of the ranchers.[3]

The small operators held up through
the blizzards and the decline in prices
better than the big ones. As a precaution
against future catastrophes, they began
acquiring title to land, fencing in their
pastures, and improving their grazing
practices. Others moved onto the plains,

[3] *Western Expansion* (New York, 1949), p. 686.

too, and started fencing in small tracts
in the 1880s. They were pioneer farmers, or "nesters," as the cowmen dubbed
them. Many were attracted thither by
the advertisements of railway companies, which by that time were extending their trackage across the plains in
several localities. The arrival of the
nesters precipitated another conflict,
which often broke out into an open
range war. As they built their fences
around their farms, the cowboys armed
themselves with wirecutters as well as
six-shooters; they cut the barbed wire
and drove their trampling herds across
gardens and fields. The scattered settlers fought back feebly and fearfully
at first, but as their numbers grew they
gained strength. Moreover, the courts
upheld them, for they had titles to their
land. This competition for the range
caused the cattlemen to obtain titles,
too, and fence in their pastures; otherwise they would be left with no space
for grazing. Simultaneously the same
railroads which brought in the nesters
crisscrossed the plains farther west and
eliminated the need for trailing the
cattle on a long drive to a shipping
point.

The proximity of the rails, the invasion by nesters, the severe seasons,
and the floundering market, all combined to work a transformation in the
cattle industry. Many small ranches
appeared amid the big ones, and several of the latter were subdivided. As
fencing became a necessity, the cattlemen were able to turn to the breeding
of improved stock. They bred and grazed
Shorthorns and Herefords, which put
on more weight in less time than the
Longhorns. They studied and applied
the best feeding and grazing practices

of the time and maintained closer cost accounting.

As the revised methods of ranching became widely adopted, the new breeds displaced the Longhorns, which declined to near extinction. That sturdy animal could stand rougher treatment, but no longer was that necessary. Instead, the new, pampered stock produced beef of better quality so much faster that they commanded a much better price in relation to the cost of care, feed, and shipping. The earlier range industry ha*' risen and declined in response to the conditions of the times, but with its passing the cattle business had not suffered an eclipse. Instead, it had staged a comeback after the turning point in the 1880s, by changing form to an industry of specialized breeds fed on privately owned, fenced ranches. In 1900, more cattle were grazing on the grasslands of the Southwest than ever before, and the only semblance of the earlier open range was on the public lands in the mountain valleys and forests, which could be leased by ranchers for limited grazing of cattle.

THE ROUGH RIDERS

Upon the outbreak of the war with Spain in April, 1898, it was only natural that Theodore Roosevelt should recruit most of his "Rough Riders" from among the cowboys of the Southwest. First, Miguel A. Otero, Governor of the Territory of New Mexico, offered his services as a volunteer officer and wired the War Department on April 26: "Can raise a battalion of mounted riflemen in about a week." Then the Secretary of War offered a military command to Theodore Roosevelt, who was serving as under-secretary in the Department of the Navy. Realizing that he was young and lacking in training, Roosevelt recommended, instead, that if Dr. Leonard Wood would serve as colonel of a regiment to be raised in the Southwest, he would accept appointment as the lieutenant colonel. As soon as recruiting was authorized, cowboys, miners, freighters, and troopers of the territorial militia hastened to enlist. New Mexico provided the largest contingent, nearly forty percent of the eleven hundred volunteers. Approximately ten percent were Easterners, derisively dubbed the "Fifth Avenue Boys," and the remainder were contributed by the states of Texas, Colorado, and California and the territories of Arizona, and Oklahoma.

Colonel Wood went at once to San Antonio, Texas, where he prepared a training camp and mustered in the recruits. When Roosevelt arrived in May he found the boys "working like beavers" and added that he had "never seen such riding." Officially this was the First Regiment of United States Volunteers; but soon the newspaper reporters were referring to the regiment as "rough riders." Because of Roosevelt's renown for spectacular deeds, his name instead of that of Colonel Wood soon was coupled with the "Rough Riders."

Early in June the men and horses entrained for Tampa, Florida, where they were to embark for Cuba on a transport ship; but unfortunately the ship could not accommodate the regiment's horses. They had to be left behind, excepting those of the officers. Undaunted, the Rough Riders fought as "dismounted cavalry" at Las Guasimas and charged on foot up San Juan Hill near Santiago. Roosevelt boasted, "I waved my hat and we went up the hill with a rush." Actually those eager beavers attacked recklessly against needless odds, as if they were trying to win the war by themselves before other troopers could catch up with them. As a result they incurred heavy casualties, about seven times as great as those of other volunteer regiments. Admittedly they did accomplish their objectives, thereby contributing materially to the quick victory that summer.

During the campaign Leonard Wood was promoted to the rank of general, and Roosevelt was advanced to his place as commanding officer; therefore it was in fact Colonel Roosevelt's regiment when it was mustered out in New York in September. Nearly a year later, in June of 1899, several hundred of the young veterans met in Las Vegas, New Mexico, for their first annual encampment and reunion. Roosevelt, then governor of New York, rode in his service uniform at the head of the parade. Then the Rough Riders watched firemen's races in a city park and followed with a demonstration of their own skill as horsemen. Before a crowd of spectators they competed in pony racing, "bronco busting," and calf roping.

Rodeos of a kind had long been associated with the cattle industry of the Southwest. First came those of the Dons in southern California, and later similar demonstrations of skill had been seen on many of the ranches and in some towns of other localities. Once, also in Las Vegas, Charles Goodnight's cowboys, while engaging in their first northward cattle drive in 1866, entertained spectators with an impromptu performance much like a modern rodeo. North Platte, Nebraska, could also claim a similar early distinction, because tryouts were held there in 1882 for roles in the Buffalo Bill Wild West Show. The next year Pecos, Texas, organized some competitive events for cowboys, and at about that time Prescott, Arizona, promoted a similar public performance. But it was the show in Las Vegas, New Mexico, in 1899, which stood out as one of the greatest of that century. Because of its association with the popular "Teddy" and his Rough Riders, it received wide publicity, and by the same token it presented some of the best talent of the Southwest. It set the pattern for the commercialized rodeos of later years; cowboys pitted their strength against rough stock in unique events which perpetuated the robust heritage of the Cattle Country.

15
STEEL TRAILWAYS

Around the prospective railroad station now represented by two platform cars coupled together, a town of wooden buildings was springing up with western rapidity. The clatter of hammers, the fitting of lumber, and calls and imprecations, in the honest English tongue, filled the air. . . . A group of Mexicans squatted in a row on the ground and gazed at El Diablo, as they called the locomotive. . . . The scene was an interesting one, for it was the meeting of two civilizations, the Latin of three centuries ago and the Anglo Saxon of today. Across the river, a mile away, the old town of adobe lay about the plaza from which the narrow and crooked streets led out into the open country — the new town, already surveyed and laid out in lots, was building along the rectangular lines of wide streets and avenues.

The Boston Herald, *July 27, 1879*

In the years following the Civil War the growth of industry in the East and the extension of the frontier in the West stimulated spectacular railway promotion and construction. In the generation preceding 1860 some preliminary achievements had prepared the way.

EARLY PROMOTION

After the inauguration of the first successful but short line back in 1830, the building of railroads had been promoted enthusiastically in Congress, in the press, and at railway conventions in the 1840s, and trunk lines had been extended westward to the Mississippi in the 1850s. The Illinois Central had established a precedent in 1851 by obtaining indirect grants of land from the public domain, but the bugaboo of States' Rights would deter any other pursuit of that precedent as long as the South was influential in the Congress. Then, as California drew immigrants to the west coast and the cattle industry built towns on the plains, enterprising men envisioned the laying of tracks across the plains and through the mountain passes to ports on the Pacific.

As early as 1845, Asa Whitney of New York had proposed the building of a railroad from the Great Lakes west to Oregon, and Sam Houston of Texas had countered by recommending a line running from Galveston to San Diego by way of the Gila River. In 1853, Senator Gwin of California presented a plan for branches starting at St. Louis, Memphis, and New Orleans to converge in Texas, whence they would form one trunk line running through Albuquerque to San Francisco. However, the bridging of the wide gaps between the settlements was hardly feasible then without federal aid, which would not be forthcoming while civil war was imminent; consequently the construction of transcontinental railways would be delayed until the times were more auspicious.

In that preliminary era before the Civil War, the first railway lines of the Southwest had been built in Texas and in California. At Harrisburg, Texas, near Houston, track was laid in 1852 for the beginning of the Buffalo Bayou, Brazos, and Colorado Railroad; but after eight years the line had been extended only to Alleyton, near the Colorado River of Texas. Simultaneously another, the Houston and Texas Central, was being built up the valley of the Brazos River toward Millican, where it arrived in 1860. Two more were added in 1859 when the Texas and New Orleans laid track from Houston to Orange on the Sabine River and the Brazoria Railroad built a line connecting Columbia on the Brazos River with the Harrisburg Railroad. These railways and a few shorter ones were serving south central Texas with a total of three hundred and six miles of track in 1860.

In California the building of railways also got a start in the 1850s, but on a scale even smaller than that of Texas. Three short lines, the California Central, the Las Mariposas, and the Sacramento Valley, had a total of seventy miles of line in operation by 1860.

Wherever the early railroads were built, they displaced the stagecoaches. The greater speed by rail made that service more desirable despite the hazards of collision with buffaloes or wagons and the frequent derailment of trains.

However, the railways did not immediately eliminate the stagecoaches, for the latter continued to provide "feeder" service from small towns to the terminals where the "iron horse" stopped for the loading of passengers and freight.

FEDERAL AID

During the Civil War, with the North in control in Washington, the central route to the Pacific won undisputed preference over the southern route and, in 1862, the Congress passed the first Pacific Railway Act. By its provisions the western portion of the line was to be built by the Central Pacific Railroad Company, which had been incorporated in California in 1861. In that company the original promoter was Theodore D. Judah, a young engineer who had previously been employed by the Sacramento Valley Railways Company. He aroused the interest of Charles Crocker, Mark Hopkins, Collis P. Huntington, and Leland Stanford, who later became the famous "Big Four" of the Central Pacific. Much of the early groundwork, however, was contributed by Judah. Because he was dissatisfied with the surveys of routes through the mountains sponsored by the government in 1853, he made his own and found a more practicable pass through the Sierra Nevada range. Then he went to Washington, where his effective lobbying obtained congressional designation of his company as the builder of the western part of the first transcontinental line.

Judah claimed that he refused to be a party to some deception in which his partners were willing to indulge in order to collect generous subsidies from the government. For that reason, he obtained options to buy them out and then went east in order to seek the participation of other capitalists. His death in New York in November, 1863, prevented the consummation of his plan for reorganization.

The Pacific Railway Act provided that the eastern part of the line was to be built by a new corporation, the Union Pacific Railroad Company. Several privately built railways were to converge at Council Bluffs, Iowa, whence the government-sponsored tracks to be laid by the new company would extend westward until they connected with those of the Central Pacific at the Nevada-California boundary. The act provided further that funds for financing the railroad would be derived from a government subsidy, first mortgage bonds, a grant of public lands, and by popular subscription to capital stock. The government granted a right-of-way from the public domain and five alternate sections of land on either side of the track for each mile built. Because those alternate sections presumably would be held for several years until the value of the land increased, the intervening squares on the checkerboard would be available in the meantime for purchase or homesteading by settlers, who then would provide some local passenger and freight traffic for the railroad.

The lands granted to the railway company would immediately give it something tangible for the security of a government loan. As soon as each section of forty miles of track was laid according to specifications, acceptance of the work by federal commissioners would qualify the company for receipt of an issue of United States bonds in the amount of sixteen thousand dollars for each mile in level country, twice that amount in rugged foothills or plateaus, and thrice as much, or forty-eight thousand dollars, in the mountain ranges. Those bonds would not be an outright gift; instead they would be a federal loan granted as a first mortgage. After completion of the line, five percent of the annual earnings were to be reserved for paying off the bonds.

Congressional legislation for the building of a transcontinental railway caused great rejoicing among railroad financiers and in the cities along the proposed route. The Congress had offered land and funds, and one jubilant proponent exlaimed that everyone was "trying to show his zeal in worshiping the road." However, hope had mounted too high too soon, for after two years not a mile of track had been laid. Then Thomas C. Durant, executive vice president of the Union Pacific Company, appealed to the Congress for the granting of more liberal terms. In response a new act was passed in 1864. It doubled the grant of land from five to ten sections for each mile and made the government bonds a second mortgage, so that the company could obtain private loans as a first mortgage.

ACROSS THE CONTINENT

Durant organized a finance company, which he called the "Credit Mobilier." By it an inside ring of financiers assured themselves double profits by holding the preferred stock and handling the construction contracts, too. The company employed Peter A. Dey as the first construction engineer, but he resigned after he found that the officers had rigged the specifications in the first contracts. In his place the company engaged General Grenville Dodge, who had demonstrated his ability as an engineer and administrator while building military railroads during the Civil War. Immediately he established the rule that he should have full charge in the field, with "no divided interests and no railroad masters in New York." Finally the long idle Union Pacific Company was ready to begin construction.

The Union Pacific was supposed to connect with some branches converging at Council Bluffs, but in 1865 those auxiliary lines had not yet been completed; therefore the new company began construction at Omaha. The first rail was spiked to the ties on July 10, and forty miles of track were laid in the next four months. Thereafter General Dodge pushed the work along more rapidly. He sent a surveying party ahead for locating the route. Next came the grading crew, which prepared the road bed, and the bridge gang followed them. Finally the tracks were laid by a corps of stalwart Irishmen, who set the wooden cross ties and spiked the steel rails to them. Bringing up the rear, on the constructed track, freight trains transported the necessary materials from the starting point on the Missouri River.

General Dodge personally supervised the investigation of alternate routes and selected one which followed up the Platte River into the mountains and crossed the divide through Lone Tree Pass. By January, 1867, two hundred and sixty miles of track had been laid to a temporary terminal in North Platte, Nebraska. That winter raids by hostile Indians were threatening to impede progress, but the government sent out three troops of cavalry and the work proceeded. By summer in 1867 the terminal camp was at Julesburg, Colorado, and by autumn the crews were housed in winter quarters in Cheyenne, Wyoming. In the year 1867 General Dodge had built two hundred and forty miles of track, or about twenty miles a month, and the directors looked forward ambitiously to a figure doubling that amount in the next year. For this final exertion they purchased a large stock of materials and sent it to Cheyenne.

The officers of the company had a strong motive for making haste. The estimates of their engineer indicated that the railroad could be built through the mountains for less than the forty-eight thousand dollars a mile which the government would lend, leaving a cash surplus. Moreover, in 1866, the Central Pacific also had been making haste and now it had obtained approval to cross the California line and build on eastward through Nevada. Thenceforth the two companies would be competing for the lucrative federal loan to be allowed for each mile of track laid in the mountains.

Good teamwork had contributed to the rapid headway made by the western portion of the line. The Central Pacific Company had as its titular executive a good public relations man, Leland Stanford, ex-governor of California. Huntington assumed Judah's former function as promoter of smooth working relations with the federal government, Hopkins was the office manager who kept the books and held a rein on his partners whenever necessary, and Crocker, an efficient superintendent of construction, could boast afterward that he was the one who actually built the railroad.

Although the Big Four already had teamed up before the first railway act was passed in 1862, they encountered difficulties which delayed the beginning of work. Even after the inducement had been doubled in the amended charter of 1864, work proceeded slowly

at first. After a full year the Central Pacific had only sixty-five miles of track. Then Crocker concluded to try Chinese laborers. His experiment in the employment of fifty of the Orientals demonstrated that the Chinese had the necessary stamina and that they were less inclined than Irish Americans to go on strike. Crocker then arranged for the importation of shiploads of Chinese laborers. At the rail head they took over the strenuous labor under the supervision of American foremen. When the track penetrated into the rugged Sierra Nevada Mountains, the Chinese workmen patiently chiseled Summit Tunnel through the hard granite. Then when the rails reached the state line in June of 1868, the company directors obtained congressional approval for building on eastward. Now the managers began straining for the race with Union Pacific through the mountainous country of Nevada and Utah.

The competing superintendents reinforced their crews of laborers and drove them on relentlessly. As the two lines approached each other, the advance surveying parties marked routes which would run parallel without meeting. In fact, the amended act failed to specify where the tracks should meet, and it appeared that the two companies might build competing railways across Utah, or perhaps all of the way across the West, in order to collect the lucrative government subsidies for both tracks. To prevent this possible duplication, the Congress had to intervene. The officers of the two companies were called to the Capitol, where they reached an agreement embodied in a special supplementary act. Promontory Point in Utah would be the meeting

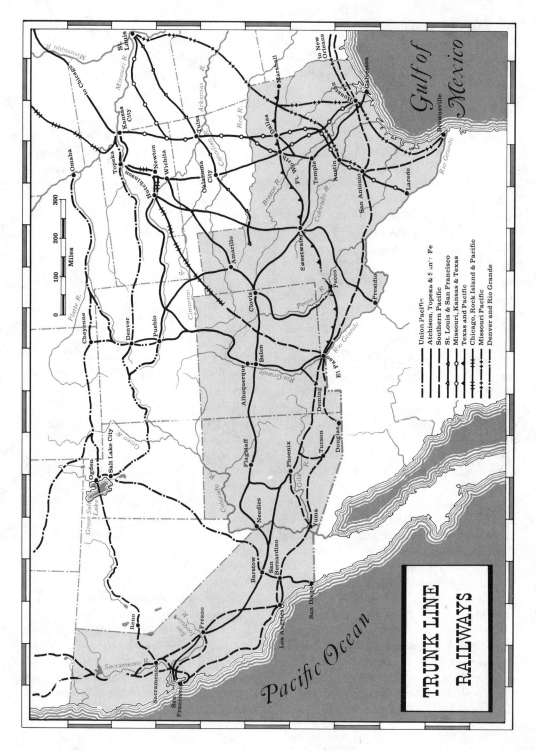

place of the two lines.

In early May, 1869, Stanford's special train reached the place where the rails would be joined, and a few days later Durant's train arrived. Then came the festive ceremonies. While the Twenty-First Infantry Band played patriotic music, the workmen laid the last rail on the wooden ties with holes bored in some for the gentle reception of special spikes moulded from Nevada silver, Idaho and Montana gold and silver, and Arizona gold, silver, and iron. After they had been tapped into place, so that they could be removed and preserved as mementos, Stanford and Durant each took a light swing at the final one, made of California gold, which General

Dodge finished tapping into its hole. The two engineers eased forward their locomotives on the finished track until their cowcatchers touched, and then they drank a toast in champagne. That signaled the outburst of a general celebration at the junction point and in eastern cities where a telegraphic signal reported the job done. At last the East and Far West had been connected by a railway that would inaugurate a new era not only in California but also in the territories which it crossed. Moreover, this spectacular achievement stimulated efforts to build other railroads over the routes already surveyed across the western half of the nation. Two of them would also serve the Southwest.

ON THE SOUTHERN ROUTE

The next transcontinental railway to be completed extended the full west-to-east length of the southwestern states and territories. It originated as the project of two companies, both of which aspired to build all of the way. One was the Southern Pacific, organized and owned by the Big Four of California. It was chartered in 1865 to build not only in California but also eastward on the old Mormon road approximating the thirty-second parallel. If it were to succeed, progress would have to be rapid, because another company, the Texas and Pacific, obtained a charter in 1871 for the building of a railroad on the same route, but westward from Marshall, Texas, to San Diego, California.

The original section of the Texas Pacific Railroad from Longview to Dallas started operation in 1873. The financial depression beginning in that

year then caused a delay until Jay Gould and Russell Sage took charge and obtained new financial support. Also, as work progressed they would receive generous grants of land from the State of Texas as well as subsidies in the form of bond issues promised by counties and towns along the way. For management of the construction they employed General Dodge, who had finished his work on the Union Pacific. As he applied his usual energetic measures, he hoped to make sufficient speed so that he could meet the Southern Pacific at Yuma on the western border of Arizona. However, the latter company had greater resources and its own efficient superintendent of construction, Charles Crocker.

On March 19, 1879, the Southern Pacific was completed to Tucson, Arizona, and in March a year later it reached El Paso. The officers of the slower-moving Texas Pacific, therefore, had to be content with an agreement connecting the two tracks at Sierra Blanca, ninety-two miles east of El Paso. An eastward extension acquired by the Texas Pacific then provided direct connection from New Orleans to California along the thirty-second parallel route. In 1884, Huntington of the Big Four reorganized the Southern Pacific Company, which leased or bought connecting lines and brought under one management a railway system extending from Portland, Oregon, and Ogden, Utah, to San Francisco, thence southward to Guadalajara in Mexico, and from Los Angeles eastward across the Southwest to New Orleans.

PROGRESS OF THE SANTA FE

Another railroad, the Atchison, Topeka, and Santa Fe, originated as a local line, but soon acquired a transcontinental goal. Actually it entered New Mexico a little ahead of the Southern Pacific, but did not immediately acquire its own tracks to the west coast. The president, Cyrus K. Holliday, originally planned to build a railroad only from Topeka, Kansas, to his home town, Atchison, and the outbreak of civil conflict delayed the building of that line. During the Civil War, he expanded his ambitions. He would extend the railroad along the old Santa Fe Trail and link the cities in Kansas with those of the Southwest.

Holliday enlisted the financial support of some Kansas and Texas capitalists, who obtained a charter from the Congress in 1863 and employed Otis Berthoude Gunn as construction engineer. After he had completed a survey from Topeka to Atchison in 1866, Thomas J. Peter replaced him and continued the advance planning.

By the terms of the charter, the Santa Fe Railroad would receive alternate sections of land for ten miles on both sides of the track for each mile built, like the Union Pacific, but in this case the land would be granted only if the track reached the Kansas-Colorado line by December, 1873. That objective seemed almost unattainable in the lean years immediately following the war. Money was scarce and capitalists were hesitant about making an investment with only a promise of land in the future as collateral. In that critical time two fortuitous developments were all that kept the project alive. One was the employment of Tom Peter, who not only invested some of his own money but also obtained funds from some eastern financiers. The other was the opportune acquisition of some Indian land at a bargain price. On the Pottawatamie Reservation three hundred and forty thousand acres had been granted to a railroad company which failed to do any building, and now the Santa Fe company purchased one-third of it for one dollar an acre. The possession of land made possible the raising of funds. Some came in the form of loans secured by the land, more accrued from the sale of shares, and additional sums were advanced by the counties through which the railroad would operate.

Finally, in October of 1868, work began on the section of the line from Atchison to Topeka, and in March the first train ran between those two cities. By September 1869, however, the line reached no farther west than Burlingame, twenty-six miles from Topeka. Even so, some confident promoters laid out the town of Newton on the route ahead, and when the railroad arrived there in 1871 it already had six thousand eager citizens. Then, with funds exhausted, the line stopped at Newton. Further extension had to be held up until capital could be built up by the profitable operation of the road already built. During the recess Tom Peter surveyed a branch to Wichita, Kansas, and after his company failed to accept this branch, he organized his own company and built it himself. Later the Santa Fe directors conceded that he had made a sound investment and leased the subsidiary track from him.

J. D. (Pete) Criley, assisted by a new engineer, Albert A. Robinson, supervised the renewed construction westward. At that time only a year remained before the offer of land would expire, and the end of the track was almost three hundred miles from the Colorado line. Then Criley reorganized the crews and spurred the men on for a race against the deadline. By concerted exertion the construction gang soon was finishing three miles of track daily, and late in December, in good time, the railroad reached the border of the Territory of Colorado. Then the acquisition of the promised grant of nearly two million acres of land could have assured continuation of construction into the Southwest if the panic of 1873 had not pulled the props out from under the financial structure and temporarily delayed the construction.

THE RACE WITH RIVALS

Despite the hard times, a loan presently was obtained with the land as security, and then construction began on the extension of the line through Colorado. As the tracks approached Pueblo, the Santa Fe encountered competition. The Kansas Pacific also had a charter for the building of a railroad on that route, and when the grading crews of the two companies crossed paths, a lively row ensued. Fortunately for the Santa Fe, the citizens of Pueblo favored that company. They sent out posses of armed men, who held strategic places along the route and enabled the Santa Fe to win the race.

Another critical race soon ensued. The old Santa Fe Trail crossed from southern Colorado into northeastern New Mexico by way of Raton Pass, which already was established as the best route for the laying of tracks over the mountains on the way to Santa Fe. Another railway, the Denver and Rio Grande, which was building south from Denver, had El Paso as its objective. Already it, too, was at Pueblo, and if it were ever to cross New Mexico, it would have to enter that territory by way of the same pass; but the narrow defile could accommodate only one right-of-way.

In Raton Pass, Richens Lacy Wootton, familiarly known as "Uncle Dick," had improved the rocky trail and now operated it as a toll road. The company which could first make a deal with Wootton and start grading a roadbed in the Pass would be the victor in this race. Agents of the rival companies came to Trinidad simultaneously, but the Santa Fe representatives, William R. Morley and Albert A. Robinson, reached Wootton first. When they offered him a cash settlement of fifty thousand dollars for his toll road, he replied that he would prefer a lifetime pass on the railroad and twenty-five dollars a month for groceries. Agreement on these terms enabled the Santa Fe men to begin work. That night they hired some laborers, equipped them with picks, shovels, and lanterns, and started turning dirt for a graded roadbed. When the Rio Grande men arrived, they saw that the Santa Fe had won the race.

In the autumn of 1878 the Santa Fe workmen laid track by Wootton's place, and on December 1 a locomotive crossed the line into New Mexico. On July 1 the track reached Las Vegas, and three days later the first train arrived at the makeshift depot at that former Mexican port of entry on the Santa Fe Trail. To the chagrin of the Spanish-American townsmen, however, the engineers had chosen a route which missed the plaza by a mile. A new Anglo-American town immediately mushroomed along the tracks across the river from Old Town. Meanwhile construction proceeded by way of Rowe and over Glorieta Pass to Santa Fe, where the townsmen celebrated with a joyous parade when the first train arrived on February 9, 1880. The original Atchison and Topeka Railroad at last had justified the addition of "Santa Fe" in its title.

The Santa Fe had come off victorious in one race with the Denver and Rio Grande only to lose out in the next encounter. The builders of the latter line,

frustrated in their desire to reach El Paso, decided to extend their tracks westward across the Rocky Mountains. The approach to the summit lay in the deep Royal Gorge of the Arkansas River at Cañon City, Colorado. The Santa Fe men also became ambitious to build in that direction, and soon the rival crews came into conflict in the Gorge. This time they built stone forts, loaded hired gunmen on locomotives, and prepared for a real battle. When it appeared that the outcome might be determined by sheer force and the loss of many lives, the directors of the two companies conferred and agreed upon a settlement on March 27, 1880. The Denver and Rio Grande would pay the Santa Fe one million four hundred thousand dollars for the construction work already completed along this route, and the Santa Fe would stay out of Denver and Leadville for at least ten years. Subsequently the Denver and Rio Grande built on westward into the mountains, where its narrow gauge tracks served mining towns in southern Colorado. Since some of the branches lay in the upper valley of the Rio Grande, this railroad finally had justification for use of the name "Denver and Rio Grande."

After losing in the competition for control of the Royal Gorge, the Santa Fe directors hoped to find some other way for extension of their tracks to the west coast. There remained one feasible route following Beale's camel trail along the thirty-fifth parallel, but it was tied up legally. A charter for construction on that route had been obtained by the Atlantic and Pacific Company. Although no building had been done, the existence of that charter blocked the way. For the time being the only chance for continuation of traffic to California would be by means of a connection with some other railroad. As described previously, the Southern Pacific was building toward El Paso in 1880, when the Santa Fe reached the capital of New Mexico. Therefore the latter company built track down the Rio Grande valley through Albuquerque in 1881 and made a junction with the Southern Pacific at Deming on March 8 of that year. This connection provided railway transportation from Kansas City to all towns in the Southwest served both by the Santa Fe and Southern Pacific.

Still the directors of the Santa Fe company wanted to run trains on their own tracks to the west coast, and one good route remained unused. Early in 1881 the Santa Fe, in partnership with the St. Louis and San Francisco Railway Company, acquired control of the nearly defunct Atlantic and Pacific company, which held the charter to lay a track along the thirty-fifth parallel. Immedi-

ately the builders began grading on that route. Rails were laid west through Gallup, New Mexico, and Winslow and Flagstaff in Arizona, but now the Southern Pacific stood in the way. The Big Four had hastily built a branch to Needles, California, in order to hold that gateway against any rival approaching from the east. The only solution would be another agreement, with the Union Pacific, for a connection at Needles and the handling of Santa Fe traffic from that point on to the coastal cities. This done, the Santa Fe inaugurated service on this route to the coast on August 21, 1883. A year later the Santa Fe leased the Needles-Mojave branch of the Southern Pacific and built an extension in 1885 over Cajón Pass and by way of San Bernardino, California, to the port of San Diego. At last Santa Fe trains could run on their own track from Kansas City to southern California, and by means of an eastern extension built to Chicago three years later, this railway then provided through service from that city to the Pacific Coast.

OTHER TRUNK LINES

While the major transcontinental railways were being built westward, the Southwest was also being criss-crossed by other trunk lines. By 1872 the Houston and Texas Central had built from Millican north to Dallas, and the Missouri, Kansas, and Texas, known as the "Katy," reached south across Indian Territory to Denison, Texas. The Missouri Pacific built a railroad from St. Louis and New Orleans to the gulf ports of Texas. Soon the International and Great Northern provided for transportation diagonally

across Texas by running a line from Longview in the east to Hearne on the Texas Pacific and thence south to Laredo on the Rio Grande. This road was absorbed later into the Southern Pacific system, as was the Galveston, Harrisburg, and San Antonio, which was extended to a point near El Paso in 1880. Another, the Fort Worth and Denver City, which built west across the Texas Panhandle to Texline in 1888, became a branch in the Burlington system. Then the Gulf, Colorado, and Santa Fe line which connected Galveston and Fort

Worth in 1881, was absorbed by the Santa Fe company five years later. The latter provided a connection with this acquisition by running a branch south from Newton, Kansas, to Fort Worth, Texas.

The Santa Fe built an alternate track from Kansas City through Indian Territory and across the Texas Panhandle to a junction with its original trunk line at Belen, New Mexico; but in conformity with the laws of Texas, this branch was incorporated in Texas as the Panhandle and Santa Fe. Later, in 1900, Arthur E. Stillwell, a Kansas City insurance man and railway promoter, conceived a plan for the building of a railway from Kansas City southwest across Kansas, Oklahoma Territory, Texas, and Mexico to Topolobampo on the Gulf of California. After several obstacles had been overcome, track was laid on most of the route which he proposed, and ultimately that portion connecting Kansas City with Presidio on the Rio Grande became a unit in the Santa Fe system. Another diagonal line, the San Pedro, Los Angeles, and Salt Lake, was completed in 1905 by

a company headed by William A. Clark, and it soon was taken over by the Union Pacific.

In the early period of railroading in the Southwest the travelers in wooden coaches drawn by steam-powered locomotives had experiences with equipment and methods which would be considered quaint by modern standards. As quoted by L. L. Waters, one engineer on the Santa Fe recalled later that,

In those days we never got any train running orders. We ran exclusively by smoke and headlight. We never had any collisions, except with buffalo. My conductor was a character. He never wore a coat, he had been a rustler and an ox skinner in the West for years and had never worn a coat since he had been there, and only one heavy flannel shirt. Our food was buffalo meat. . . . The bread came from Lawrence, Kansas, and by the time we got it, it was hard enough to knock down a buffalo with.[1]

Nevertheless, the railways provided a needed service with speed greatly improved over that of the pack train and freight wagon, and they created a marvelous spectacle for the frontiersman.

THE HARVEY SYSTEM

Rapidly many refinements were introduced, and notable among them were the services of the unique Harvey system which paralleled the Santa Fe Railroad. In 1875, when Fred Harvey took over management of the restaurant in the Topeka depot, he improved greatly the quality of food and service. Soon he added another Harvey House at Florence, Kansas, and quite rapidly he acquired other links in a chain extending along the Santa Fe Railroad

from Chicago to the west coast. He maintained luxury hotels in sixteen places, including Las Vegas, Santa Fe, and Albuquerque in New Mexico, Seligman and the Grand Canyon in Arizona, and Barstow on the Mojave Desert. In other cities his establishment was comprised of a restaurant, curio shop, and newsstand. In all of his eating places he

[1] *Steel Trails to Santa Fe* (Lawrence, Kansas, 1950), p. 290.

sought to provide the best available food and services.

Before dining cars were introduced, the trains stopped at meal time in one of the cities where a Harvey House adjoined the depot. To expedite the service, orders taken on the moving train were telegraphed ahead to the restaurant, where the dinners were prepared in advance, ready for serving promptly upon the arrival of the passengers. After dining cars were included in the trains, Harvey also managed the food service on them, with his traditionally high standards.

By several achievements Fred Harvey earned his reputation as the "civilizer of the West." In the course of time he employed close to five thousand girls in the East and Midwest and sent them out to his restaurants under the chaperonage of trusted matrons. He required that the girls sign a contract not to get married for at least one year; but sooner or later, often sooner, they were wed to Western railroaders, ranchers, and businessmen and became the mothers of well-reared youth throughout the Southwest.

In addition, by including books in the stock for sale at the newsstands, Fred Harvey stimulated the interest of many Westerners in literature. Furthermore, he contributed an improvement in the economy of some of the Indian tribes by marketing their handcrafted jewelry and rugs through his curio shops. If the wares did not come up to the desired standards, he even sent craftsmen out to some of the pueblos for supervision of their handiwork. That investment returned good dividends, as more and more tavelers became purchasers of the unique, colorful wares produced by the skilled tribesmen.

FROM PROMOTION TO REGULATION

Enthusiasm for the advantages of the new services became a rage, as the railways extended their facilities into the remoteness of the Southwest. Texas was unique in that that state possessed its own public domain, of which twenty-four million acres, or one-tenth of the area of the state, were donated to forty-one railroad companies. In that state and elsewhere one city after another voted upon itself a large indebtedness in the form of bond issues in order to secure a connection with centers of commerce by the new means of rapid transportation. Enthusiastic promoters charted numerous feeder lines, some of which were never built. In Arizona and New Mexico a few branches radi-

ated from the principal cities, but in those territories the sparse population did not justify much construction of subsidiary lines. In Texas and California, on the other hand, where the open spaces were filling up fast, a network of short lines soon crisscrossed the countryside. By 1910, all of Texas was well served by fourteen thousand miles of railroads, while California with eight thousand was not far behind.

The initial enthusiasm subsided as the patrons of the railways soberly arrived at the conclusion that they had become dependent upon an institution in which a remote and "soulless" corporation had the advantages of a natural monopoly. This awakening was reflected in the demand for regulation of railroads which swept across Texas and California. An article in the new constitution of Texas which was adopted in 1876 declared railways to be "common carriers" on "public highways," subject to regulation by the legislature "to correct abuses." Companies were required to keep their books open to inspection, and consolidation of competing lines was forbidden. In 1879, the legislature went a step further by adopting an act which regulated freight rates, and three years later, another which reduced passenger rates. Critics of the railways, who contended that such piecemeal legislation was inadequate, encouraged the young and vigorous attorney general, James S. Hogg, to assume the role of guardian of the public interest against corporate abuses. In the late 1880s he launched a campaign of prosecution of railways. He fought nonresident control, he required the companies to maintain managing offices within the state, and he forced the dissolution of a traffic pool in which nine companies had been cooperating. Then he sponsored a constitutional amendment which would establish a state regulatory commission. After the amendment was adopted, such a commission was created in 1891 under the chairmanship of John H. Reagan. This body undertook the prevention of discrimination in railway services and the regulation of passenger and freight rates. In subsequent years it became recognized as an effective agency.

Simultaneously in California the agitation for regulation of railways elicited from the Constitutional Convention of 1878 a provision for the creation of a railroad commission. After the constitution was adopted, however, the newly formed agency disappointed its sponsors. Application of effective controls proved to be difficult in a state in which a real and powerful monopoly existed in the hands of the all-pervasive Southern Pacific Company. In 1880, for example, at Mussel Slough in Tulare County, the company had offered to sell some settlers railroad lands, only to delay conveying the title in an effort to extort from them a higher price. When the settlers protested, the company initiated proceedings for their eviction. In the clash which ensued, five were killed and seven others were haled into court for resisting arrest. Of the latter, five were convicted and sentenced to terms of eight months in jail. In addition the company had been employing a lobbyist in Washington, one David D. Colton, whose correspondence which came to light after his death in 1878 revealed that he had been engaging in some rather dubious tactics in his manipulations in behalf of favorable legislation for his employers.

The Free Harbor Fight at Los Angeles illustrated further the powerful influence of the Southern Pacific. Because the port facilities at San Pedro, which served Los Angeles, had become inadequate for handling the ocean-going ships of that era, the Los Angeles Chamber of Commerce sought federal aid for improvement of the harbor. In 1892, however, Collis P. Huntington, one of the Big Four, announced that his company would make the desired improvements at the harbor of Santa Monica, nearby, where incidentally the Southern Pacific owned all of the waterfront. Obviously this proposal would influence the Congress against adoption of the Free Harbor Bill, and failure to improve the harbor at San Pedro, upon which the Santa Fe Railroad was dependent, would be a severe blow to that railroad. Therefore the Santa Fe company joined with the Los Angeles Chamber of Commerce in pressing for favorable action in Washington. When the bill came out of committee in 1896, however, Huntington's influence had prevailed. The bill had been revised so that Santa Monica, not San Pedro, would get an astonishingly large appropriation, approximately three million dollars. Then California's senator, Stephen M. White, took up the fight for an amendment in favor of the free harbor at San Pedro. When the amended bill carried, the Southern Pacific had lost in the effort to obtain federal aid for a port wherein it would have complete control.

The Free Harbor Fight had shifted the issue of regulating California's railway monopoly from the state to the national arena. Likewise, publication of a novel, *The Octopus,* in which Frank Norris described railway abuses, especially the Mussel Slough affair, aroused national concern. Then upon the death of Huntington in 1901, the merger of the Central Pacific and Union Pacific lines brought fifteen thousand miles of track into one mammoth system. That, too, called attention to the growth of a problem beyond the reach of the regulatory body of California or of any one state. Back in 1887, the Congress had established the Interstate Commerce Commission for the assumption of the larger task; but it, too, had thus far been rather ineffective. Now, finally, the adoption of more specific measures, followed by President Theodore Roosevelt's "trust-busting" campaign, made the national regulatory procedures more effective in California as well as in the remainder of the nation.

A BOON TO MINING AND MANUFACTURING

Despite the occasional abuses and the animosity which the railroads provoked, they did effect a rapid and appreciated transformation in the economy of the Southwest. Their influence upon the development of the cattle industry has been described above. They also affected profoundly another area of industrial activity—mining. Earlier efforts had been concentrated mainly upon the mining of the precious metals, gold and silver, which could bear the cost of tedious removal by pack train; but copper, coal, and petroleum could not be handled by such means. Now the railways became available for bringing in heavy equipment and hauling out the ores.

In California the figures for mineral production in the latter part of the nineteenth century show that gold and silver still remained paramount. In the output of gold only Colorado exceeded California in 1900: in silver production the coastal state ranked seventh in the Union, and copper mining was increasing. By that date the development of railway and ocean shipping had increased the production of "black gold." In the 1880s, oil fields were producing at Whittier, Summerland, and Puente Hills, and in 1893 the Los Angeles-

Salt Lake field was discovered. At the end of the century California wells were pumping over four million barrels annually, an amount surpassed in only four other states.

California also acquired a specialized industry as the result of the discovery of borax in Death Valley in 1880. The Harmony Borax Company, later reorganized as the Pacific Coast Borax Company, paid twenty thousand dollars for the claim of Aaron and Rosie Winters, the ranchers who had identified the deposits. Over the desert trail to the railway at Mojave the company hauled out the borax on large wagons drawn by two horses and eighteen mules, from which came the popular title, "Twenty Mule Team Borax Company." After 1890, however, mountain deposits yielded most of the borax, which was shipped on a spur railway line to a refinery in San Francisco.

In Texas, where very little gold ever had been found, some silver was mined and the yield continued to be fairly good in 1900. In this state the production of coal was on the increase by 1900, but more significant was the early boom in the production of petroleum. In the 1860s, a field had been opened near Nacogdoches, followed thirty years later by another at Corsicana. In 1900 the wells in those fields accounted for the major portion of the eight hundred thirty-five thousand barrels produced in Texas. The very next year that output was more than doubled by production spouting from a gusher in a new field, the "Spindletop," at Beaumont. That and other areas of drilling increased the output of the state to twenty-eight million barrels in 1905. Because the automobile age was just dawning, the demands of the market were as yet insufficient for absorption of the great production of which Texas fields were capable. After 1905 production declined until the big boom of the 1920s.

In both Texas and California the building of railways, along with the availability of fuel, stimulated the growth of manufacturing. In Texas, as Beaumont and Orange became important sawmill centers, production was exceeding a billion board feet annually by the end of the century. Fort Worth, where stockyards were built in 1890, assumed leadership in meat packing. Dallas, near Fort Worth, turned in a different direction after the establishment of textile plants made it a rising center of cotton processing.

In California, as in Texas, lumbering emerged as the early industry of significance. In Humboldt and Mendocino Counties the giant redwood trees were felled and processed to meet the demands of cities, mines, and railways. Flour milling became another early industry of importance, as did the making of wagons and carriages in numerous small shops. Textile manufacturing, sugar refining, and cigar making also appeared quite early.

In New Mexico some of the early mines were restored to production and new ones were opened in the latter part of the nineteenth century. Silver and copper were mined in Socorro County, the old placer mines on the Ortiz Grant near Santa Fe continued to produce gold, and silver strikes were made in Grant County. The production of coal, mostly from mines near Raton, Gallup, and Santa Fe, boosted the territory up to first place in the

Southwest. Then in 1880, prospectors found "The Bridal Chamber," a silver-walled cave, in Sierra County, and simultaneously the Solitaire Mine made a boom town of Kingston. Within the ensuing decade gold discoveries at the Aztec and Mystic mines created a roaring camp at Elizabethtown on the Maxwell Ranch. Meanwhile the old copper mine at Santa Rita was being worked steadily. Although the production was fairly good in the latter part of the nineteenth century, it would be increased greatly a little later, in 1910, when the Kennecott Copper Company began utilizing heavy machinery for pit mining. Even so, in 1900 New Mexico held seventh place in the Union in copper production, while the rank of this territory was tenth and eleventh, respectively, in gold and silver.

In Arizona, after the coming of the railroads, the mineral industries boomed to unforeseen magnitude. The Silver King mine near Superior began production in 1876, shortly before the advent of the Southern Pacific Railroad, and in its first decade it yielded silver valued at more than six million dollars. In 1877, another rich discovery was made at Tombstone on the desert in the southeastern part of the territory. From 1880 to 1888, the era of lush production, the Tombstone district produced gold and silver valued at over a million dollars. In time the deep shafts began to fill

with water and, although efforts were made to pump it out, the yield of rich ore never again reached the earlier mark. In the 1890s Arizona experienced a new gold rush induced by the opening of rich mines near Prescott and Yuma.

Especially significant in Arizona was the rapid increase in the mining of copper. In the 1850s an early beginning had been made, and then in the 1870s the great producers were opened in the Clarkdale, Bisbee, Globe, and Morenci districts. The richest of the mines, the Copper Queen at Bisbee, has yielded over one hundred million dollars worth of ore. In 1885, it was acquired by the Phelps-Dodge Corporation, which subsequently also bought up other rich mines in Arizona. In 1900, this company built a copper smelting plant near the southern boundary of the territory, where the new city of Douglas soon arose. By that date the production of one hundred and eighteen million pounds annually gave Arizona third place in the Union in copper production. This territory also was strong in its output of gold and silver, ranking fifth and sixth respectively. The processing of minerals contributed a large part of the twenty million dollar value added by manufacturing in Arizona in 1900, a figure much larger than that of New Mexico but less than one-twentieth of the amount reported in California.

DEVELOPMENT OF AGRICULTURE

In the late nineteenth century, while mining and manufacturing were expanding, agriculture also made rapid gains after the building of the railroads, especially in Texas and California. In fact,

the boom was promoted by the railway companies, whose directors realized that the stimulation of migration to the lands along their tracks would create needed business for the newly built lines. They ran excursion trains frequently and distributed pamphlets advertising the marvelous productivity of these lands. Some companies even sent immigration agents to the East and abroad in order to induce settlers to make their homes on the farmland along the routes of their railways.

In Texas the liberal land laws encouraged immigration. In 1876, that state still possessed about sixty million acres of public domain, and three years later the legislature offered the unappropriated lands for sale at fifty cents an acre. A revised statute of 1895 made available to each purchaser one section of arable land at two dollars an acre and three additional sections of pasture land at one dollar an acre. These inducements brought a veritable rush to the farmers' frontier, where the settlers developed methods of "dry farming" appropriate to the semiarid climate of the high plains. Although cotton and corn continued to be the staple crops in the older portion of the state, in the 1880s the farmers in the western part were experimenting successfully with the growing of sorghum, milo maize, and Kaffir corn. On the red plains of northern Texas they turned to wheat, which by 1900 became established as the principal crop of the Panhandle. The expansion of farming lifted Texas to an eminent position in agriculture by 1900, when the three hundred and fifty thousand farms in the state were yielding crops valued at about two hundred and forty million dollars. By then the population had passed the three million mark.

In New Mexico and Arizona some improvement in farming techniques appeared in the vicinity of the newer towns, but elsewhere the antiquated methods of the colonial era still prevailed. Many farmers still plowed their fields with oxen and harvested their grain with sickles. Retarding factors included the lack of large-scale irrigation projects, the long continuation of territorial status, the unimproved roads, the isolation of the countryside, the unsettled titles to much of the land, and the slow growth in population. As recently as 1900 New Mexico had less than two hundred thousand people, while Arizona had only a little over one hundred thousand. Nevertheless, a few bold ventures forecast the dawn of a new day.

In the 1890s the Pecos Irrigation and Investment Company, founded by James T. Hagerman, built three dams on the lower Pecos River in New Mexico, irrigated what was formerly range land, and attracted new settlers to the Pecos Valley. In the same decade wells were being drilled for the irrigation of farmland on higher ground in eastern New Mexico. Farther west, in the Gila Valley of Arizona, John B. Swilling and others began work on the Salt River irrigation project in 1870, and fifteen years later thirty-five thousand acres, largely in the vicinity of Phoenix, were being cultivated by virtue of water distributed by irrigation canals. In those years, too, colonies of Mormons migrated from Utah to locations in Arizona favorable for farming and by 1884 about two thousand five hundred persons had settled in and near the towns of Brigham City, St. Joseph, and Sunset. Other Mormon colonists founded Jonesville and Mesa City in the Salt River Valley, where in the early 1880s they engaged successfully in farming by digging the Utah Ditch for carrying the water to their fields. In the Arizona of the 1900s, however, small irrigation projects made arable only one hundred and eight thousand acres out of a total of seventy-two million. In this territory, as in New Mexico, the projects of that era only signaled the beginning of bigger things to come in the succeeding century.

California far surpassed the neighboring territories in early agricultural development and by 1900 was gaining rapidly on the leadership of Texas. In the 1880s a persuasive publicity campaign had attracted immigration almost equal to that of the gold rush in '49. According to Glenn S. Dumke, much of the credit for sending people to California goes to Charles Nordhoff, whose book, *California for Health and Pleasure and Residence*, contended in 1872 that "you have nowhere in the United States seen so complete a civilization." A flood of pamphlets and newspaper articles proclaimed the incomparable advantages of the climate of southern California, and real estate agents advertised bargains in tracts of land plotted all over that region. In 1886, for example, Theodore S. Van Dyke boasted: "Southern California seems to produce with proper care nearly every kind of tree, shrub, grass, herb, or tuber that is common or useful in the temperate zone, together with a large number of those of the tropics."

Another enthusiastic promoter of those days injected a claim about the purity of the air of Los Angeles, which "when inhaled gives to the individual a stimulus and vital force which only an atmosphere so pure can ever communicate."

When competing railroads engaged in a rate war that reduced the fare from Kansas City to five dollars for a limited time, settlers swarmed into the southern region and spread out into parts of the Central Valley, too. Some were organized into colonies for cooperative development of a chosen locality, but most of them came in family groups or as individuals. Before this boom collapsed in 1887, it had increased the population of California to about one million, or twice the number of 1870. As the promotional schemes folded up in the late 1880s, many of the more realistic settlers scattered over the countryside and sought a base for sound agricultural development.

Increased production of oranges and other citrus fruit developed during this era of agricultural transformation in southern California. This industry had already had a good start as early as 1875. Subsequently small irrigation projects increased the arable acreage in the south, growers introduced new varieties, and by 1890 the state had nearly one million orange trees. In addition, the favorable climatic conditions, the variety of soils, and the extension of irrigation projects made possible a statewide diversity in its agricultural products of which some of the leading crops were alfalfa, peaches, raisins, figs, prunes, grapes, wheat, the citrus fruits, and poultry and dairy products. In 1900 the seventy-two thousand farms in California were marketing products valued at over one hundred and thirty million dollars, and at that date the population had increased to about one and one-half million.

The four decades following the advent of the railroads had witnessed the beginning of a remarkable transformation in the economy of the southwestern states and territories. The wizards of finance and construction who had sent the freight and passenger trains speed-ing west on the steel trailways, whether they employed fair means or foul to achieve their goals, did ultimately merit their coveted reputation as "builders of an empire."

PRODUCTION AND POPULATION IN 1900

Population
(in thousands)

	Total	Native	Foreign born	Negroes	Non-English-speaking	Illiterate, above 10
Arizona	123	99	24	2	27	27
California	1,485	1,118	367	11	45	59
New Mexico	195	182	13	2	16	47
Texas	3,049	2,869	179	621	101	314

Mineral Production

	Copper (million lbs.)	Gold (thousand ozs.)	Silver (thousand ozs.)	Coal (thousand tons)	Petroleum (thousand bbls.)
Arizona	118	203	2,995	–	–
California	29	765	941	–	4,324
New Mexico	4	40	434	1,299	–
Texas	–	–	477	968	836

Agricultural Statistics

	No. of farms	Acres in thousands	Improved acreage	Value of farms (million $)	Value of livestock (million $)	Value of products (million $)
Arizona	5,809	1,935	13.2%	30	16	7
California	72,542	28,829	41.5%	797	67	132
New Mexico	12,311	5,131	6.4%	54	32	10
Texas	352,190	125,807	15.6%	962	241	240

Value Added by Manufacturers

Arizona, $20,439,000   California, $257,386,000
New Mexico, $2,062,000   Texas, $38,506,000

16
LAW AND DISORDER

To Murderers, Confidence Men, Thieves: The citizens of Las Vegas have tired of the robbery, murder, and the other crimes, that have made this town a by-word in every civilized community. They have resolved to put a stop to crime, if in attaining that end they have to forget the law, and resort to a speedier justice than it will afford. All such characters are therefore hereby notified, that they must either leave this town or conform themselves to the requirements of the law, or they will be summarily dealt with. The flow of blood must and shall be stopped in this community, and the good citizens of both old and the new towns have determined to stop it, if they have to HANG by the strong arm of force every violater of the law in this country. — VIGILANTES

> in Miguel A. Otero, My Life on the Frontier (New York, 1935) I, pp. 205-206.

In the 1850s the forms of government had been "Americanized" all across the Southwest, with statehood in operation in Texas and California and territorial administration instituted in New Mexico and Arizona. Local autonomy, however, while giving the citizens the means for expressing their desires and effecting progressive reforms, also provided an opportunity for unscrupulous exploitation of the human and physical resources of the raw frontier. Elimination of the corruption and accompanying violence would tax to the limit the potential for reform inherent in the democratic system.

CLEAVAGES IN CALIFORNIA

In California by the time of the Civil War a fair degree of order had been established by the vigilantes in the cities and the spontaneous and improvised government of the mining camps. Then men's interests became absorbed in the crisis of the war years. With sixteen thousand men enlisted in the Union Regiments, that many of the young and energetic were busily occupied, while for those who remained at home the war years brought full employment and artificial prosperity. Nevertheless, confidence in local government had been shaken as a result of its failings in the prewar years, and after the war that half-hearted confidence grew into a suspicion that banditry had become the profession of financiers who operated with great finesse inside the governmental framework. Evidence accumulated steadily in confirmation of that suspicion.

The record of the dealings of the Southern Pacific Railroad in the vicinity of Los Angeles has been recounted in a previous chapter. That company was also becoming the state's biggest landowner and was granting rebates in freight charges to favored shippers. In addition, the Central Pacific almost obtained control of the waterfront in San Francisco by extracting concessions from the state legislature. The inequitable distribution of land also became another source of resentment. A few ranchers owned enormous estates, some of them running to half a million acres or more, and that so much land should be withheld from settlement became a matter of aggravation among the small farmers and the landless workers. Moreover, the big proprietors employed their influence in the legislature for the obtaining of special legislation which protected their property against trespassers and assured them of the control of much of the available irrigation water. Amid these aggravating conditions, the flagrant corruption which prevailed in some of the cities, notably in San Francisco and in Sacramento, became another source of complaint.

In the early 1870s still another condition, exasperating to many Californians, was the influx of Chinese laborers who could subsist on low wages. First they had been attracted to the mines, so that as early as 1852 the state's population included twenty-five thousand Chinese. Another spurt of Oriental immigration came in the sixties, when the Central Pacific imported large numbers of them for employment in the building of the transcontinental railway. As they were laid off upon completion of the trackage, they congregated in the "Chinatown" of San Francisco and in other populous centers. Workmen, who were alarmed at this concentration of cheap labor in their midst, became advocates of the elimination of that competition by the imposition of a restriction upon further Chinese immigration.

In this new postwar era, the workingmen of the cities became the "vigilantes" who resorted to mass demonstrations in their pursuit of political reform. The Republicans, who had held dominance during the war years, soon lost popular support because of the favors granted to railroad magnates. To prevent complete defeat, the party made a concession to the reformers by turning to Newton Booth, an outspoken antimonopolist, who was elected governor in 1871. In the legislature, however, he failed to command support sufficient for the enactment of reform measures, and the opposing pressures split the Republican party. That division contributed to the victory of the Democrats in 1875, when they won two of the state's seats in the national congress and installed William Irwin as governor.

Encouraged by the Democratic victory, the laboring classes in San Francisco became vocal. They were irritated by many flagrant abuses of power; but as they resorted to street demonstrations they singled out for condemnation the one source of complaint which was immediate and visible—the Chinese. When mob violence seemed imminent in 1877, the conservative faction under the leadership of William T. Coleman organized a street patrol of a thousand armed men. Then the workingmen, aroused by the inflammatory speeches of a young Irishman, Denis Kearney, shifted from direct action to massive political organization. In San Francisco they founded their Workingmen's Party, which soon acquired adherents in other cities. This party sought legislation which would provide for the election of senators by a popular vote instead of by the legislature, it demanded state regulation of banks and industry, including the railroads, and it advocated an eight-hour day for laborers and compulsory school attendance for children.

THE NEW CONSTITUTION

The turmoil in California led to a call for a convention for the drafting of a new state constitution. In 1878, when the one hundred and fifty-two delegates had been elected, one-third of them represented the new Workingmen's Party. Of the remainder, the majority were nonpartisan advocates of reform; only eleven were Republicans and only ten Democrats.

The Constitutional Convention of 1878 embodied in the new organic law many of the demands of the agitators without changing much of the form of state government. Instead, the features which were added pertained mostly to the pressing social and economic problems. Provision was included for an eight-hour day on public works, a railway commission was authorized for elimination of abuses, a board of equalization was created in an effort to obtain fair assessment of property values, and the system of courts was reorganized with a provision that judges be popularly elected rather than appointed. In addition, legislative appropriations to private corporations were restricted, and the governor's pardoning power was diminished. The most extreme measure was the one which condemned coolie labor as "slavery" and authorized the legislature to restrict immigration and to adopt other measures for protection of the state from "dangerous and detrimental aliens."

In the referendum on adoption of the new constitution, the California electorate approved it by a very narrow margin, and, as it went into effect in January of 1880, a reaction against radicalism became immediately discernible. In fact, as an obvious precaution against any extreme interpretation of the new organic law, the voters even installed a Republican majority in the state legislature and elected a Republican governor, George C. Perkins. The popular agitation against the Chinese continued unabated until the Congress adopted an exclusion act in 1882; but in other areas the local reforming impulse awaited reactivation at a later date.

REVISION IN TEXAS

Texas had been annoyed especially by the banditti of the border back in the decade of the 1850s, and that harassment had culminated in the difficulties with Juan Cortina and his band during the Civil War. Soon afterward came the era of Radical Reconstruction, with its political turmoil, its restless former slaves, and its highway banditry, all of which led to dependence upon martial law with its excesses and popular resistance. Finally Radical rule was brought to an end by the victory of the Democrats in 1873 and the inauguration of their gubernatorial candidate, Richard Coke, in January of the next year.

The Texans then had recovered control in their own state, but the new administration had to deal with manifold difficulties. Not only were the hostile Indians as yet unsubdued on the frontier, but also Mexican bandits were terrifying the settlers along the Rio Grande. The public debt was increasing rapidly, the courts were not functioning in some localities, and the citizens were clamoring for elimination of some of the obnoxious provisions which the Radicals had written into the Constitution of 1869. The Democrats favored the imposing of more limitations on the powers of the governor, and they wanted administrative and judicial officials to be popularly elected for short terms. To effect these changes, they proposed the convening of another constitutional convention, which the voters approved in a special election in August, 1875.

Almost simultaneously with California, the Texans prepared for the drafting of a new organic law, and their convention of 1876 was controlled by the resurgent Democrats. Not one of the ninety delegates had participated in the Radical convention of 1869; moreover, only fifteen this time were Republicans and only six were Negroes. Step by step, therefore, they undid the work of the earlier body and drafted a rather lengthy, detailed instrument of government. They reduced the term of the governor from four years to two and that of the state senators from six years to four. They restricted the powers of the governor so severely that he would have no authority for supervision of other elective state administrators or of local officers. Moreover, they limited the powers of the legislature especially in matters pertaining to taxation, credit, and the public debt. They also reduced the number of courts and provided that the judges should be elected every six years for the higher courts and every four years for the inferior courts. After a battle the delegates voted down a proposed requirement that citizens should pay a poll tax as a qualification for the franchise. With much less controversy they revoked the clause of the previous Radical constitution which denied the right to secede, but they did not go so far as to insert an alternate one providing positively that Texas had such a right.

With reference to education, the delegates of 1876 eliminated the compulsory attendance law and the office of state superintendent of schools, both of which they regarded as extravagances of Radical rule, and they required that separate schools be provided for Negroes. On the other hand, they were generous to education by granting forty-five million acres of land for the support of schools and colleges and by preserving intact the perpetual state school fund which then amounted to three and one-quarter million dollars. They also abolished the controversial State Immigration Bureau and held out more direct inducements for immigration by the providing of homestead grants of eighty acres for single men and twice as much for heads of families. Their work done, they submitted their new constitution to the electorate in February, 1876, when it was adopted by a majority in the proportion of three to one. The voters also reelected Governor Coke and chose a full slate of Democrats for the filling of other offices.

BAD MEN IN TEXAS

As the Democrats came into control in Texas once more, their administrators had to contend with the problem of disorder, which by that time had been relegated mostly to the frontier. In the western part of the state the cattle country was haunted by numerous bad men, including the notorious Sam Bass. He led a gang of ruffians who had started as cattle rustlers in 1875 and soon became train robbers. Then Major John B. Jones of the Texas Rangers took charge of this bandit hunt and deputized an extra company of Rangers from among volunteers at Dallas. First he took into custody several accomplices who had been giving the outlaws aid and shelter, and soon his troopers ran down Bass and his gang in Wise County; but the ringleaders escaped.

The Rangers overtook them again at Round Rock in July, 1878, killed Bass and one other, and took as prisoners the remaining two, who were tried in Austin and sentenced to prison terms.

Other vicious gunmen remained at large in Texas. John Wesley Hardin, calculating killer, Ben Thompson, gambler and saloon proprietor, J. K. "King" Fisher, head of a gang of thieves, and others of their kind frequented the cow towns, where, according to one observer, murders and robberies occurred periodically and the saloons were filled at night with a "depraved, adventurous crowd." Against these ruffians the Texas Rangers operated courageously and effectively under the command of such capable men as Major Jones, George W. Arrington, Bill McDonald, and L. H. McNeely. They had the aid of some able sheriffs, and west of the Pecos River a profiteering saloonkeeper, Judge Roy Bean, bluffed some of the rowdies out of their evil ways or out of the country, with the Rangers lending timely assistance.

Once near El Paso, when the Rangers

were unable to maintain order alone, federal troops came to their support. In this affair in 1877 several Mexicans and Spanish Americans mobbed Charles H. Howard, who was trying to corner control of some salt deposits. After the mob had killed Howard, one of his companions, and one of the Rangers, a company of United States troops under the command of Colonel Edward Hatch marched out to San Elizario and restored order. Within a few years the agencies of the law worked westward step by step across the high plains and tamed the wild elements of the frontier. In fact, the effective campaign against lawlessness had so overcrowded the penitentiary at Huntsville by 1883 that a new one was then built at Rusk and a state prison farm was added two years later in Fort Bend County. Those outlaws who evaded arrest found it prudent to skip across the Texas line into New Mexico.

POLITICS IN ARIZONA AND NEW MEXICO

While Texas and California were putting their houses in order, the area lying between those states continued under territorial government. When it was still one unit back in the 1850s, the depredations committed by the Indians had been the most serious problem. Early in the next decade the crisis of the Civil War had provided the all-absorbing issues, and during that war, in 1863, Arizona had been separated from New Mexico. For a while thereafter the unsubdued Indians had again hindered progress, and in New Mexico this problem had been abated some ten years before the time when Arizona got relief from its Indian problem. In both territories the governors and other territorial officers of those years were Republican appointees, who as a rule had rather undistinguished records and relatively brief tenure.

In the early days in Arizona, according to Howard R. Lamar, the Spanish Americans and Southern Democrats "had the vote, but federal appointees had the power." The latter, under Governor John M. Goodwin, comprised a "Federal Ring" which indulged in speculation in mining and railroad promotion. Land-grabbing did not become a big business as it did in New Mexico, because Arizona was then a less attractive field for investment in farming and cattle-raising. A. P. K. Safford, as governor from 1869 to 1877, abetted further the activities of the Ring, while also getting credit for helping with the subjugation of the Apaches and for sponsoring the school legislation of 1870 and 1871. A later governor, Conrad M. Zulick, 1885 to 1889, came as an appointee of President Grover M. Cleveland and therefore tried to establish a Democratic ring; but he only stirred up strife, as the continuing Republican underlings counterchecked his efforts. He did, however, obtain the removal of the territorial capital from Prescott to Phoenix in recognition of the growing importance of agriculture under irrigation in the territorial economy.

New Mexico, with a population that passed one hundred thousand in the 1870s—twice that of Arizona—began to look ripe for statehood, or so some of the citizens concluded. Without authorization by the Congress, the legislature authorized the drafting of a state constitution in 1870. Although it was submitted to the electorate in 1872 and approved, it was set aside due to a legal technicality. The next effort was made in Washington. Stephen B. Elkins, formerly New Mexico's congressional delegate, endeavored to get an enabling act through the Congress, and it did carry in the House handily. In the Senate, with Southern votes seemingly assured, Elkins eagerly sought the support of Northern senators. According to L. Bradford Prince, Elkins congratulated a Northern congressman after he had made a stirring speech which Elkins had not heard. It happened that the speaker had indulged in a tirade against the South in a speech designed to keep alive war issues by "waving the bloody shirt," as was the vogue among Republicans in those years.

When the Southern friends of New Mexico saw Elkins shake the hand of the speaker, they turned against the enabling act and voted it down. By this peculiar reversal, New Mexico lost out in 1876 and only Colorado was to have the distinction of being admitted as the "Centennial State."

After the fiasco of '76 eastern interest in statehood for New Mexico lapsed for about two decades. There were several reasons, some of which were exaggerated in the reports which influenced the Congress. One was the realization that public education was not making great headway, as indicated by the revelation in 1880 that only one-fourth of the one hundred and sixty schools had been provided with buildings and that the average attendance was only a little above three thousand out of a total population of over one hundred thousand people. The use of the Spanish language in homes, schools, business houses, and courtrooms also gave many visitors the impression that this territory had not yet become properly "Americanized." Another factor which hindered seriously the economic development of New Mexico and consequently delayed statehood, too, was the unsettled status of titles to much of the land. Conflicts over land along with the arrival of many vagabonds with the coming of the railroads brought on a scourge of lawlessness which gave this frontier in the Southwest a bad reputation.

THE SCRAMBLE FOR LAND

The delay in the validation of land titles caused much of the public domain to be withheld from settlement for many years and encouraged a ruthless scramble for possession and confirmation of ownership in the settled areas. Originally the impression which seems to have prevailed was that all Spanish Americans could "sit tight" in guaranteed possession of the lands which they occupied, without filing anything. That would have precipitated a chaotic struggle for expansion of boundaries, and it would have left the owners with no legal basis for later transfer of titles. Besides, the Protocol Agreement added to the Treaty of Guadalupe Hidalgo made no such guarantee: it did provide that the titles would become legitimate by acknowledgment "before the

American tribunals." In the process of obtaining such acknowledgment, however, almost everything went wrong. A large proportion of the newly adopted citizens could not speak English and did not understand the American procedure; furthermore, they did not have ready cash for the making of surveys and the engaging of lawyers. They had to make payment in kind, that is, by signing over part of their land to the Anglo agents who offered their services. Moreover, they did not have money for payment of taxes on their property — a form of levy which they had not experienced previously. As a result, their land would be put up for sale because of tax delinquencies, and then somebody else could buy it up. These difficulties were complicated further in 1854 by congressional adoption of a donation act for New Mexico. For defense of the frontier a tract of one hundred and sixty acres would be donated to settlers who would move to this territory. That was followed in 1862 by the Homestead Act, which opened the gates wider. Under those acts many of the newcomers filed for title to land already occupied by confused Spanish Americans who had not yet validated their titles.

The combination of local factors and the dilatory response of the Congress created a fertile field for aggrandizement by unscrupulous land-grabbers. Altogether, a dismal picture is portrayed in the well-documented studies of several reputable historians — Herbert O. Brayer, Gilberto Espinosa, William A. Keleher, Howard R. Lamar, Jim Berry Pearson, and Victor Westphall. Lawyers and government men who came to this frontier early, especially to New Mexico, made land acquisition the most lucrative enterprise in the territory. Mutual interests drew them together in the Santa Fe Ring, headed by Thomas B. Catron and Stephen B. Elkins, who brought into collaboration one surveyor general after another and obtained the active support and participation of Max Frost, editor of the Santa Fe *New Mexican*. Furthermore, in all parts of the territory they engaged agents who found it profitable to do their bidding. This ring, however, did not have a monopoly, for it came into competition with the land and cattle companies which were acquiring big ranches and with many newcomers who saw an opportunity to pick up small tracts.

In the case of the Maxwell Ranch, formerly the Beaubien-Miranda Grant, soon after it had been acquired by an English company, the Secretary of the Interior, in 1874, declared it to be part of the public domain. Already there were Spanish-American settlers in Vermejo Park, and now many Anglo squatters moved in, making a total of about six hundred. To their consternation, in 1886 the United States Circuit Court confirmed the company's title to the entire two million acres. As the company agents proceeded with eviction procedures, they encountered mob resistance and riots during which some men on both sides lost their lives. Meanwhile the Santa Fe Ring seemed to side with the squatters by exerting pressure upon the legislature and the officers of the law, so that eviction notices were not served, court decisions were delayed, and even a county boundary was moved in order to change the jurisdiction. Then, after the small holders had their land put up for sale because they could not pay their taxes, an agent of the Ring bought up the tracts piece-meal and the company had to deal with the Ring.

In other instances, Spanish land grants grew by the manipulation of new owners from an original modest claim to hundreds of square miles. If Spanish owners were confirmed in their title, they found their holdings whittled away as they had to sell off part of the land year after year in order to pay their taxes on the remainder. Besides, law-yers took payment in land. For example, when the members of a grant board faced a threatening lawsuit, they had no money for the employment of an attorney; therefore their lawyer ex-tracted from them a contract whereby they would give him one-fourth or one-third of their land grant if he won the case, and usually he did. Meanwhile, as the federal survey proceeded slowly, the surveyor general, baffled by the small strips and common tracts of the settled Spanish areas, too often turned to the unsettled grasslands and made surveys of those townships which would favor the incoming cattle ranchers. Then the cattle companies took up vast tracts; one such company, alone, filed for eighty-four homesteads! By 1884, of two hundred homestead claims filed, only sixty-five met the legal require-ments. Moreover, when cases of fraud and perjury were brought into the courts, convictions could not be ob-tained. Of six hundred and forty-one such cases filed in the 1880s, only fif-teen of the defendants were found guilty, and for those filed against Max Frost the records disappeared from the court files. Of course, many of the fraudulent entries on the public domain

displaced nobody, because there had been no prior settlement.

All those years the "no man's land" in New Mexico and parts of Arizona was perpetuated by the tardiness of con-gressional confirmation of titles. In 1878, the surveyor general lamented the delay which was hindering the de-velopment of this territory. "If New Mexico was worth fighting for," he con-cluded, "then it is worth governing and caring for by decent and civilized meth-ods." Of two hundred and twelve claims received in Washington by 1891, only one hundred and forty-one had been approved and thirteen had been rejected, leaving fifty-eight still pend-ing. As claims were approved, another type of displacement occurred on those tracts which had been Spanish *sitios*, where the labor had been provided by *peones* under debt servitude. The several Spanish-American families had the privilege of small houses to live in, garden tracts to tend, and forests in which they could hunt and gather wood; but even though they and their ancestors had lived there for genera-tions, they had no title whatsoever to any land. When some newcomer bought that ranch, often he concluded that he did not need the services of those "squatters" and evicted them. They left in resentment and congregated in the towns. In Las Vegas, for one ex-ample, such displaced persons sought revenge. They put on white hoods, from which they derived their name "White Caps," and rode forth at night to shoot cattle and burn barns. Finally, by 1892, posses of armed deputies broke up those gangs and stopped their dep-redations. After all, even though their plight may have deserved sympathy, their actions plainly were illegal.

When all facets of the dealings in land are summed up, the basic cause of displacement was a sudden change in system. Where there had been a subsistence economy without land taxes and without much of a monetary medium, there appeared abruptly a new type of economy attuned to the emergent industrial revolution in the United States. It favored specialized use of the land in large tracts for profitable production in an economy utilizing money, banking, transportation, and land taxes. During the period of transition, thousands of workers were displaced, just as were those of the Enclosure Movement in England in the early stages of the Industrial Revolution there. Here, however, the displacement was even more distressing because it was complicated by a simultaneous change in legal systems and in the language employed in daily transactions. Basically the transformation made no cultural distinctions. Although Spanish Americans suffered most, a few of their literate representatives profited from the plight of their *compadres,* and in some localities large numbers of Anglo-Americans were among those ruthlessly displaced. Yet obviously those having a language handicap would be the more susceptible victims and for them recovery would be slow and difficult.

Ultimately Catron emerged as the great land baron of New Mexico. By his own boast in 1893, he had accumulated over one million acres and had a share in the ownership of two million more. By that time, however, the machinations of the Ring were on the decline. For one thing, the participants had fallen into conflicts over competing interests. More influential, however, was the effect of the railroads in opening up new arenas for speculation and in increasing the population in the central and southern part of the territory. The new breed of settlers wanted schools and security, and as early as 1884 the southern Democrats almost succeeded in moving the capital to Albuquerque in order to get it out from under the domination of the northern Republican Ring. Moreover, in that decade the Democratic President, Grover Cleveland, had sent to New Mexico as governor the high-principled Edmund G. Ross, who by his deciding vote in the United States Senate had prevented the removal of President Andrew Johnson. As he became acquainted in New Mexico, he wrote:

From the Land Grant Ring grew others, as the opportunities for speculation and plunder were developed. Cattle Rings, Public Land Stealing Rings, Mining Rings, Treasury Rings, and rings of almost every description grew up, till the affairs of the Territory came to be run almost exclusively in the interest and for the benefit of combinations organized and headed by a few longheaded, ambitious, and unscrupulous Americans.[1]

In his fight against corruption he was assisted by a conscientious surveyor general, George W. Julian, who filed most of the fraud cases. Directly they seemed to accomplish little; yet they were at least a nuisance to be contended with, and the complaints of Ross did contribute to the creation of a special court in 1891 for the more expeditious handling of land claims. He

[1] Quoted in Howard R. Lamar, *The Far Southwest, 1846–1919* (New Haven, Conn., 1966), p. 150.

was followed as governor by L. Bradford Prince, who from 1889 to 1893 turned his attention to a new line of endeavor by promoting railway construction. Then when President William McKinley appointed Miguel A. Otero in 1897, the territory had as governor a capable, affable descendant of a respected local family and an ardent champion of statehood. This, as Howard R. Lamar said, effected a veritable "revolution" in New Mexico politics.

VIOLENCE IN NEW MEXICO

Common resort to violence in the two territories had to be allayed before New Mexico and Arizona could overcome the stigma prevailing back east. Originally the Spanish society had been normally quite orderly and decorous, although it had standards for social relations and gambling which seemed immoral to newcomers of Puritan background. In the closely knit village communities the primary institutions of church and family had held the conduct of their members well in line with the accepted practices of long standing. That prevailing social adjustment was rudely disturbed by the arrival of Anglo-Americans of the rougher sort. In New Mexico in 1876 a resolute judge, Henry L. Waldo, in his instructions to a grand jury, said that "Assassination after assassination has been occurring with startling rapidity; shootings and cuttings take place around us with the most impudent and outrageous defiance of the law." Three years later, according to the Santa Fe *New Mexican,* about one hundred criminal cases were pending disposition in the courts, and Judge Prince explained that his crowded calendar resulted from the "peculiar condition of affairs in the county consequent upon the coming of the railroad, which brought in a crowd of rough characters, reckless of life and regardless of law."

Back in the 1860s and 1870s, isolated instances of shooting affrays had been increasing in number, and gambling sharks, cattle rustlers, and stagecoach bandits had begun plying their respective trades defiantly and profitably. Then when the railroads made accessible the remote localities of the Southwest, the rowdies fled to this frontier, where they could find a hiding place for burying their past while launching a new, nefarious career. As the Texas Rangers ran the bad men out of their state and the California vigilantes did likewise in their area, an undue proportion of shady characters became concentrated in New Mexico and Arizona.

In the midst of the fertile situation in New Mexico, a veritable war broke out in the cattle country of Lincoln County. On one side was John Chisum, cattle king, whose zealous guardianship over his herd of three hundred thousand head made him unpopular among the small ranchers and the nemesis of rustlers. The personification of righteousness, he had at his command a hundred stalwart cowboys. The opposing faction was led by Lawrence G. Murphy, who operated the Murphy-Dolan Store, a gambling saloon and trading post in Lincoln, the county seat. Allegedly a rustler and a shrewd profiteer, he had many hirelings among the gamblers and soldiers who frequented his store. In addition, Murphy was aligned with the Santa Fe Ring, headed by Thomas B. Catron, who then was the United States District Attorney. With this backing Murphy was able to control the sheriff of Lincoln County. A wealthy Englishman, John H. Tunstall, entered the arena as an ally of Chisum. He also owned a ranch in Lincoln County, and he advanced the capital for the opening of the Tunstall-McSween store in competition with Murphy's business. The lines were drawn, then, for the two factions to clash in the Lincoln County War.

In the summer of 1877 William Antrim, or William H. Bonney, *alias* Billy the Kid, became an employee of Tunstall. Already he had a record as a cattle rustler and a killer; yet the Englishman took a liking to the little fellow and hired him for work at his ranch. Because the competition of Tunstall's store was making inroads on Murphy's profits, the latter sent the sheriff, William Brady, with a framed-up warrant to serve on Tunstall, and the sheriff's drunken deputies murdered the Englishman without giving him a chance to defend himself. That violation of the code of the West precipitated open warfare between the two gangs.

After partisans of the deceased Tunstall had shot the sheriff in one of the battles in Lincoln County, Billy the Kid and some of his associates, aware that they were wanted now for the killing of an officer of the law, went into hiding at Fort Sumner. From that new location they sustained themselves by sallying forth frequently as cattle rustlers, while they continued the warfare. They were among fifty of McSween's men who barricaded themselves in an old building in Lincoln on July 17, 1878, when over-

taken by a posse led by a new sheriff, also working in Murphy's behalf. McSween was killed, but Billy the Kid managed to escape.

The continued warfare in Lincoln County horrified easterners and national officials; consequently President Rutherford B. Hayes sent to the territory a new governor, General "Lew" Wallace, with instructions to concentrate upon restoration of order. He visited Lincoln, established martial law, and obtained a truce; but his superficial intervention suppressed lingering animosities only temporarily. As the conflict broke into the open again, hundreds of arrests were made but very few of the suspects were convicted. Then Chisum suffered from a fresh outbreak of rustling in which Billy the Kid and some others of his former partisans participated.

The climax was contributed by a new sheriff of Lincoln County, Pat Garrett, who was elected in 1880. Because he once had been a friend of Billy the Kid, he was familiar with his habits. He knew that the outlaw was a frequent visitor at the residence of the Maxwells in Fort Sumner, where they had located after selling their big ranch up north. By hiding in a bedroom at the Maxwell home, Pat Garrett surprised and killed Billy the Kid on July 14, 1881. At that date the young outlaw was only a little past his twenty-first birthday, and he was alleged to have murdered one man for every year of his life.

In those years New Mexico had other reckless desperadoes. Cimarron was frequented by Clay Allison and "Davy" Crockett, who was thought to be a distant relative of the famous Tennesseean. One day in 1877, after Crockett had shot four soldiers, the sheriff killed him.

Then the sheriff was tried for murder, but acquitted by the jury. Las Vegas was the hangout of Dave Rudabaugh and "Doc" Holliday until both moved to Arizona. Las Vegas also was taken over in 1880 by a gang of ruffians from Dodge City. According to Milt Callon, they accounted for ten murders before the townsmen became aroused, organized a committee of vigilantes, and distributed handbills bearing a forceful warning. Then the vigilantes caught and killed four of those gunmen and ran the rest out of town. At Farmington in 1881 two men were killed and many injured in a brawl at a dance hall. One of the victims was Port Stockton, whose brother Ike gathered up a gang of gunmen and threatened to do some more killing. The local vigilantes trailed Stockton's gang to Durango, Colorado, where the ensuing battle made a shambles of that town; but Stockton escaped. In Raton, in 1882, a drunken brawl at a theater resulted in a gun battle which took the lives of four men. The crowd rushed out of the show and lynched the man who allegedly had started the trouble. At about the same time the Vicente Silva gang in Las Vegas became notorious for robbery and murder, until the leader was killed in 1893 by one of his own men. At that time Santa Fe was all worked up over the prolonged trial resulting from the murder of a prominent citizen, J. Francisco Chávez, and the local police chief, Sylvestre Gallegos. For that the Ring was blamed, and Catron defended the accused murders, but to no avail. Four were hanged.

In 1896, Albert J. Fountain, a politician and newspaper man, was murdered while traveling the lonely road from Lincoln to Las Cruces, and the county sheriff, Pat Garrett, took up the manhunt. When Oliver Lee, an influential rancher, was arrested, the territorial legislature in Santa Fe divided the county and formed a new one, Otero, in order to keep Lee from falling into Garrett's custody. When Lee came to trial at Hillsboro in 1899, all of the leading politicians were aligned on one side or the other. Lee was acquitted. At the time of that trial an outlaw, "Black Jack" Ketchum, was boldly holding up trains in the northeastern part of the territory, until a conductor shot and wounded him. He was tried and hanged in Clayton in 1901. By that date the wave of disorder finally was subsiding.

LAWLESSNESS IN ARIZONA

In Arizona the mining boom of the 1880s attracted rowdies from far and wide. Robberies of stagecoaches became so frequent that Wells, Fargo, and Company employed some special agents to guard the shipments of gold and to do some private detective work in the towns along the route. In some instances, as in the case of a bold highwayman called "Red Jack," the agents were effective in apprehending the bandits. When Tucson became the mecca of rowdies who had been run out of California, the citizens had "no law or protection from the government," according to Sylvester Mowry, who added that every man redressed his own wrongs "with pistol or knife."

Several gangs of cattle rustlers flourished in the vicinity of Tombstone.

They were managed by "Curly Bill" Brocius, "Doc" Holliday, "Old Man" Clanton, John Ringo, Frank Stillwell, and the McLowery brothers. By way of diversion they frequently shot up the town. In 1881, Curly Bill's gang waylaid a pack train belonging to a Mexican, Miguel García, and slaughtered nineteen of his men. In retaliation a band of Mexicans crossed the border and ambushed and killed Old Man Clanton and some of his gunmen.

The development of mining opened up a more lucrative field of endeavor for the surviving rustlers. They moved into Tombstone and began seizing bullion and payroll shipments, which so aroused the townsmen that they organized as vigilantes. Then Wyatt Earp, formerly marshall at Dodge City, Ellsworth, and Wichita in Kansas, became a Wells, Fargo express agent in Tombstone. After he and his three brothers had wiped out a gang of bandits under rather suspicious circumstances, the Earps were held for trial as murderers; but the jury found them innocent.

While on the subject of lawlessness in Arizona, recognition must be given to the perpetrators of a famous fraud. In 1872, Philip Arnold and John Slack claimed to have discovered a rich diamond field in the northeastern part of the territory, and they brought in "experts" who substantiated their claim. In order to make their story convincing, they had "salted" the field with a few real, imported diamonds; but they kept the exact location a secret so that only they were able to find and show off some valuable gems. After they had organized a ten-million-dollar corporation for exploitation of their "mine," some government geologists explored the area and exposed this fraudulent scheme.

An even greater fraud followed upon the diamond hoax. Its perpetrator was James Addison Reavis, a shrewd operator who conceived an unfounded claim to a great part of the Gila Valley. He presented what appeared to be valid documentary evidence that in 1748 the king of Spain had bestowed the title of "Baron of the Colorados" upon a certain Miguel Peralta de Córdoba and had awarded him a grant of land two hundred and thirty-six miles long and seventy-eight miles wide. Further, he maintained that in 1864 a descendant of the Baron had transferred ownership of the land to George Willing, an Arizona pioneer, who had given Reavis title to more than three thousand square miles lying in the south-central part of the territory. In addition, Reavis had a Mexican wife, whom he claimed to be the only living descendant of Peralta, and therefore she was also "heiress" to the tract which he had acquired. In this manner Reavis advanced a double claim to possession of some of the best land in Arizona, and he supported it with evidence so convincing that he collected rent from settlers on his land and right-of-way fees from the Southern Pacific Railroad, which crossed his estate. By means of his racket, Reavis and his wife maintained mansions in Chihuahua City, Denver, St. Louis, and Washington, D. C., in the 1880s and traveled extensively and luxuriously in the Americas and Europe.

In the 1890s closer examination by suspicious experts revealed that the paper upon which the "ancient" deeds were transcribed was less than twenty years old. Further scrutiny revealed that, in the old manuscripts in the Span-ish archives, Reavis had surreptitiously and skilfully removed some of the parchments and substituted sheets pre-pared by himself. To cap the climax, his wife turned out to be no heiress at all; she was an ordinary Mexican girl whom Reavis had married in order to promote his scheme. For his forgery and extortion Reavis was brought to trial in 1895 and sentenced to a term of six years in the penitentiary at Santa Fe. His wife returned to poverty and oblivion in Old Mexico, and after his release he went to Phoenix to spend his few remaining years.

In the latter decades of the nineteenth century range warfare between cattle-men and their rivals disturbed the peace in several localities in the Southwest, under circumstances explained in a pre-vious chapter. Arizona had one of the bloodiest of those encounters in the Graham-Tewkesbury feud. However, as noted previously, soon after 1900 such clashes had been abated by a readjust-ment within the livestock industry. The work of courageous sheriffs and vindic-tive vigilantes had also tamed down the outlaws, and their efforts had been aided by a growing population of law-abiding citizens who brought some stability to this formerly tumultuous frontier.

POLITICAL UPHEAVAL IN TEXAS

In the latter part of the nineteenth century, however, one wave of restless-ness soon was followed by another, as the Southwest became embroiled in the political agitation of the farm-labor movement and other reform efforts. When the prosperity of the early 1880s receded later in that decade, the re-versal brought distress to farmers and livestockmen, who consequently began to express grievances against banks, railroads, monetary policies, and polit-ical favoritism. In Texas that unrest first found expression during the earlier panic of the 'seventies. In Lampasas County in 1874 a group of rural resi-dents organized their local Farmers' Alliance to combat cattle kings and to catch horse thieves. Later, in 1879, this organization assumed broader objec-tives in Parker County, where it ap-peared as a means of protest against economic conditions. By 1880, several units had been founded in other parts of the state, and in that year the Alliance became incorporated as a "secret and benevolent association." As formulated in those years, the objectives were more liberal printing of paper money, prohibition of absentee land ownership, and higher taxation of railroads and land held for speculation.

After 1886, C. W. Macune, a native of Wisconsin, became the driving force in the Farmers' Alliance. First, he forged a merger with the Louisiana Farmers' Union, and by promoting the new organization as a "white man's nonpolitical secret organization," he sold farmers on establishing chapters in nearly all southern states. He also effected a consolidation with the Agri-cultural Wheel, a similar organization which had originated in Arkansas and also had organized branches in several southern states. The subsequent effort to form a merger with the Farmers' Alli-ance of Iowa and Nebraska failed to materialize at a convention which met in St. Louis in 1889; nevertheless the delegates of the two strong farm organizations and those of the Knights of Labor did achieve a unity in purpose. They would collaborate in efforts for reforms in government which would make it more responsive to the popular will and more effective in redressing the grievances of the Common Man.

Another convention in which Macune again was an active leader met in Cincinnati in 1891, and this time the delegates formed a new political party called the "Populists," or "People's Party." Its platform advocated free coinage of silver, a graduated income tax, government ownership of railroads, the abolition of national banks, and other reforms expressive of the farmers' demands.

In Texas in those same years James S. Hogg rose to ascendency as a champion of reform. While serving as attorney general in the administration of Governor "Sul" Ross, a Democrat, from 1887 to 1891, he fought for regulation of railways. Subsequently, as governor from 1891 to 1895, with Charles A. Culberson as his attorney general, he obtained more effective regulation of railways and sponsored legislation which prohibited foreigners from owning land in Texas. Then as the new Populism spread like a grass fire throughout the rural areas, the best reforming efforts of the Democrats no longer were adequate in competition with that challenge. In the gubernatorial campaign of 1894 the Populists showed surprising strength in opposition to the Democratic candidate, Culberson. Two years later, when the national convention of the Democratic Party borrowed the Populist platform and ran William

Jennings Bryan against William McKinley, the Republicans in Texas voted for Populist candidates and almost defeated Culberson. That was the zenith of the Populist movement; thenceforth the party declined rapidly.

Reform efforts did not subside after the eclipse of Populism. On the national scene Theodore Roosevelt, who became president after the assassination of McKinley in 1901, emerged as the outspoken advocate of a "square deal" for the Common Man. He contended for more popular government, conservation of resources, compulsory arbitration of labor disputes, and the breaking-up of the big monopolies. In the Midwest a young Progressive Party, headed by Robert La Follette of Wisconsin, was advocating the short ballot, primary elections, public ownership of utilities, and adoption of the initiative, referendum, and recall. On the political sidelines, the Suffragettes were campaigning vigorously for women's rights and the Prohibitionists were laboring intensively for the closing of saloons. In Texas, after the Democrats had lapsed momentarily into conservatism at the turn of the century, they now had to respond to these new extraneous pressures. Once again they assumed the leadership in statewide reform.

In 1902, the electorate in Texas adopted a constitutional amendment which required the payment of a poll tax as a qualification for voting. Although this tax worked a hardship on indigent citizens, it did in effect establish a procedure leading to the registration of voters, which constituted a badly needed reform. Three years later, during the administration of Governor S. W. T. Lanham, the legislature established specific qualifications for voting and made primary elections mandatory for the nomination of candidates for office. The reform movement received even greater impetus after the inauguration of Thomas M. Campbell as governor in 1906. During his two terms the measures which were undertaken included enforcement of pure food regulations, elimination of some abusive practices from the management of state prisons, taxation of the intangible assets of railroads and other industries, an increase in the taxes levied upon privately owned utilities, provision for the regulation of such utilities by the municipalities, and a requirement that life insurance companies invest in Texas securities three-fourths of their receipts from Texas clients. Some of those measures increased substantially the assessed value of property and the tax returns from that source; but the one regulating investments by life insurance companies led to the withdrawal of twenty-one of the companies from Texas until a revision in the requirements encouraged their resumption of operation in this state.

While enacting manifold reforms, the Campbell administration also declared war on the trusts. In that campaign the most publicized case was the one brought against the Waters-Pierce Oil Company, a subsidiary of the Standard Oil Company. The state had, in 1897, revoked the permit of the Waters-Pierce Company to engage in business in Texas, but soon H. Clay Pierce had obtained a revocation of that order by certifying that his company had terminated its affiliation with Standard Oil. When that pretense was shattered in 1905 by a court investigation in Missouri,

the Texas attorney general immediately obtained a judgment which again revoked the permit and also assessed penalties amounting to one million eight hundred thousand dollars. In similar action the penalties collected in seventy-four other antitrust cases in Texas amounted to over one million dollars. This campaign, therefore, collected a considerable sum for the state treasury, but it failed to check permanently the growth of large business combinations.

As an outgrowth of the Waters-Pierce antitrust suit, the political activities of Senator Joseph W. Bailey aroused considerable controversy, because he had been an associate and counsellor of Pierce. Nevertheless, in the contest for the selection of delegates to the National Democratic Convention of 1908, Bailey's well-organized following won a decisive victory. Hardly had the echoes of that battle faded out before the militant Prohibitionists went into action. In the election of 1910 they pressured the Democratic Party into accepting a platform plank calling for an amendment to the constitution which would impose statewide prohibition of sales of intoxicating beverages. This proposal engendered a lot of heat. The Prohibitionists enlisted the support of ex-Governor Campbell and other prominent reformers, while the opposition was headed by the incumbent governor. The amendment failed by the very narrow margin of only six thousand votes, and this social reform therefore was postponed until it became legally effective in all states but only halfheartedly observed under the federal amendment adopted in 1919. That great battle of 1911 had rather exhausted the crusading energies of the Texans; in fact, as Rupert N. Richardson has put it, the reform movement for several years thereafter enjoyed only a "wavering progress."

REFORM IN CALIFORNIA

After the turn of the century California also experienced an upsurge of reform for reasons rooted in the experience of preceding decades. After the earlier movement had led to the adoption of a new constitution in 1879, a conservative reaction set in and concern about local government subsided. Throughout the decade of the eighties the politicians soft-pedaled controversial issues and even the appeal of the Populist revolt of the succeeding decade failed to arouse many Californians. At the peak of that Populist clamor in the Midwest, the coastal state was electing a governor, James H. Budd, whose appeal to the voters, according to John W. Caughey, was based on his boast that he was young, that he was a university graduate, and that he "traveled by buckboard." Nevertheless, he turned out to be a relatively competent administrator, who emphasized economy, and his successor for the term of 1903 to 1907, George C. Pardee, also had a reputable record. The legislature, however, was controlled by machine politicians whose influence resulted in waste and favoritism in the performance of that body. The machine bosses had their origin in, and derived their power from, the larger cities, where their corrupt practices became a matter of common knowledge; therefore it was in the cities that a reform movement arose soon after 1900.

In San Francisco a political machine organized by Abe Ruef, a local attorney, flourished on "contributions" extracted from prostitutes, saloonkeepers, and operators of gambling dens. In 1901 this machine advanced a slate of candidates for city offices under the label of the "Union Labor Party." In that campaign Ruef's adherents elected Eugene E. Schmitz as mayor, whom they reelected in 1903 and 1905 against feeble reform opposition. Finally, in 1906, during an uproar over the granting of a franchise for streetcar lines with overhead trolley wires, opponents of the boss went into action. The district attorney, William H. Langdon, employed as his deputy a noted investigator of fraud, Francis J. Henry, and together they set out to expose the illegal practices of the machine leaders. Before a grand jury they submitted evidence that Ruef had pocketed over two hundred thousand dollars in bribes exacted not only from the vendors of commercialized vice but also from the treasuries of the railroad, gas, and telephone companies. During the sensational trial Henry was murdered, but Hiram Johnson and Matt Sullivan continued the prosecution successfully. They obtained the conviction of Ruef, who was sentenced to a term of fourteen years in the state prison at San Quentin. Prosecution of the wealthy payers of bribes was handicapped by the reluctance of frightened witnesses to testify and by a growing public animosity against the prosecutors that had been aroused by newspapers under the control of the defendants. Those law suits finally frittered out.

During the period, in Los Angeles a reform campaign headed by Dr. John R. Haynes obtained a new city charter in 1902 with provision for initiative, referendum, and recall, and four years later his Good Government League elected its candidates to seventeen of the twenty-three municipal offices. The mayor, A. C. Harper, however, was not one of the Good Government candidates; but soon the cleanup crew obtained proof that he was selling "protection" to purveyors of commercialized vice and forced his abdication in favor of their own candidate.

Reform organizations, springing up in more and more localities, provided roots for the growth of a concerted statewide movement. In 1907, at a convention in Oakland crusading delegates founded the Lincoln-Roosevelt League under the presidency of Frank R. Devlin. The League proposed to support the program of Theodore Roosevelt, to eliminate corruption from the state legislature, to end excessive railroad favoritism in state politics, and to require direct primaries for the nomination of party candidates. In 1907, the League installed Clinton L. White as mayor of Sacramento, and in the following year it nearly gained control of the Republican state convention when it was nominating the candidates for national offices. After this narrow escape the Republicans made a concession. They sponsored an amendment which authorized the nomination of candidates in direct primary elections, and it was adopted. Next, in 1910, the League nominated the vigorous, outspoken Hiram W. Johnson as its candidate for governor

on the Republican ticket, and after a spirited contest he won that spot on the ticket. Then the Democrats, not to be outdone, also framed a reform platform and advanced a strong candidate, Theodore A. Bell.

Obviously the Californians were going to get some reform measures one way or the other in 1910, because both parties promised the voters that they would grant the franchise to women, regulate public utilities, obtain popular election of senators, adopt an income tax, exclude the Orientals, eliminate corruption from politics, and introduce the initiative, referendum, recall, and short ballot. In that election Hiram Johnson won by a comfortable margin, and in the ensuing three years the representatives of the Lincoln-Roosevelt League enacted so comprehensive a program of reform measures that it required twenty-three amendments to the state constitution. With its platform thus enacted, the League had attained its objectives and soon receded in eminence.

When the Progressive Party nominated Theodore Roosevelt for the presidency in 1912, that party chose Hiram Johnson as his running mate, and together they carried California. However, they did not garner enough electoral votes in other states to win. Johnson then returned to the Republican Party, which seated him in the United States Senate in 1916. Thereafter politics in California reverted once more to a contest between representatives of the two major national parties. As in Texas, the reform movement had spent itself for some time to come.

PROGRESS IN NEW MEXICO AND ARIZONA

While the two states in the Southwest were engrossed in an upsurge of political idealism, the two territories were bidding again for elevation to statehood. After the rejection of New Mexico's overture in 1876, the political leaders in the territory tried again in 1889. Without waiting for the Congress to adopt an enabling act, they called for a constitutional convention, to which mostly Republican delegates were elected. They drafted a long, detailed organic law which, in effect, favored wealthy Republicans by fixing a limit on taxation. For that reason the Democrats opposed it, and because the expenditure of tax money for the support of parochial schools would be prohibited, the Catholic clergy also lent their opposition. As a result, the voters failed to approve this constitution; but the Republicans did not give up. The territorial governor, L. Bradford Prince, sent a group of twenty-nine lobbyists to Washington in 1890 in an effort to elicit favorable action; but on the way those intended spokesmen fell to arguing among themselves, and the mission failed. This fiasco revealed that there was no unanimity in the territory. Some people favored statehood because they believed that it would promote industry and business and give them a greater share in their local government. Others opposed it because the cost of state government would increase taxes and because they thought that the Spanish Americans were not ready yet to be entrusted with such responsibility.

On the subject of statehood Arizona also harbored some opponents; but in 1891 the "pros" got the upper hand and obtained the election of delegates to meet in Phoenix in a constitutional convention. It drafted an organic law which included such peculiar proposals as the one which would establish a silver currency for the payment of all state obligations and another which claimed state ownership of all rivers in the territory. Since the Congress immediately rejected Arizona's bid under that constitution, another convention met in Phoenix in 1893. It merely drafted a petition and that appeal also was rebuffed in Washington.

After 1900, several factors favored more serious consideration of the desires of the two territories. Among the political, economic, and social advances already accomplished—which raised hopes in both territories—were five which have been discussed previously: the pacification and segregation of the Indians, the advent of the railroad era, the expansion of mining, the boom in the cattle industry, and the abatement of disorder and violence. Now progress was also being made in the clarification of land titles. The Congress had created the Court of Land Claims in 1891, and in twenty years it reviewed all of the unsettled claims submitted to it. Finally title was confirmed to about two million acres of land, which was only six percent of the amount asked by the avid claimants. This tardy but conscientious concentration upon that task may have done some injustices, because clever forgeries were hard to detect; but at least it did establish recognized titles. That, in turn, encouraged economic development. Whereas *bona fide* homesteading long had been handicapped, after 1900 it grew apace. In New Mexico in one year alone, 1907, five million acres of land were taken up by homesteaders, and by 1910 the population had increased by sixty-eight percent over the figure for 1900. In Arizona by 1910 a million acres of land had been provided with irrigation, copper mining had advanced to first place in the Union, and the population had increased by sixty percent in one decade.

Meanwhile both territories had been making significant improvements in public education. As early as 1874 the legislature in Arizona had founded a system of schools with the governor serving *ex-officio* as territorial superintendent and, in 1889, a separate superintendency was created. By that date, too, more funds had been provided, a uniform series of textbooks had been adopted, and a university had been founded at Tucson in 1885. In addition, normal schools for the training of teachers were opened in Tempe in 1885 and

in Flagstaff in 1899. By 1910, the public schools of Arizona had an average daily attendance of approximately twenty thousand pupils.

In New Mexico, the effective efforts for improvement in education began with the founding of a university in Albuquerque in 1889, and four years later normal schools were established in Silver City and in Las Vegas. Meanwhile, in 1891, the legislature had enacted an improved public school law, which created a territorial system headed by a board and a superintendent. Expenditures increased from eighty-five thousand dollars in 1892 to a quarter of a million dollars seven years later. Thereafter additional funds were derived from the letting of leases on nearly three million acres of land which had been obtained in 1898 as a gift from the federal government through the efforts of Harvey B. Ferguson. By 1910, the public schools in New Mexico enrolled almost sixty thousand pupils.

THE STRUGGLE FOR STATEHOOD

In those years New Mexico usually voted Republican, which looked good to officials in Washington, where a Republican majority then usually prevailed. On the other hand, they regarded Arizona with suspicion, because many territorial leaders had been caught up in the frenzy of the "free silver heresy" of Bryan and the Populists. Besides, the trade unions were enrolling more and more of the laborers in the mines. They went on strike in Globe in 1896, in Morenci in 1903, and in Bisbee in 1907, and quite likely they would apply radical pressure on a state constitutional convention. That possibility alarmed

conservative Republicans in the East. On the other hand, President Theodore Roosevelt had a fond memory of association with his former "Rough Riders" from Arizona and New Mexico and now he was influenced in favor of statehood. The territories had another partisan in Matthew S. Quay of Pennsylvania; but his influence in the Senate was being challenged by a rival, Senator Albert J. Beveridge of Indiana, and this feud unfortunately aligned the Beveridge faction in opposition to statehood.

As the question became pressing after 1900, Beveridge as chairman of the Senate Committee on Territories took a subcommittee on a tour in the two territories and held brief closed hearings in a few cities. The committee listened to the testimony of persons selected by Beveridge; consequently it returned to Washington with the conviction that the two territories were not yet ready for statehood. Separately a committee of the House of Representatives which also conducted hearings in New Mexico and Arizona carried back a favorable recommendation. The upshot of this stalemate was that Beveridge supported a compromise proposal in 1904. By this plan, the two territories would be admitted under "jointure" as one state. Beveridge was confident that either the plan would be voted down, or else, if it were adopted, the radical tendencies in Arizona would be overwhelmed by the conservative vote of the larger population in New Mexico.

When confronted by possible jointure, the influential mine operators in Arizona naturally opposed domination of that territory by the agricultural majority in New Mexico. M. G. Cuniff argued that these two territories were as different as Texas and New Mexico, and the territorial legislature adopted a resolution which protested that jointure "humiliates our pride, violates our tradition, and would subject us to the domination of another commonwealth of different traditions, customs and aspirations."

In New Mexico the territorial governor, Miguel A. Otero, was a strong advocate of statehood; but achievement by jointure was unacceptable to him be-cause it would bring "an unnatural and unwilling alliance . . ., the coercion of two populations which are unlike in character and ambition, and largely in occupation." In recognition of these protests the Congress amended the join-ture act with provision for a referendum in the two territories. In the election in November, 1906, New Mexico approved the proposal by a vote of twenty-six thousand to fifteen thousand, largely because statehood had been delayed so long that almost any plan was acceptable. In Arizona, however, sixteen thousand voted against jointure and only three thousand for it. That killed admission as one state.

In 1908, Arizona sent to Washington a Republican delegate, Ralph H. Cameron. In party circles his election was regarded as a favorable change of heart in the territory. Soon all of Cameron's tact and persuasive powers were required to keep alive the interest of eastern Republicans, since in 1909 the labor faction had obtained control of the territorial legislature. Since 1906 New Mexico also had been represented in Washington by a capable and persevering delegate, William H. Andrews. Finally, in 1909, President William Taft concluded that he should make personal observations in the two territories, where he gathered a favorable impression. He concluded that each should be granted statehood, but, with a suspicious eye on Arizona, he advised that the conventions should exercise "due care" in the drafting of constitutions.

SUCCESS AT LAST

In June, 1910, the Congress passed an enabling act for the creation of two states instead of one. Then constitutional conventions again convened in the two capitals. In New Mexico a group of twenty-one Republicans dominated the proceedings and produced a rather conservative document. The electorate adopted it in January, 1911, by a vote of thirty-two thousand to thirteen thousand, and in the state elections in November the Democrats won a surprising victory by electing their candidate for governor, W. C. McDonald. This startling reversal was caused by the emergence of a bloc of Progressive Republicans who repudiated the party bosses and switched to the Democratic nominee. Consequently there was considerable chagrin in national Republican circles; but the procedure had gone too far for retraction. Besides, there was some cause for satisfaction in the election of Republican Senators by New Mexico. President Taft proclaimed the admission of New Mexico as a state on January 6, 1912.

In Arizona, the delegates to the constitutional convention of 1910 included only eleven Republicans against forty-one Democrats, and of the latter a majority were aggressive laborites. The Republicans, with the support of some of the conservative Democrats, were able to defeat labor proposals for the exclusion of Mexican workers and prohibition of the use of court injunctions against striking workers. On the other hand, the labor delegates did succeed in inserting some of the popular features of Progressivism, including the initiative, referendum, and recall. They even made judges subject to recall by popular vote, and in the opinion of President

Taft and conservative jurists that kind of use of the recall procedure went too far. Judges, they felt, should be free from popular pressures. Even though the electorate in Arizona approved the constitution by a vote of thirteen thousand to only four thousand, President Taft threatened to veto the resolution admitting Arizona. Promptly an amendment was adopted in another election in Arizona in December of 1911. It exempted judges from recall. In that election the voters also elected state officers, and, as could be anticipated, the Democrats won control of the legislature and elected as governor George W. P. Hunt of the labor faction. Nevertheless President Taft had gained a point, momentarily at least, so that he proclaimed Arizona admitted as the forty-eighth state on February 14, 1912. His persuasiveness was not long heeded, however, because the first state legislature resubmitted for popular approval the article providing for recall of judges, and the voters asserted their newly won sovereignty by adopting it.

Finally the two territories took their place as states alongside their two neighbors in the Southwest. Economic functions and social patterns had been transformed, territories had grown into states, disorder and violence had yielded to the more orderly processes of the law, and all across the Southwest distress and injustice had produced an upsurge of the reform which had revised the law. All of this was accomplished by evolutionary processes within the framework of the American federal system.

17
THE
MODERN SOUTHWEST

No man-made phenomenon of such tremendous power had ever occurred before. The lighting effects beggared description. The whole country was lighted by a searching light with the intensity many times that of the midday sun. It was golden, purple, violet, gray and blue. It lighted every peak, crevasse and ridge of the near-by mountain range with a clarity and beauty that cannot be described but must be seen to be imagined. It was that beauty the great poets dream about but describe most poorly and inadequately. Thirty seconds after the explosion came, first, the air blast, pressing hard against the people and things, to be followed almost immediately by the strong, sustained, awesome roar which warned of doomsday and made us feel that we puny things were blasphemous to dare tamper with the forces heretofore reserved to the Almighty.

General Thomas F. Farrell, quoted in William L. Laurence, Dawn over Zero *(New York, 1940), p. 194.*

INTEGRATION IN THE NATION

The admission of New Mexico and Arizona as states brought those parts of the old Spanish Southwest to political maturity alongside their neighbors. This consummation occurred on the eve of the involvement of the United States in the first World War, in which the four states of the Southwest contributed their resources and manpower. In fact, for each of these states the story of the participation in military achievements and of the organization of the home front would fill a separate volume. The same can be said of the contribution of the Southwest to the supreme national effort elicited by World War II, which followed only twenty years later.

In the interval between these two wars, the Southwest also shared with the remainder of the nation the industrial prosperity, the exuberance, and the social problems of the "jazz age" of the 1920s, followed by the unemployment, the business failures, and the frustration of the Great Depression of the 1930s. In the latter era the national programs of the "alphabetical" agencies which were in operation elsewhere also functioned in these four states. Local factors caused some minor deviations from the national pattern, but by and large the people of this region became well acquainted with the work of the AAA, CWA, PWA, WPA, NYA, CCC, and other relief and reform efforts. Although the New Deal may not have succeeded fully in attaining its objectives, it left a lasting economic and political imprint. That, too, could be made the subject of a full volume.

Instead of relating the national history of the past half century, this chapter will be concerned more with the effect of national forces and local achievements upon the developments *within* the Southwest in recent decades. Whereas the histories of earlier epochs describe expeditions, discoveries, battles, and institutional origins, the story since 1910 emphasizes production, transportation, federal relations, reorganization, mobility, social problems, and related political pressures.

BLACK GOLD

In the emergence of the modern Southwest, certainly one of the impressive changes in the cultural landscape was the appearance of oil derricks on the silhouette of the skyline in many localities. Oil had been discovered quite early in Texas and California, but full capitalization upon that resource had been delayed until more uses for oil would create a greater demand. After 1900 an unprecedented market for the "black gold" was created by the conversion of heating plants, the increase in the number of automobiles and trucks, the development of the diesel motor, the progress of aviation, and the utilization of more and more petroleum by-products. The price of oil increased, "wildcat" prospecting became frenzied, and several oil companies emerged as industrial giants.

In the oil boom Texas climbed quickly to first place in the Union and continued to hold that leadership. The initial area of rich production was the Spindletop field near Beaumont, which was opened in 1901, and within the next few years other fields were tapped near the Gulf coast. The major oil strike occurred at Ranger in 1917, followed by the development at Big Lake in 1923 and the discovery of the rich Yates pool in 1926 in the valley of the Pecos River. Thence exploration ventured northward successfully on the high plains, and the annual production of two hundred and fifty-seven million barrels put Texas in first place among the states in 1928. Another boom followed in 1930, when the richest field yet found was opened in eastern Texas. Soon the "black gold" was being pumped by ten thousand new wells, and the area of successful drilling continued to expand. By 1930, the ninety thousand wells in Texas were producing nearly a half of a billion barrels, or one-third of the petroleum output of the United States. The figure rose to a billion barrels annually in the early 1950s, where it has remained with little variation through subsequent years. In 1966, the output in Texas was still far ahead of that of its nearest competitor, Louisiana.

The oil boom had far-reaching effects. The new towns that mushroomed wherever new fields were opened immediately became the centers of feverish sale of leases at speculative prices and attracted a concentration of shops for the assembly and repair of equipment. This spectacular growth preceded the construction of good roads, the provision of adequate protection against fire, and the adoption of proper police and sanitary measures. Trucks mired down, fires raged out of control, disease threatened to become epidemic, and crime increased disproportionately.

Presently the Texas Rangers and local vigilance committees established order in the oil camps, and then the newcomers rebuilt the towns and obtained improved roads. As orderly development emerged in the fields, the center of financial activity shifted to Houston, the "oil capital." There, after the port had been improved and a ship canal had been built, the oil companies erected their refining plants. Wealth from this new industry also built several skyscrapers in which the oil tycoons maintained their offices. This absorption of the leading citizens of Houston in the accumulation and protection of their fortunes made many of them quite

reactionary in politics. On the other hand, the petroleum industry also had a progressive influence, in that the taxes levied upon it contributed immensely to the building of good public schools and colleges throughout the state.

The scramble for quick wealth caused excessive waste, because wells drilled too close to each other drained the underground pools rapidly. As early as 1899, state regulation had been attempted in Texas, though ineffectively; therefore, in 1917, the regulation of oil and gas production and of the laying of pipe lines was delegated to the railroad commission. Because that body had ill-defined powers, the legislature granted greater authority in the conservation statute of 1919. The only real solution lay in limitations upon production, but the efforts in that direction in 1930 were frustrated in the courts. Rapid depletion of oil resources continued to be a serious threat. For example, in eastern Texas unrestrained pumping caused the field's pressure to drop at the rate of one and two-tenths pounds daily. Other states, notably California since 1911, had also been attempting to find a solution; but restrictions in one state penalized the producers in that state if those elsewhere were not similarly checked. Therefore the governors of the southwestern states met in conference in 1931 and agreed upon an interstate compact which would prorate production. After this agreement had stood up in court tests, the railroad commission of Texas and similar bodies in the other states were able to enforce compliance with conservation measures. Within four years twenty-two states had become parties to the Interstate Oil Compact.

Many of the oil fields also produced natural gas, which soon became accepted as a convenient fuel. As early as 1910, a pipeline was laid from the Petrolia field to Dallas and Fort Worth, and after 1927, when the Panhandle gas fields were tapped, more distribution systems were built. By 1940, one-half of the households in the state were consumers of natural gas. Moreover, pipelines then had been laid into sixteen other states, and Texas was producing forty-two percent of the natural gas of the United States. Ten years later Texas continued to be well in first place in gas production; but by 1966 Louisiana had passed Texas by virtue of expanded off-shore production.

OTHER MINERAL PRODUCTS

Among other mineral products, Texas had risen to first place in the Union in the processing of asphalt—another product brought into demand by the use of motor vehicles. However, since ores were not abundant in this state, the only mineral products in which Texas ranked first in 1966 were graphite and magnesium chloride. Texas also stood near the top in sulphur, salt, cement, helium, and gypsum. In that year some prospectors claimed that they had found the lost gold mine of San Sabá, which, according to one geologist, assayed at $467.50 a ton, or the richest of any strike made in this century. If production should continue to fulfill the expectations, Texas would advance in the standings in gold production; but as of that date it was still the output of oil and gas which maintained the leadership of Texas in mineral production, with a total value of a little over five billion dollars in 1966.

California has been mentioned previously as having once been the nearest competitor of Texas in oil production. Moreover, the coast state also had early discoveries; but production did not exceed a hundred million barrels a year until the automobile came into its own in the 1920s. In response to the growing demand, new fields then were opened. In 1920, the one at Huntington Beach came in and the next year at Signal Hill and Santa Fe Springs. After this initial boom further expansion was retarded by the depression of the thirties and by the cost of transporting oil from distant California to eastern markets in competition with the lush production of Texas. Soon the spectacular growth of population in California and the attendant increase in local consumption favored a revival, and refineries were built in the vicinity of Los Angeles. By 1950, California, although pumping only about one-third as much petroleum as Texas, had advanced to second place among the states. Sixteen years later California was continuing at near the same pace, but phenomenal expansion in Louisiana had moved that state into second place.

As in Texas, the increase in oil production in California was accompanied by a growing output and use of natural gas. The volume rose from sixty-six billion cubic feet in 1920 to three hundred and twenty billion in 1936, giving this state second place in the Union at that date. However, with an increase to six hundred and sixty-four billion cubic feet in 1964, California then was outranked by the greater production of four other states.

With mineral products valued at about one and one-quarter billion dollars in 1952, California stood next to Texas in the total figures for this industry. Despite an increase to a mark above one and one-half billion dollars in 1966, California had to be satisfied with third place, due to the rapid rise of Louisiana. However, California had the advantage of greater variety. In recent years the coastal state has ranked first in the production of asbestos, boron, cement, diatomite, gypsum, mercury, sand and gravel, sodium sulfate, and tungsten. Although third in the mining of gold, the high value of this mineral made gold production a significant industry, with an annual yield around thirty-five million dollars from mines in forty counties. Since the turn of the century this has become a highly mechanized industry. The ores from lode mines were excavated and processed by complicated machinery, and the placer beds along the rivers were worked by mammoth dredges.

From Texas and California exploration for oil extended into the neighboring states of New Mexico and Arizona, and in the former some rich fields were found. The first to be opened, in 1922 and 1923, were the Hogback and Rattlesnake fields on Navajo lands in San Juan County and the Artesia field near Carlsbad. In 1926 and in 1929, others came in at Hobbs and Eunice. As soon as refineries were built to serve those fields, production increased steadily but not spectacularly. In 1955, the wells in New Mexico pumped their billionth barrel of oil, but this total for twenty-two years only approximated the yield of Texas in one year. By 1964, the annual production amounted to about one hundred and twenty-five thousand barrels, for sixth place among the states. With oil came also a good flow of natural gas, especially in San Juan County. After pipelines were laid to Santa Fe and Albuquerque in 1930 and to the west coast twenty years later, the marketing of this valuable product increased rapidly. By 1955, the total value of oil and gas produced in this state was nearly three hundred million dollars.

New Mexico continued to have a considerable return from mineral products other than petroleum and natural gas. The production of copper, principally from the old mine at Santa Rita, increased to a peak valuation of twenty-eight million dollars in 1928, and in the 1930s the yield of gold from several mines was valued around a million dollars annually. In addition, production of potash from the deposits opened at Carlsbad in 1931 increased rapidly until New Mexico held first place in the Union in the value of potassium salts mined annually. In 1955, the output of one million eight hundred thousand tons was valued at about fifty million dollars. From twelfth position among the states in mineral production of all kinds at that time, New Mexico climbed to seventh in 1964, with a total value of seven hundred and twenty million dollars. Ranking high among the other products were uranium, helium, manganese, zinc, lead, silver, molybdenum, gypsum, and coal.

In Arizona, although exploration for oil had not been very fruitful, the production of other minerals, especially copper, gave this state a relatively high standing. After 1900, the intensive exploitation of copper ores by machinery installed by the Phelps Dodge Corporation advanced Arizona rapidly until this state achieved first place in the Union in 1907, and it has maintained that position in subsequent years. By 1926, the Arizona mines were processing about three-fourths of a million pounds annually, and despite the adverse economic conditions of the Depression, that figure was doubled by 1935. Other minerals made the total valuation about fifty million dollars in 1939, and seventeen years later the total had climbed to a figure past the two hundred million dollar mark. With production of all minerals valued at about six hundred million dollars in 1966, Arizona then ranked eighth in the Union, or not far behind New Mexico. Significant among the other minerals were silver, gold, molybdenum, uranium, mercury, helium, and vanadium.

MANUFACTURING IN CALIFORNIA

The production of minerals and other factors contributed to a growth in manufacturing. Other factors included the building of railroads, previously described, along with the expansion of agriculture and the greater exploitation of water-power resources, both of which will be commented upon later. The semiarid, sunny climate prevalent in much of the Southwest also was influential, and all of these factors contributed another—growth in population. Although these inducements were sufficient in themselves to bring a steadily climbing spiral of more industries and more people in some localities, their effectiveness became stimulated even further by the concentration of war industries and training centers in favored areas of the Southwest during the two world wars.

California led the other southwestern states in industrial development. First, a noteworthy increase appeared in the refinement of oil, which came in response to the boom in petroleum production and the increase in the number of automobiles. In the twenties and thirties the rapid growth in population provided local consumers for the output of numerous other manufacturing industries. Although the earlier products—beef, wheat, and gold—continued in a favorable position, they were now accompanied by, and in some instances surpassed by, some newer ones—automobile accessories, cotton fabrics, furniture, machinery, motion pictures, tuna fish, canned and frozen vegetables, wine, and more recently, airplanes and their accessories.

Among the accretions, that of the motion picture industry was unique. The making of movies had originated in the East, but after the production of California's first commercial film, *The Count of Monte Cristo*, in 1908, the advantages of the southwestern climate and scenery attracted the other principal producers to Hollywood in the years from 1910 to 1912. They brought with them the actors and actresses who were to become the idols of that generation. Soon *The Birth of a Nation*, produced by D. W. Griffith, was grossing millions of dollars, and the era of lavish expenditures and the creation of "stars" had dawned. In the 1920s, however, the industry provoked public criticism as a result of the scandalous conduct of some of the actors and the excessive appeal to sensuality by some of the competing producers. In order to forestall censorship by a government agency, the producers voluntarily employed Will H. Hays as their "czar" for the fixing of standards and the policing of the industry. This step restored some sobriety to the industry and revived public confidence. Soon afterward, in 1927, a remarkable technical improvement made possible the synchronization of sound with the picture, and the popular reception accorded Al Jolson in the first "talkie," *The Jazz Singer,* inaugurated a new era in this industry. By 1930 it had climbed to a position among the top ten in the nation.

The beginning of telecasting in 1940 and the acquisition of television sets by more families after World War II aroused fears that the motion picture industry might be doomed. The new competition stimulated the filming of "spectacular" productions, which were projected in color on wide screens, and this improvement helped keep many movie houses open. Presently the directors seemed to run out of ideas for "spectaculars," and then it became apparent that the industry was experiencing a major transformation. Production in Hollywood and elsewhere became reoriented to the market for TV serials, documentaries, and commercials, viewed in homes across the nation, and it was the movie houses which were in trouble. Many had been forced to close their doors, and in those remaining open, a survey conducted in 1968 revealed that the audience was comprised of children and teen-agers.

In California another industry which experienced phenomenal growth was electric power production. Because the

power conducted on high tension lines from distant hydroelectric plants was inadequate to meet the demands of the booming industries, gas from the oil fields was piped in for use as fuel in large steam-power plants. In the early 1920s, those plants became absorbed into three major companies, the Great Western Power, the San Joaquin Light and Power, and the Pacific Gas and Electric Company. Later in that decade the three merged into a new company which took the title of the last-named above, which became popularly shortened to the "P G & E." By 1940, California ranked third among the states in the production of electric power, and thirteen years later this state's output of thirty-six billion kilowatt hours from both privately and publicly owned facilities was second only to that of New York. Production in the coastal state was further facilitated by the building of a nuclear power reactor on Humboldt Bay in 1963, and by that date California's output of eighty-seven million kilowatt hours advanced the state ahead of New York.

The availability of abundant electric power along with the temperate coastal climate favored the locating of several naval and military training centers in California. Those of an earlier date— Fort Ord, March Field, Fort McArthur, and Mare Island Navy Yard—were expanded, and new facilities were added when cities in California became points of embarkation for the Pacific Theatre in the second world war. Recently principal bases for both the Navy and Marine Corps have been maintained at San Diego and for the Air Force near Rosamond and Lompoc.

The location of flight centers in California contributed to a westward migration of the aviation industry, so that as early as 1935 the production in California plants was valued at almost twenty million dollars. Even greater expansion came under the impetus of World War II, when the government spent one hundred fifty million dollars on aviation in California and private investors accounted for an additional eighty million. By 1950, airplane manufacturing and services employed ten percent of the industrial workers in that state. War needs also led to expansion of shipbuilding facilities, mostly under the management of Henry J. Kaiser, whose company maintained headquarters in Oakland and built a steel mill at Fontana, near Los Angeles.

At the end of World War II, when over twelve hundred industries in California announced plans within one year for new or expanded facilities, the P G & E president, James B. Black, commented optimistically about the "permanent character" of the war boom. In 1950, the twenty percent of the workers employed in manufacturing industries was well above the figure for any other southwestern state and close to the twenty-six percent average for the nation. Two years later the value added by manufacturers almost reached seven billion dollars, a sum exceeded by only five other states. California continued to gain ground, so that by 1964 the figure had risen to seventeen billion dollars for value added, second only to New York. A big share was contributed by government expenditures, of which California was receiving seventeen percent of the total outlay of federal agencies for defense and aerospace industries.

MANUFACTURING IN TEXAS

Among the southwestern states Texas ranked next to California in manufacturing industries. The timber resources in the eastern part of the state, which previously had been drawn upon in the early production of lumber, now were utilized more and more in the manufacture of pulp and paper. After 1911 this trend was stimulated by the invention of a process for the making of sulphate paper from the fiber of yellow pine, and by 1940 the annual return from all forest products, including paper pulp, was near fifty million dollars. Another early industry, flour milling, also had expanded with the growth of the state, so that by 1940 it, too, had attained an annual production valued at about fifty million dollars. Likewise a third early industry which had continued to grow rapidly was meat packing. By 1940, it was yielding a gross return about as much as that of flour milling and timber processing combined. Likewise, textile manufactures, which had also originated before 1900, continued to grow, especially in the Dallas area.

After 1900, oil refining, one of the newcomers among the manufactures of Texas, soon became the state's leading producer, which boomed from an annual production valued at about a quarter of a million dollars in 1920 to almost a billion dollars two decades later. Other industries which have grown rapidly are the manufacturing of chemicals and cotton by-products, along with the production of iron and steel in a mill built near Houston in 1941. Also, this state, as well as California, was favored in the location of training centers, of which the larger ones were the Naval Air Field at Corpus Christi, Fort Bliss at El Paso, and Randolph Field, Lackland Air Force Base, Fort Sam Houston, and Kelly Field near San Antonio. In fact, the concentration of bases near San Antonio brought to the population of that locality a larger proportion of military personnel than in any other city, even in time of peace, and before the Air Force Academy was founded at Colorado Springs, first Kelly Field, and later Randolph Field, was called the "West Point of the Air." To this vital complex of defense establishments in Texas was added another in 1963 by the building of the mammoth Manned Space Flight Center near Houston at a cost of one hundred and twenty-three million dollars. Moreover, during and since World War II, Texas had experienced a spectacular growth in defense-related industries,

including shipyards, aviation plants, petro-chemical manufactures, synthetic rubber plants, and a tin refinery. Recently this state has also emerged as a leading producer of electric power. The output of fifty-eight million kilowatt hours in 1964 ranked Texas in third place in the Union, next to California and New York.

The manufactured products of Texas, with a value of only about a quarter of a million dollars in 1910, had grown twenty years later to a figure of about one and one-half billion dollars for value added by processing. The Great Depression halted expansion; but it experienced a spectacular revival during and after World War II, so that by 1952 the annual value was above three billion dollars, or close to one-half of the figure for California at that date. A decade later the valuation had risen to seven billion dollars, but still less than half of the figure for the rival on the West Coast.

ARIZONA AND NEW MEXICO

Arizona and New Mexico, although producers of mineral ores, were less favorably endowed in other conditions required for great growth of manufacturing industries. The cost of transportation to distant markets was prohibitive except for specialized light manufactures, and the population of the two states was not large enough to provide much of a local market. Moreover most cities in these states lacked abundant electric power at low commercial rates and did not have the supply of water essential to many large industries. Nevertheless, the presence of available space and a modest market in locali-

ties blessed with sunshine and fresh air did attract some manufactures. This trend, already apparent prior to World War II, was stimulated during and after that war.

Many young men who had been encamped for wartime training at bases near Albuquerque, Roswell, and Phoenix returned to the Southwest after the war in search of employment, and their arrival made available a supply of skilled and unskilled workers. In Phoenix the growth of manufacturing was initiated by the coming of war industries, particularly a balloon, or "blimp," factory and a large aluminum plant. By 1948, one hundred and eighty new firms had located in Phoenix, and in the succeeding decade the value of manufactures increased two and one half times. Even so, the total was still relatively low, ranking Arizona only thirty-fifth among the states. More spectacular gains followed, so that by 1963 the value added by manufacturing had passed six hundred million dollars.

In New Mexico, too, the principal source of the postwar boom was federal investment in government installations and services, located principally in Albuquerque. In 1955, federal expenditures in this state amounted to close to a half of a billion dollars, of which about forty percent was for military services. A hundred million was used by the Air Force, much of it at Sandía Base near Albuquerque, and almost twice that sum was spent by the Atomic Energy Commission on research and testing programs. With a concentration of small shops, New Mexico stood somewhat lower than Arizona in the value of manufactures, or at forty-fourth place in the Union in 1952. In the succeeding decade the figure increased from one hundred and twenty-nine million dollars to one hundred and seventy-nine million. Then, as growth tapered off, the officials of the state joined with those of Arizona, Colorado, and Utah in the organization of a regional authority for development of the Four Corners Area.

Upon the appointment of an executive director in 1968, this body was ready to launch efforts for capitalization upon the potentials for development of industry, especially in the large area around the Four Corners, with federal aid.

ATOMIC ENERGY

Previously federal expenditures in New Mexico had contributed to a spectacular and revolutionary achievement. Back in 1942, the Army had acquired a ranch school for boys at a remote mountain site known as Los Alamos, near Santa Fe, and had secretly launched work there on production of an atomic bomb. Under the direction of J. Robert Oppenheimer, a group of the best nuclear scientists in the world labored at their task for three years in the restricted city "on the Hill."

In this project the staff at the University of California collaborated. At the Radiation Laboratory in Berkeley, E. O. Lawrence had built the first cyclotron for the smashing of the atom, and then the scientists from California helped with the project in New Mexico.

The staff at Los Alamos selected a place on the sandy desert near Alamogordo as the site for testing the first bomb. In July, 1945, Army trucks transported crew and equipment to the site, where the bomb was detonated on the 16th with a demonstration of such power and brilliance as never had been witnessed before. The flash which lighted all of central New Mexico that day climaxed an achievement which not only helped speed the end of the war with Japan but also offered new peacetime possibilities so great as to suggest the ushering in of a new era in world history.

The unleashing of nuclear power made possible an industrial revolution which would be slow in unfolding; but meanwhile this scientific achievement was having immediate effects in New Mexico. For one, the Army transferred the Laboratory "on the Hill" to the newly created Atomic Energy Commission, and more federal funds were expended on research and testing projects. Los Alamos then grew into an attractive but still restricted city. Later, in 1962, the restrictions were removed, except for the laboratories. The gates were opened, property was transferred to private ownership, and the community sought "normal" readjustment.

Another effect of the revolutionary discovery was the sudden demand which it created for uranium, the mineral utilized in the releasing of nuclear energy. By an odd turn of fate, one of the relatively rich sources of uranium was the rock of the Colorado Plateau, which extends from western Colorado into southern Utah and northern Arizona and New Mexico, close to the Atomic City. The reserves of New Mexico, alone, were estimated at fifty-five million tons, or two-thirds of the nation's supply. These reserves came to light as an outgrowth of a chance discovery by one Paddy Martínez, an Indian sheepherder who found some of the yellow rock on railroad land north of Grants in 1950. Within five years, eleven major deposits of uranium ore were found in that part of the state. Feverish prospecting attracted amateurs and engineers, and one year, 1954, witnessed the incorporation of sixty-six uranium companies. Grants, New Mexico, became a new kind of a miners' boom town and the "capital" of this rich uranium district, producer of one-half of the national output, which was purchased solely by the federal government.

PRODUCTION OF LIVESTOCK

Amid the frenzy of the new atomic age, the raising of livestock, which had been one of the original industries of the Southwest, continued to be a source of economic strength. In 1955, the ranchers of these four states had a total of approximately twenty-five million head of cattle, sheep, horses, and hogs, or one-fifth of the number in the entire United States. In thirty years that represented an increase of about three million head in the Southwest, and a similar accretion of three million head was recorded in the single decade following 1955.

In the past thirty years the mechanization of agriculture had caused a decrease in the number of horses in the Southwest by over one million, yet this was one part of the nation which still had a relatively large number. As draft horses almost became extinct on farms in the Midwest, the national proportion of the number of horses in the Southwest had increased from one-seventeenth in 1925 to one-sixth thirty years later; and Texas alone accounted for about one-half of those in these four states. The survival of this domestic animal can be accounted for by the popular use of horses in cattle ranching, on dude ranches, and in rodeos.

Another livestock industry, the grazing of sheep, had grown phenomenally in Texas from 1920 to 1940, when the number of head in that state had increased from a little over three million to almost eight and one-half million.

Simultaneously the number had declined slightly in the other three southwestern states, but the great accretion in Texas had contributed a rise in the total from eight million to over twelve million. Then, however, this industry had encountered less propitious conditions caused mainly by the competition of imported wool and synthetic substitutes. The number of head in Texas dropped to about five and one-third million by 1955 and also declined slightly in the other three states of the Southwest, so that the total was a little above nine million. The general decline reduced the figure another million by 1967.

In the Southwest the raising of hogs never had been relatively profitable and declined in popularity even further in the recent era. From over two million head in 1920, the number had decreased to a little above a million in 1955, and this decline continued during the next

decade in three of the states. Only Arizona showed a small increase, from twenty-five thousand in 1955 to about thirty thousand in 1966.

The increase in the number of cattle in the Southwest more than offset the reduction in the number of horses, sheep, and hogs. In the thirty-five years following 1920 the cattle grazed in Texas increased in numbers from five and three-quarter million to eight and one-half million and in California from two million to three and one-half million. In 1955, Arizona and New Mexico each had about a million head, making a total of more than fourteen million in the four states, or about one-seventh of those in the nation. By 1966, Texas and California had registered a gain of another three million head; but at that date Arizona had only a small increase and New Mexico a slight decline, due to several years of drought on the grasslands in these latter two states.

IRRIGATION PROJECTS

In central and eastern Texas agriculture long had flourished by means of natural precipitation; and west of that area some development had been made possible by the building of small irrigation projects by Indians and later by Spaniards and Anglo-Americans. Prior to 1900, most of the facilities for irrigation were small units dependent upon the diversion of water directly from the streams into small ditches. By that date the expansion of the irrigated area was awaiting the building of large reservoirs for storage of the seasonal runoff of water, which then could be drawn upon for irrigation where and when needed. On smaller streams some reservoirs had

been built by local water companies and enterprising individuals, but the larger streams remained unutilized. That task required resources greater than private enterprise could muster, and some of the rivers complicated matters by crossing state lines. Two of them, the Colorado and Rio Grande, also bordered upon Mexico.

For projects which would provide irrigation on a large scale, only the federal government could advance the funds and cope with the complexities in interstate relations. As the nation's leaders became aware of the potential, the Congress in 1902 adopted a reclamation act which authorized the sale of federal bonds for the construction of dams, reservoirs, and other facilities. Each project would be self-liquidating, because the sale of water rights and electric power would repay the investors over a long period of years. Moreover the projects would aid control of floods by storing the seasonal runoff in large reservoirs from which it could be drained off gradually.

Under the authorization granted by the Reclamation Act, the federal government first took over and expanded some of the projects already started on a small scale by private investors. Among these were the Carlsbad and Pecos facilities in New Mexico, and then an additional dam on the Pecos River was completed in 1905. Likewise, the government improved the Salt River project in central Arizona by building Roosevelt Dam on that river, which was completed in 1911, and additional canals were provided in the broad valley below Phoenix. Next the newly created Bureau of Reclamation built Elephant Butte Dam at Hot Springs (Truth or Consequences) on the Rio Grande. Completed in 1915, this project included three hundred and sixty-three miles of canals for irrigation of land in south-central New Mexico.

In those years in the eastern part of that state and in southern Arizona, too, irrigation by means of water obtained from the underground was also proving to be feasible and possible. Deep wells, called "artesian wells," tapped sources which in some cases had sufficient pressure to cause a natural flow; but in other instances the water had to be pumped. Sooner or later most of the "gushers" also had to be provided with pumps, because the number of wells drilled after 1920 increased so fast that the underground water level fell rapidly. Subsequently irrigation by this means was regulated strictly by the Ground Water Control Act of 1931 in New Mexico and the State Underground Water Conservation Code of 1948 in Arizona.

The greatest challenge in the Southwest was offered by the Colorado River, which was fed by tributaries arising in Arizona, Colorado, New Mexico, Wyoming, and Utah, and then ran through the Grand Canyon and turned southward to form the boundary between Arizona and Nevada and California before crossing a part of Mexico to its outlet in the Gulf of California. It had a flow of fifteen million acre-feet of water a year, but seven states and Mexico could advance claims upon part of that water. Under the auspices of the Bureau of Reclamation a representative from each of the seven states met in Santa Fe, New Mexico, in 1922 for consideration of a plan for equitable sharing of this resource. In the Santa Fe Compact which they agreed upon, the four states in the upper basin—Colorado, New Mexico, Utah, and Wyoming—were conceded use of one-half of the flow of the Colorado River, while the other half would belong to the three lower states—Arizona, Nevada, and California. Arizona, however, objected to some of the provisions, refused to ratify the pact, and initiated a test case in the federal courts. Finally, in 1928, the Congress approved the terms of the compact, which was upheld by an opinion of the Supreme Court two years later. Then the Bureau of Reclamation undertook the construction of Boulder Dam, later renamed Hoover Dam, on the Colorado River where it flows in its gorge between Arizona and Nevada. It was completed in 1936, but two years passed before the All American Canal was ready to carry the released water southward for the conversion of the desert of the Imperial Valley in southern California into a productive farming region.

In the 1930s, the Gila River in Arizona was harnessed for irrigation and power production by the construction of Coolidge Dam, and the Salt River project was expanded further by the completion of dams below the Roosevelt and the addition of some others on the Verde River. In 1933, the United States concluded a treaty with Mexico embodying an agreement on a division of the water of the Rio Grande. Then, as additional projects were planned for the middle and lower course of that river, it became imperative for Colorado, New Mexico, and Texas also to agree on their shares of the water not already conceded to Mexico. In 1938, representatives of the three states adopted the Rio Grande Compact, which was based upon what was considered at that time to be the normal flow. However, during the prolonged drought of the 1950s, the shares agreed upon proved to be too generous; Colorado accumulated a water indebtedness to New Mexico, and that state in turn fell behind in its obligation to Texas.

In the thirties, before the error in estimates had caused complications, the conclusion of the Rio Grande Compact and the treaty with Mexico facilitated enlargement of the area under irrigation along the middle and lower course of the river. In those years many conservancy districts were organized in Texas, covering the drainage basins of the principal rivers in that state, and then dams were built for regulation of the

flow of water. In 1937, Buchanan Dam was completed on the Colorado River of Texas; in 1941, Possum Kingdom Dam on the Brazos; and in 1944, the Denison Dam on the Red River. The latter backed up waters and created Lake Texoma, which had a capacity exceeded by only one other reservoir in the Southwest, Lake Mead. In the fifties the treaty with Mexico also made possible work on another large project, the International Falcón Dam on the Rio Grande above Laredo, Texas. It enriched the lower valley of that river by providing water for expansion of the area under irrigation.

Back in the decade of the thirties some large projects were also undertaken in California. San Francisco obtained an improved water supply by constructing the Hetch Hetchy Dam on the Toulumne River in 1933, and Los Angeles tapped the distant Colorado River by piping water from the reservoir above Parker Dam, which was completed in 1938. Then work began in earnest on the long-envisioned, ambitious Central Valley Project. Reservoirs on the Sacramento River in the northern part of the valley would make possible the storage of the winter floodwaters of that river for diversion by canals to the arid southern part of the valley, where they could be used to irrigate far more acreage than was possible by depending solely upon the flow of the San Joaquín. As early as 1874, such a project had been proposed and, in 1921, the state legislature had responded with favorable consideration. However, because such a project would also produce electric power, the Pacific Gas and Electric Company opposed it vigorously and work was held up for a long time. Finally, in 1937, the Congress adopted this project for development by the Bureau of Reclamation. Then work was begun on Shasta Dam, which was completed in 1945. With the addition of the Delta-Mendiota Canal and the Tracy Pumping Plant, along with the Friant Dam on the San Joaquín and the Friant-Kern Canal, the driest parts of the broad valley were made productive by this Central Valley System.

COMPETITION FOR WATER

Now, back to the Colorado River. On it a major project was completed in 1952, when the new Imperial Dam provided storage for irrigation of the Yuma Mesa. Further utilization of the flow of that river, however, was impeded by a dispute which had been brewing for some time. Arizona had opposed the building of Hoover Dam and other projects which stored water for use primarily in California, but finally, in 1944, Arizona had ratified the Santa Fe Compact. The next contender was the government of Mexico, whose representatives objected to use of all of the water of the Colorado River in the United States. Mexico could advance a claim upon some of it, because that river forms the boundary between Sonora and Baja California for a short distance. By treaty, therefore, the United States agreed to allow one and one-half million acre-feet annually for use below the Border.

In 1947, California challenged the Santa Fe Compact in the federal courts and sought the adoption of a new plan whereby the courts could allocate water from time to time according to need. That seemed reasonable at the time, because the four states in the upper basin were using only about one-fourth of their allocation, whereas California was hard pressed to find water for the needs of growing industry and increasing population. Immediately, however, representatives of the four upper states sent representatives to Vernal, Utah, where, in 1948, they drafted the Vernal Compact providing for division of their share as reserved by the earlier Santa Fe Compact. The next year, after the Congress had approved the Vernal Compact, the Bureau of Reclamation drafted plans for several projects in the upper basin. In 1955, when those proposals came before the Congress, the representatives from California opposed them strenuously, while those of the upper basin defended their claims.

Among the projects proposed for the Colorado River was a large one on the San Juan, a tributary which flows through the Navajo Reservation in northwestern New Mexico. As a warning to enemies who would deprive the Navajos of the addition of three thousand irrigated farms, two thousand men of the tribe prepared to perform their sacred war dance for the first time in eighty-seven years. However, those "enemies" were vanquished without resort to the war path when the Congress approved the upper basin projects in 1956 and made the appropriations for them as sought by the Bureau of Reclamation. The next year construction began on the Navajo Dam on the San Juan River. Simultaneously work was also initiated on another of the projects located in the Southwest — the Glen Canyon Dam. It also bordered on the Navajo Reservation, but farther to the west, where the Colorado River crosses southwestward from Utah into Arizona.

On into the 1960s the competition for water continued unabated. Californians used the waters of the Colorado River and then turned it back into the channel. The Mexican government complained that this practice was intolerable, because the excessive salinity of the reclaimed water was killing the crops in the irrigated fields below the Border. In response, the United States government in 1965 agreed to construct a canal to divert the drainage water into the Gulf of California. In addition, California continued to clamor by court action for part of Arizona's share of the Colorado, a share which the latter state was not using fully. Simultaneously in the 1960s the State of California adopted a plan for diversion of much of the Feather River, in the north, through canals to the arable land of the south, at a cost of one and three-quarter million dollars.

Meanwhile a hot debate had been precipitated in 1965 by the inauguration of a Reclamation Bureau project for construction of two dams—Marble Canyon and Bridge Canyon—in the scenic part of the Grand Canyon. Conservationists launched a campaign of opposition in newspapers and magazines. David Brower, executive director of the Sierra Club of California, protested that the dams "will flood out wildlife, drown invaluable archeological and geological sites, and inundate campsites," to which Sam Goddard, former governor of Arizona, retorted that he was "deeply disturbed by the wave of unfounded, inaccurate, and what I believe to be irresponsible propaganda which was launched against the construction of the dams." When the Colorado Basin Bill finally passed in 1968, provision for these two dams had been deleted, but it did include appropriations for a giant system of pumps and aqueducts for diversion of water from the Colorado River for irrigation in central Arizona and urban needs in Phoenix and Tucson. At the same time, work was progressing on another ambitious project costing eighty-six million dollars. Three tunnels to be bored through the Rocky Mountains would divert part of the water of the upper San Juan River, a tributary of the Colorado, into the Chama River, whence it would flow into the Rio Grande. Some of the accretion would be used for irrigation, but most of it would supply the demands created by industrial growth and population increase in Albuquerque. In 1968, a mechanical "mole" completed the burrowing of the third and final tunnel through nearly thirteen miles of rock under the Continental Divide.

The desperate quest for water in the Southwest elicited another plan, entitled the North American Water and Power Alliance. This project, which would cost eight billion dollars and require thirty years to build, would tap the abundant waters of the Fraser, Yukon, and other rivers of Alaska and Canada for diversion by canals, tunnels, and existing river channels to mammoth storage basins in the intermontane trough. Other canals would carry the rare commodity southward and then east and west into the arid regions of Arizona, New Mexico, and California. In 1968, some support was mounting in both industrial and governmental circles for the launching of this promising project.

In 1959, almost fifteen million acres of land were under irrigation in the four southwestern states, and the figure was approaching one-half of all lands so improved within the entire United States. California, with seven and one-third million acres under irrigation, held first place in the Union, and Texas, which had passed the five and one-half million mark, was in second place. Projects in Arizona supplied a little over a million acres, and in New Mexico about three-quarters of a million. Especially in the latter two states a gigantic project like NAWPA, described above, was needed for further development of both agriculture and urbanization.

CONSERVATION OF RESOURCES

A nationwide movement for conservation of resources accompanied the construction of reclamation facilities. Mountains were being stripped of their timber, erosion was washing away the soil, and floods were caused by reduction of the forested area, which normally retained moisture for a slow runoff. In 1886, the Congress established the Division of Forestry in the Department of Agriculture, and five years later, it authorized the president to designate forest reserves on public lands in order to maintain the stand of timber and to improve the regularity of flow in the streams. For further protection of the headwaters of rivers, in 1911 the Congress also authorized the purchase of lands which were no longer part of the public domain.

National forest reserves were placed under the management of the Forestry Service, which was authorized to encourage flood control, to eliminate erosion, to control water use, to regulate the flow of streams, to prevent and fight fires, to propagate wildlife, and to supervise recreation in the forests. From 1906 on, permits were also issued for limited grazing of cattle in the forests, and this practice was regularized by the Taylor Grazing Act of 1934. Some of the states also set aside forest reserves, part of which were later transferred to the federal government. In Texas, for example, the State Forest Service was established in 1913, four state reserves were set aside between 1924 and 1935, and they became national forests in 1936.

Three of the four southwestern states had fruitful areas for the creation of reserves in their large acreage of forested land still publicly owned. By 1966, the national forests of California, comprised of close to twenty million acres or about nineteen percent of the area of that state, ranked second after Alaska in the extent of the public reserves. Arizona had the next largest proportion, with about fifteen percent of the area, or over eleven million acres, in national forests, and New Mexico was not far behind, with nearly thirteen percent, or nine million acres. As of that date, the average for all fifty states was only about one percent of the total areas. Texas, where forested lands were not abundant, therefore ranked below the average, with only about three-quarters of a million acres or one-half of one percent in national reserves.

The need for conservation of the soil

was also becoming critical by 1930; therefore, in 1934, this responsibility was delegated to the Soil Conservation Service created as a division of the Department of Agriculture. By volunteer solicitation of farmers and ranchers, conservation districts were formed and government field men lent technical assistance. By means of diversion dikes, strip-cropping, cover crops, contour-plowing, and hillside water "tanks," further erosion of the topsoil was prevented, dust storms were partially abated, and production of crops and forage was improved. In Texas the one hundred and fifty million acres covered in soil conservation districts by 1954 placed that state first in the Union in this endeavor, and at that time New Mexico ranked fourth, with fifty-seven million acres in such districts. Response was slower in Arizona and California.

REVOLUTION IN AGRICULTURE

Simultaneous with the rapid development of reclamation and conservation projects, the states of Texas and California, which obtained the greater benefit from them, experienced a great growth in their agricultural industries. Eastern Texas, to some extent, but much less than in earlier years, continued to be a part of the old cotton kingdom, where the remaining producers depended considerably on government controls and subsidies in their competitive industry. Cotton growing also had migrated westward to new lands which initially were not infested by the boll weevil. This expansion into drier regions, where Negro labor was not available, was facilitated by the development of irrigation and mechanization, including the power-driven cotton picker. By virtue of the expanded culture, Texas advanced to first place in the Union in cotton production. In the lower valley of the Rio Grande, where a subtropical climate prevailed, the provision of facilities for irrigation made possible specialization in the growing of citrus fruits, especially oranges and grapefruit. Meanwhile Texas also had advanced to first place among the southern states in the production of corn. In 1964, the one hundred and forty-three million acres of cultivated land in Texas produced over twenty-three million bushels of corn and four million bales of cotton.

Arizona and New Mexico also recorded gains in their farm crops; in the former alfalfa, cotton, and citrus fruits led, and in the latter wheat stood first and cotton was increasing. In the 1950s, Arizona was only slightly ahead of New Mexico in annual farm income, in which these two states held thirty-fifth and thirty-seventh places, respectively. By 1965, however, Arizona had pulled well ahead, with receipts slightly above one-half billion dollars, whereas New Mexico had barely passed the quarter billion mark.

In recent years the most spectacular gains in agriculture were experienced in California. For this state the numerous "firsts" make too long a list for recognition of all of them. Significant among the more valuable returns were those derived from citrus fruits, cotton, grapes, rice, nuts, hay, vegetables, and poultry. Farm income from all sources increased from approximately eight hundred million dollars in 1900 to first place in the Union, or about two and one-half billion dollars in 1954. A decade later the total was approaching four billion dollars annually, still first among the states; yet this income was derived from approximately the same acreage of land in farms as in Arizona and New Mexico and only one-fourth as many acres as in Texas.

The phenomenal increase in farm income in California was attributable to a remarkable agricultural revolution. Because irrigation freed the operators from their dependence upon the uncertainties of the local weather, the processes of production could be timed and scheduled with precision, and in that warm climate several crops in succession could be harvested from the same fields annually. The concentration of farm holdings in large units, along with the use of modern machinery and the employment of migratory labor in the harvesting season, created an industrial system which Carey McWilliams has described aptly as "Factories in the Field." Despite the concentration in large units, a surprisingly small proportion of the farms in California were worked by tenants exclusively. For example, only eighteen percent of the farmland was so operated in 1940, the same as it had been ten years earlier. In the Southwest only New Mexico had a lower

percentage, fifteen in 1940 as against nineteen in 1930. Texas had a much higher proportion, thirty-eight percent in 1940, due largely to the dependence upon tenants in the old cotton belt; but in that state a decrease also had been recorded, from forty-four percent ten years earlier. Arizona, on the other hand, experienced an increase in tenancy from nineteen percent in 1930 to thirty-two a decade later. More recently the dependence upon mechanization has been reflected in the decrease in the proportion of employed persons who are engaged in agriculture. In California only four of each one hundred workers were so employed in 1960 in contrast with figures of seven to nine for the other three southwestern states.

The data on income provide additional revelations concerning the agricultural economy. In 1950, about seventeen percent of the rural families on farms in the United States had an annual income of less than five hundred dollars. In New Mexico twenty-one percent of the rural farm families were in that low income category, due to the occupation of small tracts inherited by many of the Spanish Americans. In Arizona the percentage having such a low income was fifteen, in Texas fourteen, and in California only ten. Thus all three of these states fared better than the national average.

RECREATION FACILITIES

While the achievements in conservation and reclamation were contributing to an improvement in agricultural production they also contributed to the rise of another "industry" — recreation and tourism. With virgin forests pre-

served, mountain streams protected, and numerous artificial lakes created, the states built fish hatcheries in order to keep the waters well stocked, and they undertook the propagation and protection of wildlife so as to provide good hunting within limited seasons. In the forests selected sites for camping were designated, and during the Depression those facilities were improved greatly by the labor of thousands of young men enrolled in the Civilian Conservation Corps. In Arizona, for example, by 1941 the CCC had built twenty-seven camps, fifty-five thousand check dams, seven hundred and eighty-five miles of service roads, and two thousand five hundred public facilities, such as tables, benches, fireplaces, and shelters. The growing popularity of the mountain playgrounds is attested by the tenfold increase in visitors recorded in the national forests in the two decades from 1917 to 1937. In subsequent years federal appropriations made possible further improvement in facilities, and in the 'sixties supplementary aid was lent by youth employed in the "Job Corps" under the supervision of the United States Forest Service.

The creation of national parks and monuments further stimulated tourism. As early as 1864, California had made a state park of the area surrounding Yosemite Falls and, in 1900, the federal government acquired part of that tract and another in the forest of giant redwood trees for the establishment of two national parks — Yosemite and Sequoia. Two years later the Congress also created the first national monument for preservation of an ancient Indian tower, known as Casa Grande, near Phoenix, Arizona. In 1906, three more such monuments were created in the Southwest — the Petrified Forest and the Montezuma Castle cliff dwellings in Arizona and Inscription Rock at El Morro, New Mexico. In the succeeding two years four more were added — the Muir Woods in California,

the Gila and Tonto cliff dwellings in Arizona, and the Chaco Canyon Pueblo ruins in New Mexico.

The National Park Service was created in 1916 for development and management of both the parks and the monuments. Subsequently six more national parks were acquired in the Southwest: Lassen Volcanic in California in 1916, the Grand Canyon in Arizona in 1919, Carlsbad Caverns in New Mexico in 1930, King's Canyon in California in 1940, the Big Bend in Texas in 1944, and the Petrified Forest in Arizona in 1962. Year after year additional monuments also were established until the number in the Southwest had grown to thirty-three, or nearly half of those in the entire nation. Most of these parks and monuments were marvels of nature and Pueblo Indian ruins, but five were historic sites of the Spanish colonial era, and finally in 1955 the creation of a monument of old Fort Union in New Mexico added to the list a historic site of the American territorial period. By that time the report on visitation revealed that the total number registered at southwestern parks and monuments was almost eight million annually, including many, of course, who were counted several times as they traveled to one after another of the sites during the year. Among the National Parks a decade later both Grand Canyon and Yosemite attracted nearly two million visitors, while King's Canyon, the Petrified Forest, and Sequoia registered only slightly under one million each. Carlsbad Caverns and Lassen Volcanic both counted in the neighborhood of one-half million. Among the monuments, Cabrillo, a memorial to the Spanish explorer, was by far the most visited. Its registrants numbered close to a million in 1966. Not far behind, with about seven hundred thousand, was Muir Woods. Those which counted between one hundred thousand and five hundred thousand each were Bandelier, Canyon de Chelly, Death Valley, Devil's Postpile, Joshua Tree, Montezuma Castle, Organ Pipe Cactus, Pinnacles, Saguaro, Sunset Crater, and White Sands. In addition each of the four states maintained several parks and monuments which also attracted numerous visitors, and more such recreation areas were being added annually.

TRANSPORTATION AND TOURISM

The remarkable record of the Southwest in catering to sportsmen, nature lovers, and sightseers was achieved by taking advantage of automobile transportation. As early as 1905 a few courageous men in each state owned automobiles, but at that time they were able to travel only on a few local roads of dirt and gravel radiating from the larger towns. As the cars became more numerous, the counties and states improved some of the roads, and in 1916 the federal government inaugurated a program of matching funds for the development of an interstate system of improved and numbered highways. Annually more and more of the state roads were incorporated into that system. By 1953 Texas had nearly twenty-five thousand miles of highways improved by federal aid, while California had almost ten thousand miles, New Mexico four and one-half thousand, and Arizona three thousand. In the next decade the greatest gain in mileage was reported in California, with an increase to twenty-five thousand miles of federal highways by 1963.

In the Southwest the great distances between towns and from ranches to towns, along with the popularity of out-of-door recreation, made for almost universal dependence upon transportation by motor vehicles. The number of registered owners increased quite rapidly in Arizona and New Mexico and so remarkably in California and Texas that those two states moved up to first and third places in the Union. In 1953, the number of motor vehicles in California was five and one-half million and in Texas three and one-third million, while Arizona and New Mexico each had over three hundred thousand. Twelve years later those numbers had practically doubled. California's figure had increased to almost ten million and that for Texas to over five and one-half million. Arizona then had over eight hundred thousand and New Mexico five hundred thousand.

Aviation also facilitated transportation. After experimental carrying of airmail in the early 1920s, in 1928, the year following his flight across the Atlantic, Charles A. Lindbergh selected Albuquerque to serve as the initial headquarters of his Transcontinental Air Transport. That flight service later was reorganized and expanded as the Trans World Airlines (TWA). Other commercial airlines were established in the next decade, and the cities, often with federal aid, built airports for accommodation of both private and commercial flights. By 1950, a network of interstate lines bound the Southwest even more firmly into the national web, and the big airlines which served the large cities opened up channels for international contacts with a facility never dreamed of in the era of the stagecoach and the China Clipper. By 1965, the four southwestern states had close to eighteen hundred airports, and those serving the metropolitan centers had grown into veritable cities, comprised of hangars, offices, waiting rooms, shops, long concourses, and related service establishments.

While the people of the Southwest were taking to the highways and airways, those of other states came to this region in increasing numbers. A contributing factor was the practice of allowing annual vacations in almost all lines of employment. That brought a flood of tourists in summertime, and parts of the Southwest, especially at the resorts along the southern border and at the ski runs in the mountains, also grew in popularity in the winter season. Various attractions were promoted throughout these four states for catering to the tourists. At the Indian villages the tribes revived their seasonal dances, in the cattle country the towns promoted annual rodeos, in the sports arenas athletic managers scheduled "bowl" games, and in the regions noted for flowers and fruits the communities organized their annual "blossom festivals." Where none of these was appropriate, the local business leaders conceived something unique, like the "Gold Rush" at Wickenburg, Arizona, the "Frontier Daze" in Tucson, or the international festival known as "Charro Days," promoted jointly by Matamoros, Mexico, and Brownsville, Texas.

In 1915, California had two inter-national expositions, in San Francisco and in San Diego. Dallas, Texas, celebrated with a regional centennial exposition in 1936, and San Francisco promoted another world's fair three years later. More recently an extraordinary attraction was brought to Squaw Valley in California in 1960 when the Winter Olympics were conducted there. Next, in 1968, San Antonio, Texas, was optimistically promoting a "Hemisfair."

In the recent era service facilities for automobiles and their occupants arose everywhere along the improved highways, and each state in the Southwest put out more lures to get the tourists to stop a while. In this new enterprise New Mexico led all of the West in 1954, when an estimated three million cars carrying nine million passengers entered the state. In the 1960s the annual income from the tourist trade in that state alone was estimated at two hundred and eighty-five million dollars, which was about one-half that of the other leading industry, mining, and ahead of the returns from farming and manufacturing.

Unfortunately the tourist "industry" had its unpleasant aspects. Fast cars traveled on the surfaced highways at hazardous speeds, which caused accidents that took an appalling toll of lives. Especially was that true on the long stretches of arterial highways crossing Arizona and New Mexico. In 1953, the latter state acquired a new record in which it could take little pride, for it had eleven and one-half deaths per one hundred million vehicle miles, the worst of any state in the Union. Arizona with nine and eight-tenths deaths was the fifth state in the list, while Texas and California each had only about one-half as many deaths proportionately as did New Mexico. In 1955, in a desperate effort to reduce this toll, Arizona and New Mexico employed more state police officers and resorted to the use of radar detectors and unmarked patrol cars. By 1966 some improvement was made in New Mexico. With seven deaths per one hundred million miles, that state had dropped to ninth place. Arizona's seven and two-tenths held seventh rank among the states, and California still remained remarkably low; but Texas, with six and eight-tenths, was climbing rapidly in this list of leaders in needless slaughter. Obviously a reduction in the perils of travel had become urgent if tourists were to enjoy the pleasures of travel in the Southwest.

In the Spanish era an economy based upon cattle raising, agriculture, and craftwork had become characteristic of the Borderlands. In the past half century craftwork had become relegated from its earlier role as an essential accompaniment of a subsistence economy to a new role as a minor though profitable adjunct of tourism. The other two features of the earlier pattern not only survived into the modern era but also grew to greater importance, and upon them a new pattern of mining, manufacturing, and tourism became superimposed.

In the long era of transition the Borderlands continued to have a considerable degree of homogeneity; but when the region emerged as the Modern Southwest, it lost much of its separate unity and became adjusted to the economic trends in the nation-at-large. Even so, the four states with their artificial boundaries did also acquire for each its own economic and political character, strengthened by pride in local achievements.

PRODUCTION AFTER MID-CENTURY

		Ariz.	Calif.	N.Mex.	Texas	U.S.
Mineral Production	1967	$464	$1,696	$874	$5,406	$27,736
(in thousands)	1952	$232	$1,214	$288	$3,379	$13,338
Value Added by Manufacture	1967	$919	$23,123	$171	$10,861	$259,301
(in millions)	1952	$231	$8,153	$129	$3,486	$121,659
Electric Output, Kilowatt	1967	9,724	108,532	8,943	76,833	1,214,365
Hours (in millions)	1953	6,389	35,956	1,804	29,664	514,169
Farm Receipts	1967	$574	$3,989	$350	$2,984	$45,867
(in millions)	1954	$365	$2,491	$187	$1,894	$29,954
Land in Farms	1964	40	37	46	143	1,124
(in million acres)	1950	40	37	48	145	1,159
Acreage Irrigated	1964	1,125	7,599	818	6,385	37,056
(in thousands)	1954	1,177	7,048	650	4,707	29,552

PRODUCTION AFTER MID-CENTURY (Continued)

		Ariz.	Calif.	N.Mex.	Texas	U.S.
Livestock (in thousands)						
Horses	1959	51	68	43	237	2,953
	1955	55	86	61	252	3,106
Cattle	1969	1,104	4,303	1,203	9,766	109,661
	1955	945	3,583	1,140	8,501	95,433
Milk Cows	1969	55	848	39	374	14,123
	1955	53	909	52	1,031	24,408
Sheep	1969	500	1,356	840	3,949	21,111
	1955	461	2,081	1,271	5,331	30,931
Hogs	1969	51	172	48	943	57,205
	1955	25	461	52	1,087	55,002
Motor Vehicles	1968	944	11,123	589	6,180	101,048
(in thousands)	1953	359	5,504	303	3,359	56,280
Employment (%)						
Agriculture	1960	7.8	4.3	7.1	9.0	6.0
	1950	14.9	7.6	18.4	16.2	12.5
Construction	1969	5.5	5.5	7.4	6.5	5.3
	1950	4.4	7.7	11.3	8.6	6.1
Manufacturing	1960	16.1	24.2	6.4	19.6	29.8
	1950	8.8	19.6	5.9	13.5	25.9
Mining	1960	.6	3.9	6.5	3.8	1.0
	1950	4.4	.8	5.1	3.3	1.7
Personal Services	1960	16.6	16.1	18.0	14.5	14.8
	1950	8.2	6.7	6.6	7.9	6.2
Government	1960	22.6	19.1	28.6	17.9	16.6
	1950	5.3	6.3	6.6	8.3	6.2
Trade	1960	23.6	22.1	24.7	24.7	20.8
	1950	21.9	22.4	19.0	21.4	18.8
Transportation	1960	6.2	6.7	7.6	7.7	6.7
and Utilities	1950	8.9	8.2	8.2	8.2	7.8

18
PEOPLE AND POLITICS

You send me to Washington to represent you in the senate. But you do not send me there because you are interested in grave questions of national or international policy. When I come back to Arizona, you never ask me any questions about such policies; instead you ask me: "What about my pension," or "What about that job for my son?" I am not in Washington as a statesman. I am there as a very well paid messenger boy doing your errands. My chief occupation is going around with a forked stick picking up little fragments of patronage for my clients.

Henry F. Ashurst, quoted in Waldo E. Waltz, "Arizona," Rocky Mountain Politics, ed. Thomas C. Donnelly (Albuquerque, 1940), p. 283.

INCREASE IN POPULATION

The expansion of industries and extension of highways contributed to a great growth of population in California and Texas in recent decades. In fact, California has enjoyed phenomenal growth ever since the turn of the century. In each decade from 1900 to 1940 over a million people were added to those already living in the coastal state. From 1900 to 1910 the percentage of increase was sixty, to 1920 forty-four, to

1930 sixty-six, and to 1940 twenty-two. All previous gains were surpassed in the decade of World War II, when the total rose from less than seven million to ten and one-half million, for an increase of fifty-three percent. In that same decade the national growth amounted to twenty percent.

Although the Californians were hard-pressed to find an adequate supply of water and sites for more residences, nevertheless they hailed the increase with enthusiasm and anticipated an increment of another ten million in the near future. By 1965 that goal was nearly achieved. The increase in the preceding fifteen years had amounted to eight million, or seventy-six percent, advancing California finally to first place in the Union, ahead of the previous leader, New York State.

In Texas, the great spurt followed World War I, when the decade of the 1920s witnessed a growth from four million six hundred thousand to five million eight hundred thousand, or twenty-five percent. In the 1930s, however, when agriculture and manufacturing were in the doldrums, Texas added population amounting to only ten percent. Then another wholesome increase of twenty-two percent came in response to the boom accompanying World War II. This exceeded the national increase of fifteen percent for that same decade. The recent upward trend has continued so that the figure passed the ten million mark by 1965. That amounted to an increase of thirty-seven percent in the preceding fifteen years.

New Mexico and Arizona, after experiencing a rapid growth in the early 1900s, soon slowed down to a rate only a little above the national average. Finally these two states also enjoyed a mild boom in the decade of the 1940s. New Mexico gained one hundred and fifty thousand, or twenty-eight percent, from 1940 to 1950, whereas Arizona with greater industrial growth added about one-quarter of a million people, representing a gain of roughly fifty percent. In the ensuing fifteen years both states passed the one million mark. The more spectacular gain was enjoyed by Arizona, where an increase to one and one-half million in 1965 amounted to an increment of one hundred and fifteen percent since 1950. Simultaneously the growth to one million in New Mexico by 1965 represented a gain of fifty-one percent in fifteen years. Optimists in both states regarded the recent increase as the beginning of a great boom, whereas the pessimists remarked that much of the growth leaned on the uncertain prop of government spending.

In recent years even in the spacious Southwest the urban concentration of the population has become pronounced. In 1950, New Mexico recorded urbanization slightly over fifty percent, and the other three states had passed a similar milestone earlier. In the ensuing fifteen years California's proportion of city-dwellers rose to eighty-six percent, that of Arizona and Texas to seventy-five percent each, and for New Mexico to sixty-six percent. Meanwhile some of the cities of the Southwest had gained a ranking among the top twenty in the nation. By 1960, Los Angeles was in third place, Houston seventh, San Francisco eleventh, and San Diego eighteenth.

ORGANIZED LABOR

The industrialization which created improved opportunities for employment in attractive urban centers also brought some strife between labor and management. In Texas, the legislature yielded to mounting pressures by legalizing unions during the administration of Joseph D. Sayers, who was elected governor in 1898. In the ensuing upsurge of reform the lawmakers also responded with several statutes sought by organized labor. They included a workmen's compensation act, a factory safety code, a child-labor law, and a measure establishing an eight-hour day for state employees. In that era, too, the Farmers Union was founded in 1902, in response to the problems arising from overproduction, especially of cotton. Within three years this organization had enrolled one hundred and twenty thousand farmers, who on the eve of World War I obtained state provision of warehouses for the emergency storage of surplus crops.

In the port cities of Texas, where the longshoremen were organized during the First World War, they went on strike in 1920 for the closed shop and better wages. When clashes occurred between the union members and the strikebreakers employed by the steamship companies, Governor W. P. Hobby declared martial law in order to "assure open transportation." This stifled that strike, and two years later, when railroad shopmen left their jobs, Governor Pat M. Neff responded with similar drastic action. This time the resort to martial law was contested in the courts, with the result that intervention by such means was declared unconstitutional in 1926. When the longshoremen went on strike again in 1935, violence ensued, but this time the laborers and employers concluded a compromise settlement. In subsequent years, as unionization of workers gained ground, those in the oil fields joined the Congress of Industrial Organization (CIO), which emerged as the largest union in the state. Fortunately Texas

in recent years has been spared the ill effects of serious, widespread conflicts between labor and management.

Among the miners in Arizona unionization penetrated quite early and precipitated some strikes even before the turn of the century. Subsequently, as numerous workers enrolled in the Western Federation of Miners, they became more aggressive and went on strike in Bisbee in 1907 and in Globe in 1909; but the mining companies broke the strikes without conceding consequential gains for labor. Then after the laboring classes had influenced the work of the constitutional convention in 1911 and had elected a pro-labor governor, considerable progress was made during the early years of statehood, when employers granted concessions and the legislature enacted laws desired by the unions.

In Arizona the militant International Workers of the World (IWW) enrolled many of the miners, and in 1917 it called a strike in Bisbee. Because this walkout was curtailing copper production in the war emergency, the Phelps Dodge managers concluded that they would have popular support for drastic action. They arranged for a sheriff's posse to arrest twelve hundred of the strikers, then to load them on freight cars and ship them to an isolated spot in southwestern New Mexico, where they were confined in large corrals. The federal government then came to the rescue of the stranded miners by providing temporary shelter and rations at a military camp located near Columbus, New Mexico. At first the employers seemed to have won a decisive victory, because this mass deportation of wartime disrupters of production elicited applause in the antilabor press. Especially was there gratification that someone had had the courage to stifle the feared IWW. Soon, however, when Germany began exploiting this deportation as propaganda in defamation of American democracy, a reaction set in. Under pressure of this reversal, the Phelps Dodge Company agreed to accept federal mediation in labor disputes thereafter. Even so, organized labor in Arizona had suffered a setback which handicapped its effectiveness until favored by the legislation of the New Deal in the 1930s. Then the CIO organized the miners and migratory farm laborers, while the American Federation of labor enrolled the lumber workers and skilled craftsmen.

In New Mexico industrialization was advancing more slowly than in the other southwestern states, and the individualistic Spanish Americans were not very receptive to Anglo organizers; consequently unionization proceeded rather slowly. As in Arizona, the early efforts met with greater success among the miners and railroad shopmen. In 1922, the employers broke strikes by both groups; they completely routed the coal miners' union, but they did grant some concessions to the miners. Soon afterward, when the feared IWW organizers and members began invading this state from Colorado, Governor Richard Dillon sent the National Guard to Raton in 1927 to head them off. By stopping all automobiles and turning back suspicious-looking passengers,

the guardsmen probably saved New Mexico from a spell of strife; but the means employed certainly were of questionable constitutionality.

In subsequent years the trouble spot in New Mexico was in Silver City, where the United Mine, Mill, and Smelter Workers came periodically into conflict with representatives of the Kennecott Copper Company and sometimes engaged in strikes which resulted in violence. As usual, the employers and union engaged in a running contest of mutual incrimination in an effort to influence public opinion. In 1956, finally, the employers seemed to emerge triumphant when a federal grand jury in Denver indicted fourteen officials of that union under allegations that they had filed false affidavits claiming that they were not communists.

In 1967, the miners' union in New Mexico, under new leadership, joined in a coalition with twenty-five other units of copper miners, including those in Arizona, for a concerted strike against Kennecott and Phelps Dodge. This deadlock lasted for over eight months, making it the longest strike against a single industry in the nation's history. The shutdown impoverished the workers' families and cost both states millions of dollars in welfare payments, depleted personal income, and lost taxes before the settlement in April of 1968 finally gained for the workers a favorable wage settlement and greater fringe benefits.

STRIFE IN CALIFORNIA

In California, the state which led in industrialization, the strife between labor and management naturally became more acute, especially in the formative era. In the late 1800s local unions had been organized and some strikes had been called. When unions of several cities united in 1891 for greater strength, the employers in San Francisco also organized, and then the rival forces were aligned for a showdown, which soon came. Two years later, during the panic which then gripped the nation, workers on the waterfront went on strike but failed to reap any gains, because they were blamed for a mysterious explosion of a bomb in a nonunion rooming house. In 1900, strife was renewed when the Employers Council clashed with the City Front Federation. After a scourge of violence which lasted for three months and cost the lives of five men, this dispute subsided in a stalemate. Nevertheless, the unions continued to gain in strength, San Francisco became a city of "closed shops," and the Labor Party carried through its reform measures while it had undisputed control of the municipal government for a decade prior to World War I.

In Los Angeles workers also organized early, and unions called some strikes back in the 1890s; but when newspaper typesetters for the *Times* demanded recognition and better pay, Harrison Gray Otis locked them out and denounced labor unions in scathing editorials. Employers in Los Angeles then responded by forming their own organization for combating union activities. It was no surprise that when the next clash came, in 1910, it again involved the city's newspaper. After an explosion wrecked the Times building on October 1, the union leaders contended that negligence on the part of the proprietor had contributed to a gas explosion; but Otis claimed that the building had been dynamited, and a

grand jury supported his version. Private detectives employed by Otis then gathered evidence contributing to the arrest of three union leaders, who were led to believe that a plea of guilty would win them clemency. Instead, the judge gave one a life sentence and the others fifteen years in prison. After this successful public condemnation of organized labor, the unions had to operate cautiously against an aroused opposition. For long afterward Los Angeles remained a city of "open shops."

While the conflict was brewing in the City of Los Angeles, a radical union, the IWW, was organizing agricultural laborers in California. When the leaders of that union tried to obtain improved treatment for nearly three thousand migrant workers who were crowded into miserable camps near Wheatland and paid only subsistence wages, the sheriff intervened in behalf of the employers. The rioting migrant workers killed him and the district attorney. For contributing to this crime, two union leaders were sentenced to prison for life, but aroused legislators did come through then with regulations for improvement of the labor camps.

The next controversy arose in San Francisco in 1916 as the outcome of an explosion of a bomb which killed ten persons participating in a Preparedness Day parade on July 22. For alleged involvement in this crime, Thomas Mooney of the labor faction received the death sentence, but President Woodrow Wilson commuted it to imprisonment for life. Evidence that the case against Mooney had been framed up was presented to one governor after another, but through two decades none of them considered the granting of a pardon to him as politically expedient.

The mood of that era in the coastal state was reflected in the criminal syndicalism law enacted during the "red scare" which followed the First World War. That statute provided that any "doctrine or precept" favoring "crime, sabotage, acts of force" in order to bring about a change in "industrial or political control" was a criminal offense. Frequent arrests under this act in the early 1920s not only served the ostensible purpose of crushing the Communist Labor Party but also operated as an effective check on the entire labor movement, especially in Los Angeles. During this period, the Industrial Association of San Francisco raised a million dollar fund which was expended whenever needed for the breaking of strikes in that city.

Finally, after New Deal legislation came to the support of embattled labor in the 1930s, unionization again made headway in California. In 1939, when the longshoremen, organized by Harry Bridges, went on strike, they encountered the usual unyielding opposition. Although the businessman's governor, Frank Merriam, called out the National Guard for prevention of violence, this time the union persisted in its demands until it won several concessions. That was the turning point. Soon afterward a pro-labor governor, Culbert L. Olson, released the imprisoned Mooney, and by that time the industrial activity of wartime was improving the lot of the workingman. One hundred and twenty thousand of them were organized successfully in San Francisco and two hundred thousand in Los Angeles. Encouraged by favorable national legislation, the unions even reached out again for successful enrollment of agricultural laborers and bargained for improvement in their wages and working conditions. Times indeed had changed.

MUNICIPAL GOVERNMENT

The same factors which had precipitated labor organization, that is, the growth of industry and business, also contributed to revisions in the form of city governments in order to make them more efficient. First came an experiment with the commission form. In 1901, while coping with the crisis following a flood at Galveston, Texas, the heads of the several municipal departments held meetings as an emergency coordinating council. From this emerged the commission plan, which subsequently was adopted in several other cities. The next innovation cannot be claimed by the Southwest, for it was in Staunton, Virginia, in 1906, that the council employed a city manager as the responsible administrator. As this new council-manager form proved its merit, it won adherents throughout the nation, and then some city commissions also employed managers, thereby inaugurating the commission-manager form. Either way, the trend was toward the combining of the popular policy-making function of the council or commission with business efficiency and professional techniques under the administration of an employed manager. The mayor then yielded his previous administrative role and served as presiding officer of the council and legal and ceremonial head of the municipality.

Several cities in each of the four states in the Southwest revised their charters in the years before and after World War I in order to employ managers; but the era of the greatest number of adoptions was the period of greatest industrial expansion following World War II. For example, in California, from 1946 to 1954, one hundred and twenty cities adopted this plan. As a result, by the latter date California had two hundred and thirty-three municipalities and three counties which had employed professional managers. Meanwhile one hundred and ninety-five cities in Texas, seventeen in New Mexico, and fourteen in Arizona had done likewise. Altogether this movement by 1954 had encompassed over one-half of the municipalities in the Southwest having a population above five thousand, and it had won over almost universally those above twenty-five thousand. Then a mild reaction set in, as could be expected following a spurt of rapid growth. Some of the smaller cities found that they lacked the means for continued employment of qualified administrators; unpopular managers elicited criticism, and politicians clamored for restoration of "spoils." Nevertheless, the number declined only slightly, so that three hundred and seventy-two cities in these southwestern states were operating under this plan in 1960.

At the state level in these four southwestern units of government no revolutionary reform had been introduced, such as the manager plan of the cities. Commissions had been appointed to try to reduce the number of other commissions, and organizations had advocated constitutional revision; but no fundamental reorganization had been devised. Instead, each of the four states continued to function under its constitution: written in 1876 for Texas, 1879 for California, and 1911 for Arizona and New Mexico.

Through the years those lengthy documents had become much amended. Administrative bureaus had multiplied, legislation had grown in complexity, the tax structure had become a hodgepodge, and the numerous counties had become "small" and inefficient in terms of the transportation facilities of the twentieth century.

PRESSURE GROUPS

Simultaneously the population segments and economic interests of this century emerged as pressure groups which sought to obtain legislation each in its own behalf. As the moneyed interests began to feel their power, they resorted to unethical practices in some instances. For example, in California in the 1930s the flagrant "buying" of legislators led to an investigation which revealed that one "public relations counsellor," Arthur H. Samish, had collected about half a million dollars from individuals and organizations for his services in obtaining the legislation which they wanted. Because the activities of Samish appeared to be legal, the only upshot of the investigation was that he was barred from the floor for having boasted that he "owned" the legislature.

More recently, according to James A. Totten, lobbying has become "respectable" as a "necessary adjunct to the democratic process." In 1959 he estimated that for each legislator in California five lobbyists were also active in the capitol. In that state the more influential spokesmen represented fruit, oil, banking, liquor wholesalers, and Hollywood; in Texas they spoke for oil, lumber, cotton, brewers, and the Protestant churches; in Arizona for sheep, lumber, copper, and the Mormons; in New Mexico for mining, the Catholic Church, and Spanish Americans; while in all four states effective lobbies represented cattle growers, merchants, teachers, trucking companies, railroads, veterans, labor unions, public utilities, and the aged, who now were respectfully classified as "senior citizens."

In recent years another kind of pressure superseded that of earlier times. Under the aegis of the "Great Society" of the national administration headed by President Lyndon B. Johnson, more and more federal funds became available for grants to states, counties, cities,

and schools. Then almost every political unit became a pressure group, clamoring for a share of federal largesse and often for the appropriation of state money as matching funds. Modern politicians, therefore, had to acquire skill in getting grants in order to be relieved of this pressure. In the Southwest they responded remarkably well, for three of the four states in 1965 exceeded the national average of fifty-five dollars per capita in grants of federal funds. This figure did not include expenditures on military installations, but rather those funds spent for relief, employment, health, welfare, and highways. Only Texas, at fifty-two dollars per person, lagged slightly behind the national average. California drew fifty-eight dollars per person and New Mexico ninety-five dollars, while Arizona then basked in a federal outlay of three hundred and fifty dollars per capita. Subsequently this largesse has been curtailed considerably.

DEMOCRATIC TEXANS

Throughout the past half century Texas continued to be a Democratic state, at least in the filling of most local offices; but thrice in that time the conservative Democrats swung the state to the support of Republican candidates for the presidency. Soon after the turn of the century the absorbing local issues were the increased expenditures and taxes of the reform administrations. In addition, the tenant farmers were finding their plight aggravated by the mild depression which preceded the First World War, and ardent church members were maligning the brewers. Consequently, when James E. Ferguson capitalized upon the unrest by appealing to

the tenants and simultaneously retained the church and business votes by evading the liquor issue, his victory inaugurated the era of "Pa" and "Ma" Ferguson.

Some constructive legislation was enacted and harmony prevailed during the first term of Governor Ferguson, but his popularity declined as taxes increased. When he tried to dictate the selection of a president at the state university in 1917 and ordered the dismissal of some outspoken professors, the legislature investigated his own administration and brought impeachment charges against him. As a result, he was removed from office because of some revelations about irregularities, mostly fiscal. Inasmuch as his dismissal barred him from holding office again in Texas, his wife, Miriam A. Ferguson, ran in his stead five times and was twice elected, in 1925 and in 1933. In addition "Pa" ran a rather weak race as a candidate for the presidential nomination back in 1920. Meanwhile, because the Fergusons had turned conservative during the prosperous 'twenties, the way was prepared for a reformer to challenge them. Dan Moody assumed that role and won in 1927 and again in 1929; but the principal achievement of his two terms was an administrative reorganization at the state penitentiary.

In 1928, when the Democratic candidate for the presidency, "Al" Smith, was a Catholic, the Texans for the first time deserted from their traditional party and supported the California Republican, Herbert Hoover. They returned to the ranks four years later, however, by casting the state's electoral votes for Franklin Delano Roosevelt, the Democratic architect of a "New Deal." A contributing factor was the astute party choice of a Texan, John Nance Garner, as Roosevelt's vice-presidential teammate. Once before a Texan, Colonel Edward M. House, had served as personal adviser to a president, Woodrow Wilson, and now Texans were becoming eminent nationally once more. Representative Sam Rayburn became Speaker of the House, Senator Tom Connally advanced to the chairmanship of the important Senate Committee on Foreign Relations, and President Roosevelt appointed Jesse Jones of Houston as chairman of the Reconstruction Finance Corporation in 1933 and as Secretary of Commerce in 1940.

In state politics, on the other hand, the Texans were charmed into electing a radio entertainer and flour salesman, W. Lee O'Daniel, as governor in 1938. His folksy campaign appealed to the farmers, and his promise of pensions drew the vote of the senior citizens. In 1940, he won again by advocating the enactment of a sales tax in order to obtain revenue for the granting of the pensions. Finally the legislature did respond by levying taxes which would provide sufficient revenue for increasing the state's share of old age assistance to a maximum of twenty dollars a month for eligible persons over sixty-five.

In 1948 the Texans, as loyal Democrats, helped elect Harry S. Truman in his surprise victory. Wartime prosperity, however, had turned them conservative again so that they were rather unresponsive to his advocacy of a "Fair Deal," or other additional liberal legislation. Moreover, they became aroused by the prospect that their state might lose the royalties to be derived from production of oil offshore in the so-called "tidelands." Since 1937, when oil had been discovered off the coast of California, that state had granted leases and the other southwestern states concluded that they, too, had jurisdiction over their tidelands. Texas could claim devolution of the old Spanish rule of supervision over offshore waters ten and one-half miles out, instead of the three mile limit prevailing in most other states, and now exploration for oil in the tidelands promised big returns. This prospective source of revenue also interested federal officials, and in 1947 when the Attorney General asked the Supreme Court who should control the offshore leasing of wells, that Court broke tradition by rendering an advisory opinion to the effect that those rights belonged to the federal government. On the other hand, the Texans could contend that such a ruling lacked historical substantiation, and further that it was only an advisory opinion and not a decision arising from a real case with all of its martialed evidence.

In 1952, when the Republican candidate, Dwight D. Eisenhower, promised that title to the tidelands would be returned to the respective states, the "Democrats for Eisenhower," headed by Allan Shivers, the gubernatorial candidate, carried Texas for "Ike." Within a year the campaign promise was respected by congressional disclaimer to title to the tidelands, and the first two oil leases granted by the state enriched the treasury by one-half a million dollars. Subsequently Governor Shivers also became outspoken in his contention against federal invasion of "States' Rights," by which he meant specifically the rulings of the Supreme Court in behalf of Negroes and the adoption of federal regulations fixing the price of natural gas. It was at this time that Lyndon B. Johnson, formerly a Texas school teacher and an administrator of a New Deal agency, had been elected to the Senate, wherein he now had become the Democratic majority leader. He criticized the Eisenhower administration for its maintenance of "flexible" price supports for farm crops and advocated, instead, higher federal props for the farmer. He also made a strong plea for party unity, which was effective to a degree. He and Sam Rayburn wrested control of Texas Democrats from Shivers and his followers, and the party installed Price Daniel as gov-

ernor in 1956. However, in the presidential election of that year the Texans again crossed their ballots in favor of Eisenhower. Two years later Daniel won reelection handily, as did the incumbent Democratic senator, Ralph Yarborough.

When John F. Kennedy, the Democratic nominee for the presidency in 1960, selected Lyndon B. Johnson as his running mate, Johnson had to resign his seat in the Senate. In the election that fall, the Democratic team easily won election to local offices; but much to their disappointment, the vigorous campaigning of a Republican, John G. Tower, won his election to the Senate seat vacated by Johnson. The Democrats, however, continued to control the other Senate position, occupied on into the 'sixties by Ralph W. Yarborough, as well as the governorship filled by Price Daniel to 1963 and by John B. Connally, his conservative successor.

On November 22, 1963, Dallas, Texas, suffered unfortunate notoriety as the scene of the tragic assassination of the President, John F. Kennedy. One of the assassin's bullets wounded Governor Connally, but he soon recovered. Thus Lyndon B. Johnson suddenly assumed the presidency, and when he ran for a full term in the election of November, 1964, he won by a landslide, with four hundred and eighty-six votes to only fifty-two for Barry M. Goldwater of Arizona. Two years later when Governor Connally also won reelection, his seventy-three percent of the ballots cast in Texas was next to the highest majority among the governors in the nation in that election year. In the 1968 presidential election Hubert H. Humphrey, Johnson's vice president, carried this state by a very narrow margin, whereas the Democratic Lieutenant Governor, Preston Smith, garnered fifty-six percent of the vote in his victory over the Republican candidate, Paul W. Eggers. In 1970 Smith won reelection by defeating Eggers again, and another Democrat, Lloyd M. Bentsen, Jr., won a seat in the Senate in his campaign against Nixon's man, George Bush.

CRUSADING CALIFORNIANS

California, like Texas, had experienced an upsurge of reform on the eve of the First World War. Hiram Johnson, the popular prosecutor of machine "bosses," won election as governor on the Republican ticket in 1914 and obtained reelection as a Progressive two years later. In 1917, California sent him to the United States Senate, where he served until his death in 1945. As a Progressive he supported the reform legislation of Wilson and Roosevelt but disagreed with them in their foreign policies. His performance won him a reputation for being a rather disagreeable insurgent, liberal one moment, reactionary the next, and always ready with a gruff retort.

Complacency settled upon California during the prosperous decade following the first World War. The state regularly voted Republican in those years, and legislation pertained to routine matters. In the national arena, Herbert Hoover, who had become an adopted son of California, served as Secretary of Commerce under President Calvin Coolidge and won election as president in 1928.

The Depression of the 'thirties brought a startled awakening to Californians, as it did to the citizens of other states. Here perhaps the crisis became more acute with greater alacrity because certain booming industries, such as the construction trades, motion pictures, and tourism, were keenly sensitive to national trends and fell into a slump immediately. Moreover, the "Okies," the refugees from the dust bowl, swarmed into California and congregated in makeshift camps, where they suffered from hunger and disappointment until organized relief was forthcoming. The number of those refugees who were wandering around in the Central Valley was estimated at one hundred thousand in the mid-thirties. By that time California's temperate climate also had attracted another body of newcomers — the retired farmers and business people from throughout the Midwest. They were industrious and intelligent, but often their resources were rather limited, so that they had to engage in part-time employment. California therefore had a larger proportion of persons over sixty-five years of age than did the other states, and now, with time on their hands, these "senior citizens" became receptive to utopian schemes. Perhaps, as John Gunther has suggested, it was the bright sunshine which caused previously conservative Midwesterners to "go crazy" in California.

The first panacea which attracted support was "technocracy," a proposal advanced by Howard Scott of Columbia University. He contended that if the national economy were regimented by scientific planning in order to utilize all available technical improvements, then everyone would need to work only two or three hours daily and laborers could be retired with pensions at age forty-five. While this scheme was gathering some support, two others advanced in 1934 soon overshadowed it. One was the Epic crusade of Upton Sinclair, a Socialist and the author of many plays and novels. He advocated the elimination of the sales tax, the enactment of heavy income and corporation taxes, and the issuance of state "scrip" as a substitute for the money then so scarce. His proposal included the founding of state land colonies for the unemployed and the payment of pensions of fifty dollars a month to retired persons. On this program to "End Poverty in California" (Epic), he campaigned for election as governor in 1934. He did succeed in obtaining the Democratic nomination, but he lost the election to Frank Merriam, who had strong support among the businessmen.

The other panacea which blossomed in the year 1934 was the Townsend Plan, a simple solution for all economic ills. The originator, Dr. Francis E. Townsend, a retired physician, proposed that the state levy a tax of two and one-half percent on all business transactions and use the revenue for the payment of pensions of two hundred dollars a month to all persons over sixty. The aged multitude who enrolled in Townsend Clubs in California and other states did not pause to compute the mathematics of this impractical proposal, but rather adopted it with the fervor of a new religious faith. For several years afterward this plan continued to have a devoted band of followers.

Meanwhile many Californians became devotees of another scheme, which was dubbed "Ham and Eggs." A radio commentator, Robert Noble, proposed that all persons over fifty be paid a pension of twenty-five dollars every Tuesday, and an advertising agent, Willis Allen, lent promotion, but with a change to thirty dollars every Thursday. The labor unions and the Communist Party endorsed this proposal, and thousands turned out and even paid for admission to the spectacular mass meetings staged by the promoters. When the plan was made an issue in the election of 1938, over a million people voted for it; but soon the enthusiasm waned. When the proposal was submitted again in a special election the next year, it was soundly defeated.

Obviously a California which could be carried off by such radical panaceas would accept the relatively mild measures of the New Deal with little opposition. This state, therefore, voted Democratic in the national elections through 1948, thereby contributing a large bloc of electoral votes to Roosevelt and Truman. Locally, however, the Republicans were gaining ground in that same era. In 1942, they nominated as their candidate for governor the affable attorney general, Earl Warren, whose previous record was not especially distinguished, and in him they found a winner who proved also to be a capable executive. Since it was then possible in California for a candidate to file in the primary election of either or both parties, in 1946 Warren entered both the Democratic and Republican primaries and won the nomination on both tickets. That assured his reelection without a contest and, in 1950, he was victorious again. Meanwhile he had been the running mate of Thomas E. Dewey, the Republican candidate for the presidency in

1948, but in that close contest Dewey had lost to Truman. Because Joseph Knowland of the Oakland *Tribune* had contributed effectively to Warren's gubernatorial victories, the governor sent Knowland's son, William F. Knowland, to the United States Senate, where he served effectively but with personal attributes somewhat reminiscent of Hiram Johnson.

At the Republican nominating convention of 1952, Governor Warren was advanced as California's "favorite son" for the presidential candidacy, with the loyal support of Senator Knowland. The Eisenhower camp, however, won California's other senator, Richard M. Nixon. In his brief time in office Nixon had garnered some publicity as an amateur sleuth on the trail of a few ex-communists who previously had been in government employment. With Eisenhower's approval, the Republicans then nominated Nixon for the vice-presidency, and the successful campaign that year elevated the youthful Nixon to the office which had eluded Warren four years previously. A factor in the Republican victory was Eisenhower's stand on the tidelands issue, which appealed to Californians as well as to Texans. Warren also was influential in carrying California for Eisenhower, and a year later he was rewarded with appointment as Chief Justice of the Supreme Court. In the next presidential election, in 1956, the Eisenhower-Nixon team again carried California, and Warren's protégé, Thomas Kuchel, won election to the Senate. Goodwin Knight, also a Republican, became governor.

In 1958, Knowland resigned as senator in order to run as the Republican candidate for governor in California.

The popular Goodwin Knight, thus elbowed out of the gubernatorial contest, ran for election to the Senate. This maneuver by Knowland caused a rift in Republican ranks, which in turn enabled Democratic candidates to defeat both him and Knight. Clair Engle emerged victorious in the senatorial contest, and Edmund ("Pat") Brown won in the gubernatorial race.

For the presidential campaign of 1960 the Republicans nominated Nixon, California-born, as their candidate, because his eight years as President Eisenhower's cooperative teammate seemed to qualify him well for the office. In that campaign the opponents, Nixon and John F. Kennedy, appeared in several popular televised debates, and the contest was a close one. Nixon lost by a margin of only one hundred and twenty thousand votes. The victor, Kennedy, selected as his Postmaster General a Californian, J. Edward Day.

Undaunted, Nixon next challenged Pat Brown in the gubernatorial campaign of 1962, but failed to unseat that popular Democratic chief executive, although Kuchel, a liberal Republican, won reelection to the Senate. Following this defeat Nixon changed his place of residence from California to New York.

Again in 1964, Californians crossed up their ballots. They gave the state's forty electoral votes to Lyndon B. Johnson, Democratic candidate for the presidency, but elected a Republican and former song-and-dance man of the movies, George Murphy, to replace Engle in the Senate. This political success of a popular entertainer, without previous experience in government, encouraged another entertainer to venture into politics. Ronald Reagan, former actor, proved to be a popular, persuasive orator, who captured the Republican audience and emerged as the candidate for governor in 1966. Although Brown had been about as effective as any governor could be in the burgeoning coastal state, he was hurt by the "white backlash" arising from his efforts in behalf of civil rights for Negroes. Reagan's overwhelming victory catapulted him immediately into the ranks of Republican presidential prospects. Even without campaigning actively, he emerged as the state's "favorite son" for the nomination in 1968. Richard Nixon, however, won that nomination and, with Reagan's help, carried the state, long his home state, by a margin of only one percent of those voting. However, the Republican candidate for the Senate, Max Rafferty, was too reactionary for a majority of Californians. He lost to the Democratic candidate, Alan Cranston.

California's forty electoral votes, only two less than those of New York, made the coastal state a pivotal prize in any presidential campaign, or as James A. Totten has expressed it, this state had become "the national axis of the two major parties." National attention, therefore, was focused upon the California primary election of June 4, 1968, which was a critical test of the candidacy of Senator Robert F. Kennedy for the Democratic nomination as a presidential candidate. Kennedy won the election, only to be felled, mortally wounded by an assassin's bullet, on the morning following his gratifying victory. For the second time within a decade a southwestern city, this time Los Angeles, had become the scene of a momentous national tragedy.

In the general election in November of 1970 Reagan easily won reelection, but a young Democrat, John V. Tunney, son of a former boxing champion, defeated George Murphy in their contest for one of the state's two seats in the Senate.

SEESAW IN ARIZONA

In Arizona the voters helped elect the winner in each national political contest from 1912 through 1956. Within the state, however, the issues arising from economic trends and pressures shaped local trends. The initial Democratic governor, G. W. P. Hunt, who had mustered strong support among the laborers, was defeated by a Republican, Thomas E. Campbell, in 1918; but Hunt kept bouncing back. He was returned to the governor's office in 1922 in the midst of the national Republican administration of Warren G. Harding, and he won again in 1930, during the term of another Republican, Herbert Hoover.

In the era of Franklin Delano Roosevelt and the New Deal, the Democrats carried Arizona handily in the filling of most local offices. Eminent among the Democratic candidates of those years was Sidney P. Osborn, publisher, who had tried for election as governor in 1918, 1924, and 1938 before finally winning election in 1940. His reputation for honesty, individualism, and hard work contributed to his reelection in 1942 and again in 1944. Then, amid a revival of business activity, the Republicans began gaining favor. In 1950, they elected Howard Pyle, radio executive, whose record in administrative reorganization and in meeting the problems posed by a population boom won a second term for him in 1952, when Eisenhower also carried this state. Even though the governorship was returned to a Democrat, E. W. McFarland, in 1956, Eisenhower again received Arizona's electoral votes in the national race of that year. However, when McFarland sought election to the United States Senate in 1958, he lost to a Republican opponent, Barry M. Goldwater. In that election another Republican, Paul Fannin, became the state's chief executive. Richard O. Davies has interpreted this recent swing to "neoconservatism" in a state dependent upon federal economic support as a result of weak labor organization, an influx of retired persons, and the presence of opportunities "to make quick wealth."

In the closely contested national election of 1960, Nixon had the support of Goldwater in carrying Arizona. Then the victor, John F. Kennedy, appointed Stewart L. Udall of Arizona as Secretary of the Interior. Locally, the team of a Republican governor, Fannin, and a Republican senator, Goldwater, with a Democratic senator, Carl Hayden, was continued in office by the reelection of both Fannin and Hayden in 1963. The next year, when Goldwater won the Republican nomination for the presidency, his place in the Senate was taken over by Fannin. Goldwater's extreme conservatism, however, attracted only fifty-two of the nation's electoral votes. Meanwhile a Democrat, Samuel P. Goddard, Jr., had succeeded Fannin as governor; however the tide turned again in 1966 when another conservative Republican, Jack Williams, won in the gubernatorial campaign.

Despite the recent Republican upsurge in Arizona, a Democrat, Carl Hayden, had succeeded in winning reelection to the United States Senate time and again since 1927, and prior to that he had gone to Washington originally in 1912 as the state's first representative in the Congress. By 1968, his fifty-six years of service exceeded by far the years of tenure of two previous record holders, Adolph Sabath of Illinois and Sam Rayburn of Texas. Meanwhile, by virtue of his diligence and seniority, Hayden had advanced to a powerful position as chairman of the Senate Committee on Appropriations.

Finally, in May of 1968, Hayden, at the age of ninety, announced that he would not seek reelection, and immediately Goldwater came forward as a strong candidate for replacement of Hayden. In the election in November, 1968, the voters returned him to the Senate, reelected Williams as Governor, and gave Nixon a big majority in the presidential race. In 1970 both Governor Williams and Senator Fannin won reelection.

POLITICOS IN NEW MEXICO

In New Mexico around the turn of the century the Spanish-American voters, typically individualistic and conservative, could be counted on to vote Republican. In 1912, however, the newly organized Progressive Republicans broke away from the Republican Ring and threw their support to the Democratic candidate, W. C. McDonald, who therefore won election as the first governor of this state. Nevertheless, Republicans filled most local offices and the initial representatives sent to Washington were also Republicans, including, as noted earlier, Thomas B. Catron as one of the senators.

Catron's colleague in the Senate was Albert B. Fall, a prominent lawyer and rancher residing in the southern part of the state. In 1921, President Harding appointed Fall as Secretary of the Interior, and while serving in that office he became involved in the scandal arising from the lease of Teapot Dome and other oil reserves to Harry F. Sinclair and Edward L. Doheny. In 1931, for having accepted a loan which appeared to have been a bribe, Fall was sentenced to serve a year in the federal penitentiary. By a strange inconsistency in the administration of justice, the same evidence which was used in obtaining the conviction of Fall was presented in a later, separate case against Doheny for having paid a bribe, but in that trial the evidence was deemed too flimsy to incriminate Doheny and the case against him was dismissed.

The leader of the Progressive bloc in New Mexico was Bronson Cutting, a Santa Fe publisher, who had come to this state for his health in 1910. Through the ensuing twenty-five years Cutting held the balance of power in New Mexico, because neither party could win without the support of the Progressives. In 1916 that faction helped elect as governor another Democrat, Ezequiel C. de Baca, but two years later a rift in the ranks made possible the victory of a Republican, O. A. Larrazolo. Although the nation went Republican in the 1920s, in New Mexico the Progressives contributed to the election of Democrats

in 1920 and 1922, and two years later Cutting himself professed to be a Democrat. In 1926, however, when the Republicans were able to enlist the support of the Cutting faction, they elected as governor a businessman, Richard C. Dillon. He promised the voters improved highways, free textbooks, workmen's compensation, prohibition enforcement, and no increase in taxes. After the legislature had enacted most of his program, he was reelected in 1928.

Governor Dillon appointed Cutting to the seat in the Senate vacated by Catron in 1927. In Washington he became affiliated with the Progressive Republicans while also continuing in his determination to "rule or ruin" his party in New Mexico. In the words of Charles B. Judah, the Democrats had found him to be "indigestible," and now the Republicans could not assimilate him either. Therefore in 1930 he again swung his influence to the Democrats, who won in the state elections in that year. Upon the launching of extensive reform and relief measures by the Congress in 1933, Cutting became a New Dealer. As such he was in a position to obtain many benefits for his state, and he was beginning to do so, when he was killed in an airplane accident in 1935. As his successor the Democratic governor, Clyde K. Tingley, appointed an eminent Spanish-American, Dennis Chávez, who had been representing New Mexico in the House since 1930.

Back in 1915, when the citizens with Spanish surnames accounted for fifty-seven percent of the population of New Mexico, they were quite influential in politics, and Cutting had managed to win their support. Through the next three decades party leaders often became entangled in issues pertaining to the Spanish-American voters, who up to 1930 had been predominantly Republican. In the succeeding decade they were captured by the Democrats, largely by virtue of the many New Deal programs which benefited the economically depressed. Another factor, of course, was the presence of Chávez, a member of one of their distinguished families, as their representative in the Senate, where he could dispense funds and appointments. By 1950, the growth in "Anglo" population had caused the percentage of Spanish surnames to decline to thirty-seven; but by that date eastern New Mexico had been filled with migrants from Texas, who also were predominantly Democratic. From then on to win, a political leader had to command a combination of the support of "Little Texas" in the east and of the ten Spanish-American counties in the north. The uniting of those two blocs often required consummate skill; in fact, after reviewing the several conjectures advanced in explanation of the vote of the Spanish-American faction, Jack Holmes came to the conclusion that the quest for "exploratory principles in determining the nature of the state's Hispanic politics is a baffling endeavor."

New Mexico remained securely Democratic throughout the Roosevelt and Truman administrations; but in this state, as in Arizona, a Republican upsurge followed World War II. That party, strengthened by the defection of many of the younger Democrats, elected Edwin L. Mechem governor in 1950 and reelected him two years later, when New Mexico was carried by Eisenhower in the presidential contest. That

swing of the pendulum to the Republicans almost swept Senator Chávez from office. Back in 1946, he had defeated the Republican candidate for the Senate, Patrick J. Hurley, formerly an ambassador to China, by a very slim margin, and now in 1952, when the vote again was very close, Hurley claimed that fraudulent practices had been employed. The Senate committee which checked the ballots and investigated the election procedures did find many irregularities and recommended that the seat in the Senate be declared vacant; but the colleagues of Chávez in the Senate voted against accepting the committee recommendation. Chávez, therefore, retained his position.

In 1954, the revitalized Democrats succeeded in electing John F. Simms as governor, and again they returned to the Senate for his second term their candidate, Clinton P. Anderson, formerly an administrator of New Deal agencies in New Mexico and subsequently Secretary of Agriculture in the Cabinet of President Roosevelt. In 1955, he ascended to the chairmanship of the Joint Committee on Atomic Energy, a post of considerable relevance to the economy of his state.

In the election of 1956 Eisenhower again carried New Mexico, and with him Mechem again won reelection as governor. Two years later Mechem lost by a narrow margin to a Democratic candidate, John Burroughs, and Chávez easily won reelection to the Senate. In 1960, when Kennedy received New Mexico's electoral votes, Anderson retained his seat in the Senate. The state's Democrats, however, were unable to thwart efforts of Mechem for a comeback, and he again won a term as governor. Two years later a Democratic candidate, Jack M. Campbell, did manage to defeat Mechem in his bid for another reelection. After the death of Senator Chávez in November, 1962, Mechem resigned shortly before the end of his term as governor, and his lieutenant governor appointed him to serve for the remainder of the term of Chávez in the Senate.

In 1964, Lyndon B. Johnson won New Mexico's four electoral votes, and another Democrat, Joseph M. Montoya, who had been serving in the House of Representatives since 1957, succeeded Mechem in the Senate. After four years of reasonably effective leadership by Campbell, it seemed that this state might be securely restored to the Democratic camp, but not so. New Mexicans again split their tickets in 1966, when they reelected Anderson, a Democrat, to the Senate, and then chose David F. Cargo, a Republican, to succeed Campbell as governor. As one observer re-

marked, in this state and in Arizona, too, the voters had been attracted by the "more articulate and attractive campaigners." In 1968, New Mexico supported Nixon for President and narrowly reelected Cargo as governor. His opponent, Fabián Chávez, ran strongly throughout the state but failed to carry the unpredictable vote of the Spanish Americans in the northern counties.

In New Mexico in 1969 a convention of seventy delegates drafted a new constitution that lowered the voting age to twenty and provided for the grouping of state agencies in twenty departments under directors responsible to the governor. In a referendum held on December 9 the electorate, averse to granting the governor so much power, rejected this new document by the narrow margin of about thirty-five hundred votes. Two years later the electorate gave Montoya another term in the Senate, and this time they chose as governor a Democrat, Bruce King.

BORDER CONFLICTS

On the eve of the First World War New Mexico and Texas became involved in some international political incidents. In the course of the Constitutional Revolution which had erupted in Mexico in 1910, the reactionary faction gained the upper hand and installed General Victoriano Huerta in the presidency briefly, from February 1913 to July 1914. Because President Woodrow Wilson refused to recognize Huerta, he became an implacable foe of Wilson and the United States. Then one of his generals, Pascual Orozco, Jr., solicited aid in Texas for a revolutionary uprising across the border in Chihuahua. Al-

though he and four companions were shot by a posse in Texas on August 30, 1914, he had succeeded in arousing a following among Mexican aliens and Mexican-Americans, who on January 6 drafted their Plan of San Diego (Texas).

The conspirators proposed to reconquer all of the Southwest and restore it to Mexico. Although the original leaders soon were arrested, their followers organized military bands which took refuge south of the Rio Grande and engaged in frequent and destructive raids in the rural areas in the vicinity of Brownsville during the summer and autumn of 1915. Then, after President

Wilson recognized the accession of Venustiano Carranza to the presidency in Mexico, Carranza strengthened the border patrol and soon halted the depredations.

While Wilson's partiality to Carranza was bringing relief from one source of trouble, it also provoked animosity in other quarters. One of Carranza's disgruntled rivals, "Pancho Villa," whose real name was Doroteo Arango, also headed an army of insurgents who hid out in the northern mountains of Mexico, and now they began venting their ire against the United States by engaging in raids across the border. The climax came in January, 1916, when a band of nearly five hundred bandits which everyone assumed was led by Pancho Villa sacked Columbus, New Mexico, killing sixteen persons and wounding many more. Afterwards rumors persisted that the raid might have been conducted by some rivals in order to discredit Villa, who was reported to be engaged elsewhere on that day. Recently, however, Haldeen Braddy has uncovered convincing evidence that Villa directed the raid from a nearby gulch. He had ample grievances, in that the government of the United States had been favoring his rival and denying Villa munitions.

At any rate, a military expedition commanded by General John J. Pershing and supported by National Guardsmen crossed into Mexico in an effort to catch and punish Villa. This retaliatory measure antagonized the Mexicans, so that Pershing met with an unfriendly reception. Besides, the Villa band proved to be too elusive, and although a few of the bandits were tracked down, the expedition failed in its objective. After an expenditure of the lives of twelve soldiers and one hundred and thirty million dollars, the troops were withdrawn in February, 1917. Ill feeling against Villa rankled along the border for many years afterward, as evidenced by the outcry which was raised when the New Mexico legislature created Pancho Villa State Park as a tourist attraction at Columbus in 1959.

Another border conflict involved the lowlands of El Paso, known as "El Chamizal." Back in 1848 the boundary between Mexico and the United States had been located in the channel of the Rio Grande, but floods later caused the river to change its course, leaving north of the riverbank about three hundred acres that formerly had been on the other side. The government of Mexico disputed the claim of the United States to that land. In 1911, the two nations agreed to submit the question to an international tribunal; but when the commissioners rejected the claim of the United States, its government refused to accept the decision.

In Mexico the bitterness provoked by this arbitrary action of the United States refused to die out. In order, therefore, to improve relations and restore goodwill, President Kennedy entered into an agreement with the President of Mexico in June, 1963, accepting the findings of the tribunal back in 1911. To give it effect, the two nations would first join in the dredging of a new channel for the Rio Grande, again locating the disputed area on the Mexican side. That also called for cooperation in the construction of six new bridges. Then Mexico would purchase the seventy-five business buildings and three hundred residences in the transferred area, and that would require the relocating of the forty-five hundred residents of the district. In mid-December, 1968, President Lyndon B. Johnson and the Mexican President, Gustavo Díaz Ordaz, participated in the ceremonial diversion of the Rio Grande into its new channel, marking the completion of this project.

Mexicans naturally lauded the Chamizal agreement as a new milestone in inter-American relations. In El Paso, however, many displaced and dispossessed persons were dejected, and some claimed that their compensation was inadequate to cover their losses. Aware that the federal government was becoming lenient in the payment of damages to Indian tribes for its violation of treaties long ago, civic leaders in El Paso remarked that now after part of their city had been given to Mexico, no doubt the rest of it would be returned to a tribe of Indians which was laying claim to it!

In domestic politics, when the trends in the Southwest in recent years are summed up, the record is quite impressive. Texas had led off with the elevation of Colonel House to a position of eminence, followed by the influential role of Hiram Johnson of California in the Senate and the advancement of Albert B. Fall of New Mexico to a place in the Cabinet of President Harding. Soon Herbert Hoover of California became president, and then more Texans—Jack Garner, Jesse Jones, Tom Connally, and Sam Rayburn—emerged in positions of leadership. Next Earl

Warren of California became a vice-presidential candidate, a role in which "Dick" Nixon later achieved success, and then Warren became Chief Justice of the Supreme Court. Back in Texas, Lyndon B. Johnson rose to the vice-presidency and subsequently became president in his own right. Meanwhile a Californian, J. Edward Day, had served in President Kennedy's Cabinet. In 1964, finally, the Southwest provided both of the candidates in the national campaign which pitted Barry Goldwater against LBJ. Four years later Ronald Reagan appeared to be in the making as a presidential candidate. At that date Carl Hayden of Arizona and Clinton P. Anderson of New Mexico were continuing in eminent senatorial roles, and Stewart Udall of Arizona was serving in President Johnson's Cabinet. Subsequently, in 1969, Robert H. Finch of California became a member of the Cabinet of President Nixon.

As evidenced by the production of presidential candidates and other national political leaders, certainly the old Spanish Southwest had arrived at maturity and had become an influential part of the nation in the 1960s. By and large the economy and politics of the Southwest had become geared to national trends. A Modern Southwest, absorbed in national affairs, had emerged in the land of the ancient Indian tribes and the hardy Spanish colonists. In the background the heritage of the earlier era still lingered as an influential factor in the growth of the modern Atomic Age.

POPULATION AFTER MID-CENTURY

	Ariz.	Calif.	N. Mex.	Texas	U.S.
Population (in thousands)					
1968 Estimate	1,609	19,300	1,006	10,977	199,861
1960	1,321	15,863	953	9,631	179,992
1950	750	10,586	681	7,711	150,697
Population Increase, 1950-1965	115%	76%	51%	37%	28%
Population Characteristics					
Over 65 1960	6.8%	8.7%	5.3%	7.8%	9.2%
1950	5.9%	8.6%	4.9%	6.7%	8.2%
Median Age 1960	25.7	30.0	22.8	27.0	29.5
1950	26.9	32.1	24.0	27.9	30.2
Persons per 1960	3.45	3.05	3.69	3.36	3.29
Household 1950	3.43	3.01	3.7	3.4	3.38
Urban 1960	74.5%	86.4%	65.7%	75.0%	69.9%
1950	55.5%	80.7%	50.2%	58.4%	64.0%
Population Composition (in thousands)					
White 1960	1,170	14,455	876	8,375	158,831
1950	655	9,915	630	6,727	134,420
Negro 1960	43	884	17	1,187	18,812
1950	26	462	8	977	15,045
Indian 1960	83	39	56	6	524
1950	66	20	42	3	357
Chinese and 1960	4	203	0	8	702
Japanese 1950	3	143	0	3	476
Born in 1960	36	249	11	202	576
Mexico 1950	25	162	10	196	451
Foreign-born 1960	70	1,344	21	299	9,738
Totals 1950	46	985	17	277	10,161

19
AMERICANS ALL

Kids here at home grow up surrounded by barriers . . . all man-made. Neighborhood barriers, social barriers, racial barriers, political barriers, barriers of wealth. You climb over one only to find another ahead of you.

Then you find yourself at the front, thousands of miles from home. And suddenly, perhaps for the first time in your life, you realize that here on foreign soil is an outpost of America where there are no barriers. This was always the dream you had of America, a dream that never before had come quite true. . . . There are only Americans . . . at the front, only Americans purged of the artificial barriers we still make so much of here at home.

Quentin Reynolds, quoted in Beatrice Griffith, American Me *(Boston, 1948), p. 265.*

By 1900, the Southwest had emerged predominantly Anglo-American in population and culture; yet this region also had acquired some large and influential minority groups. The ancestors of two of the groups, first the Indians and then the Spaniards, had in turn been the majority people who once had regarded this land as their own. They had sought strenuously to keep it that way; but the great infiltration by others had transformed them into minority status, and then they were joined by more recent minority accretions—the Afro-Americans, the Oriental Americans, and the Mexican Americans.

All of them had contributed much of the labor which had transformed the Southwest so remarkably in the brief span of one century, and meanwhile, either overtly or unconsciously, all had also made some cultural contributions.

RESERVATION INDIANS

First in chronological order were the Indians, who officially became a minority group in 1924, when the granting of citizenship had theoretically terminated their inferior status as "wards," or "stepchildren." Meanwhile, since 1887 assimilation had been attempted under the provisions of the Dawes Act, but because the individual allotment of land as authorized by that act could not be carried out effectively in this semiarid climate, most of the reservation land remained undivided. A family could not live by farming one hundred and sixty acres of rock and cactus; therefore a majority of the Southwestern Indians remained under tribal management and tried to maintain a pastoral economy. It is true that in some instances, as in the case of the Pima, the lands were distributed; but more often the reservation pattern was modified only by the sale or lease of some of the land to ranchers, followed by the purchase of additional acreage for the reservation by the federal government.

By 1900, conditions on the reservations had degenerated badly, in part due to misunderstanding which fostered errors in reservation management and in part due to negligence which permitted exploitation of the Indians. In New Mexico, Arizona, and southern California a few boarding schools had been provided; but they too often prepared the children to be maladjusted and unhappy when they returned to the squalor of their family homes; consequently after 1892 some government-supported schools were opened on the reservations. In addition, the government gave financial aid to some mission schools, which were therefore called "contract schools." In all cases the intent was that the children should be removed from the retarding influence of their families in order to facilitate their instruction; but without an understanding of the intent the parents naturally lent poor cooperation. The schools were criticized for the bringing in of children forcibly, and the teachers in turn criticized the federal government for issuing confusing, often contradictory regulations.

A pitiably low standard of living contributed to a creeping degeneration of health. In 1912, the Public Health Service conducted a survey which revealed that an appalling percentage of the Indians were suffering from trachoma or tuberculosis or both. Immediately appropriations for medical care were increased, so that within four years there were fourteen Indian hospitals in Arizona, ten in New Mexico, and six in California. Then the expenditures on treatment were increased from about three hundred thousand dollars in 1916 to around five hundred thousand ten years later. The real need, however, was for preventive measures, which would necessitate a comprehensive economic rehabilitation accompanied by instruction in public sanitation and personal hygiene. Without such measures, the funds spent on treatment failed to check the toll of disease.

In 1926, the Department of the Interior authorized the Institute for Government Research to make a survey of conditions on the reservations in the Southwest. Because this survey was directed by Lewis Meriam, the findings published in 1928 are known as the "Meriam Report." It called attention to the deplorable conditions prevailing on the reservations and the inferior services rendered by the Bureau of Indian Affairs. Schools were inadequate, salaries were too low, living quarters were wretched, health services were substandard, the death rate of Indians from tuberculosis was several times higher than that of the nation-at-large, and some of the reservations actually faced a state of emergency.

In 1929 a new Commissioner of Indian Affairs, Charles J. Rhoades, a banker and scholar, undertook allevia-tion of some of the ills revealed by the Meriam Report, and before the end of his term of office, in 1933, he had obtained an increase in appropriations and a reorganization of the administrative service. By that time, however, the Depression had made the plight of the Indians even worse; but simultaneously it had installed in the Capitol a new national administration with a passion for experimental reforms. Then the next appointee as head of the Indian Bureau was John Collier, a social worker who had edited *American Indian Life* magazine and had long been a scathing critic of past practices.

REORGANIZATION ACT

Collier immediately inaugurated some sweeping reforms. He ordered that qualified Indians should be employed by the Bureau, that no more reservation land should be sold, and that henceforth the emphasis should be upon the providing of day schools instead of boarding schools. Then he secured a congressional appropriation for emergency relief and another one for support of an Indian Civilian Conservation Corps. The next year, 1934, he obtained the enactment of the Indian Reorganization Act, which contained these provisions: that no further distribution or alienation of tribal land would be permitted; that the existing reservations should be enlarged by purchase of contiguous areas; that the tribes should be given assistance in the drafting of constitutions providing for their own local government; that they should be authorized to establish business corporations; that the Congress would create a revolving fund from which loans could be granted for improvement of production on the reservations; that Indians should be prepared for positions of leadership among their own people; that they should be encouraged to revive their traditional cultural practices; and that this new program would be effective for each tribe only after it had been accepted in a referendum.

Immediately most of the tribes of the Southwest voted for acceptance of their "New Deal," but the largest, the Navajos, failed to adopt a constitution because their experience had made them skeptical about promises emanating from the Bureau of Indian Affairs. They continued to be governed by a traditional tribal council, which was recognized by the Congress in an act adopted in 1950. Acceptance by other tribes was followed by the tedious drafting and adopting of a constitution, which placed responsibilities for management upon the Indians themselves, with the government agents functioning as advisers.

Then the tribes obtained loans for the opening of cooperative stores, the development of their craft industries, the drilling of wells, and the improvement of farms and livestock. Now emphasis was placed upon day schools, of which thirty-two were opened on the Navajo reservation alone, by 1937, and in California the Indian Bureau entered into contracts with the state for the provision of schools. The encouragement given to the Indians to prepare for leadership resulted in the employment of more Indian teachers, so that by 1940 one-fourth of the teachers were Indians. Adult education was also promoted and bilingual textbooks were prepared. Likewise, the health service was expanded by means of an increase in appropriations to four million dollars by 1936.

Effectuation of the Indian Reorganization Act brought definite gains in education, health, and income; but an even greater improvement in economic conditions accompanied World War II. Then farm products commanded higher prices, additional opportunities for employment opened up, and the younger men, who volunteered or were conscripted for service in the Armed Forces, acquired a new concept of their role as Americans. They returned home after the war to become the leaders in a new movement for freedom and opportunity. Meanwhile conditions in time of war had caused a depletion of personnel and services in the Indian Bureau, a circumstance which actually proved beneficial to most of the tribes. As they were left more dependent upon their own resources and leadership, they responded by demonstrating that they were acquiring the ability to manage their own affairs more competently.

During the war years the income of the Navajos, for example, increased from two hundred thousand dollars in 1940 to six million seven hundred thousand in 1945. Nevertheless, they suffered a winter of destitution in 1948–1949. Although they had the largest reservation, they also had more people than any other tribe and their population was increasing rapidly. Lands which could provide no more than a bare subsistence for thirty-five thousand Indians were occupied by close to sixty thousand in 1950. They still depended mainly upon their sheep industry; but their range lands were overgrazed, and the market for wool and mutton was on the decline. In those same years many other Southwesterners were also being forced to abandon the grazing of sheep in favor of some other more lucrative enterprise.

During this crisis of the late 1940s, contributions in goods for the Navajos were forthcoming from other parts of the nation that were flown in by airlift. In addition, the government made an appropriation of eighty million dollars for emergency relief; yet many Navajos remained stolidly unimpressed by these gestures of generosity. One member of the tribal council, Sam Ahkeah, remarked cynically that the funds probably would be used "to fatten payrolls in the Indian Bureau" and openly criticized a national policy that regarded Indians as "wild pets." Instead, he argued, they should be permitted to manage and develop their own resources.

The numerous published accounts of the plight of the Navajos elicited a public reexamination of federal Indian policy. In 1950, the Bureau of the Census reported the Indian population of the Southwest to be about sixty thousand in Arizona, forty-two thousand in New Mexico, twenty thousand in California, and less than three thousand in Texas. The Navajos themselves would account for about one-half of the total number, and other surveys revealed that over one-half of their eleven hundred fam-ilies had an annual income of less than one thousand dollars. The death rate from tuberculosis was nine times higher than the national average, for dysentery thirteen times higher, for gastroenter-itis twenty-five times, and for measles nearly thirty. Moreover, where there were thirty thousand children of school age, the government schools could ac-commodate only about six thousand.

INDIAN "LIBERATION"

Revelations about the continuing state of distress led to a revision in national Indian Policy. In effect, the program of the Reorganization Act of 1934 had meant a return to segregation. Now this policy came under criticism for its emphasis upon a pastoral and agricultural existence in isolation with its deliberate encouragement for rever-sion to traditional tribal practices. That kind of a life could only retard prepara-tion for assimilation. It was strongly argued that assimilation should again be the goal, and to that end emphasis should be placed upon the develop-ment of individual competence for participation in the modern industrial economy. Consequently, in 1950, the Congress appropriated eighty-eight mil-lion dollars for a long-range program of rehabilitation and soon enacted other measures to "free" the Indians. Sub-sidies were cut, supervision was cur-tailed, the trusteeship over the several tribes was terminated, the ban on the sale of liquor to Indians was repealed, and all of the privileges and responsi-bilities of citizenship were extended to them. The southwestern states soon responded by granting Indians the right to vote and by adopting measures for integrating the adults in the state wel-fare programs and the children in the public schools. The new program, re-ferred to as "Indian Liberation," repre-sented a revival of the assimilation policy of the Dawes Act of 1887 but with implementation in a variety of ways other than by land distribution.

For Navajo pupils who could not be enrolled in distant public schools, the government built new boarding schools to accommodate over a thousand pupils and sent out trailer-schools to twenty-five sites on the reservation. By 1956, therefore, Glenn L. Emmons, Commis-sioner of Indian Affairs, could report that at last nearly all Navajo children were in school. Meanwhile Annie Wauneka, daughter of Chee Dodge, a former chief, had won the distinction of being the first woman elected to membership on the Tribal Council. As a champion of improved health serv-ices, she sought and soon obtained a program for the taking of twenty thou-sand chest X-rays, the establishment of free clinics, and a program for reeduca-tion in modern methods of prevention and treatment.

The new economic program, launched in 1950, contemplated the resettlement of many unemployed Navajos in areas where they might obtain factory jobs, but ninety percent of those removed could not speak English well and made the adjustment with great difficulty. Because about one-half of the sixteen thousand Indians who were involved in this experiment had by 1954 returned to the reservation, a program of more careful selection and preparation was introduced, with more tangible results. Under this new concept, inducements were offered in order to bring new industries to sites bordering on the reservation, and the development of irrigation facilities for some hundred thousand acres of arid land was advanced with congressional approval in 1955. Work then was launched on the construction of Navajo Dam as one of the upper Colorado River projects.

New-found sources of income aided the Navajo rehabilitation program. The "worthless" reservation land turned out to be rich in uranium which, under lease, returned over a million dollars in the decade preceding 1955. The oil wells that had earlier been drilled on reservation lands brought in eighteen million in the same period. Instead of apportioning this income as a "dole" among all members of the tribe, the council invested it in trading posts, water wells, industrial development, college scholarships, and clothing for school children. By 1955, the eighty thousand Navajos had an income of approximately thirty million dollars, or an average of four hundred and fifty dollars per person; but that amounted to only about one-fourth of the per capita income of other Americans.

Critics of the new policy contended that termination of government super-

vision was being made so abruptly that thousands of the less fortunate Indians would suffer from being thrust into the modern stream of competition without adequate preparation. On the other hand, Paul Jones, then chairman of the Navajo Tribal Council, said in 1956 that "only recently have we had the privilege of thinking for ourselves." He welcomed the new freedom and anticipated that the Indians would be fully independent within another decade.

By 1959, Navajo revenues were amounting to about thirty thousand dollars a day. The reservation had its own park system and police force, and the Tribal Council had embarked upon a twenty-five million dollar school-building program. Tribal functions employed about fifteen hundred persons, and approximately three thousand worked for the Santa Fe Railroad, in the oil fields, and in three uranium mills and six mines. Another thousand had jobs off the reservation. Soon the completion of Navajo Dam provided increased employment in agriculture and in recreational services. In many respects the reservation appeared to be a small state of its own located within Arizona and New Mexico. An inherent tendency toward segregation was offset by the election of two members of the Tribal Council to the New Mexico House of Representatives in 1964. Four years later the council had finished its work on a constitution that provided for a government much like that of a state; it was to be headed by an elected chairman and a council of seventy-four members. If and when adopted in a future tribal referendum, this new form of government would replace the one designed by the Bureau of Indian Affairs in the 1930s and formalized in 1950.

Other reservation Indians also were effecting a rapid readjustment. Some were aided by belated federal compensation for injustices of the past. In 1944, the United States Court of Claims awarded five million dollars to the Indians of California as compensation for the failure of the government to ratify the treaty of 1852 and to provide the lands as agreed upon in that treaty. Two years later the Congress created a special Indian Claims Commission for consideration of similar appeals from other tribes. For some twenty years lawyers employed by Indians throughout the nation had gathered evidence supporting five hundred and eighty-three claims — of which about one-half were granted — which involved awards of over two hundred million dollars. Some of the Southwestern tribes benefited from this work. For example, in May of 1968, the Mescaleros in New Mexico received payment of eight and one-half million dollars for their lands which had been appropriated by white settlers back in the 1880s. According to Chief Wendell Chino, after the tribe had reserved large sums for housing, scholarships, and investments, a sum of one thousand dollars was awarded each member. Thereupon neighboring cities reported a rush for purchase of pick-up trucks and household appliances, but no boisterous conduct was mentioned. Already this tribe, under the direction of its Business Council, had been making some headway on its own towards economic rehabilitation by the successful management of stores, cattle enterprises, and the Ruidoso Recreation Area. Further, in 1970, the Commission ruled that the Navajos and Hopis should receive compensation respectively for twenty-eight million and five million acres of land which originally had been theirs.

The Jicarilla Apaches on their reservation in northern New Mexico also have been making a remarkable readjustment. In the 1960s, they were farming fifteen hundred acres of irrigated land, were grossing about a third of a million dollars yearly from cattle production, and were acquiring modern homes as well as trucks and cars. Under the direction of their Tribal Council, they were also operating two profitable recreation areas and a large shopping center. The Arizona Apaches, located on the San Carlos and Fort Apache reservations, likewise were steadily improving their status by means of cattle and lumber production, management of mineral leases, and operation of recreation areas and trading posts. The four thousand Hopis, dependent mainly upon the grazing of cattle on their reservation of six hundred thousand acres, were improving their range practices and faring better than in the past. In recent years, as skilled fire fighters, they have been called upon for assistance in checking forest fires in many localities in the Southwest. Although they have long been inclined to resist the invasion of their isolation by modern civilization, recently many families have acquired radios and washing machines and nearly all faithfully and hopefully send their children to modern schools. Also in Arizona, the Pápagos, residing on one of the most desolate of all the reservations, have been methodically following their Development Plan. Under the leadership of Tom Segundo, in the 1950s they started building roads and vocational schools, drilling water wells, and purchasing labor-saving equipment. Everywhere improved conditions have encouraged a rapid growth in population. In 1960, Arizona and California each had twenty thousand more Indians than a decade earlier, while in New Mexico the increment amounted to fifteen thousand. The "vanishing Red Man" had become a legend of the past.

THE PUEBLO INDIANS

Among the residents of New Mexico were the twenty thousand Indians of nineteen pueblos, which belong in a category different from those on reservations. For one thing, they had been partially assimilated into Spanish civilization a long time ago. Soon after the American occupation they had been granted citizenship and conceded title to their own community land grants, which range in size from twelve thousand acres for Pojoaque to about four hundred thousand for Zuñi. The most famous of the pueblos, Taos, which had forty-seven thousand acres, obtained a doubling of that area in 1970 by acquiring ownership of national forest lands surrounding its sacred shrine at Blue Lake. Each pueblo maintained an independent existence under the administration of its own tribal government headed by a chief, whose symbol of authority was a silver-headed cane sent to the pueblos by President Lincoln during the Civil War; yet all have been served in recent years by the United Pueblos Agency with headquarters in Albuquerque.

The economy of the Pueblo Indians has continued to be basically pastoral and agricultural, with supplementary income from outside sources. Prior to 1930, many of the men left the villages a few months annually to hire out as laborers in mines and on the railroads. In those years, too, with the growth of tourism, the women found a market for their artistically decorated pottery and other handcrafted products. When the Depression choked off those sources of cash income, for several years the Pueblos had their backs to the wall. Many had to subsist on relief and for a time poverty and resignation prevailed.

In the years of distress some of the state and federal agencies analyzed the problems of the Pueblo Indians and inaugurated programs for an improved utilization of their resources. As an illustration, at Nambé Pueblo an experimental community school was established in 1935 under the auspices of the University of New Mexico. In it the teachers and adult pupils developed a new curriculum, based upon community needs and resources, for appropriate instruction in crafts, land management, personal health, social relations, and oral English. This pointed the way to a new method for promoting community improvements.

After World War II, agricultural income increased and the products of household industries again had a market. As a result some of the Pueblos in many respects emerged better off than their Spanish-American neighbors. For example, in San Ildefonso, the men seldom sought employment as laborers for Spanish Americans and some even hired men of the latter group to work for them. A study of this pueblo, made by

William Whitman, revealed that, while the men maintained the tradition of cooperative work on community projects, the women who made pottery for sale had caught the spirit of the American competitive, individualistic economy. Moreover, the women were enhancing their prestige by control of their earnings which could be used to pay for schooling or a truck or some other wants of modern times. In their culture, these Pueblos had evolved a fusion of Indian dances, religion, and customs, Spanish language and authoritarian spirit, and Anglo-American gadgets, clothing, and economic practices. The younger generation, on the other hand, after having been away to school or off to war, had adopted more of the customs, language, learning, and frailties, too, of the majority population.

One exceptional pueblo, La Laguna, enjoyed a phenomenal recovery from poverty after uranium deposits, which were found on the reservation in 1953, began returning a million dollars a year in royalties. The governing council invested part of the funds, distributed part, and undertook needed local improvements with the remainder. Further gains followed when one hundred and fifty persons in this pueblo obtained employment in an electronic products plant built there by an eastern firm in 1962.

Three of the nineteen pueblos have prepared written constitutions, and one, Santa Clara, has granted the franchise to women. In the others the chiefs have been chosen by a secret procedure influenced by the religious caciques. In defense of this custom, Domingo Montoya, chairman of the Inter-Pueblo Council, said that "the less the world knows about our religious life the less it will be changed." Something about the Pueblo religion seemed to harmonize with the Moral Rearmament principles, for many of these Indians became advocates of that movement. When Moral Rearmament assembled twelve hundred youth for a conference in Santa Fe in December, 1966, the chief of one pueblo and ex-chiefs of two others appeared as speakers on the program.

In the mid-1960s the United Pueblos Agency received annual grants from the Field Foundation for maintenance of offices and community services. In addition, many of the pueblos had federal grants for antipoverty programs. By these means Montoya said that they hoped ultimately "to get out from under the Bureau of Indian Affairs, which will enable us to live the way we want instead of the way others want us to." His statement, like that of other Indian leaders, expressed the widespread desire for independence and self-realization on the part of this American minority group.

SPANISH AMERICANS

In the sequence of peoples occupying the Southwest the Spanish Americans followed after the Indians. In many localities the families of Spanish ancestry had been engulfed by the great influx of other peoples in recent times. In the zone of original Spanish settlement the larger cities had become predominantly Anglo-American, yet they still had families who took pride in their

Spanish cultural heritage as well as in their creditable record as citizens of the United States. Most of them had become well assimilated, and some had accumulated wealth from ranching or business and consequently had the means and time for devotion to an avocational participation in community service.

On the other hand, many small communities continued to be predominantly Spanish American. The largest area so populated was in New Mexico, where in 1950 the northern counties had one hundred and seventeen thousand persons of Spanish descent as against only seventy thousand *extranjeros*. In fact, in seven of the counties, which were essentially rural, the Spanish-American population exceeded eighty percent of the total.

The old Spanish-American villages long had been battered by disintegrating influences, yet the people, especially those of the older generation, persisted in occupying many of them. Once their ancestors had had access to grazing lands on the mesa as well as possession of their own irrigated fields in the valley. By application of their ingenuity and hard labor in the frugal use of their limited resources they once had maintained a village life which had been nearly self-sufficient in its economy and eminently satisfactory in its social relationships. Beginning in the Mexican Period, when the urge to become more democratic led to the abolition of primogeniture, the family of a deceased landowner divided his fields among his direct heirs. A tract of land which once grew food for a family presently was cut up into narrow strips of only a few acres each for the families of sons and grandsons. Simultaneously the villages lost ownership of much or all of the common lands, as has been described previously. George I. Sanchez has explained this as an outcome of the inability of the agrarian villagers, handicapped in their knowledge of English, to compete successfully amid the complexities of the new era.

As the land base of the village economy dwindled away, many of the men supplemented their meagre income by leaving the community several months annually to work in the beet fields of Colorado or in local mines or on ranches or in railroad construction. Many moved their families to neighboring cities where they found employment, and presently some of them became successful proprietors of small business establishments. Even so, often they retained possession of a small tract in a remote village and returned frequently for visits where the pull of the ties of family and relatives was persistent.

When most opportunities for outside employment faded out during the Depression, many of the Spanish Americans had no recourse but to swallow their pride and go on relief. From that surrender many never recovered, as attested by the fact that in 1955 one in ten Spanish Americans was receiving public assistance. Twelve years later in three of the northern counties twenty-five percent of the people were on relief. Even during the Depression, however, the younger generation found limited opportunities for escape. Some enrolled in the Civilian Conservation Corps, and others received assistance from the National Youth Administration for pursuit of studies which would prepare them to be teachers, business employees, social workers, or lawyers. Interest in the legal profession was a natural outgrowth of the enthusiasm of Spanish Americans for participation in politics as an expression of their new-found freedom in the American regime. Moreover, during the Depression, when the relief agencies became the economic mainstay of so many of their people, the men who played the game of politics skillfully were those who got ahead. Advancing as a political leader with a large following of dependents had become the modern substitute for the traditional role of the "don" or the "patrón."

During World War II, new opportunities for employment became available and the competition was abated by the induction of young men for service in the Armed Forces. Many of the Spanish Americans, both men and women, served loyally, and in the retreat from Bataan, which was covered by artillery regiments from the Southwest, one-fourth of the casualties were New Mexicans, mostly Spanish Americans. After the war the educational benefits offered by the G. I. Bill became a great boon. The young "veterans" enrolled in colleges and vocational schools in far greater numbers than ever had been possible before. This served, therefore, as a major factor in the rehabilitation of the economically handicapped younger generation of Spanish Americans.

The new opportunities for the youth lay in the cities, but the countryside was not completely abandoned. In the villages of old adobe houses many families still clung to the traditional way of life while also coping as well as they could with the economic trends of the new era. Now only about one-third of their income was derived from the land; the remainder came from either relief checks or limited supplementary employment. The average family income was far too small for a wholesome standard of living, as evidenced by the prevalence of substandard homes and sanitation facilities as well as the high rate of infant mortality and deaths from tuberculosis. Moreover, the youth were deprived of stimulating advantages.

CULTURAL COHESION

In the rural Spanish-American homes the family still continued to be a strong primary group under paternal authority, and in the villages the Catholic Church served as the focal point of social activities as well as religious worship. For recreation the young and old alike enjoyed feast days, dances, wedding parties, school functions, and political rallies. The virtues of those communities have been well described by John H. Burma in his article in *Social Forces*, in which he concluded with this summary:

In a day of almost cut-throat competition, the rural Spanish-American village represents a non-communist form of co-operation between persons who live and work in a compact social group. Here a real social consciousness, even if limited in scope, shines out to the larger individualistic society.[1]

In the local public and parochial schools instruction was conducted in English, but that was almost the only place in the

[1] "Present Status of the Spanish-Americans in New Mexico," *Social Forces*, 28, 2 (December 1949), p. 138.

village community in which English was spoken. The resort to Spanish in neighborly greetings was regarded as an expression of regard for the old traditions, yet the language of the street had become a corrupted oral Spanish comprised of persistent archaisms and new fused forms, with an English word injected here and there for the modern innovations. While the Spanish-speaking people were borrowing English words to round out their vocabulary, the English-speaking newcomers were also injecting some Spanish words in their conversation.

Another mark of distinction in the more remote Spanish-American villages was membership in *Los Hermanos Penitentes*. In a previous chapter mention has been made of the obscure origin and rapid growth of that order in the Spanish colonial era. Afterward, in the Mexican Period, when most of the missions were secularized and the Franciscans withdrawn, the Brothers of Light stepped into the religious void by performing priestly rites with no effort to maintain secrecy. When Bishop Lamy came to New Mexico, he objected to the conducting of religious services by unordained laymen and therefore sought to suppress the society. Because his appeals were disregarded, the Church explicitly decreed disbandment in 1889. That ban, along with the annoying curiosity of rude newcomers, caused the order to go "underground." The fraternal rites, including the procession during Holy Week with its carrying of the cross and moderate flagellation, were performed thenceforth in strict secrecy, and members were forbidden to write or relate to outsiders anything about their rules and ceremonies. Under those circumstances the maintenance of standardized rules became impossible. Because each chapter handed down its own procedures by oral transmission, many variations appeared in local practices. Some chapters even degenerated into mere political clubs which were maintained by their leaders for promotion of solidarity in their competition with Anglo-American rivals for election to local offices.

In 1947, Archbishop Edward V. Byrne offered to give the order his sanction if the members would curtail their excesses and accept regulations formulated by the Church. Many chapters, thus regularized, became united thenceforth as approved Church auxiliaries under *El Concilio Arzobispal*, but others by refusing to submit became "renegades." In the postwar years the chapters still in existence no longer retained the practices of cruel flagellation and crucifixion, but served more as secret charitable organizations which attracted men because of the universal urge to belong to a club. According to Fray Angélico Chávez, the enrollment of members and the continued secrecy could be attributed to a local spirit of "patriotism and racial sensitivity." He concluded that the society preserved "many old Christian and old Spanish nuggets of virtue, courtesy, and folklore, which we have since squandered away."

In the cities of northern New Mexico the Spanish Americans and Anglo-Americans have continued to be somewhat exclusive in private social functions, but in the schools, in public and business functions, and in organized social endeavors, very little discrimination or prejudice, one way or the other, remained by the decade of the fifties.

In fact, in some communities, where the newcomers were members of the national majority, they found themselves to be in the minority locally, and those engaged in business or employment which served a Spanish-American clientele soon either shed or restrained any previous concepts they may have had about racial superiority. Admittedly, however, there were some newcomers who by bringing wealth with them could afford to indulge in prejudice, which usually found expression in their referring to their employees as lowly "Mexicans." Moreover, on the border of the area of Spanish-American predominance, where the invaders were numerous and often persistent in retaining the old Southern racial outlook, prejudices did prevail for several decades. Even so, by the 1950s evidences of improvement appeared in those areas, as indicated, for example, by the smoothness of integration of children in the public schools. Likewise, throughout the Southwest, the Spanish Americans were gaining acceptance in public employment. In the two years following 1966, the number of persons having Spanish surnames who obtained federal jobs in the southwestern states increased by forty-one percent, or twice the ratio of growth in the total number of federal positions in that area during those years. This trend was felt also in other lines of employment.

THE ALIANZA

Despite the steadily improving status of the Spanish Americans, they still had more than their share of economically depressed families, and it was to be expected that somebody would assume to speak for them during the rash of protest marches and riots elsewhere in the nation in the 1960s. The man who capitalized upon this opportunity was Reies López Tijerina, a native of Texas who originally had come to New Mexico wearing a white robe as the self-appointed leader of a new religious sect. In 1963, he found a cause as the militant champion of impoverished Spanish Americans who believed that their ancestors had had their land "stolen" from them by Anglo-Americans. By 1965, his organization, which he called "Federal Alliance of Land Grants," had attracted the enrollment of perhaps two thousand members who were contributing one dollar a month to a "legal fund."

López Tijerina spent some time in Mexico and Spain, where he claimed to have obtained evidence that his followers were the rightful owners of most of New Mexico, and he contended further that the Treaty of Guadalupe Hidalgo of 1848 guaranteed their continued possession of their ancestral land grants. However, he failed to show any of the evidence which he said he had found, and later he complained that the Treaty had been improperly drafted. Yet he also endeavored to have Cuba or Mexico file an appeal with the United Nations about American "violation" of that treaty. He simultaneously threatened forceful recovery of the claimed land, yet he later explained that he did not really expect to get the land that way but only to attract attention. Moreover, if he could not gain recovery of the land, he proposed that his followers would accept compensation instead. This idea apparently was derived from the work of the Indian Claims Commission, which was then operative. Later he seemed also to take a leaf from the book of the Black Power movement by conferring with Negro leaders and advocating a kind of a reverse apartheid and an assertion of superiority on the part of the Spanish Americans.

While López Tijerina was groping about for a definition of purpose, he made rousing speeches at mass meetings of members and organized contingents of them for demonstrations which evolved from a peaceable march to an armed raid. First, early in 1966 he led a small procession in a march from Albuquerque to Santa Fe for the filing of a petition with Governor Campbell. Next, in the autumn of that year he and numerous members attempted to occupy part of the Carson National Forest near Pojoaque under the contention that those members were heirs of the original Spanish owners of that land under a community grant from Spain. After attempting to "arrest" some forest rangers for "trespassing" on the members' land, López Tijerina and four others were arrested for assaulting a ranger and destroying federal property. For this Tijerina received a sentence of two years in the penitentiary and five years on probation.

After the accused men obtained their liberty while their conviction for the forest raid was being appealed, they planned a mass occupation of the former Tierra Amarilla land grant of approximately six hundred thousand acres. When about twenty selected men raided the Tierra Amarilla courthouse in an effort, as they said, to make a "citizens' arrest" of some opposing county offi-

cials, they shot up the place, wounding one deputy sheriff and badly beating another. Governor Cargo, alarmed by the report of violence, rushed the National Guard to the scene. López Tijerina and ten others were rounded up and arrested for their participation in this assault on law officers, and while they were out on bond, the deputy sheriff who had been wounded and who had identified López Tijerina as one of the raiders was dragged from his car on January 3, 1968, and beaten to death. Investigating officers could find no clue as to the identity of the killer.

Previously, on January 2, Senator Joseph M. Montoya had publicly denounced López Tijerina as an "uneducated charlatan," yet in April the late Reverend Martin Luther King appointed this Spanish-American spokesman as leader of New Mexico's contingent in the Poor Peoples' March on Washington to be conducted in June. Both the state officials of the League of United Latin American Citizens and the Archbishop of Santa Fe endorsed that march but deplored the selection of López Tijerina as the leader.

In the fall of 1968, López Tijerina filed as a candidate for governor, but state officials could not legally list his name on the ballot because he had been convicted of a felony. Although his substitute, José Alfredo Maestas, proved to be an incisive debater, he received the unimpressive total of less than two thousand votes. Undaunted, López Tijerina conducted his own aggressive legal defense in his trial in Albuquerque on three of the charges arising from the courthouse "historic event at Tierra Amarilla," as he described it. On December 13, because the jury found the evidence unconvincing, Tijerina was acquitted of those three charges; but seven other charges remained for prosecution in a later trial, and on two of those counts he was convicted in November, 1969. Meanwhile the Supreme Court of the United States had refused to hear the appeal of his conviction for assaulting a forest ranger, and Tijerina had pending another appeal of a penalty of three years in prison for burning some forest signs in June, 1968. While in jail, with his appeal bond revoked, López Tijerina resigned as president of the Alianza. He stated as his reason a disagreement over policies, and then he added, "I am tired of paying the debts for others."

In the general election in November of 1970 the Alianza again sponsored some candidates. This time Wilfredo Sedillo garnered about twenty-two hundred votes in his campaign for election as governor, thereby registering a small gain over the results in 1968. An even greater gain was recorded by William Higgs, who received about thirty-three hundred votes in his campaign for election to the Senate.

In previous chapters the circumstances involved in the adoption of the Treaty of Guadalupe Hidalgo in 1848 and the ruthless displacement of the 1880s have been described, and no doubt many of the members could establish the fact that they were descendants of families which had lost their land by legal maneuvers which they did not understand. Yet those who analyzed the problem doubted that the regaining of small strips of land would effect a lasting solution in this modern industrial era. Instead, a comprehensive program of economic redevelopment was needed, and while state and federal officials as well as foundation executives were pondering the ways by which that might be effected, the expenditure of thirty million dollars up to 1967 in the War on Poverty in New Mexico was contributing some immediate but spotty and inadequate improvements in the northern counties. Thus the destitute, essentially rural portion of the Spanish-American minority had grown impatient; but because of the tactics employed by López Tijerina and his followers, many urban members of that minority, who were effecting a satisfactory readjustment, regarded the others as misguided persons for whom they should be apologetic. On the other hand, among the Alianza's adherents in the Southwest and among observers elsewhere who were inclined to sympathize with any champion of a cause, López Tijerina acquired the stature of a courageous, persecuted folk hero.

THE NEGROES OF TEXAS

In sequential order in the Southwest after the Indians and Hispanos the next minority to emerge was the Negroes. In the era of Reconstruction those in Texas attained nominal freedom as sharecroppers on the plantations. At that time the state constitution required the segregation of Negroes in separate schools, the legislature required the payment of a poll tax as a qualification for voting, and the Negroes were frightened into subservience by the Ku Klux Klan, the Knights of the Rising Sun, and the Sons of Washington. For higher education separate facilities were added in 1879 by the founding of Prairie View State Normal and Industrial College. That institution and the public schools were continued on an inferior basis due to poor buildings, short terms, unequal distribution of funds, and inadequately trained teachers. Most churches, too, practiced segregation, and in them the Negroes again had poor facilities because they lacked the means to do any better.

Despite the sorry conditions, the Texas cotton belt actually indulged in less prejudice than did the Deep South, and in the western communities of the state, where Negroes were not very numerous, they generally were well treated. As a rule the Negro leaders of that era were inclined to be patient and to place their hope in vocational education, of which more was made available after 1912 by the founding of Negro junior colleges. Through those years Texas had only two race riots, both in 1919. The Negroes seem to have had their desire for equality aroused by their participation in World War I. Because the whites sensed this awakening and were determined to squelch it, open clashes with loss of lives occurred in both Houston and Longview in that one year. In the 1920s, terror again took over, as the second Ku Klux Klan resorted to the burning of property and the flogging or hanging of wayward blacks. By that time, too, a new way of nullifying the Negro vote had been devised. The Democratic Party excluded them from the primary elections in which the winning office holders nearly always were selected, because they had very little opposition in the regular elections.

Nevertheless the colored people of Texas were steadily gaining in economic status and increasing in numbers. By 1930, the eight hundred and fifty thousand Negroes comprised close to fifteen percent of the total population of the state. Although about two-thirds of them were small farmers, and one-eighth of the total were still sharecroppers, those who had broken such bonds now accounted for the ownership of twenty-three percent of the total number of farms. The thirty-eight percent who dwelt in the cities had employment in business and manufacturing. By 1930, too, the Negroes were maintaining four thousand of their own churches and had the promising advantages of six junior colleges, two senior colleges, adult evening classes, agricultural extension services, and several welfare associations. In 1921, a Negro from Texas, Henry Flipper of El Paso, had been appointed assistant to the Secretary of the Interior, which was the highest federal office attained by one of this minority to that date. In fact, Flipper had also been the first Negro to be graduated from West Point back in 1877. In subsequent years he had served as an officer of the Tenth Cavalry during Indian troubles on the plains and then had become a civil and mining engineer. He had been employed by Albert B. Fall as a consultant in 1908, and thus it was Fall who called him to Washington in 1921.

MIGRATION AND INTEGRATION

The migration of Negroes from Texas to other states, already under way before 1930, was offset by natural increase in that state. After that date even though the migration gained momentum, Texas also gained in numbers with an increase to nine hundred and twenty-four thousand in 1940, nine hundred and seventy-seven thousand in 1950, and over a million by 1960. This growth caused an overcrowding in some cities and rural areas, which in itself stimulated migration; but there were other reasons. One was the revolution in agriculture which reduced tenancy in Texas by the combining of small farms into large tracts for cultivation by machinery and harvesting by Mexican migrant labor. Another was the pull of localities farther west where Negroes were as yet not numerous and less prejudice existed. That pull became stronger as the rise of manufacturing offered opportunities for employment in Phoenix, Los Angeles, and San Francisco.

As the flow of Negroes westward doubled their numbers in Los Angeles during World War II, from seventy thousand to one hundred and fifty thousand, evidences of prejudice appeared and open clashes seemed imminent; but no serious riots occurred then, and after the war the process of accommodation appeared to proceed with serenity for two decades. In other western cities the migrants were also being absorbed in those years without serious conflicts. Thus by 1950 the Negro population of California had increased to four hundred and sixty-two thousand, which was almost five percent of those in the nation. Arizona then had twenty-six thousand and New Mexico eight thousand.

World War II increased the pressure upon the southern states for the conceding of equality to Negroes. One-half a million men and some women of this minority had served in the Armed Forces, where their experience under integration had set an example which the South could not ignore upon their return. Moreover, those who had remained at home had attained an improvement in economic status as a result of wartime employment, and the Negro press had loyally supported the war effort.

In Texas harbingers of a new era began appearing during the war years. Lynchings became rare, and only one race riot occurred, this time at Beaumont in 1943. In the following year the Supreme Court of the United States held that the Texas law which prohibited Negroes from voting in primary elections was unconstitutional. Then when the Democratic Party sought to conduct strictly white primaries under the principle that the party as a private association could make its own rules, many counties in Texas ignored that maneuver and allowed the Negroes to participate.

The Supreme Court intervened in 1945 in behalf of a Negro candidate who had been denied admission to the University of Missouri. The opinion of the Court was that that denial had constituted a denial of equality in educational opportunities, and this ruling affected Texas, too. In those postwar years the conditions, still prevalent in Negro education in this state, were brought to public attention by the publication of the findings of a study conducted by Truman M. Pierce. Although the enrollment record was good, the per capita expenditures for Negro pupils in the school year of 1949–1950 had been one hundred and fifteen dollars, which was thirty-eight dollars less than for each white pupil. Equality in educational facilities obviously did not yet exist; but the trend was in that direction, as evidenced by the narrowing of the gap which prevailed in figures for earlier years. Even so this progress was being made in a system which maintained segregation, and soon afterward, in 1955, the Supreme Court called for gradual integration of all pupils in the public schools. A year later another ruling banned segregation on all bus transportation systems. In New Mexico and Arizona, where the law had permitted segregation in local school systems, integration was effected promptly in those communities which had been maintaining separate schools for Negroes. In western Texas, too, integration was accomplished immediately without strife in seventy communities, and by 1956 the state had a total of one hundred and three desegregated school districts.

In eastern Texas, where Negroes were numerous, the city and county officials said that they would "study the problem," and in 1955 the whites in several cities organized local units of the Texas Citizens Council in an effort to find some means for resisting integration. Governor Shivers then seemed to lend support by advancing a new political doctrine called "interposition," by which he meant that the states could refuse to accept federal action which violated their rights. Meanwhile, however, the National Association for Advancement of Colored People won test cases which required the acceptance of Negro applicants at two state colleges, and the Dallas County Medical Society admitted Negro physicians to membership for the first time in its eighty years of existence. On the other hand, when Negro youth attempted to enroll in white schools in Alvarado, Beaumont, Mansfield, and Oliver Springs, mobs assembled and threatened violence. In Beaumont they were admitted to the college after three of the opposing pickets had been arrested; but in Mansfield, where the governor sent Texas Rangers to maintain order, the Negro applicants were transferred to another school. In Dallas the superintendent of schools testified that immediate desegregation would be "cataclysmic" and urged that twelve to fifteen years be allowed for the process of amicable accommodation "without compulsion." As integration in the schools progressed steadily thenceforth, other discriminatory practices also yielded. In 1966, for example, a federal court held that the Texas poll tax was unconstitutional, and in that same year Houston sent to the state legislature its first two Negro members in seventy-one years.

In California, however, where the accretion of Negroes had doubled their number between 1950 and 1960, the great concentration in Los Angeles was not well accommodated. An antipoverty program was launched but too slowly effectuated, and a Commission on Human Rights was appointed but too late for preventive action. In the Watts district, in August of 1965, the Negroes rioted for seemingly no immediate purpose except to vent their resentment towards whites, whom they blamed for their crowded conditions and inferior status. Police sought to intervene but were too few to prevent the mobs from wrecking, looting, and burning property throughout the district. It was, as some diagnosed it, an outgrowth of "ghetto pathology."

After the riots had spent themselves, the state government sought to alleviate the causes more energetically. In September, seven million dollars more were obtained for the War on Poverty. By December, job training and placement centers had been established and an inspector appointed for investigation of any complaints about "police brutality." Watts had established the pattern for uncontrolled, destructive rioting in Negro ghettos in other cities in the South and East in 1967 and 1968, but during that scourge Watts, with improved services and employment, remained relatively quiet, disturbed only by a gun battle in August of '68 in which police killed three persons and wounded thirty-seven. In fact, up into 1968 no other city in the Southwest had suffered an outburst of Negro frustration like that of Watts in 1965 and elsewhere later. The only other ominous rumblings appeared in Oakland, California, where militant Negro extremists organized as the "Black Panthers" and engaged in a series of skirmishes with the police. In San Francisco and Berkeley the Black Panthers were also active in the campus demonstrations of 1968 to 1969, as described in the ensuing chapter. The Negro minority, emerging first in rural Texas, had by 1968 become assertive in behalf of social justice and deserved recognition in the industrial cities all across the Southwest, and this contributed to a belated improvement in status.

ORIENTAL IMMIGRANTS

The growing West long had needed a ready supply of labor; consequently in those years when California was booming and the Negroes had not yet started arriving in large numbers, this need was met by the importation of Orientals. First to come were the Chinese, who aroused the animosity of white laborers by congregating in the cities after their work in railroad construction was finished. Labor leaders and politicians then raised such a row about Chinese immigration that they obtained passage of the Exclusion Act of 1882. Although some migrated to other states, those remaining in California multiplied until that state had fifty-eight thousand in 1950 and ninety-six thousand ten years later. A large number of them, over twenty thousand, were concentrated in San Francisco's colorful "Chinatown."

Soon after California's first "nativist" campaign had curtailed the coming of Orientals, a demand arose from the same state for the bringing in of more. This time the demand was an outgrowth of the extensive production of sugar beets in the nineties. Already Japanese laborers had been pouring into Hawaii, and after annexation of that territory by the United States in 1898, they had the privilege of migrating to the states. Moreover, that migration was encouraged by agents sent to Hawaii by labor contractors who offered to advance the cost of transportation and promised what seemed to them to be good pay. Up to 1907 about seven thousand crossed to California annually.

The newly arrived Japanese proved to be ideal farm hands. They worked hard and could be easily hired and readily fired. However, they ate cheap foods, saved their earnings, and soon leased or bought small tracts which they could farm independently. In this manner these frugal people unwittingly courted trouble, because the other small farmers felt the pinch of competition and the big growers saw their supply of labor dwindling. Again agitators fanned the flames of prejudice. Following the tragic earthquake and fire which devastated San Francisco in 1906, the Japanese were blamed for the looting which occurred, and some were mobbed and assaulted. That fall when the San Francisco school board ordered the Japanese children to attend a segregated Chinese school, the mother country protested. President Theodore Roosevelt negotiated a compromise solution by persuading the school board to retract its order and by concluding the "gentleman's agreement" whereby the Japanese government assumed responsibility for restricting the emigration of "coolies" to this country. They still could come by way of Mexico or Hawaii, but the resentment which had been aroused against them caused a diminution of the flow. In 1909, only about sixteen hundred entered the United States and a larger number returned to Japan.

The nativists of California were not content with a mere informal exclusion of the Japanese. They played up the consequences of "unfair" competition with those still there, of whom three hundred and thirty-one owned small farms in 1912. Consequently this pressure from California obtained congressional enactment of the Alien Land Law of 1913, which prevented individuals not eligible for citizenship from buying land or leasing farms for a period longer than three years.

During World War I, when Japan was an ally of the United States, agitation against the minority in this country quieted down, but it was revived in the era of hysteria and reaction which followed that war. First the California legislature outlawed contracts for sharecropping, and then under pressure from this state the Congress included a comprehensive exclusion of Orientals as one feature of the Immigration Act adopted in 1924. By that date the cumulative number of Japanese who had entered this country was two hundred and seventy-one thousand, or only eight-tenths of one percent of the total immigration, and many of them already had returned to their homeland. In 1940, two-thirds of the one hundred and twenty thousand Japanese in California were of the second generation. They were called "Nisei," whereas the original immigrants were known as "Issei." The Japanese youth, determined to become good Americans, placed much faith in education and did good work in school. Nevertheless, often they failed to find employment for which they were fitted, and meanwhile they had become out of harmony with the Oriental culture of their parents and in good measure socially isolated from other Americans.

Amid the stresses already plaguing the American Japanese, opportune material for another campaign of defamation was provided by Japan's "sneak attack" on Pearl Harbor on December 7,

1941. At the public hearings conducted in California by a congressional committee some representatives of the persistent anti-Oriental factions repeated false allegations about Japanese sabotage at Pearl Harbor, and the ensuing publicity drew even tighter the tension which then pervaded the entire western coast. The Department of Justice arrested over two thousand of the Japanese aliens, and by then, even though the official reports from Hawaii revealed that there definitely had been no sabotage, public opinion already had been too much aroused for a graceful reversal. With control of the situation transferred to the War Department, General John DeWitt ordered the evacuation of all Japanese residents from the coastal area. This he justified as a "military necessity" because those people were an "enemy race."

The Wartime Civil Control Commission, created in March, 1942, managed the evacuation and the War Relocation Authority assumed trusteeship of the property of the Japanese citizens and aliens, or what little property they had left. The frightened victims already had disposed of most of their possessions for offers under their real value. The evacuees were moved temporarily to crude "centers" in California, from which they were soon transferred to hastily constructed camps. Two were located in California, two in Arizona, and one each in Colorado, Idaho, Utah, and Wyoming. Those eight isolated camps housed one hundred and ten thousand Japanese, who in the final year of the war were released gradually. By the autumn of 1945 the camps were closed.

With the war over, the Japanese were free to go "home," but they no longer had a home. Many Nisei had demonstrated their loyalty by serving with commendable records in the Armed Forces; yet agitators in California still were enflaming public resentment against them. Around three thousand of the evacuees had been permitted to enroll in colleges, where they worked to support themselves while also maintaining a commendable record in scholarship. They were prepared, then, to move to professional employment in midwestern and eastern states. Many of the others who lacked that advantage obtained jobs as laborers on farms and in cities far removed from California. Fifty-seven thousand, or about one-half of the original number, returned to that state, where they found whatever employment they could. Some settled in communities where they were cordially, rather apologetically, welcomed. As years passed, the bitterness subsided, and by 1960 the number of Japanese in California had increased even beyond the original figure.

During the war crisis the people of this minority had experienced a severe strain, an unjustified condemnation, and a loss of property estimated at about three hundred and sixty-five million dollars. War production in California was hindered by a shortage of labor, and all of America lost prestige by permitting a persecution which John Caughey has described as "group proscription." On the other hand, those Japanese who resettled elsewhere gained a new appreciation for their merits, or as Bradford Smith put it, they were "discovering America."

The early Japanese migration to America had been accompanied by a lesser influx of other Orientals, among whom the Filipinos constituted the largest contingent. Like the Japanese, they migrated first to Hawaii, whence they were able to enter the United States without limitations. Over fifty-five thousand had come by 1935, when the Congress acted to grant the Philippines independence after a preparatory period of ten years. Thenceforth the islands were allowed a quota of only fifty immigrants annually.

Before the gates were closed, the Filipinos who had migrated to the United States were mostly young, single men, who hoped to accumulate some savings and return to their homeland. Discrimination in employment, however, restricted them to jobs as migratory workers, with no chance to save, and they were ashamed to return without that "nest egg." Adept at "stoop labor," that is, at fruit-picking and vegetable-gardening, they traveled by truck from job to job under the management of a *padrone*, or labor contractor. In the off seasons they congregated in segregated areas of Stockton and Los Angeles, where several of them bunked in one small room. As aliens they were ineligible for state or federal relief, and during the Depression this deprivation worked a severe hardship upon them.

Many of the Filipinos got some schooling by virtue of missionary scholarships, but they still remained isolated socially. Because they were often part Spanish, they considered themselves to be "whites"; yet whenever one tried to date a white girl he usually was rebuffed, sometimes with accusations about "immoral conduct." In their segregated existence they had no female companions, no family life, and no wholesome recreation.

Despite discrimination and poverty, one-third of the Filipinos fought alongside American boys as volunteers in the Armed Forces during World War II. As a result, many acquired training which they could use to advantage after the war, and those who remained in California also had better opportunities for employment during the war years. Either way, the Filipinos improved their economic status, so that some even emerged as proprietors of service shops catering to the wants of their own group. Then they founded their own community organizations for the promotion of festivals and the administration of relief, and after the California law prohibiting interracial marriages was repealed in 1948, they were freed from that form of discrimination. Although many of this minority continued to lead somewhat abnormal social lives, at least they were finding the barriers against acceptance less formidable.

MIGRANT MEXICANS

The curtailment of Oriental immigration by the Act of 1924 and by the independence of the Philippines a decade later led to an importation of cheap, migratory labor from another source — Mexico. The northward flow began in response to the shortage of labor during World War I, when crossing the border was restricted only by qualifications as to age, health, literacy, and means of support. During that war even those restrictions were often disregarded so that by 1920 two hundred and fifty thousand had crossed into Texas, eighty-nine thousand had entered southern California, sixty-two thousand had come to Arizona, and twenty thousand to New Mexico. After the war the increased demand so stimulated this migration that in the 1920s the above number for California was more than quadrupled and that for Texas and New Mexico was almost tripled, while the figure for Arizona was approximately doubled.

In the earlier years the Mexican immigrants obtained employment mostly in mining and construction work, but with the great growth of agriculture they shifted to migratory, seasonal farm employment in the decade of the 'twenties in California and a little later in Texas. Although the flow northward decreased during the Depression, a mass migration set in again when World War II created a demand for labor. Because many of those desiring to come were illiterate and unable to pay the fees required for legal admission, they entered the United States illegally. Detection was difficult along the border where the Rio Grande was shallow and flowed through a desolated, slightly populated region. Unscrupulous agents smuggled many across, while some waded or swam the river, thereby deriving the appellation of "wetbacks." By 1946, approximately one hundred and twenty thousand Mexicans had migrated illegally into the border area of the southwestern states.

A treaty with Mexico concluded in 1942 facilitated legal entrance of migratory laborers. The Mexican government would permit the *braceros* to cross temporarily into the United States and the government of this country would provide free transportation and would guarantee decent living conditions. The agreement also assured American laborers that the Mexicans would not displace other workers in this country nor cause a reduction in prevailing wages. Two hundred and twenty thousand Mexicans were imported seasonally and then returned during the five years while that treaty was in effect. On this program the government of the United States expended one hundred and twenty million dollars, which in effect served as a subsidy for the big producers of cotton, fruit, vegetables, and sugar beets.

The large number of Mexicans who migrated permanently to Texas, either legally or illegally, settled in towns along the Rio Grande, where the warm climate held down the cost of living in the winter seasons. From that home base many traveled in summer to the Colorado beet fields, or even as far as Michigan; but the larger proportion made the "big swing" through Texas during the cotton-picking season. For those located in California the route of travel was from winter quarters in southern towns up and down the Central Valley in the harvesting season.

The migrating laborers had had to find their own shelters in Texas prior to 1942, when the Farm Security Administration provided labor camps under the management of the A & M College. After the war, when the government ceased maintaining those camps, some were taken over by cities and counties and others by private proprietors. Because several were closed, many of the migrants again had to provide their own makeshift camps. For those who worked in Arizona and California, privately owned camps were established. Later, when they were required to pass government inspection, appalling conditions were found in some of them. In 1957 alone, ten percent of those camps were closed by orders from federal supervisors.

The cultural gulf between the Mexican migrants and the majority population, along with the deliberate segregation and isolation of the workers and their families by the labor contractors, fostered prejudice and discrimination, especially in Texas. On that account, in 1943, the Mexican government prohibited the consignment of contract laborers to that state under the treaty of the preceding year. Immediately the Texans established a "Good Neighbor Commission" in an effort to halt discriminatory practices against members of the "Caucasion race." In addition, the Office of the Coordinator of Inter-American Affairs, which previously had been promoting friendly relations with upper-class representatives of countries in Latin America, began also to give some attention to this domestic aspect of interrelations. Funds were channeled into scholarships for Mexican-American youth, into workshops for the training of their teachers, and into conferences on the problems of migrant laborers. It proved difficult, however, to overcome the old Southern attitudes. Conditions improved a little, but when the treaty expired in 1947 the Mexican government still had Texas on its blacklist.

In California, typical slum conditions prevailed in a "Little Mexico" that had arisen in the eastern part of Los Angeles. In it the juveniles responded to their natural urge for self-expression by acquiring a distinctive garb called "zootsuits" and by roaming the streets in gangs thus attired. In 1943, some quarrels between these gangs and sailors on shore leave precipitated an outbreak of open warfare between the "zootsuiters" and the sailors. The conflict grew to such proportions that the police were unable to quell it, but presently the "war" ran its course and faded out. Then the city council outlawed zootsuits, as if that alone were the source of the trouble. Far more effective was the appointment of a citizens' committee by Governor Earl Warren and the prompt agreement on plans for the building of a quarter-million-dollar youth center in the Mexican district of Los Angeles.

In those years, while America was at war, obviously the officials and many citizens, too, in California as well as in Texas and other parts of the Southwest realized that the treatment accorded the Mexican Americans in the border zone had become a critical factor in maintaining the friendship of the nations south of the border—a friendship which was vitally important to the cooperative war effort. Simultaneously the youth of this minority group gave ample demonstration of their loyalty. Three hundred and seventy-five thousand of them served in the Armed Forces, and in Los Angeles the Mexican Americans accounted for twenty percent of the names on the casualty lists, whereas they comprised only ten percent of the city's population.

In the postwar years the federal government made illegal entry of Mexicans more difficult by strengthening the Border Patrol. Alert officers arrested one hundred and forty-five thousand wetbacks, but instead of requiring their repatriation, the government of the United States obtained the approval of Mexico for "paroling" these *braceros* to farm employers in this country. After the expiration of the treaty for organized importation of seasonal workers, a similar program was continued under short-term agreements between the two nations. The seventy-five thousand Mexicans who were brought across the border seasonally between 1947 and 1949 were in such great demand that the numbers were increased annually until the figure rose to nearly one-half a million by 1955.

Because the officially imported *braceros* returned to Mexico with their savings after each harvest season, the growth in the number of resident Mexican Americans resulted largely from natural increase. In Texas, by 1950, they numbered about one-half a million, of whom over three hundred thousand were natives of the United States. California had even more — six hundred thousand, of whom less than one-third had been born south of the border. The one hundred thousand plus in Arizona included only twenty-five thousand recent immigrants.

ASSISTANCE WITH ADJUSTMENT

Through the years, several organizations of both outside and inside origin have sought to facilitate the adjustment of the Mexican Americans. The unions intervened first, by making some headway in the organization of migratory workers in California as early as the 1920s. Whenever they led these laborers in strikes, however, as they did in that state four times between 1928 and 1936 and occasionally elsewhere in the Southwest, they encountered defamatory propaganda and the opposition of local peace officers, who arrested the leaders. These conflicts too often aroused such antagonism against the Mexican Americans that their acculturation was further handicapped; yet the unions did ultimately gain for them some improvement in their economic status.

Other organizations have concentrated more on social action. The oldest is La Alianza Hispano-Americana, which offered low-cost group insurance while also fostering cultural adjustment. Another, the League of United Latin American Citizens, or LULACS, founded in 1929, has had a successful record in removing prejudice, opposing violence, raising funds for scholarships, seeking equality of opportunity, and encouraging loyal citizenship. Still another, the Mexican Congress, was organized in 1938, grew spectacularly at first, then faded out during the war years because many of the older, more conservative Mexican Americans concluded that its program was too radical.

Following World War II other movements arose. One was the GI Forum, which was founded in Texas in 1945 by Dr. Hermán García as a means for Hispanos to discuss and express their position on public issues. Since then it has spread across the Southwest and expanded its activities to include the promotion of many youth services. Another was a Catholic-sponsored effort launched in 1945 by the bishops of the provinces of Denver, Santa Fe, Los Angeles, and San Antonio. They formed the Bishop's Committee for the Spanish-Speaking, which launched a program for social and spiritual welfare by concentrating one year in turn on the needs of each province. In Texas, which received attention first, under the supervision of the Reverend Robert E. Lucy, Archbishop of San Antonio, two hundred and forty million dollars were allocated for expenditure on clinics, parish centers, educational programs, group insurance, and medical services.

The efforts in behalf of social and economic adjustment were accompanied by others on the educational front. After World War II, the Pan American Union and local educational institutions continued the conducting of workshops and conferences for teachers. Soon over one-half of the two hundred larger independent school districts in Texas were teaching Spanish in the elementary grades, as a means of facilitating a better mutual understanding. In 1946, a federal court in California handed down the ruling that segregation could be resorted to in public schools only when necessitated by a handicap in language on the part of some of the pupils. Two years later a Texas court rendered a similar opinion with the additional provision that segregation on account of language could be maintained only in the first year of the elementary schools.

Despite the application of legal and instructional remedies, many of the Mexican-American youth were retarded educationally as a result of their linguistic handicap. Because too few finished high school, the resultant maladjustment along with the prejudice which many still encountered caused them to compensate by seeking their own way of "belonging." In the urban ghettos many joined gangs known as "pachucos" and resorted to crime and violence. Even so their proportionate rate of involvement in misdemeanors was not much greater than that of other city youth in the post-war years of excessive juvenile delinquency.

As for the migrant farm workers of Mexican extraction, in 1964, Willard Wirtz, Secretary of Labor, exercised his option to curtail the importation of *braceros,* as was allowed in the law governing that program. Because he concluded that imported seasonal labor no longer was needed, he reduced the number to be admitted from one hundred thousand in 1964 to thirty-five hundred the next year. Immediately the growers of fruit and vegetables cried "ruin" and sought restoration of their subsidized source of cheap labor. Seven hundred high school boys were recruited to help harvest crops that year, but this proved to be no solution. Many deserted rather than live and work under the conditions prevailing on some of the farms. The next year a few of the growers acquired farms in Mexico, some went out of business, and the remainder adjusted to the new conditions. However, the closing of the border increased the number of Mexican laborers who entered illegally. In 1966 over seven thousand wetbacks filtered across the line into Arizona.

The Mexican-American migrant laborers already residing in the Southwest experienced a change in status following World War II. The younger men had served loyally in the Armed Forces, and many earned the hero's reception which was accorded them when they returned. In those years, too, the demand for labor in the factories attracted workers of this group to urban centers. Although in their city "colonia" their conditions of living often corresponded to those of other blighted "slums," even that represented some improvement over conditions previously experienced as migrant laborers. Now they were settled in one location, where they could be reached by union organizers and welfare workers and where their children could get more and better schooling. This movement to the cities was stimulated also by the mechanization of agriculture, which was reducing the need for manual harvesting. In California, for example, by 1950 thirty-five percent of the cotton was being gathered by mechanical pickers and eighty-five percent of the beets was being harvested by machine. "Stoop" labor still employed many of the migrants, however, and those engaged in grape-picking were organized by the United Farm Workers, headed in California since 1965 by César Estrada Chávez. In 1967 he sought to bring the producers to terms by promoting a nationwide boycott of the grape industry, which soon became the symbolic *la causa* of all Hispanos throughout the Southwest. The boycott was effective; by July of 1970 three-fourths of the growers had signed contracts providing for recognition of the union and an increase in daily wages.

In 1968, a comprehensive program of assistance to the Mexican-American minority was undertaken by the Ford Foundation, whose spokesman, Mitchell Sviridoff, made the announcement with this explanation:

Mexican Americans are an ethnic group beginning to move into the mainstream of our society. Their poverty, unemployment and low education have been compounded by difficulties with immigration, language, discrimination and communication among local and regional groups.[2]

[2] *The Denver Post,* June 16, 1968.

This foundation made a grant of over two million dollars for the establishment of the Mexican-American Legal Defense and Educational Fund for the handling of problems of segregation and discrimination through legal channels, and another of six hundred and thirty thousand dollars for the creation of the Southwest Council of La Raza. The latter organization had representatives from Arizona, California, Colorado, New Mexico, and Texas, who through local boards would provide technical assistance and leadership training programs related to economic redevelopment and political participation. Pride in the heritage of *La Raza* presently evoked a spirit of comradeship on the part of Mexican Americans, as expressed in their designation of themselves as *chicanos.*

It is somewhat ironic that in this recent era of industrial revolution the border zone of the old Spanish Southwest has been "reconquered" by a new wave of Spanish-speaking colonists migrating northward from Mexico. Through many centuries the region has experienced invasion by one group after another, who have contested each other in a struggle for existence. All have contributed a cultural influence and a numerous progeny, and finally a majority of the latter have emerged with a pride in citizenship and a common faith in America. Although by mid-century these Americans had not yet fully gained an ideal status in all respects, they had advanced steadily toward an improved acceptance and adjustment in the Modern Southwest.

20

CULTURAL MATURITY

Still the mind smiles at its own rebellions,
Knowing all the while that civilization and the other evils
That make humanity ridiculous, remain
Beautiful in the whole fabric, excesses that balance each other
Like the paired wings of a flying bird.
Misery and riches, civilization and squalid savagery,
Mass war and the odor of unmanly peace;
Tragic flourishes above and below the normal life.
In order to value this fretful time
It is necessary to remember our norm, the unaltered passions
The same-colored wings of imagination
That the crowd clips, in lonely places new-grown, the unchanged
Lives of herdsmen and mountain farms,
Where men are few, and few tools, a few weapons, and their
     dawns are beautiful.
From here for normal one sees both ways,
And listens to the splendor of God, the exact poet, the sonorous
Antistrophe of desolation to the strophe multitude.

The old Spanish Borderlands once had developed a relatively isolated folk culture, and then after the Anglo-American occupation the remarkable achievements were economic and political. Even so, throughout the national era there was a constant striving for cultural attainments, so that the churches, schools, means for communication and entertainment, and expression in the fine arts might measure up to the standards prevailing elsewhere in the nation. In accord with the tendency on any frontier, sometimes the effort yielded a mere imitation of an Eastern or European institution which was not suited to the needs of this region until it evolved with adaptations. Sometimes, also, the effort produced mostly buildings and statistics without much cultural essence until they, too, became oriented. The effort was not lost, however, because steadily evidence accrued that the ambitions of the transplanted pioneers were leading to creditable achievements.

GROWTH OF CHURCHES

The original pervasive cultural influence in the Southwest was contributed by the Catholic Church as an accompaniment of its spiritual leadership. The role of the Church in the early days and the later transition to religious toleration have been described in previous chapters. Then Protestantism took root, but, as mentioned previously, after the transfer of the Borderlands to the United States, the Catholic Church also enjoyed a revival. Subsequently the continued growth of Catholicism maintained the position of that church as the leading denomination. At the time of the religious census of 1936 it had one million eight hundred and seventy-five thousand members in these four states, which amounted to forty-one percent of all church members in this region and almost ten percent of the Catholic communicants in the entire United States.

Within the Southwest, California's almost one million Catholics led the other three states in numbers by 1936, but New Mexico, with slightly less than two hundred thousand, had the greater proportion of the total population, forty-one percent, who held to that faith. In Arizona, too, Roman Catholics numbering close to one hundred thousand made theirs the leading church in the state. Only in Texas were they second in strength to a Protestant denomination—the Baptists.

The migration of Southerners to Texas for more than a century had brought the state into the "Bible belt," where the conservative Southern Baptists maintained first place both in membership and in influence. The faithful members strongly opposed indulgence in dancing, playing cards, and consuming alcoholic beverages, and they denounced Catholics as well as all other church members who were lax in such discipline. All Baptist groups in Texas could count close to eight hundred thousand members in 1936, or nearly two hundred thousand more than the Catholic Church. That placed the four hundred thousand of a more liberal Protestant denomination—the Methodists—in third place.

In California, it was the Methodist Church which ranked second to the Catholics in number of members, but a rather poor second. All Methodist denominations could count close to one hundred and fifty thousand members in 1936, which was only about one-sixth of the membership of the Roman Catholic Church. Third and fourth places were held by the Baptists and Presbyterians, respectively, with around one hundred thousand each. In fact, California had become the land of many cults in religion, just as it had also fostered several fads in politics. Nearly all religious faiths had some representation and no single Protestant denomination had advanced to a position very far ahead of the others. In New Mexico, the Catholics maintained such a clear preponderance that the Methodists were able to hold second place in 1936 with only about 13,000 members. In Arizona, too, the Catholics were well ahead; but here it was the Latter Day Saints (Mormons) who had advanced into second place, with twenty-two thousand members in 1936. The following table shows the increase in membership in the four states from 1906 to 1936 compared with population growth:

	Membership (in thousands)		% Church Growth	% Population Growth
	1906	1936		
United States	35,068	55,807	57	62
Arizona	50	165	230	240
California	674	1,928	187	282
New Mexico	158	244	54	117
Texas	1,281	2,299	79	91

In the nation the increase in church membership was lagging only slightly behind the growth in population, but, of these states, only Arizona followed national trends, and so was it only in Arizona among these states, due to strong missionary activity there. Texas was catching up; but in California and New Mexico the influx in population obviously had spurted well ahead of the ability of the churches to keep up. Statistics for subsequent years give the membership of the denominations nationally, without a breakdown by states.

PAROCHIAL AND PUBLIC SCHOOLS

The role of the churches as pioneers in education in the Southwest has been elaborated upon in a previous chapter, along with the simultaneous emergence of public schools. Subsequently the growth in population required a rapid expansion of facilities, in which the trends usually corresponded with those elsewhere in the nation. By 1900, elementary schools had become available to almost all pupils, and then in the next two decades secondary schools became the area of great expansion. Meanwhile many systems were changing from the original eight-four division of the curriculum to the six-three-three plan, which included a junior high school between the elementary grades and the senior high school, and later to the middle school, or four-four-four plan. Simultaneously consolidation of districts and enrichment of the curriculum were both making headway. Colleges also grew in number and scope, and then, following the Second World War, they also experienced a great increase in enrollment, which called for another concentration upon the provision of financial means for the maintenance of adequate facilities.

EDUCATIONAL DATA AFTER MID-CENTURY

	Ariz.	*Calif.*	*N. Mex.*	*Texas*	*U.S. Total*
Public Schools					
Elementary					
Number of Schools (1966)	566	5,403	472	3,681	73,216
Number of Pupils (1968)	287,000	2,893,000	151,000	1,509,000	27,418,000
Secondary					
Number of Schools (1966)	104	1,088	199	2,137	35,597
Number of Pupils (1968)	124,000	1,689,000	122,000	1,195,000	17,543,000
Private Schools					
Elementary					
Number of Schools (1966)	116	1,275	94	559	15,340
Number of Pupils (1964)	29,000	349,000	25,000	141,000	5,400,000
Secondary					
Number of Schools (1966)	30	389	32	137	4,606
Number of Pupils (1964)	7,000	93,000	5,000	27,000	1,400,000
Years of Schooling					
1950 (aged 25+)	10.0	11.6	9.3	9.3	9.3
1960 (aged 25+)	12.1	11.3	11.2	10.4	10.6
Major Museums & Art					
Galleries (1967)	3	44	3	7	307
Junior Colleges	4	72	2	36	396
Universities & Colleges (1968)	6	87	9	59	1,375

By 1950, the educational statistics of these four southwestern states were on a par in most respects with the average figures for all the states. For example, at that time the number of persons between the ages of five and twenty-nine who were enrolled in schools and colleges in the United States amounted to forty-nine and four-tenths percent of the total population. In the Southwest both Arizona and New Mexico slightly exceeded that average, with percentages of fifty and seven-tenths and forty-nine and seven-tenths, respectively. California was within one-tenth of a percent of the national average, while Texas fell below by only

three percent. Likewise, in the number of years of schooling attained by persons over twenty-five years of age, both Texas and New Mexico had a median of nine and three-tenths, equal to the record of the nation-at-large, while Arizona and California had a superior record, with ten years and eleven and six-tenths years, respectively. Ten years later persons over twenty-five had one more year of education on the average than prevailed in 1950, and now in the Southwest it was Arizona which had the superior record, with a median of twelve years.

By 1964, the remarkable feature in the educational statistics appeared in

UNIVERSITIES ABOVE 10,000 ENROLLMENT (1967–1968)

ARIZONA:	University of Arizona	21,284
	Arizona State	21,037
CALIFORNIA:	University of California	
	Berkeley	27,749
	Los Angeles	28,000
	Santa Barbara	12,000
	California State	
	Fresno	10,190
	Los Angeles	20,000
	Long Beach	24,243
	Sacramento	12,000
	San Diego	20,037
	San Fernando	15,995
	San Francisco	18,500
	San Jose	22,364
	Southern California	17,500
	Stanford University	10,922
NEW MEXICO:	University of New Mexico	13,024
TEXAS:	University of Texas	
	Arlington	11,873
	Austin	29,841
	University of Houston	21,170
	Texas Tech.	18,080
	North Texas State	13,356
	Texas A. & M.	10,918

the record enrollment. These four southwestern states then had eight million pupils enrolled in public and private schools, not counting those pursuing higher education. That was about one-sixth of the school enrollment in the entire nation.

In the public schools local variations appeared in parts of the Southwest. Texas, for example, had developed what amounted to a dual system. Because the legislation of 1876 and 1884 allowed much local leeway, the rural communities organized districts which depended upon state funds without supplementary local taxation for the construction of buildings and the making of other improvements, whereas the cities formed independent districts which levied taxes for improvement of facilities abreast with the times. In addition, the George Peabody Fund expended one hundred and fifty million dollars between 1874 and 1900 on the maintenance of model schools in eighteen cities in Texas. Consequently a great discrepancy arose between the "independent" and "common" schools. After 1920, much effort and considerable money were expended on efforts to reduce that discrepancy, that is, by consolidating rural districts, by raising the salaries of their teachers, and by erecting needed buildings. One feature of the rural-urban contrast was the difference in expenditures upon schools for Negroes and for whites, and the trend toward equalization of those figures in recent years was only one aspect of the movement for elimination of the widely prevalent rural lag.

By mid-century the schools of Texas compared favorably with those of other southern states. In 1955 the annual expenditure for each pupil had risen to two hundred and thirty-three dollars, which was only eleven dollars less than the national average. In each of the other three southwestern states, however, the figure was around ten dollars above the national average. In California, which was more densely populated than the neighboring states, the above-average per capita expenditure maintained schools which were noted for their progressive methods and ultra-modern facilities, even though the buildings in several communities were overcrowded because of the continuing growth of population in those localities. The progressive trend in the coastal state was the outgrowth of a state curriculum study of 1925 which called for projects and activities emphasizing functional knowledge. In Texas a thorough study of the curriculum was made over a period of five years, from 1934 to 1939, with consequent revisions resulting in many improvements. Subsequently many of the differences derived from the old rural-urban dichotomy were reduced.

In the other three southwestern states, a dual system emerged, too, but under different circumstances. The Church established parochial schools wherever there were Catholics in sufficient number. In those schools the Sisters provided instruction in schools maintained by the respective parishes under standards which met the requirements of each state system. In 1964 those three states had about one private school to five public, whereas in Texas the ratio was only one to ten.

The movement towards consolidation with its attendant advantages made headway early in California, so that by 1950 Texas was maintaining about one-third more elementary schools than the coastal state to serve about four-fifths as many pupils. Fourteen years later, however, Texas had less than four thousand elementary schools as against above five thousand in California. In terms of relative size, each elementary school in Arizona, California, and Texas accommodated about five hundred pupils on the average as against only three hundred in New Mexico. Another recent trend has been the shifting of more of the burden of cost from local districts to the state and federal governments. In New Mexico, for example, by 1962 the state was providing nine-tenths of the school funds and the federal government was adding one-third of the amount spent by the state.

HIGHER EDUCATION

In facilities for higher education the population density and financial resources of California and Texas made it possible for those two states to acquire a large number of both private and public colleges and universities, whereas in Arizona and New Mexico the state-supported facilities were more numerous. In 1967, Arizona maintained five such institutions as against only one private college, and in New Mexico the ratio was six to three. By way of contrast, California and Texas each had almost an equal number of public and private colleges, and the total number was much more impressive—eighty-seven and fifty-nine, respectively. Moreover, the latter two states also led in the founding of junior colleges at a rapid pace. By 1967, California led the Union in that movement, with sixty-seven such two-year colleges, and Texas was second with thirty-seven. Prior to that date the widely scattered four-year colleges of the other two states had been considered adequate to serve the needs in higher education; yet some of the rapidly growing communities in remote locations were clamoring for the provision of such facilities, with some success. By 1967, Arizona had five junior colleges and New Mexico two.

Texas and California had the resources for support of their institutions for higher education on a more lavish scale than was possible in most other states. With funds derived from oil royalties and other sources, the University of Texas became one of the richest institutions in the nation, with a permanent fund of fifty million dollars in 1950. The University of California established a branch in Los Angeles as early as 1919 and thereafter grew rapidly into the largest university system in the nation, boasting an enrollment of thirty-seven thousand in 1954. Continued growth on the original campuses along with the addition of other branches boosted the enrollment of the California University system to eighty-three thousand by 1967 and at that date the several state colleges had an additional sixty-five thousand students. In Texas the state university system, with fewer units than that of California, then had a total enrollment of fifty-seven thousand. In both systems specialized facilities had been provided by private contributions. For example, a generous donation from James Lick in 1874 had enabled the building of Lick Observatory near San Jose by the University of California, and an even greater observatory was completed on Mt. Palomar in 1948 by virtue of a grant of six million dollars from the Rockefeller Foundation.

The colleges and universities in the other two southwestern states also became creditable institutions and even distinguished in special fields of study, regardless of the limitations of a smaller clientele and a more modest budget. Moreover, in recent years they have been less disturbed by attacks upon their academic freedom than were the state university systems in their two neighboring states, where some of the wealthier citizens seemed to be frightened by, and often desirous of curtailing, the very freedom of investigation which had contributed to the greatness of their universities.

At the University of Texas an administrative conflict came to a head in the war years, while Dr. Homer P. Rainey was president. When the Regents planted "spies" in the classrooms and then requested the dismissal of two tenured economics professors, President Rainey spoke up in defense of academic freedom. For this act of "insubordination" the Regents dismissed him in November, 1944. The faculty and student body defended his position, and the American Association of University Professors, after conducting an investigation, condemned this "attempt by a politically dominant group to impose its social and educational views" and placed this university on its list of "censured institutions" in 1946. In that same year Rainey ran for election as governor, but in this bid for statewide vindication he was defeated. Subsequently he accepted an appointment as Professor of Education at the University of Colorado.

A few years later in the case of the University of California the issue was likewise the infringement of academic freedom, but there the circumstances were different. From 1941 to 1949 a state senator, Jack B. Tenney, headed an investigating committee which denounced all liberal or progressive movements with the result, as the California press afterwards concluded, that "no apparent harm had been done to Communism, but severe damage to liberalism." Among other things, the Tenney Committee demanded the requirement of a noncommunist oath of all public employees, with the result that such an oath was adopted in Los Angeles in 1948 and in the state in 1950.

At the state university, the Regents had concluded in 1949 that it would be wise to obviate legislative meddling by adopting their own oath for the university faculty members and other employees. Most of them took the oath immediately, but thirty-two faculty members refused because they felt that such an oath would be ineffective as a deterrent to subversive teaching and would be used as a means for dismissal of instructors without recourse to a proper hearing. The Regents then proclaimed that the issue had become "disobedience" instead of "communism" and dismissed the twenty-six faculty members who still were holding out. Two years later the Third District Court held that the special oath for professors was a violation of tenure, destructive of true scholarship, and unconstitutional. Finally, in 1953, the twenty-six professors were reemployed, but with the question of their arrears in salary still subject to further litigation.

The Berkeley campus rumbled with discontent again in 1964 and 1966. On the first occasion thousands of students supported a sit-down strike as a protest against the alleged curtailment of their free speech. Actually they were disturbed about their anonymity. According to their spokesman, Mario Savio, the institution had become a "multiversity," so impersonal that it was incapable of fulfilling a true educational function. Students wore lapel buttons proclaiming that "I'm an IBM card— don't bend, fold or mutilate." In the midst of this crisis the chancellor, Dr. Clark Kerr, resigned but soon changed his mind, and Savio was jailed for contempt of court. Later, seven hundred and fifty rebellious students were fined for trespassing while participating in a "sit-in" strike.

In December of 1966, Savio, no longer enrolled as a student, led another demonstration because Navy recruiting officers were allowed to operate an information desk in the Student Union, whereas some student groups had been denied a similar privilege. Again a sit-in was broken up by police officers called in by the administration. This time the slogan of the demonstrators was "student power." They demanded not only complete control of university policies but also "sexual freedom" and withdrawal of American troops from Vietnam, or, according to Savio, they would close down the university. In response, Governor-elect Ronald Reagan promised a hard line. "If they don't like the rules, they should get out," he said. Subsequently the Regents made administrative changes, but some tension persisted. In February of 1969, another disrupting demonstration was precipitated by the scheduled appearance of the governor for attendance at a meeting of the Board of Regents.

Meanwhile, in the preceding November, violence had erupted on the campus of San Francisco State College. It had been triggered by the agitation of a member of the Black Panther organization who had been dismissed from his employment as an English instructor. In this instance, the striking students, who had been joined by several sympathetic faculty members, caused the closing of the institution for the remainder of the semester and provoked more trouble in February for the newly appointed "hard line" president, Dr. S. I. Hayakawa. Finally, in March, the administration granted the students' request for a Black Studies Department and other concessions.

COMMUNICATIONS MEDIA

The educational endeavors of schools and colleges were ably supplemented by agencies for the dissemination of news and the communication of ideas. The *Galveston News*, founded in 1842, was the first continuing newspaper in the Southwest; but soon others also appeared, in Monterey, California, in 1846, in Santa Fe, New Mexico, in 1847, and in Tubac, Arizona, in 1859. After the large infiltration of Anglo-Americans, town after town acquired a local daily or weekly newspaper, whose editor was in those years a man of considerable influence in his community and often an outspoken devotee of personal journalism. After 1900, many of the newspapers in smaller towns "folded up" in competition with the urban dailies, which were emerging as predominant throughout the trade area of the principal cities. Of one hundred and fifty-one newspapers having a large circulation in the United States in 1950, twenty-four emanated from urban centers in the Southwest. Those twenty-four could boast a total circulation of over four million copies, which amounted to almost one newspaper for each family in these four states. Many of those of less circulation were holding on, despite the competition, as attested by the presence of two hundred and seventy-five papers publishing in the Southwest in 1965. Their total circulation then was about nine million.

The newspapers of the twentieth century, by their inclusion of cartoons, comics, sports sections, feature articles, and puzzles, entered the entertainment field, along with their function as disseminators of news, opinion, and commercial information. Beginning in the 1920s the transmission of news, entertainment, and advertisements also became the function of commercial radio broadcasting. The first such station went on the air in 1920 in Pittsburgh, Pennsylvania, and the first in the Southwest followed soon afterward. In fact, a licensed experimental station had been in operation on a small scale since 1912 in San Jose, California, and eight years later that "first" for Pittsburgh soon was followed by the addition of commercial stations in Dallas, Texas, Las Cruces, New Mexico, and Oakland, California. Within two years this remarkable invention had also made possible the local reception of stations operating in Amarillo, College Station, Fort Worth, and San Antonio in Texas, in Phoenix, Arizona, and in Los Angeles, San Francisco, and Stockton in California.

By 1940, when the first station for the experimental broadcasting of television in the Southwest was authorized for construction in San Francisco, California had fifty-two radio stations on the air; Texas, fifty; Arizona, eleven; and New Mexico, eight. After World War II, the expansion into small cities and the addition of competitors in the urban centers so swelled the number of radio broadcasters that by 1965 California had five hundred and ninety-six stations; Texas, three hundred and forty-three; Arizona, sixty-nine; and New Mexico, fifty-seven. This growth was accomplished in competition with telecasting, which by that date was being done from forty-six stations in Texas, thirty-four in California, eight in Arizona, and six in New Mexico. These remarkable inventions were bringing almost every hamlet and rural home instant reception of news from all over the world as well as the standardized national entertainment features and racy commercials of the modern era.

MUSIC AND DRAMA

The Southwest, which provided a receptive audience for the "live" and recorded entertainment transmitted by modern media, also had a traditional interest in music and drama. In California, the first theater presented performances in San Francisco as early as 1850; but Galveston, Texas, could lay claim to the acquisition of the first opera house in the Southwest, built in 1871, and two years later Texas had another, in Dallas. In 1876, the Grand Opera House was opened in San Francisco, where the early appreciative patronage contributed to the popularity of several "stars" of that era—among them David Belasco, Lotta Crabtree, Laura Hope Crews, and Edna Wallace Hopper. After the turn of the century the continued interest contributed to the establishment of several outdoor theaters, notably those of the San Francisco Bohemian Club, founded in 1902, the San Gabriel Mission, starting in 1912, and the Pasadena Community Playhouse Association, organized in 1916. In Texas, the Dallas Little Theatre opened in 1921.

In music Texas won distinction in the early years as the home of an eminent native composer, Franck von der Stucken, but San Francisco could advance a claim to the sponsorship of the first symphony orchestra in the Southwest, organized in 1911. Soon California had in residence several noted composers—Ernst Bacon, Charles Wakefield Cadman, Henry Hadley, and

Arnold Schoenberg. Beginning in 1921, the Hollywood Bowl provided an appropriate and unique amphitheater for philharmonic concerts and other musical presentations, and subsequently other cities in the Southwest undertook the building of amphitheaters and the sponsorship of symphony orchestras.

Previously the emergence of California as the world's leading center of motion picture production has been described as an "industrial" achievement; yet credit must also be given to that commercial enterprise for bringing to Hollywood the nation's best talent in acting, music, playwriting, and production. Incidentally, in the early years Texas contributed more than its share of the stars — Gene Autry, Madge Bellamy, Mary Brian, Joan Crawford, Mary Martin, Tom Mix, Ginger Rogers, and Ann Sutherland. But it was California which became the crucible of innovations not only in music and drama but also in fashions and slang, which spread as fads throughout the western world. Naturally, with the rise of radio broadcasting and telecasting, many of the popular programs for those media also originated in California, featured the movie stars, and bolstered further the cultural influence of Hollywood.

ARTS AND CRAFTS

For artists the Southwest long has had the special attractions of natural grandeur, agreeable climate, abundant historic sites, and unassimilated Indians. The westward migration carried with it several pioneer artists, some of whom were widely acclaimed even before they became adopted sons of the Southwest, while others rose to eminence after they arrived. To Texas, even before the Civil War, came a number of painters, including Theodore Gentilz, Eugenie Lavender, Herman Lungkwitz, H. S. McArdle, Julian Onderdonk, and Richard Petri. Later, in 1870, this state became the place of residence of a noted German sculptor, Elisabet Ney, who became the standard-bearer of formal art on this frontier. Likewise California attracted a number of prominent artists in the early decades of statehood. Among the painters the earlier arrivals included Albert Bierstadt, Thomas Hill, Thomas Moran, Charles Nahl, William Keith, and Toby Edward Rosenthal, while among those coming later were Charles Dickman, Francis McComas, Xavier Martinez, Arthur Matthews, Gottardo Piazzoni, Bruce Porter, and William Wendt. This state, like Texas, gained distinction by the work of an eminent sculptor, Douglas Tilden, whose pupil, Robert I. Aitken, also won acclaim. As visitors in Arizona near the end of the century came several well-known artists, among them Frederick Dellenbaugh, Thomas Moran, Maxfield Parrish, Frederick Remington, and Charles M. Russell.

Artists who congregated in favored localities founded art colonies. The first such group, the Bohemian Club of San Francisco, organized in 1872, was not exactly a "colony," yet it grew into an association which became influential in the progress of art in the Bay region. Later, in 1898, Ernest L. Blumenschein and Bert Phillips, who were making sketches while on a tour originating in Denver, Colorado, settled in Taos, New

Mexico, because they had become fascinated by the colorful and historic scenes which they found in that locality. That was the beginning of the famous Taos art colony, which in its early years attracted other talented painters including Oscar Berninghaus, Irving Couse, W. H. Dunton, Victor Higgins, Joseph Henry Sharp, and Walter Ufer. This group founded the Taos Society of Artists in 1914, which has continued to have a distinguished membership down through subsequent years. The pioneer leadership in Taos and San Francisco moved others to found art colonies and art centers at Carmel and Laguna Beach, California, at Santa Fe, New Mexico, and at Tucson, Arizona.

Another trend since the turn of the century has appeared in the revival of ancient Indian arts and crafts, in which the Southwest has since become the nation's leading contributor of truly indigenous talent for artistic expression. The Navajos wove colorful and durable rugs and blankets, into which they worked their unique terraced designs. The Pueblo Indians utilized red clay and vegetable or mineral paints in the making of beautiful glazed pottery, of which María Montoya Martínez of San Ildefonso became the leading exponent. The Pueblos also molded silver rings, bracelets, buckles, earrings, necklaces, and belt conchos, which were decorated with inlaid turquoise. In Arizona the Pimas, Pápagos, and others made use of yucca fibre, cattail stems, and willow twigs in the plaiting of baskets bearing traditional decorative designs. In this manner several tribes demonstrated their resourcefulness and artistic talents in converting local materials into specialties which were sold first at Harvey Houses and later in eastern department stores as well as at roadside markets throughout the Southwest. Simultaneously the anonymously produced Navajo sand paintings excited widespread attention, and Indians of other tribes began displaying their drawings and paintings in southwestern galleries and national exhibits. Recently, too, groups of Spanish-American craftsmen in northern New Mexico have been producing hand-carved pine furniture which recreates the unique designs of the colonial period.

TRENDS IN ARCHITECTURE

The early architecture, like the crafts of the Southwest, had both Indian and Spanish antecedents. Although the flat-roofed adobe buildings were durable, attractive, well suited to the climate, and readily constructed from local materials, the Anglo-Americans at first overlooked those advantages and imported extraneous styles. In eastern Texas, they built typically southern manor houses, and elsewhere they imposed upon the landscape a great variety of incongruous importations. They copied Greek, Victorian, Gothic, and Italian Renaissance styles and decorated dwellings with the "gingerbread" ornaments characteristic of the eighties and nineties. Later, especially in the designing of public buildings, they began employing a more creditable version of the Romanesque architecture.

In the era following the First World War, each state in the Southwest acquired its characteristic style. In Texas, after the rise of the cattle industry on the frontier, the ranchers built a low, long, rambling type of residence which was copied after those of the Mexican *haciendas*. As this "ranch house" style grew in popularity, it spread to other parts of the Southwest, especially to California. Meanwhile the builders in the southern part of that state had been adopting the bungalow, which was easy to build and well suited to the climate. As that vogue swept across the nation, many Californians abandoned it in favor of a "Spanish" style which combined elements of modern functionalism with the early adobe form. Subsequently Frank Lloyd Wright of Wisconsin and Richard Neutra popularized the "International Style," which employed glass and concrete in an unornamented, functional adaptation to the age of industry. In Arizona, where Wright and his students established a training center near Phoenix in 1939, the vogue in architecture became even more completely International.

In New Mexico, the colonial Spanish design continued to be in evidence in the rural districts, and after World War I it was copied in the construction of residences and public buildings in the cities. The new style, which retained the flat-roofed adobe form, with or without the projecting *vigas*, added modern features, like brick trim, corner windows, and sometimes a gabled roof of low pitch. Because public buildings of more than one story became in effect replicas of colonial missions and earlier Indian pueblos, this style, neither entirely Indian nor Spanish, came to be known as "Pueblo." Odd as it may seem, when William George Tight, the young and imaginative president of the University of New Mexico, sought the adoption of this style of architecture on the campus, the animosities which he aroused led to his dismissal in 1910. He was only a little ahead of the times, however, for the Regents officially adopted the Pueblo style in 1927. In pursuit of that decision, many of the attractive buildings on the campus were designed by John Gaw Meem, who was retained as the University architect from 1933 to 1956.

DESCRIPTIVE LITERATURE

For literary efforts the Southwest soon became recognized as a fruitful field for factual writing, that is, history, description, reminiscences, folklore, ethnological studies, and archeological reports. In historical writing the pioneer was Hubert Howe Bancroft, who operated a book shop in San Francisco in the 1850s and acquired a private collection which ultimately grew to sixty thousand volumes. Simultaneously he began collecting manuscripts of public records and personal reminiscences from all parts of the West. Then he employed several clerks, who did the sorting, note-taking, and writing, and by these means his "history factory" produced nearly forty volumes of history, essays, and biography in the 1880s. Among them were detailed histories of the two states and two territories in the Southwest, which are especially valuable for the documentary data included in the footnotes.

In Texas the work of Bancroft was preceded by a superior historical study prepared with painstaking care by a lawyer, Henderson Yoakum, and first published in 1855. Two other lawyers, one in California and the other in New Mexico, also turned out comprehensive histories of their states which were carefully documented and at the same time more readable than Bancroft's volumes. One was Theodore H. Hittell, a contemporary of Bancroft in San Francisco, and the other was Ralph Emerson Twitchell, whose work on New Mexico was first published in the year of statehood, 1912. Soon afterward, in 1915, a voluminous work on the history of Arizona was completed by Thomas Edwin Farish.

The foundations laid by the early historians were built upon, in each of the four states, by several able scholars of later years, most of whom were professors in the colleges and universities of their states. The dean of the scholars in the university group was Herbert Eugene Bolton, who found his field of interest while employed as a member of the faculty of the University of Texas for ten years following 1901, and then he continued with his studies of the Borderlands at the University of California until 1953. He explored Mexican and Spanish archives, personally retraced the trails followed by the Spanish pioneers, turned out several volumes on the achievements of the principal explorers, and inspired many of his students to follow his work with supplementary studies of Southwestern history.

In the field of descriptive writing, many volumes were written by Spanish explorers and others who dealt with events of the early period, but those which became more widely circulated were written by outsiders who related what they had experienced during a brief sojourn in one part or another of this frontier. The less transient pioneer in popular description was Charles F. Lummis, who came to Arizona as a newspaper reporter in 1886 and studied Indian cultures while residing in the Pueblo of Isleta in the early 1890s. He became a companion of Adolph F. A. Bandelier, noted archeologist, who made the first scientific studies of Indian ruins in Arizona and New Mexico. In 1894, Lummis became editor of *Land of Sunshine*, a literary monthly review published in southern California. Altogether he wrote five books which described with clarity the quaint and attractive characteristics of life in the Southwest. His work set a precedent for others who were quick to follow with numerous popular books on the Southwest. Because many of them were turned out by descriptive writers whose talents more often leaned toward facility and flamboyancy rather than accuracy and sincerity, the works of Lummis continued for many years to be superior to those of most of his successors. Incidentally, after the publication of the archeological investigations conducted by A.F.A. Bandelier, another scientist, Edgar L. Hewett, engaged in further explorations, which he described in several popular books. Hewett also founded the School of American Research in Santa Fe in 1909.

Other pioneers in descriptive literature wrote vivid accounts of their own experiences in the Southwest, and some compiled valuable collections of materials on the experiences of others. In the 1840s, Dr. Josiah Gregg, who had migrated to New Mexico for improvement of his health, wrote an enduring description of this territory and the trade conducted by way of the Santa Fe Trail. In Texas the pioneers John J. Lynn, Noah Smithwick, and John C. Duvall recalled their adventures in the days of the Revolution and Republic, while Francis R. Lubbock left valuable reminiscences for the period of the Civil War and subsequent years. Another Texan, Z. M. Morrell, described the trials of a Baptist preacher on the frontier, and still another, Charles A. Siringo, recounted the experiences of a cowboy on the open range.

The first of many tales about outlaws was written by Pat F. Garrett, who related what he knew about the life of Billy the Kid, and by John Wesley Hardin, who described his own escapades as a Texas bad man. Army life during the dangerous days in Arizona before the turn of the century was portrayed by Martha Summerhayes, a soldier's wife, and simultaneously Miguel A. Otero combined in his personal narrative a view of social life and his experiences as territorial governor of New Mexico. For this territory, N. Howard (Jack) Thorpe prepared a valuable compilation of cowboy songs and stories, while in Texas the cowboys, Indians, outlaws, and pioneers all figured in the collections of folklore compiled by John A. Lomax and J. Frank Dobie.

In California, a series of published reminiscences spanned an entire century of history. William Heath Davis covered mainly the events of the Mexican Period, Horace Bell dwelt upon the epoch of the Civil War, and Harris Newmark contributed his narrative which continued down to 1913. In this state Henry George, an economist, produced a nonfictional work of an entirely different category. His own hard lot back in the 1860s, in contrast to the fortunes accumulated by the monopolists, stimulated his thinking about the injustices of his times. In his *Progress and Poverty,* published in 1879, he became a pioneer in the study of exploitation and advanced his famous but controversial single-tax theory. His book was widely read, and although his proposal never was adopted, the author did influence the theorizing of many other early American economists. Another influential Californian was John Muir, the naturalist, whose appealing descriptions of the scenic grandeur of western mountains contributed a strong impetus for the creation of national forests and parks.

FICTION AND POETRY

Down through the years the Southwest has been the source of some creditable fiction, much of which, like the work of the artists, was produced by visitors who came to find some local color and a theme and then departed. Even so, there were several who became adopted sons and a few who were *bona fide* natives of the region. The earliest to come were Mark Twain (Samuel Clemens) and Bret Harte; the former found his talent as a humorist while employed in newspaper work in California in the 1860s, and the latter won fame in that same decade for his stories of rough life in the mining camps. Both contributed articles to *Overland Monthly,* a pioneer literary journal published in San Francisco, and in 1868 Bret Harte became its editor.

In the 1880s, Helen Hunt Jackson penned her protests against the exploitation of the Indians and made her most persuasive appeal by means of fiction. In that same decade, when Gertrude Atherton began producing her novels of life in the Spanish colonial era, she became the first native of California to gain renown for a literary achievement. Later another native, Jack London, surpassed her in fame by virtue of his many gripping stories of men and animals living in the northern wilds. As a Socialist, he also wrote his views of the class struggle, but in that field he was less convincing than Frank Norris, who wrote emotional appeals for social reform. Meanwhile Ambrose Bierce was emerging as the leading literary figure in California in the eighties and nineties. He fabricated terrifying mystery stories and morbid tales of the Civil War, and as a contributor to the newspapers of William Randolph Hearst, he became a scathing, abusive critic of the processes of democracy and progress.

California laid claim to the novelist Robert Louis Stevenson, because he resided in that state in the eighties and nineties. Arizona likewise could take pride in the works of Zane Grey, Stewart Edward White, Owen Wister, and Harold Bell Wright. New Mexico had a share in the fame of General "Lew" Wallace, whose inspired writing of the epic *Ben Hur* was interrupted periodically by the annoying duties which required his attention while serving as territorial governor in the eighties. In

that same decade Texas was the place of abode of William Sidney Porter (O. Henry), who derived material for many of his famous short stories from his own experiences in that state. On the other hand, Mollie E. Moore became a permanent resident of Texas and won renown for her fiction of prairie and plantation, and Eugene Manlove Rhodes, famous author of western novels and short stories, resided in southern New Mexico and found his inspiration there before he moved to New York in 1896.

In the early era the Southwest produced only a few poets of merit. Mirabeau Buonaparte Lamar, once president of the Texas Republic, gained recognition for his romantic verse, and Sharlott Hall won the acclaim of the people of Arizona for her poems describing the life of pioneer settlers. California's contributions were more resplendent. First, starting back in the sixties, came "Joaquin" Miller, a picturesque character who set in his stanzas the exploits of the pioneers. He had as a contemporary Ina Coolbrith, whose lyrics portraying local color won her the honor of being selected as the poet laureate of California at the Panama-Pacific Exposition in San Francisco in 1915. Her immediate successor as California's foremost poet was George Sterling, who penned beautiful odes and sonnets in the classic form. Eminent among the poets of the Southwest in the era between the two world wars were Wytter Bynner of New Mexico, a prolific critic and lyricist, and Robinson Jeffers, a resident of California, who sang sadly of the blight of civilization.

PRODIGIOUS PRODUCTION

With the emergence of the Modern Southwest in the decades following World War I a prodigious number of persons in this region won distinction for attainments in those fields of endeavor indicative of cultural advancement. In fact, N. Scott Momaday may have made a sage observation when he had one of his fictional characters remark:

The white man takes such things as words and literature for granted, as indeed he must, for nothing in his world is so commonplace. On every side of him there are words by the millions, an unending succession of pamphlets and papers, letters and books, bills and bulletins, commentaries and conversations. He has diluted and multiplied the Word, and words have begun to close in upon him. He is sated and insensitive, his regard for language—for the Word itself—as an instrument of creation has diminished to the point of no return. It may be that he will perish by the Word.[1]

At mid-century for the listings in *Who's Who in America* these four states contributed five hundred and eleven college professors, two hundred and seventy-one clergymen, two hundred and sixty-three authors, two hundred and twenty-seven scientists, one hundred and seventy-five artists and architects, one hundred and fifty-one journalists, and sixty-two musicians.

Mere passing comments on so many men and women of recent cultural eminence in the Southwest would become a meaningless dictionary of names. For an appraisal of the relative cultural maturity of the region and its component states, a more productive interpretation

[1] *House Made of Dawn* (New York, 1969), p. 89.

may be derived from a further analysis of the listings in *Who's Who in America*. Formerly the annual editions were supplemented periodically by a pamphlet classifying the names by geographic distribution, from which an analysis for these states has been made for 1950, the year of a decennial census. At that date twenty-seven and six-tenths persons for each one hundred thousand in the United States were selected for recognition in *Who's Who in America*. The first interesting revelation, therefore, is that for these four southwestern states taken as a whole the ratio then was twenty-seven and six-tenths, exactly the same as for the nation-at-large. Thus by mid-century the Southwest had arrived at a stage of cultural maturity at least on a par with the older portion of the nation.

When the statistics for each of the four states are aligned for comparison, the cultural leadership of California becomes clearly established. That state had contributed for listing in *Who's Who in America* thirty-nine and one-tenth persons for each one hundred thousand of the total population, which was a figure well above the national average. New Mexico, with twenty-four and two-tenths, was following close upon the record of the forty-eight states, whereas Arizona's eighteen and one-tenth compared less favorably, and Texas fell considerably lower in the table, with thirteen and two-tenths.

As could be expected, the outstanding feature of the analysis presented in the accompanying table is California's abundant share of famous actors and actresses, of whom that state in 1950 had ten times the national average. More-

CULTURAL MATURITY, 1950

	U.S.	Arizona	California	New Mexico	Texas
Totals for 90 vocations	27.6	18.1	39.1	24.2	13.2
Actors and actresses	.13	0	1.4	0	0
Artists	.44	.4	.61	2.5	.04
Authors	.88	1.0	1.5	1.0	.13
Business executives	2.8	1.0	2.7	1.0	1.1
Clergymen	1.8	.93	1.6	1.2	1.1
College professors	3.1	1.0	3.3	2.3	1.9
Doctors of medicine	1.3	1.3	1.6	.44	.44
Educators	1.3	1.0	1.1	1.0	.67
Engineers	.9	1.0	1.2	.44	.28
Judges	.49	.8	.4	1.3	.27
Lawyers	1.9	1.6	1.5	3.1	1.1
Public officials	1.3	.8	.52	1.6	.58
Scientists	1.2	2.4	1.6	1.2	.5
U.S. Army officers	.74	.8	1.1	.88	1.1
U.S. Navy officers	.43	0	1.5	0	.05

over, California also had a superior ranking as the place of residence of eminent authors, college professors, physicians, engineers, scientists, and officers of the United States Army and Navy. New Mexico had an extraordinary record in the talent of its artists, authors, judges, lawyers, and public officials. Arizona excelled in its claim upon famous authors, engineers, and scientists, while Texas had more than the usual number of distinguished Army officers.

The place of birth of eminent persons in the Southwest, as recorded in the various collections of biographies, reveals a trend toward an increase in the number of natives of this region. More and more the cultural contributions have become an indigenous product. Still another trend, which does not appear in a marked manner in the published directories, is recognized by students of history and the fine arts. It is the increasing number of representatives of the large minority groups who have earned deserved honors for their achievements. For example, in the 1950s Joe Herrera (Bluebird), a Cochití Pueblo Indian, won honors for his original art not only in the United States but also abroad, and in 1969 N. Scott Momaday, a Kiowa, received the Pulitzer Prize for his novel on Indian life, *House Made of Dawn*. In the years around mid-century Indians had risen to prominence for their arts and crafts, Spanish Americans had won acclaim as artists, musicians, and public officials, Negroes had won honors in art, music, journalism, and the theater, and Orientals had forged ahead as actors, authors, and scientists. This, therefore, had become another evidence of cultural maturity in the Modern Southwest.

HERITAGE ON THE FRONTIER

On the moving frontier the pioneers became obsessed in the ordeal of making their homes, raising their families, and protecting themselves against the dangers surrounding them. They thought little about whence they and their neighbors came or their role in history. Upon the maturation of society in a given region, the proud and thoughtful citizens began to give consideration to the contributions of their ancestors and the factors which shaped their institutions. Then they gathered records, wrote histories, founded museums, and celebrated the anniversaries of great events. For a review of the American frontier a frame of reference often employed for evaluation by historians is the much-quoted thesis advanced by Frederick Jackson Turner near the beginning of this century.

Turner contended that the frontier experience of four hundred years had contributed much toward making Americans what they are. His research led him to conclude that that experience made the participants more democratic, materialistic, and exuberant than their contemporaries in a more stable society. Further, he believed that it contributed to the emergence of an "American race," modified institutions, and innovations in legislation, while also opening a "safety valve" for the escape of the impoverished and oppressed of the East.

Because Turner derived his conclusions from studies of the northeastern and midwestern Anglo-American frontiers, that is the region where his thesis admittedly is more applicable. In the Southwest, however, a frontier of a different type appeared first—that of the Spanish pioneers. Instead of advancing in a forward-moving frontier line, or zone, they ventured far out into small, concentrated outposts, or "islands" of settlement. Their experience democratized very little their authoritarian concept of society and tempered their original individualistic nature with a great degree of the kind of community cooperation required for survival. While engaged in essentially a materialistic conquest, they usually refused to admit it; instead they professed spiritual aims and continued to pay high honor to men of culture—the padres and the dons. Although they could have justified outbursts of exuberance, they were humble instead in their reverence toward God and Nature. As for nationalism, their loyalty to the King was taught and required rather than feverishly inspired, and only later, in the Mexican Period, did occasional expressions of something akin to nationalism break through.

The legislation applied on the Spanish frontier was in the main centrally promulgated for application throughout the Empire; only near the end of the colonial period were innovations sought for improvement of government and defense specifically in this locality. Although Spanish institutions were transplanted intact at first, this frontier did force some modification, as evidenced in the development of architecture, in the control of Indian pueblos, in the emergence of the Penitentes, and in the revision of folk literature. For commoners who came as soldiers and found new homes, certainly this frontier seemed to provide an opportunity to escape from the restrictions of an older environment, yet in effect many had "escaped" into new surroundings every bit as restrictive. Although by intermarriage with Indians they did produce a new race, the *mestizos*, this class remained so long submerged that consciousness of the evolution was suppressed. Only recently has the concept of "La Raza," or a new and responsible race, begun to penetrate this region from Mexico. Thus, to sum up, Turner's thesis is applicable in very few particulars.

With the penetration of this region by Anglo-Americans, they came to a frontier different from any which they had previously opened, for here it was already partially conquered. Therefore they first moved into the Spanish islands of settlement and later filled in the intervening gaps wherever that was possible. Immediately they superimposed democratic political institutions, which became more democratic in practice with the later upsurge of reform and progressivism. They found resources which fostered individualistic aggrandizement, and they emphasized material gain which in turn led them to honor the builder and the money-maker. Their expressions of Manifest Destiny certainly were exuberant; moreover the new spirit was illustrated well by the difference between the lusty cowboy and the reticent sheepherder.

In the new era, special legislation was devised for ranching, mining, Indian administration, reclamation, and conservation of resources. Opportunities for "escape" benefited the single men who came to work on ranches or in mines, but the pioneer who transplanted his family had to have some resources to bring with him. Numerous evidences of modified institutions can be cited, including Indian practices, the land system, the rodeo, and literary expression. Finally, the components had been introduced for the development of a new race even beyond the degree envisioned by Turner. By 1966 those components, however, still absorbed in problems of accommodation, were not extensively producing racial amalgamation. By and large, the Turner thesis, derived from observation of another frontier, can also be accepted as generally interpretive of this one in the American territorial period.

THE LONG VIEW

There is also another angle to the "long view." In the aboriginal region which became the present Southwest, round-headed and long-headed races, nomadic hunters and sedentary farmers, weavers of baskets and molders of pottery had intermingled throughout a long era of migrations accompanied by intercultural associations. After centuries of conflict and consequent social readjustment, of which no scholar has yet been able to combine the fragmentary records into a complete story, favored localities witnessed the emergence of the "Golden Age" of Pueblo culture with all of its remarkable attainments.

In the Middle Ages, Spain experienced an intermingling of Alans, Arabs, Basques, Jews, Sueves, and Visigoths. The peninsula which once had been a frontier of the Roman Empire was conquered by Mohammedans in the Middle

Ages and later repossessed by native Christians. Finally, after a long period of conflict, cultural interchange, and attendant social disorganization, the Golden Age of Spanish culture emerged in Iberia. For more than a century unified Spain had a record resplendent with attainments in literature and science as well as in leadership in expansion overseas.

Likewise the British Isles in the Middle Ages were overrun by Angles, Saxons, Picts, and Britons. First conquered by Romans and then by Normans, England subsequently became involved in wars with rival kingdoms on the European continent. After a long siege of internal conflicts, accompanied by the usual fusion of cultures and social disorganization, the diverse elements became integrated in the Elizabethan Age. Then a unified England became noted for the virility of its culture as well as energetic activity all around the world.

In the Borderlands which were to become the American Southwest, the Indians, Spaniards, and Anglo-Americans maintained hegemony in that order. Intermingling at a later date with the people of the three original cultures were Negro Americans, Mexican Americans, and Oriental Americans. Again the period of transition was characterized by racial conflict, cultural fusion, and social disorganization, just as had the formative eras in the land of origin of these American components. By the middle of the twentieth century evidences of cultural accommodation and maturity were beginning to appear.

In the above analogy a conclusion concerning the cultural attainments to be anticipated in the Southwest of the future may be implicit; yet there is no guarantee that history may repeat itself. All that can be concluded with certainty is that, although the record of the past has been shadowed periodically by conflict and tragedy, it is also replete with narratives of heroic deeds and remarkable achievements, and the promise of the future is subject to the molding forces which will be wielded by Americans of generations yet to come.

BIBLIOGRAPHY

INTRODUCTION

This guide to supplementary reference materials lists those sources which were especially helpful in the preparation of this book, together with many others which the student of southwestern history will find helpful in obtaining a more intimate acquaintance with the component events and trends.

Often the best analytical treatment for a specific topic will be found in articles in the professional journals. A classified bibliography of such periodical literature that appeared in the years 1942–1955 was presented in "A Guide to Literature of the Southwest" (by Lyle Saunders and Genevieve Porterfield) and was published for those years in *The New Mexico Quarterly* (Albuquerque). Usually the historical journals also have useful index volumes. Among those which should be consulted are *The American West* (Salt Lake City, 1961–), *Arizona and the West* (Tucson, 1959–), *California Historical Society Quarterly* (San Francisco, 1922–), *New Mexico Historical Review* (Santa Fe, 1926–), *Pacific Historical Review* (Berkeley, 1932–), *El Palacio* (Santa Fe, 1912–), *Panhandle-Plains Historical Review* (Canyon, Texas, 1928–), *Southern California Historical Society Quarterly* (Los Angeles, 1918–), and *Southwestern Historical Quarterly* (Austin, Texas, 1919–).

Several books which could well be cited as references for many of the chapters in this work merit advance mention here. Among the histories of the American frontier, there is one that includes an excellent survey of the prior Spanish frontier in the Borderlands: LeRoy R. Hafen and Carl C. Rister's *Western America* (New York, 1941, and its subsequent editions). Another work which is widely acclaimed for its scholarly treatment of the Anglo-American frontier, including the Southwest, is Ray Allen Billington's *Westward Expansion* (New York, 1949, and its later editions). Another authoritative and delightfully readable account is Robert E. Riegel's *America Moves West* (New York, 1930, with subsequent revisions).

Regional histories are few. Those deserving recognition for their good summaries of several aspects of southwestern history are, in addition to Richardson and Rister already mentioned in the Preface: Odie B. Faulk, *Land of Many Frontiers* (New York, 1968), W. Eugene Hollon, *The Southwest—Old and New* (New York, 1961), Paul Horgan, *Great River: The Rio Grande in North American History*, 2 vols. (New York, 1945), Paul I. Wellman, *Glory, God and Gold* (New York, 1954), and Green P. Wertenbaker (Green Peyton), *America's Heartland: The Southwest* (Norman, Okla., 1948).

Histories of the four states that emerged from the Spanish Borderlands present the story of each constituent segment from the Spanish beginnings to recent times. The pioneer among the state historians for this region was, of course, Hubert Howe Bancroft, whose volumes still are invaluable for the earlier years. They include his *History of Arizona and New Mexico* (San Francisco, 1889, and Albuquerque, 1966), *History of California*, 7 vols. (San Francisco, 1884–1890, and reprint edition), and *History of the North Mexican States and Texas*, 2 vols. (San Francisco, 1884–1889).

Other more recent histories of each of the four states that are available in many college and university libraries are:

ARIZONA: Ward R. Adams and Richard E. Sloan, *History of Arizona*, 4 vols. (Phoenix, 1930); Thomas E. Farish, *History of Arizona*, 8 vols. (Phoenix, 1915–1918); Madeline F. Paré and Bert M. Fireman, *Arizona Pageant* (Phoenix, 1965); Edward H. Peplow, *History of Arizona* (New York, 1958); Rufus K. Wyllys, *Arizona, the History of a Frontier State* (Phoenix, 1950).

CALIFORNIA: John W. Caughey, *California* (New York, 1953) and *California, the Romance of a Great State* (New York, 1940); Robert G. Cleland, *California Pageant: The Story of Four Centuries* (New York, 1946) and *From Wilderness to Empire* (New York, 1944); Zoeth S. Eldredge, *History of California*, 5 vols. (New York, 1915); Don E. Fehrenbacher, *A Basic History of California* (Princeton, N.J., 1964); Theodore H. Hittell, *History of California*, 4 vols. (San Francisco, 1885–1897); Andrew F. Rolle, *California; A History* (New York, 1963).

NEW MEXICO: Warren A. Beck, *New Mexico; A History of Four Centuries* (Norman, Okla., 1962); Charles F. Coan, *A History of New Mexico*, 3 vols. (Chicago, 1925); Erna Fergusson, *New Mexico: A Pageant of Three Peoples* (New York, 1951); Frank D. Reeve, *History of New Mexico*, 4 vols. (New York, 1961); Ralph E. Twitchell, *The Leading Facts of New Mexico History*, 2 vols. (Cedar Rapids, Iowa, 1911, and Albuquerque, 1963).

TEXAS: Carlos E. Castañeda, *Our Catholic Heritage in Texas, 1519–1936*, 6 vols. (Austin, 1953); Seymour V. Connor, *The Saga of Texas*, 6 vols. (Austin, 1965); Lewis N. Newton and Herbert P. Gambrell, *A Social and Political History of Texas*, edited by Eugene C. Barker (Dallas, 1932); William S. Pool and others, *Texas: Wilderness to Space Age* (San Antonio, 1963); Rupert N. Richardson, *Texas, the Lone Star State* (New York, 1943); Ralph W. Steen, *The Texas Story* (Austin, 1960); Clarence R. Wharton, *Texas under Many Flags*, 5 vols. (Chicago, 1930); Henderson Yoakum, *History of Texas*, 5 vols. (New York, 1856, and Austin, 1935, 1953).

A wealth of detailed information about specific historic sites in these four states also appears in guide books published for use by tourists. Among the numerous books and pamphlets of this type which are available in museums and bookstores all across the Southwest, certainly honorable mention must be accorded to those on each of the four states prepared by the Writers' Program of the Works Progress Administration—first published in New York in 1940 and 1941, with revised editions appearing subsequently.

The portion of the bibliography that follows—arranged by subtopics under the respective chapter headings—includes an extensive and representative selection of monographs and edited volumes of source materials. Limitations of space have, regrettably, prevented the inclusion of other good books on the several topics.

1: BEFORE COLUMBUS

PHYSICAL BACKGROUND: John R. Borchert and Jane McGuigan, *Geography of the United States and Canada* (Chicago, 1966); Edwin Corle, *Desert Country* (New York, 1941); Jack L. Cross, et al., *Arizona: Its People and Resources* (Tucson, 1960); Ernest L. Felton, *California's Many Climates* (Palo Alto, 1965); Herbert Gambrell, ed., *Texas Today and Tomorrow* (Fort Worth, 1961); Edmund C. Jaeger, *California Deserts* (Stanford, 1965); David Lavender, *The Rockies* (New York, 1968); C. L. White, E. J. Foscue, and T. L. McKnight, *Regional Geography of Anglo-America* (Englewood Cliffs, N.J., 1964); Alfred J. Wright, *United States and Canada* (New York, 1956); Clifford M. Zierer, *California and the Southwest* (New York, 1956); Herbert S. Zim, *Rocky Mountains* (New York, 1963).

SOUTHWESTERN ARCHEOLOGY: Charles A. Amsden, *Prehistoric Southwesterners from Basketmaker to Pueblo* (Los Angeles, 1949); Byron Cummings, *First Inhabitants of Arizona and the Southwest* (Tucson, 1953); Harold S. Gladwin, *A History of the Ancient Southwest* (Portland, Me., 1957); Edgar L. Hewett, *Ancient Life in the American Southwest* (Indianapolis, 1930); Frank C. Hibben, *The Lost Americans* (New York, 1946) and *Treasure in the Dust* (Philadelphia, 1951); Alfred V. Kidder, *Southwestern Archeology* (New Haven, Conn., 1963); John C. McGregor, *Southwestern Archeology* (New York, 1941, Urbana, 1965); Malcom J. Rogers, *Ancient Hunters of the Far West* (San Diego, Calif., 1966); Robert Silverburg, *The Old Ones; Indians of the American Southwest* (New York, 1965); Richard Wetherill, *Anasazi* (Albuquerque, 1957); Hannah Marie Wormington, *Prehistoric Indians of the Southwest* (Denver, 1947).

INDIANS, SOUTHWEST: Erna Fergusson, *Dancing Gods* (New York, 1931); Pliny E. Goddard, *Indians of the Southwest* (New York, 1931); Louis T. Jones, *Indian Cultures of the Southwest* (San Antonio, 1967); Charles F. Lummis, *Mesa, Canyon and Pueblo* (New York and London, 1925); Ruth M. Underhill, *Red Man's America* (Chicago, 1953). Also the journals of Spanish explorers, bibliography for Chapters 2 and 3.

THE PUEBLOS: Sophie Bledsoe de Aberle, *Pueblo Indians of New Mexico, Their Land, Economy, and Civil Organization* (New York, 1948); Adolph F. A. Bandelier and Edgar L. Hewett, *Indians of the Rio Grande Valley* (Albuquerque, 1937); Edgar L. Hewett, *The Pueblo Indian World* (Albuquerque, 1945); Charles F. Lummis, *The Land of Poco Tiempo* (New York, 1893; Albuquerque, 1952, 1966); Mamie Ruth T. Miller, *Pueblo Indian Culture as Seen by the Early Spanish Explorers* (Los Angeles, 1941); New Mexico Association on Indian Affairs, *Pocket Handbook: New Mexico Indians*, ed. by Bertha P. Dutton (Santa Fe, 1948); Walter C. O'Kane, *Hopis: Portrait of a Desert People* (Norman, Okla., 1953); Ruth D. Simpson, *The Hopi Indians* (Los Angeles, 1953); Stanley A. Stubbs, *Bird's Eye View of the Pueblos* (Norman, Okla., 1950); Frank Waters, *Masked Gods* (Albuquerque, 1950).

APACHES AND NAVAJOS: Sonia Bleeker, *The Apache Indians* (New York, 1951); Dane C. and Mary R. Coolidge, *The Navajo Indians* (Boston, 1930); Stanley Crocchiola (Father Stanley), *The Jicarilla Apaches* (Pampa, Texas, 1967); Jack D. Forbes, *Apache, Navajo and Spaniard* (Norman, Okla., 1960); James J. Hester, *Early Navajo Migrations and Acculturation in the Southwest* (Santa Fe, 1963); Dorothea Leighton and Clyde Kluckhohn, *Children of the People* (Cambridge, Mass., 1947);

George T. Mills, *Navajo Art and Culture* (Colorado Springs, 1959); Morris E. Opler, *Apache Life-Way* (Chicago, 1941); Ross Santee, *Apache Land* (New York, 1947); Charles L. Sonnichsen, *The Mescalero Apaches* (Norman, Okla., 1958).

ARIZONA: Paul Ezell, *The Maricopas* (Tucson, 1963); Jack D. Forbes, *Warriors of the Colorado: The Yumas of the Quechan Nation and Their Neighbors* (Norman, Okla., 1959); Edmund C. Jaeger, *Our Desert Neighbors* (Stanford, Calif., 1950); Alice Joseph, Rosamond B. Spicer, and Jane Chesky, *Desert People* (Chicago, 1949); Alfred L. Kroeber, *The Mohave* (Washington, D. C., 1925); Ruth M. Underhill, *The Pápago Indians of Arizona and Their Relatives, the Pima* (Washington, D. C., 1940); University of Arizona Bureau of Ethnology, *Indians of the Southwest; A Survey of Indian Tribes and Indian Administration in Arizona* (Tucson, 1954).

CALIFORNIA: Merriam C. Hart, *Studies of California Indians* (Berkeley and Los Angeles, 1955); Robert F. Heizer and M. A. Whipple, *The California Indians; A Source Book* (Berkeley, 1951, 1965); Alfred L. Kroeber, *Handbook of the Indians of California* (Berkeley, 1953).

TEXAS: Mary Jourdan Atkinson, *The Texas Indians* (San Antonio, 1953); George E. Hyde, *Indians of the High Plains* (Norman, Okla., 1959); Robert H. Lowie, *Indians of the Plains* (New York, 1954); Mildred P. Mayhall, *The Kiowas* (Norman, Okla., 1962); W. W. Newcomb, Jr., *The Indians of Texas* (Austin, 1961); Ernest Wallace and E. A. Hoebel, *The Comanches* (Norman, Okla., 1952).

2: THE SEVEN CITIES

COMPREHENSIVE: Herbert E. Bolton, *Spanish Exploration in the Southwest, 1542–1706* (New York, 1916) and *Spanish Exploration in the Borderlands* (New Haven, Conn., 1921); Bernard de Voto, *The Course of Empire* (Boston, 1952); Frederick W. Hodge and Theodore H. Lewis, *Spanish Explorers in the Southern United States, 1528–1543* (New York, 1907); Paul Horgan, *Conquistadores in North American History* (New York, 1963); Frederick A. Kirkpatrick, *The Spanish Conquistadores* (New York, 1949); Herbert I. Priestley, *The Coming of the White Man, 1492–1848* (New York, 1930); Edward H. Spicer, *Cycles of Conquest, 1533–1960* (Tucson, Ariz., 1962).

NÚÑEZ C. DE VACA: Adolph F. A. and Fanny Bandelier, eds., *The Journey of Álvar Núñez Cabeza de Vaca* (New York, 1905); Morris Bishop, *The Odyssey of Cabeza de Vaca* (New York, 1933); Cleve Hallenbeck, *Álvar Núñez Cabeza de Vaca, The Journey and Route . . .* (Glendale, Calif., 1940).

SOTO: Edward G. Bourne, *Narratives of the Career of Hernando de Soto*, 2 vols. (New York, 1922); R. B. Cunningham Graham, *Hernando de Soto* (London, 1903); Theodore Mayhard, *De Soto and the Conquistadores* (New York and London, 1930).

VÁSQUEZ DE CORONADO: Herbert E. Bolton, *Coronado, Knight of Pueblos and Plains* (New York, 1949; Albuquerque, 1964) and *Coronado on the Turquoise Trail* (Albuquerque, 1949); Angelico Chavez, O.F.M., *Coronado's Friars* (Washington, D. C., 1968); Arthur G. Day, *Coronado's Quest; The Discovery of the Southwestern States* (Berkeley, 1940); George P. Hammond, *Coronado's Seven Cities* (Albuquerque, 1940); George P. Hammond and Agapito Rey, *Narratives of the Coronado Expedition, 1540–1542* (Albuquerque, 1940).

DRAKE: Francis Drake and others, *The World Encompassed by Sir Francis Drake* (London, 1854, 1926); *Drake's Plate of Brass: Evidence of His Visit to California in 1579* (San Francisco, 1937); Henry R. Wagner, *Sir Francis Drake's Voyage around the World, Its Aims and Achievements* (Glendale, Calif., 1926).

OTHERS: Cleve Hallenbeck, *The Journey of Fray Marcos de Niza* (Dallas, 1949); George P. Hammond and Agapito Rey, eds., *Expedition into New Mexico Made by Antonio de Espejo, 1582–1583* (Los Angeles, 1929), *The Gallegos Relation of the Rodríguez Expedition to New Mexico* (Santa Fe, 1927), and *The Rediscovery of New Mexico, 1580–1594* (Albuquerque, 1966); Maurice G. Holmes, *From New Spain by Sea to the Californias, 1519–1668* (Glendale, Calif., 1963); W. Michael Mathen, *Vizcaíno and Spanish Expansion in the Pacific Ocean* (San Francisco, 1925); John U. Terrell, *Estevanico the Black* (Los Angeles, 1968); Henry R. Wagner, *Juan Rodríguez Cabrillo, Discoverer of the Coast of California* (San Francisco, 1941); Arthur Woodward, translator, *The Sea Diary of Fr. Juan Viscaino to Alta California, 1769* (Los Angeles, 1959).

3: NEW MEXICO

OÑATE: George P. Hammond, *Don Juan de Oñate and the Founding of New Mexico* (Santa Fe, 1927); George P. Hammond and Agapito Rey, *Don Juan de Oñate, Colonizer of New Mexico, 1595–1628*, 2 vols. (Albuquerque, 1953); Gaspar Peréz de Villagrá, *History of New Mexico*, tr. by Gilberto Espinosa and ed. by F. W. Hodge (Los Angeles, 1933; Chicago, 1966).

VARGAS: Jessie B. Bailey, *Diego de Vargas and the Reconquest of New Mexico* (Albuquerque, 1940); J. Manuel Espinosa, *Crusaders of the Rio Grande: The Story of Don Diego de Vargas* (Chicago, 1942) and *First Expedition of Vargas into New Mexico, 1692* (Albuquerque, 1940); Irving A. Leonard, *The Mercurio Volante of Don Carlos de Siguenza y Góngora: An Account of the First Expedition of Don Diego de Vargas into New Mexico in 1692* (Los Angeles, 1932).

OTHERS: Eleanor B. Adams, ed., *Bishop Tamarón's Visitation of New Mexico, 1760* (Albuquerque, 1954); L. R. Bailey, *Indian Slave Trade in the Southwest* (Los Angeles, 1968); Herbert E. Bolton, *Pageant in the Wilderness: The Story of the Escalante Expedition* (Salt Lake City, 1951); Peter P. Forrestal and Cyprian J. Lynch, eds., *Benavides' Memorial of 1630* (Washington, D.C., 1954); Charles W. Hackett, *Revolt of the Pueblo Indians of New Mexico and Otermín's Attempted Reconquest, 1680–1682* (Albuquerque, 1942); George P. Hammond and Agapito Rey, *Fray Alonso de Benavides' Revised Memorial of 1634* (Albuquerque, 1945); Oakah L. Jones, Jr., *Pueblo Warriors & Spanish Conquest* (Norman, Okla., 1966); Charles L. Kenner, *A History of New Mexican-Plains Indian Relations* (Norman, Okla., 1969); Don S. Matson and Albert H. Schroeder, eds., *A Colony on the Move: Gaspar Castaño de Sosa's Journal, 1590–1591* (Santa Fe, 1965); C. L. Sonnichsen, *El Paso, 1581–1917* (El Paso, 1968); Alfred B. Thomas, *After Coronado: Spanish Exploration Northeast of New Mexico, 1696–1727* (Norman, Okla., 1935); Alfred B. Thomas, *Forgotten Frontiers* (Norman, Okla., 1932) and *The Plains Indians and New Mexico, 1751–1778* (Albuquerque, 1940); France V. Scholes, *Church and State in New Mexico 1610–1650* and *Troublous Times in New Mexico, 1659–1670* (Albuquerque, 1937, 1942).

4: MORE BORDERLANDS

KINO: Herbert E. Bolton, *Kino's Historical Memoir of Pimería Alta*, 2 vols. (Cleveland, 1919), *The Padre on Horseback* (San Francisco, 1932), and *Rim of Christendom* (New York, 1936); Peter M. Dunne, *Pioneer Jesuits in Northern Mexico* (Berkeley, 1944); Francis C. Lockwood, *With Padre Kino on the Trail* (Tucson, 1934); F. J. Smith, J. L. Kessell, and F. J. Fox, *Father Kino in Arizona* (Phoenix, 1966); Rufus K. Wyllys, *Pioneer Padre, the Life and Times of Eusebio Francisco Kino* (Dallas, 1935).

ARIZONA: Francisco Garcés, *A Record of Travels in Arizona and California, 1775–1776*, translated by John Galvin (San Francisco, 1966); Francis C. Lockwood, *Story of the Spanish Missions of the Middle Southwest* (Santa Ana, Calif., 1934); Francis C. Lockwood and Donald W. Page, *Tucson, the Old Pueblo* (Phoenix, 1930); Jacobo Sedelmayr, *Jacobo Sedelmayr, Missionary, Frontiersman, Explorer, in Arizona and Sonora . . . 1744–1751* (San Francisco, 1955).

PORTOLÁ & SERRA: Ivy May Bolton, *Father Junípero Serra* (New York, 1952); Ray Brandes, ed., *The Costansó Narrative of the Portolá Expedition* (Newhall, Calif., 1970); Omer Englebert, *The Last of the Conquistadores, Junípero Serra, 1713–1784* (New York, 1956); Maynard J. Geiger, *The Life and Times of Fray Junípero Serra, O.F.M.* (Washington, D.C., 1959); MacKinley Helm, *Fray Junípero Serra* (Stanford, Calif., 1956); Richard F. Pourade, *The Call to California* (San Diego, 1969); Ann Roos, *The Royal Road: Father Serra and the California Missions* (New York, 1951).

CALIFORNIA: Herbert E. Bolton, *Anza's California Expeditions*, 5 vols. (Berkeley, 1930), *Fray Juan Crespi, Missionary Explorer on the Pacific Coast, 1769–1774* (Berkeley, 1927), and *Outpost of Empire* (New York, 1931); J. N. Bowman and R. F. Heizer, *Anza and the Northwest Frontier of New Spain* (Los Angeles, 1967); Peter M. Dunne, *Black Robes in Lower California* (Berkeley, 1952); Francisco Garcés, *A Record of Travels in Arizona and California, 1775–1776*, translated by John Galvin (San Francisco, 1966); Finbar Kenneally, *Writings of Fermín Francisco de Lasuén*, 2 vols. (Washington, D. C., 1965); Charles F. Lummis, *The Spanish Pioneers and the California Missions* (Chicago, 1936); Richard F. Pourade, *The Explorers* (San Diego, Calif., 1960); Herbert I. Priestley, *Franciscan Explorations in California* (Glendale, Calif., 1946); Felix Reisenberg, Jr., *The Golden Road: The Story of California's Mission Trail* (New York, 1962); F. M. Stanger and A. K. Brown, *Who Discovered the Golden Gate?* (San Mateo, Calif., 1969); Jesse D. Stockton, ed., *Spanish Trailblazers in the South San Joaquin, 1772–1816* (Bakersfield, Calif., 1957); Theodore E. Treutlein, *San Francisco Bay: Discovery and Colonization, 1769–1776* (San Francisco, 1968).

RUSSIAN EXPANSION: Gertrude Atherton, *Rezanov* (New York, 1906); Hector Chevigny, *Russian America* (New York, 1965); Raymond H. Fisher, *The Russian Fur Trade, 1550–1700* (Berkeley, 1943); Al Markov, *The Russians on the Pacific* (Los Angeles, 1955).

LA SALLE AND THE FRENCH: Isaac J. Cox, *Journeys of René Robert Cavelier, Sieur de La Salle*, 2 vols. (New York, 1922); Henry Folmer, *Franco-Spanish Rivalry in North America* (Glendale, Calif., 1953); Father Nicolas de Freytas and John G. Shea, *The Expedition of Don Diego Dionisio de Peñalosa* (Albuquerque, 1964); E. B. Osler, *La Salle* (Ontario, Canada, 1967); Francis Parkman, *La Salle and the Discovery of the Great West* (Boston, 1869, 1879, 1897, 1927; edited by W. R. Taylor, New York, 1956); John U. Terrell, *La Salle* (New York, 1968).

TEXAS: Vito Alessio Robles, *Coahuila y Texas en la Época Colonial* (Mexico, 1938); Hodding Carter, *Doomed Road of Empire: The Spanish Trail of Conquest* (New York, 1963); Carlos E. Castañeda, *The Mission Era: The Finding of Texas, 1693–1732* (Austin, 1936); Fray F. Céliz, *Diary of the Alarcón Expedition into Texas, 1718–1719*, trans. by F. L. Hoffman (Los Angeles, 1935); Odie B. Faulk, *A Successful Failure: The Saga of Texas, 1519–1810* (Austin, 1965); Noel M. Loomis and Abraham P. Nasatir, *Pedro Vial and the Roads to Santa Fe* (Norman, Okla., 1967); Father Flavius McCaleb, *Spanish Missions of Texas* (Dallas, 1954); Juan Agustín Morfi, *History of Texas, 1673–1779*, trans. by C. E. Castañeda, 2 vols. (Albuquerque, 1935); Ross Phares *Cavalier in the Wilderness* (Baton Rouge, 1952); Robert S. Weddle, *San Juan Bautista, Gateway to Spanish Texas* (Austin, 1968).

LOUISIANA: Herbert E. Bolton, *Athanase de Mézieres and the Louisiana-Texas Frontier*, 2 vols. (Cleveland, 1914); John W. Caughey, *Bernardo de Galvez in Louisiana, 1776–1783* (Berkeley, 1934); Henry Folmer, *Franco-Spanish Rivalry in North America, 1524–1763* (Glendale, Calif., 1953); Charles W. Hackett, *Pichardo's Treatise on the Limits of Louisiana and Texas*, 2 vols. (Austin, 1931–1934); Abraham P. Nasatir, *Spanish War Vessels on the Mississippi, 1792–1796* (New Haven, Conn., 1968); James L. Robertson, ed., *Louisiana under the Rule of Spain, France, and the United States, 1785–1807*, 2 vols. (Cleveland, 1911); Carl I. Wheat, *Mapping of the Trans-Mississippi West, 1540–1861*; Vol. 1, *The Spanish Entrada to the Louisiana Purchase* (San Francisco, 1957); Arthur P. Whitaker, *The Mississippi Question, 1795–1803* (New York and London, 1934) and *The Spanish-American Frontier, 1783–1795* (Boston, 1927).

5: THE COLONIAL PATTERN

COMPREHENSIVE: Edward G. Bourne, *Spain in America, 1450–1580* (New York, 1904); Dario Fernandez Flores, *The Spanish Heritage in the United States* (Madrid, 1965); George M. Foster, *Culture and Conquest: America's Spanish Heritage* (Chicago, 1960); Francis L. Fugate, *The Spanish Heritage of the Southwest* (El Paso, 1952); Charles F. Lummis, *The Spanish Pioneers* (Chicago, 1963); Herbert I. Priestley, *The Coming of the White Man, 1492–1848* (New York, 1930).

TRAVELS AND REPORTS: Lansing B. Bloom, ed., *Antonio Barreiro's Ojeada sobra Nuevo Mexico* (Santa Fe, 1928); Richard H. Dana, *Two Years before the Mast* (New York, 1840, 1909, 1940); Eugene Duflot de Mofras, *Travels on the Pacific Coast*, trans. by Marguerite E. Wilbur (Santa Ana, Calif., 1937); Pedro Bautista Pino, Antonio Barreiro, and José Agustín de Escudero, *Three New Mexico Chronicles*, trans. by H. B. Carroll and J. V. Haggard (Albuquerque, 1942).

THE MISSIONS: Kurt Baer, *Architecture of the Spanish Missions* (Berkeley and Los Angeles, 1958); Helen Bauer, *California Mission Days* (New York, 1951); John A. Berger, *The Franciscan Missions of California* (Garden City, N. Y., 1948); Carlos E. Castañeda, *The Missions at Work* (Austin, 1938); Francisco Atanasio Domínguez, *The Missions of New Mexico, 1776*, trans. and ed. by Eleanor B. Adams and Fray Angelico Chavez (Albuquerque, 1956); Edgar L. Hewett and R. G. Fisher,

Mission Monuments of New Mexico (Albuquerque, 1943); Maynard A. Geiger, O.F.M., *Franciscan Missions in Hispanic California* (San Marino, 1969); Henry W. Kelly, *The Franciscan Missions of New Mexico* (Albuquerque, 1942); Finbar Kenneally, *Writings of Fermín Francisco de Lasuén*, 2 vols. (Washington, D.C., 1965); Francis C. Lockwood, *Story of the Spanish Missions of the Middle Southwest* (Santa Ana, Calif., 1934); Father Flavius McCaleb, *Spanish Missions of Texas* (Dallas, 1954); William H. Oberste, *History of Refugio Mission* (Refugio, Texas, 1942); John L. Phelan, *The Millenial Kingdom of the Franciscans in the New World* (Berkeley, 1969); Richard F. Pourade, *Time of the Bells* (San Diego, 1961); Felix Reisenberg, Jr., *The Golden Road: The Story of California's Mission Trail* (New York, 1962); Sister Mary S. Van Well, *Educational Aspects of Missions of the Southwest* (Milwaukee, 1952); Edith B. Webb, *Indian Life at the Old Missions* (Hollywood, 1952); Francis J. Weber, *Documents of California Catholic History, 1784–1963* (Los Angeles, 1965); Robert S. Weddle, *Six Spanish Missions in Texas* (Austin, 1968); Ralph B. Wright and others, *California Missions* (Los Angeles, 1950).

ARTS AND CUSTOMS: E. Boyd, *Saints and Saint Makers of New Mexico* (Santa Fe, 1946); Arthur L. Campa, *Spanish Folk-Poetry in New Mexico* (Albuquerque, 1946), *Spanish Folksong in the Southwest* (Albuquerque, 1933), and *Treasures of the Sangre de Cristos* (Norman, Okla., 1963); Robert M. Denhardt, *The Horse of the Americas* (Norman, Okla., 1947); Roland F. Dickey, *New Mexico Village Arts* (Albuquerque, 1949); Aurelio M. Espinosa, *España en Nuevo Méjico* (Boston, 1937); José E. Espinosa, *Saints in the Valleys; Christian Sacred Images and Folk Art of Spanish Mexico* (Albuquerque, 1960); Donald R. Hannaford, *Spanish Colonial or Adobe Architecture of California, 1800–1850* (New York, 1931); Alice Corbin Henderson, *Brothers of Light* (New York, 1937); Ruth Laughlin, *Caballeros* (New York, 1931; Caldwell, Idaho, 1945); Aurora Lucero-White Lea, *Literary Folklore of the Hispanic Southwest* (San Antonio, 1953) and *Los Hispanos* (Denver, 1947); Charles F. Lummis, *The Land of Poco Tiempo* (New York, 1893; Albuquerque, 1966) and *Spanish Songs of Old Californians* (Los Angeles, 1923); Jo Mora, *Californios* (Garden City, N.Y., 1949); Nina Otero, *Old Spain in Our Southwest* (New York, 1936); Trent E. Sanford, *The Architecture of the Southwest: Indian, Spanish, American* (New York, 1950); Richard B. Stark, *Music of the Spanish Folk Plays in New Mexico* (Santa Fe, 1970); Mitchell A. Wilder and Edgar Breitenbach, *Santos: The Religious Folk Art of New Mexico* (Colorado Springs, 1943).

INTERIOR PROVINCES: Herbert E. Bolton, *Texas in the Middle Eighteenth Century* (Berkeley, 1915); Sidney B. Brinckerhoff and Odie B. Faulk, *Lancers for the King: A Study of the Frontier Military System of Northern New Spain* (Phoenix, 1965); Odie B. Faulk, *The Last Years of Spanish Texas* (The Hague, 1964); Rex E. Gerald, *Spanish Presidios of the Late Eighteenth Century in Northern New Spain* (Santa Fe, 1968); Francis C. Lockwood and Donald W. Page, *Tucson, the Old Presidio* (Phoenix, 1930); Max L. Moorhead, *The Apache Frontier* (Norman, Okla., 1968) and *New Mexico's Royal Road* (Norman, Okla., 1958); Kathryn S. O'Conner, *The Presidio La Bahía* (Austin, Texas, 1966); Marc Simmons, *Spanish Government in New Mexico* (Albuquerque, 1968); Albert B. Thomas, trans. and ed., *Teodoro de Croix and the Northern Frontier of New Spain, 1776–1783* (Norman, Okla., 1941); Donald E. Worcester, trans. and ed., *Instructions for Governing the Interior Provinces of New Spain, 1786* (Berkeley, 1951).

6: INFILTRATION

EXPLORERS AND INTERLOPERS: Thomas P. Abernathy, *The Burr Conspiracy* (New York, 1954); Ricardo Caillet-Bois, *Nuestras Corsarios: Brown y Bouchard en el Pacífico, 1815–1816* (Buenos Aires, 1930); Robert S. Cotterill, *Gutiérrez de Lara, Mexican Texan* (Austin, 1949); William H. Goetzmann, *Exploration and Empire* (New York, 1967); W. Eugene Hollon, *Lost Pathfinder: Zebulon Montgomery Pike* (Norman, Okla., 1949); James R. Jacobs, *Tarnished Warrior, Major General James Wilkinson* (New York, 1938); Virgil N. Lott and Virginia M. Fenwick, *People and Plots on the Rio Grande* (San Antonio, 1957); David Meriwether, *My Life in the Mountains and on the Plains*, ed. by Robert A. Griffen (Norman, Okla., 1965); Royal O. Shreve, *The Finished Scoundrel* (Indianapolis, 1933); Thomas B. Sweeney, *Aaron Burr's Dream for the Southwest* (San Antonio, 1955); John U. Terrell, *Zebulon Pike* (New York, 1968); Harris G. Warren, *The Sword Was Their Passport; A History of American Filibustering in the Mexican Revolution* (Baton Rouge, 1943); Richard G. Wood, *Stephen Harriman Long* (Glendale, Calif., 1966).

TEXAS: Vito Alessio Robles, *Coahuila y Texas desde la Consumación de la Independencia hasta el Tratado de Paz del Guadalupe Hidalgo*, 2 vols. (Mexico, D.F., 1945–1946); Eugene C. Barker, *The Life of Stephen F. Austin, Founder of Texas, 1793–1836* (Nashville, 1924); Claude L. Douglas, *James Bowie: The Life of a Bravo* (Dallas, 1943); May E. Francis, *Bowie's Lost Mine* (San Antonio, 1954); Sallie Glasscock, *Dreams of Empire: The Story of Stephen Fuller Austin and His Colony in Texas* (San Antonio, 1951); S. H. Lowrie, *Culture Conflict in Texas, 1821–1835* (New York, 1932); W. H. Oberste, *Texas Irish Empresarios and Their Colonies* (Austin, 1953); William S. Red, *The Texas Colonists and Religion, 1831–1836* (Austin, 1924); Marilyn M. Sibley, *Travelers in Texas, 1761–1860* (Austin, 1967); David M. Vigness, *The Revolutionary Decades: The Saga of Texas, 1810–1836* (Austin, 1965).

SANTA FE TRAIL: William Brandon, *The Santa Fe Trail* (New York, 1967); Josiah Gregg, *Commerce of the Prairies*, 2 vols. (New York, 1844; Cleveland, 1905; Chicago, 1926; Norman, Okla., 1954); David Lavender, *Bent's Fort* (Garden City, N.Y., 1954); Margaret Long, *The Santa Fe Trail* (Denver, 1954); Leo E. Oliva, *Soldiers on the Santa Fe Trail* (Norman, Okla., 1967); George C. Sibley, *The Road to Santa Fe*, ed. by Kate L. Gregg (Albuquerque, 1952); John E. Sunder, ed., *Matt Field on the Santa Fe Trail* (Norman, Okla., 1960); Stanley Vestal, *The Old Santa Fe Trail* (Boston, 1939; Kansas City, 1955); Henry P. Walker, *The Wagonmasters; High Plains Freighters* (Norman, Okla., 1966); James Josiah Webb, *Adventures in the Santa Fe Trade, 1844–1847*, ed. by Ralph P. Beiber (Glendale, Calif., 1931); David J. Weber, *The Extranjeros* (Santa Fe, 1968) and *Prose Sketches and Poems, Written in the Western Country* (Albuquerque, 1967); Otis E. Young, *The First Military Escort on the Santa Fe Trail, 1829* (Glendale, Calif., 1951).

FUR TRADERS AND TRAPPERS: Olive W. Burt, *Jedediah Smith* (New York, 1951); Kit Carson, *Autobiography*, ed. by M. M. Quaife (Lincoln, Neb., 1968); Harvey L. Carter, *"Dear Old Kit"* (Norman, Okla., 1968); Daniel E. Conner, *Joseph Reddeford Walker and the Arizona Adventure* (Norman, Okla., 1956); Hiram M. Chittenden, *The American Fur Trade of the Far West*, 3 vols. (New York, 1902, 1935); Robert G. Cleland, *This Reckless Breed of Men; The Trappers and Fur Traders of the Southwest* (New York, 1950); Edith Dorian and W. N. Wilson, *Trails West and the Men Who*

Made Them (New York, 1955); Morgan M. Estergreen, *Kit Carson* (Norman, Okla., 1962); Alpheus H. Favour, *Old Bill Williams, Mountain Man* (Chapel Hill, N.C., 1936); Lewis H. Garrard, *Wah-to-Yah and the Taos Trail* (Norman, Okla., 1955); LeRoy R. Hafen, ed., *Mountain Men and the Fur Trade of the Far West*, 4 vols. (Glendale, Calif., 1966); LeRoy R. and Ann W. Hafen, *Old Spanish Trail* (Glendale, Calif., 1954); Kenneth L. Holmes, *Ewing Young, Master Trapper* (New York, 1967); Donald Honig, *Frontiers of Fortune: The Fur Trade* (New York, 1967); George Hyde, *Life of George Bent* (Norman, Okla., 1968); Dale L. Morgan, *Jedediah Smith* (Indianapolis, 1953); Forbes Parkhill, *The Blazed Trail of Antoine Leroux* (Los Angeles, 1965); James O. Pattie, *Personal Narrative*, ed. by Timothy Flint (Cincinnati, 1831; Cleveland, 1905; Chicago, 1930); Glen Rounds, ed., *Mountain Men: George Frederick Ruxton's Firsthand Accounts* (New York, 1966); Paul C. Phillips, *The Fur Trade*, 2 vols. (Norman, Okla., 1961); Carl P. Russell, *Firearms, Traps, & Tools of the Mountain Men* (N.Y., 1967); Alson J. Smith, *Men against the Mountains: Jedediah Smith and the Southwest Expedition of 1826–1829* (New York, 1965); Stanley Vestal, *Kit Carson* (Boston and New York, 1928) and *Mountain Men* (Boston, 1937); William S. Wallace, *Antoine Robidoux, 1794–1860; A Biography of a Western Adventurer* (Los Angeles, 1953); Mark J. Weber, Jr., *Extranjeros* (Santa Fe, 1968); Iris H. Wilson, *William Wolfskill, 1798–1866; Frontier Trapper to California Ranchero* (Glendale, Calif., 1965).

CALIFORNIA: John Bidwell, *In California before the Gold Rush* (Los Angeles, 1948); H. H. Clark, *The Clipper Ship Era, 1843–1869* (New York, 1910); Susanne B. Dakin, *The Lives of William Hartnell* (Stanford, 1949); Richard H. Dana, *Two Years before the Mast*, Volume 23 of the *Harvard Classics* (New York, 1909, 1940); William H. Davis, *Seventy-Five Years in California, 1831–1896* (San Francisco, 1929); Thomas J. Farnham, *The Early Days of California* (Philadelphia, 1859; Oakland, Calif., 1947); David M. Goodman, *A Western Panorama, 1849–1875 . . . J. Ross Browne* (Glendale, Calif., 1965); George P. Hammond, ed., *The Larkin Papers*, 4 vols. (Berkeley, 1951–1953); Rockwell D. Hunt, *John Bidwell, Prince of California Pioneers* (Caldwell, Ia., 1942); Overton Johnson and William H. Winter, *Route across the Rocky Mountains* (Princeton, 1932); Robert F. Lucid, ed., *The Journal of Richard Henry Dana, Jr.* (Cambridge, Mass., 1968); George D. Lyman, *John Marsh, Pioneer* (New York, 1930); Charles F. McGlasham, *History of the Donner Party* (Truckee, Calif., 1897; Ann Arbor, 1966); Adele Ogden, *The California Sea Otter Trade, 1784–1848* (Berkeley, 1941); George R. Stewart, Jr., *The California Trail: An Epic with Many Heroes* (New York, 1962) and *Ordeal by Hunger; The Story of the Donner Party* (New York, 1936); Reuben L. Underhill, *From Cowhides to Golden Fleece* (Stanford, 1946); Douglas S. Watson, *West Wind: The Life Story of Joseph Reddeford Walker* (Los Angeles, 1934).

7: LONE STAR REPUBLIC

COMPREHENSIVE: Eugene C. Barker, ed., *The Austin Papers* (Austin, 1919, 1926) and *The Life of Stephen F. Austin, Founder of Texas, 1793–1836* (Nashville, 1924); Carlton Beals, *Stephen F. Austin* (New York, 1953); Asa K. Christian, *Mirabeau Buonaparte Lamar* (Austin, 1922); Llerena Friend, *San Houston, The Great Designer* (Austin, Texas, 1954); Herbert Gambrell, *Anson Jones, the Last President of Texas* (Garden City, N.Y., 1948); Herbert M. Gambrell, *Mirabeau Buonaparte Lamar, Troubador and Crusader* (Dallas, 1934); Sam Houston, *The Autobiography of Sam Houston*, ed. by Donald Day and Harry H. Ullom (Norman, Okla., 1954); Marquis James, *The Raven, a Biography of Sam Houston* (Indianapolis, 1929); David M. Vigness, *The Revolutionary Decades: The Saga of Texas, 1810–1836* (Austin, 1965).

THE REVOLUTION: Eugene C. Barker, *Mexico and Texas, 1821–1835* (Dallas, 1938); William C. Binkley, *The Texas Revolution* (Baton Rouge, La., 1952); Carlos E. Castañeda, *The Mexican Side of the Texas Revolution* (Dallas, 1928); David Crockett, *The Adventures of David Crockett, Told Mostly by Himself* (New York, 1934, 1955); Sam H. Dixon and Louis W. Kemp, *Heroes of San Jacinto* (Houston, 1932); Claud Garner, *Sam Houston, Texas Giant* (San Antonio, 1969); Sue Flanagan, *Sam Houston's Texas* (Austin, 1964); L. L. Foreman, *The Road to San Jacinto* (New York, 1943); Stewart H. Holbrook, *Davy Crockett* (New York, 1955); Louis W. Kemp, *The Signers of the Texas Declaration of Independence* (Houston, 1944); Walter F. McCaleb, *The Alamo* (San Antonio, 1956); Constance M. Rourke, *Davy Crockett* (New York, 1955); Richard Santos, *Santa Anna's Campaign against Texas* (Waco, Texas, 1968); James A. Shackford, *David Crockett, the Man and the Legend* (Chapel Hill, N.C., 1956); Vincent F. Taylor, *David Crockett* (San Antonio, 1955); Lon Tinkle, *13 Days to Glory; The Siege of the Alamo* (New York, 1958); Frank X. Tolbert, *The Day of San Jacinto* (New York, 1959); Odina de Zavala, *History and Legends of the Alamo . . .* (San Antonio, 1917, 1957).

THE REPUBLIC: Ephraim D. Adams, *British Interest and Activities in Texas, 1838–1846* (Baltimore, 1910; Gloucester, Mass., 1964); William C. Binkley, *The Expansionist Movement in Texas, 1836–1850* (Berkeley, 1925); Carter E. Boren, *Religion on the Texas Frontier* (San Antonio, 1968); Mary W. Clarke, *David G. Burnet* (Austin, 1969); Seymour V. Connor, *Adventure in Glory: The Saga of Texas, 1836–1849* (Austin, 1965); Fayette Copeland, *Kendall of the Picayune* (Norman, Okla., 1943); John N. Cravens, *James Harper Starr, Financier of the Republic of Texas* (Austin, 1950); Clarence B. Douglas, *The Gentlemen in the White Hats* (Dallas, 1934); George Durham, *Taming the Nueces Strip* (Austin, 1962); Claud Garner, *Sam Houston, Texas Giant* (San Antonio, 1969); Wayne Gard, *Rawhide Texas* (Norman, Okla., 1965); W. J. and Margaret F. Hammond, *La Reunion, a French Colony in Texas* (Dallas, 1957); Jim Dan Hill, *The Texas Navy* (Chicago, 1937); William R. Hogan, *The Texas Republic; A Social and Economic History* (Norman, Okla., 1946); W. Eugene Hollon and Ruth L. Butler, eds., *William Bollaert's Texas* (Norman, Okla., 1965); William J. Hughes, *Rebellious Ranger: Rip Ford and the Old Southwest* (Norman, Okla., 1964); Terry G. Jordan, *German Seed in Texas Soil* (Austin, 1966); Barnes Lathrop, *Migration into East Texas, 1835–1860* (Austin, 1949); Milton Lindheim, *The Republic of the Rio Grande* (Waco, Texas, 1964); Noel M. Loomis, *The Texan-Santa Fe Pioneers* (Norman, Okla., 1958); Thomas P. Miller, *Bounty and Donation Land Grants of Texas, 1835–1888* (Austin, 1967); Joseph M. Nance, *Attack and Counterattack: The Texas-Mexican Frontier, 1842* (Austin, 1965); Stephen B. Oates, ed., *Rip Ford's Texas* (Austin, 1963); Gerald S. Pierce, *Texas under Arms* (Austin, 1969); Rupert N. Richardson, *The Comanche Barrier to South Plains Settlement* (Glendale, Calif., 1933); Charles P. Roland, *Albert Sidney Johnston, Soldier of Three Republics* (Austin, 1964); Joseph W. Schmitz, *Texas Statecraft, 1836–1845*

(San Antonio, 1941); Stanley Siegel, *A Political History of the Texas Republic, 1836–1845* (Austin, 1956); Jesse G. Smith, *Heroes of the Saddlebags; a History of Christian Denominations in the Republic of Texas* (San Antonio, 1951); Justin H. Smith, *The Annexation of Texas* (New York, 1911); Virginia H. Taylor, *The Franco-Texas Land Company* (Austin, 1969); Walter Prescott Webb, *Texas Rangers; A Century of Border Defense* (Boston, 1934; Austin, 1965); Tom H. Wells, *Commodore Moore and the Texas Navy* (Austin, 1960); Elgin Williams, *The Animating Pursuits of Speculation: Land Traffic in the Annexation of Texas* (New York, 1949).

8: THE MEXICAN PERIOD

GENERAL: The state histories of California and New Mexico are the best sources on the events of the Mexican Period.

CALIFORNIA: Edwin Bryant, *What I Saw in California* (Santa Ana, Calif., 1936); Susanna Bryant Dakin, *A Scotch Paisano: The Life of Hugo Reid* (Berkeley, 1939); Richard H. Dana, *Two Years before the Mast* (New York, 1840, 1909, 1940); William Heath Davis, *Seventy-five Years in California* (San Francisco, 1929); Eugene Duflot de Mofras, *Travels on the Pacific Coast*, trans. by Marguerite Eyer Wilbur (Santa Ana, Calif., 1937); Job F. Dye, *Recollections of a Pioneer, 1830–1855* (Los Angeles, 1951); Thomas J. Farnham, *The Early Days of California* (Philadelphia, 1859); Alexander Forbes, *California: A History of Upper and Lower California* (London, 1839; San Francisco, 1937); Gerald J. Geary, *The Secularization of California Missions* (Washington, D.C., 1934); George P. Hammond, ed., *The Larkin Papers*, ten vols. (Berkeley and Los Angeles, 1960); George L. Hardin, *Don Agustín V. Zamorano, Statesman, Soldier, Craftsman, and California's First Printer* (Los Angeles, 1934); J. J. Hill, *History of Warner's Ranch and Its Environs* (Los Angeles, 1927); C. Alan Hutchinson, *Frontier Settlement in Mexican California* (New Haven, Conn. 1969); Myrtle M. McKittrick, *Vallejo, Son of California* (Portland, 1944); Edna D. P. Nelson, *The California Dons* (New York, 1962); Doyce B. Nunis, Jr., *The Trial of Isaac Graham* (Los Angeles, 1967); Angustias Ord, *Occurrences in Hispanic California*, trans. and ed. by Francis Price and William H. Ellison (Washington, D.C., 1956); Richard F. Pourade, *The Silver Dons* (San Diego, 1963); Alfred H. Robinson, *Life in California before the Conquest* (New York, 1846, 1925; London, 1851); William W. Robinson, *Land in California* (Berkeley, 1948); Reuben G. Thwaites, ed., *Early Western Travels*, Vols. XXVIII-IX, *Journal of T. J. Farnham* (Cleveland, 1904–1907); Jeanne Van Nostrand, *Monterey, Adobe Capital of California* (San Francisco, 1968).

NEW MEXICO: Lansing B. Bloom, ed., *Antonio Barreiro's Ojeado sobre Nuevo Mexico* (Santa Fe, 1928) and "New Mexico under Mexican Administration," in *Old Santa Fe*, Vol. I, Nos. 1–5 (Santa Fe, 1913–1914); Horace B. Carroll, *The Texas Santa Fe Trail* (Canyon, Texas, 1951); Fayette Copeland, *Kendall of the Picayune* (Norman, Okla., 1943); W. W. H. Davis, *El Gringo, or New Mexico and Her People* (Santa Fe, 1938); Thomas Falconer, *Letters and Notes on the Texas Santa Fe Expedition, 1841–1842*, ed. by Frederick W. Hodge (New York, 1930); Josiah Gregg, *Commerce of the Prairies*, 2 vols. (New York, 1844; Cleveland, 1905; Chicago, 1926; Norman, Okla., 1954); George W. Kendall, *Narrative of the Texas Santa Fe Expedition*, 2 vols., ed. by Milo M. Quaife (London, 1848; Chicago, 1929, Austin, 1935); David Lavender, *Bent's Fort* (Garden City, N.Y., 1954); Noel M. Loomis, *The Texas-Santa Fe Pioneers* (Norman, Okla., 1958); William W. Morrow, *Spanish and Mexican Land Grants* (San Francisco, 1923); Pedro Bautista Pino, Antonio Barreiro, José Agustín de Escudero, *Three New Mexico Chronicles,* trans. by H. B. Carroll and ed. by J. V. Haggard (Albuquerque, 1942); James Josiah Webb, *Adventures in the Santa Fe Trade,* ed. by Ralph P. Bieber (Glendale, 1931).

9: NEW ALLEGIANCE

COMPREHENSIVE: Alfred H. Bill, *Rehearsal for Conflict; The War with Mexico, 1846–1848* (New York, 1947); Polly Bolian, *Mr. Polk's War* (New York, 1968); Donald B. Chidsey, *The War with Mexico* (New York, 1968); Seymour V. Connor, *Adventure in Glory: The Saga of Texas, 1836–1849* (Austin, 1965); Bernard A. De Voto, *The Year of Decision, 1846* (Boston, 1943); Charles L. Dufour, *The Mexican War* (New York, 1968); Robert S. Henry, *The Story of the Mexican War* (Indianapolis, 1950); Frederick Merk, *Manifest Destiny and Mission in American History* (New York, 1966); Walter F. McCaleb, *The Conquest of the West* (New York, 1947); James K. Polk, *Diary of a President, 1845–1849,* Allan Nevins, ed. (New York, 1952); Glenn W. Price, *Origins of the Mexican War* (Austin, 1967); Antonio López de Santa Anna, *Las Guerras de Mexico con Texas y Los Estados Unidos* (Mexico, D.F., 1910); R. E. Ruiz, *Mexican War: Was It Manifest Destiny?* (New York, 1963); Charles Sellers, *James K. Polk,* 2 vols. (Princeton, N.J., 1966); Otis A. Singletary, *The Mexican War* (Chicago, 1960); George Winston Smith and Charles B. Judah, *Chronicles of the Gringos* (Albuquerque, 1968); Justin H. Smith, *The War with Mexico,* 2 vols. (New York, 1919); Nathaniel W. Stephenson, *Texas and the Mexican War* (San Antonio, 1944).

TAYLOR AND TEXAS: Vito Alessio Robles, *Coahuilo y Texas desde la Consumación de la Independencia hasta el Tratado de Paz de Guadalupe Hidalgo,* Vol. II (Mexico, D.F., 1946); Brainerd Dyer, *Zachary Taylor* (Baton Rouge, 1946, 1967); James K. Greer, *Colonel Jack Hays, Texas Frontier Leader and California Builder* (New York, 1952); William J. Hughes, *Rebellious Ranger: Rip Ford and the Old Southwest* (Norman, Okla., 1964); David Lavender, *Climax at Buena Vista* (Philadelphia, 1966); Silas B. McKinley and Silas Bent, *Old Rough and Ready; The Life and Times of Zachary Taylor* (New York, 1946); Stephen B. Oates, *Rip Ford's Texas* (Austin, 1963); Cornelius C. Smith, Jr., *William Sanders Oury* (Tucson, 1967).

KEARNY AND NEW MEXICO: Ross Calvin, *Lieutenant Emory Reports* (Albuquerque, 1951); Dwight L. Clarke, *Stephen Watts Kearny, Soldier of the West* (Norman, Okla., 1961); Philip St. George Cooke, *Conquest of New Mexico and California* (New York, 1878; Chicago, 1964); George R. Gibson, *Journal of a Soldier under Kearny and Doniphan,* ed. by R. P. Bieber (Glendale, Calif., 1935); John T. Hughes, *Doniphan's Expedition, Containing an Account of the Conquest of New Mexico* (Topeka, 1907); Abraham R. Johnston, Marcellus B. Edwards, and Phillip G. Ferguson, *Marching with the Army of the West,* ed. by R. P. Bieber (Glendale, Calif., 1936); William A. Keleher, *Turmoil in New Mexico, 1846–1868* (Santa Fe, 1952); David Lavender, *Bent's Fort* (Garden City, N.Y., 1954); Susan Shelby Magoffin, *Down the Santa Fe Trail and into Mexico,* ed. by Stella M. Drumm (New Haven, 1926); Jacob S. Robinson, *Journal of the Santa Fe Expedition under Colonel Doniphan*

(Princeton, N.J., 1932); George F. A. Ruxton, *Adventures in the Rocky Mountains* (London, 1847) and *Ruxton of the Rockies,* comp. by Mae Reed Porter and L. R. Hafen (Norman, Okla., 1950); James H. Simpson, *Journal of a Military Reconnaissance from Santa Fe, New Mexico, to the Navajo Country . . . 1849* (Philadelphia, 1852); Ralph E. Twitchell, *The Military Occupation of New Mexico* (Chicago, 1963).

FRÉMONT AND CALIFORNIA: Frederick S. Dellenbaugh, *Frémont and '49* (New York, 1914); Richard H. Dillon, *J. Ross Browne, Confidential Agent in Old California* (Norman, Okla., 1965); Alice Eyre, *The Famous Frémonts and Their America* (Los Angeles, 1950); John C. Frémont, *Narratives of Exploration and Adventures,* ed. by Allan Nevins (New York, 1928); Guy G. Giffen, *California Expedition, Stevenson's Regiment of First New York Volunteers* (Oakland, 1951); Norman A. Graebner, *Empire on the Pacific* (New York, 1955); John A. Hawgood, ed., *First and Last Consul: Thomas Oliver Larkin and the Americanization of California* (San Marino, Calif., 1962); Werner H. Marti, *Messenger of Destiny: The California Adventures, 1846–1847, of Archibald H. Gillespie* (San Francisco, 1960); Allan Nevins, *Frémont, Pathmarker of the West* (New York, 1939); Charles Preuss, *Exploring with Frémont* (Norman, Okla., 1958); Fred B. Rogers, *William Brown Ide, Bear Flagger* (San Francisco, 1962); Irving Stone, *Immortal Wife* (New York, 1944); Arthur Woodward, *Lances at San Pascual* (San Francisco, 1948).

COOKE AND ARIZONA: Philip St. George Cooke, *Conquest of New Mexico and California* (New York, 1878; Chicago, 1964); P. S. G. Cooke, W. H. C. Whiting, and F. X. Aubry, *Exploring Southwestern Trails, 1846–1854,* ed. by R. P. Bieber (Glendale, Calif., 1938); F. A. Golder, T. A. Bailey, and J. L. Smith, *The March of the Mormon Battalion* (New York and London, 1928); A. W. Gressinger, *Charles I. Poston, Sunland Seer* (Globe, Ariz., 1961); Henry Standage, *The March of the Mormon Battalion* (New York, 1928); Otis E. Young, *The West of Philip St. George Cooke, 1869–1895* (Glendale, Calif., 1955).

10: ACROSS THE SOUTHWEST

GOLD RUSH: Charles Bateson, *Gold Fleet for California: Forty-Niners from Australia and New Zealand* (East Lansing, Mich., 1964); Ralph P. Bieber, ed., *Southern Trails to California in 1849* (Glendale, Calif., 1937); J. Ross Browne, *A Dangerous Journey, California 1849* (Palo Alto, Calif., 1950); John A. Caughey and others, *Rushing for Gold* (Berkeley, 1949); Donald B. Chidsey, *The California Gold Rush* (New York, 1968); John Dillon, *Fool's Gold: A Biography of John Sutter* (New York, 1967); Robert Eccleston, *Overland to California on the Southwestern Trail* (Berkeley and Los Angeles, 1950); George W. B. Evans, *Mexican Gold Trail* (San Marino, Calif., 1954); Grant Foreman, *Marcy & the Gold Seekers* (Norman, Okla., 1939); Theressa Gay, *James W. Marshall: The Discoverer of California Gold* (Georgetown, Calif., 1967); William S. Greever, *The Bonanza West: The Story of the Western Mining Rushes, 1848–1900* (Norman, Okla., 1963); Benjamin B. Harris, *The Gila Trail: The Texas Argonauts and the California Gold Rush* (Norman, Okla., 1960); *Journal of Forty-niners, Salt Lake to Los Angeles,* ed. by L. R. and Ann W. Hafen (Glendale, Calif., 1954); John H. Kemble, *The Panama Route, 1848–1869* (Berkeley, 1943); Oscar Lewis, *Sea Routes to the Gold Fields* (New York, 1949) and *Sutter's Fort* (Englewood Cliffs, N.J., 1966); Jay Monaghan, *Australians and the Gold Rush* (Berkeley and Los Angeles, 1966); Rodman W. Paul, *The California Gold Discovery* (Georgetown, Calif., 1966); John E. Pomfret, *California Gold Rush Voyages, 1848–1849* (San Marino, Calif., 1954).

THE MINES: John W. Caughey, *Gold is the Cornerstone* (Berkeley, 1948); Julian Dana, *The Sacramento, River of Gold* (New York, 1939); George P. Hammond, ed., *Digging for Gold without a Shovel* (Denver, 1967); Rockwell D. Hunt, *California in the Making* (Caldwell, Ida., 1954); Remi Nadeau, *Ghost Towns and Mining Camps of Calfornia* (Los Angeles, 1965); Rodman W. Paul, *California Gold . . .* (Cambridge, Mass., 1947; New York, 1965); Glenn C. Quiett, *Pay Dirt* (New York, 1936); Charles H. Shinn, *Mining Camps; A Study of American Frontier Government* (New York, 1947, 1965); Otis E. Young, Jr., *How They Dug the Gold* (Tucson, 1967).

BOUNDARY AND SURVEYS: Richard A. Bartlett, *Great Surveys of the American West* (Norman, Okla., 1962); Odie B. Faulk, *Too Far North . . . Too Far South* (Los Angeles, 1967); John Galvin, ed., *Western America in 1846–1847: The Original Travel Diary of J. S. Abert* (San Francisco, 1966); P. N. Garber, *The Gadsden Treaty* (Philadelphia, 1923); William H. Goetzmann, *Army Exploration of the American West, 1803–1863* (New Haven, Conn., 1959); George Griggs, *History of the Mesilla Valley, or the Gadsden Purchase* (Las Cruces, N.M., 1930); Robert V. Hine, *Bartlett's West: Drawing the Mexican Boundary* (New Haven, Conn., 1968); Ivor D. Spencer, *The Victor and the Spoils: A Life of William L. Marcy* (Providence, R.I., 1960); Amiel W. Whipple, *A Pathfinder in the Southwest*, ed. by Grant Foreman (Norman, Okla., 1941).

EXPRESS: Lucius Beebe and Charles Clegg, *U. S. West: The Saga of Wells Fargo* (New York, 1949); Alden Hatch, *American Express* (Garden City, N.Y., 1950); Noel M. Loomis, *Wells Fargo* (New York, 1969); Oscar O. Winther, *Express and Stagecoach Days in California* (Stanford, Calif., and London, 1938) and *Via Western Express and Stagecoach* (Stanford, 1945).

CAMEL EXPERIMENT: Stephen Bonsal, *Edward Fitzgerald Beale, Pioneer in the Path of Empire, 1822–1903* (New York, 1912); Harlan D. Fowler, *Camels to California* (Stanford, 1950); A. A. Gray, F. P. Farquhar, and W. S. Lewis, *Camels in Western America* (San Francisco, 1930); May Humphrey Stacey, *Uncle Sam's Camels* (Cambridge, Mass. 1929).

STAGECOACH LINES: Roscoe P. and Margaret B. Conkling, *The Butterfield Overland Mail*, 2 vols. (Glendale, Calif., 1947); J. V. Frederick, *Ben Holladay, Stagecoach King* (Glendale, Calif., 1940); LeRoy R. Hafen, *The Overland Mail, 1849–1869* (Cleveland, 1926); W. Turrentine Jackson, *Wagon Roads West, 1846–1869* (Berkeley, and Los Angeles, 1952); Walter B. Lang, *The First Overland Mail*, 2 vols. (Washington, 1940, 1945); Ellis Lucia, *The Saga of Ben Holladay* (New York, 1959); Alexander Majors, *Seventy Years on the Frontier*, ed. by Prentiss Ingraham (Chicago, 1893; Columbus, Ohio, 1950); Ralph Moody, *Stagecoach West* (New York, 1967); Waterman L. Ormsby, *The Butterfield Mail*, ed. by Lyle H. Wright and Josephine M. Bryan (San Marino, Calif., 1954); Richard F. Pourade, *The Colorful Butterfield Overland Stage* (Palm Desert, Calif., 1966); Stanley Vestal, *Wagons Southwest* (New York, 1946).

PONY EXPRESS: Roy S. Bloss, *Pony Express; The Great Gamble* (Berkeley, Calif., 1959); Arthur Chapman, *The Pony Express* (New York, 1932); Ralph Moody, *Riders of the Pony Express* (Boston, 1958).

11: AMERICANIZATION

GOVERNMENT: Merritt P. Allen, *William Walker, Filibuster* (New York, 1932); George Durham, *Taming the Nueces Strip* (Austin, Texas, 1962); Joseph Ellison, *California and the Nation, 1850–1869* (Berkeley, 1927); William H. Ellison, *California, A Self-Governing Dominion, 1849–1860* (Berkeley, 1950); Theodore Grivas, *Military Governments in California, with a Chapter on Their Prior Use in Louisiana, Florida, and New Mexico* (Glendale, Calif., 1963); Calvin Horn, *New Mexico's Troubled Years* (Albuquerque, 1963); William Lindheim, *The Republic of the Rio Grande* (Waco, Texas, 1964); William O. Scroggs, *Filibusters and Financiers* (New York, 1916); Edward S. Wallace, *Destiny and Glory* (New York, 1957); John E. Weems, *Men without Countries: Three Adventurers of the Early Southwest* (Boston, 1969); S. H. Willey, *The Transition Period of California, 1846–1850* (San Francisco, 1950); David A. Williams, *David C. Broderick* (San Marino, Calif., 1969); Rufus K. Wyllys, *The French in Sonora, 1850–1854* (Berkeley, 1952).

DEFENSE: Averam B. Bender, *The March of Empire; Frontier Defense in the Southwest* (Lawrence, Kansas, 1952); James A. Bennet, *Forts and Forays*, ed. by Clinton E. Brooks and Frank D. Reeve (Albuquerque, 1948); Sherbourne F. Cook, *The Conflict between the California Indians and White Civilization* (Berkeley, 1943); Stanley Crocchiola (Father Stanley), *Fort Union, New Mexico* (Canadian, Texas, 1953) and *Satanta and the Kiowas* (Borger, Texas, 1968); Edward E. Dale, *The Indians of the Southwest* (Norman, Okla., 1949); Robert W. Frazer, *Forts of the West* (Norman, Okla., 1965) and *Mansfield on the Condition of the Western Forts, 1853–1854* (Norman, Okla., 1963); Herbert M. Hart, *Old Forts of the Far West* (Seattle, 1965); Harry M. Henderson, *Colonel Jack Hays, Texas Ranger* (San Antonio, 1954); William A. Keleher, *Turmoil in New Mexico, 1846–1868* (Santa Fe, 1952); George A. McCall, *New Mexico in 1850*, ed. by Robert W. Frazer (Norman, Okla., 1968); James Pike, *Scout and Ranger*, ed. by C. L. Cannon (Princeton, N.J., 1932); Francis P. Prucha, *A Guide to the Military Posts of the United States, 1789–1895* (Madison, Wis., 1964); Rupert N. Richardson, *The Comanche Barrier to South Plains Settlement* (Glendale, Calif., 1933); James H. Tevis, *Arizona in the 1850s* (Albuquerque, 1950); Walter P. Webb, *The Texas Rangers, a Century of Frontier Defense* (New York, 1935); Paul I. Wellman, *Death on the Desert, the Fifty Years War for the Great Southwest* (New York, 1935); Donald W. Whisenhurst, *Fort Richardson* (El Paso, 1968).

LAND: Robert H. Becker, *Diseños of California Ranchos: Maps of Thirty-Seven Land Grants, 1822–1846* (San Francisco, 1964); Herbert O. Brayer, *Pueblo Indian Land Grants of the "Rio Abajo," New Mexico* (Albuquerque, 1939) and *William Blackmore*, Vol. I., *Spanish Mexican Land Grants of New Mexico and Colorado* (Denver, 1948); Gilberto Espinosa, *El Rio Abajo* (Pampa, Texas, n.d.); Albert J. Diaz, *Land Grants, New Mexico* (Albuquerque, 1960); William Keleher, *Maxwell Land Grant: A New Mexico Item* (Santa Fe, 1942; New York, 1965); Aldon S. Lang, *Financial History of the Public Lands in Texas* (Waco, Texas, 1932); Thomas L. Miller, *Bounty and Donation Land Grants of Texas, 1835–1888* (Austin, 1967); William W. Morrow, *Spanish and Mexican Private Land Grants* (San Francisco, 1923); Jim B. Pearson, *The Maxwell Land Grant* (Norman, Okla., 1961); Richard F. Pourade, *Historic Ranchos of San Diego* (San Diego, 1969); William W. Robinson, *Land in California* (Berkeley, 1948); Victor Westphall, *The Public Domain in New Mexico, 1854–1891* (Albuquerque, 1965).

SCHOOLS: Frederick Eby, *The Development of Education in Texas* (New York, 1925); Pauline Jackson, *City of the Golden Fifties* (Berkeley, 1941); Marian Russell, *Land of Enchantment: Memoirs . . .* , ed. by Garnet M. Brayer (Evanston, Ill. 1954).

CHURCHES: Paul Bailey, *Jacob Hamblin, Buckskin Apostle* (Los Angeles, 1948); Paul Bailey, *Sam Brannon and the California Mormons* (Los Angeles, 1953, 1959); Sister Richard Marie Barbour, *Light in Yucca Land* (Santa Fe, 1952); Willa Cather, *Death Comes for the Archbishop* (New York, 1927); Fray Angelico Chavez, *The Old Faith and Old Glory* (Santa Fe, 1946); W. W. H. Davis, *El Gringo, or New Mexico and Her People* (Santa Fe, 1938); Leslie R. Elliott, ed., *Centennial History of Texas Baptists* (Dallas, 1936); William Glover, *The Mormons in California* (Los Angeles, 1954); Thomas Harwood, *History of New Mexico Spanish and English Missions of the Methodist Episcopal Church from 1850–1910*, 2 vols. (Albuquerque, 1908–1910); William J. Howlett, *Life of the Right Reverend Joseph Machebeuf* (Pueblo, Colo., 1908); Edward D. Jervey, *The History of Methodism in Southern California and Arizona* (Nashville, 1960); William S. Red, *A History of the Presbyterian Church in Texas* (Austin, 1936); Jean B. Salpointe, *Soldiers of the Cross* (Banning, Calif., 1898: Albuquerque, 1968); Louis H. Warner, *Archbishop Lamy, an Epoch Maker* (Santa Fe, 1936).

12: SECESSION AND REUNION

COMPREHENSIVE: Full coverage for each state may be found in the various state histories. For general treatment, consult: Ray C. Colton, *The Civil War in the Western Territories* (Norman, Okla., 1959); Robert W. Frazer, *Forts of the West* (Norman, Okla., 1965); Bruce Grant, *American Forts Yesterday and Today* (New York, 1965); Francis P. Prucha, *A Guide to the Military Posts in the United States, 1789–1895* (Madison, Wis., 1964); Arthur A. Wright, *The Civil War in the Southwest* (Denver, 1965).

CONFEDERATE TEXAS: Donald Day and Harry H. Ullom, *The Autobiography of Sam Houston* (Austin, 1964); Llerena Friend, *Sam Houston, the Great Designer* (Austin, 1954); Harry M. Henderson, *Texas in the Confederacy* (San Antonio, 1955); Marquis James, *The Raven, A Biography of Sam Houston* (Indianapolis, 1929); Ludwell H. Johnson, *The Red River Campaign; Politics and Cotton in the Civil War* (Baltimore, 1958); Catherine W. McDowell, ed., *Now You Hear My Horn* (Austin, 1968); Stephen B. Oates, *Confederate Cavalry West of the River* (Austin, 1961); James Pike, *Scout and Ranger*, ed. by P. L. Cannon (Princeton, N.J., 1932); Fletcher Pratt, *Civil War on Western Waters* (New York, 1956); May M. and R. F. Pray, *Dick Dowling's Battle* (San Antonio, 1936); Ben H. Proctor, *Not without Honor: The Life of John H. Reagan* (Austin, 1962); Charles P. Roland, *Albert Sidney Johnston, Soldier of Three Republics* (Austin, 1964); Frank X. Tolbert, *Dick Dowling at Sabine Pass* (New York, 1962); Ernest Wallace, *Texas in Turmoil: The Saga of Texas, 1849–1875* (Austin, 1965); John L. Waller, *Colossal Hamilton of Texas* (El Paso, 1968); Walter Prescott Webb, *The Texas Rangers* (Austin, 1965); Lyman L. Woodman, *Cortina, Rogue of the Rio Grande* (San Antonio, 1950); Marcus Wright, *Texas in the War, 1861–1865* (Hillsboro, Texas, 1965).

UNION CALIFORNIA: Joseph Ellison, *California and the Nation, 1850–1869* (Berkeley, 1927); Francis P. Farquhar, ed., *Up and Down California in 1860–1864; The Journal of William H. Brewer* (Berkeley and Los Angeles, 1967); Herbert M.

Hart, *Old Forts of the Far West* (Seattle, Wash., 1965); Aurora Hunt, *The Army of the Pacific* (Glendale, 1951); Elijah R. Kennedy, *The Contest for California in 1861* (Stanford, 1943); Charles W. Wendte, *Thomas Starr King, Patriot and Preacher* (Boston, 1921).

CAMPAIGNS IN NEW MEXICO: Alwyn Barr, *Charles Porter's Account of the Confederate Attempt to Seize Arizona and New Mexico* (Austin, 1964); Reginald S. Craig, *The Fighting Parson* (Los Angeles, 1959); Stanley F. L. Crocchiola (Father Stanley), *Civil War in New Mexico* (Denver, 1960); Chris Emmett, *Fort Union and the Winning of the Southwest* (Norman, Okla., 1965); Martin H. Hall, *Sibley's New Mexico Campaign* (Austin, 1960); Max L. Heyman, *Prudent Soldier: A Biography of Major General E.R.S. Canby, 1817–1873* (Glendale, Calif., 1959); Ovander J. Hollister, *Boldly They Rode* (Denver, Colo., 1949); William A. Keleher, *Turmoil in New Mexico, 1846–1868* (Santa Fe, 1952); Robert Lee Kerby, *The Confederate Invasion of New Mexico* (Los Angeles, 1958); James C. McKee, *Narrative of the Surrender of a Command of United States Forces at Fort Fillmore* (Houston, 1960); Theophilus Noel, *A Campaign from Santa Fe to the Mississippi* (Shreveport, 1965; Houston, 1961); Charles R. Sanders, *A History of Sibley's Texas Brigade* (Richmond, Va., 1961): U.S. War Department, *Confederate Victories in the Southwest* and *Union Operations in the Southwest*, ed. by Calvin Horn and William Wallace (Albuquerque, 1961).

THE CARLETON COLUMN AND ARIZONA: Pauline Henson, *Founding a Wilderness Capital: Prescott, A.T., 1864* (Flagstaff, Ariz., 1965); Aurora Hunt, *The Army of the Pacific* (Glendale, Calif., 1951) and *Major General James Henry Carleton, 1814–1873* (Glendale, Calif., 1958); Francis C. Lockwood, *Life in Old Tucson, 1854–1864* (Tucson, 1953); Sylvester Mowry, *Arizona and Sonora* (New York, 1864); J. Morris Richards, *The Birth of Arizona, the Baby State* (Phoenix, 1940); Benjamin Sacks, *Be It Enacted: The Creation of the Territory of Arizona* (Phoenix, 1964).

RECONSTRUCTION IN TEXAS: Edwin A. Davis, *Fallen Guidon: The Forgotten Saga of General Jo Shelby's Confederate Command* (Santa Fe, 1962); Joseph Hergesheimer, *Sheridan, a Military Narrative* (Boston, 1931); Blair Niles, *Passengers to Mexico* (New York, 1943); William C. Nunn, *Texas under the Carpetbaggers* (Austin, 1962); Joseph H. Parks, *General Edmund Kirby Smith, C.S.A.* (Baton Rouge, 1954); Charles W. Ramsdell, *Reconstruction in Texas* (New York, 1910; Gloucester, Mass., 1964); Carl C. Rister, *Border Command: General Phil Sheridan in the West* (Norman, Okla., 1944); Andrew F. Rolle, *The Lost Cause: The Confederate Exodus to Mexico* (Norman, Okla., 1965); John L. Waller, *Colossal Hamilton of Texas* (El Paso, 1968).

13: INDIANS SUBDUED

COMPREHENSIVE: L. R. Bailey, *Indian Slave Trade in the Southwest* (Los Angeles, 1966); Edward E. Dale, *The Indians of the Southwest* (Norman, Okla., 1949); J. P. Dunn, *Massacres of the Mountains* (New York, 1886; 1958); Robert W. Frazer, *Forts of the West* (Norman, Okla., 1965); Bruce Grant, *American Forts Yesterday and Today* (New York, 1965); Herbert M. Hart, *Old Forts of the Far West* (Seattle, 1965); John K. Herr, *The Story of the United States Cavalry, 1775–1942* (Boston, 1953); Francis P. Prucha, *A Guide to the Military Posts of the United States, 1789–1895* (Madison, Wis., 1964); Frank G. Roe, *The Indian and the Horse* (Norman, Okla.,

1955); U.S. National Park Service, *Soldier and Brave: Indian and Military Affairs in the Trans-Mississippi West* (New York, 1963); Robert M. Utley, *Frontiersmen in Blue: The United States Army and the Indian, 1848–1865* (New York, 1967); Paul I. Wellman, *Death on the Desert: The Fifty Years' War for the Great Southwest* (New York, 1935).

ARIZONA: John Bigelow, *On the Bloody Trail of Geronimo* (Los Angeles, 1968); Sonia Bleeker, *The Apache Indians, Raiders of the Southwest* (New York, 1951); Ross Calvin, *River of the Sun* (Albuquerque, 1946); Woodworth Clum, *Apache Agent* (Boston, 1936); William T. Hagan, *Indian Police and Judges: Experiments in Acculturation and Control* (New Haven, Conn., 1966); J. G. Hayes, *Apache Vengeance* (Albuquerque, 1954); Virginia W. Johnson, *The Unregimented General: A Biography of Nelson A. Miles* (Boston, 1962); Charles F. Lummis, *General Crook and the Apache Wars*, ed. by T. L. Fisk (Flagstaff, Arizona, 1966); Don Schellie, *Vast Domain of Blood* (Los Angeles, 1968); Martha Summerhayes, *Vanished Arizona*, ed. by M. M. Quaife (Chicago, 1939); Don L. Thrapp, *Al Sieber, Chief of Scouts* (Norman, Okla., 1964) and *The Conquest of Apacheria* (Norman, Okla., 1967); Edward Wilson, *An Unwritten History: A Record from the Exciting Days of Early Arizona* (Santa Fe, 1966); Norman B. Wiltsey, *Brave Warriors* (Caldwell, Ida., 1963).

CALIFORNIA: Sherbourne F. Cooke, *The Conflict between the California Indians and White Civilization* (Berkeley, 1943); Robert Eccleston, *The Mariposa Indian War, 1850–1851*, ed. by C. G. Crampton (Salt Lake City, 1957); R. F. Heizer and M. A. Whipple, *The California Indians: A Source Book* (Berkeley and Los Angeles, 1965); Keith A. Murray, *The Modocs and Their Wars* (Norman, Okla., 1958).

NEW MEXICO: Lynn R. Bailey, *The Long Walk: A History of the Navajo Wars, 1846–1868* (Los Angeles, 1964); Sonia Bleeker, *The Apache Indians, Raiders of the Southwest* (New York, 1951); Stanley F. L. Crocchiola (Father Stanley), *Fort Stanton* (Pampa, Texas, 1964); Chris Emmett, *Fort Union and the Winning of the Southwest* (Norman, Okla., 1965); Maurice Frink, *Fort Defiance and the Navajos* (Boulder, Colo., 1968); Aurora Hunt, *Major General James Henry Carleton, 1814–1873* (Glendale, Calif., 1958); William Keleher, *Turmoil in New Mexico, 1846–1868* (Santa Fe, 1952); Frank McNitt, *Navajo Expedition . . . Lieutenant James H. Simpson* (Norman, Okla., 1964); Lawrence K. Murphy, *Indian Agent in the Southwest: William Arny's Journal, 1870* (Santa Fe, 1967); James D. Shinkle, *Fort Sumner and the Bosque Redondo Reservation* (Roswell, N.M., 1965); C. L. Sonnichsen, *The Mescalero Apaches* (Norman, Okla., 1958); Captain J. G. Walker and Major O. L. Shepherd, *The Navajo Reconnaissance, A Military Exploration of the Navajo Country in 1859* (Los Angeles, 1964).

TEXAS: Grant Foreman, *Advancing the Frontier* (Norman, Okla., 1933); J. Evetts Haley, *Fort Concho and the Texas Frontier* (San Angelo, Texas, 1952); George E. Hyde, *Rangers and Regulars* (Columbus, Ohio, 1952) and *Indians of the High Plains* (Norman, Okla., 1959); Grace Jackson, *Cynthia Ann Parker* (San Antonio, 1959); William H. Leckie, *The Military Conquest of the Southern Plains* (Norman, Okla., 1963); Mildred P. Mayhall, *Indian Wars of Texas* (Waco, 1965) and *The Kiowas* (Norman, Okla., 1962); W. W. Newcomb, Jr., *The Indians of Texas* (Austin, 1961); Wilbur S. Nye, *Carbine and Lance; The Story of Old Fort Sill* (Norman, Okla., 1937); Robert S. Reading, *Arrows over Texas* (San Antonio, 1967); Rupert N. Richardson, *The Comanche Barrier to South Plains Settlement* (Glendale, Calif., 1933) and *The Frontier of Northwest Texas, 1846–1876* (Glendale, Calif., 1963); Carl C. Rister,

Border Command; General Phil Sheridan in the West (Norman, Okla., 1944), *Fort Griffin on the Texas Frontier* (Norman, Okla., 1956), and *The Southwestern Frontier, 1865–1881* (Cleveland, 1928); Ernest Wallace, *Ranold S. Mackenzie on the Texas Frontier* (Lubbock, Texas, 1965); Ernest Wallace and E. A. Hoebel, *The Comanches* (Norman, Okla., 1952); Derek G. West and others, *The Battles of Adobe Walls and Lyman's Wagon Train* (Canyon, Texas, 1964).

GOVERNMENT POLICY: Helen Hunt Jackson, *A Century of Dishonor* (New York, 1881, 1964); Oliver La Farge, *As Long as the Grass Shall Grow* (New York and Toronto, 1940); Henry E. Fritz, *The Movement for Indian Assimilation, 1860–1890* (Philadelphia, 1963); Lawrence C. Kelly, *The Navajo Indians and Federal Indian Policy* (Tucson, 1968); Loring B. Priest, *Uncle Sam's Stepchildren: The Reformation of United States Indian Policy* (New Brunswick, N.J., 1942); P. J. Rahill, *The Catholic Indian Missions and Grant's Peace Policy, 1870–1884* (Washington, D.C., 1953); S. Lyman Tyler, *Indian Affairs: A Study of the Changes in Policy of the United States toward Indians* (Provo, Utah, 1964).

14: THE CATTLE INDUSTRY

CATTLE INDUSTRY: Oren Arnold and John P. Hale, *Hot Irons: Heraldry of the Range* (New York, 1940); Lewis Atherton, *The Cattle Kings* (Bloomington, Ind., 1961); Robert G. Cleland, *The Cattle on a Thousand Hills; Southern California, 1850–1870* (San Marino, Calif., 1941); Edward E. Dale, *The Range Cattle Industry* (Norman, Okla., 1930); J. Frank Dobie, *Cow People* (Boston, 1964) and *The Longhorns* (Boston, 1941); Harry S. Drago, *Great American Cattle Trails* (New York, 1965); Wayne Gard, *The Chisholm Trail* (Norman, Okla., 1954); Gene M. Gressley, *Bankers and Cattlemen* (New York, 1966); J. Evetts Haley and Erwin E. Smith, *Life on the Texas Range* (Austin, 1953); Jo Mora, *Californios* (Garden City, N.Y., 1949); Louis Pelzer, *The Cattlemen's Frontier . . .* (Glendale, Calif., 1936); Mari Sandoz, *The Cattlemen from the Rio Grande across the Far Marias* (New York, 1958); John T. Schlebecker, *Cattle Raising on the Plains* (Lincoln, Neb., 1963); Earl A. Swessinger, *Texas Trail to Dodge City* (San Antonio, 1950); Charles W. Towne and Edward N. Wentworth, *Cattle and Men* (Norman, Okla., 1955); George A. Wallis, *Cattle Kings of the Staked Plains* (Denver, 1965); Stephen R. Wilhelm, *Cavalcade of Hooves and Horns* (San Antonio, 1958).

SHEEP INDUSTRY: L. G. Connor, *A Brief History of the Sheep Industry in the United States* (Washington, D.C., 1921); Earle R. Forrest, *Arizona's Dark and Bloody Ground* (Caldwell, Ida., 1952); Winifred Kupper, *The Golden Hoof; The Story of the Sheep of the Southwest* (New York, 1945); William J. Parish, *The Charles Ilfeld Company* (Cambridge, Mass., 1961); Charles W. Towne and Edward N. Wentworth, *America's Sheep Trails* (Ames, Iowa, 1945).

THE COWBOY: E. Douglas Branch, *The Cowboy and His Interpreters* (New York and London, 1926); Edward E. Dale, *Cow Country* (Norman, Okla., 1943, 1965); Philip Durham and Everett L. Jones, *The Negro Cowboy* (New York, 1965); Sydney E. Fletcher, *The Cowboy and His Horse* (New York, 1951); Joe B. Frantz and Julian E. Choate, *The American Cowboy* (Norman, Okla., 1955); Stan Hoig, *The Humor of the American Cowboy* (Caldwell, Idaho, 1958); John A. Lomax, comp., *Cowboy Songs and Other Frontier Ballads* (New York, 1946); Vincent P. Rennert, *The Cowboy* (New York, 1966); P. A. Rollins, *The Cowboy, His Characteristics, His Equipment, and His*

Part in the Development of the West (New York, 1924, 1930, 1936); S. J. Sackett, *Cowboys and Songs They Sang* (New York, 1967); Bradford Scott, *The Cowpuncher* (New York, 1942); C. L. Sonnichsen, *Cowboys and Cattle Kings* (Norman, Okla., 1950); Howard N. Thorp and Neil M. Clark, *Pardner of the Wind, Story of the Southwestern Cowboy* (Caldwell, Ida., 1945); Fay E. Ward, *The Cowboy at Work* (New York, 1958); Clifford P. Westermeier, ed., *Trailing the Cowboy* (Caldwell, Ida., 1955).

HORSES: Robert M. Denhardt, *The Horse of the Americas* (Norman, Okla., 1947); J. Frank Dobie, ed., *Mustangs and Cow Horses* (Dallas, 1965); George C. Franklin, *Wild Horses of the Rio Grande* (Boston, 1954); Walker D. Wyman, *The Wild Horse of the West* (Caldwell, Ida., 1946).

BISON: E. Douglas Branch, *Hunting the Buffalo* (New York and London, 1929); Wayne Gard, *The Great Buffalo Hunt* (New York, 1959); George B. Grinnell, *When Buffalo Ran* (Norman, Okla., 1966); Mari Sandoz, *The Buffalo Hunters* (New York, 1954); Paul I. Wellman, *The Trampling Herd* (New York, 1959).

RANCHES: H. F. Burton, *History of the J. A. Ranch* (Austin, 1927); Robert G. Cleland, *Irvine Ranch of Orange County, 1810–1950* (San Marino, Calif., 1952); Robert G. Cleland, *The Place Called Sespe* (San Marino, Calif., 1940, 1957); Calhoun Collins, *The McKittrick Ranch* (Bakersfield, Calif., 1958); Cordia S. Duke and Joe B. Frantz, *Six Thousand Miles of Fence* (Austin, 1961); Paul W. Gates, *California Ranchos and Farms* (Madison, Wis., 1967); Frank Goodwyn, *Life on the King Ranch* (New York, 1951); J. Evetts Haley, *Charles Goodnight, Cowman and Plainsman* (Boston, 1936), *George W. Littlefield, Texan* (Norman, Okla., 1943), and *The XIT Ranch of Texas* (Norman, Okla., 1953, 1967); W. C. Holden, *The Spur Ranch* (Austin, 1934); William Keleher, *Maxwell Land Grant; A New Mexico Item* (Santa Fe, 1942, New York, 1965); Tom Lea, *The King Ranch*, 2 vols. (Boston, Mass., 1957); Henry D. and Frances T. McCollum, *The Wire that Fenced the West* (Norman, Okla., 1965); Lorrin L. Morrison, *Warner; The Man and the Ranch* (Los Angeles, 1962); Lewis Nordyke, *Cattle Empire; The Fabulous Story of the 3,000,000 Acre XIT* (New York, 1949); William M. Pearce, *The Matador Land and Cattle Company* (Norman, Okla., 1964); James Rowe and others, *King Ranch* (Corpus Christi, 1953); Lester F. Sheffy, *The Francklyn Land & Cattle Company* (Austin, 1963); A. Ray Stephens, *The Taft Ranch: A Texas Principality* (Austin, 1963); Dulcie Sullivan, *The L. S. Brand* (Austin, 1968); Walter A. Tompkins, *Santa Barbara's Royal Rancho* (Berkeley, 1960); George A. Wallis, *Cattle Kings of the Staked Plains* (Dallas, 1957).

THE ROUGH RIDERS: Henry Castor, *Theodore Roosevelt and the Rough Riders* (New York, 1954); Chris Emmett, *In the Path of Events with Colonel Martin Lalor Crimmins, Soldier, Naturalist, Historian* (Waco, Texas, 1959); Herman Hagedorn, *Leonard Wood, A Biography* (New York and London, 1931); W. H. Hobbs, *Leonard Wood, Administrator, Soldier, and Citizen* (New York, 1920); Ralph Keithley, *Buckey O'Neill* (Caldwell, Ida., 1949); Theodore Roosevelt, *The Rough Riders* (New York, 1899, 1924); Clifford P. Westermier, *Who Rush to Glory: The Cowboy Volunteers of 1898* (Caldwell, Ida., 1958).

15: STEEL TRAILWAYS

COMPREHENSIVE: Richard A. Bartlett, *Great Surveys of the American West* (Norman, Okla., 1962); Ira G. Clark, *Then Came the Railroads: The Century from Steam to Diesel in the Southwest* (Norman, Okla., 1958); Gilbert C. Fite, *The Farmers'*

Frontier, 1865–1900 (New York, 1966); Billy M. Jones, *Health-Seekers in the Southwest, 1817–1900* (Norman, Okla., 1967); Glenn C. Quiett, *They Built the West* (New York, 1934); Robert E. Riegel, *The Story of the Western Railroads* (New York, 1926); Fred A. Shannon, *The Farmer's Last Frontier: Agriculture, 1860–1897* (New York, 1945); Richard Steinheimer and Donald Sims, *Western Trains* (San Marino, Calif., 1966).

THE UNION PACIFIC: Grenville M. Dodge, *How We Built the Union Pacific Railway* (Omaha, 1903; 1965); Robert W. Fogel, *The Union Pacific Railroad* (Baltimore, 1960); Robert L. Fulton, *Epic of the Overland* (San Francisco, 1924; Los Angeles, 1954); John D. Galloway, *The First Transcontinental Railroad* (New York, 1950); Wesley S. Griswold, *The Work of Giants: Building the First Transcontinental Railroad* (New York, 1962); Stanley P. Hirshson, *Grenville M. Dodge* (Bloomington, Ind., 1967); James McCague, *Moguls and Iron Men: The Story of the First Transcontinental Railroad* (New York, 1964); H. K. White and Nelson Trottman, *History of the Union Pacific* (New York, 1923).

TO SANTA FE: Samuel H. Adams, *The Harvey Girls* (New York, 1942); Robert G. Athearn, *Rebel of the Rockies: The Denver and Rio Grande Western Railroad* (New Haven, Conn., 1963); Glenn D. Bradley, *The Story of the Santa Fe* (Boston, 1920); Donald Duke and Stan Kistler, *Santa Fe: Steel Rails through California* (San Marino, Calif., 1966); William Griever, *Arid Domain: The Santa Fe and Its Western Grant* (Stanford, 1954); F. G. Curley, *New Mexico and the Santa Fe Railway* (New York, 1950); James Marshall, *Santa Fe: The Railroad that Built an Empire* (New York, 1945); L. L. Waters, *Steel Trails to Santa Fe* (Lawrence, Kansas, 1950); E. D. Worley, *Iron Horses of the Santa Fe Trail* (Dallas, Texas, 1965).

THE CENTRAL AND SOUTHERN PACIFIC: George T. Clark, *Leland Stanford* (Stanford and London, 1931); C. B. Glasscock, *Bandits and the Southern Pacific* (New York, 1929); Oscar Lewis, *The Big Four: The Story of Huntington, Stanford, Hopkins, and Crocker, and the Building of the Central Pacific* (New York, 1938); Charles H. Matson, *The Story of Los Angeles Harbor* (Los Angeles, 1935); Neill C. Wilson and Frank J. Taylor, *Southern Pacific, The Roaring Story of a Fighting Railroad* (New York, 1952).

TEXAS RAILROADS: Lynn R. Bailey, *The A. B. Gray Report: Survey of a Route on the 32nd Parallel for the Texas Western Railroad, 1854* (Los Angeles, 1963); V. V. Masterson, *The Katy Railroad and the Last Frontier* (Norman, Okla., 1952); Robert S. Maxwell, *Whistle in the Piney Woods: Paul Bremond and the Houston, East and West Texas Railway* (Houston, 1963); Richard C. Overton, *Burlington Route* (New York, 1965) and *Gulf to Rockies* (Austin, Texas, 1953); St. Clair G. Reed, *A History of the Texas Railroads and Transportation Conditions under Spain, Mexico, the Republic, and the State* (Houston, 1942).

CALIFORNIA: John E. Baur, *The Health Seekers of Southern California, 1870–1900* (San Marino, Calif., 1959); William M. Camp, *San Francisco, Port of Gold* (New York, 1947); Vincent P. Carosso, *The California Wine Industry, 1830–1895* (Berkeley, 1951); Julian Dana, *The Sacramento, River of Gold* (New York, 1939); A. Bray Dickinson, *Narrow Gauge to the Redwoods* (Los Angeles, 1967); Richard V. Dodge, *Rails of the Silver Gate* (San Marino, Calif., 1960); Glenn S. Dumke, *The Boom of the Eighties in Southern California* (San Marino, Calif., 1944); Rudolf Glanz, *The Jews of California: From the Discovery of Gold until 1880* (New York, 1960); Robert V. Hine, *California's Utopian Colonies* (San Marino, 1953); Hank

Johnson, *The Railroad That Lighted Southern California* (Los Angeles, 1966); Frank M. King, *Pioneer Western Empire Builders* (Pasadena, 1946); Oscar Lewis and Carroll D. Hall, *Bonanza Inn, America's First Luxury Hotel* (New York, 1939); Bruce A. MacGregor, *South Pacific Coast* (Berkeley, Calif., 1968); Clarence P. Milligan, *Death Valley and Scotty* (Los Angeles, 1942); D. F. Myrick, *Railroads of Nevada and Eastern California*, Vol. I (Berkeley, 1962); Remi A. Nadeau, *City Makers; The Men Who Transformed Los Angeles from Village to Metropolis . . . 1868–1876* (New York, 1948); Richard F. Pourade, *The Glory Years* (San Diego, 1960); Dan Ranger, *Pacific Coast Shay* (San Marino, Calif., 1964); Felix Riesenberg, Jr., *Golden Gate, the Story of San Francisco Harbor* (New York, 1940); Andrew F. Rolle, *An American in California; The Biography of William Heath Davis, 1822–1909* (San Marino, Calif. 1956); Wallace Smith, *Prodigal Sons: The Adventures of Christopher Evans and John Sontag* (Boston, 1951); Frank M. Stanger, *Sawmills in the Redwoods* (San Mateo, Calif., 1967); Ruth C. Woodman, *The Story of the Pacific Coast Borax Company* (Los Angeles, 1951).

TEXAS: Leavitt Corning, Jr., *Baronial Forts of the Big Bend* (Austin, 1967); Samuel W. Geiser, *Horticulture and Horticulturists in Early Texas* (Dallas, 1945); Frank Goodwyn, *Lone Star Land* (Dallas, 1955); J. Evetts Haley, *Charles Schreimer, General Merchandise: The Story of a Country Store* (Austin, 1944); W. C. Holden, *Alkali Trails; or Social and Economic Movements of the Texas Frontier, 1846–1900* (Dallas, 1930); Billy M. Jones, *The Search for Maturity: The Saga of Texas, 1875–1900* (Austin, 1965); Robert L. Martin, *The City Moves West* (Austin, 1969); Coleman McCampbell, *Saga of a Frontier Seaport* (Dallas, 1934); Virginia Madison, *The Big Bend Country* (Albuquerque, 1955); Rupert N. Richardson, *The Frontier of the Northwest Texas, 1846–1876* (Glendale, Calif., 1963); J. Lee and Lillian J. Stambaugh, *The Lower Rio Grande Valley of Texas* (San Antonio, 1954); Kenneth W. Wheeler, *To Wear a City's Crown* (Cambridge, Mass., 1968).

ARIZONA AND NEW MEXICO: Rex Arrowsmith, *Mines of the Old Southwest* (Santa Fe, 1963); Opie R. Burgess, *Bisbee Not So Long Ago* (San Antonio, 1967); Joseph Chisholm, *Brewery Gulch* (San Antonio, 1949); Robert G. Cleland, *History of Phelps Dodge, 1834–1950* (New York, 1952); Sims Ely, *The Lost Dutchman Mine* (New York, 1953); Andrew K. Gregg, *New Mexico in the Nineteenth Century* (Albuquerque, 1968); Michael Jenkinson, *Ghost Towns of New Mexico* (Albuquerque, 1967); Fayette A. Jones, *Old Mining Camps of New Mexico, 1854–1904* (Santa Fe, 1964); J. H. McClintock, *Mormon Settlement in Arizona* (Phoenix, 1921); Nell Murbarger, *Ghosts of the Adobe Walls* (Los Angeles, 1968); Dorothy J. Neal, *The Cloud-Climbing Railroad* (El Paso, 1967); Ed Newsom, *Wagons to Tucson* (Boston, 1954); Stuart A. Northrop, *Minerals of New Mexico* (Albuquerque, 1940) and *Mining Districts of New Mexico* (Albuquerque, 1942); W. J. Parish, *Charles Ilfeld, Sedentary Merchant in the Arid Southwest, 1865–1884* (Cambridge, Mass., 1949); Barry Storm, *Lost Arizona Gold* (Quincy, Ill., 1953); Harold W. Weight, *Lost Mines of Old Arizona* (Twentynine Palms, Calif., 1959); Rufus K. Wyllys, *Men and Women of Arizona* (Phoenix, 1940); Marcia R. Wynn, *Desert Bonanza: The Story of Early Randsburg* (Glendale, Calif., 1963).

16: LAW AND DISORDER

VIGILANTES AND CALIFORNIA: Gertrude F. H. Atherton, *Golden Gate Country* (New York, 1945); Yellow Bird, *The Life and Adventures of Joaquin Murieta* (Norman, Okla., 1955); Stanton A. Coblenz, *Villains and Vigilantes* (New York, 1936, 1957); John M. Myers, *San Francisco's Reign of Terror* (Garden City, N.Y., 1966); Adelaide Smithers, translator, and John Galvin, ed., *The Coming of Justice to California: Three Documents* (San Francisco, 1963); George R. Stewart, *Committee of Vigilance: Revolution in San Francisco, 1851* (Boston, 1964); Sardis W. Templeton, *The Lame Captain: The Life and Adventures of Pegley Smith* (Los Angeles, 1965); Alan C. Valentine, *Vigilante Justice* (New York, 1956); Mary Floyd Williams, *History of the San Francisco Committee of Vigilance of 1851* (Berkeley, 1921).

BAD MEN AND THE TEXAS RANGERS: Robert J. Casey, *The Texas Border and Some Borderliners* (Indianapolis, 1950); Clarence B. Douglas, *The Gentlemen in the White Hats* (Dallas, 1934); O. G. Fisher and J. C. Dykes, *King Fisher, His Life and Times* (Norman, Okla., 1966); Wayne Gard, *Sam Bass* (Boston, 1936; Lincoln, Neb., 1969); James K. Greer, *Colonel Jack Hays, Texas Frontier Leader and California Builder* (New York, 1952); J. Evetts Haley, *Jeff Milton, A Good Man with a Gun* (Norman, Okla., 1948); John W. Hardin, *The Life of John Wesley Hardin* (Seguin, Texas, 1926); Harry M. Henderson, *Colonel Jack Hays, Texas Ranger* (San Antonio, 1954); W. J. Hughes, *Rebellious Ranger* (Norman, Okla., 1964); Bonita K. Lackey, *Stories of the Texas Rangers* (San Antonio, 1955); W. B. Lewis, *Life and Adventures of Sam Bass* (Dallas, 1878); Virginia Madison, *The Big Bend Country* (Albuquerque, 1955); Charles L. Martin, *A Sketch of Sam Bass, the Bandit* (Norman, Okla., 1956); Jack Martin, *Border Boss: Captain John R. Hughes—Texas Ranger* (San Antonio, 1942); Leon C. Metz, *John Selman, Texas Gunfighter* (Hastings, N.M., 1966); Lewis N. Nordyke, *John Wesley Hardin, Texas Gunman* (New York, 1957); C. L. Sonnichsen, *I'll Die Before I'll Run* (New York, 1951), *Roy Bean, Law West of the Pecos* (New York, 1943), and *Ten Texas Feuds* (Albuquerque, 1957); Walter P. Webb, *Texas Rangers: A Century of Border Defense* (Boston, 1936; Austin, 1965).

DISORDER IN NEW MEXICO: Ramon F. Adams, *A Fitting Death for Billy the Kid* (Norman, Okla., 1960); Ed E. Bartholomew, *Black Jack Ketchum* (Houston, 1955); William Brent, *The Complete and Factual Life of Billy the Kid* (New York, 1964); Mary Hudson Brothers, *Billy the Kid* (Farmington, N.M., 1949); Walter N. Burns, *The Saga of Billy the Kid* (New York, 1943); Manuel C. De Baca, *Vicente Silva and His Forty Bandits* (Washington, D.C., 1947); O. S. Clark, *Clay Allison of the Washita* (Houston, 1954); Agnes M. Cleaveland, *Satan's Paradise* (Boston, 1952); Kyle S. Crichton, *Law and Order Limited: The Life of Elfego Baca* (Santa Fe, 1928); Stanley L. Crocchiola (Father Stanley), *Clay Allison* (Denver, 1956), *Dave Rudabaugh* (Denver, 1961), and *Desperadoes of New Mexico* (Denver, 1953); Erna Fergusson, *Murder and Mystery in New Mexico* (Albuquerque, 1948); Arrell M. Gibson, *The Life and Death of Colonel Albert Jenkins Fountain* (Norman, Okla., 1965); J. W. Hendron, *The Story of Billy the Kid* (Santa Fe, 1948); Calvin Horn, *New Mexico's Troubled Years* (Albuquerque, 1963); Aurora Hunt, *Kirby Benedict, Frontier Federal Judge* (Glendale, Calif., 1961); Frazier Hunt, *The Tragic Days of Billy the Kid* (New York, 1956); W. H. Hutchinson, *Another Verdict for Oliver Lee* (Clarendon, Texas, 1965); William A. Keleher, *The Fabulous Frontier: Twelve New Mexican Items* (Santa Fe, 1945) and *Violence in Lincoln County* (Albuquerque, 1957); Robert N. Mullin, ed., *Maurice G.*

Fulton's History of the Lincoln County War (Glendale, Calif., 1968); Frederick W. Nolan, ed., *The Life and Death of John Henry Tunstall* (Albuquerque, 1965); Miguel Otero, *My Life on the Frontier*, 2 vols. (Albuquerque, 1936–1939) and *The Real Billy the Kid* (New York, 1936); A. W. Poldervaart, *Black Robed Justice* (Santa Fe, 1948); Charles L. Sonnichsen, *Tularosa, Last of the Frontier West* (New York, 1960); Kent L. Steckmesser, *The Western Hero in History and Legend* (Norman, Okla., 1965).

LAND TITLES: See Bibliography for chapter 11.

LAWLESSNESS IN ARIZONA: Ed Bartholomew, *Wyatt Earp*, 2 vols. (Ft. Davis, Texas, 1968); Glenn G. Boyer, *Suppressed Murder of Wyatt Earp* (San Antonio, 1967); E. H. Cookridge, *The Baron of Arizona* (New York, 1967); William A. Dupuy, *Baron of the Colorados* (San Antonio, 1940); Jonathan H. Greene, *A Desperado in Arizona, 1858–1860* (Santa Fe, 1966); Asbury Harpending, *The Great Diamond Hoax...*, ed. by James H. Wilkins (Norman, Okla., 1958); Jess G. Hayes, *Sheriff Thompson's Day* (Tucson, 1968); Hiram C. Hodge, *Arizona As It Was* (Chicago, 1963); Pat Jahns, *The Frontier World of Doc Holliday* (New York, 1957); John M. Jeffrey, *Adobe and Iron: The Story of the Arizona Territorial Prison at Yuma* (La Jolla, Calif., 1969): Stuart N. Lake, *Wyatt Earp, Frontier Marshall* (Boston, 1931, 1956); Douglas Martin, ed., *Tombstone's Epitaph* (Albuquerque, 1951); John M. Myers, *The Last Chance: Tombstone's Early Years* (New York, 1950); Donald M. Powell, *The Peralta Grant: James Addison Reavis and the Barony of Arizona* (Norman, Okla., 1960); C. L. Sonnichsen, *Billy King's Tombstone, the Private Life of an Arizona Boom Town* (Caldwell, Ida., 1942, 1951); Edward Wilson, *An Unwritten History: Exciting Days of Early Arizona* (Santa Fe, 1966); Bruce A. Woodward, *Diamonds in the Salt: Diamond Hoax Chicanery* (Boulder, Colo., 1967).

POLITICS AND REFORM IN TEXAS: Robert C. Cotner, *James Stephen Hogg: A Biography* (Austin, 1959); James T. DeShields, *They Sat in High Places; the Presidents and Governors of Texas* (San Antonio, 1910); Marion H. Farrow, *The Texas Democrats, Early Democratic History in Texas* (San Antonio, 1944); Frank Goodwyn, *Lone Star Land* (Dallas, 1955); Robert Lee Hunt, *A History of Farm Movements in the Southwest, 1873–1925* (College Station, Texas, 1935); John A. Lomax, *Will Hogg, Texan* (Austin, 1950); Seth S. McKay, *Seven Decades of the Texas Constitution of 1876* (Lubbock, Texas, 1943); Roscoe C. Martin, *The People's Party in Texas* (Austin, 1933); E. T. Miller, *A Financial History of Texas* (Austin, 1916); D. H. Smith, *Mr. House of Texas* (New York and London, 1940).

POLITICS AND REFORM IN CALIFORNIA: Walton Bean, *Boss Ruef's San Francisco* (Berkeley, 1952); Edith Dobie, *Political Career of Stephen M. White* (Stanford, 1927); W. H. Hutchinson, *Oil, Land, and Politics: The California Career of Thomas Robert Bard*, two volumes (Norman, Okla., 1965); J. Gregg Layne, *The Lincoln-Roosevelt League, Its Origin and Accomplishments* (Los Angeles, 1943); George E. Mowry, *The California Progressives* (Berkeley, 1951); Gerald D. Nash, *State Government and Economic Development: A History of Administrative Policies in California 1849–1933* (Berkeley and Los Angeles, 1965).

TERRITORIES TO STATES: George H. Kelly, *Legislative History of Arizona* (Phoenix, 1926); Howard R. Lamar, *The Far Southwest, 1846–1919: A Territorial History* (New Haven, Conn., 1966); Robert W. Larson, *New Mexico's Quest for Statehood* (Albuquerque, 1968); Irving McKee, *"Ben Hur" Wallace* (Berkeley and Los Angeles, 1947); David Meriwether, *My Life in the Mountains and on the Plains*, ed. by Robert A. Griffen (Norman, Okla., 1965); Joseph Miller, *Arizona: The Last*

Frontier (New York, 1956); Miguel Otero, *My Nine Years as Governor of the Territory of New Mexico, 1897–1906* (Albuquerque, 1940); J. Morris Richards, *The Birth of Arizona, the Baby State* (Phoenix, 1940); Paul A. F. Walter, *Colonel José Francisco Chaves, 1833–1904* (Santa Fe, 1927); Rufus K. Wyllys, *Men and Women of Arizona* (Phoenix, 1940).

17: THE MODERN SOUTHWEST

COMPREHENSIVE, STATE AND REGIONAL: Henry G. Alsburg and Harry Hanson, editors, *Arizona, the Grand Canyon State* (New York, 1966); Ross Calvin, *Sky Determines* (Albuquerque, 1948, 1965); William T. Chambers and Lorrin Kennamer, *Texans and Their Land* (Austin, 1963); Robert G. Cleland, *California in Our Time* (New York, 1947); Jack L. Cross and others, *Arizona, Its People and Resources* (Tucson, 1961); George M. Fuerman, *Reluctant Empire* (Garden City, N.Y., 1957); Morris E. Garnsey, *America's New Frontier: The Mountain West* (New York, 1950); Paul E. Griffin, *California, the New Empire State* (San Francisco, 1957); John Gunther, *Inside USA* (New York, 1947); Rockwell D. Hunt, *California Firsts* (San Francisco, 1957); David W. Lantis and others, *California, Land of Contrast* (Belmont, Calif., 1963); Seth S. McKay and Odie B. Faulk, *Texas after Spindletop: The Saga of Texas, 1901–1965* (Austin, 1965); Haniel Long, *Piñon Country* (New York, 1941); Carey McWilliams, *California, The Great Exception* (New York, 1949) and *Southern California Country* (New York, 1946); Lewis Nordyke, *The Truth about Texas* (New York, 1957); Richard F. Pourade, *Gold in the Sun* (San Diego, 1963); W. J. Redgrave, *California, the State That Has Everything* (Greenlawn, N.Y., 1962); Elton M. Scott, *Texas Today* (Norman, Okla., 1963); Ralph W. Steen, *Twentieth Century Texas* (Austin, 1942); Walter P. Webb, *Handbook of Texas*, 2 vols. (Austin, 1952); Green P. Wertenbaker, *The Face of Texas* (New York, 1961); Clifford M. Zierer, *California and the Southwest* (New York, 1956).

MINERAL INDUSTRIES: Kenneth Alexander, *Death Valley, U.S.A.* (Cranbury, N.J., 1969); Maurice Cheeck, *Legal History of Conservation of Gas in Texas* (New York, 1938); James A. Clark and Michael T. Halbouty, *Spindletop* (New York, 1952); Robert G. Cleland, *History of Phelps Dodge* (New York, 1952); Gerald Forbes, *Flush Production; The Epic of Oil in the Gulf Southwest* (Norman, Okla., 1942); F. W. Galbraith, *Minerals of Arizona* (Tucson, 1941); Lucille Glasscock, *A Texas Wildcatter* (San Antonio, 1952); R. E. Hardwicke, *Legal History of Conservation of Oil in Texas* (New York, 1938); Boyce House, *Oil Boom* (Caldwell, Ida., 1941); H. C. Hoover, *Ore Deposits of the Western States* (New York, 1933); W. H. Hutchinson, *Oil, Land, and Politics, the California Career of Thomas Robert Bard*, two volumes (Norman, Okla., 1965); Marquis James, *Texaco Story, the First Fifty Years, 1902–1952* (New York, 1953); Ira B. Joralemon, *Romantic Copper* (New York, 1935); Ruth Sheldon Knowles, *The Greatest Gamblers* (New York, 1959); Frank F. Latta, *Black Gold in the Joaquin* (Caldwell, Ida., 1949); Isaac F. Marcosson, *Anaconda* (New York, 1957); Ruel McDaniel, *Some Ran Hot* (Dallas, 1939); David Nevin, *The Texans* (New York, 1968); Stuart H. Northrop, *Minerals of New Mexico* (Albuquerque, 1942); Carl C. Rister, *Oil! Titan of the Southwest* (Norman, Okla., 1949); E. H. Sellards, *Texas Mineral Resources* (Austin, 1946); T. R. Stockton, R. C. Henshaw, and O. W. Graves, *Economics of Natural Gas in Texas* (Austin, 1952); Frank J. Taylor and Earl M. Welty, *Black Bonanza* (New York, 1950); Jack K. Wagner, *Gold Mines of California* (Berkeley, 1970); C. A. Warner, *Texas Oil and Gas* (Houston, 1939); Gerald T. White, *Formative Years in the Far West: A History of Standard Oil Company of California* (New York, 1962) and *Scientists in Conflict: The Beginnings of the Oil Industry in California* (San Marino, Calif., 1968).

COMMERCIAL ENTERPRISE: Robert K. Arnold and others, *The California Economy, 1947–1980* (Stanford, 1961); Charles M. Coleman, *P. G. & E. of California* (New York, 1952); Jack L. Cross and others, *Arizona: Its People and Resources* (Tucson, 1966); W. G. Cunningham, *Aircraft Industry* (Los Angeles, 1951); Thomas E. Dabney, *The Man Who Bought the Waldorf; The Life of Conrad N. Hilton* (New York, 1950); Donald Deschner, *The Films of W. C. Fields* (New York, 1967); George N. Fenin and William K. Everson, *The Western, from Silents to Cinerama* (New York, 1962); Herbert Gambrell, ed., *Texas Today and Tomorrow* (Ft. Worth, 1961); Lewis Jacobs, *The Rise of the American Film; A Critical History* (New York, 1939); Benjamin B. Hampton, *A History of the Movies* (New York, 1928); Tom Lee McKnight, *Manufacturing in Arizona* (Berkeley and Los Angeles, 1962); William J. Parish, *The Charles Ilfeld Company* (Cambridge, Mass., 1961); Frank C. Platt, compiler, *Great Stars of Hollywood's Golden Age* (New York, 1966); John T. Schlebecker, *Cattle Raising on the Plains, 1900–1961* (Lincoln, Neb., 1968); Harold Stearns, *The Stage and the Movies in America, a Reappraisal* (London, 1937); Charles F. Talman, *The Realm of the Air* (Indianapolis, 1931).

ATOMIC ENERGY: J. W. Campbell, *The Atomic Story* (New York, 1947); George Fitzpatrick, ed., *This Is New Mexico* (Santa Fe, 1948); Leslie R. Groves, *Now It Can Be Told* (New York, 1962); Lansing Lamont, *Day of Trinity* (New York, 1965); Daniel Lang, *Early Tales of the Atomic Age* (Garden City, N.Y., 1948); W. L. Lawrence, *Dawn over Zero; The Story of the Atomic Bomb* (New York, 1946).

RECLAMATION AND AGRICULTURE: George W. and Helen P. Beattie, *Heritage of the Valley* (Pasadena, Calif., 1939); Ernest L. Bogart, *The Water Problem of Southern California* (Urbana, Ill., 1934); Peter Briggs, *Water: The Vital Essence* (New York, 1967); Luther Burbank, *The Harvest of the Years* (Boston, 1927); Willie A. Chalfant, *The Story of Inyo* (Chicago, 1922); Clarke E. Chambers, *California Farm Organizations* (Berkeley, 1952); Charles T. Clark and James E. Willis, *The Highland Lakes of Texas* (Austin, 1967); Robert E. Clark, *New Mexico Water Resources Law* (Albuquerque, 1964); Erwin Cooper, *Aqueduct Empire* (Glendale, Calif., 1969); Robert De Roos, *The Thirsty Land; The Story of the Central Valley Project* (Stanford, 1948); Laura Gilpin, *The Rio Grande, River of Destiny* (New York, 1949); Allen G. Harper, Andrew Cordova, and Klervo Oberg, *Man and Resources in the Middle Rio Grande Valley* (Albuquerque, 1943); Harold Hoffsomer, ed., *The Social and Economic Significance of Land Tenure in the Southwestern States* (Chapel Hill, N.C., 1950); W. Eugene Hollon, *The Great American Desert* (New York, 1966); Norris Hundley, Jr., *Dividing the Waters: A Century of Controversy between the United States and Mexico* (Berkeley and Los Angeles, 1966); Claude B. Hutchison, ed., *California Agriculture* (Berkeley, 1946); P. L. Kleinsorge, *The Boulder Canyon Project* (Palo Alto, 1941); Karl F. Kraenzel, *The Great Plains in Transition* (Norman, Okla., 1955); Dean E. Mann, *The Politics of Water in Arizona* (Tucson, 1963); A. W. McKay, *The California Fruit Growers Exchange System* (Washington, D.C., 1950); Carey McWilliams, *Factories in the Field* (Boston, 1939); Janet Nickelsburg, *California—Water and Land* (New York, 1964); Walter E. Packard, *The Economic Implications of the Central Valley Project* (Los Angeles, 1942); E. Louise Peffer, *The Closing of the Public Do-*

main; Disposal and Reservation Policies, 1900–1950 (Stanford, 1951); Roy Robbins, *Our Landed Heritage, the Public Domain* (Princeton, N.J., 1942); Paul B. Sears, *Deserts on the March* (Norman, Okla., 1947); M. H. Saunderson, *Western Land and Water Use* (Norman, Okla., 1949); J. Lee and Lillian Stambaugh, *The Lower Rio Grande Valley of Texas* (San Antonio, 1954); Donald C. Swain, *Federal Conservation Policy, 1921–1933* (Berkeley and Los Angeles, 1963); John U. Terrell, *War for the Colorado River*, Vol. I, *The California-Arizona Controversy* (Glendale, Calif., 1966); Wallace Smith, *Garden of the Sun* (Fresno, Calif., 1950); Stewart L. Udall, *The Quiet Crisis* (New York, 1963); Nathan L. Whetten, *Rural New Mexico* (Chicago, 1948); David O. Woodbury, *The Colorado Conquest* (New York, 1941).

FOREST POLICY: Marion Clawson and Burnell Held, *The Federal Lands; Their Use and Management* (Baltimore, 1957, 1967); Raymond F. Dassmann, *The Destruction of California* (New York, 1965); William D. Douglas, *Farewell to Texas* (New York, 1967); Holway R. Jones, *John Muir and the Sierra Club: The Battle for Yosemite* (San Francisco, 1965); Jim Morley, *Muir Woods* (Berkeley, 1968); John Muir, *Gentle Wilderness: The Sierra Nevada*, edited by David Brower (San Francisco, 1964); Roy Robbins, *Our Landed Heritage, the Public Domain* (Princeton, N.J., 1942); Shirley Sargent, *Galen Clark: Yosemite Guardian* (San Francisco, 1964).

RECREATION: Edward M. Ainsworth, *Beckoning Desert* (Englewood Cliffs, N.J., 1962); Marion Clawson, *The Economics of Outdoor Recreation* (Baltimore, 1966); Charles G. Crampton, *Standing Up Country: The Canyon Lands of Utah and Arizona* (New York, 1964); Mabel Crosby and Eve Ball, *Bob Crosby, World Champion Cowboy* (New York, 1967); Devereux Butcher, *Our National Parks and Monuments* (Boston, 1956); Arthur H. Carhart, *Fishing in the West* (New York, 1952); Michael Frome, *National Park Guide* (New York, 1967); J. Donald Hughes, *The Story of Man at Grand Canyon* (Grand Canyon, 1967); Paul C. Johnson, ed., *National Parks of the West* (Menlo Park, Calif., 1965); Max Kegley, *Rodeo: The Sport of the Cow Country* (New York, 1942); Nelson B. Keyes, *The Real Book about Our National Parks* (Garden City, N.Y., 1957); William S. Lee, *The Great California Deserts* (New York, 1963); Francois Leydet, *Time and River Flowing: The Grand Canyon* (San Francisco, 1964); Norman Lobsenz, *The First Book of National Monuments* (New York, 1959); Clifford L. Lord, *Keepers of the Past* (Chapel Hill, N.C., 1965); Janet Nickelsburg, *California's Climates* (New York, 1964); Jack O'Connor, *Hunting in the Southwest* (New York, 1945); Lee Owens, *American Square Dances of the West and Southwest* (Palo Alto, 1949); Earl S. Pomeroy, *In Search of the Golden West: The Tourist in Western America* (New York, 1957); Harold V. Ratliff, *Towering Texans, Sport Sagas of the Lone Star State* (San Antonio, 1950); M. S. Robertson, *Rodeo* (Berkeley, 1961); Rube Samuelson, *The Rose-bowl Game* (New York, 1951); Edward B. Scott, *The Saga of Lake Tahoe* (Crystal Bay, Nev., 1957); Hart Stilwell, *Hunting and Fishing in Texas* (New York, 1946); Freeman Tilden, *Interpreting Our Heritage* (Chapel Hill, N.C., 1967) and *The National Parks* (New York, 1961); Herbert E. Ungnade, *Guide to the New Mexico Mountains* (Denver, 1965); Clifford P. Westermier, *Man, Beast, Dust; The Story of the Rodeo* (Denver, 1947); John R. White and Samuel J. Pusateri, *Sequoia and King's Canyon National Parks* (Stanford, 1949).

18: PEOPLE AND POLITICS

LABOR AND WELFARE: Ira B. Cross, *A History of the Labor Movement in California* (Berkeley, 1935); Harry Elsner, Jr., *The Technocrats: Prophets of Automation* (Syracuse, 1967); John A. Ford, *Thirty Explosive Years in Los Angeles County* (San Marino, Calif., 1961); Curt Gentry, *The Frame-up; The Tom Mooney-Warren Billings Case* (New York, 1967); Margaret S. Gordon, *Employment Expansion and Population Growth: The California Experience, 1900–1950* (Berkeley and Los Angeles, 1954); Abraham Holtzman, *The Townsend Movement: A Political Study* (New York, 1963); David Nevin, *The Texans* (New York, 1968); Louis B. and Richard S. Perry, *A History of the Los Angeles Labor Movement* (Berkeley and Los Angeles, 1963); Duane Robinson, *Chance to Belong; Story of the Los Angeles Youth Project, 1943–1949* (New York, 1949); Grace H. Stimson, *Rise of the Labor Movement in Los Angeles* (Berkeley and Los Angeles, 1955); E. A. Williams, *Federal Aid for Relief* (New York, 1939).

GOVERNMENT AND POLITICS: Charles C. Alexander, *Crusade for Conformity: The Ku Klux Klan in Texas, 1920–1930* (Houston, 1962); Patricia C. Armstrong, *A Portrait of Bronson Cutting through His Papers, 1910–1927* (Albuquerque, 1959); Ernest R. Bartley, *The Tidelands Oil Controversy* (Austin, 1953); Wilbourn E. Benton, *Texas: Its Government and Politics* (Englewood Cliffs, N.J., 1961); Robert E. Burke, *Olson's New Deal for California* (Berkeley, 1953); Paul Casdorph, *The Republican Party in Texas, 1865–1965* (Austin, 1965); James A. Clark and Weldon Hart, *The Tactful Texan: A Biography of Governor Will Hobby* (New York, 1958); William Costello, *The Facts about Nixon; An Unauthorized Biography* (New York, 1960); Thomas C. Donnelly, *The Government of New Mexico* (Albuquerque, 1947) and *Rocky Mountain Politics* (Albuquerque, 1940); Rowland Evans and Robert Novak, *Lyndon B. Johnson: The Exercise of Power* (New York, 1967); David Farrelly and Ivan Hinderacker, *The Politics of California* (New York, 1951); Philip Geyelin, *Lyndon B. Johnson and the World* (New York, 1967); Leonard E. Goodall, ed., *Urban Politics in the Southwest* (Tempe, Ariz., 1967); Leroy C. Hardy, *California Government* (New York, 1964); Gladwin Hill, *Dancing Politics ... California* (Cleveland, 1968); Jack E. Holmes, *Politics in New Mexico* (Albuquerque, 1967); Bernard L. Hyink and others, *Politics and Government in California* (New York, 1963); Will Irwin, *Herbert Hoover* (New York, 1929); Clyde E. Jacobs and John F. Gallagher, *California Government* (New York, 1966); Frank H. Jonas, ed., *Politics in the American West* (Salt Lake City, 1969); Charles B. Judah, *Governor Richard C. Dillon* (Albuquerque, 1948) and *The Republican Party in New Mexico* (Albuquerque, 1949); Don Lohbeck, *Patrick J. Hurley* (Chicago, 1956); Stewart MacCorkle and Dick Smith, *Texas Government* (New York, 1964); Bruce B. Mason and Heinz R. Hink, *Constitutional Government in Arizona* (Tempe, Ariz., 1963); Seth S. McKay, *Texas and the Fair Deal* (San Antonio, 1954) and *Texas Politics, 1906–1944* (Lubbock, Texas, 1951); Brett H. Melendy and Benjamin F. Gilbert, *The Governors of California: Peter H. Burnett to Edmund G. Brown* (Georgetown, Calif., 1965); Roy D. Morey, *Politics and Legislation: The Office of Governor in Arizona* (Tucson, 1965); George E. Mowry, *The California Progressives* (Chicago, 1963); S. D. Myers, Jr., and J. Alton Burdine, *Government Reform in Texas* (Dallas, 1936); Milton Nahm, *Las Vegas and Uncle Joe* (Norman, Okla., 1965); Gerald D. Nash, *State Government and Economic Development: A History of Administrative Policies in California, 1849–1933* (Berkeley and Los Angeles, 1965); Burl Noggle,

Teapot Dome: Oil and Politics in the 1920s (Baton Rouge, 1962); Spencer C. Olin, Jr., *California's Prodigal Sons* (Berkeley, 1968); William C. Pool and others, *Lyndon Baines Johnson: The Formative Years* (San Marcos, Texas, 1967); Emma M. Shirley, *The Administration of Pat M. Neff, Governor of Texas, 1921–1925* (Waco, Texas, 1938); C. W. Taylor, *Public Administration in Arizona* (New York, 1942); Bascom N. Timmons, *Jesse Jones, the Man and the Statesman* (New York, 1956); Henry Tobias and Charles Woodhouse, *Ethnic Minorities in Politics* (Albuquerque, 1968): H. A. Turner and J. A. Vieg, *The Government and Politics of California* (New York, 1960); John D. Weaver, *Warren: The Man, the Court, the Era* (Boston, 1967); Oliver D. Weeks, *Texas Presidential Politics in 1952* (Austin, 1953).

BORDER AND DEFENSE: Lansing B. Bloom, ed., *New Mexico in the Great War* (Santa Fe, 1927); Haldeen Braddy, *Cock of the Walk; Qui-qui-ri-qui! The Legend of Pancho Villa* (Albuquerque, 1955) and *Pershing's Mission in Mexico* (El Paso, 1966); Robert J. Casey, *The Texas Border and Some Borderliners* (Indianapolis, 1950); Clarence C. Clendenon, *Blood on the Border* (New York, 1969) and *A Study in Unconventional Diplomacy* (Ithaca, N.Y., 1961); Horacio Estol, *Realidad y Leyenda de Pancho Villa* (Mexico, D.F., 1956); Martin Luis Guzman, *Memoirs of Pancho Villa*, translated by Virginia H. Taylor (Austin, 1965); Mary O. Handy, *History of Fort Sam Houston* (San Antonio, 1951); Larry A. Harris, *Pancho Villa and the Columbus Raid* (El Paso, 1949); Stacy C. Hinkle, *Wings and Saddles* (El Paso, 1967); Sheldon B. Liss, *A Century of Disagreement: The Chamizal Conflict, 1864–1964* (Washington, D.C., 1965); Florence C. and Robert H. Lister, *Chihuahua* (Albuquerque, 1966); Frederick Palmer, *John J. Pershing, General of the Armies; A Biography* (Harrisburg, Pa., 1948); Ernest P. Schuster, *Pancho Villa's Shadow* (New York, 1947).

19: AMERICANS ALL

AMERICAN INDIANS: Sophie Bledsoe de Aberle, *Pueblo Indians of New Mexico, Their Land, Economy, and Civil Organization* (New York, 1948); Sonia Bleeker, *The Mission Indians of California* (New York, 1956); William A. Brophy and Sophie D. Aberle, *The Indian: America's Unfinished Business* (Norman, Okla., 1966); Edward E. Dale, *The Indians of the Southwest* (Norman, Okla., 1949); Fred Eggan, *Social Organization of the Western Pueblos* (Chicago, 1950); Carlos B. Embry, *America's Concentration Camps: The Facts about Our Indian Reservations Today* (New York, 1956); Laura Gilpin, *The Enduring Navaho* (Austin, 1968); Grenville Goodwin, *Social Organization of the Western Apache* (Tucson, 1969); Edmund C. Jaeger, *Our Desert Neighbors* (Stanford, Calif., 1950); Alice Joseph, Rosamond B. Spicer, and Jane Chesky, *The Desert People: A Study of the Pápago Indians* (Chicago, 1949); Lawrence C. Lekky, *The Navajo Indians and Federal Indian Policy* (Tucson, 1968); Oliver La Farge, ed., *The Changing Indian* (Norman, Okla., 1942); Charles H. Lange, *Cochití: A New Mexico Pueblo* (Carbondale, Ill., 1968); Dorothea C. Leighton and Clyde Kluckhohn, *Children of the People* (Cambridge, Mass., 1947); Oscar H. Lipps, *The Case of the California Indians* (Chemawa, Oregon, 1933); Francis C. Lockwood, *The Apache Indians* (New York, 1938, 1948); Alice Lee Marriott, *Indians of the Four Corners* (New York, 1952) and *The Valley Below* (Norman, Okla., 1949); Joseph Miller, *Arizona Indians, the People of the Sun* (New York, 1941); Franc J. Newcomb, *Navaho Neighbors* (Norman, Okla., 1966); James E. Officer, *Indians in School* (Tucson, 1956); Walter C. O'Kane, *Hopis: Portrait of a Desert People* (Norman, Okla., 1953); Morris E.

Opler, *Apache Life-Way* (Chicago, 1941); Elsie C. Parsons, *Pueblo Indian Religion*, 2 vols. (Chicago, 1939); Dorothy F. Robinson, *Navajo Indians Today* (San Antonio, 1966); Ross Santee, *Apache Land* (New York, 1947); Ruth D. Simpson, *The Hopi Indians* (Los Angeles, 1953); Anne M. Smith, *New Mexico Indians* (Santa Fe, 1966); Charles L. Sonnichsen, *The Mescalero Apaches* (Norman, Okla., 1958); Edward H. Spicer, ed., *Perspectives in American Indian Culture Change* (Chicago, 1961); Leslie Spier, *Yuman Tribes of the Gila River* (Chicago, 1933); Stanley Steiner, *The New Indians* (New York, 1968); Stanley A. Stubbs, *Birds-Eye View of the Pueblos* (Norman, Okla., 1950); Laura Thompson, *Culture in a Crisis: A Study of the Hopi Indians* (New York, 1950); Ruth M. Underhill, *The Navajos* (Norman, Okla., 1956) and *The Pápago Indians of Arizona and Their Relatives the Pima* (Washington, D.C., 1940); University of Arizona Bureau of Ethnology, *Indians of the Southwest; A Survey of Indian Tribes and Indian Administration in Arizona* (Tucson, 1953); Evon Z. Vogt and Clyde Kluckhohn, *Navajo Means People* (Cambridge, Mass., 1952); Ernest Wallace and E. A. Hoebel, *The Comanches* (Norman, Okla., 1952); Frank Waters, *Book of the Hopi* (New York, 1963); William Whitman, 3rd., *The Pueblo Indians of San Ildefonso: A Changing Culture* (New York, 1947).

SPANISH AMERICANS: John H. Burma, *Spanish Speaking Groups in the United States* (Durham, N.C., 1953); Arthur L. Campa, *Treasures of the Sangre De Cristos: Tales and Traditions of the Spanish Southwest* (Norman, Okla., 1963); Kyle Crichton, *The Proud People* (New York, 1944); Alex M. Darley, *Passionists of the Southwest* (Glorieta, N. M., 1968); George M. Foster, *Culture and Conquest: America's Spanish Heritage* (Chicago, 1960); Charles Gibson, *The Spanish Tradition in America* (Columbia, S.C., 1968); Nancy L. Gonzalez, *The Spanish American of New Mexico* (Los Angeles, 1967); Alice Corbin Henderson, *Brothers of Light* (New York, 1937); Michael Jenkinson, *Tijerina* (Albuquerque, 1969); Oliver La Farge, *Behind the Mountains* (Boston, 1956); Ruth Landes, *Latin Americans of the Southwest* (St. Louis, 1965); Ruth Laughlin, *Caballeros* (New York, 1931; Caldwell, Ida., 1945); Carey McWilliams, *North from Mexico* (Philadelphia, 1948); Office of the Coordinator of Inter-American Affairs, *Spanish-Speaking Americans in the War; The Southwest* (Washington, D.C., 1943); George Mills and Richard Grove, *Lucifer and the Crucifer: The Enigma of the Penitentes* (Colorado Springs, 1956); Peter Nabakov, *Tijerina and the Courthouse Raid* (Albuquerque, 1969); Nina Otero, *Old Spain in Our Southwest* (New York, 1916); Leonard Pitt, *The Decline of the Californios* (Berkeley and Los Angeles, 1966); Julian Samora, ed., *La Raza: Forgotten Americans* (South Bend, Ind., 1968); George I. Sanchez, *Forgotten People; A Study of New Mexicans* (Albuquerque, 1940, 1967); Lyle Saunders, *Spanish Speaking Americans and Mexican-Americans in the United States* (New York, 1944); Robert H. Talbert, *Spanish-Name People in the Southwest and West* (Ft. Worth, 1955); Antonio Vigil, *The Coming of the Gringo* (New York, 1970); Carolyn Zelany, *Conflict and Accommodation in a Dual Ethnic Community in New Mexico* (New Haven, Conn., 1942).

AFRO-AMERICANS: Harry A. Bailey, *Negro Politics in America* (Columbus, Ohio, 1967); Earl Brown and George R. Leighton, *The Negro and the War* (New York, 1942); Jerry Cohen and William S. Murphy, *Burn, Baby, Burn!* (New York, 1966); Henry O. Flipper, *Negro Frontiersman*, ed. by Theodore D. Harris (El Paso, 1963); Edward E. Lewis, *The Mobility of the Negro* (New York, 1931); David Loth and Harold Fleming, *Integration North and South* (New York, 1956); D. G. Mandebaum, *Soldier Groups and Negro Soldiers* (Berkeley and Los Angeles, 1952); Gunnar Myrdal,

An American Dilemma: The Negro Problem and Modern Democracy, 2 vols. (New York, 1944); Truman M. Pierce, *White and Negro Schools in the South* (Englewood Cliffs, N.J., 1955); Budd Schulberg, *From the Ashes: Voices of Watts* (New York, 1967); Texas State Department of Education, *Negro Education in Texas* (Austin, 1931).

ORIENTAL AMERICANS: American Council on Public Affairs, *The Displaced Japanese Americans* (Washington, D.C., 1944); Gunther Barth, *Bitter Strength: A History of the Chinese in the United States, 1850–1890* (Cambridge, Mass., 1964); Leonard Bloom and Ruth Riemer, *Removal and Return: The Socio-Economic Effects of the War on Japanese-Americans* (Berkeley, 1949); Allan R. Bosworth, *America's Concentration Camps* (New York, 1967); Ping Chiu, *Chinese Labor in California, 1850–1880; An Economic Study* (Madison, Wis., 1963); Daniel and Samuel Chu, *Passage to the Golden Gate* (New York, 1967); Roger Daniels, *The Politics of Prejudice: The Anti-Japanese Movement in California* (Berkeley and Los Angeles, 1962); Yamato Ichihashi, *Japanese in the United States* (Stanford and London, 1932); Bruno Lasker, *Filipino Immigration to Continental United States and Hawaii* (Chicago, 1931); Carey McWilliams, *Prejudice: Japanese-Americans, Symbol of Racial Intolerance* (Boston, 1944); Stuart C. Miller, *The Unwelcome Immigrant: The American Image of the Chinese* (Berkeley, 1969); Elmer C. Sandmeyer, *The Anti-Chinese Movement in California* (Urbana, Ill., 1939); Bradford Smith, *Americans from Japan* (Philadelphia, 1948); Edward K. Spicer and others, *Impounded People* (Tucson, 1969); Betty Lee Sung, *Mountain of Gold: The Chinese in America* (New York, 1967); Dorothy S. Thomas, *The Salvage* (Berkeley, 1952); Dorothy S. Thomas and Richard Nishomato, *The Spoilage* (Berkeley, 1946); Taro Yashima, *The New Sun* (New York, 1943).

MEXICAN AMERICANS: John H. Burma, *Spanish Speaking Groups in the United States* (Durham, N.C., 1953); Ernesto Galarza, *Merchants of Labor: The Mexican Bracero Story* (Santa Barbara, Calif., 1967); Manual Gamio, *The Mexican Immigrant* (Chicago, 1930); Claud Garner, *Wet Back* (New York, 1947); Pauline R. Kibbe, *Latin Americans in Texas* (Albuquerque, 1946); Ruth Landes, *Latin Americans of the Southwest* (St. Louis, 1965); Peter Matthiessen, *Sal Si Puedes: César Chávez* (New York, 1969); Carey McWilliams, *Factories in the Field: The Story of Migratory Labor in California* (Boston, 1939), *Ill Fares the Land* (Boston, 1942; New York, 1967), and *North from Mexico* (Philadelphia, 1948); Selden C. Menefee, and John N. Webb, *Mexican Migratory Workers of South Texas* (Washington, D.C., 1941); D. W. Meinig, *Imperial Texas: Interpretive Essay in Cultural Geography* (Austin, 1969); Julian Nava, *Mexican Americans, Past, Present, and Future* (New York, 1969); Office of the Coordinator of Inter-American Affairs, *Spanish-Speaking Americans in the War; The Southwest* (Washington, D.C., 1943); Mary Kidder Rak, *They Guard the Gates* (Evanston, Ill., 1941); Duane Robinson, *Chance to Belong; Story of the Los Angeles Youth Project, 1943–1949* (New York, 1949); Arthur J. Rubel, *Across the Tracks: Mexican-Americans in a Texas City* (Austin, 1966); Julian Samora, ed., *La Raza: Forgotten Americans* (South Bend, Ind., 1966); George I. Sanchez and Lyle Saunders, *Wetbacks* (Austin, 1949); Lyle Saunders, *The Spanish Speaking Population of Texas* (Austin, 1949); Stanley Steiner, *La Raza: The Mexican Americans* (New York, 1970); Robert H. Talbert, *Spanish-Name People in the Southwest and West* (Ft. Worth, 1955).

20: CULTURAL MATURITY

CHURCHES: Carter E. Boren, *Religion on the Texas Frontier* (San Antonio, 1968); Fray Angelico Chavez, *The Old Faith and Old Glory* (Santa Fe, 1946); Leslie R. Elliott, ed., *Centennial History of Texas Baptists* (Dallas, 1936); Leland D. Hine, *Baptists in Southern California* (Valley Forge, Pa., 1966); Edward D. Jervey, *The History of Methodism in Southern California and Arizona* (Nashville, 1960); Arthur B. Kinsolving, *Texas George: The Life of George Herbert Kinsolving, Bishop of Texas, 1892–1928* (Milwaukee and London, 1932); Nancy Barr Mavity, *Sister Aimee* (New York, 1931); John B. McGloin, S.J., *California's First Archbishop: The Life of Joseph Sadoc Alemeny, O.P., 1814–1888* (New York, 1966); Sister M. Lilliana Owens, *Carlos M. Pinto, S.J., Apostle of El Paso* (El Paso, 1951); Edward L. Parsons, *The Diocese of California: A Quarter Century, 1915–1940* (Austin, 1958); William S. Red, *A History of the Presbyterian Church in Texas* (Austin, 1936); Sister Blandina Segale, *At the End of the Santa Fe Trail* (Milwaukee, Wis., 1948); David H. Stratton, *The First Century of Baptists in New Mexico, 1849–1950* (Albuquerque, 1954); Louis H. Warner, *Archbishop Lamy, an Epoch Maker* (Santa Fe, 1936); Francis J. Weber, *California's Reluctant Prelate: The Life and Times of the Right Reverend Thaddeus Amat, C.M.* (Los Angeles, 1964).

EDUCATION: Edward L. Barrett, Jr., *The Tenney Committee* (Ithaca, N.Y., 1951); Edward M. Burns, *David Starr Jordan, Prophet of Freedom* (Stanford, 1953); Paige W. Christiansen, *Of Earth and Sky: A History of New Mexico Institute of Mining and Technology* (Socorro, N.M., 1964); Roy W. Cloud, *Education in California* (Stanford, 1952); Charles W. Cooper, *Whittier: Independent College in California* (Los Angeles, 1967); Frederick Eby, *The Development of Education in Texas* (New York, 1925); William W. Ferrier, *Origin and Development of the University of California* (Berkeley, 1930); David P. Gardner, *The California Oath Controversy* (Berkeley and Los Angeles, 1967); A. M. Gustafson, *John Spring's Arizona* (Tucson, 1966); Dorothy Hughes, *Pueblo on the Mesa; The First Fifty Years of the University of New Mexico* (Albuquerque, 1939); Rockwell D. Hunt, *History of the College of the Pacific* (Stockton, 1951); J. R. Kelly, *History of New Mexico Military Institute, 1891–1941* (Albuquerque, 1953); Carey McWilliams, *Witch Hunt: The Revival of Heresy* (Boston, 1950); Ernest C. Moore, *California's Educators* (Los Angeles, 1950); New Mexico Education Survey Board, *Public Education in New Mexico* (Santa Fe, 1948); Sister Lilliana Owens and others, *Jesuit Studies: Jesuit Beginnings in New Mexico, 1867–1882* (El Paso, 1950); George S. Perry, *The Story of Texas A & M* (New York, 1951); George R. Stewart and others, *The Year of the Oath* (New York, 1950); Stephen B. Weeks, *Education in Arizona* (Washington, D.C., 1918); Tom Wiley, *Politics and Purse Strings in New Mexico's Public Schools* (Albuquerque, 1968).

PRESS AND RADIO: Sam Acheson, *35,000 Days in Texas; A History of the Dallas News and Its Forbears* (New York, 1938); John Bruce, *Gaudy Century: The Story of San Francisco's Hundred Years of Robust Journalism* (New York, 1948); W. C. Holden, *Alkali Trails; Or Social and Economic Movements of the Texas Frontier, 1846–1900* (Dallas, 1930); E. C. Kemble, *A History of California Newspapers* (New York, 1927); Estelle Lutrell, *Newspapers and Periodicals of Arizona, 1859–1911* (Tucson, 1950); Joe Ann Schmitt, *Fighting Editors* (San Antonio, 1958); Carl I. Wheat, *The Pioneer Press of California* (Oakland, Calif., 1948).

THE THEATER: Lucius Beebe and Charles Clegg, *Cable Car Carnival* (Oakland, Calif., 1951); Robert E. Cowan, *Forgotten Characters of Old San Francisco* (Los Angeles, 1938); Ronald L. Davis, *A History of Opera in the American West* (Englewood Cliffs, N.J., 1965); Pauline Jacobson, *City of the Golden Fifties* (Berkeley, 1941); Edgar M. Kahn, *Cable Car Days in San Francisco* (Stanford, 1940); G. R. McMinn, *The Theater of the Golden Era* (Caldwell, Ida., 1941); Constance Rourke, *Troupers of the Gold Coast* (New York, 1928); Evelyn Wells, *Champagne Days of San Francisco* (New York, 1939).

THE ARTS: John Adair, *The Navajo and Pueblo Silversmiths* (Norman, Okla., 1944); Dury B. Alexander and Todd Webb, *Texas Homes of the Nineteenth Century* (Austin, 1966); Charles A. Amsden, *Navajo Weaving* (Albuquerque, 1952); Bainbridge Bunting, *Taos Adobes: Spanish Colonial and Territorial Architecture of the Taos Valley* (Santa Fe, 1964); Van Deren Coke, *Taos and Santa Fe: The Artists' Environment, 1882–1942* (Albuquerque, 1963); Roland F. Dickey, *New Mexico Village Arts* (Albuquerque, 1949); Dorothy Dunn, *American Indian Painting of the Southwest and Plains Area* (Albuquerque, 1968); C. R. Ferguson, *You May Meet These Artists in Santa Fe and Taos* (Santa Fe, 1950); Esse Forrester-O'Brien, *Art and Artists in Texas* (Dallas, 1935); Donald B. Goodall and Gibson A. Danes, *Charles Umlauf, Sculptor* (Austin, 1967); Lloyd Goodrich, *John Sloan* (New York, 1952); Paul Horgan, *Peter Hurd* (Austin, 1965); Harold Kirker, *California's Architectural Frontier: Style and Tradition in the Nineteenth Century* (San Marino, Calif., 1960); Mabel Dodge Luhan, *Taos and Its Artists* (New York, 1947); Estelle Lutrell, *Mission San Xavier del Bac* (Tucson, 1923); Alice Marriot, *María the Potter of San Ildefonso* (Norman, Okla., 1948); Eugene Neuhaus, *William Keith, the Man and the Artist* (Berkeley, Calif., 1938); Franc J. Newcomb, *Hosteen Klah; Navaho Medicine Man and Sand Painter* (Norman, Okla., 1964); Joaquin Ortega, ed., *New Mexico Artists* (Albuquerque, 1952); Pauline A. Pinckney, *Painting in Texas* (Austin, 1967); John E. Pomfret, *The Henry E. Huntington Library and Art Gallery* (San Marino, Calif., 1969); Trent E. Sanford, *The Architecture of the Southwest, Indian, Spanish, American* (New York, 1950); John Sloan, *New Mexico Artists* (Albuquerque, 1949); Howard Swan, *Music in the Southwest* (San Marino, Calif., 1952); Clara Lee Tanner, *Southwest Indian Craft Arts* (Tucson, 1968); Frank Waters, *Leonard Gaspard* (Flagstaff, 1964).

LITERATURE: Oren Arnold, *Roundup of Western Literature* (Dallas, 1949); Adolph F. A. Bandelier, *A Scientist on the Trail* (Berkeley, 1949); John F. Bannon, S.J., *Bolton and the Spanish Borderlands* (Norman, Okla., 1964); Melba B. Bennett, *The Stone Mason of Tor House: Robinson Jeffers* (Los Angeles, 1966); Joan Benson, *Mark Twain's Western Years* (Stanford, 1938); Ray Allen Billington, *America's Frontier Heritage* (New York, 1966) and *The Frontier Thesis: Valid Interpretation of American History* (New York, 1966); Edwin R. Bingham, *Charles F. Lummis, Editor of the Southwest* (San Marino, Calif., 1955); Winston Bode, *A Portrait of Pancho: The Life of a Great Texan, J. Frank Dobie* (Austin, 1965); Mary G. Boyer, *Arizona in Literature* (Glendale, Calif., 1934); Edgar M. Branch, *Clemens of the Call* (Berkeley, 1969); John W. Caughey, *Hubert Howe Bancroft, Historian of the West* (Berkeley, 1946); J. Frank Dobie, *John C. Duval, First Texas Man of Letters* (Dallas, 1965) and *Southwestern Lore* (Austin, 1927); Ronnie Dugger, ed., *Three Men in Texas: Bedichek, Webb, Dobie* (Austin, 1967); Edwin W. Gaston, *Eugene Manlove Rhodes* (San Antonio, 1968); John W. Gaston, Jr., *The Early Novel of the Southwest* (Albuquerque, 1962); David J. Harkness, *The Southwest and West Coast in Literature* (Baton Rouge, 1954); Wilson M. Hudson, *Andy Adams: His Life and Writings* (Dallas, 1964); Wilbur

R. Jacobs, John W. Caughey, and Joe B. Franz, *Turner, Bolton, and Webb* (Seattle, 1965); Anne Roller Josler, *Our Mountain Heritage; Silverado and Robert Louis Stevenson* (Stanford, 1950); Albert Kaiser, *The Indian in American Literature* (New York, 1953); Dallas Kenmore (pseudo), *Fire-bird, a Study of D. H. Lawrence* (New York, 1952); Charles H. Lange and Carroll L. Riley, *The Southwestern Journals of Adolph F. Bandelier, 1880–1882* (Albuquerque, 1966); Aurora Lucero-White Lea, *Literary Folklore of the Hispanic Southwest* (San Antonio, 1933); William McCann, *Ambrose Bierce's Civil War* (Chicago, 1956); Mabel Major, *Signature of the Sun; Southwest Verse, 1900–1950* (Albuquerque, 1950); Mabel Major, Rebecca W. Smith, and T. M. Pearce, *Southwest Heritage: A Literary History with Bibliography* (Albuquerque, 1948); Richard O'Connor, *Ambrose Bierce: A Biography* (Boston, 1967); Ruth Odell, *Helen Hunt Jackson* (New York, 1939); T. M. Pearce, comp., and A. P. Thomason, ed., *Southwesterners Write* (Albuquerque, 1946); Anne M. Peck, *Southwest Roundup* (New York, 1950); George S. Perry, *Roundup Time, A Collection of Southwestern Writers* (New York and London, 1943); Martin S. Peterson, *Joaquin Miller, Literary Frontiersman* (Stanford, 1937); May Davison Rhodes, *The Hired Man on Horseback* (Boston, 1938); Martin Shockley, ed., *Southwest Writers' Anthology* (Austin, 1967); C. L. Sonnichsen, *The Southwest in Life and Literature* (New York, 1962); George Sterling, ed., *Continent's End, an Anthology of Contemporary California Poets* (San Francisco, 1952); A. Wilbur Stevens, ed., *Poems Southwest* (Prescott, Ariz., 1968); George R. Stewart, *Bret Harte, Argonaut and Exile* (Boston, 1931); Ernest W. Tedlock, *D. H. Lawrence* (Albuquerque, 1963); Franklin D. Walker, *A Literary History of Southern California* (Berkeley, 1950) and *San Francisco's Literary Frontier* (New York, 1939); Stanley T. Williams, *The Spanish Background of American Literature*, Vol. I (New Haven, Conn., 1955).

INDEX

Barrios y Jáuregui, Jacinto de, 68
Barstow (Ariz.), 294
Bartleson, John, 112
Bartlett, John R., 187, 188
Bass, Sam, 307
Baylor, John R., 209, 227
Baylor University, 216
Beale, Edward Fitzgerald, 188–189, 210
Beale, John Charles, 103
Bean, Roy, 307
Bear Flag Republic, 170, 171
Bear Springs (Ariz.), 166
Beaubien, Carlos, 108, 154, 168
Beaubien-Miranda Land Grant (N. Mex.), 154, 270, 310
Beaumont (Tex.), 298, 387, 388
Becknell, William, 105, 108
Beckwith, E. G., 187
Belasco, David, 407
Belen (N. Mex.), 294
Bell, Horace, 412
Bell, John, 225
Bell, Peter H., 196
Bell, Theodore A., 321
Bell Ranch (N. Mex.), 279
Bellamy, Madge, 408
Beltrán, Bernaldino, 30
Benavides, Alonso, 38
Benedict, Kirby, 148
Benicia (Calif.), 200, 218
Bennett, James A., 212
Bent, Charles, 107, 165, 168
Bent, William, 107, 163
Bentsen, Lloyd M., Jr., 360
Berkeley (Calif.), 335, 389, 405–406
Bernalillo (N. Mex.), 10, 25, 35, 47
Bernal Springs (N. Mex.), 231
Berninghouse, Oscar, 409
Bidwell, John, 112
Bierce, Ambrose, 413
Bierstadt, Albert, 408
Big Bend National Park, 345
Big Lake (Tex.), 327
Big Sandy River, 35
"Billy the Kid," 314, 412
Birch, James, 190
Bisbee (Ariz.), 299, 323, 352
Bison; see Buffalo
Black, James B., 333
Black Panthers, 389, 406
Blackburn, Ephraim, 92
Blue Lake, 378
Blumenschein, Ernest L., 408
Bodega Bay, 62, 111
Bohemian Club, 407, 408
Bolton, Herbert Eugene, 10, 17, 52, 96, 411
Bonneville, Benjamin L. E., 212

Bonney, William H., 314
Booth, Newton, 305
Borax, 298
Bosque, Fernando del, 43
Bosque Redondo, 249–250, 272
Boulder Dam, 338
Bowie, James, 103–104, 118–123
Braceros, 393, 394, 396
Bradburn, John Davis, 117, 118
Brady, William, 314
Brannon, Sam, 202
Brazoria Railroad, 284
Brazos River: and La Salle, 64; Nolan, 92; Austin, 103, 104; Indians, 208; cattle 279; railroad, 284; conservancy, 339
Breckenridge, John C., 225
Brian, Mary, 408
Bridge Canyon Dam, 341
Bridges, Harry, 355
Brigham City (Ariz.), 300
Brocius, "Curly Bill," 316
Broderick, David C:, 203
Brower, David, 341
Brown, Aaron V., 190, 191
Brown, Edmund, 362–363
Brown, Jacob, 160
Browne, J. Ross, 235
Brownsville (Tex.), 160: and gold rush, 180; Cortina, 206–207; in Civil War, 238, 239, 240; "Charro Days," 347; border trouble, 367
Bryan, William Jennings, 318, 323
Bucareli y Ursua, Antonio María, 57, 58
Buchanan, James, 205
Buchanan Dam (Tex.), 339
Budd, James H., 320
Buena Vista, Battle of, 162, 167
Buffalo: and Indians, 12, 16; and Spaniards, 22, 26, 30; robes, 106; slaughtered, 255, 271
Buffalo Bayou, Brazos and Colorado Railroad, 284
"Buffalo Soldiers," 257
Bureau of Indian Affairs: and Calif., 209, 210; Jacksboro affair, 256; and Clum, 259, 262; and health, 373; reduced services, 374, 376
Bureau of Reclamation, 338, 340
Burke Act, 264
Burleson, Edward, 128
Burlington railway system, 293
Burnet, David G., 103, 116, 121, 124
Burr, Aaron, 96–97
Burroughs, John, 366
Bush, George, 360

Bustamante, Anastasio, 117
Bustamante, Juan Domingo de, 50, 51
Bustamante, Pedro de, 10
Bustamante y Tagle, Bernard, 48
Butterfield, John, 190–191, 193
Bynner, Wytter, 413
Byrne, Edwin V., 382

Cabeza de Vaca; see Núñez
Cabildo, 39, 46, 50, 69, 87, 136
Cabrillo; see Rodriguez Cabrillo
Cabrillo National Monument, 345
Cadillac, Antoine de la Mothe, 65
Cadman, Charles Wakefield, 407
Cahuenga Pass (Calif.), 145, 172
Cajón Pass (Calif.), 59, 172, 293
Calhoun, James S., 204, 210
Calhoun, John C., 133, 175
California; see topic sought
California Central Railroad, 284
California Stage Company, 190
Call, Daniel, 100
Camel experiment, 188–189
Cameron, Ralph H., 324
Camino Real, 38, 50, 59, 61, 62, 66, 107, 162
Camp Apache (Ariz.), 261
Camp Grant (Ariz.), 257, 258, 259
Camp Moore (Ariz.), 212
Camp Supply (Okla.), 256
Camp Verde (Ariz.), 259
Camp Verde (Tex.), 188
Camp Wright (Calif.), 223
Campbell, B. H., 278
Campbell, Jack M., 384, 367
Campbell, James, 269
Campbell, Thomas E., 363
Campbell, Thomas M., 319
Campeachy (Tex.), 99
Campo, Andrés do, 27
Canadian River, 26, 68, 71, 104, 277
Canby, Edward R. S., 224, 229, 230–232, 235, 255
Candelaria, Juan, 270
Cañon de Chelly, 249; National Monument, 346
Captain Jack, 255
Caravans: to N. Mex., 38, 39; supplies, 75, 77; on Santa Fe Trail, 105, 146, 163; to Calif., 181
Carey, Asa B., 232
Cargo, David F., 367, 384
Carleton, James H.: quoted, 203; in Calif., 223; expedition, 229; in Ariz., 234–235; in N.

Carleton, James H. *(Cont.)*
Mex., 235; and Indians, 248–250
Carlsbad (N. Mex.), 330, 338
Carlsbad Caverns National Park, 345
Carmel (Calif.), 409
Carmelite Priests, 29
Carranza, Venustiano, 368
Carrillo, José Antonio, 138, 198, 203
Carson, Christopher, 109–110, 169, 172, 212, 248
Carson National Forest, 384
Casa Grande (Ariz.), 7, 345
Castaño de Sosa, Gaspar, 31
Castillero, Andrés, 143
Castillo, Diego del, 43
Castillo Maldonado, Alonso del, 19
Castro, Henri de, 131
Castro, José, 143, 170, 171
Castroville (Tex.), 131
Catholic Church: crusade in Spain, 20; Inquisition, 38, 40; N. Mex. parishes, 40, 51, 147; in La., 69; Texas parishes, 69; and Jesuits, 52; and Franciscans, 77–81; colonial art, 83; social influence, 81; state church, 81; in Tex., 122; diocese in Calif., 144; and "Know Nothing" party, 196, 203; schools and colleges, 217; revitalized, 218–220; Navajo schools, 252; as pressure group, 357; and Spanish Americans, 381; and Penitentes, 382; and Mexican Americans, 395; recent growth, 399; parochial schools, 403
Catron, Thomas B., 310–311, 314, 365
Cattle: with Oñate, 33; at missions, 53, 62, 82; with Anza, 57; with Ramón, 66; colonial, 76, 77; at *presidios*, 88; early Tex., 104, 267; early Calif., 111, 266–267; brands, 267, 276; Indian, 253; number in 1850 and 1900, 220, 349; range industry, 269–279; map of trails, 273; transformation, 279–281; rustlers, 313, 315; recent production, 337, 349; in national forests, 342; of Indians, 377
Cavendish, Thomas, 29
C. de Baca, Ezekiel, 365
Central Pacific Railroad Company, 285, 304
Central Valley (Calif.): altitude, 1; explored, 62; express, 184;

Central Valley (Calif.) *(Cont.)*
Stage line, 190; banditry, 203; in Civil War, 222; boom, 301; irrigation, 339–340; and "Okies," 360; and Mexican labor, 393
Chaco Canyon (N. Mex.), 7; National Monument, 345
Chama River, 35, 48, 341
Chambers, William, 98
Chamuscado; see Sánchez
Chapman, Joseph, 100
Chapuis, Jean, 68
Chaves, Jose Antonio, 147
Chávez, César Estrada, 397
Chávez, Dennis, 365–367
Chávez, Francisco, 268
Chávez, Fabián, 367
Chávez, J. Francisco, 249, 251, 315
Chávez, Manuel M., 232
Chemical industries, 333, 334
Chicanos, 397
Chico, Mariano, 140–141
Childress, H. M., 271
Chiles, Joseph B., 112
Chinese: trade, 91, 111; labor, 287, 304; Chinatown, 304; agitation, 305; exclusion, 305, 389; attainments, 415
Chino, Wendell, 377
Chino Ranch (Calif.), 270
Chisholm, Jesse, 274
Chisum, John, 279, 313–314
Chivington, John M., 231–232
Chorpenning, George, 184, 191
Chouteau, Auguste Pierre, 99
Christian Brothers, 217, 219
Churches; see name of denomination
Cimarron (N. Mex.), 212, 253, 270, 314
Cimarron River, 100, 104, 107
Citizenship: by treaty, 176; for Pueblos, 253, 378; reservation Indians, 264, 265, 372; Negroes, 244
Citrus fruit, 301, 343
City manager plan, 355–356
Ciudad Juárez (Mex.), 42, 129, 238
Civil War: and stage lines, 193; Calif., 222–224; Tex., 224–227, 236–241; N. Mex., 227–234, 235, 236; Ariz., 227–228, 235; map, 233; and cattle, 270
Civilian Conservation Corps, 345, 373, 380
Clanton, N. H., 316
Clark, Edward, 226
Clarkdale (Ariz.), 299
Clarksville (Tex.), 216
Clay, Henry, 97, 116

Clayton (N. Mex.), 315
Clemens, Samuel, 192, 194, 412
Cleveland, Grover M., 308, 312
Clum, John P., 259–262
Coal, 298, 330
Cochise, 212–213, 259, 261
Cochití Pueblo, 8, 45, 415
Coke, Richard, 244, 306
Coleman, William T., 305
College of California, 217
College of the Pacific, 217
College Station (Tex.), 407
Collier, John, 373
Coloma (Calif.), 179
Colorado; see topic sought
Colorado City (Ariz.), 235
Colorado Plateau, 1, 2, 336
Colorado River: Indians, 13; exploration, 21, 23, 24, 25, 59, 109; Oñate, 37; Kino, 53; Anza, 57, 59; Garcés, 59; Yuma crossing, 57, 59, 60; Kearny, 172; Mormon Battalion, 174; cession, 176; gold rush, 180–181; Aubry, 185; Yuma city, 186; Sitgreaves, 187; camels, 189; boundary, 204; defense, 212; Civil War, 223, 231–234; navigation, 235; sheep, 270; reservations, 257; irrigation, 338–339, 340
Colorado River of Tex., 44, 129, 284, 339
Colt revolver, 275
Colton, David D., 296
Columbia (Tex.), 284
Columbus (N. Mex.), 352, 368
Colyer, Vincent, 258
Comadurán, Antonio, 173
Comancheros, 76
Comanches; see Indians
Comandante general, 60, 70, 88–89
Comisario, 34, 38, 80
Commerce: early N. Mex., 38, 68, 71, 105, 214; colonial, 77; early Calif., 91, 111–112, 184; early Tex., 91, 104–105, 119, 132; and gold rush, 182; in Civil War, 226, 239
Communist Labor Party, 355
Compromise of 1850, 200
Concho (Ariz.), 270
Concho River, 44
Conchos River, 30–31
Conejos River, 95
Confederacy; see Civil War
Congregational Church, 218
Congress of Industrial Organizations, 352
Connally, John B., 359
Connally, Tom, 358

119, 123, 127
Jackson, Helen Hunt, 255, 413
Jaeger, Louis J. F., 181
James, Edwin, 100
James, John, 269
James, Thomas, 104
Japanese, 389–392, 415
Jeffers, Robinson, 398, 413
Jefferson, Thomas, 93, 97
Jeffords, Thomas, 259
Jémez Pueblo, 8
Jenkins, John, 202
Jesuits (Society of Jesus), 52–54, 77
Job Corps, 345
Johnson, Andrew, 240, 242, 250, 312
Johnson, J. Neeley, 203
Johnson, Hiram, 320–321, 360, 362
Johnson, Lyndon B., 357, 359, 362, 367, 369
Johnson Ranch (N. Mex.), 232
Johnston, Albert Sidney, 126, 222, 224
Jolson, Al, 332
Jones, Anson, 132–134
Jones, Jesse, 358
Jones, John B., 307
Jones, Paul, 376
Jones, Thomas Ap Catesby, 144
Jonesville (Ariz.), 300
Jordan, S. W., 129
Jornada del Muerto, 38, 166, 268
Joshua Tree National Monument, 346
Juárez, Benito, 238, 241
Judah, Theodore D., 285
Julian, George W., 312
Junior Colleges, 401, 404
Jusepe, 31, 36

Kaiser, Henry J., 333
Kansas Live Stock Company, 272
Kansas-Nebraska Act, 188
Kansas Pacific Railroad, 271, 291
Kautz, August V., 259, 262
Kearney, Denis, 305
Kearny, Stephen Watts, 156, 162–166, 169, 171–173, 209
Keith, William, 408
Kelly Field (Tex.), 334
Kemper, Samuel, 97–98
Kendall, George Wilkins, 129, 149, 150, 151, 153, 269–270
Kendrick, James, 91
Kenedy, Mifflin, 279
Kennecott Copper Company, 299, 353
Kennedy, John F., 359, 362, 364, 366, 368

Kennedy, Robert F., 363
Kern River, 110
Kerr, Clark, 405
Ketchum, "Black Jack," 315
King, Bruce, 367
King, David Starr, 222
King, James, 202
King, Martin Luther, 384
King, Richard, 279
King's Canyon National Park, 345
Kingston (N. Mex.), 299
Kino, Eusebio Francisco, 52–54, 57
Kitchen, Peter, 186
Knight, Goodwin, 362
Knights of the Golden Circle, 225
Knights of Labor, 318
Knights of the Rising Sun, 385
"Know Nothing" Party, 196, 203
Knowland, Joseph, 362
Knowland, William F., 362
Koslowski Ranch (N. Mex.), 232
Ku Klux Klan, 243, 385, 386
Kuchel, Thomas, 362

Labor Unions, 351–355, 395, 397
Lackland Air Force Base, 334
La Fitte, Jean, 99, 101
La Follette, Robert, 318
La Grange (Tex.), 216
Laguna Beach (Calif.), 409
Laguna Pueblo (N. Mex.), 9, 47, 379
Laguna Salada (Calif.), 57
Lake Mead, 338, 339
Lake Texoma, 339
La Lande, Baptiste, 95, 98
Lamar, Mirabeau Buonaparte, 126, 127–129, 152, 413
Lampasas County (Tex.), 317
Lamy, Juan B., 219, 382
Land: as Spanish motive, 20; *encomiendas*, 33, 39, 41, 46, 74; grants, 74–75; mission, 82, 138–140; presidial, 88; in Tex., 102, 103, 117, 126, 129, 131, 133, 197, 207, 214, 243, 244, 300; in Calif., 137, 154, 176, 210, 214–215; in N. Mex., 154, 176, 215–216, 253, 304, 310–313, 322–323, 380, 383–385; for schools, 216–217, 323; for Indians, 251, 252, 254; in severalty, 264; open range, 274; in ranches, 278–281; for railroads, 283–286; in Ariz., 308, 316; recent Indians, 372, 378
Lane, William Carr, 204
Langdon, William H., 320

Language, Indian, 8, 15; also see English and Spanish
Lanham, S. W. T., 318–319
Laperouse, Conte de, 91
La Raza, 397, 417
Laredo (Tex.), 130, 293, 339
Larios, Juan, 43
Larkin, Thomas A., 111, 158, 169, 170, 198
Larrazolo, O. A., 365
La Salle, Cavelier Sieur de, 63–64, 93
Las Animas land grant, 154
Las Cruces (N. Mex.), 315, 407
Las Mariposas Railroad, 284
Lassen Volcanic National Park, 345
Lasuén, Fermín Francisco de, 61, 62
Las Vegas (N. Mex.): founded, 107; and Armijo, 153; in Mexican War, 164, 168; and Fort Union, 211; in Civil War, 230; 231; and sheep, 270; and Rough Riders, 282; early rodeos, 282; Santa Fe railroad, 292; Vigilantes, 303; and Harvey system, 294, 295; and bandits, 311, 315; and normal school, 323
Latter Day Saints; see Mormons
Laureano de Zubiría, José Antonio, 147
Lavendar, Eugenie, 408
Lawrence, E. O., 335
Lawton, H. W., 263
League of United Latin American Citizens, 384, 395
Lee, Oliver, 315
Lee, Robert E., 207, 239
Leftwich, Robert, 103
León, Alonso de, 64–65
Leroux, Antoine, 187
Lewis, William H., 232
Leyba, Fernando de, 70
Leyva de Bonilla, Francisco, 31, 36
Lick, James, observatory, 404
Limestone County (Tex.), 244
Lincoln, Abraham, 193, 203, 221–222, 225–226, 229, 378
Lincoln County (N. Mex.), 313–314
Lincoln-Roosevelt League, 321
Lindbergh, Charles A., 346
Literature, 84, 295
Livestock production, 220, 336–337, 349
Llano Estacado, 2, 26, 129, 199, 250, 252
Lomax, John A., 412
London, Jack, 413
Lompoc (Calif.), 332

Otero, Miguel A., 281, 303, 313, 324, 412
Otero County (N. Mex.), 315
Otis, Harrison Gray, 354
Ouray (Ute), 253
Outlawry; see Disorder
Overland Mail, 184, 190–194

Pacheco y Heredia, Alonso de, 40
Pacific Coast Borax Company, 298
Pacific Gas and Electric Company, 332, 339
Pacific Railway Act, of 1862, 284–285; of 1864, 286
Pacific Telegraph Company, 193
Padilla, Juan de, 25, 27
Padres, José María, 137, 139
Palace of the Governors, 38, 136, 151, 204
Palma, Salvador, 57, 58, 60
Palmito Ranch, Battle of, 239
Palo Alto, Battle of, 160
Paloú, Francisco, 59
Panama-Pacific Exposition, 413
Pancho Villa State Park, 368
Panhandle, of Texas, 278, 293, 294, 329
Panhandle and Santa Fe Railroad, 294
Paper production, 333
Pardee, George C., 320
Paredes y Arillaga, Mariano, 157, 162
Parker County (Tex.), 317
Parker, Cynthia Ann, 128
Parker Dam, 339
Parker, John, 128
Parrish, Maxfield, 408
Partido system, 268
Pasadena Community Playhouse, 407
Patterson, James, 98
Pattie, James Ohio and Sylvester, 108–109, 146
Paul, Gabriel R., 231, 234
Peabody, George F., 402
Pease, Elisha M., 196, 243
Pecos Pueblo, 8: and Coronado, 25–27; and Espejo, 31; and Castaño, 31; and Zaldívar, 35; and Oñate, 36; and Vargas, 45; Indian Trade, 47
Pecos (Tex.), 307
Pecos Irrigation and Investment Company, 300
Pecos River: exploration, 9, 19, 44, 146; development, 272, 279, 300, 307, 327, 338
Pelham, William, 215

Peña, Cosmé, 141
Peñalosa, Diego de, 40, 63
Penitentes, 80, 382
Peones, 75, 214, 251, 268, 311
Peoples Party, 318, 320, 323
Peralta, Battle of, 234
Peralta, Pedro de, 37
Peralta de Córdoba, Miguel, 316
Perea, Estevan de, 38, 39
Pérez, Albino, 148–149
Pérez, Demetrio, 148
Pérez, Ignacio, 101
Pérez, Juan, 34, 58
Pérez de Almazán, Fernando, 67
Pérez de Villagrá, Gaspar, 32, 34
Perfecto de Cos, Martín, 119–120
Perkins, George C., 306
Perry, John T., 272
Pershing, John J., 368
Peter, Thomas J., 290, 291
Petri, Richard, 408
Petrified Forest National Park, 345
Petrís de Cruzate, Domingo, 44
Petroleum: early production, 297, 298; statistics in 1900, 302; Tex., 298, 327–328, 333; Calif., 297–298, 329; N. Mex. 330, 376; Tidelands, 358, 359
Petrolia (Tex.), 329
Phelps Dodge Corporation, 299, 331, 352–353
Phillips, Bert, 408
Phoenix (Ariz.): and irrigation, 300, 341; capital, 308, 323; industry, 334; Negroes, 387; early radio, 407; in architecture, 410
Piazzoni, Gottardo, 408
Picacho Pass (Ariz.), 234
Pico, Andrés, 172
Pico, Pío, 138, 145, 169
Picurís Pueblo, 8
Pierce, Franklin, 175
Pierce, H. Clay, 319
Pigeon Ranch (N. Mex.), 232
Pike, James, 225
Pike, Zebulon Montgomery, 95–96, 98
Pilar (Tex.), 67
Pimería Alta, 53, 55
Piñeda; see Álvarez
Pinnacles National Monument, 346
Pino, Juan Estevan, 149
Piper, Edward, 269
Pizarro, Francisco, 22, 23
Placer mining, 179–180
Placeres, 110, 146

Placerville (Calif.), 184, 191
Plum Creek (Tex.), 128
Poets, 413
Poinsenay, 262
Poinsett, Joel F., 114, 119
Point Isabel (Tex.), 160
Pojoaque (N. Mex.), 151, 381, 384
Politics; see Government
Polk, James K., 133, 157–176
Ponce, Antonio, 167
Ponce de León, Juan, 18
Ponce de León, Pedro, 34
Pony express, 191–193
Poor People's March, 384
Popé, 41, 42, 44
Population: Pueblos, 10, 50; colonial N. Mex., 51; Calif. missions, 62; colonial Calif., 62; Tex. missions, 67; colonial Tex., 67; Tex. colonists, 103, 104; aliens in N. Mex., 110; aliens in Calif., 112; Argonauts in Calif., 191, 220; data in 1850, 220; in 1900, 302; growth, 350–351; data in the 1960s, 370; of Indians, 375, 378; Spanish Americans, 380; Negroes, 387; Japanese Americans, 390; Mexican Americans, 395
Populism; see Peoples' Party
Porter, Bruce, 408
Porter, David D., 188
Porter, William Sidney, 413
Portolá, Gaspar de, 56
Posada, Alonso de, 40
Possum Kingdom Dam, 339
Poston, Charles D., 186
Potash, 330
Pottery, 6, 7, 9, 378, 409
Powers, James, 103
Prairies Land and Cattle Company, 279
Prairie View State Normal and Industrial College, 386
Pratte, Bernard and Sylvestre, 108
Precipitation, 2, 5
Presbyterian Church, 218, 399–400
Prescott (Ariz.), 235, 299, 308
Presidio (Tex.), 294
Presidios: location, 56, 57, 59, 61, 65, 66, 67, 70, 118, 142; land, 74; functions, 87–88; reorganized, 88–89
Price, Sterling, 166, 168
Price, William, 256
Primogeniture, 21, 380
Prince, L. Bradford, 309, 313, 322
Professions, 414–415

464